The most consistently useful book I've owned in many years. This is technical writing at its best: lucid prose that explains and exemplifies the vast capabilities of QuickTime on the Web, then goes on to inspire a flood of ideas that can be explored right away because the enclosed CD includes great sample code, media, and essential tools, including QuickTime Player Pro.

> —Dr. Frank Lowney
> *Director, Electronic Instructional Services*
> *Georgia College & State University*

Its broad possibilities make QuickTime the technology to tell a captivating tale. With such a technology you need proper guidance to successfully relay your message; *QuickTime for the Web* is the book to do so. Whether you are a novice or an expert, this book will guide you through all the important aspects, with intricate real-world examples, as well as inspire new ways of authoring. With its engaging writing, it's a joy to read and . . . the best reference manual on the subject.

> —Mario Piepenbrink
> *QuickTime Evangelist*
> *Bluevilla*

Since QuickTime is an always evolving technology and now has support for MPEG-4 and a number of other features, it's great to have this third edition available. . . . As in the first two editions, this *QuickTime for the Web* offers easy and thorough explanations. This edition will always be on my desk at hand's reach and not tucked away in a bookshelf.

> —Francesco Schiavon
> *Digital Media Deployment Instructor*
> *Vancouver Film School, Interactive Media*

QuickTime for the Web, third edition, is a fantastic resource for anyone who works with new media. It's a must-have reference for anyone who wants to use digital computer media at any level, beginner or expert. I've learned more glancing through this book than I could ever hope to gather from various other sources or glean from my own experience. This book will open your eyes to all the possibilities that QuickTime enables.

> —Jim Longo
> *Cofounder*
> *Rhythm Division*

An impressively thorough reference that also functions well as a general introduction to a complex and extensive technology. Unlike many "authorized" texts, this up-to-date book reveals all the tricks and gotchas with exactly the encyclopedic level of detail that the subject deserves. Everyone working on the internet/multimedia axis should have a copy.

—Brennan Young
Multimedia Programmer

The title *QuickTime for the Web* doesn't really do this book justice. Although QuickTime and targeting it for the Web is the main focus of the book, it's about a whole lot more than that. I'd say it's *the* book to read for all that is QuickTime. The wealth of information just about QuickTime is incredible. And oh, by the way, it has a lot of great information about related technologies like streaming, Flash, SMIL, etc. . . .

The book . . . is different from most technical books of its kind. It's easy to read, contains some humor, is written by someone who knows the technology well, and above all you can tell the author is excited about what you can do with QuickTime.

I'd rate this as a must-read for anyone doing anything with QuickTime. It contains everything you need to know to deploy QuickTime content and more. It also does a great job of explaining what specific tools you'll need to build the QuickTime content of your choice.

—Brad Behrendt
President, Digital Prairie Systems
www.theprairie.com

QuickTime for the Web unleashes the power of digital media. This comprehensive guide is an excellent ready reference to the extensive visual, audio, and interactive capabilities of QuickTime. From basic concepts through clear how-to examples and a wealth of tips, the author covers all aspects of creating and delivering QuickTime media for the Web. This edition extends a keystone work to include the myriad of new features in the QuickTime 6 release.

—Steven M. Cox, Ph.D.
Interactive New Media Developer
virtualthink.com

QuickTime
for the Web
for Windows
and Macintosh

Third Edition

Apple

MORGAN KAUFMANN PUBLISHERS

AN IMPRINT OF ELSEVIER SCIENCE

AMSTERDAM   BOSTON   LONDON   NEW YORK
OXFORD   PARIS   SAN DIEGO   SAN FRANCISCO
SINGAPORE   SYDNEY   TOKYO

Acquisitions Editor	Tim Cox
Publishing Services Manager	Simon Crump
Editorial Coordinator	Stacie Pierce, Richard Camp
Associate Project Manager	Brandy Palacios
Project Management	Elisabeth Beller
Cover Design	Laurie Anderson
Cover Image	Wilhelm Scholz/Getty Images
Text Design	Rebecca Evans and Associates
Illustration	Traci Auer, Cherie Plumlee, and Apple
Composition	Nancy Logan
Copyeditor	Ken DellaPenta
Proofreader	Daril Bentley
Indexer	Steve Rath
Printer	The Maple-Vail Book Manufacturing Group

Morgan Kaufmann Publishers
An imprint of Elsevier Science
500 Sansome Street, Suite 400
San Francisco, CA 94111
www.mkp.com

Library of Congress Control Number: 2003106923
ISBN: 1-55860-904-0

This book is printed on acid-free paper.

Contents

Preface

Why QuickTime?

QuickTime is the best and most popular way to put sound and video on websites and CD-ROMs. QuickTime is a free download and works equally well on Windows and Macintosh systems. QuickTime uses open standards like MPEG-4 that let you create, send, and play multimedia files that work transparently with other media players.

You can deliver QuickTime movies using any Web server, regardless of its operating system; put QuickTime movies (and QuickTime itself) on CD-ROM; or use QuickTime to send streams with live video, audio, text, and hyperlinks, across a campus LAN or over the World Wide Web.

But QuickTime is more than just movies. It lets you create background music, slideshows, distance learning courses, interactive virtual reality tours, games, even small applications that work over the Internet, all without any C or Java programming (or any programming at all).

Your website can bark like a dog, show live video, present slideshows with music and cross-fade transitions, or include working financial and scientific calculators—just using QuickTime.

QuickTime enables you to integrate recorded video and sound with live audio and video streams, still images and animated graphics, scrolling titles and credits, MIDI, real-time effects, 3D virtual reality, multiple languages, subtitles and closed captions, Flash animation, and user interactivity—all optimized for delivery over the Internet, LAN, or disk.

There are other technologies for playing streaming audio and video—you can use RealPlayer or Windows Media Player, for example—and other technologies for playing animated graphics—such as Flash Player—but QuickTime is more than a player application. QuickTime is a complete media architecture that provides high-quality image and sound capture, graphics creation, import from other formats, mixing, editing, compositing, archiving, compression, runtime animation and interaction, and Internet delivery. QuickTime media can be optimized for any bandwidth—

DVD, high-speed corporate or campus LANs, CD-ROM, the Web, and yes, third-generation cell phones.

QuickTime is an enabling technology. It's used "under the hood" of many professional tools, including Adobe Premiere, Discreet Cleaner, and Final Cut Pro. Many professionals—even those who deliver their final product in Real or Windows Media format—first create, edit, and archive their work in QuickTime.

Artists who create work in Flash often use QuickTime in postproduction, to add interactivity or non-Flash media types such as VR or MIDI, then deliver their final product as QuickTime movies.

There were over 100 million downloads of QuickTime 5 last year, most of them by Windows users. Millions more installed QuickTime from CD or bought computers with QuickTime preinstalled. QuickTime 6 has taken off like wildfire.

Why use QuickTime? Here are seven good reasons.

▶ Quality

QuickTime movies don't restrict you to any particular compression format. This means that you can capture and edit your work at the highest possible resolution, allowing you to create a "master copy" of your movie for archive purposes (or for very high-end playback), without worrying about the final file size or Internet bandwidth requirement.

You can then export copies of your movie using any of QuickTime's many compressors, choosing the one that delivers the best quality for your content at a given bandwidth. QuickTime supports a rich set of compressors, some from Apple and some from other sources, including MPEG-1 and MPEG-2 audio and video, MP3 audio, MPEG-4 video and AAC audio, QDesign Music 2, Sorenson 3 video, Qualcomm Purevoice for speech, and dozens of others.

QuickTime compressors are plug-in modules that anyone can write, so you aren't limited to the compressors Apple provides—if you prefer the DivX video and Ogg Vorbis audio compressors, for example, you can plug them in and use them (and yes, if you have the skill, you can write your own). This opens QuickTime to cutting-edge video compression from companies like XygoVideo and Streambox.

It also means that QuickTime gives you the highest-quality output of any multimedia format—the sharpest video and clearest audio at a given bandwidth. For some examples, check the QuickTime movie trailers at www.apple.com/trailers/.

Cinematographers and studios prefer to show their work on the Internet in QuickTime. These are among the highest-quality movies anywhere on the Internet. You'll get a detailed look at how to create this kind of magic in Chapter 12, "Just Like in the Movies."

World-Class Streaming

Streaming audio and video allow you to deliver live feeds over the Internet or a LAN. You can watch and hear things as they happen. You can also use streams to send video on demand, allowing viewers to access movies stored on your server as if they were local files. For example, you can provide a live broadcast of a lecture or keynote address over a campus LAN while storing a copy that people can view later. When they view it later, they can skip around in the movie without waiting for the file to download, just as if it were on a local disk.

QuickTime provides world-class streaming for those who need it. You can stream QuickTime audio, video, and text; MPEG-4 files; and MP3 playlists, at virtually any bandwidth over virtually any network. You can send QuickTime streams using Windows, Linux, Mac OS, Solaris (and other servers) to Windows, Macintosh, and Linux clients. The source code is available from Apple and can be compiled for still other platforms—also free, as open source. The server software is free by download, just like the player. No license fees.

QuickTime can also send and play IceCast-compatible MP3 streams that can be played by WinAmp, iTunes, and others, as well as true MPEG-4 streams and files that work with any ISO-compliant player.

All Macintosh computers now come with the additional ability to encode and broadcast live QuickTime and MPEG-4 streams over standard IP networks, including the Internet. A typical Macintosh can send 200–400 simultaneous streams directly, or relay an unlimited number through a streaming server running on any operating system.

Software is also available from third parties to broadcast live or stored audio and video in QuickTime format using either Windows or Macintosh computers, ranging from simple "send one stream now" applications to full-blown mobile television studios with multiple feeds, graphic overlays, and camera-to-camera transitions, for under $1000.

Independent reviews comparing Windows Media, Real, and QuickTime found that QuickTime streaming servers offer the highest quality, easiest setup, and lowest cost, particularly for large enterprises. QuickTime allows you to send as many simultaneous streams as you like with no license fee.

Other streaming servers, in contrast, can cost tens of thousands of dollars in license fees alone.

In addition, QuickTime allows you to mix streaming media with other media in the same movie. There are beautiful examples of music streams embedded in customized players using sprites, still images, and even virtual reality. The streams, the unique player "skin," and the hyperlinked sprite buttons can all be part of the same QuickTime movie. This book shows you how in Chapter 17, "Mixing It Up: Streaming and Nonstreaming."

▶ Progressive Download

Streaming is perfect for live events, but the quality of streaming over the Internet is limited by bandwidth. The pipe just isn't big enough to carry DVD-quality movies in real time.

But streaming isn't the only way to deliver movies. As an alternative, QuickTime can deliver movies using progressive download, also called Fast Start for the Web. This allows you to send movies that are higher quality than streaming bandwidth would allow. The movie is buffered locally as it arrives and is played from the buffer while it downloads. Dropped bits are retransmitted, so nothing is lost in transmission. The movie may pause while waiting for the network, but the network connection does not limit the movie quality, it only lengthens the transmission time.

With QuickTime, you can actually deliver better-than-television quality audio and video over the Internet. If your movie fits inside the available bandwidth, it plays in real time, just like streaming movies. If there isn't enough bandwidth, the movie pauses while the buffer fills, then continues.

And while streaming is limited to video, audio, and text, a Fast Start movie can contain any of the over 200 media types that QuickTime supports, including interactive sprites, virtual reality, Flash animation, and real-time effects. There's literally nothing else like it.

▶ Rich Media

QuickTime supports more different kinds of media, in more different formats, than any other multimedia platform (for a full list, see Appendix E, "QuickTime Media Types").

This lets you create presentations that simply aren't possible in any other format. For example, imagine adding a Flash logo and an MP3 sound track to a series of JPEG images, to create a slideshow with transitions that are precisely synchronized with the sound track, branded with your logo. It's a snap in QuickTime. Want to add a clickable link that opens your website in a browser? Another snap. Want to swap that MP3 sound track for an AAC track? Dead easy. Want to include a virtual reality tour of your studio? You can do that, too.

If all you want is a sound track and a video track, QuickTime is one good choice among two or three candidates. When you want it all, Quick-Time is the best, often the only, choice. And let's face it: sooner or later, you *will* want it all.

By the way, QuickTime media handlers are components, just like sound and video compressors. So you can plug in a third-party component and use non-Apple media types in QuickTime movies. For example, you can use Pulse 3D animations, BeHere 360-degree immersive movies, Zoomify detail-on-demand images, even Axel real-time ray-trace rendering, in the same movie with any other QuickTime media. Just plug in the appropriate media handler. If your movie is on the Web, and someone needs one of these components to view it, QuickTime offers to download and install it for them automatically.

No other technology offers more than a small fraction of the media types available in QuickTime, and the QuickTime media palette is constantly growing. New media types are added, almost on a monthly basis, through the efforts of Apple engineers, standards bodies such as MPEG, and the work of creative third parties (like you).

▶ Durability

How long do you want your work to last? A week? A year? Ten years or longer? It matters what format you choose.

Do you remember vinyl records, 16 mm home movies, 8-track tapes? Okay, maybe you're not that old. How about WordStar files on floppy disk, Commodore video cartridges, or NetShow files? The fact is, digital storage formats, both physical and software, disappear more rapidly all the time.

In contrast, QuickTime celebrated its 10th birthday last year. At the party, people brought movies they made a decade ago using QuickTime 1.0. They loaded them onto a computer running QuickTime 5.12, the latest version at that time, and the movies played beautifully—in most cases, they played better in the current version of QuickTime than they ever had before.

This doesn't happen by accident. The QuickTime team is dedicated to adding new features and capabilities to QuickTime in ways that don't break existing movies or applications. In many cases, new features become available later transparently, without modifying the movie or program. For example, QuickTime 1.0 had no ability to play movies in full-screen mode, but a QuickTime 1 movie plays just fine in full-screen mode using QuickTime 6. Programs that supported QuickTime compression were suddenly able to save movies in MPEG-4 format. No other existing multimedia technology has this kind of track record, nor is it likely to.

But QuickTime offers more than just stability. A key part of durability is *reuseability*—you need to be able to update your existing work over time, adding an MP3 or AAC sound track, for example, or substituting one logo for another. And you need to be able to repurpose your work—combining existing graphics or video with new text or music, or with entirely new media types. You need to be able to take your movies apart and recombine them with new or pre-existing material, keeping them current without starting from scratch.

QuickTime lets you do that. Most other multimedia formats are closed boxes—you can pour your work into them, but you can't get your work back out again. Once you've converted your audio to Real format, for example, you can't pull the sound track back out, add a JPEG slideshow, and then export it as Windows Media or QuickTime. No way.

QuickTime, on the other hand, lets you save high-quality versions of your work, from which media can be extracted, reused, recombined, saved, and exported to other formats at any time. In fact, you can often reuse QuickTime media without recompressing it, allowing you to reuse compressed Web-based material without degrading the quality—a godsend when you no longer have access to the original.

If you want your work to be playable—and reusable—down the road, QuickTime is your best friend.

▶ Interactivity

QuickTime movies can take your audience beyond the passive experience of television—*way* beyond. QuickTime movies can include sprites that react to their environment—bouncing off the walls, for example. And the environment can change as a result of events—keyboard and mouse input, the current point in the movie timeline, calculations, interactions among sprites, with other media tracks, even with other movies. A QuickTime sprite can be programmed to take over 100 different *kinds* of actions.

Your movie can load URLs in a browser window, synchronized to the movie timeline, for example. Or the movie can pause, or jump to a specified point in its timeline, based on user input. Sound tracks or text tracks can be enabled or disabled to add subtitles or commentary. The current language for the movie can be changed, automatically selecting an appropriate video or text track. New movies can be loaded and played as a sprite action. Text can be input or displayed. Math calculations can be performed. Data can be exchanged with Web-based services using XML. Animated creatures can shoot photons at each other in simulated mayhem. All these actions, and many, many, more, can be combined in literally infinite ways. You can actually use QuickTime sprite actions to build lightweight portable applications that run over the Internet and work equally well on Macintosh and Windows computers.

In addition, QuickTime 6 supports all the actions and events for Flash 5, so you can import Flash tracks complete with actions. You can also add QuickTime actions to Flash media, whether or not the media already has native Flash actions. That means you can use Flash to create great-looking interactive graphics and just drop them into QuickTime movies, then add QuickTime-specific actions.

When it comes to interactivity, no other multimedia format even comes close.

Open Standards

Standards are dull by nature, but standards are actually one of the most exciting reasons to use QuickTime—because standards create whole new industries.

What do competing neighborhood video stores, disk manufacturers, electronics stores, and electronics manufacturers all have in common? DVD disc format and MPEG-2 compression. They can all bring something to market knowing it will work with the other parts.

That allows, even encourages, competition. Quality and variety go up, prices go down, and things just work. You don't have to look at a DVD to see which company's DVD player it works in. The neighborhood store doesn't worry about which brand to stock.

But when you adopt a vendor's proprietary format, you adopt the vendor. For good or ill, you're stuck with them. If the vendor decides to change formats or fees, you're at their mercy. If they drop support for the format or go out of business, you're out of luck.

When you adopt a standard format, you know that multiple vendors can step up to provide the services you need. In a pinch, you can even do it yourself, or hire someone—either in-house or as a contractor—to do what needs doing. The standard is there for anyone to work with.

Consider Apple's industry-leading commitment to MPEG-4. Other companies created "MPEG-4" compressors for use inside their proprietary media. QuickTime has that too, of course, but it also reads and writes native MP4 files that can be exchanged with other MP4 servers and players. Because it's an open standard, everyone—Internet service providers, telecom switch makers, cell phone designers—can add things to the MP4 mix. And they have. Soon you'll be able to listen to MP4 on portable audio players, watch MPEG-4 movies on disc players, and get MPEG-4 messages on your cell phone. And that's just the tip of the iceberg. This is rapidly coming together as a whole that's far more than the sum of its parts.

▶ Oh Yeah, and Another Thing . . .

QuickTime offers a near-universal browser plug-in for multimedia. Put almost any kind of multimedia on your website and QuickTime can play it. No need to have multiple plug-ins for live audio, high-quality video, Flash animations, MP3, and MPEG-4. Using QuickTime, you can write one version of your HTML and have it perform consistently on all popular browsers and platforms. One plug-in is all you need. It's a free download, and over 100 million computers have it already. You can get a free license from Apple to include it on your CD-ROMs.

All recent versions of QuickTime include low-bandwidth compressors with high-quality audio and video that will play over the Web in real time, no special server software needed.

QuickTime supports media types that go far beyond audio and video, and more are being added constantly. Recent additions include MPEG-4 video, AAC audio, 3GPP text for cell phones, and JPEG 2000 images.

The pro version of QuickTime Player, included with this book, can convert almost any kind of multimedia content into QuickTime format. You can use it to compress all kinds of media, optimizing for delivery over dialup, fast Internet access, LAN, or CD-ROM. You can even create movies that deliver alternate versions of the same content to people viewing them at different connection speeds or in different languages.

You want more? There's more. But frankly, it would take a whole book to tell you about it.

Fortunately, you now have that book.

▶ So What's in This Book?

In the first few chapters, we'll introduce you to QuickTime—show you how to import existing media into QuickTime movies, how to embed movies in Web pages, and how to deliver them from an ordinary Web server. Then we'll introduce you to real-time streaming.

In the subsequent chapters, we'll look at creating movies that use sound (including MP3 and AAC), MIDI music, still images, motion video (including MPEG-4), and text (including 3GPP), and show you how to compress them and optimize them for CD, LAN, or the Web. Then we'll show you how to send those movies as real-time streams.

After that, we'll show you how to create movies using more exotic media—such as sprites and Flash—and how to wire your movies for interactivity. Then we'll show you how to mix exotic and interactive media with real-time streams in the same movie, and deliver it over the Web.

Finally, we'll show you how to use QuickTime to create immersive virtual reality worlds and 3D objects; how to add sounds, sprites, and image overlays to these VR worlds; and how to put them into Web-based presentations.

To help you through it all, we've included a CD-ROM with plenty of examples, including lots of cut-and-paste HTML and JavaScript. The CD works equally well on Windows or Macintosh computers.

The CD also includes QuickTime Pro (a $29.95 value); free tools from Apple Computer, such as MakeRefMovie, Plug-in Helper, and MakeEffectMovie; and trial or lite versions of software from other vendors, including Totally Hip's LiveStage Pro, Channel Storm's LiveChannel, SoundsaVR, and Spike.

For updates, additions, and corrections to this book, hit the Web at
`developer.apple.com/techpubs/QuickTime/QTBooks/QT4WebBook.htm`

or follow the link at

`www.mkp/companions1558609040`

Ready? Let's do it!

Acknowledgments

I'm grateful to all the groups and individuals who have made significant contributions to this book.

I'm deeply indebted to many people at Apple Computer—I wish I could name them individually.

Apple's QuickTime engineering team provided invaluable assistance, answered endless questions, painstakingly reviewed my drafts, and quietly created all of this amazingly cool stuff.

Apple's crack Web team (www.apple.com) provided a great deal of help, particularly with sample content, compression, and wired movies.

Apple's technical publications group worked long and hard in more ways than I can enumerate. Editing, proofreading, illustrating, and creating original content for the CD come to mind, but they only begin the list.

Many thanks to the team at Morgan Kaufmann who worked so hard and with such enthusiasm to make this book a success. Special thanks to Tim Cox, Stacie Pierce, Elisabeth Beller, Richard Camp, and Sherri Dean.

Sample content, demos, and tools for the CD were contributed by Jeff Harris, Michael Shaff, Matthew Peterson, Ian Mantripp, Guillaume Iacino, Ken Loge, Peter Hoddie, Erik Fohlin, Steve Cox, Peter Bisset, Cliff Walker, Peter Hoddie, Christofer Yavelow, Ken Turkowski, David Egbert of Retiarius Enterprises, Janie Fitzgerald of Axis Productions, Christoph Cantillon of Azine Software, Brennan Young, Robert West, Bill Meikle, Audio Integration, and a number of creative people at Apple.

Additional software on the CD was provided by Channel Storm, Totally Hip Software, Squamish Media Group, and Apple. Streaming content for the third edition was contributed by: TheBasement Studios, Australia; and RadioIO.

Special thanks to Ken Waagner of Smartly-Dunn Ltd. for permission to use the Wilco streaming player; Ken rocks, and so does Wilco.

Belated thanks to Paul Kent of Mactivity for his generosity and support.

Many contributors to earlier editions included new or revised material for the third edition as well, for which they have my continuing gratitude.

And thanks, mom. It's nice to be here.

Introduction

There are some basic concepts that you should be familiar with so you can read the rest of this book without getting a headache. (Well, that's the idea, anyway.) This chapter covers three fundamental topics:

- **What's a QuickTime Movie?**

  Think you already know? Check it out.

- **What's QuickTime?**

  What you get, what it does, what it runs on.

- **Delivery: Local, Streaming, and Fast Start**

  Three very different ways to deliver QuickTime.

What's a QuickTime Movie?

If we think about it at all, most of us expect a movie to contain moving pictures and synchronized sound. A QuickTime movie is a lot more versatile than that. Of course, it *can* be a moving picture with synchronized sound, but it can just as easily be a series of still images with synchronized text, or invisible background music, or a talking Web tour with a graphic control panel of your own design.

- **A QuickTime movie is a file that tells the computer what kind of media to present and when to present it.**

  The media can be video, sound, MIDI music, text, animated sprites, still images, transition effects, even a series of website addresses. QuickTime has media handlers that will show the video, play the sounds, synthesize music from MIDI instructions, render text on the user's screen, animate sprites and test for user interaction, create a cross-dissolve, or load a series of websites in a browser frame. QuickTime can synchronize all of these activities, creating a multimedia experience that the word "movie" doesn't adequately describe.

- **A QuickTime movie is made up of one or more tracks—video tracks, sound tracks, text tracks, or other track types.**

  Each track points to media of a particular type. You can have multiple tracks of the same type, such as multiple sound tracks or multiple video tracks.

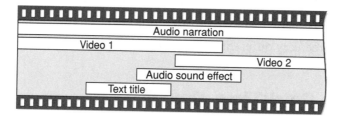

- **Tracks are sychronized to a timeline and arranged in time and space.**

  The movie timeline is used to synchronize all the media, so sound and video, for example, stay in precise synch. Tracks can begin and end anywhere in the movie timeline, so one track can follow another—seamlessly or with any amount of overlap or delay. Visual tracks can be arranged in space as well as time. For example, a pair of video tracks could be sequential (play in the same space but at different times), or play at the same time—side by side, one above the other, picture-in-picture, or overlapping with various kinds of transparency. Visual tracks are arranged in layers, so you can choose which track is "on top" of another.

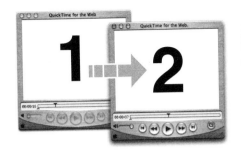

Sequential   **Side-by-side**   **Superimposed**

- **Track characteristics can change when a movie plays.**

  Most track characteristics, such as video layer or audio volume, can change as a result of user interaction or runtime calculations. For example, there can be alternate sound or text tracks in English, French, and Chinese, with the movie set to enable the correct tracks for the user's system automatically, or a movie can contain buttons to enable subtitles or change languages, or superimpose a video track with the dialog in sign language.

- **You create a QuickTime movie by adding and arranging tracks.**

  You make a QuickTime movie by adding tracks that point to the media you want to use. You edit a QuickTime movie by arranging the tracks—when they start and end, which parts of the media they use in what order, any events they should respond to or actions they should take, and how they overlap in time and space.

- **QuickTime tracks use samples, not frames.**

  A QuickTime movie doesn't have a fixed frame rate. Each track has one or more media samples. Each sample has a start time and a duration. A single QuickTime movie can contain both NTSC and PAL video tracks, for example, playing side-by-side—one at 30 samples a second and the other at 25. And they can play on a background track consisting of a single JPEG sample with a duration equal to the whole movie!

- **Tracks don't contain media samples—they just point to them.**

  The tracks in a movie tell QuickTime what media to play and when to play it, but a track doesn't actually contain any media samples—it just points to them. The actual samples can be elsewhere in the same file, or in a different file (on the same computer or a network file server), or somewhere on the Internet. They can even be part of a live stream.

- **You can edit a QuickTime track without modifying the media that it points to.**

QuickTime allows nondestructive editing. You can edit a track to delete all but the first and last parts of a video file, for example, and only those parts will be displayed when the movie plays, but the video file itself remains intact. For example, a hard disk can contain dozens of different movies created using a single media file stored on a CD-ROM. The movies just point to different parts of the media file arranged in different orders. A QuickTime movie is not the sample data—it is the organizing principle that tells the computer where the data is, what it is, and what to do with it.

■ **When you save a QuickTime movie, you can either save a small movie that points to the media data in other files, or you can make the movie self-contained.**

If you save a movie normally, the sample data is not copied into the movie file. If you make the movie self-contained, the resulting movie file contains copies of all the media samples used, interleaved for smooth delivery. Only the samples that are actually used in the movie are copied into the file.

Saved as normal
(Movie points to media data in other files.)

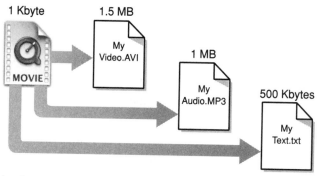

Saved as self-contained
(Movie contains copies of all media data used
by its tracks, interleaved for smooth delivery.)

If the movie points to media data in other files, the path to those files must remain intact for the movie to play. The path can be a URL or a directory path and filename.

- **QuickTime media data can be compressed in a variety of ways.**

You can use QuickTime to compress media when saving a movie, or to play back compressed media, or to translate compressed media from one format to another. Almost any kind of media can be compressed, and different kinds of compressed media can be used in the same QuickTime movie.

For example, still images may be in GIF, JPEG, or PNG format, among others; video may be compressed using Cinepak, Sorenson, MPEG-4, or other video codecs; and audio may be compressed using QDesign, MP3, Qualcomm PureVoice, AAC, or other audio codecs. Tracks using different compressors can coexist in the same movie.

You can save multiple copies of a movie using different compression techniques. You might create a highly compressed version for delivery over slow Internet connections, for example, and a less compressed but better-looking version for delivery over faster connections. You can generate movies of widely different size and quality from the same source by using different compressors, or even by using different settings for the same compressor.

- **You can import and export existing media from other formats.**

For example, you can import CD audio tracks, AVI or MPEG-4 movies, FLIC animations, MP3, or MIDI music files directly into QuickTime. Once you've imported these files, you can deliver them over the Internet in QuickTime movies. You can also edit them, compress them in various ways, and combine them with other media.

You can also export media from a QuickTime movie to other formats. For example, you could import a MIDI file into a QuickTime movie music track, then export the music track as an AIFF or WAV sound file.

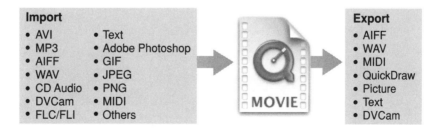

QuickTime can be extended to import and export additional media types. For example, you can add MPEG-2 export to create DVDs, or MPEG-1 export to create VCDs. For a full list of media types that QuickTime imports and exports natively, see Appendix E, "QuickTime Media Types."

We'll look at using all these features of QuickTime movies in various projects throughout the book. They can be combined in some surprising ways.

▶ What's QuickTime?

QuickTime is a file format, a set of applications and plug-ins, and a software library with an application programming interface (API). A what, a what, and a *what*? Right. Let's look at those three items, shall we?

QuickTime File Format

The QuickTime file format is the QuickTime movie file, and it's completely platform-independent. You can deliver QuickTime movies from any kind of file server or Web server: UNIX, Solaris, Linux, Mac OS, Windows NT—you name it. You don't need to use a Macintosh or a Windows computer to send QuickTime movies over the Web or over a LAN.

QuickTime movies are extremely versatile data structures that can contain almost any combination of media using almost any kind of compression, as described in "What's a QuickTime Movie?" (page 1).

The QuickTime file format is an open standard. It has been adopted by the Motion Picture Experts Group as the basis for the MPEG-4 file specification. You can download the file format specification from

developer.apple.com/techpubs/quicktime/quicktime.html.

Applications and Plug-ins

The applications and plug-ins that come with QuickTime are the Quick-Time browser plug-in (and ActiveX control, for Windows), QuickTime Player, and PictureViewer (for Windows and versions of the Mac OS that don't include Preview). These applications allow people to play QuickTime movies and view still images inside a Web browser or from the desktop.

QuickTime plug-in   **QuickTime Player**

Apple provides applications and plug-ins that run on Mac OS X and 32-bit Windows computers (Windows 98/2000/NT/ME/XP). Other programs, such as Acrobat, Word, Flash, and Cleaner, can also play QuickTime movies if the QuickTime software library is installed.

Browser Plug-in (and ActiveX)

When you put a QuickTime movie on your Web page, people need the QuickTime browser plug-in to play it (some browsers also require an ActiveX control, which is part of the QuickTime plug-in). This provides a user interface for watching the movie in a browser. A movie playing in the QuickTime plug-in looks something like this:

Volume control — Plug-in settings

Position indicator

Play button — Time slider — Step buttons

The browser plug-in (and ActiveX control) can be controlled from HTML or JavaScript.

QuickTime Player

QuickTime Player provides a way to play QuickTime movies outside of a Web browser. Like the plug-in, it can play movies, MP3, and a variety of other file types from a hard disk or CD, over a LAN, or off the Internet. QuickTime Player can be used to play live Internet streams and Web multicasts without using a browser. You can even launch QuickTime Player to show full-screen movies from a link in a Web page.

The pro version of QuickTime Player, included on the CD in the back of this book, allows you to create, edit, compress, and save QuickTime movies, in addition to playing them. It also allows you to import from other file types, such as AVI or MIDI files, into QuickTime movies, and to save them or to translate from one file type to another, such as converting from MP3 to AIFF sound.

QuickTime Player runs on Mac OS X and most 32-bit Windows systems (Windows 98 and later). On a Mac it looks like the following illustration:

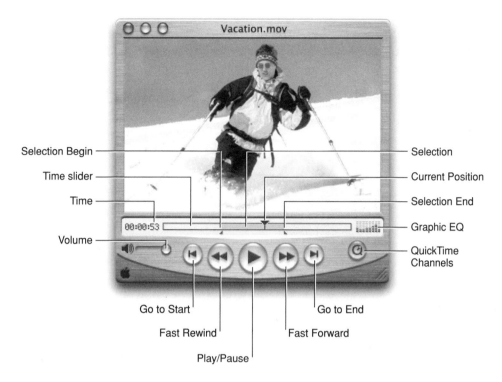

We'll show you how to use QuickTime Player to do various things, such as importing a series of JPEG images into a slideshow or adding a sound track and titles to a movie, as we go along. For a full summary of Quick-Time Player's features and controls, see Appendix A, "QuickTime Player Pro Editing Features."

QuickTime API

QuickTime includes a set of software libraries and an application programming interface (API) that C and Java programmers can use to create applications that use QuickTime. These applications typically display, create, or edit QuickTime movies. Examples include Adobe Premiere, Apple's Final Cut Pro, Discreet's Cleaner, Totally Hip's LiveStage Pro, and Macromedia Director, to name just a few.

Some applications that use the QuickTime API are Macintosh-only, some are Windows-only, and some run on either platform. It's up to the author. The CD in the back of this book contains demo versions of some of these programs.

Like the applications and plug-ins, the QuickTime API is available for both the Mac OS X and 32-bit Windows operating systems. For further information about the C interface to the QuickTime API, see *Discovering QuickTime* by George Towner/Apple Computer, Inc., published by Morgan Kaufmann. For more about the Java interface, see *QuickTime for Java, 2nd Edition* (forthcoming) by Tom Maremaa and William Stewart/Apple Computer Inc., also to be published by Morgan Kaufmann.

Who Gets What

The applications, plug-ins, and software libraries are all available from Apple Computer and can be downloaded over the Web free of charge. They are installed automatically when you install QuickTime. You can download QuickTime from `www.apple.com/quicktime/download/`, or you can install it from the CD in the back of this book.

A pro license for QuickTime, which adds editing, export, saving, and compression features to QuickTime Player, is also available for purchase over the Web. It costs $29.99 US. *You* don't have to buy it, though; it's included on the CD.

If you need to play MPEG-2 video in QuickTime, it's available as a separate download from Apple. MPEG-2 playback isn't included in the standard QuickTime download or on the CD in this book for licensing reasons.

The API that lets you write new QuickTime programs in C or Java is also available from Apple and can also be downloaded over the Web free of charge, but it's not automatically included with QuickTime. To get it, you need to download a Software Developers Kit (SDK), available at `developer.apple.com/sdk/`.

If you like, you can license QuickTime from Apple and include it on CDs that you create, so your users don't have to download it over the Web. There is currently a free version of the license available, so you can include QuickTime on your CD free of charge. You need to fill out a license agreement; the forms are on the Apple website at `developer.apple.com/mkt/swl/agreements.html`.

For additional licensing details, see Appendix F, "Including QuickTime on Your CD."

▶ Delivery Methods: Disk, Streams, Web Server

You can deliver QuickTime movies to people in three very different ways: as files on a disk or CD; from a Web server; or as real-time streams. You don't necessarily have to choose one method—one of the nice things about QuickTime is that you can mix and match. But it will help you to understand the rest of this book if you know a few things about each method up front.

Local Delivery

One way to deliver QuickTime movies is to put them on a disk of some kind—a CD, a file server, or the viewer's hard disk.

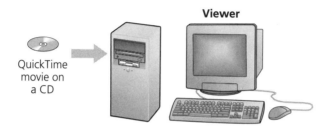

Viewer

QuickTime
movie on
a CD

People typically play these movies by double-clicking them. The operating system knows they're QuickTime movies by their file type or file extension (the file extension for QuickTime movies is .mov). The operating system launches the QuickTime Player application, which plays the movie.

It's also possible to embed QuickTime movies in HTML Web pages and put your website on a disk. People view these local Web pages with their browsers, and the QuickTime movies are played by QuickTime's browser plug-in. The plug-in can also open movies by launching QuickTime Player, as described in "Targeting QuickTime Player" (page 115).

Whether it's on the desktop or in a browser window, when a movie is played from a file on disk, it's called a local movie. This can be a slight misnomer if the movie is on a LAN file server, but the mechanism for getting and playing the movie—file access—is the same.

The big advantage of putting a QuickTime movie on a disk is bandwidth. You can have large-format visuals, high frame rates, and use compressors that give the best possible output. For full-screen movies with CD-quality sound tracks, this is often the way to go.

The obvious *dis*advantage of putting a movie on a disk is the disk itself; either you have to actually send something physical to the user, or the user has to download a large file to a local disk before playing it.

Streaming Server Delivery

Another way to deliver QuickTime movies is from a streaming server using real-time streams. This is often called streaming audio or video.

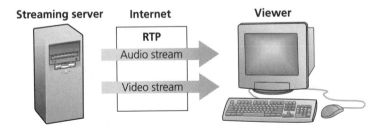

Streams

Streams are what happens when you send a movie across a network and watch it in real time. In other words, if a movie is one minute long, it takes exactly one minute to deliver it over the network—it doesn't go any faster, no matter how quick the network is. It doesn't go any slower, either—if the network connection isn't fast enough, parts of the movie simply don't get through.

Ordinary Web servers are not set up to send real-time streams. To send streams, servers need special software—streaming server software, to be exact. We'll come back to that in a moment.

Because they're sent in real time, streams can originate from a live source, such as a video camera, a microphone, or the audio output of a CD player. Streaming is the only way to send live audio or video transmissions over the Internet in real time.

Streams can also originate from QuickTime movie files on a streaming server, but the audience doesn't download a copy of the file when you stream a movie. The viewer's QuickTime Player or plug-in just displays the data as it arrives, then discards it—it isn't stored locally. Consequently, there is no copy of the movie on the viewer's computer.

Another thing that distinguishes streams from file downloads is the ability to skip around. When you stream a movie file, you don't have to start at the beginning or watch the whole thing. You can stream a clip starting and ending anywhere in the movie. This is really nice for instructional material organized into distinct sections.

Streaming Server

A streaming server is any computer running software that can send streams over a network in real time. There are different protocols for sending real-time streams, each requiring different server software. Real and Windows Media streams, for example, use proprietary schemes that require server software only available from Real or Microsoft, respectively.

QuickTime streaming uses Real-Time Transport Protocol (RTP) and Real-Time Streaming Protocol (RTSP). These are both open standards—not proprietary schemes—so you can send QuickTime streams using server software from several different vendors, including Apple, Real, IBM, Channel Storm, and others. You can even use free open source software. (And if you already have a Real server, you might be surprised to find that it includes a free QuickTime server!)

Apple provides free streaming software bundled with Mac OS X Server. Other companies provide QuickTime server software for Windows, Linux, and various flavors of UNIX. Apple also provides an open source version of the streaming server software at no cost; it's been successfully compiled on a variety of UNIX, Linux, and other platforms, and precompiled binaries are available for Windows and BSD UNIX.

If you want to send streams, but don't have your own server, there are also service providers, such as Bopjet.com, who can host your streaming content, just as there are hosts for ordinary Web pages.

Streaming QuickTime Movies

To stream a QuickTime movie, you first need to save it specifically as a streaming movie, which you can do using QuickTime Player (or other software, such as Cleaner). You then put the movie on a streaming server.

People need the URL of the movie to view it, so you typically embed the URL in a Web page, which we'll discuss in detail shortly.

The URL for a streaming movie uses Real-Time Streaming Protocol (RTSP://). The QuickTime plug-in uses RTSP to request the movie from the streaming server, and the movie is sent to the plug-in using RTP streams.

Note RTSP and RTP are not the same. The movie is *requested* over RTSP. It is *delivered* over RTP.

It sounds complicated, but it really isn't; the Web page lives on a Web server, the streaming movie lives on a streaming server, and the QuickTime plug-in uses the URL from the Web page to get the movie from the streaming server, as shown in the following illustration.

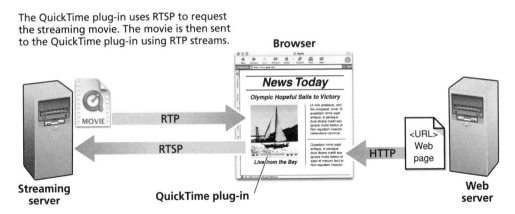

The QuickTime plug-in uses RTSP to request the streaming movie. The movie is then sent to the QuickTime plug-in using RTP streams.

The advantages to streaming are obvious: movies play in real time, you can send live transmissions as well as stored files, and people can skip around without downloading the intervening material. In fact, the movie file is not downloaded to the viewer, making it much harder to copy without your permission.

The disadvantage of streaming is usually lower movie quality. The data rate of your movies *must* be less than the Internet connection speed of your audience, or a streaming movie doesn't play at all. In addition, streaming protocols don't retransmit lost packets; they're just lost. If you're sending streams over a campus or corporate LAN, these aren't serious problems—you have lots of bandwidth and little or no packet loss.

On the Internet, it's another story. Compressing a movie until its data rate is lower than your slowest user's connection speed can dramatically lower its quality. And over the Internet, packet loss is common; some of the data is just not going to get through.

Fortunately, it's possible to compress a movie at different data rates and have QuickTime automatically send the best version for a viewer's connection speed. That way you can provide high-quality movies to people with fast connections and still not leave anyone out. This is explained in Chapter 8, "Alternate Realities: Language, Speed, and Connections."

Finally, real-time streaming is limited to sound, video, text (including hypertext links), and MIDI music. Other media types, such as sprites, VR, or Flash, can't be sent as real-time streams.

Happily, QuickTime lets you mix nonstreaming media with streaming media in the same movie. We'll show you how in Chapter 17, "Mixing It Up: Streaming and Nonstreaming."

Web Server Delivery

So far, we've looked at two ways to deliver multimedia—local files and real-time streams. Most multimedia players force you to choose one or the other—if you want to send Flash or Shockwave, the audience has to wait for it to download; if you want to send Real or Windows Media, you have to accept the lower quality, data loss, and limited media types that go with real-time streams.

QuickTime offers another way. QuickTime allows you to send Fast Start movies over the Internet. These movies are delivered over a network just like Web pages, using HTTP (hyper-text transport protocol). Lost packets are retransmitted, so there is no data loss.

Of course, you could use HTTP (or FTP) to transfer the files, then let people play them locally. But this is something better—Fast Start for the Internet (also called progressive download) lets your audience play the movie *while* it downloads.

A Fast Start movie has the data that QuickTime needs to start it playing at the beginning of the file. Consequently, QuickTime can start to play the movie as soon as the first part of the file has downloaded, typically within a few seconds of starting the transfer. If the Internet connection is faster than the movie's data rate, the movie plays smoothly as it arrives, just like a streaming movie. No waiting.

If the connection isn't quite fast enough to play the movie in real time, there is a delay equal to the difference—in other words, if your one-minute movie takes a minute and five seconds to download, there is a five-second delay before the movie starts playing. Of course, if your one-minute movie takes an *hour* to download, the delay gets pretty serious, but the viewer can play the part that has already arrived at any time, which often helps—especially if your movie opens with something interesting to look at (can you say "text prologue"?).

You still need to compress your movie appropriately for the expected connection speed, but you no longer have to aim at the lowest common denominator—people on slow connections experience a delay, but they're not shut out. And you can create multiple versions for people with different connection speeds.

People normally watch Fast Start movies in a Web browser using the QuickTime plug-in, but it's also possible to play Fast Start movies over the Web using QuickTime Player. You can do this either by entering a URL directly into QuickTime Player, or by putting the right tags in a Web page to launch QuickTime Player, as you'll see in "Targeting QuickTime Player" (page 115).

The big advantage of using a Web server to show your movies is that people can watch them from anywhere, anytime, with minimum effort on your part. You don't have to pay postage to send them a disk, they don't have to wait for the file to download before the show starts, and you don't need a streaming server or any special software. You can put movies in ordinary Web pages and send them to the world.

If your audience has fast enough connections, they can watch the movies in real time. People with slower connections just have to wait a little longer (okay, sometimes a *lot* longer, but that's life on the Internet).

The main limitation of Internet delivery is bandwidth, whether you're streaming or downloading. Uncompressed full-screen movies use millions of *bytes* per second, while most Internet connections are measured in thousands of *bits* per second. Consequently, movies that play smoothly over the Internet tend to be highly compressed, use only part of the screen, and show only a few frames per second. Optimizing a movie to look good, while keeping the data rate low enough for the Internet, is an art.

We'll look closely at that art in "Secrets of the Apple Compressionist" (page 342).

Which Should You Choose?

Depending on what you're trying to accomplish, you may want to deliver your movies as disk files, as real-time streams, or as Fast Start movies over the Web. But QuickTime doesn't force you to choose a single method.

QuickTime movies can be self-contained, but they can also point to data in local files, on Web or FTP servers, or in real-time streams. This lets you combine delivery methods, by including streaming media in a Fast Start movie, for example.

Each method has its strengths, and each calls for different techniques to get the best results. We'll examine these more closely in the course of the book, but here's a general summary:

- Put demanding, high-bandwidth movies on a disk when practical.

- Live events, sensitive material you don't want copied, and long material that viewers will skip around in should go on a streaming server.

- Everything else should be delivered as Fast Start movies over the Internet.

- Most streaming movies can be enhanced by wrapping them in a Fast Start movie to add things that can't be streamed, such as chapter lists and media skins. (Such as *what*, you ask? Hey, we're just getting started.)

Now that you've got the conceptual framework, we're ready to get into the specifics: exactly what you can do and exactly how to do it.

Shall we dance?

First Things First:
Installing QuickTime

Before you can do anything with QuickTime, you need to install it. This chapter explains

- how to install QuickTime from the CD
- how to register and unlock QuickTime Pro
- how to set your Internet connection speed
- how to configure QuickTime Player
- how to get the latest updates over the Internet

As a rule, all this just works. If you have any trouble, see Appendix B, "QuickTime Configuration." It covers

- how and when to adjust the QuickTime settings
- how to configure the QuickTime plug-in
- how to configure your browser

Minimum System Requirements

- **For Windows 98/ME/2000/XP**

  Pentium or compatible processor, 32 MB RAM, SoundBlaster or compatible sound card. Latest version of DirectX recommended.

- **For Mac OS**

  PowerPC processor, 32 MB RAM, Mac OS 8.6 or later. Mac OS X *strongly* recommended (I mean, really, *really* strongly.)

Note If you are running a version of the Mac OS prior to Mac OS X, QuickTime 6.03 will be installed. The minimum system requirement for QuickTime 6.2 is Mac OS X.

▶ Installing QuickTime from the CD

Open the plastic flap in the back of the book using a sharp knife, scissors, your teeth, or an entrenching tool. Just don't scratch the CD, chip your teeth, or cut yourself.

Your QuickTime Pro serial numbers are printed on a slip of paper behind your CD.

Put the CD in your computer. Open the Software folder, then the Quick-Time folder. Double-click the QuickTime Installer.

Apple's installer lets people save time by downloading only the parts of QuickTime that they need. The choices currently are Minimum, Recommended, and Custom.

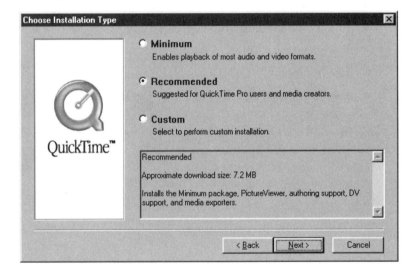

Important Since you're installing QuickTime from a CD, you should do a Custom install. Choose Select All to get absolutely everything. (You need *everything*.)

You can also use the Custom selection to uninstall QuickTime later, if you need to do that at some point.

▶ Registering QuickTime Pro

You'll be prompted to register QuickTime during the installation process. This is where you enter the name and serial number on the card that came with the CD. Entering a valid name and serial number gives you a QuickTime 6 Pro license, which unlocks QuickTime Player's editing, authoring, and enhanced playback features. Enter the name and serial number *exactly* as shown, including all spaces, dashes, letters, and numbers. It's easy to mistake some letters for numbers, and vice versa (0, 5, 6, and 8 look quite a bit like O, S, G, and B in certain fonts).

Note A name and serial number should be printed on the slip of paper behind the CD in this book. Put it somewhere safe. There are two serial numbers: one for Mac OS and one for Windows. Use the one that's appropriate. Enter the name and serial number *exactly as shown* to unlock QuickTime Pro. (You can enter whatever you like as your organization, but the name and serial number *must* be entered as a matched pair.)

The pro version of QuickTime does not require a separate installation. When you enter your name and serial number in the registration window, it unlocks the pro features of QuickTime. It does not change the name of QuickTime Player or change the product name in the About QuickTime window, however. To verify your QuickTime 6 Pro license, choose Registration in your QuickTime Settings control panel. You will see the words "Pro Player Edition" and a version number of 6.0 or higher.

If you don't register QuickTime during the installation, you can do it later through the QuickTime Settings control panel.

Apart from that, installation is a simple matter of clicking OK when prompted, then restarting your computer when installation is complete.

▶ Setting Your Connection Speed

You'll be asked to select a connection speed during installation. This setting tells QuickTime how fast your Internet connection is. Choose the setting closest to your actual connection speed. If your 56K modem typically connects at 29K, for example, choose 28.8K/33.6K.

QuickTime looks at this setting when it plays a movie that has alternate versions compressed at different data rates. It plays the highest-quality version of the movie that will play over the connection chosen here.

Once QuickTime is installed, you can open the QuickTime Settings control panel (it's with the rest of your Windows or Mac OS control panels) to change the speed setting at any time.

If you make a movie that plays different versions depending on the user's connection speed, you can change the setting here to test them all from your machine.

Configuring QuickTime Player

Most of the preferences for QuickTime Player are matters of personal taste, and the defaults are fine, but there's one that you need to set explicitly to do the exercises in this book. You need to tell QuickTime Player to open movies in a new window instead of replacing the contents of the current window. That way you can have multiple movies open at once—a must for cutting and pasting between movies.

To set the Player preferences, launch QuickTime Player. If you're connected to the Internet, the Hot Picks movie will open automatically. Pay no attention (well, gawk if you want to, but that's not why we're here).

For Windows, Mac OS 8, or Mac OS 9, choose the Edit menu, Preferences, Player Preferences. For Mac OS X, choose the QuickTime Player menu, Preferences. Check the "Open movies in new players" box. Click OK.

Well OK, then.

Updating to the Latest Version

The CD in this book contains QuickTime 6.1 for Windows, 6.2 for Mac OS X, and 6.03 for older versions of the Mac OS. Apple regularly improves QuickTime, so you should upgrade to the latest version. Fortunately, upgrading is very easy. In fact, there are four different ways to do it.

On the Mac OS, you can use the Software Update control panel to check for, and download, new system software of all kinds, including QuickTime.

In addition, the QuickTime folder on your hard disk contains a QuickTime Updater program. Double-click the Updater to check for a new version of QuickTime over the Internet and optionally download it.

Alternatively, you can choose Update Existing Software in the Help menu of QuickTime Player. It does the same thing.

Finally, just use QuickTime when you're connected to the Internet. QuickTime will periodically check for updates, notify you if there are any, and offer to get them for you. (There's a good chance that this will happen the first time you run QuickTime Player after installing it from the CD.)

This last method is QuickTime's smart update feature, and it's been around since QuickTime 4. Consequently, anyone who has QuickTime and uses the Internet will probably have a recent version of QuickTime when they visit your website.

Software updates can be small or large. QuickTime has a modular architecture, and the update process will get only the modules that have changed since your current version. People who do a minimum install get an update only for the modules they installed.

Starting with QuickTime 5, the smart update feature has been extended to cover missing components. When someone tries to play a QuickTime movie that requires a component they don't have (perhaps because they did a minimum install), QuickTime tells them that something is missing and offers to get it for them. If they say "yes," QuickTime downloads and installs the missing part. Similarly, if you're using Explorer for Windows and don't have the right ActiveX control, you'll be prompted to get it when you load a Web page that needs it (such as Start.htm on the CD).

Since you just installed everything, your first update will probably be a few megabytes. Fortunately, you've got a thick book to read while it downloads.

Note Some copies of this book may contain later versions of QuickTime, such as QuickTime 6.3 for Windows and Mac OS, on the CD. Whenever possible, the CD will be updated to the latest version of QuickTime for each print run.

Bust a .Mov

By now you have a pretty good idea what QuickTime is, you've installed it, and you're ready—possibly eager—to rock and roll. We'll start with a quick explanation of how multimedia gets delivered over the Internet and how to play a QuickTime movie from a Web page.

Then we'll show you how to import your existing media—still images, sound files, digitized video clips, and so on—into QuickTime movies. This will give you some hands-on experience with the editing features of Quick-Time Player.

You can choose to have QuickTime play most of these files over the Internet either as QuickTime movies or in their native file format (such as JPEG, AIFF, or AVI). We'll show you how to do both, and we'll look at the advantages of importing your media files into QuickTime versus delivering them as is.

Finally, we'll show you how to save QuickTime movies so they're self-contained, cross-platform, and ready for Internet delivery.

▶ Multimedia and the Web

Browsers come with a built-in ability to display styled text and some types of graphic images, such as GIF and JPEG. To play other kinds of media, such as movies, MP3, MIDI, or virtual reality, browsers use plug-ins.

Browsers and MIME Types

When a browser encounters a file type that it can't display, it looks for an application or plug-in that handles that type.

But how does a browser know what type of file it has encountered? Well, if the browser gets the file over the Web, it asks the Web server, and the Web server replies with a header that contains the file type (such as "text/html" or "video/quicktime").

Okay, so how does the Web server know the file type? The Web server has a look-up table that associates file types with file extensions, so it knows that .mov files are QuickTime movies, .doc files are Microsoft Word documents, and .mp3 files are MPEG-1, layer 3 audio. In Internet parlance, this is called the file's MIME type (Multi-purpose Internet Mail Extension, in case you wondered).

The point is, the Web server identifies files by their file extensions, so it's critical that you use the right file extension when you put a multimedia file on a Web server. For a QuickTime movie, the right extension is .mov.

In some cases, you can also specify a file's MIME type directly in your HTML, and that's generally a good idea. If the Web server contradicts you, however, the browser may choose to believe the server instead of your HTML, so you definitely want the Web server on your side.

If there is no entry in the look-up table for a particular file extension, the Web server usually assumes it's a text file and tells the browser to display it as text—which can lead to some very odd-looking Web pages. If your movies display as garbled text, that may be the problem.

Note As new media types are invented, a system administrator needs to make new entries in the Web server's look-up table. Many system administrators have never done this, however, because new Web servers comes with the current MIME types already in their look-up tables. But the tables *are* extensible, and webmasters can add support for new types at any time. For details, see Chapter 6, "What Webmasters Need to Know."

Browsers have similar look-up tables of their own, so they know how to deal with files on local disks.

When you install a new browser plug-in, it adds the MIME types and file extensions it supports to the browser's look-up table and registers itself as the plug-in for those types. That's how browsers know what plug-in to use for a particular file type.

Unfortunately, it's possible for more than one plug-in or application to register for the same MIME type, and it's difficult or impossible for you to know which one will be called when you create a Web page. Lots of different plug-ins can play MP3 or AIFF files, for example.

As a Web author, this creates a problem for you: you don't know what plug-in or application will be used, how much space it needs on the page (if any), what it looks like, or what its capabilities are. Can it autoplay? Will it play the file as it downloads? Can you set the default volume or make it loop? Is it displaying an advertisement for someone else's product?

To see this for yourself, open the Italy1 folder, inside the Projects folder on your CD. Double-click the file Italy.mp3, or drag it onto your browser. The file may be played by QuickTime, Windows Media Player, Music Matchbox, iTunes, or something else. It's really impossible to predict. The only thing you know for sure is that it won't be consistent. It will work well on some computers, badly or not at all on others. When you care how your website looks and behaves, this is really unacceptable.

So, how can you control which plug-in or application gets used for your media? You have to talk to the browser using HTML, specifically the <EMBED> tag.

Note There's also an <OBJECT> tag, which does pretty much the same thing as the <EMBED> tag—we'll examine both in the next chapter.

Unfortunately, there is no way to directly specify in the <EMBED> tag that a particular plug-in should be used to play a file. All you can do is specify a file with a particular MIME type. The browser can pick any plug-in or application that says it handles that type. To target a particular plug-in, you have to specify a file whose type is registered *only* by that plug-in.

That's the secret.

Fortunately, there are three file types that only QuickTime can play— QuickTime movie files (.mov), QuickTime image files (.qtif), and MacPaint files (.pntg). If you pass any of these files to a browser using the <EMBED> tag, the browser should always open them with the QuickTime plug-in.

Note Some older versions of Windows Media Player registered for the .mov file type. This caused problems at the time and required cumbersome workarounds. Recent versions of WMP no longer do this, however, and versions 4 and later of QuickTime automatically correct it. The problem, commonly called "media hijacking," appears to have gone away, at least for now.

Try this. Go back to the Italy.mp3 file in the Italy1 folder. This time, open the file in QuickTime Player and Save As Italymp3.mov on your hard disk. Double-click the new .mov file, or drag it onto a browser. It now plays using QuickTime. Every time.

That means you know exactly how your Web page will look and behave when you pass your media as .mov files. What's more, you can control what QuickTime does with files to a remarkable degree by passing commands directly to QuickTime from your HTML.

We'll get into the details in the next two chapters, but here's a short sample that shows how to play a QuickTime movie from a Web page. It works equally well with all the major browsers (and most of the minor ones) on Mac and Windows, as long as the user has QuickTime installed.

```
<EMBED SRC="My.mov" height=16 width=320
  type="video/quicktime" />
```

Pretty simple, no? You give the name of the source file, the height and width of the user interface, and the MIME type. To see this work, drag the file `PlayMovie.html` from the Italy1 folder onto your hard disk—put it in the same folder as `Italymp3.mov`—then open the Web page using your browser. It should load the `Italymp3.mov` file and display a simple audio controller 16 pixels tall.

Note If you didn't open `Italy.mp3` in QuickTime Player, and saved it to your hard disk as `Italymp3.mov`, you need to do it now, so that `PlayMovie.html` will work.

Once you've convinced the browser to open the QuickTime plug-in, you can talk directly to the plug-in from your HTML. And that opens a world of possibilities.

On the way to exploring those possibilities, you should learn how to create QuickTime movies from existing files on your hard disk: JPEG images, MP3 audio files—that sort of thing.

▶ Importing Media into QuickTime

To make a QuickTime movie from an existing media file, open the file with QuickTime Player. If it opens and plays, you can deliver it as a QuickTime movie.

Note You can open most files in QuickTime Player by choosing Open Movie from the File menu. For text files or PICT images, choose Import.

As you highlight files in the Open File dialog box, the confirmation button reads either Open, Convert, or Convert... (with three dots).

- If the button reads Open, the file is already a QuickTime movie.
- If the button reads Convert, QuickTime can create a movie that points to data in the highlighted file, or create a self-contained movie that cop-

ies the data without altering it. The QuickTime plug-in can play these files over the Internet in their native file format.

- If the button reads Convert... , QuickTime needs to create a new file in order to make a movie from the data in the highlighted file. You'll be prompted to save the converted file with a new name.

If you opened the original file using Open or Convert, choose Save As (not Save) from the File menu.

At this point, no matter how you opened the media file, you'll see the Save File dialog box shown in the following illustration.

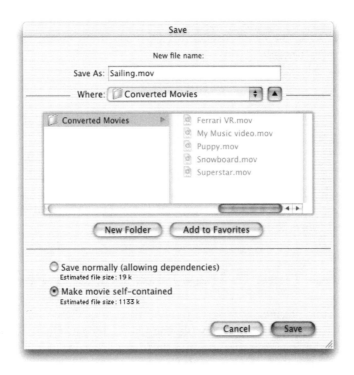

Click the "Make movie self-contained" button. Choose a filename with the .mov extension so your Web server knows that it's a QuickTime movie.

You now have a QuickTime movie that contains a copy of the data in your original file. Note that the data in your file has not been altered or recompressed. If your file was an .mp3, .mp4, or .jpg, for example, the audio and video data are unchanged—there is no loss of quality or information. QuickTime has simply copied the data into a movie file and created a movie header that describes it.

What's the difference between your original file and the new Quick-Time movie file? The QuickTime file has a movie header that adds a few Kbytes to the file size, and the file opens in QuickTime—in the QuickTime Player application when double-clicked, and in the QuickTime plug-in when embedded in a Web page.

In addition, now that your file is a QuickTime movie, you can edit it in QuickTime Player—add new tracks to it, such as your logo and a link to your website, combine it with other media files, or compress it using any of QuickTime's many codecs. We'll explore these options throughout the book. Here's a quick example to get you started.

Example   Adding a background image to an audio file

1. Use QuickTime Player to open the file `Italy01.jpg` (in the Italy1 folder in the Projects folder).

    Copy (Edit menu). Close (don't save).

2. Now open `Italy.mp3` in QuickTime Player.

    Select All (Edit menu). Add Scaled (Edit menu).

3. Save As `Italy2mp3.mov` (self-contained).

Congratulations. You've just added a JPEG background image to an MP3 file and saved them as a QuickTime movie. Double-click the movie, or drag it onto a browser, and you'll see QuickTime display the image while it plays the audio.

▶ Using QuickTime to Play Files in Other Formats

Once you convince a browser to open the QuickTime plug-in, you can ask QuickTime to play a file—any file you like, as long as QuickTime can play it.

And there are good reasons to do this. For example, you might want to deliver MP3 downloads in .mp3 file format, so people can easily transfer them to portable MP3 players. But you might also want to use the Quick-Time plug-in to play the files over the Web, because QuickTime can play the MP3 file *while* it downloads—and because you want some control over your Web page: what the audio controller looks like, how much space it takes up, whether the music should autoplay or loop, and so on.

So you need to get the browser to load the QuickTime plug-in, then tell QuickTime to play the MP3 file.

Here's how:

1. Start with a small file in a format that only QuickTime handles. Feel free to use `Tiny.mov`, `Tiny.pntg`, or `Tiny.qtif` from the Bustamov or Italy1 folder on the CD.

2. Embed this file in your Web page. If you use `Tiny.mov`, the HTML starts out looking like this:

```
<EMBED SRC="Tiny.mov" TYPE="video/quicktime"
  HEIGHT="16" WIDTH="200" />
```

When a browser reads this `<EMBED>` tag, it sees that a QuickTime movie is being loaded and passes it to the QuickTime plug-in.

3. Now add a line to your `<EMBED>` tag with the QTSRC parameter, to tell the QuickTime plug-in which file you *really* want to play, so your tag looks like this:

```
<EMBED SRC="Tiny.mov" TYPE="video/quicktime"
  HEIGHT="16" WIDTH="200"
  QTSRC="Italy1.mp3" />
```

The QuickTime plug-in sees that you really want to play `Italy1.mp3`, not `Tiny.mov`, so it loads `Italy1.mp3` from the Web server (or in this case, the CD) and plays it. The browser doesn't decide which plug-in gets the MP3 file—you do. To see this in action, drag the file `Playmp3.html` (in the Italy1 folder) onto your browser.

Important   The SRC and TYPE parameters must specify a file type that only QuickTime handles. The SRC file must be a real file of the type you specify in the TYPE parameter. Some file servers, and some browsers, verify the SRC file's existence or type. Even though the file is not played by QuickTime, it is downloaded by the browser (so keep it small).

As you would expect, this technique works with any file type that QuickTime can play, including SMIL `.smil` files, Flash `.swf` files, and MPEG-4 `.mp4` files. You can even use QTSRC to play a QuickTime movie.

Streaming QuickTime movies are an example of movies you might want to specify using QTSRC. Streaming movies use the RTSP protocol, so they usually have a URL that begins with RTSP://. The viewer's browser might not know what to do with a URL that starts with RTSP—or it might send RTSP URLs to RealPlayer or Windows Media Player by default—but the browser will happily invoke the QuickTime plug-in to play `Tiny.mov` or `Tiny.qtif`, and QuickTime will happily play the streaming movie—just set QTSRC equal to the streaming URL.

This technique can even be used to prevent other plug-ins from playing QuickTime movies—use a `.qtif` or `.pntg` file as the SRC, and pass the `.mov` file in QTSRC. This is not generally something you need to worry about, however.

Note If you're concerned about another plug-in taking over the .mov file type, you can use QTSRC to embed all your multimedia files, whether you've converted them to QuickTime movies or not. Using a QuickTime image file or a MacPaint file in the SRC parameter *always* causes the browser to load the QuickTime plug-in, if QuickTime is installed.

By the way, don't worry about what the SRC file looks like when you use QTSRC—the browser won't load the SRC file unless QuickTime is installed, and QuickTime won't show the SRC file if there is a QTSRC specified, so no one will see the SRC file. The browser will download the SRC file though, so make sure the file actually exists and is a type that only QuickTime can play. It's also important to use a small file—the smaller the better.

▶ When To .Mov It

You can make a browser use the QuickTime plug-in either by importing your media into QuickTime movies or by using the QTSRC parameter. Both methods give you control when embedding files that multiple plug-ins can handle.

So the real question is, when should you import your media into a QuickTime movie and when should you leave it in its native format?

In general, you probably want to provide a file in its native format if you want to make it portable to other software or external devices. You might want your audience to be able to transfer a file to their MP3 or MP4 player, for example, or a device that can play WAV files but not QuickTime movies. If your final destination is not QuickTime Player or the QuickTime plug-in, keep the file in its native format and use QTSRC to have QuickTime play it as it downloads.

The main advantage to delivering your files as QuickTime movies is that you can edit them and enhance them in significant ways. For example, it's easy to add an image to an MP3 file, as you saw in "Example: Adding a background image to an audio file" (page 30). You can just as easily add a URL. Think about that—what if all your MP3 files displayed an image of the artist, the words "Don't steal music," and a clickable link to buy the music? Would file swapping eventually become a way to *enhance* music sales, the way radio airplay does now? Maybe not, but it's an interesting possibility.

With QuickTime, there are *lots* of possibilities.

▶ Saving Movies

So far, you've been given a few examples that instructed you to "Save As (self-contained)," without any explanation of what the options were. Let's rectify that now. How you save a movie can make a big difference in what gets saved. The differences can be subtle, but they can also be radical—particularly in the movie's file size and behavior over the Internet. It's important to choose the right method for your needs.

There are three ways to save a movie in QuickTime Player:

- Save
- Save As (self-contained)
- Save As (allowing dependencies)

The obvious difference between Save and Save As, of course, is that Save overwrites the current movie file, while Save As creates a new file.

Note If you're creating a new movie—by importing media from another format, for example—there *is* no existing movie file to overwrite, so Save does the same thing as Save As: it creates a new file.

Save As

When you choose Save As (or save a movie for the first time), QuickTime creates a Fast Start movie file that can play as it downloads over a network. You have the choice of making the movie self-contained or allowing dependencies.

Making the movie self-contained creates a file with a movie header at the beginning, followed by copies of all the sample data used in the movie—video frames, sound samples, and so on—interleaved for smooth delivery. Everything you need is in one file. This is generally how you want to save a QuickTime movie. The file can be extremely large, as it contains all the audio, video, VR, or other media that it needs.

Allowing dependencies, on the other hand, creates a very small file that contains only the movie header. This movie header contains references to the media samples, but the new movie file contains no sample data itself. When the movie is opened, it resolves the references and locates the sample data. It can't play unless it can resolve the references and read the data from its original source, wherever that may be.

The big difference here is that self-contained movies copy the data they need into the movie file, while movies with dependencies have references to data that exists somewhere else.

Let's see how this works in practice.

1. Launch QuickTime Player and open the file Italy.mp3 (in the Italy1 folder). Select All. Copy.

2. Paste, Paste, Paste (choose Paste in the Edit menu—or press the key equivalent—three times).

3. Save to your hard disk as Small3.mov. Allow dependencies.

4. Save As to your hard disk as Big3.mov. Make the movie self-contained.

Play the movies. They both play the same tune three times. Check the file sizes. Small3.mov is only a few kilobytes, much smaller than Italy.mp3. Big3.mov, on the other hand, is just over three times the size of Italy.mp3 because it contains three copies of the data. Eject the CD and try to play Small3.mov. It should fail. Big3.mov should still play just fine, however.

Both kinds of movies can play as they download over a network, but self-contained files often play more smoothly because the media data is interleaved for playback.

Note This is most noticeable when a movie depends on data in more than one file, or when a movie presents data in a sequence other than the original file's storage order.

There's only one kind of self-contained movie file, but files with dependencies come in different flavors. How QuickTime resolves a reference depends on the *kind* of reference. Three common ways to create a reference to sample data are by opening a local file, opening the URL of a file, or opening the URL of a stream.

Local File References

When you save a movie that's dependent on data in a local file, QuickTime typically saves a reference to the full path and filename of the data file, along with the location where each sample is stored within that file.

If you move either the data file or the movie file (or both), the path to the data generally changes. QuickTime will attempt to fix this by looking for the data file, by name, in the directory that contains the movie file. If this fails, the user may be asked whether to abort or try to help locate the missing file.

If the data file can be found, but has been edited in a way that changes the location of any sample, the results are unpredictable—what happens when you attempt to interpret a series of random bytes as audio, or video, or a URL? Something bad, that's for sure.

Generally speaking, you don't want any of this to happen, so you don't want to create a movie with local file dependencies for delivery over the Internet.

Still, there are reasons to save this kind of movie. You can make a large number of different movies from a single set of data—various editing "cuts" of the same film, for example—without duplicating the source material. Or, if you have several gigabytes of MP3 files that you want to deliver as QuickTime movies, you might prefer movie files that take up only a few kilobytes each, rather than doubling your needed disk storage by making the movie files self-contained.

You *can* deliver this kind of movie over the Internet, but there are extra housekeeping chores involved and it's pretty easy to screw it up. Use this technique only if you have a good reason.

If you do deploy this kind of movie over the Web, here are some tips to make things simpler and more reliable:

- Keep the movie file in the same directory as all of its data files.

- Don't mix upper- and lowercase letters in file or directory names (avoid names like Italy.mp3—use italy.mp3 instead). I broke this rule because I made the files as examples for a book—it was more important to make filenames easy to read by people than easy to maintain.

- If any data file has a modification time or date later than the movie file that depends on it, discard the dependent movie and create a new one. The data is probably not where the movie thinks it is.

URL File References

When you choose Open URL from QuickTime Player's File menu, you can enter the URL of a media file anywhere on the Internet or local IP network, then save it as a movie with dependencies; this creates a movie file with a URL pointing to the data, instead of a local path and filename.

This can be quite handy, especially for Internet movie delivery. The movie file is small and can be moved freely without invalidating the URL. It's much less fragile than a movie with local file dependencies.

The movie file itself can be copied and shared without copying the data it depends on, which remains on the server the URL points to. This leaves you, the author or distributor, in control—you can remove the data, limit access to it by password, or use common network tools to monitor who watches it and when.

Important To create a URL data reference, be sure the data file is available *only* through the URL— if the Web server is also on your local network, and there is a valid path to the data file using the local file system, you may get a file reference instead of a URL reference.

Streaming URLs

If you open a stream in QuickTime Player, any movie you save will have a URL data reference to the stream. This is a great way to create a movie that mixes streams with other kinds of media—something we'll spend a whole chapter on later (see Chapter 17, "Mixing It Up: Streaming and Non-streaming.")

Well, that covers Save As. Now, what about plain old Save?

Save

When you choose Save from QuickTime Player's File menu, QuickTime writes a new movie header to the existing movie file. It does not copy or delete any sample data. This can have some surprising results, depending on the movie file.

Note If there is no open movie file, QuickTime does a Save As—described in "Save As" (page 33).

Recall that when you create a movie allowing dependencies, you create a file with no sample data, just a movie header. If you open this movie, make changes, and Save, the movie header is overwritten. Pretty much what you'd expect.

But if you open a *self-contained* file, make changes, and Save, things get a lot more interesting:

- If you delete material from the movie, the file doesn't get any smaller, because no sample data is deleted. If the new movie header is longer than the original, the file may actually get bigger.

- If you add material from another source, your movie is no longer self-contained. It's partly self-contained, but it also has dependencies. Woo-hoo!

- If you copy material that's in the movie file already, the file is still self-contained, but it doesn't get much bigger. The copies are just references to data inside the file, and you can have multiple references to the same data.

- Recall that a self-contained movie has a header followed by sample data. If you make changes that cause the movie header to become larger, and it no longer fits in front of the media data, the movie header is appended to the end of the file. This is the kicker. The movie header is stored at the front of the file so QuickTime knows what to do with the data that follows. If the header is at the end of the file, QuickTime can't play the file while it downloads over a network. It doesn't know if the file contains audio, video, a mixture, or something else, until the header arrives at the end of the file.

This may all sound pretty confusing, so let's try some concrete examples. Use QuickTime Player to open Italy.mp3 again. This time save it as a self-contained movie named Big1.mov.

Notice that you now have a movie file slightly larger than Italy.mp3. Use your file system to make a copy of the file and name it Slow3.mov. Open the new file (Slow3.mov), Select All, Copy. Paste, Paste, Paste. Save.

Check the file size. It's only slightly larger than Big1.mov, even though it plays the tune three times and is self-contained. Compare that with Big3.mov, the self-contained movie with three copies of the data. Three times the music, and about the same file size. Cool.

Now for the bad news. If you put Slow3.mov on a Web server, it won't play as it downloads. Adding those copies made the movie header bigger, and the new version didn't fit at the front of the file, so QuickTime put it at the end.

Ready to get really crazy? Open Slow3.mov and Save As Fast3.mov, allowing dependencies. You now have a Fast Start movie that depends on a slow-start movie. If you put Fast3.mov and Slow3.mov in the same folder on a Web server, Fast3.mov will play while it downloads data from Slow3.mov. If you ever get in a jam by Saving a movie (instead of Saving As), and suddenly people are looking at the QuickTime logo while the file downloads, instead of watching the movie as it arrives over the network, this is a quick fix.

Not that you'll ever need it, of course. You can just replace the glitched movie. Because you always back up your files, and you never throw away the original source material. Right?

Right.

Note Some Macintosh files can have both a data fork and a resource fork, but Windows and UNIX files don't have resource forks. In the ancient days of QuickTime 1.0, the header data for a movie was stored in the movie file's resource fork. Before you could put a movie on a UNIX Web server or a Windows CD, you had to move everything into the data fork. There was a utility program named `FlattenMoov` that did this, so using it was often called "flattening" a movie. QuickTime now stores the movie header in the data fork by default, so movies no longer need to be flattened in this sense. It's history.

What's in a Name?

On your computer, a file can probably have blank spaces or characters other than numbers and letters in its name. But a movie intended for the Web must have a name that doesn't confuse the Web server's file system, the viewer's file system, or any browsers.

For example, a movie named `My Movie` cannot be used on most Web servers, and a link to `<A HREF="My Movie">` will fail on a variety of browsers and operating systems. One problem is the blank space; another is the lack of a file extension. Use `MyMovie.mov` instead, or better still `mymovie.mov`.

Your computer may not be case-sensitive—you can name a file `MyMovie.Mov` and link to it with `<A HREF="mymovie.mov">`. This works fine locally, but the link will fail if the movie is put on a disk that uses the case-sensitive UFS file system, which is what most Web servers use.

Here are some useful rules for naming movies:

- Use a short name and a three-letter file extension separated by a period; for example: `MyMovie.mov`.

- Use lowercase `.mov` for the file extension.

- Use only *one* period (`.`) in the filename, just before the file extension.

- Use only letters (a–z) and numbers (0–9) in the actual name.

- Never begin a filename with a number; use `Movie1.mov` rather than `1Movie.mov`.

- Never, never, include a blank space, a colon (`:`), a vertical bar (`|`), a forward slash (`/`), or a backslash (`\`) in a filename. These characters have special meaning to some operating systems.

- If you capitalize any letters in the filename, be sure all links to the movie use *exactly the same capitalization*. `MyMovie.mov` is not equal to `mymovie.mov`. It may work on your computer, then fail when you upload the files to your Web server.

Settings You Can Save

Some of the user settings that you can choose in QuickTime Player's Movie menu are saved along with the movie. You can use these settings to control the way a movie is displayed when it's played in QuickTime Player (you'll use other techniques to control the QuickTime plug-in, with the following two exceptions).

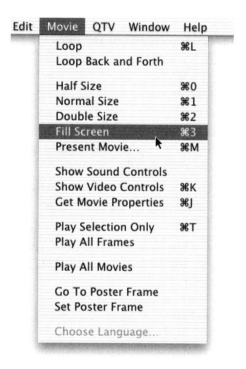

The following two settings are applied whether a movie is played in the QuickTime plug-in *or* QuickTime Player:

- **Half Size**—movie plays at half its normal height and width. The data rate of the movie is unchanged.

- **Double Size**—movie plays at twice its normal height and width. For movies compressed with the Sorenson 3, MPEG-4, or H.263 video codecs, this can be a good way to increase the display size of the movie without increasing its data rate or file size.

The Half Size and Double Size settings affect movie playback in the plug-in, but the plug-in gets its display area from the browser, so be sure to allocate the right amount of space in the HEIGHT and WIDTH parameters for a half-size or double-size movie. The controller size doesn't change, so the correct height is (MovieHeight x Size) + 16. Don't just double the old height.

Note New in QuickTime 6.1, "Full Screen" replaces the old "Fill Screen." The movie plays scaled up to fill the screen without changing its aspect ratio. The screen resolution is *not* changed. This is not a setting that can be saved. To create a QuickTime movie that plays in full-screen mode by default, see "Full-Screen Movies" (page 106).

The following settings are applied *only* if the movie is played in Quick-Time Player:

- **Loop**—when the movie reaches the end, it starts over again in a continuous loop.

- **Loop Back and Forth**—when the movie reaches the end, it plays backward to the beginning; when it reaches the beginning, it plays forward again, playing back and forth endlessly.

- **Play Selection Only**—only the part of the movie selected in the control bar plays; if either kind of looping is also set, the selection loops instead of the whole movie.

- **Play All Frames**—every video frame is displayed, no matter how long it takes; QuickTime will not drop frames if it gets behind. Audio is muted when this is selected.

Tip To make a QuickTime movie autoplay even when it's launched in QuickTime Player (equivalent to AUTOPLAY="True" for the plug-in), open the Properties window (Get Movie Properties), choose Auto Play from the right pop-up menu, and click the checkbox. This setting is saved with the movie.

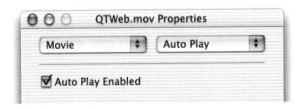

And that should be all you need—probably more than you need—to know about choosing plug-ins, importing media into QuickTime, and saving movies. Don't worry if your head is spinning a little—you can always refer back to this stuff if you need to.

Basic Training: Putting QuickTime in a Web Page

The most fundamental part of using QuickTime on the Web is putting QuickTime movies in a Web page. You've already seen how to make this work when QuickTime is installed on the viewer's computer. This chapter will show you how to make it work whether QuickTime is installed or not. In the next chapter, we'll look at ways to achieve striking effects by combining QuickTime and HTML. Later in the book, we'll look at ways to create radically different kinds of QuickTime movies and deliver them over the Web. All these things will draw on the basic skills covered in this chapter: getting a QuickTime movie into a user's computer through a Web page in a way that's reliable, attractive, and flexible.

This chapter covers five basic topics:

- adding a working Get QuickTime button to your Web page
- embedding a QuickTime movie with the <EMBED> tag
- adding the <OBJECT> tag for ActiveX
- using clickable posters to launch movies
- opening movies using a hypertext link (the <A HREF> tag)

▶ "Get QuickTime" Button

The easiest and friendliest way to let your audience know that they need QuickTime is to simply say, "You need QuickTime to see this. It's a free download. Click here to get it," and provide a clickable link to the Quick-Time download site.

There are ways to detect whether or not your visitors have QuickTime and, if they don't, either prompt them to download it or take them to an alternate Web page. We'll cover a few such methods in detail, but a Get QuickTime button is a good fallback no matter what else you do. Clever is good. Clever with a simple, sturdy backup is better.

Apple provides a GIF image that you can use as a button. It's in the Basic folder of the CD as getquicktime.gif.

Link it into your Web page like this:

```
<A HREF="http://www.apple.com/quicktime/download/">
<IMG SRC="getquicktime.gif" WIDTH="88" HEIGHT="31"
   BORDER="0" ALT="Get QuickTime (free download)"></A>
```

You can cut and paste this HTML directly from the file GetQT.txt, also in the Basic folder of the CD. The GIF needs to be in the same folder as the Web page to work exactly as shown.

If the GIF is in a different folder from your Web page, include the relative path to it in the SRC parameter. For example:

```
IMG SRC="../Images/getquicktime.gif"
```

This is so simple it would be silly *not* to do it.

Embedding with the <EMBED> Tag

The primary way to deliver QuickTime content over the Internet is to embed it in a Web page with the <EMBED> tag. This works with essentially all of the current browsers and operating systems, and it gives you near-total control over the appearance of the page and the behavior of the QuickTime plug-in.

The following illustration shows an example of a movie embedded in a Web page (Embed.htm in the Basic folder of the CD). Embedding the movie allows you to specify the movie's position on the Web page, and the Web page itself gives you control over the images, text, and links that surround the movie. Generally speaking, this gives you a lot more creative control than a typical player application does.

The <EMBED> tag can be used anywhere in a Web page. It's similar to the <IMG> tag—it takes a SRC parameter, which specifies what to display, as well as HEIGHT and WIDTH parameters, which tell the browser how much space to give it on the page. There are a few optional parameters you can add to control the browser in other ways. In addition, the <EMBED> tag lets you pass parameters directly to the QuickTime plug-in, and that permits all kinds of interesting things.

Basic <EMBED> Parameters

The browser understands several <EMBED> tag parameters, but most of them aren't needed. You can generally get by with a simple

```
<EMBED SRC="MyMovie.mov" WIDTH="320" HEIGHT="256">
```

replacing MyMovie.mov with the name of your movie, and setting HEIGHT and WIDTH to the size of your movie (in pixels).

Important   Add 16 to the height of the movie to allow room for the QuickTime movie controller.

Two other <EMBED> parameters you should use are PLUGINSPAGE, which should point to the QuickTime download page, and TYPE, which should be set to "video/quicktime" for movie files. Another frequently used parameter is HIDDEN, which you can use for background sounds.

Let's look at the basic <EMBED> parameters more closely.

SRC

The SRC parameter tells the browser what file to load. If the movie is in the same folder as the Web page, set the SRC parameter to the movie's filename:

```
<EMBED SRC="MyMovie.mov" WIDTH="320" HEIGHT="256" />
```

If the movie is in a different folder, include the relative path to the movie as well:

```
<EMBED SRC="../Movies/MyMovie.mov" WIDTH="320"
  HEIGHT="256">
```

Alternatively, you can include the full URL of the movie:

```
<EMBED
  SRC="http://www.myisp.com/mystuff/movies/MyMovie.mov"
  WIDTH="320" HEIGHT="256" />
```

Tip It's generally best to use a relative URL because it makes your website more portable.

HEIGHT and WIDTH

The HEIGHT and WIDTH parameters tell the browser how much space to allocate on the Web page for QuickTime. Set them to the size of the movie in pixels.

Important Add 16 to the height of a movie to make room for the controller. For example, set HEIGHT="256" for a movie 240 pixels high:

```
<EMBED SRC="MyMovie.mov" WIDTH="320" HEIGHT="256" />
```

For a sound-only movie, use a height of 16 for the controller and any width that looks good on your Web page. A WIDTH of 180 works well for most pages. (If you set the HEIGHT and WIDTH both to 16 for a sound-only movie, the controller is minimized to a single Play/Pause button.)

```
<EMBED SRC="Sound.mov" WIDTH="180" HEIGHT="16">
```

Important Never set `HEIGHT` or `WIDTH` to less than 2, even if the movie is hidden. It can trigger a bug in some browsers.

Tip To find the height and width of a QuickTime movie, open the movie using QuickTime Player. Choose Show Movie Info from the Window menu. This opens an Info window. The size of the movie is shown as Width x Height.

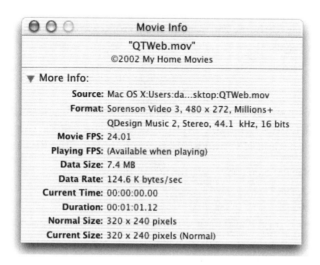

In this illustration the movie is 240 pixels high, so set the `HEIGHT` parameter to 256 to allow space for the controller:

```
<EMBED SRC="QTWeb.mov" WIDTH="320" HEIGHT="256" />
```

PLUGINSPAGE

Use the `PLUGINSPAGE` parameter to direct people to the QuickTime download site if they don't have the QuickTime plug-in.

```
<EMBED SRC="MyMovie.mov" WIDTH="320" HEIGHT="256"
  PLUGINSPAGE="http://www.apple.com/quicktime/download" />
```

TYPE

Use the `TYPE` parameter to tell the browser the MIME type of your file. For QuickTime movies (`.mov` files) this should be `"video/quicktime"`.

If your movie is sent from a Web server that doesn't correctly identify .mov files as QuickTime movies, this parameter can help the browser do the right thing. In your HTML, the TYPE parameter looks like this:

```
<EMBED SRC="MyMovie.mov" WIDTH="320" HEIGHT="256"
  TYPE="video/quicktime"
  PLUGINSPAGE="http://www.apple.com/quicktime/download" />
```

For brevity and easier reading, we'll leave the PLUGINSPAGE and TYPE parameters out of the examples in this book, unless we want to draw special attention to them. But it's a Really Good Idea to include them in all of your Web pages.

HIDDEN

The HIDDEN parameter is used to hide the movie. Its default is False, so if you want QuickTime to play a sound in the background, set HIDDEN= "True". Set both HEIGHT and WIDTH to 2 when using the HIDDEN parameter:

```
<EMBED SRC="BgSound.mov" WIDTH="2" HEIGHT="2"
  HIDDEN="True" />
```

Important Some browsers crash if HEIGHT or WIDTH is less than 2, so that's the minimum safe size.

Since the movie is hidden, you also need to set some parameters for the QuickTime plug-in. Just add them to the <EMBED> tag; the browser ignores any tags it doesn't understand, and the tags are passed to the plug-in. You need to pass AUTOPLAY="True" and CONTROLLER="False" to the plug-in, so the movie plays automatically without a controller:

```
<EMBED SRC="BgSound.mov" WIDTH="2" HEIGHT="2"
  HIDDEN="True" CONTROLLER="False" AUTOPLAY="True">
```

Tip Some versions of Netscape browsers for Windows don't give any time to hidden movies. If it's crucial that your background sound play in Netscape 6 for Windows, for example, don't use the HIDDEN parameter. If you set the height and width to 2 x 2 pixels and embed the movie at the end of a sentence, it will generally pass for a period (.) at the end of the text.

Those are the basic <EMBED> parameters for the browser, plus a couple for the plug-in. Now let's look at the rest of the browser parameters.

Full List of Browser <EMBED> Parameters

- SRC="[*path/*]Filename"

  Specifies the name of the movie. Just use the filename if the movie and the Web page are in the same folder. Otherwise, include the relative path or the full URL.

- HEIGHT="*Height*"

  Sets the vertical space on the page allotted to the plug-in. Use the height of the movie in pixels, plus 16 for the controller.

- WIDTH="*Width*"

  Sets the horizontal space on the page allotted to the plug-in. Use the movie width in pixels, or any width you like for a sound-only movie.

Important Never set HEIGHT or WIDTH to a value less than 2.

- HIDDEN="True" | "False"

  If "True", the plug-in isn't displayed; use this for invisible background sound. (You'll also need to set some plug-in parameters to make the sound play without a controller.) Some versions of Netscape don't play embedded sounds if they are hidden. One workaround is to leave a 2 x 2 pixel artifact, disguised as a period at the end of a sentence.

- PLUGINSPAGE="http://www.apple.com/quicktime/download/"

  Specifies where to get the plug-in if the user doesn't have it. Very useful.

- TYPE="*MIMEtype*"

  Specifies the MIME type of the file (such as video/quicktime or image/x-quicktime). The MIME type is normally supplied by the Web server or implied by the file extension and doesn't need to be specified. Specify the MIME type if you're not certain that your Web server will supply it. It couldn't hurt.

Tip If you specify a QuickTime image file (.qti or .qtif) in the SRC parameter, set TYPE="image/x-quicktime". For a MacPaint image (.pntg), set TYPE="image/x-macpaint".

- ALIGN="Left" | "Right" | "Top" | "Bottom"

  Sets text alignment on the page with respect to the plug-in area.

  Use of this parameter is *not* recommended.

Some people have reported that their browsers do not reliably display media when the ALIGN parameter is used in the <EMBED> tag. Its use is *not* recommended.

- BORDER="*BorderWidth*"

  Draws a border around the plug-in, *BorderWidth* pixels wide.

- FRAMEBORDER="Yes" | "No"

  Specifies a border or no border (default).

- HSPACE="*HorizMargin*"

  Sets the margin, in pixels, to the left and right of the plug-in.

- VSPACE="*VertMargin*"

  Sets the margin, in pixels, above and below the plug-in.

- NAME="*ObjectName*"

  Specifies the name of the object loaded by the plug-in. This is only for JavaScript to use. (Don't confuse this with QuickTime's MOVIENAME parameter.)

- CACHE="True" | "False"

  Turns disk caching on or off for this movie (in some Netscape browsers).

- PALETTE="Foreground" | "Background"

  For Windows computers, tells the plug-in to use the foreground palette or background palette. Default is the background palette.

That's pretty much all there is to know about using the <EMBED> tag to talk to a browser. Mind you, we haven't scratched the surface of what you can make QuickTime do using the <EMBED> tag—that fills the whole next chapter.

▶ Adding the <OBJECT> Tag

The <OBJECT> tag takes care of two shortcomings of the <EMBED> tag. The most serious problem is that recent versions of Internet Explorer for Windows (versions 5.5 SP2 and later) ignore the PLUGINSPAGE parameter inside the <EMBED> tag. Whether this is a bug or a design feature is unclear. The problem is, viewers who don't have QuickTime aren't offered a download window (by recent versions of IE for Windows)—the browser just says it can't play the media.

Note This affects only Windows users who *don't* have QuickTime. If QuickTime is installed, the <EMBED> tag works perfectly, even in current versions of IE for Windows. There is a widespread notion that the <EMBED> tag doesn't work with ActiveX controls—this is not correct. The <EMBED> tag works with ActiveX controls—only the PLUGINSPAGE parameter is unsupported.

A less serious problem, which we've already discussed, is that the <EMBED> tag doesn't let you specify a particular plug-in, which requires you do to a little dance with the browser to get the plug-in you want, when more than one plug-in registers for the same media type.

A solution for both of these problems is to use the <OBJECT> tag to tell IE for Windows to use the QuickTime ActiveX control. This allows you to direct any kind of media to QuickTime—without concern about the server or browser MIME type settings. If the QuickTime ActiveX control is not installed, IE for Windows will offer to get it automatically, so this solves the PLUGINSPAGE problem as well.

This is a classic browser/OS dependency. If you're experienced with HTML, you've dealt with this kind of thing before. You need to set a variable to "0" for one browser and to "No" for another. So you do both.

In this case, doing both means using the <OBJECT> tag for Internet Explorer for Windows, and the <EMBED> tag for everyone else. Fortunately, you can wrap an <EMBED> tag inside an <OBJECT> tag.

If a browser can execute the <OBJECT> tag, it will skip the <EMBED> tag. Browsers that don't understand or can't execute the <OBJECT> tag ignore it and use the <EMBED> tag instead.

This may sound confusing (it may even *be* confusing), but it's really just a matter of adding the <OBJECT> tag to your HTML page. Some HTML editors, such as Adobe GoLive6, do this for you automatically. There are also freeware and shareware tools that you can download to wrap your <EMBED> tags in the equivalent <OBJECT> tags.

If you need to do it yourself or want to check your HTML generator's work, here's how it works:

The <OBJECT> tag takes a WIDTH and a HEIGHT parameter, just like the <EMBED> tag. Instead of a PLUGINSPAGE parameter, it accepts two parameters that identify the needed ActiveX control—CLASSID and CODEBASE.

The CLASSID parameter uniquely identifies the QuickTime ActiveX control as the plug-in to use. The CODEBASE parameter tells Explorer for Windows where to get the control if it's not already installed.

The SRC parameter, and any other parameters you want to pass, uses a slightly indirect syntax. Each parameter gets its own <PARAM> tag, and inside the tag are two parameters:

- **NAME**—the name of the parameter, such as SRC
- **VALUE**—the value of the parameter, such as MyMovie.mov

With the <OBJECT> and <PARAM> tags wrapped around the <EMBED> tag, it ends up looking like this:

```
<OBJECT WIDTH="100" HEIGHT="100"
  CLASSID="clsid:02BF25D5-8C17-4B23-BC80-D3488ABDDC6B"
  CODEBASE="http://www.apple.com/qtactivex/qtplugin.cab">

<PARAM NAME="src" VALUE="My.mov">

<EMBED WIDTH=100 HEIGHT=100 SRC="My.Mov">
</EMBED>

</OBJECT>
```

Let's examine this little bit of HTML, shall we? The WIDTH and HEIGHT allocate space on the page and should reflect your movie's dimensions, including the controller. The CLASSID and CODEBASE must be entered exactly as shown. To prevent typing errors, copy the text from ClassID.txt, in the Basic folder on the CD.

Set the VALUE parameter in the <PARAM> tag to the URL of your movie. You can use a relative or absolute URL.

The <EMBED> and </EMBED> tags are required, as all browsers except IE for Windows ignore <OBJECT> tags that include a CLASSID parameter.

You can add any other <EMBED> tag parameters to the <OBJECT> tag using separate <PARAM> tags. You don't need to pass a PLUGINSPAGE to the <OBJECT> tag, however, as the CODEBASE takes care of this. Similarly, you don't need to pass both an SRC and a QTSRC—the CLASSID specifies the QuickTime ActiveX control, so you can specify the URL of anything QuickTime can play in the SRC, regardless of its MIME type.

Here's a more complex example:

```
<OBJECT WIDTH="180" HEIGHT="16"
  CLASSID="clsid:02BF25D5-8C17-4B23-BC80-D3488ABDDC6B"
  CODEBASE="http://www.apple.com/qtactivex/qtplugin.cab">

<PARAM NAME="src" VALUE="Hot.mp3">
<PARAM NAME="autoplay" VALUE="true">
```

```
<EMBED WIDTH=180 HEIGHT=16
  SRC="UNeedQT.pntg" TYPE="image/x-macpaint"
  QTSRC="Hot.mp3"
  AUTOPLAY="True"
  PLUGINSPAGE="http://www.apple.com/quicktime/download/">
</EMBED>

</OBJECT>
```

Note that the <EMBED> tag uses SRC and TYPE to invoke the QuickTime plug-in, QTSRC to specify an MP3 file to play, and PLUGINSPAGE to direct people without QuickTime to the download site.

The <OBJECT> tag uses CLASSID to invoke QuickTime, passes the MP3 filename in the SRC parameter, and points to the ActiveX control using CODEBASE.

The main choice you face as a Web author is whether to bother about this at all. If you simply use the <EMBED> tag as described previously, Internet Explorer for Windows won't offer to download the QuickTime ActiveX control when people need it, but otherwise things will work fine. You just have to rely on your Get QuickTime button or your own QuickTime detection code (described in the following chapter) to prompt users to download QuickTime if they need it.

Wrapping an <OBJECT> tag around the <EMBED> tag is more work, of course, but it has some advantages. It prevents any other plug-in or application from taking over the .mov file type in Internet Explorer for Windows (the most common place for problems of this sort in the past). It presents users who need QuickTime with a familiar Windows dialog box to download the ActiveX control. It even allows users with older versions of Quick-Time to view your content in the latest version of Internet Explorer (the current ActiveX control is backward compatible with QuickTime 3 and later).

Of course, once your viewers *have* the QuickTime ActiveX control, most of these advantages go away.

If you're creating a new Web page or have the ability to write a script that will update existing pages automatically, by all means wrap your <EMBED> tags in an <OBJECT> tag for ActiveX. If that seems like too much work, just add an <OBJECT> tag on your home page (or the gateway page to your QuickTime content). That will ensure that visitors who come through the front door have the QuickTime ActiveX control—taking care of 90% of the potential problems with minimum fuss on your part.

Tip If you find the syntax of the <EMBED> and <OBJECT> tags a little daunting, there are inexpensive, and even free, tools that will wrap your <EMBED> tag in the appropriate <OBJECT> tagset, or even create both the <EMBED> and <OBJECT> tags for you. Open your browser and search for Pageot, TagMagker, or QT-HTML.

The <OBJECT> Tag and HTML Standards

If you're not interested in W3C standards or HTML history, skip ahead to "Linking with the <A HREF> Tag" (page 56). If you're an HTML purist, however, this section is dedicated to you.

The <EMBED> tag is not part of the W3C standard for HTML, but the <OBJECT> tag is. So why am I telling you to use <EMBED> and suggesting that the use of <OBJECT> is optional? Why not just use <OBJECT>?

For a very short period, it was indeed possible to write an <OBJECT> tag that worked the same way in Explorer and Netscape, on Windows and Macintosh. Had this happy time lasted, it might have been universally adopted. It did not last.

Internet Explorer for Windows uses the CODEBASE and CLASSID parameters to specify an ActiveX registration number (available only from Microsoft) and a location where an ActiveX control is located. Since ActiveX codes and registrations apply only to the Windows operating system, these are essentially proprietary "extensions" of the <OBJECT> tag. They are not part of the W3C specifications, and browsers other than IE for Windows generally ignore an <OBJECT> tag that contains these parameters.

With the release of IE for Windows 5.5 (SP2), it was no longer possible to write an <OBJECT> tag that would work cross-platform and cross-browser. The standard is currently complex, open to much interpretation, and implemented differently on different browsers and operating systems (and even on different versions of the same browser on a given OS). We need to use HTML that works cross-platform and cross-browser.

When is a standard not a standard? When implementations of the standard are not interoperable—things that work on one implementation don't work on the others.

And that's exactly where we are today.

Well, tomorrow is another day, so we may yet see the <OBJECT> tag become a universal standard. If that day comes, we should indeed change our Web pages to use the new standard.

And since the phrase "tomorrow is another day" is the last line of *Gone with the Wind*, I'll conclude by paraphrasing Scarlett O'Hara: let's think about that tomorrow.

▶ Using a Poster Movie

Okay, you know how to embed a movie in a Web page, in a way that takes people to the QuickTime download site when needed. The only problem now is, the movie starts to download when the Web page loads.

Unless the viewer wants to see or hear the movie, this is a waste of time and bandwidth—yours and the viewer's. It's better to let your audience choose when to download a movie.

The standard way to do this is to use a poster movie. A poster movie is typically a still image displayed on the Web page by the QuickTime plug-in. When a viewer clicks the image, QuickTime downloads a movie.

For an example, open `Poster.htm` (in the Basic folder) in a browser window. There is a still image taken from a movie—a poster—that you can click to play the movie.

While a poster movie is usually a single image from the main movie, you can also use a small looping clip or any other QuickTime movie as a poster. One reason to use a single image is that it has a very short load time, which makes your page more responsive. A text movie is also small and fast-loading though, and scrolling text can be very effective.

You can make any QuickTime movie into a poster movie by adding an `HREF` parameter to the movie's `<EMBED>` tag. Set the `HREF` parameter to the movie you want to play when the poster is clicked.

In its simplest form, the HTML looks like this:

```
<EMBED SRC="Poster.mov" HEIGHT=yy WIDTH=xx
    HREF="Actual.mov" TARGET="myself" />
```

Of course, you would add the `TYPE` and `PLUGINSPAGE` parameters, and perhaps wrap the `<EMBED>` tag in an `<OBJECT>` tag.

The only new elements here are the `HREF` parameter, which loads a new movie, and the `TARGET` parameter, which specifies where the movie goes. The two most common targets are `myself`, which loads the new movie wherever the poster is, and `quicktimeplayer`, which loads the new movie in QuickTime Player.

Important   When you pass a relative URL in the `HREF` parameter, the URL is relative to the current *movie* (in this case `Poster.mov`), *not* relative to the Web page the poster movie is embedded in!

That's a poster movie in its simplest form, but you generally want to add some refinements, such as using a scene from your movie as a poster, turning the controller off for the poster and turning it back on for the real movie, or perhaps launching QuickTime Player.

Here's how to make a poster from a scene in a movie:

1. Open the movie in QuickTime Player.

2. Choose Select None (Edit menu).

3. Move the time slider to the scene you want to use, and click in the display area. This selects a single frame from the movie.

   If you want to use a short clip instead of a still image, hold down the Shift key and drag the time slider to the end of the clip. This selects a clip.

4. Copy. Close (don't save).

   If you want to edit your poster in an application such as Photoshop, launch the application, open a new image canvas (Photoshop will use the size of the image you just copied as the default image size), and Paste. Edit to your heart's content. When you're done, flatten any layers, Save, open the edited image in QuickTime Player, and Copy.

5. Choose New Player from the File menu. Paste. Your selection is now a new movie.

6. Save As (self-contained) `Poster.mov`.

You're done.

Embed the poster image in your Web page as a movie (a very small movie), adding the HREF parameter to tell the QuickTime plug-in to load and play the real movie if the user clicks the poster:

```
<EMBED SRC="Poster.mov"
  CONTROLLER="false"
  HEIGHT=yy+16 WIDTH=xx
  BGCOLOR="white"
  TARGET="myself"
  HREF="<Actual.mov> E<CONTROLLER="true" AUTOPLAY="true">"
/>
```

It's important to turn off the movie controller for the poster movie—you want people to click the poster, not try to play it, and clicking on the controller won't trigger the HREF.

If you've made a poster image that's 16 pixels taller than the movie, the height of your poster will be perfect for the actual movie plus controller. If not, set the height to the movie height plus 16. Some space will show around the poster in this case, so you should set a background color to mask it.

By setting the TARGET parameter to "myself", you're telling the plug-in to load the actual movie over the poster movie, replacing it. Click the poster and it becomes a movie.

The HREF parameter has some odd-looking syntax in this example because it contains some nested parameters within it. This is covered thoroughly in the next chapter, so without explaining too much, I'll just point out that the first value is the URL of the actual movie. If the poster movie and the actual movie are in the same folder on the server, all you need is the filename. There are also a pair of values that are passed to the target movie, as if they were in an <EMBED> tag for that movie—CONTROLLER is TRUE, so the viewer can pause, rewind, adjust the volume, and so on, and AUTOPLAY is TRUE, so the movie loads and plays, instead of loading and waiting.

To see this in action, open the Basic folder and load Poster.htm in your browser.

As a final reminder, you would also include the TYPE and PLUGINSPAGE parameters, and perhaps surround the <EMBED> tag with an <OBJECT>.

Launching QuickTime Player from a Poster Movie

It's possible to use a poster movie to play your QuickTime movies (or other media files) in QuickTime Player instead of the browser plug-in. This is handy because QuickTime Player can do some things that the plug-in can't, such as playing movies in full-screen mode.

To make a poster that launches QuickTime Player, set the TARGET parameter to quicktimeplayer. Since the new movie will load in the QuickTime Player application, instead of replacing the poster, the height and width of the poster don't need to be the same as the movie height and width, and you don't need to restore the movie controller in the plug-in after the poster is clicked. This simplifies things a little. The HTML looks like this:

```
<EMBED SRC="Poster.mov"
  CONTROLLER="false"
  HEIGHT=yy WIDTH=xx (height and width of poster)
  TARGET="quicktimeplayer"
  HREF="Actual.mov"
/>
```

To see this in action, see Poster2Player.htm in the Basic folder of the CD.

If you want the movie to autoplay or loop in QuickTime Player, you can store these characteristics in the movie itself. For details, see "Saving Movies" (page 33).

▶ Linking with the <A HREF> Tag

A frequently asked question at this point is, why do we need the <EMBED> tag? Can't we just link to a QuickTime movie using a standard hypertext link, like this:

```
<A HREF="Demo.mov">Demo Movie</A>
```

Won't that play a QuickTime movie from a Web page?

Generally speaking, yes it will. But it's rarely a good idea to do this. Here's why:

- **No prompt for download**

  Unlike the <EMBED> tag and <OBJECT> tag, a text link doesn't accept a PLUGINSPAGE parameter or a CLASSID parameter, so if a visitor doesn't have QuickTime, the link will simply fail—it won't prompt the viewer to download the plug-in or ActiveX control.

- **No communication with QuickTime**

  You can't pass any parameters to QuickTime through a text link—you give up the ability to use HTML to control autoplay, looping, sound level, or anything else.

- **No control over the environment**

  Depending on the browser type, version, operating system, and user settings, a movie opened from a text link may play in any of several ways. Often the movie is played in an otherwise empty browser window with the default background color (gray or white). Sometimes the movie plays in a new window just big enough for the movie and controller. Sometimes the movie plays in QuickTime Player. Sometimes it doesn't play at all, even though QuickTime is installed—the browser may just download the movie and hope the user knows what to do with it.

- **No QTSRC**

  You can't tell the browser one thing, then tell QuickTime something else. That means you can't make the browser use QuickTime to play MP3, SMIL, RTSP streams, or anything other than QuickTime movies.

- **Leftovers, unreliable file handling**

  If the browser chooses QuickTime Player instead of the plug-in, it will download the entire movie to the user's hard disk and leave it there. It may call QuickTime Player while the movie is downloading, but often it will wait until the download is complete. Some browsers will download the file and do nothing with it. The user has to delete the movie manually and may not even know where the browser has put it.

- **No return address**

  When the browser gives a movie to the plug-in, the plug-in gets the movie's URL. That movie can then use relative URLs to reference other movies. If the browser downloads the file and calls the player application, QuickTime Player gets the movie from a local file—it doesn't know the movie's URL and can't do anything with relative URLs from the movie. That's one reason you should launch QuickTime Player from a poster movie—the plug-in can pass a URL to the player.

See `Link.htm` in the Basic folder of the CD for an example of a Web page with a simple text link to a movie. An illustration of a QuickTime movie opened using this way follows, but it won't necessarily look like that on your computer. If you can, try opening `Link.htm` using different browsers and operating systems, or even different computers with the "same" software. You may be surprised at the variety of responses.

Having said all that, there are sometimes situations that force you to use a plain hypertext link as your point of departure. The simplest answer is to create a small HTML file that contains only a header and the <EMBED> tag, then link to that. With a little work, you can generate such a file on the fly using a server-side script. There are other, more complex techniques as well. For details, see "Launching QuickTime Player from a Text Link" (page 100).

Okay, enough basics. Let's have some fun.

Special Delivery: QuickTime + HTML

By this time you should have the basics under your belt: you know what a QuickTime movie is, you can convert existing multimedia into QuickTime movies, and you can embed a movie in a Web page.

Now it starts to get enjoyable. Let's look at some advanced techniques for embedding QuickTime in a Web page—taking advantage of the Quick-Time plug-in, Plug-in Helper, and the HTML-friendly features of Quick-Time movies.

This chapter covers

- cool stuff you can do with QuickTime (plug-in and ActiveX)
- complete list of QuickTime <EMBED> tag extensions
- tips for adding the <OBJECT> tag parameters
- QuickTime and URLs
- Plug-in Helper
- copy protection
- different ways to launch QuickTime Player
- full-screen movies
- embedding multiple QuickTime movies on a Web page
- detecting QuickTime

Fun with QuickTime

The QuickTime plug-in has a lot of special features that you can control from HTML. You can tell the QuickTime plug-in to start playing a movie automatically or to wait until the user clicks the Play button. Or you can tell the QuickTime plug-in not to let users save the movie to disk, giving you some basic copy discouragement. Or you can hide the movie controller, set the default audio volume, have the plug-in play a series of movies one after another . . . but wait! There's more!

The QuickTime plug-in has over 30 special features that can be controlled from HTML, and these features can be combined in hundreds of ways. You control the special features by inserting parameters in the <EMBED> and <OBJECT> tags.

Note The basic techniques for putting a QuickTime movie in a Web page, using the <EMBED> and <OBJECT> tags, and the parameters that control the browser, were covered in Chapter 4, "Basic Training: Putting QuickTime in a Web Page.")

This section describes some particularly cool features of the plug-in in detail. Only the <EMBED> tags are shown in these examples, and the TYPE and PLUGINSPAGE parameters have been left out for brevity.

Some Particularly Cool Features

Autoplay

As John Brunner once wrote, "It's supposed to be automatic, but actually you have to push this button." You can simplify the user interface by having the QuickTime movie start playing automatically. The user doesn't have to do anything. This is especially effective with audio of the human voice. People are singularly amazed when they click into a website and it just starts talking.

AUTOPLAY="True" | "False" (the default is "False")

Example
```
<EMBED SRC="My.mov" HEIGHT="256" WIDTH="320"
    AUTOPLAY="True">
```

Your viewers can set their own default value for autoplay using their QuickTime settings, so set this to False if you want to be 100% certain that the movie won't start until the user clicks a button.

A new feature of autoplay for QuickTime 5 is the ability to start a movie playing when the network download has reached a certain point in the movie timeline.

Normally, QuickTime will start the movie when it calculates that it has downloaded enough to play the whole movie without interruption (the remaining data will arrive by the time it's needed). If the data transfer rate slows, QuickTime may have to pause during playback while more of the file downloads. This can cause "false starts" or stuttering. You can prevent most problems of this sort by setting the movie to autoplay after a few seconds have downloaded, rather than right away. The syntax is

```
AUTOPLAY="@HH:MM:SS:FF"
```

where HH = hours, MM = minutes, SS = seconds, and FF = 30ths of a second.

Note If your Web page opens the movie in QuickTime Player instead of the browser plug-in, you can make the movie autoplay by clicking the Auto Play Enabled checkbox in the movie properties window, as described in "Settings You Can Save" (page 39).

Audio Volume

By default, the QuickTime plug-in plays audio at full volume, which is 100% of the loudness the user has selected in the computer's Sound control panel. You can use the VOLUME parameter to create quiet background music or barely perceptible whispering. Note that MIDI at full volume is generally louder than recorded sound, so setting the volume to 75% is a good way to play MIDI sounds at the expected level.

```
VOLUME="Percent" (0-300)
```

Example
```
<EMBED SRC="MyMIDI.mov" HEIGHT="16" WIDTH="180"
    AUTOPLAY="True" VOLUME="75">
```

Values of greater than 100 can be used to overdrive the audio. This should be done cautiously because it can create distortion and clipping, not to mention annoyance.

Tip If you choose to include looping background music on your site, set a low volume. That way, fewer people will want to strangle you.

Play Something Else, Man

You can tell the QuickTime plug-in to play a different file than the one specified by the SRC parameter of the <EMBED> tag. This is crucial because the browser uses the SRC parameter to decide which plug-in to use. If the SRC parameter specifies a QuickTime movie (.mov), QuickTime image (.qti), or a MacPaint image (.pntg), the browser will choose the Quick-Time plug-in. You can then use the QTSRC parameter to tell the plug-in to play a QuickTime movie, Flash (.swf), MIDI, MP3, or other file type. This is discussed in more detail in Chapter 3, "Bust a .Mov," and Chapter 4, "Basic Training: Putting QuickTime in a Web Page."

QTSRC="*Filename*"

Example `<EMBED SRC="UNeedQT.qtif" TYPE="image/x-quicktime" HEIGHT="16" WIDTH="180" QTSRC="Hot.mp3">`

Set QTSRC to the name of the file you really want the plug-in to play. You can include a relative path or the full URL.

Important If you use a relative path, make it relative to the movie or image file specified in the SRC parameter, *not* relative to the HTML page that contains the <EMBED> tag.

Another important feature of the QTSRC parameter is that the QuickTime plug-in can get the specified URL using its own HTTP, RTSP, or file handling processes. This means that it works properly with RTSP URLs used for streaming movies and with local files that the browser itself might mishandle. It also means you can set a maximum download speed with the QTSRCCHOKESPEED parameter, described next.

The browser still downloads the file indicated by the SRC parameter, even though the plug-in ignores it. This is basically wasted bandwidth, so specify a small throw-away image in the SRC parameter. A good choice is UNeedQT.qtif, which you can find in the Basic folder of the CD. By the way, the SRC parameter has to point to a real file, or the browser gets confused.

Slow Down!

Okay, normally you want the movie to download faster, not slower. But a large movie can bring your server to its knees when someone downloads it using a T1 connection, even though 20 people could watch the same movie simultaneously using 56K modems. That's because the viewer with the T1 connection is using 1.5 megabits per second of bandwidth, the same as twenty-four 56K modems.

So if a movie has a data rate of less than 56,000 bits per second, for example, you might want to limit the download speed to a little over 56K— people can still watch the movie as it downloads, but someone with a fast Internet connection won't hog all your server's bandwidth.

You limit the bandwidth for a movie by setting its choke speed. The parameter is QTSRCCHOKESPEED. This parameter is applied only to movies specified by the QTSRC parameter, as described in "Play Something Else,

Man" (page 61). If the browser does the download, you can't control it using the QTSRC choke speed.

QTSRCCHOKESPEED="*MaxSpeed*" (in *bits* per second)

Example ```
<EMBED SRC="UNeedQT.qti" TYPE="image/x-quicktime" HEIGHT="16"
    WIDTH="180" QTSRC="Hot.mp3"
    QTSRCCHOKESPEED="130000">
```

Use a choke speed setting a little higher than the data rate of the movie to allow for network overhead. For a 128 Kbits/sec MP3, for example, set the choke speed to 130000 so people with fast connections can hear it in real time, but people with *really* fast connections won't use up all your Web server's bandwidth.

You can also set QTSRCCHOKESPEED="movierate" and QuickTime will do its best to use only as much bandwidth as needed to play the movie smoothly.

**Tip**  As of this writing (QuickTime 6.1) QTSRCCHOKESPEED limits only the download speed of the actual movie file specified by QTSRC. Any data contained in external files, including alternate-data-rate movies, is unaffected. Consequently, this parameter is used mainly with self-contained movies.

## Click Here, Play There (Poster Movies)

You can associate a URL with a QuickTime movie, so the URL loads when someone clicks inside the movie's display area. This lets you do a number of interesting things. The URL can specify a Web page, a JavaScript function, or a second movie. If the URL specifies a Web page, that page can include an embedded movie of its own.

You can specify a target for the URL, so it loads in another frame or another window. You can also target the URL to replace the current movie in the QuickTime plug-in, or to load in the QuickTime Player application, launching it if necessary.

This last feature is particularly useful. You can embed a movie for the plug-in, typically a single image with no controller, and tell the plug-in to launch a different movie in QuickTime Player when someone clicks the image. An example of this is Poster2.htm (in the SpecialDelivery folder on the CD), shown in the following illustration.

HREF="*url*" TARGET="FrameName" TARGETCACHE="True" | "False"

*Example* ```
<EMBED SRC="Poster.mov" HEIGHT="256" WIDTH="320"
    CONTROLLER="False" HREF="Actual.mov"
    TARGET="quicktimeplayer">
```

Clicking the poster movie loads the actual movie in QuickTime Player.

The TARGET parameter is optional. It works just like the TARGET parameter in an <A HREF> tag; it can specify a frame or a window, and it can be used to create a new window with a given name. It also supports three special values:

- **myself**—causes the URL to replace the current movie in the plug-in
- **quicktimeplayer**—loads the URL in the player application
- **browser**—loads the URL in the default browser window, even if the movie is playing in QuickTime Player

Important The special values are case-sensitive in some versions of QuickTime, so use all lowercase.

If you set TARGET="myself", the image is transformed into a movie when the user clicks it.

You can also use the HREF parameter to trigger a JavaScript function and pass data to it when someone clicks the movie:

```
<EMBED SRC="ClickMe.mov" HEIGHT="256" WIDTH="320"
  HREF="javascript:openMovie('HugeMovie1.htm')">
```

Note A bug in Explorer 4.5 caused it to ignore HREF parameters that began with javascript:, but this was fixed in subsequent versions.

If you want the URL specified in the HREF parameter to load automatically, instead of waiting for a mouse click, include the AUTOHREF="True" parameter. (The AUTOHREF parameter requires QuickTime 4.1 or later.)

```
<EMBED SRC="UNeedQT4.qti" TYPE="image/x-quicktime"
HEIGHT="2" WIDTH="2" HIDDEN="True"
HREF="Actual.mov" TARGET="quicktimeplayer" AUTOHREF="True" >
```

Important If you use a relative URL in the HREF parameter, it must be relative to the *poster movie,* not relative to the current Web page.

Start and End Times

You can tell the plug-in to play just part of a movie by setting the start time, the end time, or both. You might do this to create a series of buttons, each of which plays a different clip from the same movie. This technique is most useful with streaming movies or local movies.

```
STARTTIME="StartTime" ENDTIME="EndTime"
```

Example
```
<EMBED SRC="Long.mov" HEIGHT="176" WIDTH="120"
    STARTTIME="00:01:10:0" ENDTIME="00:02:10:0"
    AUTOPLAY="True">
```

Times are in Hours:Minutes:Seconds:Fractions relative to the start of the movie (00:00:00:0). The fractions are expressed in 1/30ths of a second. For 30 frames-per-second video, each fractional time unit is one frame. The example above plays one minute of Long.mov, starting one minute and ten seconds into the movie. You can specify just a start time or just an end time.

The timecode is expressed as HH:MM:SS:FF, *not* HH:MM:SS.FF (the separator is a colon, not a decimal point). This is different from the timecode displayed by QuickTime Player's Info window, which uses the decimal point between seconds and fractions.

You normally want to set AUTOPLAY="True" when you specify a start or end time, so the clip just plays; otherwise the user might try to position the controller to play a different clip. When you specify a start or end time, the viewer cannot play any earlier or later part of the movie.

Note Setting start and end times for a clip is useful for real-time streaming movies or local movies on a disk—it's less useful for Fast Start movies over the Internet because the whole movie downloads, not just the specified clip, and the user must wait until the movie has downloaded to the beginning of the clip. For Fast Start (progressive download) movies, it's better to break the movie into a series of smaller movies.

Play a Series of Movies

You can tell the QuickTime plug-in to play a series of movies, one after the other. When the current movie finishes, the next movie in the list starts. This can be a good way to deliver a long movie; users never need to store more than a small piece of it on their computers at any time.

QTNEXT*n*="<*Filename*> T<*Target*>" or "GOTO*n*"

Example　<EMBED SRC="First.mov" HEIGHT="176" WIDTH="120"
　　QTNEXT1="<Second.mov> T<myself>"
　　QTNEXT2="<Third.mov> T<myself>">

You have to append a number between 1 and 255 to each QTNEXT. They execute in numerical order.

Note that you must place angle brackets around the <*Filename*> and T<*Target*> values, and quotes must surround both values jointly:

"<*Filename*> T<*Target*>"

Set <*Filename*> to the name of the file you want to play next. You can include a relative path or the full URL.

The T<*Target*> parameter is optional. It specifies where the movie plays. If it's not specified, the next movie replaces the current browser window or frame, and any subsequent QTNEXT statements are lost.

The special value of T<myself> targets the QuickTime plug-in and is normally the value you want; the next movie replaces the current movie, and subsequent QTNEXT statements are executed in turn. The target can also be the name of a browser window or frame. If no window or frame of that name exists, a new browser window with that name is created.

You can also specify T<quicktimeplayer> as a target, which opens the movie in QuickTime Player.

Each QTNEXT statement has an index number, which is the order in which the movies play. If you specify a QTNEXT1, then a QTNEXT5, and then a QTNEXT10, for example, the three of them execute in numerical order, and their index numbers are 1, 5, and 10. Want to keep your sanity? Number the QTNEXT statements in simple numerical order: 1, 2, 3, ...

The special index value of 0 is assigned to the original movie named in the SRC parameter (or the QTSRC parameter, if it was specified).

Why have index numbers? Because instead of a filename, you can specify GOTO*n*, where *n* is the index of the QTNEXT you want to go to. You normally do this to create a simple loop:

```
<EMBED SRC="First.mov" HEIGHT="176" WIDTH="120"
  QTNEXT1="<Second.mov> T<myself>"
  QTNEXT2="<Third.mov> T<myself>"
  QTNEXT3=GOTO0 >
```

This example plays First.mov, then Second.mov, then Third.mov, then goes back to First.mov (index 0), in an endless loop. You can use values other than 0 to cause QTNEXT statements to play in arbitrary order, or to start looping from some midpoint. For example,

```
<EMBED SRC="Intro.mov" HEIGHT="176" WIDTH="120"
  QTNEXT1="<First.mov> T<myself>"
  QTNEXT2="<Second.mov> T<myself>"
  QTNEXT3=GOTO1 >
```

would play the Intro.mov just once, then play First.mov and Second.mov in an endless loop.

Note A bug in QuickTime 4.1 caused GOTO0 to play the most recent movie instead of the first movie in the sequence, although any subsequent movies in the sequence played correctly. The workaround is to specify the original movie at the beginning *and* end of the loop, and use GOTO1 instead:

```
<EMBED SRC="First.mov" HEIGHT="176" WIDTH="120"
  QTNEXT1="<Second.mov> T<myself>"
  QTNEXT2="<Third.mov> T<myself>"
  QTNEXT3="<First.mov> T<myself>"
  QTNEXT3=GOTO1 >
```

This sequence plays correctly whether the bug is present or not.

Tell Viewers What They Can Save

The QuickTime plug-in has a couple of options that control how viewers can save movies, or not save them: KIOSKMODE and DONTFLATTENWHENSAVING.

You can provide basic copy protection for your movie by setting KIOSKMODE to True. The plug-in disables its Save As Source and Save As QuickTime Movie commands, and doesn't allow drag-and-drop saving to the desktop.

Of course, this isn't foolproof protection, but it will stop honest people and discourage opportunists. You can get stronger protection using other techniques, as described in "Copy Protection" (page 95).

```
KIOSKMODE="True" | "False"
```

Example
```
<EMBED SRC="DontCopyMy.mov" HEIGHT="176" WIDTH="120"
  KIOSKMODE="True">
```

That's it for KIOSKMODE.

The DONTFLATTENWHENSAVING parameter is a little more complicated because you have to understand movie flattening. When a movie is flattened, all references to sample data (audio, video, and so on) are replaced with actual copies of the data. If the data is copied from external files into the movie file, this makes the movie self-contained. If the references are to data already inside the movie file, flattening replaces internal references with internal copies. In either case, it makes the movie file larger.

Unless you've copy-protected a movie, your viewers can save a copy of your movie using the QuickTime plug-in. You can control whether or not the QuickTime plug-in saves a flattened copy of the movie using this flag. By default, the Save As Source command saves without flattening, and the Save As QuickTime Movie command saves and flattens.

Most movies on the Web are already flattened, so it doesn't matter which you choose. But for some movies it can make a big difference.

If the movie on your Web server isn't self-contained, you can prevent people from making a working copy of the movie by setting the DONTFLAT TENWHENSAVING parameter in the <EMBED> tag. If the viewer then saves the movie from a browser, data in external files isn't copied. The saved movie won't play unless those files are present on the user's computer (which they won't be).

If you've created a movie with a lot of internal references, you should set the DONTFLATTENWHENSAVING parameter for a different reason. If it isn't set, all the references will turn into copies when the movie is saved, resulting in a huge file. For example, let's say you've made a movie using a 60 Kbytes audio sample that's referenced two hundred times. With internal references, the file is a little over 60 Kbytes in size; flattened, it swells to 12 MB. So tell the plug-in DONTFLATTENWHENSAVING.

Example   <EMBED SRC="DontCopyMy.mov" HEIGHT="176" WIDTH="120"
                DONTFLATTENWHENSAVING>

Combined Operations

You can combine plug-in features in an almost unlimited number of ways. For example, let's say you want a movie to play in QuickTime Player without requiring the viewer to click a poster movie, and you'd like to precede the movie with a little fanfare of trumpets. You can do this by combining the HIDDEN, CONTROLLER, AUTOPLAY, and QTNEXT parameters.

Example   <EMBED SRC="Fanfare.mov" HEIGHT="2" WIDTH="2"
                HIDDEN="True" AUTOPLAY="True" CONTROLLER="False"
                QTNEXT1="<Player.mov> T<quicktimeplayer>" >

This causes Fanfare.mov to play automatically in the background when the HTML page loads in a browser. As soon as Fanfare.mov finishes, Player.mov loads in the QuickTime Player application, outside the browser.

▶ Complete List of QuickTime Plug-in Parameters

The QuickTime plug-in accepts the following parameters. Many of them are discussed in more detail in the section, "Some Particularly Cool Features" (page 60). These parameters are passed to the QuickTime plug-in or

ActiveX control in the <EMBED> tag and can optionally be passed to the ActiveX control alone as <PARAM> tags within an <OBJECT> </OBJECT> tagset. Here's an alphabetical list of parameters, followed by their definitions:

Table of <EMBED> Tag Parameters

ALLOWEMBEDTAGOVERRIDES	MOVIEQTLIST
AUTOHREF	NODE
AUTOPLAY	PAN
BGCOLOR	PLAYEVERYFRAME
CONTROLLER	QTNEXT
CORRECTION	QTSRC
DONTFLATTENWHENSAVING	QTSRCCHOKESPEED
ENABLEJAVASCRIPT	QTSRCDONTUSEBROWSER
ENDTIME	SAVEEMBEDTAGS
FOV	SCALE
GOTO*n*	STARTTIME
HOTSPOT*n*	TARGET
HREF	TARGETCACHE
KIOSKMODE	TILT
LOOP	URLSUBSTITUTE
MOVIEID	VOLUME
MOVIENAME	

- ALLOWEMBEDTAGOVERRIDES="True" | "False" (default is False)

  If True, plug-in parameters can be overridden by subsequent commands (ordinarily a parameter can be set only once). This allows you to set a parameter to a default value for older versions of QuickTime, then override that value with a better setting that newer versions can understand. For example, older versions of QuickTime understand the AUTOPLAY settings True and False. Newer versions also understand the setting @HH:MM:SS:FF (a point in the movie timeline). If you pass this modern value, older versions of QuickTime will ignore it, leaving the AUTOPLAY parameter unset. These older versions of QuickTime do not understand ALLOWEMBED TAGOVERRIDES, however, so you can use this HTML to set older versions to True and newer versions to a point in the movie timeline:

```
<EMBED SRC=my.mov  HEIGHT=yy  WIDTH=xx
  AUTOPLAY=TRUE
  ALLOWEMBEDTAGOVERRIDES=TRUE
  AUTOPLAY=@00:01:30:00
  ALLOWEMBEDTAGOVERRIDES=FALSE />
```

Note Always set ALLOWEMBEDTAGOVERRIDES to False after performing any overrides. If this setting is left True, all settings can be overridden by user defaults or other lower-priority methods.

- AUTOHREF="True" | "False" (default is False)

  If True, causes any URL specified in the HREF parameter to load immediately, without waiting for a mouse click.

- AUTOPLAY="True" | "False" | "@HH:MM:SS:FF" (default is user-selected)

  Sets the movie to automatically start when the Web page loads, or to not start automatically, or to start only when download reaches a specified point in the movie timeline.

  In QuickTime 5.01 and later, AUTOPLAY can accept a timecode, and the movie will autoplay only when the download reaches that point in the timeline. Use this to prevent "false starts" over the Internet. The syntax is

  AUTOPLAY="@HH:MM:SS:FF"

  where HH = hours, MM = minutes, SS = seconds, and FF = 30ths of a second. Versions of QuickTime prior to 5.01 will not autoplay if a timecode is used.

Important The timecode is expressed as HH:MM:SS:FF, *not* HH:MM:SS.FF (the separator is a colon, not a decimal point). This is different from the timecode displayed by QuickTime Player's Info window, which uses the decimal point.

- BGCOLOR= "*#rrggbb*" | "*ColorName*"

  If the rectangle specified by HEIGHT and WIDTH is larger than the movie, this sets the background color for the rectangle. You can specify the color as a hexadecimal triplet of red, green, and blue values.

  QuickTime 4 and later also accepts names in place of some RGB values:

Color name	RGB value
BLACK	#000000
GREEN	#008000
SILVER	#COCOCO
LIME	#00FF00
GRAY	#808080
OLIVE	#808000
WHITE	#FFFFFF
YELLOW	#FFFF00
MAROON	#800000
NAVY	#000080
RED	#FF0000
BLUE	#0000FF
PURPLE	#800080
TEAL	#008080
FUCHSIA	#FF00FF
AQUA	#00FFFF

Note   QuickTime attempts to interpret any other color name as a hexadecimal number, so "ORANGE," for example, is equivalent to #00A00E. That's a color, but it isn't orange.

- CONTROLLER "True" | "False"

  Include a visible controller with the movie (or not). Default is True unless the movie is a .swf (Flash animation) file or a VR movie (a panorama or object movie). Flash and VR default to no visible controller in the QuickTime plug-in.

- CORRECTION="None" | "Full" (VR only, default is Full)

  Shows a VR panorama with no correction for warping (fastest) or provides full correction for horizontal and vertical warping.

Note   The CORRECTION value "Partial" is no longer supported and maps to "Full" in Quick-Time 4 and later.

- DONTFLATTENWHENSAVING

  If specified, the plug-in does not make copies of data that is included in the movie by reference. If the movie is on a Web server and references external media, this prevents viewers from saving a working copy of the movie using the plug-in. If a movie contains internal references, such as the same audio clip referenced hundreds of times, setting this flag prevents the movie from swelling up like a tick when saved.

- ENABLEJAVASCRIPT="True" | "False" (default is "False")

  If you want to control a QuickTime movie using JavaScript functions, you need to enable JavaScript for that movie by setting ENABLEJAVA SCRIPT="True". For details, see "QuickTime and JavaScript" (page 534).

- ENDTIME="*Time*" (*Hours:Minutes:Seconds:Thirtieths*)

  If set, causes the movie to stop playing at the specified point in the movie. The user will not be able to play the movie beyond the specified point. See also STARTTIME (page 76). Note that the separator between *Seconds* and *Thirtieths* is a colon, not a decimal point.

- FOV="*Angle*" (VR only)

  Sets the initial vertical field of view in degrees (and therefore sets the zoom) for a VR movie. The valid range for "*Angle*" is dependent on the movie.

Example   FOV="22.25"

- GOTO*n*

  See QTNEXT (page 75).

- HOTSPOT*n*="*Url*" TARGET*n*="*FrameName*" (VR only)

  Links the specified VR hotspot to a URL. The TARGET parameter is optional. See TARGET (page 77).

- HREF="*Url*"

  Clicking in the display area of the movie loads the specified URL. The URL can be a Web page, a QuickTime movie, or a JavaScript function. You can use this in conjunction with the TARGET parameter to cause the URL to load in another frame or window, in the QuickTime plug-in itself, or in the QuickTime Player application. See also TARGET, AUTOHREF.

Note   If you pass a relative URL in the HREF parameter, it must be relative to the currently loaded movie, not relative to the current Web page.

- KIOSKMODE="True" | "False"

  If True, the plug-in does not allow the user to save a copy of the movie.

- LOOP="True" | "False" | "Palindrome" (default is False)

  If True, the movie loops endlessly. If Palindrome, the movie loops back and forth, first playing forward, then backward.

- MOVIEID="*n*" (integer value)

  Assigns an integer ID to the movie. This permits the movie to be targeted by wired actions in another movie. Similar to MOVIENAME, but MOVIEID allows the movie to be targeted from a movie that doesn't know this movie's name. A number is also easy to create as the result of a calculation.

- MOVIENAME="*Name*"

  Assigns a name to a movie. This permits the movie to be targeted by wired actions in another movie. For example, one movie can act as a controller for other movies, starting them, stopping them, skipping to a particular time, activating certain tracks, and so on.

Note MOVIENAME is not the same as the NAME parameter. Use NAME to target an embedded movie by name from a JavaScript function; use MOVIENAME to target wired sprite actions between movies.

- MOVIEQTLIST="*QTList as XML*"

  Creates a default movie QTList, in XML format. If your movie has wired actions that use a QTList, such as loading a series of movies from a QTList, this tag allows you to supply the initial movie list as part of your HTML. Note that there can be a movie QTList and as many track QTLists as there are tracks. This command sets only the movie QTList. If the movie contains an embedded movie QTList, it is overwritten by the QTList set here.

Example
```
<Embed src=my.mov height=yy width=xx MovieQTList=
  "<myDataBase>
    <myRecord>
      <lastname>Bailey</lastname>
      <firstname>Bill</firstname>
      <phone>555-1212</phone>
    </myRecord>
  </myDataBase>"
/>
```

- NODE="*n*" (VR only)

  Specifies the initial node for a multinode VR scene.

- PAN="*Angle*" (VR only)

  Sets the initial pan angle, in degrees, for a VR movie. The valid range depends on the movie and is 0–360 for full cylinders or cubes.

- PLAYEVERYFRAME= "True" | "False" (default is False, except for .swf)

  If True, the plug-in does not drop frames, even if it gets behind. The movie may play at a slower than normal rate, but it plays every frame. The sound is muted when PLAYEVERYFRAME is True.

- QTNEXT*n* = "<*url*> T<*Target*>" (*n* = 1–255) or "GOTO*x*" (*x* = 0–255)

  Specifies a list of movies to play, with an optional target. The target can be a frame, a window, <myself>, or <quicktimeplayer>. Both <*url*> and T<*Target*> must be enclosed by angle brackets. If a target is specified, the target and the URL together must be surrounded by quotes. Multiple QTNEXT*n* statements can be included in a single <EMBED> tag. The value of *n* is an integer from 1 to 255. Each QTNEXT*n* executes in numerical order. The GOTO*x* statement causes a branch to the matching QTNEXT*n*. To branch to the original movie named in the SRC or QTSRC parameter, specify GOTO0 (Gee-Oh-Tee-Oh-Zero).

Note If you use a relative URL in a QTNEXT parameter, it must be relative to the currently loaded movie, not relative to the current Web page or relative to the first movie. Each URL in a series is relative to the previous URL.

- QTSRC="*url*"

  Causes the plug-in to ignore the URL specified by the SRC parameter and to play the file specified by "*url*". Useful for playing nonmovie files with the QuickTime plug-in and for specifying rtsp:// URLs. You can use the QTSRCCHOKESPEED parameter to limit the HTTP or FTP bandwidth used by a file specified with QTSRC. Note that the browser still downloads the file specified in the SRC parameter, but the plug-in ignores it.

- QTSRCCHOKESPEED="*MaxSpeed*" (in bits per second) or "movierate"

  Specifies the maximum HTTP or FTP bandwidth used to download a file specified in the QTSRC parameter. Useful to limit server load when a large movie is downloaded by viewers with fast Internet connections. Also useful for reserving bandwidth for RTP streaming when loading a movie over HTTP that contains both streaming and nonstreaming tracks.

Note As of this writing (QuickTime 6.1), QTSRCCHOKESPEED limits the download speed of data only in self-contained movies. Any data contained in external files, including alternate or reference movies, is unaffected.

- QTSRCDONTUSEBROWSER="True" | "False" (default is False)

  If True, the URL specified in the QTSRC parameter is loaded using Quick-Time's internal methods, instead of using the browser to fetch the file. This prevents the browser from caching the file, which speeds access to local movies and can help prevent copying movies over the Web. Currently, URLs using RTSP:// or data:// protocols default to QuickTime, and other protocols default to the browser.

Note　As of this writing (QuickTime 6.1), QTSRCDONTUSEBROWSER affects download of only the actual movie specified in QTSRC. Any data contained in external files, including alternate or reference movies, may be loaded through the browser.

- SAVEEMBEDTAGS="True" | "False" (default is False)

  Tells the plug-in to apply the current <EMBED> tag parameter values to a new movie. This causes a movie specified in an HREF, HOTSPOT, or QTNEXT parameter to be played using the current plug-in settings. This overrides any setting embedded in the specified movie by applications such as Plug-in Helper. If this parameter is False, some current parameters may still be inherited, and others may be reset to their defaults when the new movie loads.

- SCALE="ToFit" | "Aspect" | "*n*" (default is 1)

  Scales movie to fit the rectangle allocated in the <EMBED> tag, or scales to the best fit while keeping the movie's aspect ratio, or scales by a factor of *n*. For example, to play a movie at double its normal size, set SCALE="2"; to play a movie at half size, set SCALE="0.5".

- STARTTIME="*Time*" (*Hours:Minutes:Seconds:Thirtieths*)

  If set, causes the movie to start playing at the specified offset into the movie's timeline. See also ENDTIME (page 73). The user will not be able to play parts of the movie prior to this point in the timeline. Note that the separator between *Seconds* and *Thirtieths* is a colon, not a decimal point.

  STARTTIME is normally used with movies stored on a streaming server or a local disk, as these movies allow random access into the file. It's not terribly useful for Fast Start movies on the Internet, as the movie has to download everything from the beginning to the specified STARTTIME before it can play the clip. For Internet delivery, it's generally better to save the movie as a series of self-contained clips.

- TARGET[*n*]="*FrameName*" (or "myself", "quicktimeplayer", or "webbrowser")

  Causes the URL associated with a HOTSPOT or HREF to load in the named frame. If you match a TARGET with a HOTSPOT, append the same value *n* to TARGET that you used to identify the hotspot. If set to myself, the URL replaces the current movie. If set to quicktimeplayer, the URL loads in the QuickTime Player application. If set to webbrowser, the URL loads in the default browser window, launching the default browser if necessary. See also HOTSPOT, HREF, TARGETCACHE.

- TARGETCACHE="True" | "False"

  If set to True, a URL loaded using the TARGET parameter is stored in cache.

- TILT="*Angle*" (VR only)

  Sets the initial vertical tilt angle, in degrees, for a VR movie. The valid range is dependent on the movie, but is typically –42.5 to +42.5 for a cylinder.

- URLSUBSTITUTE*n*="<*String*>:<*SubstituteURL*>"

  Replaces every instance of *String* with *SubstituteURL* inside any HREF tracks, sprite action URLs, or VR hotspot URLs. Both *String* and *SubstituteURL* must be surrounded by angle brackets, and the two must be separated by a colon. The value *n* may be any integer from 1 to 999 and may be omitted if only one URLSUBSTITUTE parameter is specified. Use this parameter to repurpose QuickTime movies with embedded URLs without editing the movies.

- VOLUME="*Percent*" (0–300)

  Sets audio volume from 0 to 300% of the user's sound setting. Values greater than 100 may cause distortion and clipping.

Plug-in Parameters and the <OBJECT> Tag

The HTML examples in this chapter, and in most of this book, use the <EMBED> tag alone rather than showing an <OBJECT> tag wrapped around the <EMBED> tag. Like the PLUGINSPAGE parameter, the <OBJECT> tag is omitted to make the code examples shorter and easier to understand.

You will probably want to add the <OBJECT> tag to some—perhaps even all—of your Web pages, however. The process is described in detail in Chapter 4, "Basic Training: Putting QuickTime in a Web Page," and for the most part it's very straightforward.

But now that you've had a chance to see the variety of plug-in parameters for QuickTime, it's probably a good idea to review the most important points and clear up some possible ambiguities.

These are the basic steps you need to take:

- Add an `</EMBED>` tag as a marker after the `<EMBED>` tag.
- Put the `<OBJECT> </OBJECT>` tags around the `<EMBED> </EMBED>` tags.
- Insert the `HEIGHT`, `WIDTH`, `CLASSID`, and `OBJECTCODE` parameters inside the `<OBJECT>` tag.
- Create a `<PARAM>` tag for every plug-in parameter in the `<EMBED>` tag.

These are two important points to remember:

- You don't need to use `QTSRC` in the `<OBJECT>` tag to get QuickTime to play something—the `CLASSID` takes care of that. If your `<EMBED>` tag uses `SRC=` `"a.mov"` and `QTSRC="b.mov"`, you can use just the `<PARAM>` tag: `<PARAM NAME="src" VALUE="b.mov" >`. It does no harm to use `QTSRC` inside an `<OBJECT>` tag; it just isn't necessary to get the QuickTime ActiveX to play a file.
- Don't create `<PARAM>` tags for `HEIGHT` or `WIDTH`. They go inside the `<OBJECT>` tag.

Here are some tips to help you resolve issues that some people have found confusing:

- Pass the `HIDDEN` parameter inside a `<PARAM>` tag, even though it's technically a browser parameter, not a plug-in parameter.
- If your HTML includes a `TARGET` parameter, it needs its own `<PARAM>` tag; but if the target is part of a URL, it doesn't need one.

  For example,

  `HREF="url" TARGET="frame"`

  becomes

  `<PARAM name="href" value="url">`
  `<PARAM name="target" value="frame">`

  whereas

  `HREF="<url> T<frame>"`

  becomes

  `<PARAM name="href" value="url T<frame>" >`

- Any time there's an equal sign (=) in your <EMBED> tag, you need a separate <PARAM> tag. All the values to the right of an equal sign can be passed in a single <PARAM> tag.

If you follow these guidelines, you should be able to construct a valid <OBJECT> tagset around any <EMBED> tag.

⏵ QuickTime and URLs

As you can see, a number of the QuickTime <EMBED> tag parameters take URLs as values. On the Internet, all things are connected by URLs—strings of characters that describe the location of a data source, usually a file or a stream. Some URLs contain the absolute path to a file. Others imply some of the path, giving directions relative to the URL of the current document. But URLs can contain more than just path and filenames—they can specify protocols and can carry embedded data or even programming commands. They can also specify a target destination in addition to a source address.

QuickTime understands a variety of path descriptions and protocols and can use URLs to carry data and instructions as well. It makes particularly strong use of the targeting function, directing traffic to browser windows, frames, the QuickTime plug-in, or QuickTime Player.

The syntax can be very fussy for these things, and a lot of how they work is not obvious, so we should probably go over it now.

I'm afraid this does get pretty technical. If you're not in the mood just now, feel free to skip ahead to "Plug-in Helper" (page 87). But make a mental note to come back later. Understanding this will save you a lot of head-pounding later on.

Protocols

QuickTime supports the standard protocols for data transfer—HTTP: and FTP: for movie and data files; File: for local files; and RTSP: and RTP: for real-time streams. It also supports the less commonly known Javascript: and data: protocols, which we'll look at in a moment.

If you load a movie using a given protocol, subsequent URLs with no specified protocol are assumed to use the same. For example, if you tell QuickTime

```
<EMBED SRC="ftp://ftp.server/path/My.mov"
  HREF="MyOther.mov">
```

QuickTime will assume that it should load MyOther.mov using FTP because that was the last protocol specified.

Javascript: Protocol

The Javascript: protocol lets you call JavaScript functions and pass data (but it relies on the browser to carry the message). Here's an example:

```
<EMBED SRC="poster.mov"
  HREF="javascript:openMovie('Movie1.htm')" >
```

This executes a JavaScript function and passes data to it when the poster movie is clicked.

Notice that the JavaScript protocol uses a colon, but no forward slashes, also that parameters are passed to functions in parentheses, and that you need to use single quotes to delimit individual parameters within the parentheses.

QuickTime can execute a JavaScript function, and pass data to it, any time it generates a URL: in <EMBED> tag, movie, and track HREF parameters; QTNEXT statements; VR hotspots; HREF tracks; text track HREF parameters; wired sprite actions; Flash actions; and so on.

Note A bug in Internet Explorer 4.5 caused it to ignore URLs that began with JavaScript:, but it works fine in subsequent versions.

data: Protocol

The data: protocol has some interesting uses in QuickTime. The syntax is

```
data:type/encoding,
```

followed by the actual data. Here's an example:

```
<EMBED SRC="a.mov" HEIGHT=60 WIDTH=240
  QTSRC="data:text/plain,A self-contained text movie!" >
```

This creates a small self-describing QuickTime text movie. To see it in action, check out DataText.htm in the SpecialDelivery folder of the CD.

QuickTime supports plain text and Base64-encoded data. Yes, you can put a movie or image in Base64 format and embed it right in the URL, if that's the kind of thing you like to do.

You need to use Base64 to pass binary data, or text that includes quotes, angle brackets, or anything that will make the browser think you're talking to it.

Addressing

QuickTime now supports absolute, relative, and root-relative addressing in both the plug-in and the player application. But there are some things to watch out for. Let's go over the different addressing modes and any Quick-Time-related gotchas.

Absolutely

An absolute address is any URL that begins with a protocol identifier—`ftp://`, `http://`, `file:///`, `data:`, and so on. The identifier is normally followed by the domain name, or the literal IP address, of a server for the file or stream. Some protocols, such as RTP and RTSP, can be used only with absolute addresses.

In general, absolute addressing works throughout QuickTime with no quirks.

Macintosh developers will find producing a cross-platform CD that uses absolute addressing with the `File:` protocol is extremely difficult, however. You just don't know if the CD is MyCD, or D: or E: or F:—Windows developers will already be familiar with this. One solution is to use root-relative addressing, which we'll look at next.

Root Relativity

Root-relative addressing gives directions to a file from the root directory of the current server—or the current disk, for local files. The protocol is implied: whatever protocol was used to load the current document. Root-relative addresses all begin with a forward slash. For example:

```
<EMBED SRC="/users/~bob/movies/my.mov"
```

Depending on the Web server, the "root" directory may be the actual root directory of the disk, or the Web folder that holds all the website files, or even the top-level directory for a user area.

Root-relative addressing is great for CDs. You can link a movie to a particular file using root-relative addressing and use the same movie in any directory—it will still point to the file. The cross-platform problems of absolute addressing on local disks go away with root-relative addressing.

QuickTime supports root-relative addressing in any URL.

Relatively Speaking

Relative addressing describes the path to a file, relative to another file—generally the file you loaded last. The protocol is implied: same as last time.

In QuickTime 5 and later, relative addressing should work throughout QuickTime (earlier versions had limited support for relative URLs in QuickTime Player, with full support only in the plug-in).

Using relative addressing in QuickTime can be tricky, however. You specify a relative path in a SRC parameter just as you would expect—relative to the current Web page. But it's the browser that fetches the SRC file, not QuickTime.

The browser passes the URL along to QuickTime, but that's the *only* URL QuickTime gets. The browser doesn't pass along the URL of the current Web page. For QuickTime, the SRC movie *is* the current document.

Consequently—and I can't stress this enough—all subsequent URLs must be relative to the *currently loaded movie*. The SRC movie gets downloaded, even if it's not displayed, so a relative URL in the QTSRC parameter must be relative to the SRC URL.

If you have relative addresses in the SRC, QTSRC, and HREF parameters of your <EMBED> tag, SRC is relative to the Web page, QTSRC is relative to SRC, and HREF is relative to QTSRC. This can get very confusing, but there are simple steps you can take that will simplify things.

If you put your movies in the same folder as the Web pages that use them, any relative path is the same from the Web page or the movie. No more complications. The relative path from Web page to movie is just a filename. If at all possible, organize your site this way.

If you must put your movies in a different directory from your HTML, at least put all the movies that link to each other in one folder. If all your linked movies are in the same folder, the relative path from movie to movie is always just the filename. Only the SRC parameter contains the path from the HTML folder to the movie folder.

For example, if you write this:

```
<EMBED SRC="../../MOVIES/a.mov" HREF="b.mov"
```

the browser uses the SRC address to find a.mov, then passes the movie's absolute address to QuickTime. If the viewer clicks the movie, QuickTime will look for b.mov in the same folder as a.mov.

Here's the most common type of mistake:

```
<EMBED SRC="../../MOVIES/a.mov" HREF="../../MOVIES/b.mov"
```

QuickTime treats the second URL as being relative to the first. This will make QuickTime look for `b.mov` in `../../MOVIES`, *starting* from `../../MOVIES/`. Can you say, "file not found"?

Similarly, for relative addressing in a series of QTNEXT parameters, each URL is relative to the one before. That's no big deal *if* the movies are all in the same folder. If they're not, just remember to go slow and check your path to make sure each link goes from the current movie to the new movie.

Oh, in case you're wondering, if a movie is loaded in-line using the `data:` protocol, it doesn't *have* a URL—it's inside one. You can't use relative URLs if the current movie was stuffed inside a URL itself.

Addresses and #Names

A URL can end in a name that specifies an anchor within a file, such as `/Web /Tutorial.html#step1`. This specifies a point within the file named `step1`, named using an `<A>` tag, such as `<A NAME="step1"> </A>`.

Clicking a link that ends with a name normally causes a browser to scroll the display window to the named point in the specified file. Unlike most URLs, a browser will not generally report an error if it cannot find a named point—it just scrolls to the end of the file.

A name can be appended to any URL—absolute, relative, and so on. If a URL consists solely of a name, such as `HREF="#step1"`, the current file is implied. QuickTime can send URLs that end in names, or pass them to a browser or JavaScript function, but names in URLs generally have no meaning for QuickTime itself—you can't use a named anchor to jump to a point in the movie timeline or a node in a VR movie, for example.

Perhaps most significantly, you cannot use a URL with a name to jump to a particular point in a QuickTime SMIL file, at least not as of QuickTime 6.1.

Note Internet Explorer 5 for the Macintosh has some very odd behavior if you use a URL in one frame to open a file in another frame to a particular point, such as

`HREF="OtherFile.html#step3" TARGET="OtherFrame"`

The file should load in the target frame, scrolled so that the named anchor is at the top of the window (or as far down as you can scroll in the file). Sometimes this happens, but IE5/Mac often scrolls to the wrong position, especially if the file is already loaded in the target frame. This has nothing to do with QuickTime, but it does prevent movies that use this technique from working on some machines.

Targeting

In HTML, a hypertext link can include a TARGET parameter that tells the browser to open a file in a particular frame or window. If the named frame or window doesn't exist, the browser creates a new window and names it accordingly. A few reserved names have special meanings, such as _top and _parent, allowing you to target a window or frame structurally, rather than by name.

QuickTime supports this kind of targeting. A movie playing in one frame can load a series of Web pages in adjacent frames, for example. QuickTime also supports a few additional target types. We'll look at what these targets do, then look at ways to attach targets to QuickTime URLs.

Target Types

QuickTime extends URL targeting to include these additional choices: myself, quicktimeplayer, webbrowser.

The quicktimeplayer target allows you to launch movies in QuickTime Player from the QuickTime browser plug-in.

The webbrowser target allows you to open a URL in the user's default browser from a movie running in the QuickTime Player application.

The myself target allows you to replace the movie currently playing in the plug-in, without refreshing the surrounding Web page.

All other targets are treated as frame or window names.

QuickTime Player and the QuickTime plug-in handle some of the target types a little differently. Here's a summary of the behavior of the player application and the plug-in in response to each target type.

QuickTime Player

- If no target is specified, or the target is myself or quicktimeplayer, the URL loads in a QuickTime Player window—either a new window or the current window, depending on the user's settings (there is currently no way to override the user settings). If a new Player window is opened, the current movie continues to play. If an HTML file is encountered, it is opened in the default window of the user's default browser, launching the browser if necessary.

- If the target is webbrowser, the URL loads in the default browser window, launching the default browser if necessary. The current movie continues to play.

- If some other target is specified, and the default browser has an open window or frame with that name, the URL loads there. Otherwise, a browser window with that name is created, launching the default browser if necessary. The target name is passed to the browser, so targets such as _blank or _top can have special meaning. The current movie continues to play.

QuickTime Plug-in

- If no target is specified, or the target is webbrowser, the URL loads in the current browser window or frame, replacing the current movie and any Web page that contains it.

- If the target is myself, the new URL replaces the current movie in the QuickTime plug-in. The URL should point to a QuickTime movie or some other file that QuickTime can play. The surrounding page is unaffected.

- If the target is quicktimeplayer, the new URL opens in QuickTime Player, launching it if necessary. If QuickTime Player is already active, the URL may open in a new player window or the current window, depending on user settings. The movie in the plug-in continues to play.

- If some other target is specified, and the browser has an open window or frame with that name, the URL loads there. Otherwise, a browser window with that name is created. This is useful for opening an adjunct Web page or image in another frame. The target name is passed to the browser, so targets such as _blank or _parent can have special meaning. The current movie continues to play.

Specifying a Target

Starting with QuickTime 5, you can attach a target to nearly any QuickTime URL using this syntax:

```
"<url> T<target>"
```

Notice that the URL and the target are each surrounded by angle brackets, and that the two are jointly surrounded by quotes. This is required. Also, the URL must come first, followed by a space, an uppercase T, and the target.

Here are some examples:

```
QTNEXT="<http://www.server.com/movie.mov> T<myself>"
HREF="<../HTML/webpage.html> T<frame2>"
HOTSPOT13="<Waterfall.mov> T<quicktimeplayer>"
```

Earlier versions of QuickTime used different targeting methods for different types of URLs. HREF used TARGET, HOTSPOT*n* used TARGET*n*, QTNEXT used the current syntax, and some other URL types could not be targeted.

The old methods are still supported for compatibility reasons, but going forward you can use this one method to attach a target to any QuickTime URL that can be targeted in QuickTime 5 or later.

There are two QuickTime URLs that you cannot target: SRC and QTSRC. Both have a fixed target: the QuickTime plug-in. Trying to add a target to SRC will confuse the browser (the browser sees it before QuickTime). Attempting to target QTSRC will cause QuickTime to display the broken movie icon.

Passing Plug-in Data in URLs

QuickTime 5 introduced a URL extension that allows you to specify a separate set of <EMBED> tag parameters for each movie as part of its URL. This provides much of the functionality of Plug-in Helper (described next) and is generally easier to use and more flexible than embedding the settings inside a movie using Plug-in Helper.

In addition, URL extensions can be added to the HTML automatically by any script that can output a text file. The syntax is

```
"<URL> T<Target> E<ParamA=Value ParamB=Value ...>"
```

The T< > parameter is optional. The E< > parameter can enclose any of the QuickTime <EMBED> tag parameters. For example:

```
<EMBED SRC=Movie1.mov HEIGHT=256 WIDTH=320
   CONTROLLER=False
   HREF="<Movie2.mov> T<myself>
        E<CONTROLLER=True AUTOPLAY=True>"
/>
```

This example tells the QuickTime plug-in to play Movie1.mov with no controller, leaving the AUTOPLAY parameter unspecified (controlled by user preferences).

If the viewer clicks inside the movie's display area, the HREF parameter tells the plug-in to load Movie2.mov. The URL extensions T< > and E< > tell the plug-in to replace the current movie (T<myself>) and to autoplay with a controller (E <CONTROLLER=True AUTOPLAY=True>).

Note that the URL itself is surrounded by angle brackets, and quotes surround the URL and all its extensions jointly.

Parameter values set using this method take precedence over any values embedded in a movie using Plug-in Helper (described next).

Currently the E< > URL extension is recognized only by the QuickTime plug-in. This extension is ignored when a URL is part of a movie played in QuickTime Player.

Plug-in Helper

Plug-in Helper is a tool you can use to enhance QuickTime movies for the Internet. Its main purpose is to put plug-in parameters, such as AUTOPLAY and CONTROLLER, inside a movie. When the QuickTime plug-in plays that movie, it's as if you had put the parameters in the <EMBED> tag or passed them in the E< > URL extension.

That's handy because with HREF and QTNEXT you can specify more than one movie in a single <EMBED> tag. With Plug-in Helper, each movie can have its own permanent set of plug-in parameters, so that you can set

CONTROLLER="False"

in a poster movie, for example, and

CONTROLLER="True"

in the movie it links to.

It's also nice to take some settings out of the highly visible HTML and put them inside the movie structure for privacy. For example, you can put QTNEXT1="../Secret/Next.mov" inside a movie without ever putting the URL of Next.mov in your HTML.

Most plug-in parameters for a movie can be set two different ways: directly in the HTML—either in the <EMBED> tag or as part of an E< > URL extension—or using Plug-in Helper. What happens if you set a parameter one way in HTML and another way using Plug-in Helper?

The sequence is HTML first, Plug-in Helper second, user preferences third (the AUTOPLAY parameter can also be set by user preferences). The first method to set a parameter fixes its value. Any values not specified by one method can still be set by another method.

Starting with QuickTime 5, movies loaded into the plug-in through HOTSPOT, HREF, or QTNEXT can have their parameters explicitly set in HTML by the SaveEmbedTags parameter or by the E< > URL extension. In many cases, this is a better solution than putting the settings in the movie itself using Plug-in Helper. For details, see SAVEEMBEDTAGS (page 76) and "Passing Plug-in Data in URLs" (page 86).

Plug-in Helper also has some features that aren't in the <EMBED> tag. You can use Plug-in Helper to prevent the movie from being edited or saved, and you can permanently associate URLs with the movie, so clicking the movie activates a link even if the movie is playing in QuickTime Player (or playing in someone else's website).

Note   Bear in mind that Plug-in Helper sets only parameters that QuickTime understands, not the parameters that the browser deals with, such as SRC, HIDDEN, HEIGHT, or WIDTH. Those parameters can be passed only in HTML.

There are two versions of Plug-in Helper, one for the Mac OS and one for Windows. Use the version that's right for you. They're both in the Tools folder on the CD.

You can open a movie in Plug-in Helper by choosing Open from the File menu, or you can drag the movie onto Plug-in Helper. There's a checkbox for copy-protecting the movie, a text-entry box for plug-in settings, and a pair of text-entry boxes for HREF links, as shown in the following illustration. It's pretty easy to use.

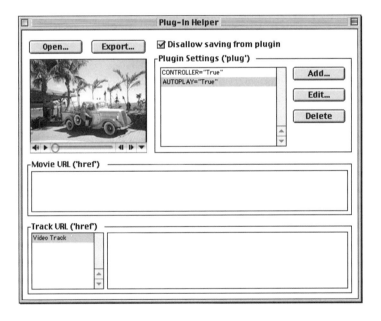

The checkbox for copy protection applies to a movie whether it's played by the plug-in, QuickTime Player, or any other application that uses the QuickTime API for editing and saving movies. If this box is checked,

QuickTime will not allow the movie to be saved or edited. For more information, see "Copy Protection" (page 95).

The parameters you enter in the Plugin Settings text box affect only the QuickTime plug-in; they won't affect a movie when it's played by Quick-Time Player. The only exceptions are MOVIENAME and MOVIEID, which Quick-Time Player also recognizes. For practical examples of using the Plugin Settings box, see "Adding URL Links to Movies" (page 89) and "Making a Poster Movie with Plug-in Helper" (page 92), immediately following this section.

Tip If you need to store settings in a movie that's played by QuickTime Player, see "Settings You Can Save" (page 39).

The URLs you enter in the HREF text boxes are active in either the Quick-Time plug-in or QuickTime Player. We'll look at the HREF text boxes in detail next.

When you're ready to save your changes, click the Export button. You have to give the movie a new name or a new location at this point. If you try to overwrite the movie you just opened, it doesn't work (Plug-in Helper just beeps).

Adding URL Links to Movies

You can embed links to various URLs inside a movie using Plug-in Helper. This makes the links independent of any HTML, so multiple movies specified by a single <EMBED> tag can each have their own links. The links travel with the movie, even if someone "borrows" the movie for their own website.

This also allows you to create links that work when a movie is playing in QuickTime Player. QuickTime Player can be told to load the URL itself, if it's the URL of something QuickTime can play, or it can open the URL in a browser window, launching the browser if necessary.

The URL can specify a movie, a Web page, or some other file. It can be targeted to load in a window or frame of the browser, to replace the current movie, or to load in QuickTime Player.

There are three areas in the Plug-in Helper window where you can add URLs: the Plugin Settings text box, the Movie URL text box, or the Track URL text box. Each has a slightly different behavior.

Plugin Settings Text Box

Adding a URL to the Plugin Settings text box causes the URL to load when someone clicks the display area of the movie, as long as the movie is loaded in the QuickTime browser plug-in. You add a URL in the Plugin Settings box using this syntax:

```
HREF="<Url> T<Target>"
```

The specified URL can be relative or absolute. If you use a relative URL, it must be relative to the *movie,* not relative to the Web page the movie is embedded in.

The T<*Target*> parameter is optional. If no target is specified, the URL loads in the current browser window or frame, replacing the current movie and any Web page it's embedded in.

If a target is specified, it can be a browser window, a frame, or the special values quicktimeplayer or myself. If the window or frame specified doesn't exist, a new browser window of that name is created. If the target is myself, the URL replaces the current movie inside the plug-in, leaving the surrounding Web page in place.

The URL loads when someone clicks in the display area of the movie. This could be the display area of any video track, sprite track, or text track. It doesn't work with audio-only movies, however, and clicking the movie controller doesn't load the URL either.

If you also specify AUTOHREF="True" in the Plugin Settings box, the URL loads immediately, without playing the current movie or waiting for a mouse click.

Starting with QuickTime 5, it's also possible to assign plug-in parameters to a movie as part of the movie's URL. In other words, you can specify the URL of a movie and also tell the QuickTime plug-in to, for example, autoplay or loop the movie. This also works with URLs entered in the Plugin Settings text box. For details, see "Passing Plug-in Data in URLs" (page 86).

Movie URL Text Box

Adding a URL to the Movie URL text box causes the URL to load when someone clicks the display area of the movie, whether the movie is loaded in the QuickTime browser plug-in or QuickTime Player.

The syntax for adding a URL in the Movie URL text box is different from the Plugin Settings text box. Enter just the URL—don't include an HREF= string. For example, enter

```
http://www.server.com/path/filename
```

not

```
HREF="http://www.server.com/path/filename"
```

If you specify a target for the URL, you need to use angle brackets and quotes:

```
"<http://www.server.com/path/filename> T<myself>"
```

The URL loads when someone clicks in the display area of the movie. This could be the display area of any video track, sprite track, or text track. It doesn't work with audio-only movies, and clicking the movie controller doesn't load the URL.

Adding a URL in the Movie URL text box creates a link that works both in the QuickTime plug-in and QuickTime Player, but the target parameter may be resolved differently. QuickTime Player's default target is itself, but if you link to a Web page, QuickTime Player will direct it to the default browser window, opening the default browser if necessary. The Quick-Time plug-in's default target is the browser window or frame that contains the plug-in.

If the movie is played in the QuickTime browser plug-in, the URL can include E < > URL extensions to pass data to the plug-in, specifying how the movie should be played.

For additional details, see "QuickTime and URLs" (page 79).

Track URL Text Box

A track URL is similar to a movie URL, but you can enter a different track URL for every video track in the movie, whereas you can have only one movie URL.

The syntax for a track URL is the same as for a movie URL. It's just that the track URL is activated when someone clicks inside the display area of a particular video track, rather than anywhere in the movie. The video tracks appear by name in a scrolling list—click one to associate a URL with it, then enter the URL.

Since tracks can be arranged in time and space, this lets you activate a different URL depending on where or when the user clicks. Track URLs work only with video tracks, not with sprite or text tracks.

The QuickTime plug-in and QuickTime Player respond to track URLs just as they do to a movie URL.

Important You can't combine track URLs with a movie URL. Choose one or the other. If you specify both, the movie URL takes precedence, and any track URLs are ignored. Sprite tracks and VR tracks already interpret mouse clicks internally, so they don't trigger URLs set in the Plugin Settings, Movie URL, or Track URL boxes. You can set URL triggers directly in a sprite track or VR track, however, as you'll see when we explore those track types.

Making a Poster Movie with Plug-in Helper

Here's a practical example of how to use the Plugin Settings text box in Plug-in Helper. Suppose you want to embed a still image in your Web page that loads and plays a movie when someone clicks the image. Suppose further that you want the movie to load and play right where the image is. You can do this, and you can use Plug-in Helper to get it right. Here's how:

1. Make a QuickTime movie that contains just the still image. Let's call it Poster.mov. You can do this by opening an image in QuickTime Player and saving it as a self-contained movie. Or you can click on any frame in a movie, choose Copy, New, Paste, and then Save.

2. Embed the poster movie in your Web page and set the HREF and TARGET parameters so the real movie loads when someone clicks the image:

```
<EMBED SRC="Poster.mov" HEIGHT=176 WIDTH=120
  HREF="Other.mov" TARGET="myself">
```

The problem now is that you don't want the poster movie to have a controller; you want people to click the poster, not try to play it. But you *do* want the second movie to have a controller, and you want it to autoplay. So:

3. Pass the CONTROLLER="False" parameter in the <EMBED> tag for the poster movie:

```
<EMBED SRC="Poster.mov" HEIGHT=176 WIDTH=120
  CONTROLLER="False"
  HREF="Other.mov" TARGET="myself" >
```

4. Use Plug-in Helper to put the `CONTROLLER="True"` and `AUTOPLAY="True"` parameters inside the other movie, as shown in the following illustration:

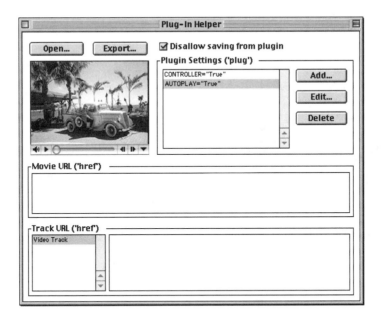

The resulting Web page has a poster movie (with no controller), linked to a movie that plays automatically and has a controller, as shown in the following illustration. You can see this in action by using your browser to open `Poster.htm` in the SpecialDelivery folder of the CD.

Clicking on the poster movie loads
the actual movie with a controller
and begins to autoplay.

An alternative method to accomplish the same thing without using Plug-in Helper would be to pass these parameters to the new movie using a URL extension, like this:

```
<EMBED SRC="Poster.mov" HEIGHT=176 WIDTH=120
  CONTROLLER="False"
  HREF=
  "<Other.mov> T<myself> E<controller=true autoplay=true>" >
```

Bear in mind that you can't set a separate height or width for the two movies using Plug-in Helper; the HEIGHT and WIDTH settings tell the browser how much space to give the plug-in, and the plug-in itself can't change them. So you have to choose one setting that works for both the poster and the movie.

Remember that the controller adds 16 pixels to the height of the movie, so set HEIGHT equal to at least the movie height plus 16. Ideally, the poster image should be exactly 16 pixels taller than the movie. If the poster is larger or smaller than the movie plus the controller, set HEIGHT and WIDTH to the larger dimensions and set an appropriate background color using the BGCOLOR parameter in the <EMBED> tag. Black is an effective background color for most movies.

If you want the second movie to load in the QuickTime Player application instead of replacing the image in the Web page, set the TARGET parameter to quicktimeplayer instead of myself.

If you want to get really clever (and who doesn't?), you can create a poster that turns into a movie when you click it, then morphs back into a poster when the movie's done. For details, see "Poster Movies" (page 111).

That pretty much covers the basics of Plug-in Helper. We'll look at other uses for Plug-in Helper throughout the book, but they all use the same checkbox and set of text boxes that we've just covered.

▶ Copy Protection

There are several things you can do to give your movies a degree of copy protection—nothing that would stop the federal government (or a determined teenager with unlimited time and equipment), but enough to keep honest people honest, and average would-be copiers baffled:

- You can set a movie characteristic that prevents the movie from being edited or saved by any QuickTime application.
- You can deliver your movies as real-time streams.
- You can encrypt the media.
- You can deliver a movie with URL data references and a compressed header. ("A what and a *what*?" you may ask. Exactly.)

Note Here's a word to the wise. There's a lot of interest in securing movies and, yes, there are a lot of useful tricks, but, no, there is no 100% foolproof method—someone can always point a movie camera at the screen, capture the packets as they stream across the network, or pilfer the bits from the screen and audio buffers. So far, no encryption scheme has proven to be unbreakable. Of course, there are new "digital rights management" schemes in development all the time, so stay tuned. But for now there is simply no way to show your movies over the Internet that will absolutely prevent any form of copying, despite what anyone may claim.

- **Disallow Saving**

  Clicking the "Disallow saving from plugin" checkbox in Plug-in Helper is one of the simplest and most effective forms of QuickTime copy protection.

  QuickTime won't save a movie if the "Disallow saving from plugin" checkbox is set with Plug-in Helper. All QuickTime applications, including QuickTime Player and Plug-in Helper, recognize the disallow saving setting and will not copy or save the movie once this attribute is set.

  Of course, if people get copies of your protected movie from the browser cache, or by accessing your server directly, they can duplicate them using their file systems. But these copies also have the disallow saving attribute. People still can't cut, change, or edit your movies.

Important   Make a backup copy of your movie *before* you turn copy protection on using Plug-in Helper. You cannot edit and save the movie afterward.

- **Use Real-Time Streams**

  People have a hard time copying your movie file if you never send it to them. With real-time streams, you don't send the actual file—just streams of media. QuickTime doesn't store the streams locally as a movie. It displays the media and discards it.

  Only very sophisticated users, equipped with packet-sniffing technology, are able to intercept and copy these data streams. It takes additional sophistication to reconstruct a movie from them. For well over 99.9% of the population, it's simply impossible.

  The trade-off is that it takes a bit of extra effort for you to deliver QuickTime movies as real-time streams. It isn't difficult, mind you, but there are a couple of extra steps.

  Also, by their nature real-time streams can deliver only as high quality an experience as the viewer's bandwidth permits. People on slow or unreliable connections can't view high-bandwidth streaming content and may find the quality of low-bandwidth material unacceptable.

  Of course, streaming also has advantages that balance these drawbacks, such as the ability to jump to any point in a movie without downloading the intervening material.

  For this and other reasons, streaming is the most common approach to copy protection.

For more information, see Chapter 7, "What about Streaming?," and Chapter 14, "Gently down the Stream."

- **Encrypt the Media**

  The traditional approach to copy protection is encryption. This is moderately effective for copy-protecting physical media, such as DVDs, and can be very effective at keeping any kind of data from being intercepted and copied by people who don't have the encryption key.

  The problem is, you generally have to supply the encryption key to the viewer. If the viewer wants to make copies, you can't usually prevent it except by legal action.

  QuickTime has built-in support for encryption using media keys—only viewers who have the key can view the media. It's very similar to the way you unlock QuickTime Pro's editing features. Currently, only Sorenson video has implemented media key protection as an option for their codecs.

  Other vendors, such as Sealed Media, market encryption systems for various multimedia types, including QuickTime movies, that conceal the key from the viewer. These systems provide moderate to strong protection for any QuickTime media, at a cost. They typically require the user to install special software to allow them to see your movies, and they are not free. This approach may work well with confidential information on a LAN or intranet, or for high-value pay-per-view material, but it is not well suited to copy-protecting movies delivered over the Internet to the nonpaying public.

- **URL Data References**

  Remember that QuickTime movies can point to data in other files, including files on the Internet that are not movies themselves. For example, you can open QuickTime Player, choose Open URL from the File menu, and type in the URL of any JPEG or MP3 on the Internet. It opens as a QuickTime movie.

  When you use the Open URL command and save the resulting QuickTime movie allowing dependencies, it creates a very small movie with a URL data reference—a reference to media data that it gets over the Internet.

  If you set the disallow saving property in the movie, QuickTime will not allow anyone to edit the movie or save it as a self-contained file, so even though they can play the media from your server, they can't save it. People can copy this tiny movie using their file system, but all they're really saving is a pointer to your media. When the movie is played, it always gets its data over the Internet. If you remove the data or restrict access to it, these copies no longer play.

Unfortunately, it isn't that hard to learn the URL of the media file as it travels over the Internet. This means a hacker can copy the media file. If the media file can be played locally, your movie has been cracked.

But what if the media file isn't a playable file? What if it's an unlabeled, interleaved, mish-mash of video frames, sound samples, and things too horrible to imagine, some assembly required, with no instructions?

Sure, we can do that.

Here's a recipe for creating a small movie file with data in a nonplayable file somewhere on the Internet. The movie file can be copied, and so can the data file, but the movie file always gets its data from your Internet server, and the data file is not a playable movie.

1. Create a self-contained movie.

2. Make a copy of the movie, setting the copy's file extension to `.bin`, and put the copy on a Web server.

3. Open the `.bin` file using QuickTime Player's Open URL command. Save (allow dependencies). Let's call this `Pointer.mov`.

Important   Do not save as a self-contained movie! That copies the data instead of pointing to it.

4. Drag `Pointer.mov` onto the NoSaveQT icon (in the Tools folder of the CD). This creates a save-disabled movie you can distribute.

5. Drag the local copy of your `.bin` file onto the KillMovie icon (also in the Tools folder of the CD). This makes your `.bin` file nonplayable.

6. Copy the unplayable version of the `.bin` file onto your Web server, overwriting the earlier version.

You now have a small movie that you can embed in a Web page and otherwise distribute freely. It will always get its data from your Web server. If you remove the data, the movie will not play. If you restrict access to the data, only those with access can play the movie. The data file cannot be played locally, so copying it accomplishes nothing.

This is probably the easiest and most effective way to copy-protect a Fast Start QuickTime movie for delivery over the Internet.

- **Jujitsu**

  Sometimes the best answer is jujitsu; instead of fighting the force, redirect it to your benefit. Add your logo to the movie and include a live link back to your website. QuickTime makes it simple to do both.

  Go further—add a media skin, so the movie plays in your own branded player, replete with your logo and a click-through to your website.

  Every copy of the movie becomes free advertising for your company or your product.

  Why copy-protect a rock video when every copy is a clickable link to buy the CD it's promoting? It's better than airplay—the viewer is never more than one mouse click away from the cash register.

  People love to copy things. Use viral marketing to make this force of nature your friend. QuickTime makes it easy to brand your movies and link them to your website.

  Okay, enough about copy protection. Let's look at some other things you can do with QuickTime and HTML.

Launching QuickTime Player

It's possible to write HTML that will play your QuickTime movies (or other media files) in the QuickTime Player application instead of the plug-in. This is handy because QuickTime Player can do some things that the plug-in can't, such as playing movies in full-screen mode.

The usual way to launch QuickTime Player is to use a poster movie—a QuickTime movie, usually a single image, that launches QuickTime Player in response to a mouse click. The poster can also be set to launch QuickTime Player automatically, without requiring a mouse click.

Starting with QuickTime 5, it's possible to launch QuickTime Player directly from a text link, which is sometimes preferable to a poster movie.

Launching the Player from a Poster

This is pretty well covered in "Using a Poster Movie" (page 53), and particularly in "Launching QuickTime Player from a Poster Movie" (page 55), but we'll go over it again briefly. A poster movie is a QuickTime movie that responds to a mouse click by playing another movie. In this case, that movie is targeted to open in QuickTime Player.

You can make any QuickTime movie into a poster movie by adding an HREF parameter to the movie's <EMBED> tag. To make the movie open in QuickTime Player, just add TARGET="quicktimeplayer" as well. For example:

```
<EMBED SRC="Poster.mov" HEIGHT="240" WIDTH="320"
  HREF="Main.mov" TARGET="quicktimeplayer"
  CONTROLLER="False" >
```

This example embeds Poster.mov in a Web page. If the viewer clicks in the display area of Poster.mov, QuickTime plays Main.mov in QuickTime Player.

That's all there is to it.

Launching QuickTime Player from a Text Link

Sometimes it's inconvenient to use a poster movie to launch QuickTime Player. It involves another production step, for one thing, and the viewer needs to have QuickTime installed just to see the poster. Starting with QuickTime 5, it's possible to launch QuickTime Player directly from a text link.

It's done using a special MIME type. Why another MIME type? Because there's no HTML command to open a particular application. All you can do is link to a file—the browser chooses a plug-in or an application that has registered for that file extension or MIME type. External player applications, such as RealPlayer, Windows Media Player, and QuickTime Player, each register a unique MIME type that only they play. You launch a particular player by linking to a file of the appropriate type.

For QuickTime Player, you use a QuickTime Media Link file, file extension .qtl, MIME type application/x-quicktimeplayer. Your text link is an ordinary HTML hyperlink, and it looks like this:

```
<A HREF SRC="MyMovie.qtl"> Click Here for a QuickTime
  Movie </A>
```

Important For this to work, your Web server *must* be configured to associate the .qtl file extension with the correct MIME type:

```
.qtl = application/x-quicktimeplayer
```

A QuickTime Media Link file can be either a special text file or an actual QuickTime movie.

If you change the file extension of any QuickTime movie from .mov to .qtl, it becomes a QuickTime Media Link. It's still a movie, but a browser won't pass .qtl files to the QuickTime plug-in, or any other plug-in—only to QuickTime Player. Because when QuickTime 5 or later is installed, it registers QuickTime Player as the only application for .qtl files (MIME type application/x-quicktimeplayer).

Alternatively, you can create a specially formatted text file that tells QuickTime Player what movie to play and how to play it (full-screen, looping, and so on).

Either way, there are a few drawbacks you should be aware of when using .qtl files.

This is a relatively new MIME type, so you may need to add it to your Web server's look-up table. That only takes a minute if it's actually *your* Web server, but if not, you may have to convince someone who isn't sure what a MIME type is that it's a good idea. And that *can* be tiresome. Never fear, all of today's streaming media were new MIME types once. After a while, all webmasters will know about .qtl files, or their Web servers will come with the MIME type already listed in the tables. But as an early adopter, you may have to educate some people.

Also, when you load a movie using this technique, the browser downloads the movie to the user's hard disk as an ordinary file—not as a temporary cache item—which is probably not what you want as a default behavior. What's more, some browsers wait for the whole file to arrive before calling QuickTime Player.

Fortunately, there's a pretty good solution for these problems. QuickTime supports several kinds of reference movies—small files, typically less than 1 Kbyte, that point to movies by filename or URL. QuickTime plays a reference movie by getting whatever it points to and playing that. Only the small reference movie downloads as a file.

It usually takes less than a second to download the reference movie, and the movie it points to—the real movie—can play *while* it downloads. Only the tiny reference movie is left on the viewer's disk. That does leave "mouse droppings" on the viewer's disk, of course. But that's better than elephant . . . uh, hmm . . . suppose we start again with a different metaphor? Anyway. No copy of your actual movie is saved to disk, unless you allow saving *and* the viewer explicitly chooses to save the movie.

You can make a .qtl reference movie two different ways: create a reference movie using QuickTime Player and change the file extension to .qtl, or create a .qtl file directly.

Making a Reference Movie with QuickTime Player

Just follow the bouncing ball:

1. Put your actual movie on your Web server.

2. Open QuickTime Player, choose Open URL in the File menu, and enter the URL of your movie, such as

   `http://www.myserver.com/movies/MyMovie.mov`

3. Your movie should open. If it autoplays, stop it and rewind it to the beginning.

4. Choose Save (not Save As). This creates a tiny reference movie that's basically a wrapper around the URL of the actual movie. Quit.

This creates a reference movie with the .mov file extension. You can use this movie as stand-in for your actual movie. Embed it in a Web page, pass it around on a CD, whatever. Change the file extension to .qtl so browsers will play it with QuickTime Player instead of using a plug-in.

Making a QuickTime Media Link (.qtl) File

A QuickTime Media Link (.qtl) file is a special kind of text file. It uses XML syntax, but don't worry—you don't need to know anything about XML to use it.

You can create a .qtl file directly from QuickTime Player, or you can use a text editor (or a script) to create it as text.

Creating .qtl Files Using QuickTime Player

Probably the easiest way to create a .qtl file is to use QuickTime Player:

1. Open a movie in QuickTime Player by choosing Open URL from the File menu.

2. Choose Export from the File menu, then choose Movie to QuickTime Media Link from the pop-up menu.

Important Always open a movie using Open URL when creating a QuickTime Media Link. If you open a movie by double-clicking, using the Open command, or by drag-and-drop, it will have a URL in the format `file://localhost/Volumes/Disk/Path/Filename`. Probably not what you had in mind.

3. Click the Options button in the ensuing Save File dialog box. You'll see a dialog box like the one in the following illustration.

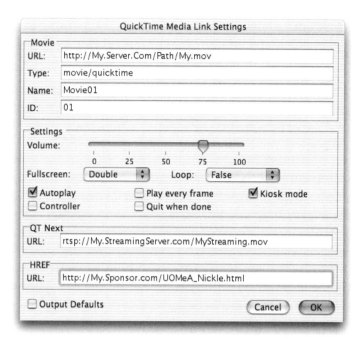

Well, it won't look exactly like that. All the fields except the URL will be blank, and all the checkboxes, pop-up menus, and sliders will be set to their defaults. But the illustration shows you some of the extra features you can set from this dialog. Nice, eh?

You can change the URL if you want the .qt1 file to point to a different movie, or you plan to put the movie on a different server. But be sure to use an *absolute* URL, not a relative URL.

Important You can't use relative URLs in .qt1 files. When the browser passes a .qt1 file to Quick-Time Player, it doesn't include the URL of the file. The browser puts the .qt1 file on a local disk and passes it to the player from there. A relative URL would be relative to wherever the browser put the file—probably the desktop. Use absolute URLs.

Click OK to generate a .qt1 file that points to the specified URL and tells QuickTime Player to play the movie it finds there with the parameters you've set.

As you can see, you can set the name and ID of the movie, the volume, various full-screen modes, and a number of other parameters, including a follow-up movie and a URL to open if the viewer clicks the movie's display area.

QuickTime has defaults for most of these parameters, and if some of your settings match the defaults, QuickTime Player doesn't normally include them in the .qtl file. If you want all your settings included in the .qtl file, whether they match the default settings or not, check the Output Defaults box.

If you like, you can edit the .qtl file using a text editor to see what parameters are set, or to change settings without going through QuickTime Player again. By coincidence, this is explained in the section immediately following.

Creating .qtl Files As Text (XML)

You can create a QuickTime Media Link file by typing three lines of text using a text editor, word processor, or any script that can generate a text file. Actually, you can copy and paste the first two lines because they're always the same.

It's XML, and the syntax may seem a little cryptic if you're unfamiliar with it, but the process is very simple. If your movie is named My.mov, your text file looks like this:

```
<?xml version="1.0"?>
<?quicktime type="application/x-quicktime-media-link"?>
<embed src="http://www.myserver.com/Movies/My.mov" />
```

Important   Don't leave out the /> at the end of the third line! This is XML, not HTML.

The first two lines tell QuickTime that this is a reference movie. Put the URL of your actual movie in the src parameter on the third line.

The URL can use HTTP, RTSP, FTP, or any protocol QuickTime supports. It's generally best to use HTTP for a movie on a Web server, and you definitely want to use RTSP for movies on a streaming server. You can't use relative URLs over the Internet though—the browser gives the file to QuickTime from the local disk; it doesn't tell QuickTime the file's original URL. Use absolute URLs.

Save this file as plain text with the .qtl file extension.

A nice feature of this kind of reference movie is that you can pass additional instructions to QuickTime Player in the third line. The player understands the following commands:

- autoplay="true" | "false" (@timestamp is not yet supported)
- controller="true" | "false"

- `fullscreen="normal" | "double" | "half" | "current" | "full"`
- `href="url"`
- `loop="true" | "false" | "palindrome"`
- `playeveryframe="true" | "false"`
- `qtnext="url"`
- `quitwhendone="true" | "false"`

Just place these commands inside the `<EMBED>` tag on the third line of the `.qtl` file. Here's an example:

```
<embed src="http://a.server.com/aMovie.mov" autoplay="true" />
```

You may have noticed two commands for QuickTime Player that don't have equivalents in the HTML parameters for the plug-in—`quitwhendone` and `fullscreen`.

The `fullscreen` command tells QuickTime Player to use the whole screen to display the movie, using a black background if the movie does not perfectly fit the screen dimensions. For more about full-screen movies, see "Full-Screen Movies" (page 106).

The `quitwhendone` command tells QuickTime Player to quit when the movie ends, effectively returning the viewer to the browser. When combined with the `fullscreen` command, this can create a seamless experience in which the QuickTime Player application is almost invisible—the viewer clicks a link, the screen goes black and a movie plays, then the browser window comes back exactly as it was. To see an example, load `Fullscreen.mov` in your browser (it's in the SpecialDelivery folder of the CD).

The remaining commands behave like their HTML `<EMBED>` tag equivalents, with the minor exception of `autoplay`, which doesn't yet support the new `autoplay="@hh:mm:ss:ff"` delayed-start feature. It's either true or false.

If you create a `.qtl` file using QuickTime Player (Export > Movie to QuickTime Media Link), it creates a text file exactly like this. If you check the Output Defaults box, the text file will include every parameter that can be set. This makes a handy template to work from—all the syntax and spelling are taken care of; just change the parameter values and save with a new name.

Speaking of names, you probably noticed that you can rename a `.mov` file with the `.qtl` file extension. The reverse is also true—you can change a `.qtl` file's extension to `.mov` and QuickTime will still play it. The main difference is that a browser will pass a `.qtl` file to QuickTime Player and a `.mov` file to the QuickTime plug-in. They're two completely different file types, mind you, but QuickTime knows that they like to exchange names, so it checks for that.

Important   This is *not* how files normally behave. Changing a file's extension is generally a Very Bad Idea—renaming a file to most other file extensions will make it unplayable. Similarly, renaming other files and giving them the `.mov` file extension can cause problems of the worst sort.

You can create other kinds of reference movies in QuickTime, including reference movies that cause QuickTime Player to load different movies based on the viewer's language or Internet connection speed. We'll look at the other kinds of reference movies—and some fairly amazing things you can do with them—in the following chapters. Right now let's look at the main reason you would want to launch QuickTime Player instead of using the plug-in: full-screen movies.

Full-Screen Movies

One serious limitation of playing movies in a browser window is, well, playing a movie in a browser window. You don't know how big it is, or if it's wider than it is tall. It's usually cluttered with menus and toolbars, and it generally distracts attention from your movie and interferes with your ability to connect to an audience.

Linking to a player application doesn't always solve the problem. The player also has an interface that may distract viewers, and you still have the viewer's desktop peeking around the sides, along with task bars, control strips, and what-have-you.

Besides, sometimes you don't want *any* interface—no menus, no windows, no control bars—just your beautiful movie, filling the screen or floating on a black background.

Okay. Let's do that. Just set the full-screen mode in the movie, and QuickTime Player will do the rest. There are several ways to set full-screen mode, and a few different kinds of full-screen modes you can set. Let's look at the modes first, then talk about the methods of setting them.

Full-Screen Modes

There are currently five different full-screen modes that you can invoke from a Web page:

- **normal**—movie plays at its normal size

- **double**—movie is scaled up to double its normal size

- **half**—movie is scaled down to half its normal size

- **current**—movie plays at the size it was when last saved, which allows you to stretch or scale the movie to a custom size, then display it in full-screen mode

- **full**—scales the movie up or down, as necessary, to fill the screen as completely as possible while preserving the movie's aspect ratio

Note Versions of QuickTime prior to 6.1 may change the monitor resolution of a Macintosh temporarily while playing a movie in full-screen mode. Later versions of QuickTime no longer do this.

In all cases, the screen is cleared to black, the movie is centered on the screen, and it plays automatically. In some cases the movie fills the entire screen; in other cases there are black borders from movie edge to screen edge.

There are never any menus or controls. The movie plays until it ends or the viewer presses the Esc key. If the movie is set to loop, it plays repeatedly until the viewer presses Esc.

If the movie is also set to quit when done, QuickTime Player quits at the end of the movie.

If the viewer presses the Esc key during the movie, QuickTime Player drops out of full-screen mode—the movie is paused and displayed at the size at which it was last saved. If the viewer then restarts the movie, it plays normally, rather than in full-screen mode.

The movie can also drop out of full-screen mode if it is playing while downloading and the download can't keep up, forcing QuickTime to pause the movie. There are a few ways to prevent this from happening. They all involve techniques that we'll cover later in the book, but here they are:

- You can deliver a movie who's data rate is lower than the available bandwidth. You'll learn how to automatically select the right movie for a viewer's connection speed in Chapter 8, "Alternate Realities: Language, Speed, and Connections."

- You can save the movie so that it doesn't fast start—it won't play until the whole file is available. This is explained in "Saving Movies" (page 33).

- You can put a low-bandwidth image or animation at the front of your movie and leave it there for several seconds, so the download gets well ahead in the movie timeline. Text is ideal for this, as you need some time to read it anyway. If the text is slowly scrolling, it's clear that the movie is playing, not hung. You'll learn how to put this kind of text into a movie in Chapter 13, "Text! Text! Text!"

- You can use wired sprites to monitor the movie's current time and the amount of movie time that has downloaded. If you're about to run out of data, the sprite can slow the movie's play rate to a virtual halt without actually stopping it, effectively pausing while the download gets ahead. We'll cover wired sprites in Chapter 15, "An Animated Approach," and Chapter 16, "Getting Interactive."

How to Set Full-Screen Mode

There are several different ways to set full-screen mode, but they fall into two broad categories: methods that set full-screen mode externally, without changing the movie itself, and methods that modify the movie internally so that it plays in full-screen mode by default.

One of the external methods you already know—you can write a three-line text file that plays a movie in full-screen mode. For details, flip back to "Making a QuickTime Media Link (.qtl) File" (page 102).

A very similar method is to create a SMIL presentation. SMIL is another XML-based way to pass movie URLs to QuickTime. I won't get into the details here—we'll cover that in Chapter 18, "SMIL for the Camera." If all you want to do is play a single movie in full-screen mode, use the three-line method just described instead—it's simpler.

Use SMIL if you want to create a full-screen presentation composed of separate elements, such as a series of JPEGs and an audio file, without importing them all into QuickTime and editing them together.

The other methods of setting full-screen mode make a change to the movie itself.

If you have a Macintosh, by far the easiest way to make full-screen movies is to use AppleScript. There are scripts already written for you on the CD that came with this book—just drop a movie, or a folder full of movies, onto the script and stand back. The documentation for the scripts is on the CD as well. It's all in the AppleScript folder.

Another method that's almost as easy is to use one of the four full-screen movies in the SpecialDelivery folder of the CD: fullnormal .mov, fulldouble.mov, fullcustom.mov, or fullfull.mov. Here's how to use them:

1. Open your movie in QuickTime Player.

2. Select All. Copy. Close (don't save).

3. Open the full-screen movie with the desired mode: normal, double, custom, or full.

4. Add. Save As (self-contained).

Your new movie is a copy of your original movie with full-screen mode set.

The next method is either complex and expensive or completely trivial, depending on your other needs. You can use one of the more capable QuickTime application programs—Cleaner 5, Media Cleaner Pro 4, or LiveStage Pro—to set the full-screen mode in a movie.

These are powerful tools, and most serious QuickTime authors have at least one, if not all three.

If you already have one of these programs, it's as simple as clicking a tab and checking a box. You can set full-screen mode when making a movie in any of these programs. You can also use any of them to add full-screen mode to your existing movies. In Cleaner or Media Cleaner, click "Don't Recompress" to set a mode in an existing movie. In LiveStage, just open the movie, click the checkbox, and save.

If you don't already have one of these programs, prepare to spend a little money and a moderate amount of time learning something complex and interesting (you've gotten this far—obviously you have the aptitude). You'll be rewarded for your efforts.

And that concludes our discussion of full-screen movies.

Putting Multiple Movies on a Page

Sometimes you want to put multiple QuickTime movies on a single Web page. This presents a problem. Like most problems, there's a way to solve it that's simple, obvious, and wrong:

```
<EMBED SRC="HugeMovie1.mov" HEIGHT=136 WIDTH=160> <BR>
<EMBED SRC="HugeMovie2.mov" HEIGHT=136 WIDTH=160> <BR>
<EMBED SRC="HugeMovie3.mov" HEIGHT=136 WIDTH=160>
```

Don't do this. If you put multiple movies on your Web page using multiple <EMBED> tags you'll run into the following problems:

- Every <EMBED> tag on the page loads a copy of the plug-in, which requires its own block of memory. It adds up.
- All the movies download at once, right along with your Web page. It takes forever.
- All the movies try to load into memory at once. Oops.

To see an example of this approach, load `MultiMovie1.htm` (in the Special-Delivery folder on the CD).

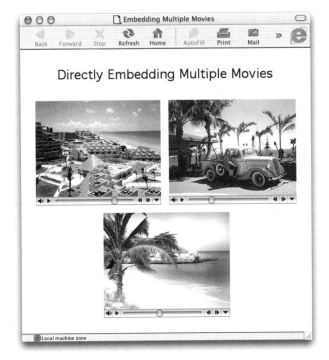

You might use this approach successfully for a page with a few small movies or in a controlled environment—two or three short audio loops, for example, or short movie clips on an intranet page for users with a known amount of RAM.

For pages delivering several large movies or MP3 files over the Internet, this is a recipe for trouble.

Fortunately, there are other solutions. You can use poster movies, target the movies to QuickTime Player, target the movies to a common frame or window, or you can use a little JavaScript.

Poster Movies

Poster movies are described in "Using a Poster Movie" (page 53) and "Making a Poster Movie with Plug-in Helper" (page 92). To embed multiple poster movies on a page, try this:

```
<EMBED SRC="Poster1.mov" HREF="HugeMovie1.mov"
  TARGET="myself" HEIGHT=136 WIDTH=160> <BR>
<EMBED SRC="Poster2.mov" HREF="HugeMovie2.mov"
  TARGET="myself" HEIGHT=136 WIDTH=160> <BR>
<EMBED SRC="Poster3.mov" HREF="HugeMovie3.mov"
  TARGET="myself" HEIGHT=136 WIDTH=160> <BR>
```

This still loads multiple copies of the plug-in, but each copy initially shows an image rather than a whole movie. This shortens the load time for your page and doesn't require a lot of RAM initially.

To see an example of this approach, load MultiMovie2.htm (in the Special-Delivery folder on the CD). It's shown in the following illustration.

Clicking a poster movie loads the actual movie.

- Multiple copies of the plug-in are loaded.

- Each movie loads into memory only when it is played.

- Each movie continues to occupy memory after it has played.

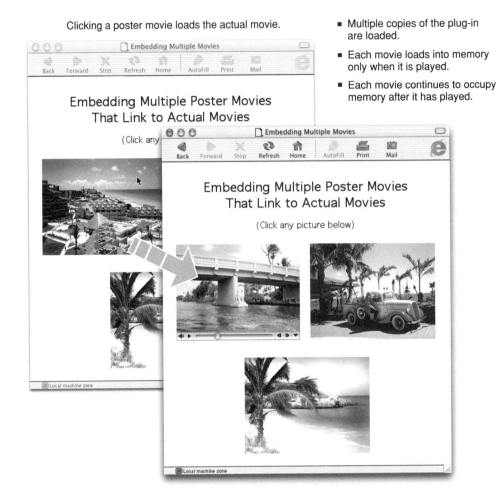

Unfortunately, each movie still loads into RAM when the user clicks a poster and continues to use RAM after it's done playing. After the second or third movie, there may not be enough RAM to play any others, and there's no easy way for the user to close the open movies.

You can get around this by having each movie turn back into a poster when it finishes. You do this by adding an HREF track to the end of the movie. HREF tracks are discussed in detail in "HREF Tracks" (page 394), but here's a little preview.

1. Create a one-line text file, using a text editor or word processor, that reads

```
A<poster.mov> T<myself>
```

using the actual name of your poster movie in place of poster.mov. Save this as a *plain-text file* with a .txt file extension, such as link.txt. Close it.

2. Drag your new text file onto QuickTime Player. It should open as a movie.

3. Select All. Copy. Close.

4. Open your real movie. Go to the end and click in the last frame. Paste. This adds the text to the end of your movie as a new text track.

5. Change the name of the new text track to HREFTrack—choose Get Movie Properties to open the Properties window, choose the last text track in the window's left pop-up menu, choose General in the right pop-up menu, click Change Name, and enter HREFTrack (exactly like that, mixed case, no spaces).

6. Choose Enable Tracks from the Edit menu and turn HREFTrack OFF.

7. Choose Save As (self-contained). This creates a new movie that replaces itself with Poster.mov when it finishes.

8. Use Plug-in Helper to set the CONTROLLER="True" and AUTOPLAY="True" parameters inside your new movie, as shown in the following illustration:

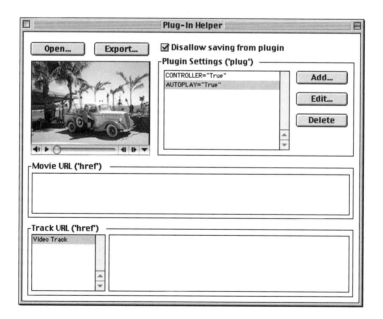

9. Use Plug-in Helper to add a CONTROLLER="False" statement to the poster:

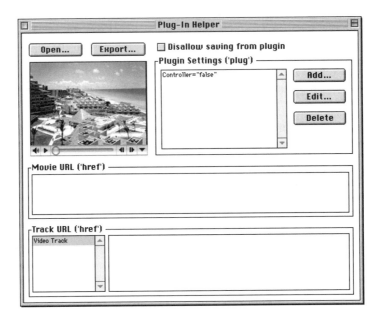

10. Change the HREF parameter in your <EMBED> tag to link the poster to your new movie. It should look something like this:

```
<EMBED SRC="Poster1.mov" HREF="NewMovie1.mov"
  TARGET="myself" HEIGHT=136 WIDTH=160>
```

11. Repeat for each movie.

When you load the page in your browser, it displays the posters without controllers. When you click a poster, it loads the movie indicated in the HREF parameter of the <EMBED> tag. The movie has a controller and auto-plays because you added those features using Plug-in Helper. Right at the end, the movie has an HREF track that replaces the movie with the poster again.

To see this in action, load MultiMovie3.htm (in the SpecialDelivery folder on the CD).

Clicking a poster movie loads and plays the actual movie. When the movie is finished playing, it reverts back to the poster movie.

- Multiple copies of the plug-in are loaded.

- Each movie loads into memory only when it is played.

- Each movie frees up memory after it has played.

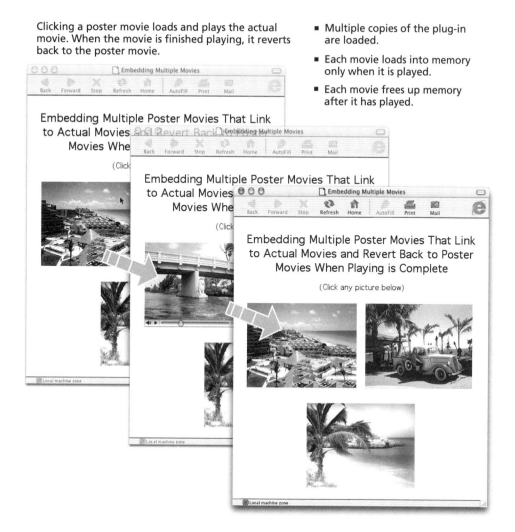

Targeting QuickTime Player

Alternatively, you can have your poster movies target QuickTime Player. A user who runs short on RAM can simply close any open movies. The HTML looks like this:

```
<EMBED SRC="Poster1.mov" HREF="HugeMovie1.mov"
   TARGET="quicktimeplayer" HEIGHT=136 WIDTH=160> <BR>
<EMBED SRC="Poster2.mov" HREF="HugeMovie2.mov"
   TARGET="quicktimeplayer" HEIGHT=136 WIDTH=160> <BR>
<EMBED SRC="Poster3.mov" HREF="HugeMovie3.mov"
   TARGET="quicktimeplayer" HEIGHT=136 WIDTH=160> <BR>
```

To see an example of this approach, load `MultiMovie4.htm` (in the Special-Delivery folder on the CD).

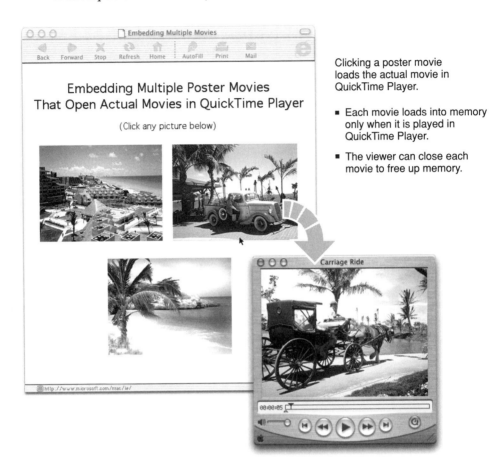

Clicking a poster movie loads the actual movie in QuickTime Player.

- Each movie loads into memory only when it is played in QuickTime Player.

- The viewer can close each movie to free up memory.

One nice thing about this approach is that the movie can be larger than the space allocated to the plug-in or even larger than the browser window. If you like, it can even play in full-screen mode. For details, see "Full-Screen Movies" (page 106).

Targeting a Frame or a Window

If you prefer, you can target a frame or a window instead of targeting QuickTime Player. If each poster targets the same frame or window, only one movie loads into memory at any time.

You can either create a frameset with a designated frame for playing movies, or you can let the browser create a new window to play movies in.

In either case, write a small HTML page for each movie, with that movie embedded in it:

```
<HTML>
<HEAD>
<TITLE>Movie In Window</TITLE>
</HEAD>
<BODY>
<DIV ALIGN="Center">
<H1>Huge Movie 1</H1>
<EMBED SRC="HugeMovie1.mov" HEIGHT=136 WIDTH=160 AUTOPLAY="True">
</DIV>
</BODY>
</HTML>
```

Use the URL of the page you just wrote in the poster's HREF parameter, and target a frame or a window. Specify the same target for all the movies:

```
<EMBED SRC="Poster1.mov" HREF="HugeMovie1.htm"
  TARGET="MovieFrame" HEIGHT=136 WIDTH=160> <BR>
<EMBED SRC="Poster2.mov" HREF="HugeMovie2.htm"
  TARGET="MovieFrame" HEIGHT=136 WIDTH=160> <BR>
<EMBED SRC="Poster3.mov" HREF="HugeMovie3.htm"
  TARGET="MovieFrame" HEIGHT=136 WIDTH=160> <BR>
```

When the user clicks a poster, the HTML page with the corresponding movie loads and plays in the named frame. If there is no frame with that name, the browser creates a new window. When the user clicks a different poster, a new movie plays in the same place. The old movie and the old copy of the plug-in are dismissed from memory, so only the current movie uses any RAM.

To see an example of this approach, load MultiMovie5.htm (in the SpecialDelivery folder on the CD).

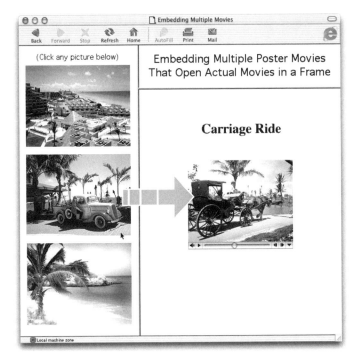

Clicking a poster movie loads the actual movie in a designated frame.

- Only the current movie playing is loaded into memory.

- As new movies are selected, the old movie is dismissed from memory.

If you use this technique, you can reduce memory requirements and speed up page loading even further by using ordinary HREF anchors instead of poster movies. After all, you're just linking to another Web page. The links can be text:

```
<A HREF="HugeMovie1.htm" TARGET="MovieFrame">Play Movie 1</A> <BR>
<A HREF="HugeMovie2.htm" TARGET="MovieFrame">Play Movie 2</A> <BR>
<A HREF="HugeMovie3.htm" TARGET="MovieFrame">Play Movie 3</A> <BR>
```

or images:

```
<A HREF="HugeMovie1.htm" TARGET="MovieFrame">
  <IMG SRC="Movie1.gif"></A> <BR>
<A HREF="HugeMovie2.htm" TARGET="MovieFrame">
  <IMG SRC="Movie2.gif"></A> <BR>
<A HREF="HugeMovie3.htm" TARGET="MovieFrame">
  <IMG SRC="Movie3.gif"></A> <BR>
```

If you're using a frameset, and MovieFrame is an existing frame, that's where each movie plays. To see an example of this approach, load MultiMovie6.htm (in the SpecialDelivery folder on the CD).

Clicking a button loads the actual movie in a designated frame.

- Only the current movie playing and its plug-in are loaded into memory.
- As new movies are selected, the old movie and its plug-in are dismissed from memory.

If there is no frame named `MovieFrame`, a new window is created with that name. The movies play in this window. To see an example of this approach, load `MultiMovie7.htm` (in the SpecialDelivery folder on the CD), shown in the following illustration.

Clicking a button loads the actual movie in a window.

- Only the current movie playing and its plug-in are loaded into memory.
- As new movies are selected, the old movie and its plug-in are dismissed from memory.

Unfortunately, you cannot control the size or the attributes of a window created from the HTML TARGET parameter. The window will have the size and characteristics of the default window for the user's browser, which may not be what you had in mind at all.

If you want your movies to play in a floating window whose size and characteristics you control, you need to use JavaScript.

Creating a Window with JavaScript

The script that specifies the size and attributes of the target window goes in the head of your main HTML page. Here's an example page:

```html
<html>
<head>
<title>JavaScript Movie Page</title>
<script language="JavaScript">
<!-- hide from old browsers
  function openMovie(url)  {
  windOptions =
      "toolbar=0,location=0,directories=0, status=0," +
  "menubar=0,scrollbars=0,resizable=0,width=320,height=240";
  moviewin = window.open(url, "movie", windOptions);
  moviewin.focus();
  }
  // -->
</script>
</head>
<body>
<a href="javascript:openMovie('HugeMovie1.htm')">
  Movie1</a><BR>
<a href="javascript:openMovie('HugeMovie2.htm')">
  Movie2</a><BR>
<a href="javascript:openMovie('HugeMovie2.htm')">Movie3</a>
</body>
</html>
```

The JavaScript function openMovie(url) opens a 320 x 240 window with no distracting bells and whistles: no Back or Home buttons, no What's Cool button, no scroll bars, no nothing—just a simple window. The window is named moviewin, and it's opened on top of any existing windows. The window is created only when someone clicks one of the movie links.

It's filled with the specified HTML page, which should contain an embedded movie.

The movie links can be text, as shown in the previous example, or GIF or JPEG images. To see an example of this approach, load `MultiMovie8.htm`.

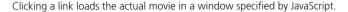
Clicking a link loads the actual movie in a window specified by JavaScript.

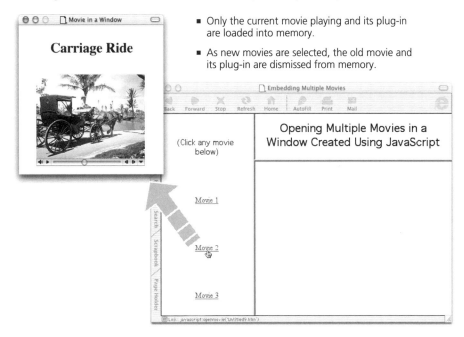

- Only the current movie playing and its plug-in are loaded into memory.
- As new movies are selected, the old movie and its plug-in are dismissed from memory.

Detecting the QuickTime Plug-in

Experiencing your website depends on the QuickTime plug-in (a term that includes the QuickTime ActiveX control), so you want to be sure your visitors have it. If they don't, you want to redirect them to a download page or to alternative content pages.

Detecting browser plug-ins tends to be a black art, due to inconsistencies among browsers, operating systems, ActiveX, JavaScript, and VBScript. The easy and reliable way is to use QuickTime to detect itself.

You can do this by embedding a QuickTime movie in your main page that automatically sends people with QuickTime to the desired content page—just add HREF and AUTOHREF parameters to the movie's <EMBED> tag. Add an HTML refresh tag to your Web page to automatically redirect people without QuickTime—either to a download page or an alternative content page.

Here's a small HTML page (in the SpecialDelivery folder of the CD as Redirect.htm) that detects whether the viewer has QuickTime 4 or later and redirects the browser accordingly. It works with Internet Explorer or Netscape browsers, versions 3 and later, on Mac OS or Windows (95/98/NT/2000/ME).

```
<HTML>
<HEAD>
<TITLE>Detect QuickTime</TITLE>
<META HTTP-EQUIV="Refresh" CONTENT="30;URL=GetQT.htm">
</HEAD>

<BODY>
<DIV ALIGN="Center">

<OBJECT WIDTH="160" HEIGHT="120"
  CLASSID="clsid:02BF25D5-8C17-4B23-BC80-D3488ABDDC6B"
  CODEBASE="http://www.apple.com/qtactivex/qtplugin.cab">

<PARAM NAME="src" VALUE="letsgo.mov">
<PARAM NAME="href" VALUE="HasQT.htm">
<PARAM NAME="autohref" VALUE="true">
<PARAM NAME="controller" VALUE="false">
<PARAM NAME="autoplay" VALUE="true">
<PARAM NAME="qtnext1" VALUE="HasQT.htm">

<EMBED SRC="GetQT.pntg" TYPE="image/x-macpaint"
  HEIGHT="120" WIDTH="160"
  ALT="You need QuickTime: www.apple.com/quicktime/download"
  QTSRC="Letsgo.mov" HREF="HasQT.htm" AUTOHREF="True"
  CONTROLLER="False" AUTOPLAY="True"
  QTNEXT1="HasQT.htm"
  PLUGINSPAGE="http://www.apple.com/quicktime/download">
</EMBED>

</OBJECT>

<P>
If you have QuickTime 4 or later, you should automatically
  be taken to our <A HREF="HasQT.htm>main page</A> in 1-2 seconds.
</P>
<P>
```

```
If you need to install or configure QuickTime, you should
  automatically be redirected to our
<A HREF="GetQT.htm">download page</A> within 30 seconds...
</P>
</DIV>
</BODY>
</HTML>
```

What It Does

If viewers have QuickTime 4.1 or later, this page immediately takes them to HasQT.htm.

If viewers have QuickTime 4.0, this page displays Letsgo.mov for half a second, then takes them to HasQT.htm.

If viewers don't have QuickTime, the browser should alert them and offer to get it for them. Netscape browser and Mac OS browsers take them to www.apple.com/quicktime/download/. Internet Explorer for Windows prompts them to automatically install the QuickTime ActiveX control. The ActiveX control then offers to download the rest of QuickTime.

If viewers have an old version of QuickTime, they should see GetQT.pntg for a few seconds, then be automatically redirected to the GetQT.htm Web page. If they are using Internet Explorer for Windows, they will be prompted to download the QuickTime ActiveX control first.

If viewers get impatient waiting for the redirect, those with QuickTime 4 or later can click the Letsgo.mov movie and jump to the main content page; those who need to get QuickTime can click the text link to the GetQT.htm page.

How It Works

If viewers are using Internet Explorer for Windows, the <OBJECT> tag's CLASSID and CODEBASE parameters tell the browser to use the QuickTime ActiveX control (and tell where to get it if it's not installed). If the Quick-Time ActiveX control is present, it executes the plug-in parameters that follow and takes the viewer to HasQT.htm. If it's not present, Explorer offers to get it.

If viewers have QuickTime 4.1 or later, the QuickTime plug-in will correctly interpret the parameters

```
HREF="HasQT.htm" AUTOHREF="True"
```

to automatically load `HasQT.htm` in the default browser window.

If viewers have QuickTime 4.0, the QuickTime plug-in will correctly interpret the parameters

```
QTSRC="Letsgo.mov" AUTOPLAY="True" QTNEXT1="HasQT.htm"
```

to load `Letsgo.mov`, play it automatically, then go to `HasQT.htm` when the movie ends.

The movie `Letsgo.mov` is a one-frame movie only 1 Kbyte in size and a half-second in duration, so this should happen in the blink of an eye. If not, viewers can click the `Letsgo.mov` movie; the QuickTime plug-in will interpret the parameter

```
HREF="HasQT.htm"
```

and go to `HasQT.htm` immediately.

If viewers don't have QuickTime, the `PLUGINSPAGE` parameter will cause most browsers to bring up an alert window offering to take them to `www.apple.com/quicktime/download/`. Internet Explorer for Windows will offer to download the QuickTime ActiveX control, which will offer to get the rest of QuickTime.

If viewers have a really old version of QuickTime, all the `<EMBED>` parameters will be ignored except `SRC`, `HEIGHT`, and `WIDTH`, so the plug-in should display `GetQT.pntg` instead of `Letsgo.mov`. `GetQT.pntg` is an image that directs viewers to the QuickTime download site.

The special tag

```
<META HTTP-EQUIV="Refresh" CONTENT="30;URL=GetQT.htm">
```

in the page header should automatically redirect viewers to the `GetQT.htm` Web page after 30 seconds, whether they can see `GetQT.pntg` or not. This also acts as a fallback in case the browser ignores the `PLUGINSPAGE` parameter.

The 30-second delay before the refresh makes sure that viewers who *do* have QuickTime have ample time for the QuickTime plug-in to load, even if their computer is having a bad hair day.

The manual link at the bottom of the page gives impatient viewers a quick way to the download page if they don't have QuickTime, and it acts as a fallback in case the browser fails to execute the automatic refresh.

Despite being only 25 lines of HTML, this page provides belt-and-suspenders redundancy. I have yet to see it fail under any circumstances.

`GetQT.pntg`, `GetQT.htm`, `DetectQT.htm`, and `Letsgo.mov` can all be found in the SpecialDelivery folder of the CD. You're welcome to use them on your own website.

Variations

The example page redirects viewers who have QuickTime to a page named HasQT.htm. You should edit both instances of HasQT.htm to point to your main content page.

The example page redirects viewers who need QuickTime to a page named GetQT4.htm. This is a short Web page that explains that the viewer needs QuickTime to experience your website, explains that it's a free download, and includes a link to the Apple download site. GetQT.htm is also in the SpecialDelivery folder of the CD. You're welcome to use it as is or edit it to fit in better with your website.

Alternatively, you can edit the example to point to your own version of a download page, or to an alternate version of your main page that doesn't use QuickTime content, or directly to Apple's QuickTime download page.

If you're redirecting viewers without QuickTime to a non-QuickTime page, delete the PLUGINSPAGE parameter from the <EMBED> tag.

It's also possible to use a combination of JavaScript and VBScript to detect QuickTime, but it's somewhat dependent on the user's browser, operating system, and QuickTime version. For details, see "Useful Java-Scripts" (page 169).

6

What Webmasters
Need to Know

So far, we've explored things from the perspective of an HTML author, and the HTML we've been looking at should work fine from your local disk. But for the HTML to work properly over the Internet, it has to be stored on a working Web server. The person who configures the Web server is, of course, the webmaster.

If you're a webmaster, there are just a few things you need to know to deliver QuickTime movies from your Web server. That information is covered here. If you aren't a webmaster, forward this information to the person who administers the Web server at your company, or to the ISP (Internet Service Provider) that hosts your website.

This chapter has two sections:

- **MIME Types and File Extensions**

  QuickTime can use HTTP or FTP to deliver multimedia content, so all the webmaster really needs to do is associate a few file extensions with the right MIME types, and your Web server is ready for QuickTime. This section lists the file extensions and MIME types.

- **Server Features and Server Load**

  No special server features are needed to deliver QuickTime over HTTP or FTP, but sometimes adding QuickTime movies to a website can cause spikes in server load. These can be smoothed by passing the right parameters to the QuickTime plug-in. This section explains how.

QuickTime can also use RTP and RTSP to deliver multimedia streams, live transmissions, and reflected multicasts. That *does* require some special server software. To learn more, see Chapter 7, "What about Streaming?"

▶ MIME Types and File Extensions

There are really only four things that you have to do in order to deliver QuickTime movies reliably from your Web server:

- Map the .mov file extension to the video/quicktime MIME type.
- Map the .qti and .qtif file extensions to the image/x-quicktime MIME type.
- Map the .pntg file extension to the image/x-macpaint MIME type.
- Map the .qtl file extension to the application/x-quicktimeplayer MIME type.

First .Mov

All QuickTime content can be delivered as QuickTime movies using the .mov file extension—movies, still images, slideshows, recorded sound, MIDI music, MPEG audio and video, Flash animations, MP3, even text. This is the preferred way to deliver multimedia content using QuickTime.

The Fab Four

The .qti, .qtif, and .pntg file extensions are used for QuickTime still image files. These files are often used to ensure that browsers will invoke the QuickTime plug-in, in cases where some other application has registered for QuickTime movie (.mov) files.

The .qtl file extension is used to create links directly to QuickTime Player, instead of the QuickTime browser plug-in.

All the Rest

QuickTime can also play content using the following file extensions and MIME types:

MIME type	File extension	Description
video/quicktime	mov, qt	QuickTime movie
image/x-quicktime	qti, qtif	QuickTime image
image/x-macpaint	pntg, pnt	MacPaint image
application/ x-quicktimeplayer	qtl	QuickTime Player movie
application/smil	smi, sml, smil	SMIL presentation
video/x-msvideo	avi	Video for Windows, OpenDML
video/x-dv	dif, dv	DV digital video and audio
video/mpeg, video/x-mpeg	mpg, mpeg, m1v, mpm, mpv	MPEG-1 video
audio/mpeg, audio/x-mpeg	mpg, mpeg, mp2, mpa, m1a, m1s	MPEG-1 audio, layers 1 and 2
audio/mpeg, audio/x-mpeg	mp3	MPEG-1 audio, layer 3
audio/mpegurl, audio/x-mpegurl	m3u	MP3 playlist
audio/basic	au, snd, ulw	8-bit audio
audio/aiff, audio/x-aiff	aif, aiff, aifc	AIFF audio
audio/wav, audio/x-wav	wav	WAV audio
audio/x-sd2	sd2	Sound Designer II
audio/midi, audio/x-midi	mid, midi, smf, kar	MIDI music, karaoke
video/flc	flc, fli	Autodesk Animator
application/ x-shockwave-flash	swf	Flash animation
image/gif	gif	Animated GIF
x-world/x-3dmf	3dmf, 3dm, qd3d, qd3	QuickDraw 3D Metafile
image/x-sgi	sgi	Silicon Graphics image
image/x-photoshop	psd	Adobe Photoshop
image/x-bmp	bmp	Windows bitmap
image/x-targa	tga	Targa image
image/tiff, image/x-tiff	tif, tiff	TIFF image
image/png, image/x-png	png	PNG image
application/sdp	sdp	Streaming session announcement
video/mp4, audio/mp4	.mp4 .mpeg4	MPEG-4 audio, video
image/jpeg2000	.jp2	JPEG 2000 image

If media is embedded in any of these formats, you need to associate the corresponding file extension and MIME type for your Web server.

Note With the exception of the MIME types `image/x-quicktime`, `image/x-macpaint`, and `application/x-quicktimeplayer`, the user's browser may be configured to handle the MIME types in this table with a plug-in other than QuickTime, but the QuickTime plug-in can play them all.

Configuring Your Server

Most Web servers come with the common MIME types and file extensions already configured. The `.qtif`, `.qtl`, and `.pntg` file extensions aren't very common, so you'll probably need to add them to the server's MIME type table. The exact steps vary depending on your Web server software, but in general you should run your Web server's `admin.app` and look for any menu choice that includes the word "MIME." On an Apache server, you can add a MIME type using the `addtype` command.

Here's how to configure the MIME types on three common Web servers:

Apache

1. Be sure you log in with administrator privileges.
2. Change directories to <apache_root>/httpd/conf.
3. Edit the file `srm.conf`.
4. Add these lines to the end of the file (or wherever the `AddType video/*` entries are):

   `AddType video/quicktime mov`

   `AddType image/x-macpaint pntg`

   `AddType image/x-quicktime qti qtif`

   `AddType application/x-quicktimeplayer qtl`

Important Make sure the file still ends with a blank line.

5. Quit the editor (save changes).
6. Restart the Web server.

Webstar

1. Open the Admin application.
2. Choose Suffix Mapping from the Configure menu. In steps 3–6, set Action to BINARY, and set File Type and Creator to *.

3. Set File Suffix to .mov, MIME type to video/quicktime. Click Add.

4. Set File Suffix to .pntg, MIME type to image/x-macpaint. Click Add.

5. Set File Suffix to .qti, MIME type to image/x-quicktime. Click Add.

6. Set File Suffix to .qtl, MIME type to application/x-quicktimeplayer. Click Add.

7. Click Update.

Microsoft Internet Information Server 4

1. Open the Microsoft Management Console (in the Internet Service Manager).

2. Choose Properties for the appropriate website.

3. Choose HTTP Headers and click the File Types button.

4. Add these file extensions and MIME types:

   .movvideo/quicktime

   .pntgimage/x-macpaint

   .qtiimage/x-quicktime

   .qtlapplication/x-quicktimeplayer

5. Click Apply.

Server Features and Server Load

No special server features are required to deliver QuickTime content from your Web server via HTTP or FTP. The user's QuickTime plug-in simply requests an HTTP or FTP file and plays the content as it arrives over the Web. If there isn't enough bandwidth to play the content as it comes in, the user's plug-in caches the file locally and plays it when enough has arrived.

It is also possible to stream or multicast QuickTime content using the real-time protocols RTP and RTSP. This *does* require special server software: either a broadcaster, a streaming server, or both. This is discussed in Chapter 7, "What about Streaming?" and Chapter 14, "Gently down the Stream."

The server load for delivering QuickTime content over HTTP or FTP is the same as that for delivering a graphic image the size of the QuickTime file. No additional server load is experienced.

Because Web pages are typically rather small, and QuickTime movies are typically pretty large, adding QuickTime movies to a website can cause spikes in server load when users with fast connections download these large files. You can smooth the load, often without affecting other viewers, by setting the choke speed for the QuickTime plug-in.

The QuickTime choke speed is set in the HTML of the page requesting the file. This is not a server setting. Most Web servers have a setting that allows you to specify the maximum bandwidth for any connection, but this restricts the maximum bandwidth for every user and every file. The QuickTime choke speed allows you to specify a restricted bandwidth for a given file transfer, without requiring you to restrict the maximum connection rate for your users globally.

As webmaster, you may or may not be in a position to modify existing Web pages for your site. If you are, here's what you need to know; if you're not, here's what the HTML authors need to know.

HTTP downloads normally run at the maximum bandwidth available. The choke speed, set by the QTSRCCHOKESPEED parameter, lets you specify a maximum HTTP bandwidth for a movie. If you set QTSRCCHOKESPEED = "56000", for example, the download speed is limited to 56K, and someone viewing the movie with a T1 connection won't suddenly use 1.5 megabits of your bandwidth.

Using the QTSRCCHOKESPEED parameter is a little tricky. A QuickTime movie is normally specified by the SRC parameter of the <EMBED> tag. The browser itself gets this file from your server, and the browser always gets files as fast as it can.

Fortunately, you can tell the browser to download a tiny dummy image, just a few hundred bytes, while passing QuickTime the name of the movie in the QTSRC parameter. If you also tell QuickTime QTSRCDONTUSEBROWSER, the QuickTime plug-in uses its own HTTP handler to get the QTSRC movie, and you can control the bandwidth using the QTSRCCHOKESPEED setting.

To add a choke speed setting to the <EMBED> tag for a movie, you change the SRC parameter to a QTSRC parameter, add a new SRC parameter that points to a dummy image, and add the QTSRCDONTUSEBROWSER and QTSRC-CHOKESPEED parameters and the maximum bandwidth to use. The HTML changes from this:

```
<EMBED SRC="Movie.mov" >
```

to this:

```
<EMBED QTSRC="Movie.mov" SRC="Dummy.qti"
    QTSRCCHOKESPEED="56000" QTSRCDONTUSEBROWSER >
```

If you specify a choke speed of slightly more than the QuickTime movie's actual data rate, it will still download fast enough for users to play it as it comes in, so viewing won't be affected.

You can find out a movie's data rate by opening it in QuickTime Player and choosing Get Info from the Movie menu. Try setting the choke speed about 15% higher than the movie's data rate and see if it plays smoothly. If it doesn't, increase the choke speed until it does.

You can also set QTSRCCHOKESPEED="movierate", and QuickTime will do its best to use only as much bandwidth as needed to play the movie smoothly.

The dummy image needs to be an actual QuickTime image file, but it can be very small. You're welcome to use the UNeedQT.qti file from the Basic folder on the CD. It's tiny.

QTSRCCHOKESPEED works with HTTP 1.1 or later Web servers that support byte-range requests. For more details on the QTSRC and QTSRCCHOKESPEED parameters, see Chapter 5, "Special Delivery: QuickTime + HTML."

Note   As of this writing (QuickTime 6.1), QTSRCCHOKESPEED limits the download speed of data only in self-contained movies. Any data contained in external files, including alternate movies, is unaffected.

What about Streaming?

By now, you should have a pretty good handle on delivering QuickTime movies from a disk or a typical Web server. With that understanding in hand, let's take a closer look at a different delivery method: streaming.

If you're already familiar with Windows Media or Real Media, you probably think of streaming as simply playing movies over the Internet. As you've seen in the previous chapters, however, QuickTime can play movies over the Internet perfectly well without streaming. So what makes streaming different?

We'll begin with a brief recap of streaming concepts that were covered in the introduction. Then we'll look at some of the pros and cons of using streaming to deliver your QuickTime movies. Finally, we'll glance under the hood at how streaming works.

This chapter is an introduction to streaming and covers the basic steps of preparing streaming movies and embedding them in a Web page. We'll take a deeper look at streaming, including setting up a streaming server, in Chapter 14, "Gently down the Stream."

▶ What It Is

Streaming is what happens when you send movies across a network and display them in real time. If a movie is one minute long, it streams over the network in one minute—if the user has a faster connection, the extra bandwidth is unused; if the user has a slower connection, some data is lost.

Because things happen in real time, a stream can originate from a live source, such as a camera or microphone, or the output of a CD player or mixer.

A stream can also originate from a file on a server, but what gets sent are not files, but media streams. You can start streaming from any point in a movie timeline and stop streaming at any other, skipping the parts that aren't played.

▶ What It's Not

Streaming isn't the only way to send movies over the Internet—two other methods are file transfer (send the movie as a file, then play it locally) and QuickTime's Fast Start (also known as progressive download), which lets you play the movie while it downloads.

Streaming is not the same as downloading a movie file.

For one thing, a stream can originate from a live source, so there may be no file. For another, the user doesn't get a copy of the movie—streams are made of data packets that are assembled into sound and video, displayed briefly, then discarded. No movie file is created on the viewer's computer.

▶ Why It's Cool

Because it happens in real time, streaming can deliver live content, such as a concert, a lecture, a radio broadcast, or a sporting event, right as it happens.

And when lots of people are watching something at exactly the same time, it's possible to send a single copy of the information over a network, instead of sending individual copies to each viewer. This is called broadcasting or multicasting. It isn't generally available on the Internet, but it *is* generally available on corporate and campus networks.

Even when a movie is streamed from a file on a server, because no file is downloaded, streaming can deliver long movies without occupying any disk space on the viewer's computer.

Because no file is transferred, you don't generally need to worry about copy protection. Streaming a movie prevents any but the most dedicated and well-equipped hacker from making a digital copy (pointing a camera at the screen still works, but hey).

Another cool thing—the streaming server can act as a remote video player; the user can skip back and forth in a movie by asking the server to start streaming from different points in the movie's timeline. You can watch the last 10 minutes of an hour-long presentation without waiting as the first 50 minutes download, or review any part of a lecture without downloading the rest.

What's more, Fast Start QuickTime movies can include streaming tracks. This allows you to add live video or live audio to an existing movie, or add a recently updated text track from a streaming server, such as a stock ticker. It also allows you to put high-bandwidth material on a hard disk or a CD, and to add in current data from a server as streaming tracks.

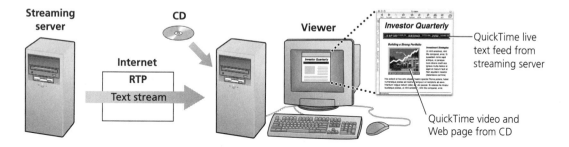

You'll learn exactly how to do all of these things in Chapter 14, "Gently down the Stream," and Chapter 17, "Mixing It Up: Streaming and Non-streaming."

What You Need

In most cases, you need three things to deliver streaming content over the Internet: a streaming server, a broadcaster (for live streams), and a little extra effort.

Streaming Server

If you want to send streams to people over the Internet, you need a streaming server. Just as you need a Web server for HTML pages, and a mail server for email messages, you need a streaming server to send real-time streams. Each kind of server handles specific protocols. Web servers handle HTTP, mail servers handle SMTP, and streaming servers handle RTSP and RTP.

The streaming server responds to requests for streaming movies, and it transmits streams to individuals in response to those requests. The requests are handled using RTSP (Real-Time Streaming Protocol), and the streams are sent using RTP (Real-Time Transport Protocol).

A streaming server can create streams from QuickTime movies stored on a disk. It can also send copies of any live streams that it has access to.

For small sites, a single computer can run Web server software, mail server software, and streaming server software. For larger jobs, one or more computers are dedicated to act purely as streaming servers. The Mac OS X Server operating system includes streaming server software. QuickTime streaming server software for other operating systems can be downloaded at no cost, and high-performance QuickTime streaming server software and hardware are available from several vendors, including Apple.

Broadcaster

If you want to stream live events, such as live television or live radio, you need a broadcaster. A broadcaster is software that creates streams from live sources such as microphones, cameras, or live audio and video feeds.

Digitizing a live source, compressing it, and creating an RTP stream from it, all in real time, is a lot of work for one computer. Consequently, a broadcaster is usually run on a separate computer from a streaming server.

The broadcaster sends a single stream of audio and a single stream of video to an IP address, which could be the address of an individual computer—for a remote presentation to a classroom or boardroom, for example—or it could be a multicast address that allows everyone on a LAN to watch the same stream. Most commonly, it sends the stream to the IP address of a streaming server. People who want to receive the streams get them from the streaming server. This keeps the broadcaster from getting overworked, even when you're serving thousands of streams across the Internet.

Mac OS X includes a QuickTime broadcaster—if you have a recent vintage Mac, you already have a broadcaster. Broadcaster software is also available for Windows, Macintosh, and other platforms from several vendors, including Sorenson, Abstract Plane, and Channel Storm.

There are also combination broadcaster/server software packages available, such as Channel Storm's Live Channel.

A Little Extra Effort

It takes a little extra effort to deliver streaming movies compared with Fast Start movies, but not a lot.

To create streams from movies stored on disk, the streaming server needs some hints to tell it when to send which bits. You can add these hints to a movie by opening it in QuickTime Player, choosing Export from the File menu, then choosing Movie to Hinted Movie from the pop-up menu. This adds hint tracks to the movie—one hint track for each media track. If you're exporting a movie using QuickTime Player, or compressing a QuickTime movie using an application such as Discreet Cleaner or Squeeze, you typically have the option of having hint tracks added at the same time.

You can then put the hinted movie on a streaming server. Give people the URL of the movie, and you're ready to stream.

For live streams it's a little different. Instead of creating a hinted movie, you normally create a small movie that contains the URL of the live streams. It isn't hard. You just open the streams in QuickTime Player using Open URL, then Save.

Alternatively, you can have QuickTime open an announcement file for the streams. Most broadcasters can create an announcement file (sometimes called an SDP file) for you automatically. Upload the announcement file to your streaming server. It goes in the same folder as the streaming movies. It has the file extension .sdp.

Once you've got either a hinted movie or an announcement file on the streaming server, you're ready to stream.

Embedding a Streaming Movie in a Web Page

You can open a streaming movie in QuickTime Player by choosing Open URL from the File menu and typing in the URL. The URL of a streaming movie starts with the RTSP protocol identifier and looks something like this:

```
rtsp://YourStreamServer.com/YourPath/YourMovie.mov
```

Of course, you'd probably prefer to put a link to your streaming movie on a Web page, rather than circulate the URL and ask people to type it into QuickTime Player. There are several ways to embed streaming movies in a Web page, which we'll examine in detail in "Streaming and QTSRC" (page 425), but briefly, the HTML looks like this:

```
<EMBED SRC="UNeedQT.qti" HEIGHT="256" WIDTH="320"
  QTSRC="rtsp://YourStreamServer.com/YourPath/YourMovie.mov">
```

If your movie is in the streaming server's default movie directory, you don't need to specify a path—just the server and filename. You need to use QTSRC because a browser may be configured to pass all RTSP URLs to another application, such as RealPlayer.

Similarly, you can embed the URL of an announcement file in a Web page to give people access to the live stream. The HTML for that looks something like this:

```
<EMBED SRC="UNeedQT.qti" HEIGHT="256" WIDTH="320"
    QTSRC="rtsp://YourStreamServer.com/YourPath/Announcement">
```

Important   Leave off the .sdp file extension when you embed the URL.

If your announcement file is LiveStream.sdp, for example, and it's in the default movies folder of www.StreamServer.com, the URL is

```
rtsp://www.StreamServer.com/LiveStream
```

The path to the default movies folder is implied, and the .sdp file extension must be omitted.

Another way to embed a live stream in a Web page is to create a tiny movie that points to the stream. Open the stream in QuickTime Player by using the Open URL menu item in the File menu. Just type in the announcement file's URL. Save it as a self-contained movie, and put the movie on your Web server. It's only a few kilobytes. Embed it in a Web page as you would a Fast Start QuickTime movie. When people play the movie, the streaming server sends them copies of the live streams it points to. This is described in detail later, in "Live Streaming" (page 445).

You can even make a QuickTime movie that points to an RTSP file using a text editor! Just write a one-line text file consisting of the characters RTSP-text followed immediately by the address of the file. For example:

```
RTSPtextrtsp://www.streamer.com/MySDPFile
```

or

```
RTSPtextrtsp://www.streamish.com/MyHintedMovie.mov
```

Save this file as plain text, but give it the .mov file extension. You can play this file using QuickTime Player or embed it in a Web page as if it were a QuickTime movie. When it plays, QuickTime will use the RTSP address to open a streaming session. Who would have guessed?

More Information

For more information about setting up streaming servers, creating streaming movies, and embedding them in Web pages, see Chapter 14, "Gently down the Stream," and Chapter 17, "Mixing It Up: Streaming and Non-streaming."

When Do You Need It?

If you want to send live broadcasts over the Internet, or even over an intranet, you need streaming. It's *the* way to send audio or video of events while they're happening. For everyone else, it's an open question. Should you put your QuickTime movies on a streaming server, or should you send Fast Start movies from an ordinary Web server? Have a look at the pros and cons of streaming and nonstreaming delivery, listed below. It's perfectly all right to use both, and in many cases that's the best answer.

Streaming Pros

- Can send live transmissions.
- Can be used for broadcast and multicast (send one stream to many viewers). Great for campus or corporate LANs.
- Provides random access to long movies.
- Uses no space on the viewer's disk.
- Never uses more bandwidth than it needs.
- Doesn't give the viewer a copy of the movie file.

Streaming Cons

- If movie data rate exceeds the connection speed, the movie plays poorly or not at all.
- Usually some packet loss over the Internet, reducing quality.
- Currently limited to audio, video, MIDI, and text (other media types, such as Flash and VR, can't be streamed).
- Doesn't always go through firewalls or NAT (multiple computers sharing a single IP address, common when sharing a DSL or cable modem).
- Requires a streaming server and/or a broadcaster.

Fast Start Pros

- The movie gets through no matter how slow the connection is. It can play over any speed connection, given enough time.
- Lost or damaged packets are retransmitted until they get through. There is no quality lost in transmission.
- No problems with firewalls or NAT.
- If connection is fast enough, movie plays as it downloads.
- Can use all QuickTime media, including sprites, Flash, and VR.
- No special server software needed.

Fast Start Cons

- Can't broadcast or multicast.
- Can't send live transmissions.
- Can't skip ahead; the user must download the whole movie.
- Puts a copy of the movie file on the viewer's disk.

Fortunately, this is QuickTime; you don't have to make a hard-and-fast choice between streaming and Fast Start. You can stream live events and send stored movies using Fast Start, for example. Or you can use alternate movies to send streams to people with fast connections and Fast Start movies to people with connections that are too slow for good streams. (Alternate movies are described in the next chapter.)

You can also send Fast Start movies over HTTP and put streaming tracks inside them. When the movies are played, QuickTime gets the Fast Start parts from your Web server and the streaming parts from your streaming server. This can happen even while the Fast Start movie is still downloading. Use this technique to mix things that *must* stream, such as live feeds, with things that can't stream, such as sprites and Flash. This is discussed in Chapter 17, "Mixing It Up: Streaming and Nonstreaming."

▶ How It Works

You really don't have to know how streaming works to use it. Streaming is a relatively new technology, though, so you might want to peek under the hood. If you're curious, read on.

Streams are sent using RTP. RTP is similar to the familiar HTTP and FTP protocols, but there are important differences.

- **HTTP and FTP (Nonstreaming)**

  HTTP and FTP are file transfer protocols: packets are sent with checksums, there is feedback from the receiving computer, and lost or damaged packets are retransmitted. If the connection speed is less than the movie's data rate, the movie still gets across; it just won't play smoothly as it comes in.

  File transfer takes however long it takes; a one-minute QuickTime movie might download in one minute, one second, or one hour, depending on the size of the file and the speed of the connection.

- **RTP (Streaming)**

  RTP transmits data in real time; a one-minute movie is sent over the network in exactly one minute. Lost or damaged packets are not retransmitted; the receiver has to be able to deal with loss in a reasonable manner. If the connection speed is lower than the data rate of the movie, the transmission breaks up and the movie plays poorly or doesn't play at all. With a fast connection, the extra bandwidth is untouched. This creates a predictable server load per stream, no matter how fast the user's connection.

- **Streams**

  Streams are data sent in real time using RTP. Starting with QuickTime 4, QuickTime Player and the QuickTime plug-in can receive and play streams. QuickTime streaming is standards-based, so the streams don't have to be QuickTime movies; any stream that conforms to the IETF standards works just fine.

  Streams can be sent in one of three ways: unicast, broadcast, or multicast.

- **Unicast**

  Unicast transmission means sending one stream to each receiver. If a thousand people are watching, the server sends a thousand streams. It's not a particularly efficient use of bandwidth, but different viewers can watch different parts of the movie, or watch different movies, at the same time. Viewers can start the movie whenever they like, and they can all independently pause, rewind, or skip ahead.

  Viewers communicate with the unicast server using RTSP. That's different from RTP, which is a one-way stream. Viewers use RTSP to request a stream, pause it, or start streaming from a different part of the movie.

QuickTime translates the user's interaction with the onscreen movie controller into the right RTSP requests automatically. Of course, if the stream is a live transmission, viewers can't skip around; they can either request a copy of the stream or not. Unicast is how most things are sent over the Internet.

Viewers normally open a unicast movie by opening an RTSP URL. The URL may be wrapped in a tiny QuickTime movie and embedded in a Web page, or it may be specified in a Web page using the QTSRC parameter. It can also be stored in QuickTime Player's Favorites window. Or, if users know the URL, they can enter it directly into QuickTime Player using the Open URL command.

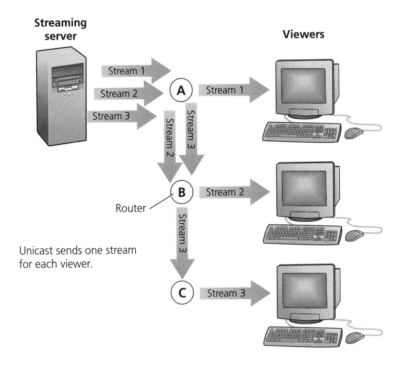

■ **Broadcast**

Broadcast transmission means sending one copy of the stream over the whole network. You do this by sending a single stream to an IP address that the network recognizes as a broadcast address. This is a good way to send a presentation to 50 viewers simultaneously over a local area network (LAN). Most small LANs support broadcasting, but large LANs may not carry broadcasts across different segments, and many LAN administrators get severely bent out of shape when broadcast addresses are used. The Internet does *not* allow broadcasting.

A broadcast is like a television transmission: viewers can't fast-forward, rewind, or pause. Viewers don't communicate with the server of a broadcast; they just decide whether or not to pay attention to packets that are already present on the network.

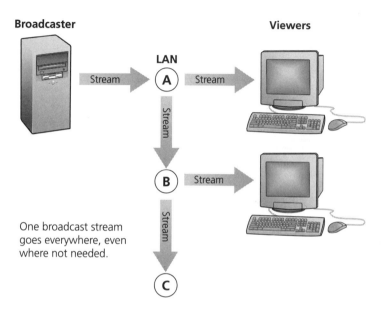

■ Multicast

Multicast transmission means sending exactly one copy of the stream, down only the branches of the network where one or more viewers are tuned in. The idea is to make the most efficient use of bandwidth possible. The broadcaster sends a single stream to an IP multicast address, and routers replicate the stream as needed. This requires fairly sophisticated router software. There are routers that support multicasting over the Internet; they form a virtual network called the Multicast Backbone, or MBone. If you're at a university or other large institution, you may be on the MBone, but most Internet users are not. On a small LAN, using a multicast IP address often has the same effect as using a broadcast IP address (with the possible exception of the effect on the network administrator). On larger LANs, using multicast instead of broadcast ensures that the stream doesn't use any unnecessary bandwidth by straying onto LAN segments where no one is watching.

Large LANs often include routers that support local multicasts. If your LAN doesn't support broadcast across segments, it may support multicast instead.

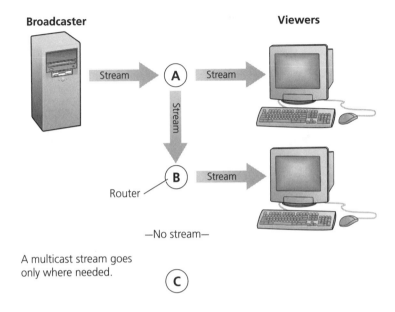

A multicast stream goes only where needed.

The viewer of a multicast has no control over what's presented. Again, the choice is simply to watch or not to watch. The viewer's computer talks directly to a router to get a copy of the stream. QuickTime Player and the QuickTime plug-in can talk to routers and can receive multicasts if a local router supports them.

- **SDP**

    Viewers normally find out about multicasts by downloading a Session Description Protocol (SDP) file. The SDP file is a text file that describes what will be streamed and gives the information needed to tune in. QuickTime Player and the QuickTime plug-in can open SDP files as if they were movies. In fact, you can embed an SDP file in a Web page *as* a QuickTime movie by adding the .mov file extension and inserting the characters SDP text at the beginning of the file (one space between "SDP" and "text"—no carriage return).

- **Saving Movies**

    When a viewer saves a streaming movie while watching it with Quick-Time Player or the QuickTime plug-in, what's actually saved are the

URL of the stream, the current point in the movie's timeline (except for live transmissions), and the user settings, such as sound volume. When the user opens this saved movie, QuickTime opens the stream and restores the settings. The movie's actual data is never copied; it lives on the server.

This is nice if you want people to see your movie but don't want to give away free copies. (Of course, someone who *really* wants to make a copy can usually find a way.)

Movies saved this way are really small (often less than 1K). You can pass them around, embed them in Web pages, or use them to create reference movies. You don't have to worry about copyrights; the copyrighted material stays on the streaming server, and the owner can choose whether or not to stream it when someone plays the movie. All you're copying is the URL.

You can also add tracks with Fast Start or local media to movies saved this way, allowing you to mix streaming content with content on a disk or a Web server. For details, see Chapter 17, "Mixing It Up: Streaming and Nonstreaming."

■ **Reflectors**

Streaming often involves computers that act as reflectors. Reflectors are typically used to translate from broadcast or multicast to unicast transmission modes.

For example, a live transmission might be sent out over a university LAN as a multicast. One of the computers or routers on the LAN could act as a reflector, sending the stream out over the MBone as an Internet multicast. QuickTime streaming servers connected to the MBone could act as further reflectors, offering the streams as unicasts to anyone who asks for them, making the transmission available to anyone on the Internet. (For this to work, the streaming servers need to have an SDP file for the multicast in their movies directory.)

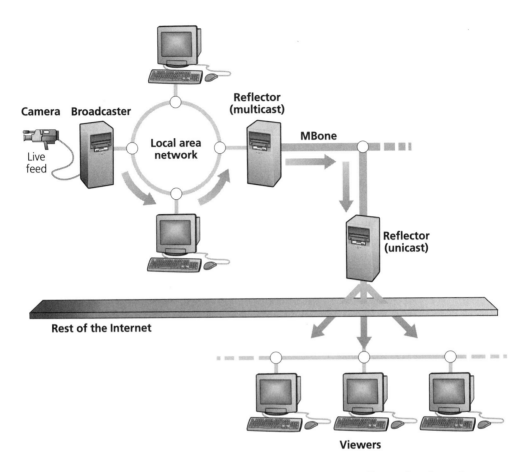

As another example, a typical scenario at a radio station is to have one computer digitize the signal, compress it for the Internet, and broadcast it over an Ethernet LAN. This computer is the broadcaster. Digitizing and compressing a signal in real time is CPU-intensive, so the broadcaster sends only a single stream. A reflector on the same LAN sends copies of the stream out over the Internet to everyone who asks for it. This second computer is both a reflector and a streaming server, and could also have recent broadcasts stored on disk, allowing people to listen to programs over the Internet that they missed over the air.

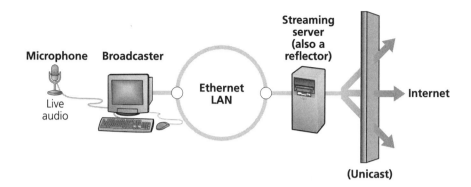

Reflectors can also be used to spread the load of serving multiple unicasts. A streaming server that can send 2000 simultaneous streams might be supported by a pair of reflectors, allowing 6000 people to watch or listen simultaneously. To add reflectors, configure the broadcaster to send its stream to a multicast IP address, so multiple reflectors can see the stream, and put a copy of the announcement SDP file on each reflector.

- **RTSP and TCP/IP**

  The RTSP control information for unicasts is sent over TCP/IP (Transmission Control Protocol/Internet Protocol) transport, just like HTTP and FTP downloads. Consequently, pretty much anyone who can receive Web pages can request a movie.

- **RTP and UDP**

  Actual streams are normally sent using RTP protocol. RTP uses low-level UDP (User Datagram Protocol) transport. UDP is faster and more efficient than TCP/IP, but it doesn't have any mechanism for reporting lost packets, so streaming over the Internet almost always involves some data loss.

- **Firewalls**

  Many companies have firewalls between their local network and the Internet. It's common for these firewalls to permit TCP/IP to pass through, but to block UDP. Consequently, viewers behind a firewall may not be able to receive streaming movies, even though they can request them over RTSP.

Apple provides software called a proxy server for RTP/RTSP as source code that will work with most popular firewalls to help solve this problem. You can find it, and more information about firewalls and streaming, at Apple's website:

`www.apple.com/quicktime/resources/qt4/us/proxy/`

If your company is running an older version of the popular SOCKS proxy software, upgrading to version 5 or later should solve the problem.

If you can't find a proxy server that works with your firewall, it's possible to wrap the streaming packets inside TCP/IP packets. This is described in "Streaming Transport" (page 711).

- **NAT**

  Sometimes small networks share a single modem for Internet access. This usually involves Network Address Translation (NAT). Streaming over RTP involves port addresses that confuse some NAT software. Most NAT vendors are now addressing this issue. If you have trouble receiving streaming movies, and you use NAT, call the makers of your NAT software or check their website for an update.

  If your NAT vendor doesn't support RTP yet, it's possible to wrap the streaming packets inside TCP/IP packets, which use port addresses that NAT is prepared to deal with. This is described in "Streaming Transport" (page 711).

- **HTTP Tunneling**

  QuickTime Streaming Server version 2.0 and later supports HTTP tunneling, which wraps the RTP packets that carry streams inside ordinary HTTP packets. When streams are sent this way, they use the standard HTTP port address (80), so they can make their way through pretty much any firewall or NAT software without difficulty.

  To enable HTTP streaming from the server, just click the appropriate checkbox (and make sure no other process is running on port 80, such as a Web server). For details, see Chapter 14, "Gently down the Stream."

  The viewer's QuickTime plug-in should configure itself automatically to use HTTP tunneling if needed. The viewer can turn HTTP tunneling on manually using the QuickTime Settings control panel, as described in "Streaming Transport" (page 711).

  There's more network bandwidth overhead when streams are wrapped in HTTP packets, so you need to use a slightly lower data rate to stream over a given connection using HTTP tunneling. Fortunately, people behind firewalls or NAT usually have high-bandwidth connections.

Alternate Realities: Language, Speed, and Connections

So far, we've shown you how to embed Fast Start or streaming movies in a Web page and how to control the QuickTime plug-in from HTML. Now we'll show you how to make QuickTime automatically show the right movie to each viewer.

QuickTime can automatically select one movie from a set of alternates, based on things like the viewer's Internet connection speed, CPU horsepower, operating system, or QuickTime version.

In addition, a single QuickTime movie can contain alternate tracks, one of which is selected based on the viewer's language.

By combining alternate movies and alternate tracks, you can create Web pages with QuickTime movies that automatically select the right version for the viewer—people with 28.8K modems get a slideshow, people with cable modems get a wide-screen streaming movie with stereo sound; French viewers get a French sound track, and Japanese viewers get Japanese subtitles—all from the same HTML.

This chapter shows you how to make alternate movies based on connection speed, operating system, and QuickTime version, and how to make alternate tracks based on language. You can combine the two, by making a movie with alternate language tracks, for example, then saving multiple versions of the movie optimized for different connection speeds.

▶ Alternate Movies

Web designers face some hard choices when it comes to multimedia. Do you stick to the lowest common denominator, creating simple websites that load quickly over 28.8K modems, or create dazzling websites that require a fast Internet connection? Or do you take the middle road, creating websites that work well at 56 Kbits/sec, but that simultaneously frustrate people with slower connections and bore people with faster ones?

Well, why choose? You can design your main Web page so it loads quickly at 28.8 Kbits/sec and add the dazzle using QuickTime alternates. You can have an alternate movie for every connection speed in the Quick-Time Settings control panel. The right movie is selected automatically—the viewer doesn't have to choose, and you don't have to write a lot of special HTML.

Similarly, you can make alternate QuickTime movies that autoselect based on CPU speed. People with 100 MHz Pentium or PowerPC computers get movies compressed with undemanding codecs that play smoothly on their systems, while people with 1 GHz dual-processor computers get the highest-quality audio and video possible, even though it takes a fast computer to decompress them in real time.

QuickTime 3 and later can automatically select from a set of alternate movies based on Internet connection speed, operating system, or CPU speed. This is done by creating a reference movie that refers to the alternates and specifies the criteria. Earlier versions of QuickTime don't recognize alternate movies, but it's possible to include a default movie inside the reference movie that they will recognize. Earlier versions of QuickTime will play the default movie. (Viewers whose browsers are configured to use Windows Media Player for .mov files also see the default movie.)

The default movie also plays if none of the criteria for the alternates is met. In other words, you can specify an alternate that requires QuickTime 5 or later, and a default. All versions of QuickTime prior to 5 will play the default.

Creating movies for different connection speeds generally starts with making the highest-quality movie you can, then saving different versions of the movie compressed at lower data rates.

To get lower data rates, you typically use some combination of the following:

- smaller display size
- lower frame rate
- more audio and video compression
- fewer audio channels
- lower audio sampling rate

We'll go into the details of compression and sampling in the audio and movie chapters.

In some cases, creating an alternate movie for lower data rates can go beyond saving the original movie with different settings. You might substitute a series of still images for a movie, for example, or replace a recorded music track with a MIDI track. If you're willing to spend the time, you can create movies that are genuinely optimized for each connection speed.

You can set a priority for each alternate, designating one as first choice, another as second choice, and so on. QuickTime plays the highest-priority movie that it can. If your highest-priority movie requires streaming, for example, or a particular codec, and the viewer doesn't have that codec or has too slow a connection for the stream, QuickTime falls back through the alternates until it finds the best version of the movie that a viewer can play.

The lowest-priority alternate should probably be a still image that plays on any version of QuickTime or any plug-in that thinks it can play Quick-Time movies. Feel free to use GetQT.mov, in the Alternates folder of the CD, as your ultimate fallback movie.

Tools for Making Reference Movies

You can make reference movies based on Internet connection speed, CPU speed, or other criteria, using applications programs such as Discreet Cleaner (formerly Media Cleaner Pro). If you use Cleaner, you can create the reference movie and the alternate movies at the same time—just specify the source movie, the compression settings for each alternate, the playback requirements for each alternate (connection speed, QuickTime version, and so on), and a default movie. The rest is automatic. Cleaner refers to the reference movie as a master movie.

If you just need an inexpensive tool for redirecting users to different movies or Web pages, based on QuickTime version, operating system, or Internet connection speed, the QuickTime Detection Pack from Qtilities.com is sharp-looking, easy to use, and priced at under $10 US (www.qtilities.com).

This book includes a small application program called MakeRefMovie (in the Tools folder on the CD) that can make a reference movie from a set of alternates (you need to create the alternates separately). It also allows you to set priorities that define the alternate movies as a series of fallbacks in case the viewer can't play a particular alternate, and to specify a default that gets embedded in the reference movie.

Another tool you can use to create reference movies is XMLtoRefMovie (also in the Tools folder of the CD). This tool was contributed by Peter Hoddie (www.hoddie.net), and it's way cool. It's ideal for creating reference movies based on the URLs of a set of streaming movies, or generating reference movies from a script. This tool is Macintosh-only.

Let's take a closer look at creating reference movies using MakeRef-Movie, then we'll look at XMLtoRefMovie in more detail.

Using MakeRefMovie

This section will show you how to use MakeRefMovie and should serve as a useful guide for using any similar tool.

Begin by creating or assembling a set of movies for each connection speed you want to support. You can have as few as two alternates.

If some of your alternates are streaming movies, you can either make Fast Start movies that point to them, and use the Fast Start movies as the alternates for the reference movie, or enter the URL of the streaming movies directly in MakeRefMovie. It's easier to add the URLs into MakeRef-Movie directly, but you may need to make Fast Start movies that point to streaming movies for other reasons (such as adding plug-in parameters using Plug-in Helper).

To make a Fast Start movie that points to a streaming movie, open the streaming movie in QuickTime Player by choosing Open URL from the File menu and typing in the URL:

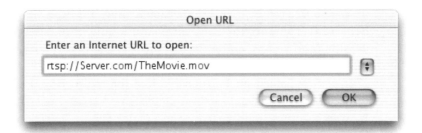

Once the streaming movie opens, choose Save As from the File menu, pick a name, and save as a self-contained movie. That's it.

In any case, put all your alternates into a folder together.

Launch MakeRefMovie. You'll be prompted to give the reference movie a name and location. Be sure to specify the folder with your alternate movies as the location.

Drag each alternate movie into the MakeRefMovie window. Set the minimum connection speed for each one. The following illustration shows MakeRefMovie in action.

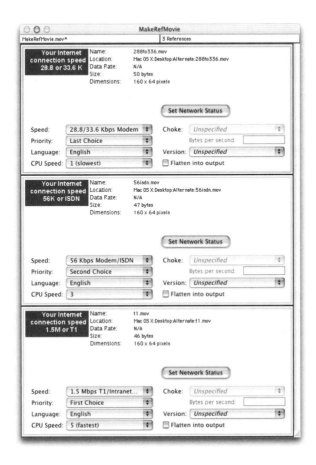

You can also use the Add URL command in the Movie menu to add a movie to the list of alternates. This lets you add movies on distant servers without having to create a local movie that points to them.

If one of your movies requires a component that isn't part of the minimal Internet download for QuickTime, there will be a note in italics beside the preview of that movie, such as *"Requires cross-fade effect component."* When you create your alternate movie, the presence of this component will be added to the other selection criteria for this movie.

If you want one of the movies to be the default movie for people who don't have QuickTime 3 or later, click the "Flatten into output" box for that movie.

For movies delivered over the Internet, the default movie should probably be a very small movie directing people to get the latest version of QuickTime. The default movie is flattened into the reference movie, so the browser downloads it even if an alternate movie is used. Keep the default movie small to minimize wasted bandwidth.

If you're delivering your movies on a CD or intranet, you might consider creating a default movie using older codecs that work with earlier versions of QuickTime, such as the Cinepak video codec and IMA 4:1 audio codec.

When you've set the minimum speed for all the alternates, you can save the reference movie. Once it's saved, copy your reference movie and all of the alternate movies into a single folder on your Web server. Finally, embed the reference movie in a Web page in the usual way:

```
<EMBED SRC="Multispeed.mov" HEIGHT=176 WIDTH=120>
```

If your alternate movies are of different sizes, set HEIGHT and WIDTH to the largest movie size, plus 16 pixels for the controller, and set an attractive background color (BGCOLOR) to fill in the space around the smaller movies.

The following illustration shows a Web page with a multiple data rate reference movie. It can be found in the Alternates folder on the CD as Whatspeed.htm. Open it with your browser. Adjust your Internet connection speed setting to see the different movies.

The version of MakeRefMovie on the CD allows you to designate alternates based on other criteria as well—such as CPU speed, language, or QuickTime version. Enjoy.

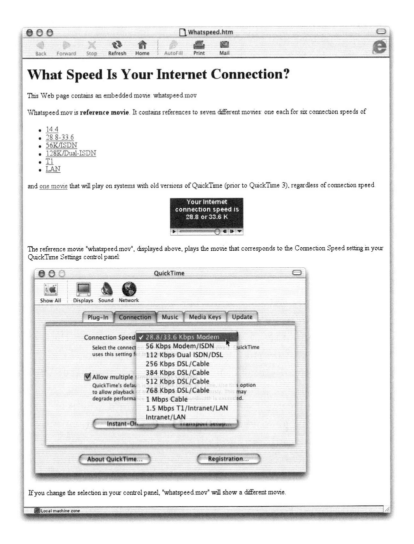

Using XMLtoRefMovie

Unlike MakeRefMovie, XMLtoRefMovie has no user interface. Instead, you create an XML-syntax file using a text editor or the output of a script. Drag the file onto XMLtoRefMovie and you're done—it creates a reference movie based on the contents of the file.

What's that? You *want* a user interface? Okay, you can have one. David Egbert of Retiarius Enterprises (www.retiariusenterprises.com) has thoughtfully provided a GUI for XMLtoRefMovie, named QTRM Maker.

You can find a copy in the Tools folder. For the latest version, check the Retiarius website.

You don't need to have copies of the alternate movies on disk to use XMLtoRefMovie; you can specify the alternates by URL. That can be a real time-saver for streaming movies—you don't need to create Fast Start movies from the streams to use as alternates.

Full documentation on XMLtoRefMovie can be found in the Tools folder (just open xmldocs.htm in your browser), but it basically works like this—you use a text editor or script to create a text file that looks something like the following:

```
<qtrefmovie>
    <refmovie src="test_28.mov" data-rate="28.8 modem" />
    <refmovie src="test_56.mov" data-rate="56k modem" />
    <refmovie src="test_t1.mov" data-rate="t1" />
</qtrefmovie>
```

The file starts with <qtrefmovie>, ends with </qtrefmovie>, and has one or more <refmovie /> elements.

Each <refmovie /> element has a src parameter that specifies a movie. The movie can be specified using a local filename or a URL (the URL can be any protocol QuickTime supports, including http://, ftp://, file:///, and rtsp://).

Each <refmovie /> element can contain a selector, such as data-rate, language, or cpu-speed, and a priority. This determines who gets to see which movie and sets the fallback order.

One of the <refmovie /> elements can be designated as the default. This movie will be copied into the reference movie that XMLtoRefMovie creates.

Save the text file with the .qtrm file extension and drag it onto XML-toRefMovie. This creates a reference movie with the same base filename but the .mov file extension (dragging MyRefMov.qtrm onto XMLtoRefMovie creates MyRefMov.mov).

That's it.

XMLtoRefMovie can also check for the presence and version of Quick-Time components by name. That quickly gets outside the scope of this book and into the QuickTime API for programmers, but there's a table listing some likely candidates in the next section, "Checking for QuickTime Components" (page 163), as well as a sample XML file on the CD that you can use to create a reference movie that plays one of two alternates based on the viewer's operating system (Mac OS or Windows). Check out MacWin.htm, in the Alternate folder on the CD.

Embedding Alternate Movies in a Web Page

There really isn't anything special to embedding alternate movies in a Web page—use a tool such as MakeRefMovie or XMLtoRefMovie to create a reference movie that points to the alternates, and embed the reference movie as you would an ordinary QuickTime movie.

Bear in mind, though, that the reference movie itself will load into an audience member's computer only for a moment, to be replaced almost immediately by the appropriate alternate. This has a couple of practical consequences.

If the viewer chooses Save after loading an alternate (assuming you allow saving), it's the alternate that's saved, not the reference movie.

If you need to modify the movie itself, by adding an auto-rotate sprite or using Plug-in Helper for example, you need to modify each alternate—modifying the reference movie will have no effect. (Parameters you pass to the movie through your HTML, in the EMBED or OBJECT tags, are passed to the alternate, so everything works as you would expect.)

If you drag your alternates into MakeRefMovie, they need to be on the server in the same folder as the reference movie—that's where it's going to look for them. If you entered URLs into MakeRefMovie or XMLtoRefMovie, the alternates need to be at the specified URLs for the same reason.

Note Okay, this sounds pretty obvious, but it must be easy to forget or something. If your reference movie stops working suddenly, check that first.

Alternate Tracks

A QuickTime movie can contain groups of two or more tracks that act as alternates. Alternate tracks can be different tracks of the same type, such as two sound tracks in different languages, or they can be different kinds of tracks, such as a voice-over in one language and text subtitles in another.

Alternate tracks can be selected based on the language setting of the viewer's computer, or they can be selected based on other criteria, such as Internet connection speed or CPU speed—just like alternate movies.

In fact, you can use alternate tracks the same way you use alternate movies. Viewers see only the part that's right for them. For local movies delivered from a disk, it doesn't matter whether you use alternate movies or alternate tracks; QuickTime accesses only the parts it needs. Over the Internet, there's an important difference. Browsers don't know how to request just certain parts of a file over HTTP, so they download whole movies, even if QuickTime needs only some of the data. Because alternate tracks are part of the same movie, they all download together as long as the movie is self-contained and delivered over the Internet. Consequently, alternate movies are a better method than alternate tracks for Internet delivery.

If you want to deliver movies with alternate tracks over the Internet and download only the tracks that the user will actually use, you need to create movies that aren't self-contained, so the alternate tracks are in separate data files.

If you're providing alternate text tracks based on language, it's generally fine to use alternate tracks rather than alternate movies, even over the Internet. Text tracks are normally only a few kilobytes each, so you can load half a dozen in a few seconds.

Making Alternate Tracks with QuickTime Player

This section shows you how to use QuickTime Player to create movies with alternate tracks based on the viewer's language.

Start by creating or assembling the alternate tracks. Creating alternate language tracks generally involves either recording voice-overs in each desired language or creating text tracks to use as subtitles. Details of recording speech for the Internet are covered in Chapter 10, "Now Hear This: Audio." Creating subtitles is covered in Chapter 13, "Text! Text! Text!"

Save each alternate track as a self-contained movie, and put all the alternates together in a single folder.

If your movie was created in one language, and you're adding alternate language voice-overs, you'll want to extract the original voice track, save it as a self-contained movie, and put it in with the rest of the alternate tracks. Make a new copy of the original movie, also self-contained, without the original voice track.

If the original voice track is already mixed as part of a composite sound track, you face some hard choices. You can use subtitles for other languages instead of voice-overs, or you can have alternate tracks that substitute just the voice-overs for the whole sound track, or you can create a new sound track to use with the alternate voice-overs.

Tip If you're creating movies from scratch, always keep the voice, music, and sound effects in separate tracks. That way you can use a different compressor optimized for each type of sound. You can also make substitutions, such as adding a foreign-language voice track or swapping a MIDI track for recorded music, without a lot of unnecessary pain.

Put a copy of your original movie, self-contained and minus any tracks that are now stored as alternates, in the folder with the alternates. Open this movie in QuickTime Player. Choose Get Movie Properties from the Movie menu, and leave the Properties window open.

For each alternate track, perform the following steps:

1. Open the alternate track in a new QuickTime Player window.

2. Select All. Copy. Close the window.

3. Go to the beginning of the original movie.

4. Hold down the Option key and choose Add from the Edit menu.

5. In the left pop-up menu of the Properties window, choose the newly added track. In the right pop-up menu, choose Alternate:

6. Click the Set button for Language and choose the language of this track from the list:

7. If this is the first alternate, go to the next step. For all subsequent alternates, click the Set button for Alternate and choose the previous alternate from the menu. In other words, if you are adding Text Track 2, set it as the alternate to Text Track 1; when you add Text Track 3, set it as the alternate to Text Track 2, and so on.

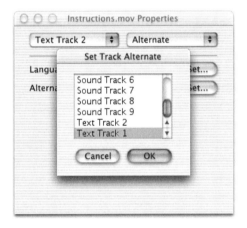

8. Save the movie, allowing dependencies.

Saving the movie after adding each track provides an incremental backup as you go along. Allowing dependencies keeps the alternate track data in separate files.

When you play the movie, only the track that matches your computer's language setting is played. To see or hear a different track, use the Choose Language command in QuickTime Player's Movie menu to select a different language—this is a good way to test each track after adding it.

Once you've added all the tracks, you can put the movie, along with all of the alternate track files, into a single folder on your Web server. You can then embed the multiple-language movie in your Web page as usual. When the Web page is viewed, only the tracks in the viewer's language are downloaded.

An example of a movie with alternate language tracks for English, French, and Spanish can be found in the Alternates folder of the CD as Languages.htm. Open it with a browser. It displays the movie Multilingual.mov in QuickTime Player. Only the track that matches your computer's language setting is displayed. To see the other tracks, use the Choose Language command in the Movie menu.

Checking for QuickTime Components

As you know by now, QuickTime uses components of various kinds as modules to perform common tasks, such as obtaining a video image, in a specific way, such as decompressing JPEG- or MPEG-encoded data.

Note This section covers some pretty technical stuff about QuickTime components that most people simply don't need to worry about. If you find yourself bored or puzzled, feel free to skip ahead to the next chapter. This section is mainly for people who *enjoy* being geeks.

Some components come from non-Apple sources, and some components are used by a relatively small number of people, compared with QuickTime as a whole. To make downloading QuickTime as convenient as possible, Apple provides a minimum installation option for people on slow Internet connections. The minimum installation doesn't include all of the many QuickTime components. In addition, new versions of QuickTime add new components, or sometimes new versions of existing components.

What all this means is, you can create a movie that uses a component your audience might not have, even if they have some version of QuickTime. Maybe they have an older version, or they did a minimum install, or the component is supplied by another company.

Happily, QuickTime will offer to get any missing component it knows about, whenever the user tries to play a movie that needs it (QuickTime knows about all Apple-supplied components, and all third-party components that are registered with Apple's component download program).

In addition, MakeRefMovie will check your alternate movies for components it recognizes as being outside the minimum installation, and add a requirement for those components to its selection criteria. XMLtoRef-Movie can also require particular components, or particular versions, but you need to specify the component type and subtype, something you're unlikely to know.

In any case, you may not want to screen out people who need a particular component—you might prefer to have QuickTime prompt them to download it. It often takes only a few seconds. You might also want to test for all the exotic components your site uses at once, rather than prompting the user to get them as needed.

If you know what components your viewers need to have, you can create a small text file that gives QuickTime the list of components, and QuickTime will offer to download anything the user doesn't have.

The text file looks like this:

```
<?xml version="1.0"?>
<?quicktime type="application/x-qtpreflight"?>
<qtpreflight>
<component type="ctyp" subtype="subt"/>
</qtpreflight>
```

where "ctyp" and "subt" are the actual four-character codes for a component's type and subtype.

This is an XML file. Save it as plain text, but with the .mov file extension, so the browser treats it as a QuickTime movie. Embed it in your Web page like an ordinary movie, but with HEIGHT and WIDTH both set to 2 (the file opens an empty movie that you don't really want to display).

The first three lines in the file are always the same. They let QuickTime know that this is an XML file of type qtpreflight. The last line is always the same. It closes the <qtpreflight> element. In between is the list of components to check for. You can have multiple <component /> elements in your file, and QuickTime will test for all of them.

For example, here's an XML file that checks for the Sorenson 3 video decompressor and the QuickTime for Java component:

```
<?xml version="1.0"?>
<?quicktime type="application/x-qtpreflight"?>
<qtpreflight>
<component type="imdc" subtype="SVQ3"/>
<component type="null" subtype="qtj "/>
</qtpreflight>
```

Note that the type and subtype are four-character codes. They are case-sensitive, and a blank space is a significant character. These values must be exactly four characters long, including any spaces.

If any components are missing, QuickTime will check to see if they are available for download. QuickTime will then open a dialog box, either offering to install them or informing the user that the needed component is not available.

Components are typically packaged in groups for download. For example, the text importer is currently part of the authoring package, so all the authoring components are downloaded and installed if the text importer is needed. If you specify several components in the same package, the package downloads only once.

Following is a list of some components that you might want to check for. Note that the type field identifies the kind of operation the component performs, and the subtype generally identifies the kind of data it operates on. For example, all image decompressors are of type "imdc", and all image compressors are of type "imco". A JPEG compressor or decompressor is of subtype "jpeg", while a Sorenson 3 compressor or decompressor is of subtype "SVQ3".

Component	Type	Subtype
Sorenson 3 video	"imdc"	"SVQ3"
QDesign Music 2 audio	"sdec"	"QDM2
MPEG-4 video	"imdc"	"mp4v"
Lens Flare effect	"imdc"	"lens"
Blur effect (effects generally)*	"imdc"	"blur"
Text importer*	"eat "	"TEXT"
MIDI or QuickTime Music*	"mhlr"	"musi"
ZyGoVideo video*	"imdc"	"ZyGo"
QuickTime for Java*	"null"	"qtj "

*Not in minimum installation

All effects (cross-fades, slides, wipes, and so on) are also of type "imdc". The subtype depends on the effect. You can dig up the subtype for most effects on Apple's website at developer.apple.com/techpubs/qtdedocs/RM/rmEffects.htm.

9 ▶

It's in the Script: Basic JavaScript

Sometimes you need to modify your HTML to work around differences in browsers and operating systems. And sometimes you need to do something that HTML just doesn't do. A little JavaScript can help.

You can use JavaScript to determine which browser and operating system a visitor has. The same script can then write out the proper HTML for that visitor. For example, you might use the <OBJECT> tag for Internet Explorer on the Windows OS and the <EMBED> tag for any other browser or OS. JavaScript can also do some things that HTML can't, such as opening a new window with a specific size and attributes. In some circumstances, you can use JavaScript to detect whether QuickTime is installed.

This chapter introduces you to some JavaScript basics, then provides three sample scripts that you can use:

- a script to detect a user's operating system, browser type, and browser version
- a script that opens a special player window for QuickTime
- a script that attempts to detect whether QuickTime is present

You can also use JavaScript to control QuickTime, to do things like play a movie when the mouse passes over an object. We'll look at using Java-Script to control QuickTime in "QuickTime and JavaScript" (page 534).

▶ JavaScript Basics

You can use the included scripts in your Web pages without needing to know much about JavaScript; if you're new to JavaScript, the following information should provide the necessary orientation.

A complete JavaScript tutorial is outside the scope of this book; to learn more, just type "JavaScript tutorial" into any Internet search engine. The Web will guide you to a wealth of information.

JavaScript is a simple scripting language that can be embedded in a Web page. (It really has nothing to do with Java; the name is misleading.)

JavaScript is interpreted by the user's browser when it opens a Web page. Because it talks to the browser, JavaScript can be used to dynamically generate HTML inside a Web page. In effect, JavaScript tells the browser, "In situation X, use this HTML; in situation Y, use that HTML." This allows you to write a single Web page that uses different HTML depending on things like the user's browser type.

JavaScript can also be used to add interactivity to a Web page. In this case, actions are taken depending on circumstances that change with user activity, such as the position of the mouse pointer.

In many cases, these kinds of things can also be accomplished without JavaScript by running special programs on your Web server known as Common Gateway Interface (CGI) scripts. The main advantages of Java-Script are

- JavaScript runs on the user's computer; there is no server load.
- JavaScript doesn't need a server; it can work from a CD-ROM.
- JavaScript can do some things that CGI scripts just can't do.

JavaScript functions are written inside the head of the HTML document. Functions can be triggered by various events, such as the page loading or a mouse click.

A JavaScript function can be used instead of a URL inside an <A HREF> tag—when a user clicks the link, the browser executes the JavaScript function instead of loading a URL.

You can also specify a JavaScript function in most places where Quick-Time expects a URL, such as in the HREF and QTNEXT parameters—as long as the movie is played by the QuickTime plug-in, any user functions are defined on the Web page that the movie is playing in, and the link is targeted so that the browser handles the URL (in other words, the URL is not targeted to quicktimeplayer or myself). For details, see "QuickTime and JavaScript" (page 534).

◉ Useful JavaScripts

Here are some scripts that can come in handy when you're writing Web pages that use QuickTime.

Identify OS, Browser Type, and Version

Here's a short script that captures the user's operating system (Win or Mac), browser (NN, IE, or Safari), and version (3x, 4x, 5x, or 6x). You can drop it into your Web page between the <HEAD> tag and the <TITLE> tag.

```
<Script language="JavaScript">

OSName = "unknown";
bName = "unknown";
bVer = "unknown";

// The OS is appended to the version somewhere
if (navigator.appVersion.indexOf("Mac") > 0) OSname = "Mac";
if (navigator.appVersion.indexOf("Win") > 0) OSname = "Win";
// Browsers set their names to Netscape or Microsoft
// as a default--real names are stored in the version
if (navigator.appName.substring(0,8) == "Netscape")
bName = "NN";
if (navigator.appName.substring(0,9) == "Microsoft")
bName = "IE";

// Look in version to see if this is really Safari
if (navigator.appVersion.indexOf("Safari") > 0)
bName = "Safari";

// Get the integer part of the version number
// and add "x" (3x, 4x, 5x, etc.)
Bver = parseInt(navigator.appVersion) + "x";
</script>
```

An HTML page that includes this script can be found in the JavaScript folder of the CD as BrowserOS.htm.

Open a Window for QuickTime

Here's a script that creates a function named openqtwin. When invoked, this function opens a 240 x 120 window named qtwin. Again, this script should be placed between the <HEAD> and </HEAD> tags on your Web page.

```
<script language="JavaScript">
<!--
  function openQTwin(url)  {
  qtwin = window.open(url,"song",'toolbar=0,location=0,
    directories=0,status=0,menubar=0,scrollbars=0,resizable=0,
    width=240,height=120');
  qtwin.focus();
  }
  // -->
</script>
```

You can set height and width to whatever value you need. Note that all the text between "qtwin =" and the following ");" must be on a single line (no carriage return) with no spaces, so the line really looks more like this:

```
qtwin = window.open(url,"song",(...)
  width=240,height=120');
```

This function creates the window only if it doesn't already exist, so no matter how many times it's called, it creates only one window. The line "qtwin.focus();" puts this window on top of your Web page, even if it was previously hidden. The window appears over the upper-left corner of your Web page, so design the page accordingly.

You can use this window to display QuickTime content. If you have multiple QuickTime movies embedded in a single page, this allows you to load and display one movie at a time, automatically closing any previous movie.

To use this function, put the following bit of script in the body of your Web page:

```
<a href="javascript:openQTwin('MyMovie.mov')">Play
  MyMovie</a>
```

When someone clicks the words "Play MyMovie," the window is activated or created, and MyMovie.mov is loaded into it.

Note Many websites currently use JavaScript's ability to open a window to create "pop-ups" for advertising. Like the old use of the <FLASH> tag, this is so annoying that it will probably die out when advertisers realize it makes people hate them, but in the meantime people have begun to use "pop-up blockers" in self-defense. As you've probably guessed by now, a pop-up blocker can prevent JavaScript from opening a window for you.

For a more sophisticated effect, embed the movie in a small Web page that displays properly in the new window, and use the URL of the Web page instead of the movie:

```
<a href="javascript:openQTwin('MyMovie.htm')">Play
  MyMovie</a>
```

This lets you put text and graphics in the new window along with the movie. It also lets you use an <EMBED> tag to control how the plug-in behaves inside the new window (to make the movie autoplay for example, or to add an HREF to a page where the viewer can buy something). The HTML for a small Web page that plays an audio movie might look like this:

```
<HTML>
<HEAD>
<TITLE>Now Playing</TITLE>
</HEAD>
<BODY BGCOLOR="#FFFFFF">
<EMBED SRC="MyAudio.mov" HEIGHT=16 WIDTH=200
  AUTOPLAY="True" >
<br>
<B>"My Audio"</B> by Me<BR>
<HR>
<DIV ALIGN="Center">
<a href="javascript:window.close()">Close this window</a>
</DIV>
</BODY>
</HTML>
```

An example page that uses this JavaScript function is JavaJuke.htm, in the Audio folder of the CD.

Using JavaScript to Detect QuickTime

Using JavaScript to detect a plug-in is something of a black art. You need to take into account the user's operating system, browser type, and browser version; you need to use JavaScript, VBScript, and ActiveX objects; and even then it won't always work.

The easiest and most reliable way to detect QuickTime is to use Quick-Time itself—this is described in "Detecting the QuickTime Plug-in" (page 121).

Still, in some circumstances it's possible to detect a plug-in by using a combination of JavaScript and VBScript. Here's how it works:

- **Internet Explorer (Windows)**

  You can use VBScript and ActiveX to detect QuickTime 4.1.1 or later.

- **All Others**

  - Netscape browsers (all versions, all operating systems)
  - Internet Explorer (version 5 or later, Mac OS)
  - Safari

  You can use the JavaScript plugins object to detect QuickTime.

It turns out that you can use both VBScript and JavaScript in the same HTML document (if you're careful). This means that by combining Java-Script, VBScript, and ActiveX, you can detect QuickTime (any version) in a Netscape browser (any version, any OS), Internet Explorer (version 5 or later for the Mac OS), and other browsers, including Safari, and you can detect QuickTime (version 4.1.1 or later) in Internet Explorer (any version for Windows).

You *can't* use scripts to detect old versions of QuickTime (prior to 4.1.1) in Windows using Internet Explorer, unless the QuickTime ActiveX control is installed.

Tip   Adding an <OBJECT> tag with the QuickTime ClassID and Codebase will prompt these people to download the ActiveX control, which is quite small and works with QuickTime 3 and later. Once they have the QuickTime ActiveX control, the detection scripts will work.

You also can't use scripts to detect QuickTime using older versions of Explorer for the Mac (prior to IE 5), but all Mac OS computers come with QuickTime installed, so that's a case where you don't really need to check.

The good news is that you *can* detect QuickTime using scripts, as long as the user has a semi-recent browser or a recent version of QuickTime. A lot of legacy cases also work—older versions of Navigator are fine, as are older versions of QuickTime on the Mac OS.

Here's an HTML page that uses VBScript and JavaScript together to detect QuickTime (in the JavaScript folder of the CD as DetectQT.htm):

```
<HEAD>
<TITLE>Test for QuickTime</TITLE>

<SCRIPT LANGUAGE="Javascript">
   var haveqt = false;
</SCRIPT>

<SCRIPT LANGUAGE="VBScript">
On Error  Resume Next
Set theObject =
  CreateObject("QuickTimeCheckObject. QuickTimeCheck.1")
On Error  goto 0

   If IsObject(theObject) Then
      If theObject.IsQuickTimeAvailable(0) Then
      'Just check for file
         haveqt = true
      End If
   End If
</SCRIPT>

<SCRIPT LANGUAGE="Javascript">
   if (navigator.plugins) {
      for (i=0; i < navigator.plugins.length; i++ ) {
         if (navigator.plugins[i].name.indexOf
         ("QuickTime") >= 0)
            { haveqt = true; }
      }
   }
</SCRIPT>
</HEAD>
```

```
<BODY bgcolor="#ffffff">
<H1>Check for QuickTime</H1>

<SCRIPT LANGUAGE="Javascript">
dload = "http://www.apple.com/quicktime/download/"
mytag = "You need <a href=" + dload + ">QuickTime</a>"

if (haveqt)
 mytag = '<EMBED SRC="hotfire.mov" width=120 height=51>';

document.write(mytag);
</SCRIPT>

</BODY>
</HTML>
```

If you want to assume that Mac OS users with older versions of Explorer have QuickTime (a safe assumption), you can add the following bit of script:

```
if ((navigator.appVersion.indexOf("Mac") > 0)
   && (navigator.appName.substring(0,9) == "Microsoft")
   && (parseInt(navigator.appVersion) < 5) )
   { haveqt = true; }
```

An HTML page that includes this test can be found in the JavaScript folder of the CD as DetectQTplus.htm.

Note   Most visitors to your website are probably using Internet Explorer on a Windows computer. As an alternative to using a script to detect QuickTime, you can simply embed a small QuickTime movie using the <OBJECT> tag, as described in Chapter 4, "Basic Training: Putting QuickTime in a Web Page." This causes the browser to look specifically for the QuickTime ActiveX control and to offer to download and install it if needed. This loads only the ActiveX control, which is a small download. If QuickTime is not installed, the ActiveX control will then offer to get the rest of the QuickTime software. The ActiveX control works with QuickTime 3 and later, so viewers who already have QuickTime can download just the control.

10

Now Hear This: Audio

At this point, you should be fairly adept at putting QuickTime movies on a Web page. Now let's take a closer look at some of the media you can create and deliver using QuickTime. First let's look at audio: what you can do with it, how to create it, how to compress it, and how to get the most out of it.

This chapter covers

- interesting things you can do with audio
- recorded music
- MP3
- MIDI
- looping and stuttering
- compression, bandwidth, and sampling
- audio codecs
- recording for the Web
- popular audio formats

Interesting Ways to Use Audio

Audio is one of the most overlooked ways to enhance a website. You can use QuickTime audio to make your Web page talk, sing, explode, or play music, while letting users control the volume or stop the sound at will.

QuickTime includes codecs that let you provide extremely high-quality sound on a CD (or for download), or extremely low-bandwidth audio that plays in real time over typical dialup connections.

In some cases you can have your cake and eat it too: MIDI music, speech compressed with the Qualcomm PureVoice codec, and music compressed with the QDesign Music Codec all deliver good-quality sound that plays in real time over typical connections.

Here are some of the interesting things you can do with QuickTime audio; we'll examine each one in detail:

- audio greetings
- background music
- ambient sounds
- stories and speech

Where it's appropriate, we'll recommend using a particular codec, sampling rate, or sample size. If you want a more detailed discussion of the choices, skip ahead to the sections "Making It Fit: Sampling, Bandwidth, and Compression" (page 208) and "Audio Codecs" (page 215).

Audio Greetings

Every home page can benefit from a simple audio greeting. It's small, it's personal, and it gives people notice that they've arrived somewhere special.

To be a real greeting, it needs to play within a few seconds of the user's arrival, so you need to use either a short sound or a low-bandwidth codec, preferably both.

The greeting can be speech, a sound effect, or a few bars of music, either recorded music or MIDI. Examples of all four are on the CD, in the Audio folder, as `Greetings.htm`.

The HTML is simple:

```
<EMBED SRC="Greeting.mov" HEIGHT="2" WIDTH="2"
   HIDDEN="True"
   CONTROLLER="False" AUTOPLAY="True">
```

Since the greeting is short and plays only once, no user interface is needed, so we set `HIDDEN="True"` and `CONTROLLER="False"`. We also specify `AUTOPLAY="True"` so the greeting plays automatically.

Tip Since you're only allocating a 2 x 2 pixel area, you can omit the HIDDEN parameter if you like. Some versions of Netscape for Windows don't play hidden audio. Just position the movie somewhere inconspicuous, or at the end of a sentence, where it looks like a period.

To avoid annoying your users, consider making a duplicate of the home page without the greeting, and make any links to the home page from elsewhere in your site point to the duplicate page. That way users hear the greeting only when they first arrive. This is only important if navigating your site involves frequent returns to the home page, where the greeting might become tiresome.

The examples below show you how to use QuickTime Player to prepare your greeting for delivery over the Web as a QuickTime movie.

Spoken Greeting

For best audio quality, start with an uncompressed digitized recording using at least a 22 kHz sampling rate (44.1 or 48 kHz is even better) with 16-bit samples. File formats that support acceptable quality include Quick-Time (.mov), AIFF (.aif), WAV (.wav), and Sound Designer II.

Open the audio file with QuickTime Player and export it as a Quick-Time movie. Click the Settings button to set the sampling rate and compressor. Choose a rate of approximately 22 kHz (use 22.05 if the original recording is 44.1), click the Mono radio button, and choose a compressor from the pop-up menu.

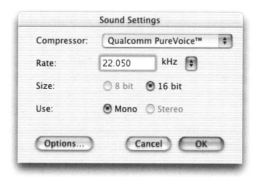

For a spoken greeting that streams over a dialup connection, the Qual-comm PureVoice compressor is ideal (choose full rate, not half rate). For cable or DSL, QDesign Music 2 at 32 or 48 Kbits gives a fuller sound. For a higher-bandwidth connection, such as an intranet or CD-ROM, use IMA

4:1 compression or no compression at all. You can hear an example of a spoken greeting by opening Greetings.htm (in the Audio folder on the CD).

Sound Effect Greeting

Maybe a more effective greeting for your website would be a brief explosion, the sound of a low-flying jet, or a few notes of bird song.

The sampling rate and sample size needed for good quality depends on the sound effect; in general, a noisier sound, like an explosion, can use a lower sample size and sampling rate. Higher-pitched sounds require higher sampling rates.

Using stereo doubles the size of the file, but it can also create the effect of movement by shifting the sound from one speaker to the other.

Choose your sound effect, then experiment with different sample sizes and sampling rates. The best compressor for sound effects over the Web is probably the QDesign Music Codec. For higher-bandwidth delivery, try IMA 4:1 or no compression at all.

For an example of a Web page with a sound effect as a greeting, open Greeting2.htm in the Audio folder of the CD.

Musical Greeting

Most memorable music, from Beethoven to the Rolling Stones, has at least one "hook" that can set a mood instantly. A short musical hook can be a very effective greeting for your website.

There are two distinct ways to embed music in a website: as a sound sample or as a MIDI file. MIDI uses much less bandwidth, but it's more limited in the kinds of sound it can reproduce. If your greeting is a few notes of piano or flute, use MIDI. If it's a guitar riff with fuzz, reverb, and screaming vocals in the background, use a sound sample.

For sampled-sound music, you should start with the highest-quality recording you can get: 16-bit stereo samples at 44.1 or 48 kHz. Make a direct digital copy from CD or DAT to an AIFF or WAV file if you can. If you have a Mac, you can make a digital copy of an audio CD track using QuickTime Player or iTunes. For Windows, you can do it with a shareware program like Audiograbber or CD Copy.

If you have to play the recording into the sound input of your computer, the optimal sampling rate for recording is generally 44.1 kHz. Save as an uncompressed AIFF or WAV file.

Open the sound file with QuickTime Player, select the part you want to use as a greeting, and export it as a QuickTime movie. At this point, you can make the file a lot smaller by choosing a 22 kHz sampling rate or Mono instead of Stereo (use 22.05 kHz if your source is 44.1 kHz).

The optimum music compressor for the Web is the QDesign Music 2 Codec. It offers high fidelity and low bandwidth (up to 100:1 compression). You'll get more compression by specifying lower data rates. Try a few different rates, and choose the lowest that sounds good to you.

You can get good quality with some compression by choosing the IMA 4:1 compressor, and this is compatible with older versions of QuickTime. If you downsample to 22 kHz and use the IMA compressor, you can get 8:1 compression and quite good sound. If you also drop from stereo to mono, it's 16:1.

If you have a sound file in MP3 format, you can use that; it gives 6:1 compression and excellent sound at 256 Kbits, or 12:1 compression and decent sound at 128 Kbits. This will still be far less than the 100:1 compression possible with the QDesign codec, so use a very short clip, or the user will be gone before your greeting plays.

Starting with QuickTime 6, the AAC compressor is available. This is the sound format used in MPEG-4 and on many DVDs. It gives better sound than MP3 at the same bandwidth, or the same sound quality at about 70% of the bandwidth.

For delivery via CD, no compressor is necessary, even for 44 kHz stereo music. If the greeting is only a few seconds long, no compressor is needed for delivery over an Ethernet LAN either.

An example of a musical greeting can be found in Greetings.htm (in the Audio folder of the CD).

Background Music (MIDI)

Background music is usually provided in MIDI format. MIDI is like electronic sheet music—it specifies the notes, the timing, and the instruments; the music is generated by the user's computer. MIDI can deliver long and complex pieces of music using small files and little bandwidth.

Of course, you can also use recorded music, sampled digitally, as background. With MP3 or AAC encoding, or the QDesign Music Codec, you can also get good quality, relatively small file size, and fairly low bandwidth, though nowhere near as low as MIDI.

If your visitors have dual-ISDN connections (128 Kbits/sec) or faster, you can deliver near–FM-quality recorded music as background using MP3, AAC, or the QDesign Music 2 set for around 100 Kbits/sec compression.

Note QuickTime doesn't come with an MP3 encoder, so you need to use another program such as iTunes or Musicmatch Jukebox to do the initial encoding for MP3.

To deliver recorded background music over dialup connections, use the QDesign Music 2 Codec set for 40 Kbits or 20 Kbits compression. Bear in mind that increasing the compression lowers the sound quality. Don't use MP3 below 128 Kbits. It sounds awful.

MIDI is generally the better choice for background music. It has a very clean sound that plays over dialup connections with no compression artifacts. The downside is that some people find MIDI *too* clean and describe it as sterile sounding. There's no doubt that you can get a sound with more character from recorded music. But recorded music really wants more bandwidth than you can normally spare for background sound.

As usual, with QuickTime you can have the best of both worlds. You can save multiple versions of a recorded song at different data rates and use alternate movies so the listener hears the highest-quality sound that will play over his or her connection in real time. Include a MIDI version for users with connections too slow to hear a good recording. Alternate movies are described in "Alternate Movies" (page 151).

You have the option of delivering your background audio using Fast Start movies from your Web server or as audio streams from a streaming server. If you're using a MIDI file as background, it's probably best to use Fast Start—MIDI is low bandwidth and sensitive to packet loss. If you want to use a live audio feed from your radio station or nightclub, streaming is the only way to go. Recorded background music works fine either way.

The first example in this section shows you how to embed a Fast Start audio movie.

```
<EMBED SRC="Bground.mov" HEIGHT=2 WIDTH=2 AUTOPLAY="True"
  HIDDEN="True">
```

Omit the HIDDEN tag if you don't mind a 2-pixel blemish and need to be sure the audio will play on all versions of Netscape for Windows. To use a stream instead, change the SRC parameter to point to a dummy image on your Web server and include the URL of the stream by adding a QTSRC parameter.

```
<EMBED SRC="UNeedQT4.pntg" TYPE="image/x-macpaint"
  HEIGHT=2 WIDTH=2 AUTOPLAY="True" HIDDEN="True"
  QTSRC="rtsp://StreamServer.com/path/Bground.mov">
```

This is explained in more detail in Chapter 14, "Gently down the Stream."

One of the biggest decisions you face as a website designer using background music is whether to include a movie controller. The controller may call attention away from other parts of your Web page, which is the opposite of "background." I can absolutely promise you, however, that you will annoy a significant number of people if you include music but don't provide a way to turn it off or adjust the volume.

I suggest using a controller unless the music selection is short, doesn't loop, and is set to play at a low volume. You can minimize the controller to just a Play/Pause button by setting `HEIGHT="16"` and `WIDTH="16"`. Alternatively, you could provide a No Background Music button that links to a version of the page without music.

Here's the HTML to play a background music file once, at low volume (70%), with no controller:

```
<EMBED SRC="Bground.mov" HEIGHT=2 WIDTH=2 AUTOPLAY="True"
  HIDDEN="True" VOLUME=70>
```

Here's the HTML to play background music endlessly, at moderate volume (80%), with a controller that allows the user to stop, start, or change the volume:

```
<EMBED SRC="Bground.mov" HEIGHT=16 WIDTH=150
  AUTOPLAY="True" VOLUME=80 LOOP="True">
```

Set `HEIGHT` to 16 for a sound with a controller. Set `WIDTH` to any convenient size, but ordinarily not less than 140. Use a larger value for the width to allow accurate positioning of the slider in a long piece of music.

Tip Use a height and width of 16 x 16 to restrict the controller to a small Play/Pause button.

Here's some HTML that plays a file continuously in the background, at the default volume, until the user smashes the computer with a brick:

```
<EMBED SRC="AnnoyingBground.mov" HEIGHT=2 WIDTH=2
  AUTOPLAY="True" HIDDEN="True" LOOP="True">
```

Tip MIDI can generate full-scale sound, so it often sounds louder than recorded sound, which is rarely full scale. If your MIDI uses full-scale tones, `volume=75` is similar to the default volume for typical sampled sound.

For more about MIDI, see "Getting the Most Out of MIDI" (page 195). You can hear examples of looping and nonlooping background music at different preselected audio volumes in BgMusic.htm in the Audio folder of the CD.

There's also a collection of royalty-free sound clips that are designed to play as loops in the Imaginationmusic folder, inside the Audio folder. Check it out!

Ambient Sounds

Merriam-Webster's Collegiate Dictionary defines ambience as "a feeling or mood associated with a particular place, person, or thing." The sound of running water and calling birds, or the crackle of high-voltage lines and the thrum of passing cars, or perhaps the distant thump of artillery and the spatter of small-arms fire, can add a distinct ambience to a website or a CD. A significant factor in the success of a CD like Myst is its use of ambient sound to add character to virtual places.

It's easy to create an endlessly looping mechanical background sound, but creating a natural-sounding loop of wind or waves, or a random-seeming interval between intermittent sounds, is more difficult.

For examples of ambient sound, load Ambient.htm from the Audio folder on the CD.

The examples below all set HIDDEN="True". To add a sound controller, delete this parameter, while setting HEIGHT=16 and WIDTH=150 (or some reasonable width for your page).

Repetitive Sound

Repetitive ambient sound is a simple audio loop. It works well if your background sound is mechanical in nature. This kind of sound tends to become tiresome very quickly, so use it sparingly.

Begin with a short audio sample, such as a 3-second .wav file, that sounds good in a loop.

1. Open the file with QuickTime Player.

2. Choose Export from the File menu, then choose Movie to QuickTime Movie. Click the Options button, then the Settings button under Sound.

3. Use 16-bit samples unless the sound is essentially noise.

4. Choose a 22 kHz sampling rate (use 11 kHz for noise).

5. Choose Mono unless the sound uses a stereo effect.

6. Choose the highest compression that produces acceptable sound (probably QDesign or IMA 4:1).

7. Embed the sound in your Web page at the desired volume:

```
<EMBED SRC="Ambient.mov" HEIGHT=2 WIDTH=2 HIDDEN="True"
    AUTOPLAY="True" LOOP="True" VOLUME=50>
```

A low volume (VOLUME=50) is generally desirable. You may hear an artifact when the sound loops. Read the section "Looping and Stuttering" (page 203) for solutions.

Note   There is a collection of royalty-free sound clips designed to play as loops in the Imaginationmusic folder, inside the Audio folder of the CD.

Chaotic Sound

Chaotic ambient sound is also an audio loop, but if properly executed the random nature of the sound (running water, falling rain, rushing wind, crackling fire) disguises the fact that the sound is a loop. It sounds continuous and random.

Begin with an audio sample of chaotic sound, such as a .wav file. A file length of 5 seconds or longer makes it harder for the ear to recognize a loop, but a shorter file downloads faster.

1. Carefully edit the sample using a sound editor so that there is no obvious "hiccup" when the file loops. A sound editor with a visual interface makes this easier.

2. Open the file with QuickTime Player.

3. Choose Export from the File menu, then choose Movie to QuickTime Movie. Click the Options button, then the Settings button under Sound.

4. Use 16-bit samples.

5. Choose a 22 kHz sampling rate.

6. Choose Mono, unless the sound uses a stereo effect.

7. Choose the QDesign Music 2 compressor if your target is the Web. For CD, use the IMA 4:1 compressor or leave uncompressed. (The Qualcomm PureVoice compressor introduces quite a bit of noise, but sometimes that works with this kind of sound, and it gives terrific compression. Give it a try.)

8. Embed the sound in your Web page using the <EMBED> tag:

```
<EMBED SRC="Ambient.mov" HEIGHT=2 WIDTH=2 HIDDEN="True"
    AUTOPLAY="True" LOOP="True" >
```

You may wish to set a low volume as well (VOLUME=50).

Tip You can sometimes get a smoother looping effect by setting LOOP="Palindrome", which causes the sound to play forward, then backward, instead of simply repeating. This works better with some sounds than others. See "Looping and Stuttering" (page 203) for more tips.

Intermittent Sound

Intermittent ambient sound is typically created by running one or more audio loops, each with intermittent sounds but with a different period. If properly executed, the changing intervals and overlaps between sounds disguise the fact that the sounds are made of interlocking loops. It simply sounds random.

1. Begin with one or more audio samples of intermittent sound, such as two .aif files. Each file should begin with a different amount of silence and should feature sound at staggered intervals. It's ideal if the sounds use a stereo effect by coming sometimes from one speaker and sometimes from the other.

2. Open each file with QuickTime Player.

3. Choose Export from the File menu, then choose Movie to QuickTime Movie. Click the Options button, then the Settings button under Sound.

4. Use 16-bit samples, unless the sound is essentially noise.

5. Choose a 22 kHz sampling rate (use 11 kHz for low-frequency rumbles).

6. Choose Stereo if the sounds use a stereo effect.

7. Use the QDesign Music compressor if your target audience is the Web. For CD, use IMA 4:1. (The Qualcomm PureVoice compressor is ideal if the sound is human voices.)

8. Embed the sounds in your Web page using a series of <EMBED> tags:

```
<EMBED SRC="Ambient1.mov" HEIGHT=2 WIDTH=2 HIDDEN="True"
    AUTOPLAY="True" LOOP="True" >

<EMBED SRC="Ambient2.mov" HEIGHT=2 WIDTH=2 HIDDEN="True"
    AUTOPLAY="True" LOOP="True" >
```

You may want to set a moderate volume as well (VOLUME=50). See "Looping and Stuttering" (page 203) for more tips.

Playing multiple movies simultaneously makes significant demands on the processor and requires a fair amount of memory. Be sure to test your Web page using the slowest machine and least amount of memory that you intend to support. To reduce demands, use a small number of movies (two or three) and make each movie small. You might want to synchronize the movies by creating a SMIL framework. See Chapter 18, "SMIL for the Camera." You can also create a movie containing a group of other movies, synchronized to suit your taste, using QuickTime's new movie tracks. Only a few application programs make it easy to create this kind of movie; one is LiveStage Pro, from Totally Hip software (www.totallyhip.com).

An alternative to using multiple movies is to make a single movie with each ambient sound loop as a track. Tracks don't loop independently in QuickTime, but it's possible to paste in hundreds of copies of a given loop end-to-end as references (one copy of the audio data referenced many times). Each reference uses only a few bytes, and each reference acts as one loop of that data. Different tracks can contain many loops of different lengths. Eventually the whole movie loops. The structure of such a movie is shown in the following illustration.

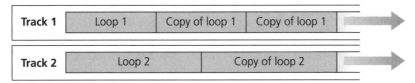

A movie that creates the effect of independently looping tracks

This technique is described in more detail in "Looping and Stuttering" (page 203).

Stories and Speech

The human voice is a magical instrument, and talking websites stun and amaze people, even today. I'm serious. Try it and see.

Fortunately, the human voice can be recorded cleanly at much lower sampling rates than music, and it also compresses very well. Consequently, a CD-ROM can easily hold 4 hours of high-quality uncompressed speech and up to 40 hours of compressed speech. Using the Qualcomm PureVoice speech codec, you can send the spoken word over a typical dialup Web connection in real time, with surprisingly good quality and enough spare bandwidth for a slideshow.

Internet delivery of the spoken word can revolutionize distance learning, particularly when lectures are synchronized with slides, animation, or URLs. It allows time-shifting as well as access from anywhere in the world.

Another speech application is a "talking book" that a person can read visually while hearing it read aloud. HTML and QuickTime make it easy to present text and audio together in an attractive manner.

An example of this on the CD is an excerpt from the poetry CD-ROM *Life Near 310 Kelvin,* by Greg Keith (www.slgbooks.com/310kelvin/). To see and hear it, run the file Speech.htm in the Audio folder of the CD, or visit the website.

Another example of effective use of the spoken work on the Internet is the live reading by poet Claire Braz-Valentine at

http://homepage.mac.com/clairebraz/

This particular reading combines controversial politics, poetry, and humor, in a way that never fails to stir people up. It also combines a low-bandwidth slideshow with the reading and plays nicely over a dialup modem. This kind of Internet content is never boring.

To prepare the spoken word for delivery over the Web or CD-ROM, use a 22 kHz sampling rate, 16-bit samples, and mono (unless you have more than one person reading and a stereo effect is desirable). The choice of codecs depends on your situation:

- Using no compression gives the highest quality and allows you to put up to 4 hours of speech on a CD-ROM (2 hours in stereo).

- 2:1 aLaw or 2:1 uLaw gives high quality and reduces the file size by 50%. Use one of these codecs if you need to save space on a CD-ROM.

- IMA 4:1 gives good quality and reduces the file size by 75%, enough to allow a reasonable download but not enough to play in real time over the Web with a dialup connection.

  MP3 or AAC encoding gives good audio quality around 100 Kbits/sec for speech, which will play in real time over DSL or cable modems.

- Qualcomm PureVoice gives moderate quality and typically reduces file size by 90%. Use this to deliver speech in real time over dialup modems or to put truly huge amounts of speech on a CD-ROM.

Embed the audio movie with a controller, so the listener can adjust the volume, pause the reading, or listen to part of it again. Set AUTOPLAY ="True" so your Web page just starts talking.

```
<EMBED SRC="Speech.mov" HEIGHT=16 WIDTH=150
    AUTOPLAY="True">
```

If you anticipate that the listener will want to listen to particular passages within the audio, set a wider WIDTH to make it easier to position the slider control accurately. For long pieces, consider adding a chapter list, as described in "Adding a Chapter List to a Movie" (page 390). This is particularly useful for distance learning applications.

Recorded Music on the Web

The Web has created a whole new distribution channel for music. Users can buy music by the song (with the opportunity to hear a sample before making a purchase) and have custom CDs mailed to them. Or they can download music directly over the Web and burn their own audio CDs at home using inexpensive CD-R/W technology. Popular compression formats like MP3 provide near-CD quality at 6:1 compression, and near-FM quality at 11:1 compression for faster downloads.

The ability to offer samples over the Web is especially important for alternative, small-label, or individually published musicians who aren't getting airplay on the radio. It's fairly easy to create a website to promote your music, with photos of your band, video clips, a jukebox of sample songs, a schedule of upcoming performances, plus snail-mail and email addresses to order CDs or just to send encouragement to the band.

But even the 11:1 compression of MP3 requires a 1 MB download to hear a 1-minute song. This is a good way to deliver a song someone knows they want, but it's not a good way to let someone browse through your songs looking for something they like. Not unless they have a very fast Internet connection.

You'll generally want to make two versions of each song available; a CD-quality or near–CD-quality file for sale or download, and a more compressed version that plays in real time over a dialup connection.

If you're selling tracks off your CD, you'll probably want to deliver your high-quality version using a lossless compressor (such as Zipit or Stuffit), so it can be decompressed to true CD quality. Another possibility is 256 or 384 Kbit MP3 format. If you're giving it away in hopes of selling it on CD, you might prefer 128 Kbit MP3, so there's more value to be gained from the CD.

The more-compressed version for immediate listening should always be prepared using the QDesign Music Codec at the lowest bit rate that sounds acceptable. If you like, you can compress the song at different rates and use alternate movies to deliver the highest bit rate the user's connection can handle.

The following section will show you how to prepare recorded music for delivery over the Web or on a multimedia CD-ROM, and how to create an online jukebox by embedding recordings in a Web page.

❯Warning   It may be illegal to post recorded music on your website unless you either own the copyright or have arranged to pay royalties to the owner.

Start with the Best

Begin with the highest-quality recording you can get. If you can make a digital copy directly from CD or DAT to a WAV or AIFF file, this is ideal.

On a Macintosh, QuickTime Player can be used to open a track directly from an audio CD: Just insert the CD into your computer's CD-ROM drive, launch QuickTime Player, choose Open from the File menu, and browse to the CD track you want. Save the audio to disk as an AIFF file without compressing it. On a Windows PC, you can capture a CD track to an AIFF or WAV file using shareware programs like Audiograbber and CD Copy.

If you're going to compress your files to MP3, there are rippers for both PC and Macintosh that will go directly from CD to MP3 at various bit rates, including MusicMatch Jukebox (for Windows and Macintosh) and iTunes (Mac only).

For a song that will be compressed and downloaded over the Web, it may be acceptable to generate the WAV or AIFF by playing a CD or a DAT into the sound input of your computer, but a true digital copy sounds better. Be sure to record at a 44.1 kHz sampling rate, in stereo, with 16-bit samples.

Prime Cut

There are four good options for compressing the high-quality version of a song for download: lossless file compression of uncompressed audio, MP3, AAC, and QDesign.

For a song that can be burned directly onto an audio CD, use uncompressed audio and a lossless file compression program like Zipit or Stuffit (create .zip files for Windows users, .sit files for Macs). Expect anywhere from 2:1 to 5:1 compression. Be sure the uncompressed audio is 44.1 kHz 16-bit stereo or it won't burn to an audio CD.

To create a file that can play on any MP3 player, use an MP3 compression program like SoundJam, iTunes, Music Match Jukebox, Media Cleaner Pro, or Wav2mp3. Expect compression of 5:1 (384 Kbit), 6:1 (256 Kbit), or 11:1 (128 Kbit). Users who have QuickTime can play an MP3 as it downloads. If they have a 128 Kbits/sec or faster connection, low bit rate MP3 can play in real time. Users with slower connections can play whatever has already arrived at any point in the download, without interrupting the download process.

AAC compression provides either better sound quality or more compression than MP3 (about 30% smaller files at the same quality). You can play back AAC files using QuickTime or any MPEG-4 compliant player. To allow playback by programs other than QuickTime, export the file to MP4 format (Export, Movie to MPEG-4).

For a song that will always be played using QuickTime, use QuickTime Player to compress the file by choosing Export (Movie to QuickTime Movie). Select the AAC or QDesign 2 codec at 128 Kbits/sec for sound quality that exceeds MP3 at the same bit rate.

For even higher quality at a given bit rate, use the Professional Edition of the QDesign Music 2 Codec, available from QDesign. Expect 10:1 to 15:1 compression for maximum quality. You can set any bit rate you like, and use the lowest bit rate that still sounds right. Listeners with a connection greater than or equal to the data rate can play the song as it downloads.

Faster, Faster

You generally also want to create a version of each song that can play in real time, or with a minimum of delay, over a dialup connection.

Open the song with QuickTime Player. You may want to edit the file at this point to make only an excerpt available for browsing.

Choose Export from the File menu and choose Movie to QuickTime Movie. Click the Options button, then click Settings under Sound. Choose 44 kHz, in Stereo, with 16-bit samples.

The optimum compressor for the Web is the QDesign Music 2 Codec. The QDesign compressor provides an Option button that lets you select the exact bit rate of the final product. A bit rate of 24 Kbits/sec plays smoothly over almost any dialup connection, and 40 Kbits/sec is reliable over most 56K modems. Try a few different rates and choose the lowest that sounds good to you. As an alternative, try the AAC compressor (requires QuickTime 6 or later for playback).

If you want to use real-time streams, rather than Fast Start movies, export the audio as a hinted movie and upload it to a streaming server, as described in Chapter 14, "Gently down the Stream."

You may want to create multiple versions of the song, each compressed at a lower bit rate, and create an alternate reference movie that plays the best version the listener's connection can handle. See Chapter 8, "Alternate Realities: Language, Speed, and Connections," for details.

Put It on the Page

This section shows you how to build a Web jukebox that includes a high-quality version of each song for download and a more compressed version that can play in real time over a visitor's connection.

The highest-quality version can be a `.zip` or `.sit` file, an MP3 or MP4 file, or a QuickTime movie. The more compressed version is always a QuickTime movie.

Making a Web jukebox means creating a Web page that provides access to multiple QuickTime movies, each of which can be several megabytes in size. Techniques for embedding multiple QuickTime movies in a single page are discussed in "Putting Multiple Movies on a Page" (page 109). This example uses JavaScript to create a floating player window for the songs, so only one song loads into memory at a time.

The JavaScript function in this example loads an HTML page into the player window. A small HTML page is created for every song, and the song is embedded in this page using the <EMBED> tag.

The main page for this example can be found as JavaJuke.htm in the Audio folder on the CD. The HTML for the main page looks like this:

```
<HEAD>
<TITLE>JavaScript JukeBox</TITLE>

<script language="JavaScript">
<!--
function openSong(url)  {
songwin = window.open(url,"song",'toolbar=0,location=0,
  directories=0,status=0,menubar=0,scrollbars=0,resizable
  =0,width=240,height=60');
songwin.focus();
}
// -->
```

```
</script>
</HEAD>

<BODY BGCOLOR="#FFFFFF" TEXT="#000000">
<H1><BR><IMG SRC="juke.gif" ALIGN="Middle">QuickTime Java JukeBox</H1>
<HR>
<H2>Today's Hot Picks</H2>

<TABLE Border=1 Cellpadding=3>
<TR>
<TD ALIGN="Center"><B>Listen Now</B></TD>
<TD ALIGN="Center"><B>Download MP3</B></TD>
</TR>
<TR>
<TD><a href="javascript:openSong('JavaSong1.htm')">
  Helena Bucket</a></TD>
<TD><a href="javascript:openSong('JavaSongmp1.htm')">
  Helena Bucket</a></TD>
</TR>
<TR>
<TD><a href="javascript:openSong('JavaSong2.htm')">
  Slay Ride</a></TD>
<TD><a href="javascript:openSong('JavaSongmp2.htm')">
  Slay Ride</a></TD>
</TR>
</TABLE>

</BODY>
</HTML>
```

Here's how the jukebox looks when no player window is open:

The small HTML pages that load in the player window are also in the Audio folder as JavaSong1.htm, JavaSongmp1.htm, and so on. The HTML for a page that loads an MP3 file in the player window looks like the following:

```
<HTML>
<HEAD>
<TITLE>Song in MP3</TITLE>
</HEAD>
<BODY BGCOLOR="#FFFFFF">
<EMBED SRC="UNeedQT4.pntg" TYPE="image/x-macpaint"
  QTSRC="HitSong.mp3" HEIGHT=16 WIDTH=200 AUTOPLAY="True">
<BR>
<B>"Helena Bucket"</B> by Helen Buckette<BR>
<HR>
<DIV ALIGN="Center">
<A HREF="javascript:window.close()">Close this window</a>
</DIV>
</BODY>
</HTML>
```

This example uses the QTSRC parameter to make the browser play the MP3 with the QuickTime plug-in.

To let the browser pick an MP3 plug-in on its own, just delete the QTSRC parameter and put the URL of the MP3 in the SRC parameter.

To play a song compressed with the QDesign Music Codec and saved as a QuickTime movie, just put the URL of the .mov file in the QTSRC parameter.

To play a song as a real-time stream, pass the URL of the stream in the QTSRC parameter:

```
QTSRC="rtsp://StreamServer.com/StreamingMovie.mov"
```

When a player window is open, it floats over the upper-left corner of the jukebox, which is why the jukebox has a graphic in that corner.

The exact placement of the window varies somewhat from browser to browser, so design your page accordingly.

Clicking a song opens the player window.

I Want My MP3

MP3 is the audio compression format that almost conquered the world. It stands for the Motion Picture Experts Group MPEG-1, layer 3 audio (not

MPEG-3). An MP3 file contains audio compressed in MP3 format. It may also contain tags that identify the song title, artist, and so on.

There are a number of free MP3 player programs for Macintosh and Windows computers, including QuickTime Player and the QuickTime plug-in. One nice feature of QuickTime as an MP3 player is that it plays as much of the file as has downloaded whenever the listener likes. On fast connections, people can listen and download in real time.

MP3 uses a perceptual codec, which means it compresses the audio by throwing away the parts that people either can't hear or don't notice. Some people hear and notice more than others, so people do argue whether it's "CD quality" or not. Almost everyone agrees that 128 Kbit MP3 sounds almost as good as FM radio, however, and that 256 Kbit MP3 sounds better than FM or cassette. Some people can tell 384 Kbit MP3 from a CD, and others can't, so let's just call it "near-CD quality" and leave it at that.

Uncompressed CD audio is made of two 16-bit digital samples, one each for the left and right channel, at 44,100 samples per second. That's about 1.5 million bits per second. That means MP3 compressed at 128 Kbits per second downloads 10 times faster than uncompressed CD audio.

That makes MP3 a good format for downloading music, but over a 28.8K modem it still takes 13 minutes to download a 3-minute song. MP3 can play in real time, but only over very fast connections. If you want to stream music or download it in real time over dialup connections, you need to use another compressor. Many MP3 download sites make a second version of songs available in a more compressed format, so people can hear a piece of music before committing to a long download.

With QuickTime, you can deliver MP3 downloads side by side with more compressed versions of the same songs, and they can all be played with one plug-in. The more compressed versions can be delivered in Fast Start format from an ordinary Web server, or they can be delivered as real-time streams. For examples, see "Recorded Music on the Web" (page 187).

There's a variant of MP3 that uses variable bit rate (VBR) compression and compresses audio even more efficiently. QuickTime 4.1 and later can play VBR-encoded MP3 and can also play real-time streams that use MP3 compression. Of course, you still need a fast connection to hear MP3 in real time.

As far as QuickTime is concerned, MP3 is just another audio compression format. If you're making a QuickTime movie, you can use MP3 audio the same way you use uncompressed audio or sound compressed using other codecs. You can open MP3 files in QuickTime Player, edit them, add them as sound tracks to QuickTime movies, save them, or recompress them using various codecs.

QuickTime Player and the QuickTime plug-in are good MP3 players, and QuickTime Player can be used as an MP3 editor, but you need a separate encoder to create new MP3s. To make a new MP3 you need a program such as iTunes or MusicMatch.

An alternative to MP3 is the new MPEG-4 audio standard: AAC audio. It offers about 30% more compression than MP3 with the same audio quality, or better sound at the same compression. QuickTime Player Pro includes an AAC audio compressor and can create AAC-compressed audio files in .mov or .mp4 format (QuickTime can play the audio from either file format). At this writing, MP3 players are far more common than MP4 players, but don't be surprised to find CD and DVD players that can handle audio in CD-audio, DVD-audio, MP3, and MP4 formats available in the near future.

Getting the Most Out of MIDI

To get the most out of MIDI, you need to know a little about what MIDI is and how QuickTime supports it. You also need to know how to import MIDI into QuickTime. Once you've got your MIDI content into Quick-Time format, you can optimize it for Web playback by using QuickTime Player.

A Little about MIDI and QuickTime

MIDI, which stands for Musical Instrument Digital Interface, is like electronic sheet music. It describes the notes, the instruments, and the performance. Performance includes the exact timing, changes made to knobs or pedals during the performance, and how hard the musician plays each note. The actual sound is not recorded in a MIDI file; it has to be reproduced from the description by a synthesizer.

Because a synthesizer creates the sound for MIDI playback, the sound is very clean—there are no compression artifacts. On the other hand, MIDI can't capture all the nuances of sound that a recording can.

MIDI describes instrumental music. The only way to include vocals in a MIDI music track is by embedding a vocal sample in the file and treating it as an instrument, which isn't really the same. QuickTime also supports karaoke, or MIDI music synchronized with text. More about that shortly.

MIDI data is very compact. Long and complex pieces of music are described by surprisingly small files. This makes it ideal for background music on a Web page, a sound track for an Internet slideshow, or as the last fallback for alternate movie sound tracks.

Each MIDI file contains a MIDI sequence, which consists of a series of MIDI events. Typical events are the beginning and end of musical notes, or changes in controls such as knobs and foot pedals.

Note   A musical note in MIDI format is described by a set of numbers that indicate the MIDI channel, the note's pitch, and the note's attack velocity. Normally, the MIDI channel corresponds to a particular instrument that plays the note, the pitch tells the instrument what note to play, and the attack velocity controls the volume. The instrument could be a piano, an electric guitar, a drum set, or something very different, so the pitch and attack velocity are interpreted accordingly. A musical note in MIDI format starts with a Note On event and ends with a Note Off event.

A MIDI system generally consists of a sequencer part and a synthesizer part. The sequencer captures or plays back MIDI sequences, and the synthesizer interprets MIDI events to create the appropriate sounds.

QuickTime includes a playback MIDI sequencer in software. It can read a MIDI file, generate MIDI events, and send them to a synthesizer, but it can't capture MIDI sequences from a keyboard or MIDI input.

If the user has an external MIDI synthesizer, QuickTime can send the events out the appropriate hardware port, such as a serial or USB port, to control the external MIDI equipment. Generally speaking, only professional musicians have external MIDI synthesizers hooked to their computers. Consequently, QuickTime includes a synthesizer in software.

The QuickTime synthesizer is the default output device for MIDI. You can select another synthesizer, if one is available, by changing the Music setting in your QuickTime Settings control panel.

Starting with QuickTime 5, you can add a "soft synth" to your computer by dropping a Sound Forge or Down-Loadable Sound (DLS-2) file into your QuickTime Extensions folder (inside the QuickTime folder on your hard disk). If you create music that relies on the special qualities of your soft synth, you need to distribute the Sound Forge or DLS-2 file with the music, either as a download or as part of an installation from your CD—as of this writing, you can't embed it in a QuickTime movie.

The General MIDI specification defines 128 instruments, such as piano, guitar, flute, violin, and various drum kits, that can be emulated by a MIDI synthesizer. It also defines some sounds you might not think of as instruments, such as a whole string ensemble or applause. Any of these instruments can be assigned to play any part in a MIDI sequence.

Many computer sound cards support General MIDI, and some MIDI players depend on the user's sound card to act as a MIDI synthesizer. Unfortunately, different sound cards implement the General MIDI specification in different ways—the guitar on one card sounds very different from the guitar on another card.

QuickTime doesn't depend on the user's sound card to emulate MIDI instruments. It includes a General MIDI synthesizer in software, so a MIDI file played by QuickTime sounds about the same on any computer. Of course, the sound quality varies somewhat depending on the sound card, amplifier (if any), and speakers. But that's just as true for playing a CD as for synthesizing a MIDI sequence.

In addition, QuickTime has licensed the Roland GS instrument set, so a MIDI file played with QuickTime not only sounds the same on different machines, it actually sounds pretty decent.

Making or Getting a MIDI Sequence

QuickTime Player doesn't create MIDI sequences. You need to import an existing MIDI file. You can use a MIDI file from a commercial source or from the World Wide Web, or you can create the MIDI sequence using other software.

One way to create a MIDI sequence is by playing an instrument, such as a keyboard with MIDI output, into a sequencer program such as Cakewalk, Opcode Vision, Studio Vision Pro, or Mark of the Unicorn's Performer. You can connect a MIDI instrument to your computer through a serial or USB port adapter, available at most computer or music stores. You can play up to 16 instruments into a single MIDI port simultaneously. Or you can play each part, such as the lead guitar, rhythm guitar, bass, piano, and drum parts, through the same MIDI port one at a time, then assign each part to a MIDI instrument using the sequencer software. This is a good way for a group or a single musician to create a MIDI sequence. You can even play all the parts using the same instrument when you create them, then play them back as different instruments. Assign each part to a General MIDI instrument, save the result as a standard MIDI file, and you can then import it into QuickTime Player.

Other software, such as Band in a Box and EasyBeat, let you create a MIDI file using your computer keyboard and mouse interactively. Musical talent is definitely helpful, but these programs are set up to enable nonmusicians to create decent-sounding music by combining programmed riffs and loops. This is a good way for creative computer geeks to create original MIDI files.

If you use EasyBeat, you can export directly to QuickTime music format, bypassing MIDI. This gives you access to the full range of QuickTime instruments (over 200) instead of restricting you to the General MIDI set of 128.

If you have sheet music, you can enter the score into a program like Coda, assign each part to a General MIDI instrument, and output it to a MIDI file.

Note There is currently no way to convert recorded music into MIDI. It's theoretically possible, but so are a lot of things. The current state of the art in commercial software can create a MIDI sequence from a recording of a single instrument playing one note at a time. Good for flute, limited for guitar or piano, useless for converting a recording of a band or orchestra.

Of course, you don't necessarily have to create your own MIDI sequences. There's a lot of MIDI freely available for download on the Web. Some artists ask you to give them credit on your Web page or send them a postcard; others are happy just to share their talent with the world. Mind you, the fact that someone has posted a MIDI version of a song for download doesn't always mean they own the copyright. Check to make sure it's an original composition by the artist, or that it's in the public domain, and that the artist has given permission for you to post this MIDI version on your website. Don't worry; even with these constraints, you'll find a lot to choose from.

One good place to find royalty-free MIDI is

`http://files.midifarm.com/midifiles/General_MIDI/`

(especially the classical section).

Importing MIDI into QuickTime

When you open a MIDI file in QuickTime Player, it creates a movie with a music track. In the Mac OS X operating system, that's all there is to it.

In Windows or Mac OS 8/9, you'll be prompted to give the movie a name and decide where to store it. The dialog boxes are shown in the following illustrations.

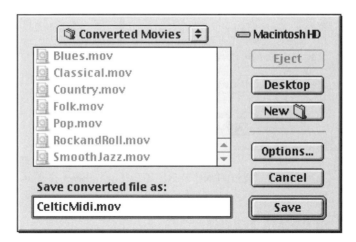

Click Options to open the Standard MIDI Import dialog box, which allows you to add silence to the beginning or end of the music track, or to make the track playable by QuickTime 2.0.

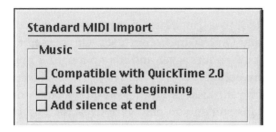

Importing Karaoke

You can also import a karaoke file (.kar) into QuickTime. This creates a movie with both a music track and a text track. The tracks are synchronized so that the appropriate text is displayed, and the appropriate syllables are highlighted, as the music plays. Once again, on the Mac OS X operating system, that's all there is to it.

On Windows or Mac OS 8/9, when you import karaoke, you get the Standard MIDI Import dialog box, with an additional Text options button that lets you choose the font, size, style, and color of the text.

See Chapter 13, "Text! Text! Text!," for more about text styles.

Editing Music Tracks

In QuickTime, a *music track* is distinct from a *sound track;* music tracks contain descriptive data such as MIDI, whereas sound tracks contain digitized audio.

For most practical purposes, you can treat a music track as a low-bandwidth sound track. You can edit a music track by cutting and pasting, you can add it to a QuickTime movie, or you can convert it to digitized audio using any QuickTime compressor. Of course, if you convert it to digitized audio it gets a lot bigger and it's no longer a music track. And no, it doesn't get any better.

You can do a different kind of editing on QuickTime music tracks by assigning different instruments to play various parts, and by customizing selected instruments. Choose Get Movie Properties from the Movie menu, choose Music Track from the left pop-up menu, then choose Instruments from the right pop-up menu.

You'll see a list of instruments used in the music. To assign a different instrument to a part, double-click the instrument you want to change. This brings up the New Instrument For Part dialog box.

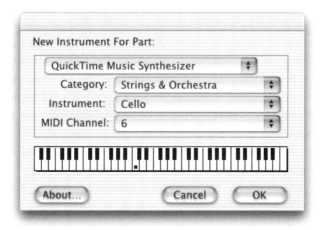

Choose a new instrument using the Category and Instrument pop-up menus. You can hear what the new instrument sounds like by clicking the piano keys.

By default, QuickTime uses the best synthesizer available on the listener's computer. You can choose the QuickTime Music Synthesizer from the pop-up menu to make sure the music track is played by QuickTime's software synthesizer on all machines.

A QuickTime music track can also contain some digitized audio. This is sometimes called a sample or a patch, and the synthesizer uses this digitized audio as the voice for an instrument. The instrument is then played using standard MIDI events. To use a digital audio sample as a custom instrument sound, arrange your desktop so the icon for the audio sample and the music track's Properties window are both visible, then drag the icon for the sample onto the instrument you want to replace.

Use this technique to make an instrument from a human voice or a barking dog, or to capture a unique instrument sound, such as breathy saxophone or a fuzzed-out electric guitar.

Currently, you can use this technique to add digital audio to a music track only in System 7 Sound format (.snd or .sfil). Of course, you have many more options if you use a Sound Forge or DLS-2 sound font. The main reason you might want to use this technique instead is that an audio sample embedded this way travels with the movie—the listener doesn't have to download a separate sound font.

You can convert an audio sample from another format to System 7 Sound using QuickTime Player. Open the sample, choose Export from the File menu, and choose Sound to System 7 Sound from the pop-up menu. You can choose the sample rate and sample size from the pop-up menu, or click the Options button to choose a sample size, sample rate, and compressor.

System 7 Sound format supports uncompressed audio, aLaw, uLaw, MACE, and IMA compression, but you can only use uncompressed audio as a custom instrument.

Adding a digital sample increases the size of the music track considerably. The following table shows how many kilobytes an audio sample adds, assuming you use 16-bit mono samples. The size doubles for stereo samples and is half as large for 8-bit samples.

Sampling rate, kHz	Kilobytes per second
44.1	88
22.05	44
11.025	24

By the way, kids, these are kilo*bytes*, not kilobits. Big, big, big.

Any digital samples have to be downloaded completely before the music track can play that instrument's part. This generally causes a delay before a Fast Start movie can play over the Web.

Optimizing MIDI for QuickTime and the Web

Synthesizing music is more CPU-intensive than playing uncompressed digital audio, so it's a good idea to limit yourself to one music track per movie (one music track playing at a time, that is).

For smooth playback on older computers, limit the music track to three or four instruments playing at any time.

For smooth start-up, have QuickTime preload the music track. In Quick-Time Player, choose Get Movie Properties from the Movie menu; choose the music track in the left pop-up menu; choose Preload from the right pop-up menu; and click the Preload checkbox. Save as a self-contained movie.

Use the General MIDI instrument set when you create MIDI for Quick-Time.

Convert the MIDI file to QuickTime and save it as a .mov file. This filters out nonstandard MIDI files and ensures that QuickTime can play this file.

The .mov file extension encourages browsers to play the file using Quick-Time.

Play it back on your computer using QuickTime's internal synthesizer so you know how it will sound. Assign different instruments to a given part to get the sound you want. Use a sound sample to create a custom instrument if you need to.

Embed the file in your Web page with the VOLUME parameter set to about 75 if your MIDI volume goes to full scale. This is roughly equivalent to normalizing recorded sound at –3 dB.

Looping and Stuttering

Sometimes you hear a pause when a movie loops, and sometimes a movie that autoplays over the Web stutters at the beginning, rather than playing smoothly from the start. This section shows you how to work around these problems to create a more seamless presentation for your audience.

Looping

You can't loop QuickTime tracks independently—all the tracks are synchronized to the same timeline. If one track goes back to the beginning, they all go. To use sound loops in QuickTime, you need to loop whole movies. If you need to have multiple independent loops, or include both looping and nonlooping media, you must use multiple movies. There are two simple ways to make a QuickTime movie loop:

- For the QuickTime plug-in, set the LOOP parameter to True, either in your HTML or by using Plug-in Helper.

- For movies played by QuickTime Player, open the movie in QuickTime Player, choose Loop in the Movie menu, then save the movie.

In either case, you'll sometimes hear a pause when the movie ends and starts over (this is more likely to happen on a Macintosh than on a Windows computer). For short audio loops, this may be a problem.

If the audio track is fairly short, try setting the cache hint. This tells QuickTime to cache the audio track, reducing the time required to make it loop. To set the cache hint, choose Get Movie Properties from the Movie menu, then choose the audio track from the Properties window's left pop-up menu and choose Cache Hint from the right pop-up menu, as shown in the following illustration.

You can also set the music track to preload using this screen, which can prevent stuttering. This loads the track into memory, if possible. That's fine for MIDI, but not always a great idea for multimegabyte sound files.

Another approach to looping is to use multiple references to the sound data. QuickTime allows you to have multiple references to the same audio data inside a movie, and each reference uses only a few bytes. QuickTime can play a string of references, one after the other, quite smoothly. For a small increase in file size, you can paste a hundred references end-to-end, effectively looping the audio a hundred times without a pause.

A 2-second movie that loops may have a pause every 2 seconds. The same 2 seconds of audio, copied a hundred times inside a movie that loops, pauses only once every 3½ minutes—longer than most people spend on a Web page.

The trick to making this work is to save the movie without flattening it. If you flatten the movie, each reference is replaced with a copy of the data, which makes the file 100 times larger.

To save a movie without flattening it, you just save normally (allowing dependencies). This is the default behavior when you choose Save from the File menu, and it is an option if you choose Save As. Here's the recipe:

1. Save your short audio loop as a self-contained movie.

2. Make a copy of the file, just in case.

3. Open the movie. Select All. Copy.

4. Paste, Paste, Paste . . . (as many times as you like).

5. Choose Save (or Save As, allowing dependencies). If you choose Save As, be sure to save the new movie in the same folder as the original.

If you choose Save, you create a self-contained movie with internal references. If you choose Save As (allowing dependencies), you create a new movie that references the data in the original movie. The differences are worth considering.

If you choose Save As, you need to put both the new movie and the original movie on your Web server together because the new movie depends on the original. Be sure to upload both movies to the same folder on your Web server.

If you choose Save, the movie is self-contained. This is more convenient for uploading. However, editing a movie and choosing Save does not guarantee that the movie will play in Fast Start mode over the Internet. When you choose Save, parts of the movie that QuickTime needs to start it playing may be saved at the end of the file. If this happens, the entire file must be downloaded before it can play. For a 2-second audio file, this may not cause a significant delay. For a larger file, it may be important.

If making the movie self-contained is more important, use Save. If making it a Fast Start movie is more important, use Save As.

In either case, the audio sample should repeat smoothly as many times as you pasted it. There may be a short pause when the whole movie loops, but that won't be often.

You can use this technique with more complex movies as well, but it takes extra care. You first need to save a self-contained (flattened) version of the movie, one that has at least one copy of all the sample data. Open this movie, copy and paste as many references as you like, and save using the Save command (or Save As, allowing dependencies).

QuickTime Player is a fine tool for editing single-track movies this way, or for editing all the tracks at once, but it's hard to edit individual tracks in QuickTime Player, so you might want to use another movie editor that lets you edit individual tracks on a multitrack timeline instead.

To edit an individual track from a complex movie in QuickTime Player:

1. Extract the track (this creates an untitled movie).
2. Edit the extracted track (by adding references, for example).
3. Select All in the extracted track. Copy. Close (don't save).
4. Delete the original track from the movie (Delete Tracks).
5. Add the edited track back into the movie (choose Add in the Edit menu).
6. Save.

Be sure to make a backup copy after every successful track edit.

Stuttering

Stuttering is a problem that sometimes occurs when a Fast Start movie is set to autoplay in a browser. You hear the movie start, pause, then start again. There are generally two things that can cause this, and there are solutions for both.

A movie set to autoplay starts when QuickTime calculates that it can play without interruption. QuickTime measures how fast the file is downloading and calculates how long it will take for the download to complete. When the time remaining is less than the movie duration, it starts the movie. In other words, QuickTime starts playing a 1-minute movie as soon as it calculates that the download time remaining is less than 1 minute.

If the connection speed is faster than the movie's data rate, the total download time is shorter than the movie's playing time, so the movie starts right away.

If you've ever watched the status window in your browser during a download over the Web, you've seen that the download speed tends to jump around, especially at the beginning. One reason for this is that files often contain small headers that your modem can compress on the fly, creating a short burst of faster-than-normal throughput. When this happens, QuickTime may calculate that the download time will be short, start the movie, then suddenly run out of data. It then waits until data is flowing fast enough to try again.

Setting AUTOPLAY="False" generally prevents a download-spike stutter, but this requires a controller as well as a user action to start the movie.

Inserting a second of silence at the beginning of the movie usually prevents an audible stutter caused by a download spike. The movie may still stutter, but you can't hear it happen.

Another way to prevent stuttering is to tell QuickTime to preload the entire audio track before playing the movie—choose Get Movie Properties from the Movie menu, then choose the audio track from the Properties window's left pop-up menu and choose Preload from the right pop-up menu. Click the Preload checkbox. This technique works best with music tracks (MIDI) or very small sound tracks.

Starting with QuickTime 5, you can eliminate stuttering by telling QuickTime not to autoplay the movie until a certain amount has been downloaded. It's done by giving a time value to the AUTOPLAY parameter, instead of True or False. Here's an example:

```
<EMBED SRC="sound.mov" HEIGHT=16 WIDTH=200
  AUTOPLAY="@05:0" >
```

This tells the QuickTime plug-in to autoplay sound.mov after 5 seconds worth has successfully downloaded. You're essentially telling QuickTime how much of the movie to buffer. Note the 5:0 at the end—that says 5 seconds, 0 thirtieths.

Important   If you pass @05:0, it means 5 seconds. If you just pass @05, it means 5 *thirtieths* of a second. Big difference. And the separator is a colon, not a decimal point.

Versions of QuickTime prior to 5.0 will treat the timestamp as False. This may be what you want. The movie won't play until the viewer pushes a button, so it probably won't stutter. Of course, it also won't autoplay.

If you want older versions of QuickTime to autoplay as always, but want newer versions to use a timestamp, you can do that too. The code is simple, but the logic is a little convoluted. It's also a perfect illustration of how to use the new AllowEmbedTagOverrides parameter. It works like this:

```
<EMBED SRC="sample.mov" WIDTH="190" HEIGHT="256"
  AUTOPLAY="true"
  ALLOWEMBEDTAGOVERRIDES="true"
  AUTOPLAY="@00:02:20.0"
  ALLOWEMBEDTAGOVERRIDES="false" >
```

First we set AUTOPLAY = "true" for earlier versions of QuickTime. Next we set ALLOWEMBEDTAGOVERRIDES=true so we can set AUTOPLAY again, this time using a timestamp. Older versions of QuickTime don't recognize ALLOW EMBEDTAGOVERRIDES, so they ignore it—they also ignore the attempt to set AUTOPLAY to a new value. Once a parameter is set, it's set (unless you allow <EMBED> tag overrides).

Finally, we set ALLOWEMBEDTAGOVERRIDES="false" so that AUTOPLAY won't be overridden by the value stored in the user's local preferences. That's the key to getting predictable behavior out of ALLOWEMBEDTAGOVERRIDES—turn it on, use it, turn it off.

Stuttering can also occur when playing a movie from a disk or CD in a browser. In this case, it's usually caused by the browser not handling local files properly. A browser normally downloads files from the Web, caches them on disk, and hands them off to a plug-in if necessary. Local files are a special case; since they're already on disk, caching them to disk is a waste of time and bandwidth. If the browser doesn't realize this, and the computer doesn't have enough bandwidth to play the movie and copy it to disk at the same time, it stutters.

The solution is to use the QTSRC parameter. Pass a very small image in the SRC parameter for the browser to download and cache, and pass the real movie in the QTSRC parameter, while specifying QTSRCDONTUSE-BROWSER="True". QuickTime uses its own file handler to get the movie, bypassing the browser and eliminating the stutter.

Making It Fit: Sampling, Bandwidth, and Compression

To deliver the best-sounding audio over the Web, you need to understand some things about sampling, bandwidth, compression, and sound in general.

A Little about Sound

Sound is how your brain interprets changes in air pressure around your ears. Well, that plus low-frequency vibrations that come in through your bones, or the soles of your feet (hey, nice speakers).

Audio recording generally uses microphones. A microphone translates the changes in air pressure into changes in voltage. If you run that voltage into a speaker, the speaker cone moves back and forth and translates the voltage back into air pressure. Put your head in front of the speaker, and it turns back into sound.

If you amplify the voltage, the sound coming out of the speaker can be louder than the sound going into the microphone, and you can be heard in a concert hall or a stadium.

If you translate those voltage changes into a more durable medium, like magnetic fields on a tape, or grooves on a vinyl record, you can play the sound back later. That's called analog recording, and it's a multibillion dollar industry.

Sampling

To make a digital recording, you measure the changing voltage at regular intervals and record a number that represents the voltage at that moment. To play it back, you use a device that takes a number as an input and produces the corresponding voltage as an output.

The more often you measure the voltage, the more accurately you can record the changes. High-pitched sounds are the result of more frequent changes, so you have to measure more often to record them. How often you measure is called the sampling rate.

The sampling rate is given in kilohertz (kHz), and 1 kHz = 1000 measurements a second. Audio CDs use a sampling rate of 44,100 measurements a second, or 44.1 kHz, and they can record just about any sound that you can hear.

When you record digitally, you use a number to represent the voltage. The more bits there are in the number, the more accurately you can record the voltage level. Audio CDs use 16-bit numbers, so they can represent the range of sound, from dead silent to ear-splitting, as a number between 0 and 65,535. That's not as sensitive as the human ear, but it's close.

If you draw the changing voltage on paper as a wiggly line, then overlay a piece of graph paper, you can see how digital sampling works. Think of the vertical lines on the graph paper as the sampling rate. Every time the voltage line crosses a vertical graph line, you take a measurement. The horizontal graph lines are the possible values for the measurement; pick the one closest to the voltage line and that's your sample value:

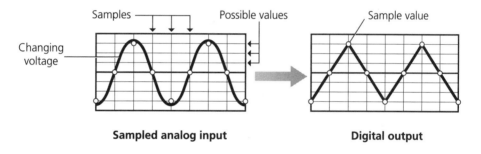

Sampled analog input   **Digital output**

As your sampling rate goes up, the sample events get closer together, and you measure more often. As the number of bits per sample goes up, the horizontal graph lines get closer together, and your measurements get more accurate:

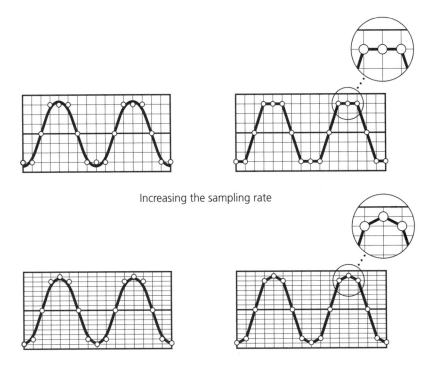

Increasing the sampling rate

Increasing the sampling rate and sample size

When you make a digital recording, or save an audio track in Quick-Time, you choose a sampling rate and a sample size. A higher sampling rate and a larger sample size result in better sound.

Unfortunately, a higher sampling rate means storing more numbers, and more sample bits means bigger numbers, so a more accurate digital recording makes a bigger file on your disk. Downloading a bigger file takes longer. And playing a bigger file in a given amount of time requires more bandwidth.

Bandwidth

This gets complicated, but don't panic. File size is measured in bytes. A byte is eight bits; 1024 bytes is a kilobyte; and 1024 kilobytes is a megabyte. So a kilobyte is roughly eight thousand bits, and a megabyte is roughly eight million bits. I'm using round numbers on purpose, because . . .

Bandwidth is measured in bits per second, not bytes. Many transmission systems include start and stop bits along with the data bits, so a byte can use more than eight bits of bandwidth. Modems compress data on the fly if they can, so other times a byte uses *less* than eight bits of bandwidth. And just to make it really ugly, there are exactly 1000 bits in a kilobit, not 1024. And there are exactly one million bits in a megabit, not 1024 x 1024. Confusing? You bet.

I'm bothering you with this because you're going to get bitten by it. The files on your disk are measured in kilobytes or megabytes, modems and T1 lines are rated in kilobits or megabits, and when you try to do the math, it doesn't work. A 56K modem won't download a 56K file in one second, nor in eight seconds. A *modem* K is a thousand **bits**, a *file* K is 1024 **bytes**, and with start bits, stop bits, and compression, a byte can use either more or less than eight bits of bandwidth.

If you want to make audio that can stream or download in real time, you need to calculate how much bandwidth the file needs. But if the file is transmitted by modems over the Internet, your calculations will be inexact. You need to use rules of thumb and leave some slop. Here are some rules of thumb, complete with slop (the column labeled "Safe bet" is deliberately conservative):

Connection	Rated	Typical throughput	Safe bet
14.4K modem	14.4 Kbits/sec	1.2 Kbytes/sec	1 Kbytes/sec
28.8K modem	28.8 Kbits/sec	2.4 Kbytes/sec	2 Kbytes/sec
33.6K modem	33.6 Kbits/sec	3 Kbytes/sec	2.5 Kbytes/sec
56K modem	53 Kbits/sec	4.8 Kbytes/sec	4 Kbytes/sec
Single ISDN	56 or 64 Kbits/sec	6 Kbytes/sec	5 Kbytes/sec
Dual ISDN	128 Kbits/sec	12 Kbytes/sec	10 Kbytes/sec
DSL	384 Kbits/sec	35 Kbytes/sec	30 Kbytes/sec
T1	1.54 Mbps	150 Kbytes/sec	50 Kbytes/sec
Cable modem	6 Mbps	300 Kbytes/sec	50 Kbytes/sec
Intranet/LAN	10 Mbps	350 Kbytes/sec	35 Kbytes/sec
100Base-T LAN	100 Mbps	500 Kbytes/sec	50 Kbytes/sec

Your mileage may vary, of course. You'll find that up to dual ISDN, the user's connection is normally the limiting factor. For DSL and T1, the server or the Internet is often the limiting factor. Cable modems and LANs are networks, and throughput varies wildly, depending mainly on how many people are using the network at that moment. A 10 Mbps LAN has a higher bandwidth than a 6 Mbps cable modem, for example, but a typical company LAN is much busier.

Making It Fit

Your operating system can tell you how large a file is. Divide the file size in kilobytes by the length of the audio in seconds, and that's how much bandwidth you need to stream or download in real time. Chances are, you need more than you've got.

There are lots of ways to make an audio file smaller. Open the file in QuickTime Player and you have several options:

- You can cut a selection from the music and save it as a smaller file, obviously, and that's often a good idea.

- You can mix the left and right channels together, converting the file from stereo to mono, which cuts the file size in half. For speech, most sound effects, and music played over a computer's built-in speaker, this is also a good idea.

- If the sound uses 16-bit samples, you can reduce the sample size to 8 bits. This also cuts the file size in half, but it degrades audio quality sharply. This is usually a bad idea, but if telephone-quality sound is good enough for your purposes, 8-bit samples are all you need.

- You can reduce the sampling rate. This can shrink the file by as much as 5:1. It also reduces the audio quality, but not as sharply as going to 8-bit samples. Here are some common sampling rates and the quality you can expect at each rate:

Sampling rates	Quality
44 kHz	CD
22 kHz	FM radio
11 kHz	AM radio
8 kHz	Telephone

At 11 kHz or 8 kHz, dropping the sample size to 8 bits may not decrease the quality very noticeably; it's worth a try, anyway.

- You can compress the file with an audio codec. This can give you anywhere from 2:1 to 100:1 compression. In many cases, you can get 10:1 compression with little noticeable drop in quality. All the QuickTime audio codecs are described in detail in "Audio Codecs" (page 215).

You can apply any of these techniques using QuickTime Player. Here's how:

1. Open the audio file, use the time slider and the Cut command to edit out any unwanted parts, then choose Export from the File menu.

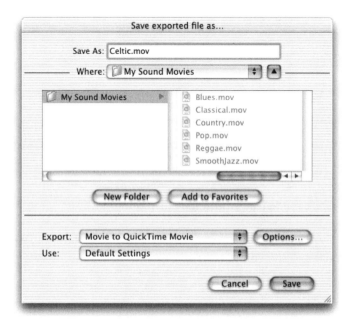

2. Choose Movie to QuickTime Movie and click the Options button.

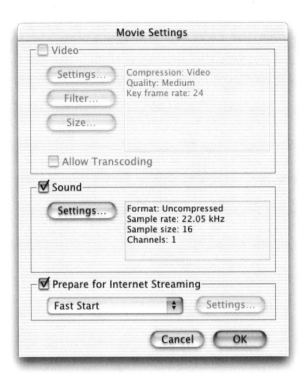

3. Click the Settings button in the Sound section.

You now have access to the sampling rate, sample size, mono or stereo mode, and the compressor to use.

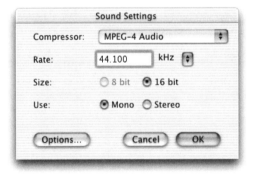

You can reduce the sampling rate or sample size, or drop from stereo to mono. This will reduce the file size and bandwidth needs, with a corresponding drop in quality.

It would be nice if you could improve the sound quality at this stage by increasing the sample rate and sample size, or turn a mono recording into stereo by clicking the button, but you can't. Sorry, amigo, it just doesn't work that way.

At this point, you can also choose a compressor from the Compressor menu. When you choose certain compressors, the Options button becomes active and you can make further settings.

If you're going to make multiple versions of the audio file using different compressors, or using different compressor settings, save an uncompressed copy first, then export each compressed version from the uncompressed copy.

Important Never compress a file that has already been compressed if you can help it. Compressing an already-compressed file normally results in a drastic loss of quality.

Now let's talk about those compressors.

▶ Audio Codecs

Codec is a shortening of "compressor/decompressor," and that's generally what you want: a compressor to squeeze the file and a decompressor to play it back. QuickTime includes a number of codecs.

QuickTime also includes some stand-alone decompressors. These are useful for playing back files that were compressed with other programs. In some cases, such as MP3, the inventor of the codec gives the decompressor away but licenses or sells the compressor. You have to buy special software to compress audio files using these codecs, but people can play them back using the free software that Apple distributes (QuickTime Player and the QuickTime plug-in). Decompression is automatic in QuickTime; you open a file, and if it's compressed with a codec that QuickTime understands, it plays.

QuickTime has a modular architecture, so when a new codec like AAC comes along, it's fairly easy to plug it in. This section discusses all the audio codecs that QuickTime currently includes, but you should check the QuickTime website for new additions. The codecs are listed in the table below, then each is discussed in detail. An "x" in the table means the compressor or decompressor is included as part of QuickTime.

Codec	Decompressor	Compressor
Uncompressed	n/a	n/a
AAC (MPEG-4 audio)	x	x
ADPCM	x	
aLaw 2:1	x	x
GSM	x	
IMA 4:1	x	x
MACE 3:1	x	x
MACE 6:1	x	x
MPEG-1, layer 2	x	
MP3 (MPEG-1, layer 3)	x	
QDesign Music	x	
QDesign Music 2	x	x
Qualcomm PureVoice	x	x
uLaw 2:1	x	x

Uncompressed

Uncompressed audio sounds the best. If you have the disk space and bandwidth, this is the way to go. When using a compressor, always start with uncompressed audio if possible. If you need to filter or process audio from a CD, save it as an uncompressed audio file, do the filtering or processing, *then* do any compression.

Uncompressed audio normally uses 8-bit or 16-bit samples—use 16-bit for CD quality, 8-bit for telephone quality. You can also export audio in the following uncompressed formats:

- 24-bit integer
- 32-bit integer
- 32-bit floating point
- 64-bit integer

These formats actually make audio files larger. Storing the audio samples as larger numbers makes it possible to do sophisticated audio filtering and processing with minimal round-off errors. If you have software that works with audio in these formats, by all means use it for filtering and processing, then use QuickTime to convert the audio back to a smaller format for distribution.

AAC (MPEG-4)

The Advanced Audio Codec (AAC) is part of the MPEG-4 specification. It's an evolutionary improvement over the MP3 codec. It is capable of encoding 5.1 surround sound (five independent speakers and a subwoofer), although the current QuickTime implementation is limited to two-channel stereo.

The AAC codec is an improvement over MP3, but it remains to be seen whether it will rapidly supplant the older format. There's a lot of hardware, software, and music collections built around MP3, and AAC is currently only about 30% better.

QuickTime 6 and later can play, edit, and create AAC audio. You can use AAC-encoded audio in QuickTime movies or export from QuickTime to .mp4 file format. QuickTime can play AAC-encoded .mp4 audio files.

One unusual feature of the AAC encoder is that it creates only certain bit rates from audio with a given sampling rate, so you may not be able to select 100 Kbit encoding, for example, and may have to choose between 96 Kbit and 112 Kbit. For more about using this compressor in QuickTime, see "All About MPEG-4" (page 768) in Appendix H, "New in QuickTime 6."

ADPCM

The ADPCM codec is mainly used in digital telephone systems to squeeze two voice channels onto a digital circuit designed to carry just one. It's sometimes used to compress WAV files. It uses a nonlinear scale to squeeze 12 bits of dynamic range into an 8-bit sample, essentially by disregarding small differences in loud sounds. It gives about a 2:1 compression and produces slightly better than telephone-quality audio.

QuickTime can read and play ADPCM, but doesn't create it unless you have software that includes an ADPCM compressor component.

aLaw 2:1

The aLaw codec is used to digitize land line telephone calls in Europe and other parts of the world. It gives 2:1 compression by scaling a 16-bit audio signal down to 8 bits.

This is a good codec if you need to compress the human voice for a CD or an intranet and want to keep quality high. It doesn't give a lot of compression, but it can often compress speech without audible degradation. It doesn't work as well for music or sound effects.

GSM

The GSM codec is used to compress voice for digital cellular telephones in Europe and much of the world. It delivers high audio quality and moderate compression for speech.

GSM is an undemanding codec that doesn't require much CPU time to compress or decompress. This, and the fact that it's a worldwide standard, have made it a popular codec for the audio channel of Internet video conferences and webcasts.

QuickTime can play back GSM-encoded audio, and some conferencing software includes QuickTime-compatible GSM encoders, but QuickTime itself does not include a GSM compressor.

IMA 4:1

The IMA 4:1 codec is a good general-purpose audio codec. It works well for music, speech, or sound effects. It gives high quality and 4:1 compression, so it's great for CD or intranet delivery, but not really for the Web, at least not over dialup connections. If you also drop from stereo to mono, you get 8:1 compression, which starts to get into MP3 territory.

It's an undemanding format to decompress, so it works well on older computers (pre-PowerPC or pre-Pentium).

This codec is backward-compatible with QuickTime 2 and later. If your target audience includes Windows 3.1 users (rather than Windows 95 or later), or users with old and tired computers, this is probably the best codec to use.

If you use a more advanced codec, you might want to provide an alternate version compressed with IMA 4:1 for the less fortunate.

MACE

MACE is an obsolete codec that was once popular on Macintosh computers. There is a version that gives 3:1 compression and introduces some audible noise, and a version that gives 6:1 compression and makes a lot of noise.

QuickTime 3 and later can play MACE audio on Windows; all versions of QuickTime can play MACE audio on Macintosh computers. Use this codec only if you need to distribute audio that was previously compressed with MACE and you can't recompress the original audio.

MPEG-1, Layer 2

The audio track of an MPEG-1 movie is usually MPEG-1, layer 2 audio. Sometimes an MPEG-1 file contains only layer 2 audio. These files are typically found on the Web as .mpg or .mpeg files.

This is an old codec, not particularly efficient or high fidelity. It's of interest mainly because of all the old MPEG-1 files floating around out there, and because it's used for the sound track in video CDs (VCD).

QuickTime can play MPEG-1, layer 2 audio. QuickTime can export layer 2 audio to other formats if the audio is in a file by itself. If the audio is multiplexed in a single file with MPEG-1 video, QuickTime cannot export the audio (use a tool such as bbDeMux or Proteron Drop Decoder). QuickTime does not edit or create MPEG-1, layer 2 audio.

MP3

MP3 is a very popular codec for downloading music over the Web. It delivers near-CD quality and 5:1 to 11:1 compression, depending on the bit rate. MP3 stands for Motion Picture Experts Group MPEG-1, layer 3 audio.

Its popularity and high audio quality make this codec a good choice for music downloads, CD delivery, or intranet delivery. MP3 does not deliver enough compression for people to hear sound in real time over dialup connections. A good dual-ISDN connection or faster is required for real-time play of 128 Kbit MP3, which is the most common bit rate. Higher bit rates are commonly used for "ripping" MP3 audio from CD for use in an MP3 player; 256 Kbit and 384 Kbit provide near-CD quality at 1/3 to 1/5 the file size.

QuickTime can edit and play MP3 audio, but QuickTime Player does not include an MP3 compressor. To create MP3 audio, you have to use a compressor program such as iTunes or MusicMatch.

For more about MP3, see "I Want My MP3" (page 193).

QDesign Music

The QDesign Music 2 Codec is a breakthrough compressor. It can deliver 10:1 compression with quality that is arguably better than MP3. It can deliver 90:1 or 100:1 compression with quality that is surprisingly good. It is unrivaled as a low-bit-rate music codec. You can specify any target data rate, and the QDesign Music 2 Codec compresses the audio to that rate.

The original QDesign Music Codec requires QuickTime 3 or later to decompress. The improved QDesign Music Codec 2 requires QuickTime 4 or later. QuickTime includes decompressors for both versions, but can only create compressed audio in the newer format. There is a pro version of the QDesign codec available from QDesign that gives more user control and produces even higher-quality sound. The most recent version, 2.1, is optimized for fast compression on G4 processors.

QDesign is a perceptual codec, meaning that it compresses sound by discarding the parts that people can't hear or don't notice. Additional compression is accomplished by discarding the parts people notice least, producing a smooth drop-off in quality at decreasing bandwidth.

You can greatly reduce the CPU load for QDesign decompression by using a lower sampling rate or by using mono instead of stereo.

This is the best codec to use for delivering music in real time over a dialup connection. The QDesign codec is suitable for Fast Start audio or streaming audio. QDesign is significantly better sounding than MP3 at low bit rates.

The QDesign codec works best for music, but it also works well for sound effects and speech. If you're working with speech alone, the Qualcomm PureVoice codec is often better and less demanding.

QuickTime can play, edit, or create QDesign Music 2 audio tracks. The encoding quality of QuickTime Player is limited using the standard encoder.

Getting the Most Out of QDesign

To get the *most* out of QDesign, you should upgrade to the Professional Edition, available from QDesign (www.qdesign.com). The pro version gives better sound, allows finer control over settings, and enables batch processing of files.

That said, you can get a lot out of the free version of QDesign included with QuickTime. There are two ways to access the QDesign Music Codec settings in QuickTime Player. The easiest way is to use the pop-up Settings menu when you choose Export and Movie to QuickTime Movie. The

QDesign settings appear in the lower pop-up menu, as shown in the next illustration.

The choices labeled "Streaming . . . Music" all use the QDesign codec. As you can see, there are choices for specific bit rates and sound types. The appropriate sample rate, sample size, and mono/stereo selections are made automatically, as follows:

- The 20 Kbits/sec choices create audio that streams over most 28.8K modems, even under worse-than-normal conditions.

- The 40 Kbits/sec choices create audio that streams over most 56K modems.

- Use the 100 Kbits/sec choices for dual-ISDN or faster connections.

- The High and Low Motion settings are used when a movie contains video as well as audio. High Motion selects the H.263 video codec, while Low Motion selects the Sorenson video codec.

- At 40 Kbits/sec you have a choice of stereo or mono. The mono setting reproduces the sound more accurately, but the stereo setting has two sound channels for stereo separation and effects. Pick the attribute that's most important for your sound.

All of these settings create a movie that's ready for real-time streaming. If you want to deliver the audio as a real-time stream, just put the exported movie on a streaming server and embed its URL in your Web page, as described in Chapter 14, "Gently down the Stream."

If you want to deliver the audio as a Fast Start movie directly from your Web server, open the movie after you export it and delete all hint tracks using the Delete Tracks command in the Edit menu, then save as a self-contained movie.

Alternatively, you can adjust the QDesign codec parameters using the Sound Settings panel, as described in "Making It Fit" (page 212). Choose the QDesign codec from the pop-up compressor menu, then adjust the sample rate, sample size, and mono/stereo settings until you find the best trade-off between quality and data rate. As a guide, choosing an 11 kHz sample rate, with 16-bit stereo samples, creates a file that needs 2.9 Kbytes/sec of bandwidth, suitable for a good 33.6K modem connection or faster.

It's worth noting that the QDesign codec uses less CPU time to decompress audio if you use a lower sample rate or use mono instead of stereo. The CPU requirements drop off in a nearly linear fashion, so it takes half as much CPU time to decompress 22 kHz audio as 44 kHz audio, and half as much to decompress mono as stereo.

If you adjust the codec using the Sound Settings panel, you can either export the movie for Fast Start or create a movie ready for real-time streaming. In either case, choose Export from the File menu. For a Fast Start movie, choose Movie to QuickTime Movie from the Export pop-up menu; for a streaming movie, choose Movie to Hinted Movie instead.

Qualcomm PureVoice

The Qualcomm PureVoice codec was originally designed to compress voice for digital cellular telephones. Consequently, it's optimized to work with voice at an 8 kHz sampling rate. It delivers good quality at low bit rates and moderate quality at astonishingly low bit rates. This is the optimum codec for sending speech over the Web.

The Qualcomm PureVoice codec is optimized for human speech, but its ability to deliver audio over a 14.4K modem, with bandwidth to spare, makes it inviting for other sounds as well. Music and sound effects sound muddy at maximum compression with this codec, but they may require as little as 0.85 Kbits/sec of bandwidth (850 bytes a second). If you need your audio to play smoothly over a 9600 baud modem, this is the codec to use.

The Qualcomm codec always uses 16-bit samples in mono. It can use several sampling rates, but is optimized for an 8 kHz rate. It has a half rate option, which sacrifices quality for bandwidth, and an option to optimize for streaming. *Always* use an 8 kHz sampling rate when compressing audio for real-time streaming with the Qualcomm codec.

The easiest way to access the Qualcomm codec settings in QuickTime Player is through the two pop-up menus that appear in the Save dialog box when you choose Export from the File menu. If you choose Movie to QuickTime Movie from the Export menu, the Qualcomm settings appear in the lower menu:

The choices labeled "Streaming . . . Voice" all use the Qualcomm codec. As you can see, there are choices for specific bit rates:

- The 20 Kbits/sec choices create audio that streams over most 14.4K modems, even under worse-than-normal conditions.

- The 40 Kbits/sec choices create audio that streams over nearly any 56K modem.

- Use the 100 Kbits/sec choices for ISDN or faster connections.

All of these choices create a movie that's ready for real-time streaming. If you want to deliver the audio as a real-time stream, just put the exported movie on a streaming server and embed its URL in your Web page, as described in Chapter 14, "Gently down the Stream."

If you want to deliver the audio as a Fast Start movie directly from your Web server, open the movie after you export it and delete all hint tracks using the Delete Tracks menu command, then save it as a self-contained movie.

You can also adjust the Qualcomm codec parameters using the Sound Settings panel, as described in "Making It Fit" (page 212). Choose the Qualcomm codec from the Compressor pop-up menu, then adjust the sample rate setting. Typical data rates for some common settings are shown below.

Sample rate	Typical data rate	Suitable target connection
8 kHz	17 Kbits/sec	28.8K modem or faster
11 kHz	23 Kbits/sec	33.6K modem or faster
22 kHz	47 Kbits/sec	56K modem or faster
44 kHz	94 Kbits/sec	Dual-ISDN or faster

The higher sampling rates give a crisper sound, especially with music. You can get twice as much compression at any sample rate by clicking the Options button and using the Half Rate setting. Half rate at 8 kHz creates audio with a typical data rate of 9 Kbits/sec.

The Options button also allows you to optimize the compressed file for streaming.

If you adjust the codec using the Sound Settings panel, you can either export the movie for Fast Start or create a movie ready for real-time streaming. In either case, choose Export from the File menu. For a Fast Start movie, choose Movie to QuickTime Movie from the Export pop-up menu; for a streaming movie, choose Movie to Hinted Movie instead.

uLaw 2:1

The uLaw codec is used to digitize land line telephone calls in the United States, Japan, and some other parts of the world. It gives 2:1 compression by scaling a 16-bit audio signal down to 8 bits. It's very similar to the aLaw codec.

This is a good codec if you need to compress the human voice for a CD or an intranet and want to keep quality high. It doesn't give a lot of compression, but it can often compress speech without audible degradation. It doesn't work as well for music or sound effects.

Recording for the Web

There are some things you can do to optimize an audio recording session for the Web. To begin with, make an extra effort to reduce noise in the recording process. If you're going to put audio on the Web, you're going to have to compress it. Compressors are less efficient at compressing noise; they work best with a clean signal. Compressors also *introduce* noise, so if you want the final output to sound good, start clean.

Ideally, record in a professional studio and transfer the audio to your computer in digital format: AIFF, CD, or DAT with digital output. Second best is to play from a DAT using audio out, or from the studio's line-level audio output, directly into your computer's audio input. Don't dub to cassette as a transport medium if you can possibly help it.

Doing It Yourself

Creating a home recording studio for music falls outside the scope of this book, but here are a few tips. Don't record to audio cassette; it's noisy. Recording to DAT or directly to your computer's disk is better. If you're recording to a multitrack tape, mix down to a stereo output connected directly to your computer's audio input.

Hi-fi stereo video cassette isn't as good a source as CD or DAT, but it's better than audio cassette. Mini-DV audio is also pretty good. But if you're shooting with a camcorder, don't use the camera's built-in microphone for sound. It picks up noise from the camera motor and the environment. Invest in small wireless clip-on microphones that your actors can wear, or use a boom mike controlled by a sound expert.

If your sound editing software can do it, normalize your recording at 70%, or –3 dB. If not, aim for a maximum level of –3 dB when you're adjusting the recording level. Full-scale audio is likely to distort when you compress it, so leave some overhead.

If your computer has a video capture card, it may include audio capture circuitry that's better than your computer's sound card. If you have a high-end audio capture card, use it.

You may need an impedance matcher between the computer and the sound source. They're not very expensive, and they can prevent a lot of problems. Going from a high-impedance output to a low-impedance input makes the signal hot and may overdrive circuitry. Going from a low-impedance output to a high-impedance input provides a weak signal, and turning up the gain to compensate adds noise.

Low $\Omega \rightarrow$ High Ω (weak signal, noise)
High $\Omega \rightarrow$ Low Ω (hot signal, may overload circuitry)

A computer's sound input is generally 20–50 kΩ. Most line-level outputs are 50 kΩ. If the output impedance is 50 kΩ, and the input impedance is 20 kΩ, the signal will be a little hot, so if you don't have an impedance matcher, you may need to turn the output level down or attenuate the input level.

A microphone typically has a 250 Ω output (*not* 250 **kΩ**). It will present a very weak signal to your computer's sound input unless you use an impedance matcher, a preamp, or both. Just cranking up the input gain will introduce noise.

Tip   You may be able to connect a headphone output jack directly to your sound input jack (they typically use the same kind of connector). Even though headphone output is typically 30–50 Ω (*not* **kΩ**), the signal is intended to drive a physical speaker and is therefore hotter than line level, so the actual signal level is frequently right on.

Make sure the sound equipment and your computer are plugged into the same electrical circuit and are properly grounded; otherwise you may hear a loud hum.

Voice-Overs and Narration

Voice recording is much less demanding than music. You can record a professional-sounding voice-over or narration without a studio (though using a studio is not a bad idea).

Most Macintosh computers made in the last few years, and any Windows PC with a good sound card, can make a clean voice recording. You'll need recording software with adjustable recording levels (don't use an autovox recording application like SimpleSound). You can invest in high-end hardware and software, such as Deck II, or high-end software alone, such as Bias Peak, or use a shareware program such as Sound-Effects; they all work fine for recording and editing voice. Sound Studio is easy to use and inexpensive, and Pro Tools Free is, well, free.

Audio uses much less RAM or disk space than video, especially at 22 kHz in mono. You'll need about 2.6 MB per minute, or about 125 MB an hour. If your software records to RAM, rather than directly to disk, make sure you have enough RAM for the entire reading—virtual memory should be fast enough for audio capture, but it's possible to have a recording drop out when paging from RAM to disk, so it's a good idea to quit all other applications before recording.

You'll need to invest in a real microphone—the kind they sell in music stores, not the kind they sell in computer stores. Expect to pay at least $100. You want a directional microphone with a cardioid pattern. You can use a dynamic microphone or a condenser type; you generally get better frequency response from a condenser, but it requires an additional power source, such as a phantom power module.

You'll also need to buy some hardware to interface the microphone to your computer's audio input. You need a preamp or an impedance matcher (possibly both), a cable from the microphone connector to your computer's sound input socket, and possibly power for the microphone. The total cost shouldn't be much over $200. If the interface gear seems overly pricey at the music store, try a discount consumer electronics store such as Radio Shack; they may have an inexpensive mixer with a microphone input, a preamp, and a line-level output. This is mainly a cabling problem.

Note No audio input on your computer? See "USB Audio" (page 228).

You'll also need a microphone stand. You'll get much better results if your narrator records from a standing position; sitting compresses a person's diaphragm. You'll need a pop screen in front of the microphone as well. You can make one from a coat hanger and an old nylon stocking, or you can get a nice-looking one that clamps to the microphone stand, from a music store.

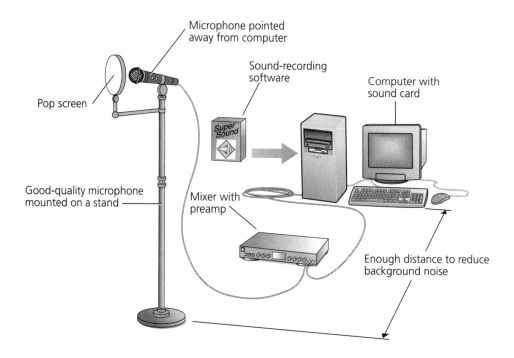

Voice-over/narration recording setup

Record at 22 kHz, 16 bits, in mono. Point the microphone away from the computer so it doesn't pick up the noise of the spinning hard disk and fan. Use a long cable and put the microphone in a quieter room if necessary.

Edit and filter the results as needed with your recording software. You normally want a little silence at the beginning and end, with a fade-in at the beginning and a fade-out at the end to prevent an audible click or pop. Normalize the peak audio level to 70% or –3 dB.

Compress any audio recording only *after* you've edited and filtered it. Save an uncompressed copy.

USB Audio

If your computer has a USB port, but no sound input jack, you need to add either a sound capture card or a USB audio adapter.

USB audio adapters come in three flavors: dirt cheap, CD quality, and professional.

- Dirt cheap adapters, such as the Griffin iMic, cost from $20 to $40, vary widely in quality (no published audio specs), but are usually just good enough for voice recording. They feature a miniature input jack with mic- and/or line-level impedance in mono or stereo.

- CD-quality adapters, such as the Onkyo U33 or Roland/Edirol UA3D, cost from $50 to $200 and provide CD-quality input (16-bit audio up to 44.1 or 48 kHz). They feature RCA jack inputs and either mini-stereo or S/PDIF optical inputs, both line- and mic-level impedance, and audio input level control. Good for pro voice or semi-pro music recording.

- Professional adapters, such as the Roland/Edirol UA-5 or Apogee Mini-Me, provide 24-bit audio capture at all sampling rates up to 96 kHz, feature S/PDIF optical and coaxial inputs, as well as 1/4-inch and/ or XLR microphone input with phantom power. The less expensive adapters (starting around $300) have RCA inputs as well. The more expensive adapters (starting around $1000) have soft-limit compressor/ limiters that allow a wider dynamic range of input without clipping or dropouts. Great stuff, if you can afford it, but for 24-bit stereo at 96 kHz, a card is a better choice than a USB adapter—the data rate is right at the limit for standard USB. For lower sampling rates, or mono, these adapters are outstanding.

▶ Popular Audio Formats

There are several popular audio formats floating around on the Web. The QuickTime plug-in can play most of them, and QuickTime Player can convert most of them to QuickTime movie files. Some of them may be useful to you for delivering audio that can be played by QuickTime as well as by other plug-ins or applications.

Unless otherwise noted below, you can import audio files in any of these formats using QuickTime Player, then export them to AIFF audio or QuickTime movies, using any of the codecs listed in "Audio Codecs" (page 215).

- **AIFF**

  Audio Interchange File Format. Widely used on the Web and Macintosh.

  - File extension: `.aiff` or `.aif`
  - MIME type: `audio/aiff`, `audio/x-aiff`

Accepts a wide variety of compression algorithms, including aLaw, uLaw, IMA, MACE (3:1 and 6:1), QDesign Music, and Qualcomm PureVoice. Can also contain MIDI data. Compressed AIFF generally requires QuickTime for playback. Some compression types require QuickTime 3 or later.

Uncompressed AIFF is supported by nearly all audio players and can be converted to WAV format losslessly.

- **WAV**

Proprietary Microsoft format widely used on the Web and in Windows.

- File extension: `.wav`
- MIME type: `audio/wav, audio/x-wav`

Standard supports compression in several formats: uncompressed 8-bit and 16-bit, ADPCM (2:1 compression of 8-bit samples with nonlinear scaling to give 12-bit dynamic range), IMA 4:1, uLaw, and aLaw. Quick-Time and Windows Media players can play all listed compression types. Windows Media Player may support additional Microsoft compressors. Most other players support only uncompressed types or a limited subset. QuickTime creates only uncompressed WAV files.

- **Sound Designer II**

Proprietary format created by Sound Designer II program. Popular with musicians and recording artists. Sound Designer II files can be used by many audio programs. Macintosh only.

- Uncompressed 8-bit and 16-bit sound.

- **MIDI (including Karaoke)**

Musical description format that specifies notes, timing, and instruments. Music is synthesized from the description either by software in the user's computer or by an external MIDI synthesizer.

- File extension: `.mid, .smf, .kar`
- MIME type: `audio/midi, audio/x-midi`

There's a tremendous amount of MIDI on the Web. It's also widely used by musicians. Bear in mind that MIDI audio files are not digitized audio, but musical descriptions that specify notes, intervals, and preferred instruments. As such, they require far less bandwidth than other audio formats and are inherently clean; most compression introduces noise, but MIDI does not. This format can be used only for some kinds of audio (instrumental music, basically) and specifies only the score and the arrangement, not the actual sound. The same MIDI file can sound very different when played using different sound cards.

When reading a karaoke file (MIDI music with a synchronized text track), QuickTime creates a movie with a music track in MIDI format and a QuickTime text track.

QuickTime includes software that synthesizes music from MIDI. Quick-Time movies can include MIDI tracks. QuickTime can convert a MIDI file into digital audio in AIFF format, with or without compression. QuickTime does not capture MIDI sequences from external sources.

- ## MOD

  MOD is very similar to MIDI, in that it specifies pitch, meter, and repetitions for instrument tracks. It differs in principle by including digital samples for each voice instead of just specifying an instrument type.

  - File extension: .mod

  The MOD format was originally developed on the Amiga, but continues to be developed and supported on other platforms, including Macintosh and Windows. There are a fair number of MOD files on the Web. There is no actual specification or standard for MOD, however, and different programs vary somewhat in the way they handle things.

  MOD is more flexible than MIDI in many respects, allowing the author to control the sound more accurately while maintaining many of MIDI's advantages, including high compression. It is hampered mainly by its ad hoc nature and lack of a real standard.

  QuickTime does not currently support MOD audio. There are programs that convert MOD files to near-equivalent MIDI files (such as MIDI-MOD), which QuickTime can then read.

- ## RealAudio

  Proprietary format created by RealNetworks. It provides highly compressed audio with good quality and can generally stream over a dialup connection.

  - File extension: .ra, .ram, .rpm
  - MIME type: audio/x-pn-realaudio, audio/x-pn-realaudio-plugin

RealAudio is a common form of streaming audio on the Web. It is roughly similar in quality and data rate to audio compressed with QuickTime using the QDesign Music Codec or the Qualcomm Pure-Voice codec.

Most of the features of RealAudio require proprietary software on the server, which must be purchased from RealNetworks, but it is possible to do a limited type of streaming with RealAudio from an ordinary HTTP server.

Only the RealPlayer application can play this media. QuickTime cannot play or create RealAudio files.

■ **MPEG-1 (layer 1 and 2 audio)**

Motion Picture Experts Group, layer 1 and 2 audio. Used on video CDs. Once fairly common on the Web, particularly in newsgroups, this format has been largely superseded by MP3.

- File extension: .m1a, .m1v, .m64, .mp2, .mpa, .mpg, .mpm, .mpv
- MIME type: audio/mpeg, audio/x-mpeg

MPEG provides audio compression up to 6:1 with very high quality. It supports sample rates of 32, 44.1, and 48 kHz only. Players are available for most platforms, including Macintosh, Windows 3.1, Windows 95/98/NT, and many flavors of UNIX.

QuickTime 3 and later can open and play MPEG layer 1 and layer 2 sound, and save an MPEG file as a QuickTime movie, on Macintosh computers. Starting with QuickTime 5, this capability is available on Windows as well. QuickTime provides decompression only; it cannot create MPEG-compressed MPEG-1 audio files from other sources.

QuickTime Player provides very limited editing of MPEG-1 files; new tracks can be added, but QuickTime treats the whole stream as a single sample—you cannot cut or copy part of it.

If MPEG-1, layer 2 audio is multiplexed with MPEG-1 video, Quick-Time cannot demultiplex and export the audio—performing an export from QuickTime results in a video-only movie.

MPEG-1, layer 2 compression can be added to QuickTime with third-party extensions such as the Hueris MPEG compressor.

- **MP3**

  Motion Picture Expert Group, MPEG-1, layer 3 audio. Very popular format for near–CD-quality audio on the Web and for portable audio players. Many DVD and CD players now support MP3 audio on ISO-9660 format CD-ROMs.

  - File extension: .mp3, .mpu
  - MIME type: application/mp3, audio/x-mpegurl

  MP3 audio offers good compression (up to 12:1) with very gradual loss of quality. The compression is not audible to most listeners at higher data rates (256 Kbit or 384 Kbit).

  MP3 audio does not offer enough compression to stream over dialup or even ISDN connections, but it is an excellent format for downloading. MP3 players are available as freeware or shareware on all popular computer platforms.

  QuickTime includes MP3 editing and playback. MP3 compression can be performed using programs such as iTunes, AudioCatalyst, or Media Cleaner Pro. QuickTime can play MP3-compressed audio in QuickTime movies as well as .mp3 files (MPEG-1 file format).

  M3U and PLS files are generally MP3 playlists, which QuickTime can also play, as described in the next bullet item.

- **IceCast/ShoutCast**

  Common format for streaming MP3 audio. No published specification, just generally observed conventions. Very popular for "dorm room radio" and other nonlicensed Internet radio formats, partially because it makes it easy to broadcast without a registered domain name; an IP address is all that's needed.

  - File extension: .pls or .m3u

  QuickTime can play IceCast/ShoutCast streaming audio by opening a playlist file or entering the URL of a playlist in QuickTime Player's Open URL dialog box, but substituting the icy:// protocol identifier for the html:// identifier. Most MP3 players, including iTunes and MusicMatch Jukebox, can also play IceCast/ShoutCast streams. QuickTime Streaming Server and Darwin Streaming Server can stream MP3 playlists using IceCast protocol and .pls playlists. For details, see "Playlists," (page 442).

- **MP4 audio**

  One of the newest audio formats on the Web is the MPEG-4 file format with AAC-encoded audio. This is an audio encoding format similar to and slightly better than MP3. MPEG-4 files can contain audio, video, text, animation, and other media types. The MPEG-4 file format is based on the QuickTime file format, with a few modifications.

  - File Extension: .mp4
  - MIME Types: `video/mpeg4, audio/mpeg4, application/mpeg4-iod`

  QuickTime can play and create MPEG-4 files in .mp4 format, and can also use MPEG-4 AAC audio compression for sound tracks in Quick-Time movies.

  MPEG-4 files can be played by any ISO-compliant MP4 player, such as QuickTime Player, RealPlayer, or Envivo's MP4 player.

Note The term "MPEG-4" has sometimes been misused to describe proprietary `.wmv` or `.asf` files that contain audio or video encoded using an MS-MPEG-4 (DivX) encoder. These are Windows Media files, not MPEG-4 files. A few `.wmv` players have gone so far as to label themselves "MP4 players," despite the fact that they cannot play `.mp4` audio files.

  True MP4 players may, or may not, support additional formats, such as Windows Media, Real Audio, or QuickTime. QuickTime can play true MPEG-4 files as well as QuickTime audio, and can use MPEG-4 compressed audio in QuickTime movies.

- **AU**

  Sun/NeXT audio format. Fairly common on UNIX systems.

  - File extension: `.au, .snd`
  - MIME type: `audio/basic`

  Java can play AU sounds directly, as can many audio players, including QuickTime 2.5 or later. The standard supports uncompressed 8-bit and 16-bit, as well as 8-bit aLaw and uLaw compression. Many players support only 8-bit uncompressed. Some also support 8-bit uLaw compressed (often incorrectly called PCM). QuickTime 3 or later supports aLaw and uLaw compression, as well as 8-bit and 16-bit uncompressed audio.

- **SND**

  Macintosh System 7 Sound format. Still sometimes used on Macintosh, with some Web presence.

  - File extension: .snd, .sfil

  This standard supports several formats and compression types used by the Macintosh Sound Manager, including 8-bit and 16-bit samples, sample rates of 44.1, 22.05, and 11.025 kHz, stereo and mono, uncompressed, aLaw, uLaw, MACE, and IMA compression.

  Uncompressed .snd files can be used as digital samples in QuickTime music tracks.

  Requires QuickTime 2.5 or later for Windows. Supported by all Macintosh computers with System 7 or later.

- **MACE**

  Macintosh Audio Compression and Expansion format, a compression algorithm used for AIFF files. Often given the .aifc file extension to distinguish it from uncompressed AIFF. Only found on a few Macintosh computers and Mac-oriented websites. Largely obsolete, and replaced by superior compression algorithms.

  - File extension: .aifc
  - MIME type: audio/aiff, audio/x-aiff

  Provides 3:1 or 6:1 compression of 8-bit or 16-bit audio using a somewhat noisy algorithm. MACE 3:1 compression discards all audio frequencies above 10 kHz. MACE 6:1 compression discards all audio frequencies above 5 kHz.

  Requires QuickTime 2.5 or later on Macintosh, QuickTime 3 or later on Windows.

- **Ogg Vorbis**

  Open source (Vorbis) audio compressor/decompressor, part of the open software movement, this compression scheme is widely felt to have better sound at lower bit rates than MP3.

  - File extension: .ogg
  - MIME type: application/org

  The distinctive quality of this compressor/decompressor is that it is free of all license or patent fees. You can download the source code and write your own implementation. There are Ogg Vorbis audio codec components available as free downloads for QuickTime 6 on Macintosh and Windows. Apple does not provide this codec, nor is it part of the component download program at this time, so if you use this compressor in your Web movies, you need to direct people to a current download site.

Show Me
Something
Good—Images

Audio is great, but let's look at making some QuickTime movies we can see as well as hear. Still images are a good media type to start with, for a number of reasons.

It turns out QuickTime can do some fairly amazing things using still images, particularly when they're combined with other media. Still images can be linked together into slideshows, for example, with music or voice-over narration (or both), real-time transition effects between slides, and hotspots with URL links.

Still images can also be added to existing QuickTime movies in some surprisingly useful ways. A still image can be used as a backdrop for scrolling credits, or as the background for a whole movie, or as a clear, sharp image of your logo floating on top of full-motion video. Because you send a single image with a long duration, this saves tons of Internet bandwidth.

In addition, working with still images will teach you how to use Quick-Time Player to edit movies, resize images, set graphics modes, put video tracks side by side, composite tracks with different types of media (such as video and sound), and change or scale the duration of a clip. Good things to know.

This chapter covers

- the thrill of using still images

- importing (and exporting) images with QuickTime

- creating slideshows using QuickTime Player

- adding transition effects to movies

- making QuickTime slideshows in other applications, including iPhoto, PowerPoint, LiveSlideShow, iMovie, and Keynote

237

- adding sound to a slideshow
- adding URL links to slideshows
- adding a still image as a movie background
- adding a logo to a movie
- alpha channels, transparency, and translucence
- color and gamma
- popular image formats

The Thrill of Still Images

Let's talk about something really exciting: still images. You already use JPEGs and GIFs in your website. In many cases, these static images are substitutes for video. But with QuickTime, still images don't have to be static images.

When you think about it, video is really just a fast slideshow, where each slide is shown for 1/30th of a second. Because QuickTime lets you display images in a sequence, each for a variable amount of time, you can create QuickTime slideshows that deliver the impact of video but at higher resolution, using much less bandwidth.

A typical slideshow image is on screen for 2, 10, or even 30 seconds, depending on what's being shown. If you transmit that image only once, instead of 30 times a second, that's a difference of at least 60:1 and as much as 900:1. That means you can increase your image resolution by a factor of 10 and still lower your data rate by at least 85% using a slideshow.

And slideshows don't have to be boring. QuickTime lets you combine your slides with music, speech, and other media, and use real-time transition effects between slides. The results are a striking improvement over a static Web page, but can play in real time over dialup modems. (For an example, see Italydialup.mov in the Images folder of the CD.)

Still images can also be combined with video, often with striking effect. Let me expand on that—in fact, let me rant for a moment. One of the saddest sights on the Web is a tiny, grainy, talking-head video of someone giving a great presentation—behind the presenter you can glimpse a giant screen full of important notes, diagrams, or beautiful images—indistinctly visible as vague shapes in a tiny video, even when the camera points directly at the slides.

Hey! Why aim a video camera at a slide, then compress it until you can't read it, or even see it clearly, just so you can send 30 copies a second of the *same image?*

Why not send *one* crystal-clear 1024 x 768 copy of the image—once—and leave it on screen for as long as the presenter does? Split the screen with a small talking-head video if you like, or superimpose the video over a corner of the slide. The computer has a high-resolution screen.

Why don't most video experts understand this? Because you can't do it with video or television—you're stuck with NTSC or PAL resolution at 25 or 30 frames a second, and you can't show a high-resolution image, period. Splitting the screen just makes it worse. And Internet video is usually lower resolution than television for bandwidth reasons.

But you can combine high resolution and low bandwidth with Quick-Time. And how. This can revolutionize your presentations. Consider distance learning—you can deliver notes, slides, and outlines with crystal clarity, side by side with your lectures if you like, over dialup modems. For business or sales, Internet presentations can be nearly as powerful as personal presentations, better in many cases than a videotaped presentation.

Okay, enough ranting. Let's actually do it.

Importing (and Exporting) Images

You can bring a still image into QuickTime just by opening it in Quick-Time Player and saving it, or pasting it into a movie and saving that. Either way, you get a QuickTime movie with at least one video track.

Video tracks containing still images can be edited by cutting and pasting. They can also be copied and added into other movies. They each have a duration, and that duration can be changed.

QuickTime can open most common image formats: Windows bitmap, FlashPix, GIF, animated GIF, JPEG, Flash, MacPaint, Photoshop (layers included as overlaid tracks), PICS, PICT, TIFF, SGI, TGA, QTIF, and PNG, to name a few. You can create images to use in QuickTime with any graphics program that can export to one of these formats.

Opening a single image in QuickTime Player creates an untitled movie with a video track containing a single frame with a duration of 1/15 second. (A layered Photoshop image opens as multiple overlaid video tracks, with each layer in its own track, all sharing the same 1/15 second duration—layer order and transparency are preserved.)

Note If you open an animated GIF, QuickTime creates one frame for each GIF frame, with the duration specified in the GIF. This is really an animation, not a still image, so animated GIFs are discussed in Chapter 15, "An Animated Approach."

A Word about Exporting Still Images

You can export the video track of a QuickTime movie as a still image in a variety of formats. Choose Export from the File menu—a pop-up menu lets you choose an export method. Three of the methods create still images: Movie to BMP, Movie to Picture, and Movie to Image Sequence.

- **Movie to BMP**

  Creates a Windows bitmap (.bmp) file from the currently displayed frame. Can be grayscale or color, with bit depths from 8 (256 colors) to 24 (millions of colors).

- **Movie to Picture**

  Creates a PICT format image from the currently displayed frame. Supports various codecs, some of which are useful for still images—Animation, BMP, Cinepak, Component Video, Graphics, Intel Indeo, Intel raw, None, Photo JPEG, Planar RGB, PNG, Sorenson video, TGA, TIFF, and Video, for example. (Other codecs are appropriate only for motion video and should *not* generally be used when creating still images—DV-NTSC, DV-PAL, H.261, and H.263.) Additional quality and compression options are available, depending on the codec chosen.

- **Movie to Image Sequence**

  Creates a still image from every frame in the video track—a single image if the video track contains a single frame—in a variety of formats: BMP, JPEG, MacPaint, Photoshop, PICT, PNG, QTIF (QuickTime Image File), SGI (Silicon Graphics Image File), TGA (Targa Image File), or TIFF. Additional quality and compression options depend on the format you choose.

You can also export a still image as video in any of the formats that QuickTime supports (QuickTime movie, AVI, DV, and so on), using any of the compressors supported by the video format you choose. This can be handy for exporting an image to a video editor such as iMovie.

▶ Creating Slideshows Using QuickTime Player

QuickTime Player is neither the easiest nor the most powerful tool for creating QuickTime slideshows, but it is one of the most flexible. And using it to create slideshows can teach you a lot about QuickTime and editing movies in QuickTime Player.

The easiest way to create a slideshow in QuickTime Player is the Open Image Sequence command (in the File menu). This command creates a movie by importing all the images in a folder. The images need to have sequential filenames and should all be the same size, or at least the same aspect ratio.

Here's what you do:

1. Create a folder.

2. Drag all the images you want to use into the folder.

3. Give the images a common root name followed by a sequence number, such as `Image01.jpg`, `Image02.jpg`, `Image03.jpg`.

   If you have ten or more slides, use a leading zero for slides 1–9 (**01**, **02**, and so on). If you have a hundred or more slides, use two leading zeroes for slides 1–9 and a single leading zero for slides 10–99 (**001**, **002**, . . . , **0**10, **0**11, . . . , **0**99, 100). Why? Because alphabetically, it's the *first* number that counts—10 comes *before* 2 or 3, because 10 starts with a 1, but 10 comes *after* 02 and 03, because 02 and 03 start with a 0.

Important   Make the sequence number the *only* number in the filename. Don't use filenames like `July1st01.jpg` or `3D-mice1.gif`. Extra numbers in the filenames confuse the sequence importer.

Tip   It can be a real pain to rename a large number of files, particularly with sequential numbers. Use a freeware or shareware utility such as File Buddy.

4. Choose Open Image Sequence from the File menu in QuickTime Player.

5. Select the first image in the sequence and click Open.

6. In the dialog box that appears, choose a frame rate for the movie.

QuickTime creates a movie with a single video track, making a video frame from each image in the folder. All the frames have the same duration, which can be as little as 1/30 of a second or as much as 10 seconds, depending on the frame rate.

Example   Launch QuickTime Player, choose Open Image Sequence from the File menu, and navigate to the ItalySlides folder, in the Examples folder on the CD. Choose the first slide in the folder. Experiment with different frame rates.

The first image determines the height and width of the video track; all the subsequent images are scaled to that height and width. This works best when all the images have the same dimensions to begin with (or at least the same aspect ratio).

You'll generally get better results by cropping or scaling the images to the same height and width using a graphics program such as Photoshop before you import them. Alternatively, you can add a solid background to smaller images instead of scaling them, so all images are on the same size "canvas" (to use Photoshop terminology). If you have iPhoto, it can scale your images and export a slideshow to QuickTime. See "iPhoto" (page 251).

As an alternative to using the Open Image Sequence command, you can create a slideshow by opening individual images in QuickTime Player, copying them, and pasting them together in any order you like. This requires a lot more clicking and mousing around, but opening images individually lets you use images of different sizes without scaling them—the video track expands to make room for the largest image you paste in—and you can use files without renaming them sequentially.

Images opened individually have a default duration of 1/15 second, so you'll probably need to change the duration later; see "Setting Image Duration" (page 243).

A third alternative is to open individual slides using the Open Sequence command. Create a folder called Import. Drag each image into the folder, do an Open Image Sequence on that single image, then drag it back out again. It's not as convenient as opening them all at once, or even opening them using the Open command, but you can mix filenames or image dimensions, and you can set an independent duration for each image (up to 10 seconds). This creates a one-frame movie for each image. Open the movies (or leave them open as you do a series of imports) and use Copy and Paste to put them together in any order you like.

Setting the Slide Sequence

When you use the Open Image Sequence command, the slides are initially arranged according to the sequence numbers in the filenames. You can change the order by selecting frames in QuickTime Player, cutting them, clicking a movie frame at the point where you want to reinsert them, and pasting. Use the same technique to rearrange slides you've put into a sequence by cutting and pasting (or exporting from another program).

You can also add individual images to an imported image sequence. Import the sequence, then open another image using the Open, Import, or Open Sequence command. Copy, click in the imported sequence where you want to insert the image, and Paste. Open as many additional images as you like, and paste them into the sequence where you will.

Tip If the images are of different sizes, there will be blank space around the smaller images. You can fill this with a solid color, texture, or image by adding a background to the movie, as described in "Adding a Still Image as a Movie Background" (page 267).

When you paste an image into a movie, it gets inserted before the currently selected frame in the sequence. This is a little disconcerting because nothing seems to happen when you paste. You have to back up a frame (Left Arrow key) to see what you've pasted.

The exception is the last frame of the movie. If you click on the last frame, then paste in an image, the new image is put at the end of the movie sequence.

So how do you paste an image just prior to the last frame? Indirectly. You paste it in at the end, then cut the next-to-last frame and paste *it* in at the end.

Setting Image Duration

QuickTime Player provides mechanisms for changing the duration of a single image or a sequence of images. Some of these mechanisms are very powerful. But changing image durations with the QuickTime Player interface can be awkward. If you'll be doing a lot of this, get an editing program that lets you lay out the images on a timeline, such as LiveStage or GoLive, then adjust the slide durations by dragging or by entering a value.

That said, you can easily make the duration of a particular image *shorter* in QuickTime Player. Just select as much as you want removed, hit the Delete or Backspace key, and presto, it's gone. For more information about making selections in QuickTime Player, see Appendix A.

There are a couple of methods you can use to increase an image's duration in QuickTime Player: Copy and Paste, or Add Scaled.

Copy and Paste

You can select all or part of an image's current duration using the selection controls, then choose Copy, then Paste. This extends the duration of the image by the amount of time selected.

There are some drawbacks to this technique. At most, a Paste operation doubles the duration of an image. If you want to increase the duration from 2/15 of a second to 2 seconds, for example, you need to paste 15 times (or repeat the Copy operation between pastes to select increasingly larger durations).

Bear in mind that each time you paste, you create another data reference. If you flatten the movie later, each reference is replaced by a copy of the image data, creating multiple stored copies of the same image.

That's not a very efficient way to increase the length of time an image is displayed. But it is easy.

Add Scaled

The other way to extend an image's duration is to use the Add Scaled command. This is a powerful technique—you can use it to lengthen or shorten the duration of a single image or a whole sequence of images. It's ideally suited to synchronizing an image sequence with other media, such as narration or music.

To use Add Scaled, follow these steps:

1. Copy or cut something whose duration you want to change.

2. Select something that has the desired duration.

3. Choose Add Scaled from the Edit menu.

This adds whatever you cut or copied as a new track (or tracks), precisely synchronized with whatever was selected when you chose Add Scaled. This is ideal for adding a video track and scaling it to exactly match a piece of music, for example, or for adding a background image to a whole movie.

It's not an ideal technique for changing a slide's duration from 2 seconds to 10 seconds, however. For one thing, it adds the image in a new video track elsewhere in the timeline, parallel to your selection, rather than extending its duration in place. So after adding it, you need to extract the new track, copy it, and paste it back where it belongs. In addition, this technique requires that you already have something 10 seconds long to scale the image to.

To help with this, there's a movie named Timeline.mov, in the Images folder of the CD. It's visually calibrated so that you can easily choose a duration from 1/30 of a second to 10 minutes. Here's how to use it to change the duration of an image:

1. Open your slideshow movie, select the image (or image sequence) whose duration you want to change, and choose Copy.

2. Open Timeline.mov, select the duration you want, and choose Add Scaled.

3. Delete the text track (Delete Tracks in the Edit menu). This gets rid of the visible timeline.

4. Choose Select All, then Copy, and close the movie (don't save!).

5. Click inside your slideshow movie. The original image or image sequence should still be selected. Replace it by choosing Replace in the Edit menu.

Hey, I said it was awkward. But it works.

Arranging Tracks Spatially

You can display more than one image at a time by arranging the images spatially, such as side by side or overlapping. You do this by organizing your images into tracks, then setting the spatial properties of each track.

For example, to create a slideshow that displays two images at a time, side by side, follow these steps:

1. Open all the images that will appear on the left side and arrange them in sequence as a slideshow movie.

2. Open the images that will appear on the right side of your presentation in a new movie and arrange them in sequence. You probably want the same number of images, with the same durations, so the left and right sides advance in step, but it's not required.

3. Choose Select All in the movie with the right-side images, then Copy.

4. Click in the first movie and Select All. Add Scaled. This adds the two slideshows together and ensures that they have exactly the same duration. The slides you added are on top of the other slides, covering them.

   Now you need to move the slides you added to the right. You do this by selecting their video track and adjusting its size and position.

5. Choose Get Movie Properties from the Movie menu. If each slideshow movie is a single video track, the slides you added are in Video Track 2, so choose Video Track 2 from the left pop-up menu (if the movie you added has multiple tracks, choose the video track at the bottom of the list and work your way up).

6. Choose Size from the right pop-up menu. It should look something like the following illustration.

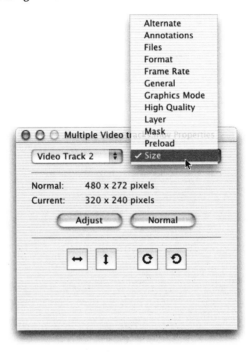

7. Click the Adjust button. Red handles should appear on the image of the video track.

8. Click the image to activate its window.

9. Hold down the Shift key, click inside the image (but *not* on any of the red handles), and drag the track to the right until the image underneath is completely revealed (the Shift key lets you drag sideways without drifting up or down). When you release the mouse button, the movie window expands to show your two tracks side by side.

10. Click the Done button.

If there are multiple video tracks on the right side, repeat steps 6–10 as needed.

Your new slides should now be positioned to the right of the first slides. When you play the movie the slides in both tracks should advance together, similar to the following illustration (which shows three tracks).

Example   Use the Open Image Sequence command twice to create two slideshows from the folder ItalySlides (in the Examples folder on the CD). Copy one and add it to the other. Open the Movie Properties window, choose Video Track 2, and follow steps 6–10 in the previous list.

You can use the same technique to position visible tracks above or below each other when they contain motion video, sprites, or text. Dragging a track while pressing the Shift key allows you to move the track straight to the right or left, or straight up and down. Dragging without the Shift key allows you to move the track freely. You can position multiple tracks this way to create any arrangement you like.

Tip   If you need to reposition a small graphic element (32 x 32 pixels or smaller), the red handles overlap, making it *very* difficult to grab. Choose Double Size or Fill Screen in the Movie menu to temporarily enlarge the movie. Reposition the video track as needed, then restore the movie to normal size.

If you arrange video tracks so they overlap, you can select which one is on top by choosing Layer from the right pop-up menu in the Info window. The layer with the smallest number is on top, and you can change it. It's okay to use negative numbers. To make the image on top partly transparent or translucent, change its graphics mode—see "Transparency and Alpha Channels" (page 271).

As you probably noticed, you can also use the Size dialog box to scale a video track, making it larger or smaller. Scaling a video track can make an image larger without increasing the file size or bandwidth. How much impact this has on the quality of the image depends on the compressor and the subject matter, but you can usually increase the size by at least 25% without much quality loss.

Conversely, scaling the video track down reduces the image size but doesn't reduce the file size or data rate, so it's rarely a good idea (though it does tend to make it look sharper). You can get better results and smaller file size by scaling images down in a graphics program like Photoshop or GraphicConverter before importing them into QuickTime.

Adding Transition Effects

You can add transition effects, such as cross-fades or wipes, between slides. QuickTime has dozens of built-in effects, with hundreds of possible variations (wipe from the upper-left corner, wipe from the top, and so on). Each transition typically adds about 2 Kbytes to your file.

Tip Once you add transitions to a file, it becomes difficult or impossible to change the slide order or change a particular slide's duration except by recreating the slideshow. When you change the duration of any part of the movie, any transition effects are slowed down or speeded up accordingly.

It's easy to add transitions using applications such as GoLive, or to create slideshows with built-in transitions using programs such as LiveSlide-Show or iPhoto, but for the moment lets look at two free tools from Apple that can add transitions to just about anything (they're in the Tools folder on the CD): MakeEffectMovie and MakeEffectSlideShow.

MakeEffectMovie

MakeEffectMovie takes whole movies as inputs and creates a new movie consisting of the two source movies joined by a transition effect.

When you launch MakeEffectMovie, it prompts you for a source movie twice. It creates a transition from the first movie you specify to the second movie, so select them in the order you want them to appear.

Once you've specified the source movies, you're prompted to pick an effect. If the effect has adjustable parameters, the appropriate controls are displayed. A preview of the effect runs constantly in the lower-left corner, so you can see what changing the parameters does.

When you have the effect and parameters you want, click OK. Make-EffectMovie creates a small movie (not self-contained) of the transition effect. You can create a series of movies, one for each pair of slides, and paste them together end to end. When you're happy with the result, Save As (self-contained). You now have a slideshow with transitions.

Unfortunately, when you do this you paste most slides twice—once as the first source for a transition and once as the second source for another transition. This doubles the file size and bandwidth needed for the slides.

MakeEffectMovie is ideal for joining two movie clips together with a transition effect. Cut the last two seconds of the first clip and the first two seconds of the next clip into separate movies, join them using MakeEffect-Movie, and paste them between the now-shortened clips. The trouble with using it for a slideshow is that you can't shorten the segments and use the trimmings to create a transition because each "clip" is a single frame.

Use this tool in a slideshow if you want to add transition effects between only occasional slides, or if file size and bandwidth aren't a problem (a slideshow on CD, for example). This tool makes it relatively easy to add any kind of transition anywhere in a movie, and you can use different transitions between different slides.

MakeEffectSlideShow

The MakeEffectSlideShow utility (in the Tools folder of the CD) creates a slideshow with real-time transitions effects, such as cross-fades or wipes, between all the slides. You can specify any QuickTime transition effect you like, and that effect is used between all the slides. You can manually specify each image in the series, so filenames don't need to be sequential, and the files don't need to be in the same folder. All the images should be the same size, though.

The interface is very crude, but it's also simple. After you launch Make-EffectSlideShow, choose Make Effect Movie from the Testing menu. You'll be presented with an Open File dialog. Navigate to your first slide and press the Convert button. Nothing appears to happen, but you have added a slide to the show. Repeat until you have clicked Convert once for each image in the slideshow, then press the Cancel button.

You'll be presented with an effect dialog box. Choose the effect you want and set any parameters the way you like them—experiment, it's free. When you're ready, click OK. Give the movie a name and put it where you can find it.

Example Launch MakeEffectSlideShow, choose Make Effect Movie from the Testing menu, and open a few random images in the ItalySlides folder on the CD (you won't see them open). Click Cancel, then choose the Explode transition. Save to your desktop and Quit. Find the movie on your desktop and play it.

MakeEffectSlideShow creates a small QuickTime movie that references all your slides. Unless you plan to keep all the slides where the reference movie can find them, you'll want to choose Save As (self-contained) to copy the slides into a movie file when you're happy with the results.

If you open the properties window of the movie created by MakeEffect-SlideShow (choose Get Movie Properties, in the Movie menu), you'll see it has three video tracks: one with all the slides used as a first source, one with all the slides used as a second source, and an effects track (very small). If you extract video tracks 2 and 3 (Extract Tracks, Edit menu), you'll see that most slides appear in both tracks, but the first slide is only in track 2, and the last slide is only in track 3.

If you save this as a self-contained movie, the file will be about twice as large as the same slideshow without transitions because most of the slides are copied into both tracks.

Okay, you may be saying to yourself, that's really easy. Why would I ever use QuickTime Player and MakeEffectMovie instead of Make-EffectSlideShow? The main reason is flexibility—MakeEffectSlideShow uses one effect for all slides and you can't easily change a slide's duration. QuickTime Player lets you set the duration of slides individually and rearrange slides freely, and MakeEffectMovie lets you use more than one kind of transition effect.

Now that you mention it though, there are easier ways to do *all* these things (but some of them aren't free). Let's look at a few.

▶ Making QuickTime Slideshows in Other Applications

There are a few programs, such as Totally Hip's LiveSlideShow and Apple's iPhoto, that create QuickTime slideshows directly from still images. We'll look at some of the nonobvious features of these programs to help you get the most from them. Other programs, such as PowerPoint for Mac OS or Keynote, create what are essentially slideshows in their own format, which they can then export as QuickTime movies. The quality and features of the exported movie can vary a great deal, depending on how it's done. We'll give you some tips.

Note It's also pretty easy to create QuickTime slideshows using the SMIL language and a text editor, as described in Chapter 18, "SMIL for the Camera."

iPhoto

Possibly the easiest way to create a QuickTime slideshow is with iPhoto. You can use any size images, with any names. Drag them into an "album," use the View menu to select a manual arrangement, and drag the slides into any order you like. Click the SlideShow button, choose a slide duration, set the slides to loop (or not loop), and choose any sound track from your iTunes collection. When you're happy with your slideshow, choose Export from the File menu and pick QuickTime.

Pick an image size, and all your slides will be scaled up or down to it without messing up the aspect ratio (unlike opening an image sequence in QuickTime Player). Choose whether or not to include the sound track, and change the slide duration if you like. Click Export and you're done.

This creates a compact slideshow with background music and lovely cross-fade transitions between slides. You can't select a different effect, unfortunately, but it's a good default.

Another limitation is that all the slides have the same duration, and modifying any slide's duration messes up all the cross-fade transitions. If you want to use iPhoto to create slideshows, you just have to live with a fixed slide duration and cross-fade transitions for all slides.

You may have noticed that when you loop a slideshow in iPhoto, the images and sound track loop independently, which is ideal. When you export to QuickTime, however, any sound track is repeated as necessary until all the slides are displayed, then cut off. If you loop the movie, the sound breaks at the end and starts over with the slides.

That's not ideal, but you can fix it pretty easily. Export the slideshow to QuickTime without sound and add the sound track using QuickTime Player, as described in "Adding Sound to a Slideshow" (page 260).

Finally, although iPhoto creates a compact, self-contained QuickTime file, it is not a Fast Start movie. That's fine for local or CD delivery, but not good at all for the Internet—if you embed it in a Web page, people will see a QuickTime logo until the entire file has downloaded. Fixing this is slightly tricky. If you just open the Movie in QuickTime Player and Save As (self-contained), the file size doubles or triples.

Note That's because QuickTime is using each image two or three times—as a slide, and as one or two sources of a transition effect. When you flatten the movie, these references all become copies, and you have two or three copies of each slide.

The solution is to create a URL reference movie, as described in "URL File References" (page 35)—put your slideshow on a Web server, open it using Open URL in QuickTime Player, and Save. This creates a tiny movie that contains the URL of the slideshow and a copy of the slideshow's movie header information. Embed this tiny movie in any Web page, or distribute it any way you like. When the movie is played, it opens the URL to your slideshow movie. It will start playing almost immediately, as soon as it starts to get data from your Web server.

LiveSlideShow

Totally Hip's LiveSlideShow, available for both Mac OS and Windows (for around $49), is probably the most powerful slideshow creation program around. You can easily create slideshows using a drag-and-drop interface, rearrange slides freely, insert unique transitions between any two slides, independently set the duration of any slide or transition, add sound to any slide, add background music to the entire slideshow, or (if you have audio input hardware) record a voice-over directly in LiveSlideShow.

It includes built-in sprite buttons to advance to the next or previous slide, go to the beginning or end, open a URL in your default browser, and more. It also includes several prebuilt themes (background, frame, and so on) and can help you create a "skinned" version of QuickTime Player for your slideshow (in QuickTime, the skin travels with your movie, so a skinned movie always plays in its own custom player).

The user interface is pretty simple and self-explanatory, but there are a few nonobvious things that you should be aware of:

- The first thing you should do when creating a LiveSlideShow project is to set the slideshow dimensions (Options menu) to accommodate your largest image. Otherwise it will scale your images into a small 400 x 300 default window. LiveSlideShow will want to add a background, so you might want to set dimensions that leave a little room around the edges of your largest image.

- You will get more predictable results if your images are all the same size to begin with. The program does automatic scaling, and it's better than QuickTime Player's Open Image Sequence command (it preserves the aspect ratio), but it's not as robust as iPhoto.

- If you click and drag the frame around an image to scale it or move it, you scale or move all the images in the slideshow—you're really changing the video track's size, position, and scaling, and all the slides share the video track.

- You can type captions for each slide, and even use scrolling text, but there is a single text track for the whole movie—if you change the size or position of the text frame in any slide, you change it for all slides.

Once you realize these minor quirks are there, they're pretty easy to live with.

LiveSlideShow is currently the only program I know of that can create a slideshow with a single copy of each slide in a self-contained, Fast Start movie. All other programs, including those from Apple, create either large files with multiple copies of each slide or compact files that don't fast start over the Internet, requiring you to make URL reference movies for Web delivery. I can't figure out how they do it, quite frankly. To quote Darth Vader: "Impressive . . . "

LiveSlideShow doesn't scale the slideshow duration to the background music—when the show ends, the music just cuts off. You might want to add background music to the slideshow using QuickTime Player instead, as described in "Adding Sound to a Slideshow" (page 260). Unlike other slideshows, you can edit the output of LiveSlideShow and Save As (self-contained) without increasing the file size by making duplicate copies of the slides. What can I say? These guys are smart.

When you export your movie from LiveSlideShow, the default is a QuickTime movie with no controller (apart from any sprite control buttons you chose to add). To display the normal QuickTime Player controls, or to edit the slideshow in QuickTime Player, you need to change the movie's Controller setting: open the Movie Properties window, choose Movie in the left pop-up menu, choose Controller in the right pop-up, and select Movie Controller instead of None. You'll need to do this to add sound to the slideshow using QuickTime Player, for example. You can change the controller back to None when you're done editing, if you like.

Video Editors—iPhoto, FinalCut Pro, and Others

If you have a Mac, it's very tempting to build your slideshow in iMovie or FinalCut Pro because they have well-thought-out interfaces for editing. It's easy to drag in photos, give them each a duration, synchronize them with audio, and add transitions. You can even use the Ken Burns effect—panning and zooming across a still image, bringing it to life and showing more detail than would otherwise be possible.

Even if you don't have a Mac, you may feel a similar temptation to create your slideshow in a video editor you know and like, then export it to QuickTime.

Unfortunately, unless you're working with slides that are in DV format to begin with, or you're creating a video DVD or exporting to a DV tape of some sort (mini-DV, digital 8, DVC-Pro, and so on), it's generally a bad idea to use a video editor to create QuickTime slideshows.

Video editors generally have a fixed resolution and frame rate, and often a fixed compression scheme, such as DV compression. The resolution is low for a modern computer screen (less than 640 x 480), and the frame rate is very high for a slideshow (25 or 30 frames a second).

Your 1024 x 768 JPEGs and 1600 x 1200 digital photos won't look all that great scrunched into DV format, and they use a lot more bandwidth at 30 frames a second than at 1 frame every 2 seconds. The transition effects aren't exported as QuickTime effects, either—they're rendered as bitmaps and compressed into video frames—so you need a pretty high frame rate for them to look decent.

Don't get me wrong. Video is great stuff for DVD or broadcast, and it has a real place on the Web, especially with broadband. It's just not a good format for slideshows, which are an ideal medium for dialup connections. For slideshows, you want high resolution, variable frame rate (a single image on screen for as long as you want), and QuickTime transition effects rendered on the viewer's computer as the movie plays (not pre-rendered on your computer and transmitted over the Internet as a series of images).

Unfortunately, the Ken Burns effect is not available as a QuickTime effect—at least not yet. You can do something quite similar using sprites, however, as we'll see in Chapter 16, "Getting Interactive."

PowerPoint

Presentation programs such as PowerPoint create what are essentially slideshows. Some versions of PowerPoint can export to QuickTime, but they don't export slideshows. They export QuickTime video.

If you've ever watched a PowerPoint presentation on videotape, you've seen the problem. The video camera can't capture the slides very well. Now imagine compressing that video and sending it over the Internet. Not pretty, and not an efficient use of bandwidth.

PowerPoint also features animated slide transitions, which can be quite effective. These transitions may be lost when you export to QuickTime. They require a fairly high frame rate to look good if they are successfully exported.

All that said, simply exporting to QuickTime can be a useful tool for creating a movie to distribute over a LAN or on CD. For export to the Web, there is a better approach, as we'll see shortly.

PowerPoint 2001 and later for the Mac can export directly to Quick-Time. You can build your slideshow, record a voice-over for each slide and have the slide's duration automatically adjust itself, and specify Quick-Time transitions between slides, all in Powerpoint. Then choose Make Movie. It works beautifully, at least for local delivery. For an example, see ppSlides.htm in the Images folder of the CD.

It's not optimized for the Web, however. You need to choose a frame rate, which generally needs to be at least 1 per second for the slides to change roughly when they should. That typically makes the file 2–3 times larger than it needs to be, as you're resending the same image every second a slide is on-screen. If you want to preserve animated slide transitions, you need a higher data rate (typically 10–15 frames per second), which requires even more bandwidth. Still, for local, CD, or LAN delivery, it works fine—choose a high frame rate (12–15 frames per second) and a low-loss video compressor, such as Animation set to high quality.

Tip It's not a good idea to embed QuickTime movies in the presentation, then convert the presentation to QuickTime. Remove embedded QuickTime from your presentation, export your presentation to a QuickTime movie, then add your QuickTime content using a QuickTime editor. QuickTime Player is a fine editor for this kind of job.

An alternative to exporting from PowerPoint, if you have a Mac handy, is to import your PowerPoint presentation into Keynote, *then* export to QuickTime. This fixes a lot of the shortcomings in PowerPoint's native export to QuickTime, and it's usually very easy. If your PowerPoint presentation imports into Keynote cleanly, the rest is a piece of cake. See "Keynote" (page 257) for details.

If you're working in the Windows OS, or don't have a copy of Keynote, and you want to optimize your PowerPoint presentation for the Web, export your slides as images, instead of exporting to QuickTime directly. Pull the images into QuickTime as a slideshow, then add any transitions or audio in QuickTime itself.

Here's how to convert an ordinary PowerPoint presentation into a Web-ready QuickTime slideshow using QuickTime Player.

1. Open the presentation in PowerPoint and choose Save As.

2. Choose a graphics format that QuickTime can open, such as GIF, JPEG, or PNG, depending on your content. (Don't use PICT.)

Tip A typical PowerPoint slide with text and graphics saves well as a GIF or PNG. If the slide includes photos or uses more than 256 colors, JPEG may be a better choice.

3. Click the Options button and make sure you're saving the whole presentation, not just one slide.

4. Enter a name for the presentation and save it. This creates a folder with the name of the presentation. Inside the folder are a series of graphic files named Slide1, Slide2, and so on.

The slides are the default size created by PowerPoint, which may not be the size you want. You can scale the slides before importing them into QuickTime using a graphics program such as Photoshop, GraphicConverter, or DeBabelizer. If you use Photoshop, it's easy to create an action that resizes all the images in a folder. Alternatively, you can resize the slides after you import them by adjusting the video track's display size, as described in "Arranging Tracks Spatially" (page 245).

Note   You can get some versions of PowerPoint to generate smaller or larger slides by changing your screen resolution before saving the presentation, but this doesn't give you very fine control.

You can now create a QuickTime slideshow from the images in the folder, either by choosing Open Image Sequence in QuickTime Player or by opening the individual images and pasting them together, as described in "Creating Slideshows Using QuickTime Player" (page 241).

You may want to add a voice-over for each slide, then combine the slides into a movie as described in "Voice-Over or Narration" (page 263).

To insert a QuickTime movie into a slide, add the slide to the movie as a background image, as described in "Adding a Still Image as a Movie Background" (page 267). This creates a new movie with the slide as the background for the QuickTime movie.

If you *aren't* adding a different-length voice-over or QuickTime movie for each slide, you can open the images in QuickTime Player using the Open Image Sequence command, as described in "Creating Slideshows Using QuickTime Player" (page 241). This automatically creates a slideshow movie from the presentation. All the slides have the same duration, based on the frame rate you choose when you open the image sequence. You can change the duration of individual slides, as discussed in "Setting Image Duration" (page 243).

If only a few slides contain a movie or voice-over, you can cut those slides out, add the movies or voice-overs, then paste them back in.

Tip If you have LiveSlideShow, from Totally Hip Software, you can easily assemble your images into a slideshow, set individual slide durations and transitions, add narrations, and save as a Web-ready QuickTime movie. That's the easy way to accomplish everything we've talked about so far. This is a particularly attractive option on the Windows OS, where direct export from PowerPoint to QuickTime is currently unavailable.

You can add music, sound effects, or narration, as described in "Adding Sound to a Slideshow" (page 260).

PowerPoint presentations that include hotspots, animations, or QuickTime movies are harder to convert. It's generally best to create a stripped-down version of the presentation without those elements, import it into QuickTime as described above, and add hotspots, animations, and QuickTime movies using the techniques described later in this book.

Sometimes it's easier to go ahead and create a new presentation, using a program that exports directly to QuickTime, such as Keynote, LiveSlideShow, GoLive, Flash, MovieWorks, or LiveStage Pro.

Another alternative is to use a service, such as Web Presenter:

`www.webpresenter.net`

They can combine audio or video of you giving a presentation with your slides, add wired sprites and chapter lists, and package the whole thing as a Web-ready QuickTime movie. For an example, see `WebPresenter.htm` (in the Images folder of the CD).

Keynote

Apple's new Keynote presentation software creates beautiful slides and features head-turning 3D transitions. As you might expect, it also does a very good job of exporting to QuickTime. If you choose the correct options, Keynote will create a movie with one frame for the duration of each slide. The transition effects are rendered video, not QuickTime effects, but they're rendered intelligently to minimize bandwidth, and this allows the use of 3D transitions that aren't yet part of QuickTime.

Open your presentation in Keynote and choose Export from the File menu. You'll have a choice of exporting to QuickTime, PowerPoint, or PDF. Choose QuickTime and click the "Next . . ." button.

You'll see a dialog box with two panels, each with a pull-down menu, as shown in the following illustration.

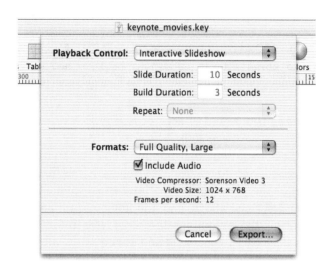

You can set the playback control to either Interactive Slideshow or Self-Playing Movie. If you choose Interactive Slideshow, Keynote creates a QuickTime movie that automatically pauses at each slide (press the Play button or the Space bar to go to the next slide, showing any animated transition). If you choose Self-Playing Movie, Keynote generates an ordinary QuickTime movie; in this case, you need to specify the duration for your slides.

The lower pop-up menu allows you to choose "Full Quality, Large," "CD-ROM, Medium," "Web, Small," or "Custom . . . "

The actual dimensions of the QuickTime slideshow that these choices create depend on the pixel dimensions of the Keynote presentation. "Full Quality" is the same size as the presentation, while "CD-ROM" and "Web" are progressively smaller.

For uncomplicated 1024 x 768 slides without sound, the labels are quite conservative—a "Full Quality" slideshow will play nicely from CD, on a LAN, or over DSL; a "CD-ROM" slideshow will play over most dialup modems (data rate: 4 Kbytes/sec); and a "Web" slideshow is suitable for transmission by telegraph (well, maybe not, but a 1200 baud modem would probably work).

Adding audio makes a huge addition to the data rate, of course. You can export audio from the Keynote presentation and/or add the audio using QuickTime Player afterwards. It's a bit easier to tweak for maximum performance if you add the audio later, as described in "Adding Sound to a Slideshow" (page 260).

The default video compressor and frame rates are excellent choices for most slides. If you have a good understanding of video codecs, you may want to make other choices; if so, be sure to choose a frame rate of 12 or higher. Don't worry, it won't actually create 12 video frames for each second a slide is on the screen. It specifies a maximum frame rate for effects.

Keynote doesn't export video at a fixed frame rate. If there are no animated transitions, it creates a movie with one frame per slide. Each frame has the duration you set as the Slide Duration in the export dialog. If there are transitions, it renders them at the chosen video frame rate, 12 fps by default. If you choose a very low frame rate, such as 1 frame per second, Keynote doesn't bother to export the animated transitions.

As long as you choose a high enough frame rate to show the transitions, you can pick any compressor and pixel dimensions you like, and Keynote will create a perfectly optimized QuickTime slideshow.

Still Others

I'm happy to report that, these days, it seems like everybody and their dog have the ability to export QuickTime slideshows. I'll list just a few to give you a sense of the variety.

- GoLive 6 has an excellent general-purpose QuickTime editor. And it makes slideshows. It's not obvious, but it does. Here's how:

  First, create a movie (Files > New Special > QuickTime Movie). Open the timeline editor (Movie menu) and drag in a picture track from the Object palette. Now check out the Inspector palette—there's a Slideshow tab! It sets up a slideshow much like iPhoto's (well, no sound, but you can add that later). Switch to the Image tab and you can import a folder full of images (be sure to check the Images Constrain Proportion checkbox). You can then drag the image and transition samples to change their durations. Fun! Don't export—that renders to video. Just Save As. Adding transitions doubles or triples the file size.

- eZediaMX and eZediaQTI can create fabulous QuickTime slideshows with drag-and-drop simplicity.

- MovieWorks Deluxe can create QuickTime slideshows, among many, many, other things.

- Qtilities QT Slide Controller doesn't actually create QuickTime slideshows, but it adds a lot of controls for presenting them.

- PicturePreview is a handy $10 bit of shareware that organizes and converts still images between any QuickTime formats, and of course, it does slideshows.

- iSlideShow is a really neat bit of shareware that doesn't make the kind of slideshows we're talking about. It makes beautifully (if slowly) rendered, high-frame-rate, ultra-high-bandwidth movies of slideshows. Playback in QuickTime is noticably smoother than video produced using iMovie or most other effects-rendering software. But you wouldn't put its output on the Web, or even most LANs.

▶ Adding Sound to a Slideshow

It's easy to add sound to a slideshow. You can add a MIDI music track, a recorded music track, sound effects, a voice-over narration, or a combination of these.

It's generally best to add sound to a slideshow near the end of production, after you add any transition effects. That way your audio won't be garbled by a transition effect, and you can scale the slideshow as a whole to exactly match the audio.

Obviously, adding sound increases the bandwidth needed to watch the slideshow in real time without a download delay. MIDI is the most efficient way to add sound. Recorded speech is also very bandwidth efficient and can be a tremendous addition. Recorded music, on the other hand, is bandwidth intensive—it works fine in local slideshows or over relatively fast connections such as DSL, but to make it play over dialup you will have to work hard and be very clever.

What's your bandwidth budget? Start with the slowest connection you plan to support in real time. If it's dialup, that's between 4000 and 5000 K/sec for most people. Divide by 10 as a rule of thumb to get a file size in kilobytes. So 4–5 Kbytes/sec for dialup. If your slides are on screen for an average of 4 seconds each, that's 16–20 Kbytes per image. Not exactly high-res stuff, but enough for simple slides. If your slides are on screen for 10–15 seconds, it's more like 40–75 Kbytes per image, which can be a nice full-screen image. That's with no sound.

If your slideshow is mainly about the images, figure out your minimum acceptable quality for a given connection speed, do the math, and whatever is left is your audio budget. If the slides are visual support for what's primarily an audio presentation, a lecture with notes, for example, it works the other way—set aside the bandwidth you need to get acceptable audio quality, and whatever's left is your video budget.

Music

A MIDI music track adds only a few kilobytes to a slideshow and requires only a few hundred *bits* per second of bandwidth. A slideshow with MIDI can easily be made to stream over a dialup modem. Recorded music requires more bandwidth and a larger file than MIDI, but it can capture sound with more character and can include vocals. For a review of bandwidth requirements and compressors for audio, see "Making It Fit: Sampling, Bandwidth, and Compression" (page 208).

In any case, once you've picked the right music, the main choice is whether to scale the slideshow's duration to match the music, or to trim the music to the length of the slideshow.

It's generally easier to scale the image duration to fit the music. Here's how:

1. Pick a piece of music of about the right length for your slideshow.

2. Open the music file in QuickTime Player; this creates an audio movie with a sound track (or a music track if you opened a MIDI file).

3. Open the slideshow in QuickTime Player. Select All. Copy.

4. Click in the audio movie. Select All. Add Scaled.

5. Save as a self-contained movie.

That's it. You now have a slideshow synchronized to your audio. The duration of the slides has been scaled to exactly match the music. The slideshow can be made either longer or shorter this way. If the slides have different durations, their durations are scaled so their length relative to each other remains the same.

You can use this same technique to add a single image to an audio-only movie, so your MP3 includes a picture of the musicians, for example. A single GIF or JPEG doesn't add much bandwidth to your audio files, but it adds a visual kick that most music sites don't have. Add a series of slides and you've got low-bandwidth MTV.

Trimming the music to match the slides is harder. You can take the music and use Add Scaled to make it fit the slides, but that makes the music play either faster or slower, which is probably not what you want.

The only real option for making the music longer is to copy some of it and paste it into the middle or onto the end. Obviously, this works better with some kinds of music than with others.

You can make a piece of music shorter simply by cutting off the end. The problem is that you tend to create an abrupt finish. You can improve on this by opening the music file in an audio editing (or MIDI sequencing) program and fading the last few seconds gradually to silence.

Cutting the end off a piece of music, or pasting on a little extra, makes the music close to the length you want, but it's hard to get an exact fit to the video that way. Once you're close, you can either scale the video to match the audio, as described previously, or you can trim the audio to exactly match the video.

Here's how to exactly trim the audio:

1. Open the slideshow. Select All. Copy.

2. Open the music file in QuickTime Player. Move the Time slider to zero. Choose Select None from the Edit menu.

3. Choose Add from the Edit menu. This adds the video to the audio. The part of the movie that has both audio *and* video is selected.

4. Choose Trim. This trims the movie to just the part that's selected. Any extra audio is deleted.

You can use Add Scaled to make something shorter or longer, but you can use Trim only to make something shorter.

If the audio is a little too short, you can trim the video to match. Follow the steps above, but add the audio to the video before you choose Trim. The Trim command removes the unselected part of the movie, and whatever you add is automatically selected; so add whatever is shorter, audio or video, to whatever is longer.

If you fit the video to the audio using Add Scaled, the duration of every slide is changed proportionally; if you use Trim, the end of the video is cut off, but the rest is unchanged.

Sound Effects

Adding a sound effect to part of a slideshow is easy.

1. Open the sound file in QuickTime Player, Select All, and choose Copy.

2. Open the slideshow and click the image you want the sound effect added to.

3. Adjust the position indicator in the Time slider if you want to add the sound effect before or after the image first appears.

4. Choose Add.

5. Save as a self-contained movie.

You're done.

Voice-Over or Narration

A slideshow with a narration is a very effective way to deliver information. In the boardroom or at the university, that's how it's done. Using still images and Qualcomm-compressed voice, you can deliver information the same way over the Web at data rates that will play in real time over dialup connections.

Typically, some slides contain a lot of information or stay on the screen while a lot gets said, while other slides are up for just a few seconds. You bring up a slide, say what you have to say, then go to the next. Creating this effect using LiveSlideShow is easy, and it's not hard to do in GoLive. Doing it with QuickTime Player takes a little more work. Here's how:

1. Begin by recording a narration for each slide. See "Recording for the Web" (page 225) for tips on recording a voice-over. Save the narration for each slide as a separate file. If your recording software can do it, add a half second fade-in from silence at the beginning and fade-out to silence at the end of each narration.

Tip If you're going to add transition effects, leave a second or two of silence at each end of the narration, so the sound tracks can overlap during the transitions without talking over each other.

2. Open a narration in QuickTime Player, open the corresponding image in another player window, copy the image, click in the narration movie, choose Select All, and Add Scaled. This creates a short movie that shows a single image for the whole narration. Do this for every slide.

3. Save these movies as you go, allowing dependencies. They take up only a few kilobytes each.

4. When you have every slide and its narration as a movie, create a new movie in QuickTime Player by choosing New in the File menu. Open

each small movie, select all, copy, close, and paste into the new movie. When all the slides are in the order you want, save as a self-contained movie.

When you create a slideshow using this technique, each slide in the final movie is in its own video track. If you added the slides in order, the first slide is Video Track 1, the second slide is Video Track 2, and so on. You can use Plug-in Helper to make each image into a hotspot to a different URL if you like.

If you want to consolidate all the images and narrations into one sound track and one video track, you can export the slideshow as a Quick-Time movie. Bear in mind that this will recompress the images. For details, see "Determining the Number of Video Tracks" (page 265).

▶ Adding URL Links

You can wire a slideshow so that a URL loads when the viewer clicks an image. The URL can be a Web page, a JavaScript function, or a QuickTime movie, and you can target the URL to load in a particular browser frame or window, to load in QuickTime Player, or to replace the current slideshow in the browser plug-in.

The easiest way to add a URL is to use an HREF parameter in the <EMBED> tag. This creates a single link for the whole movie. This technique is described in Chapter 5, "Special Delivery: QuickTime + HTML."

You can also incorporate URLs in the slideshow itself, using Plug-in Helper. This lets you create links that work even if your movie is played in QuickTime Player or in someone else's Web page. You can add a single link for the whole slideshow this way, or you can create links for individual video tracks. If you created the slideshow by pasting together individual images with sound tracks, each image will be in a separate video track and can have its own link. Adding links with Plug-in Helper is described in "Plug-in Helper" (page 87).

You can also add a series of URL links to your slideshow by creating an HREF track, as described in Chapter 13, "Text! Text! Text!" Other ways to add links and actions to your images are described in Chapter 16, "Getting Interactive." Be sure to check the section "Interactive Tools Galore" (page 489). Lots of cool new stuff.

Determining the Number of Video Tracks

If all the images are imported using Open Image Sequence, this creates a QuickTime movie with a single video track. Rearranging slides by cutting and pasting doesn't change this.

When you cut and paste from different movies, however, QuickTime Player may create a new video track any time you paste—usually when you add an image with different dimensions or compression format, or if you paste something with more than one track (such as a slide with a sound track). You may want to keep these as multiple video tracks, or you may prefer to consolidate them.

If you have multiple tracks, you can use Plug-in Helper to assign a different URL to each track, which could be convenient if you're using the slideshow to create click-through advertisements with multiple destinations.

To see if you have multiple video tracks, choose Get Movie Properties from the Movie menu and check the left pop-up menu. It will either show a single selection named Video Track or a series of choices named Video Track 1, Video Track 2, and so on.

Single video track

Multiple video tracks

You can combine multiple video tracks into one by exporting the image sequence to video—choose Export from the File menu, then choose Movie to QuickTime Movie. To choose a compressor, click the Options button, then the Settings button under Video.

If you export the images to video, QuickTime recompresses all the images using the same compressor. Choosing the right compressor is critical for maintaining image quality.

If your original images are GIFs, the compressor that's most similar is the Graphics compressor. Use the Best quality setting with no key frames or specified frame rate.

For JPEG images, choose the Photo JPEG compressor. Use the Best quality, Best frame rate, and Best key frames settings.

When you export to video, you have to choose a frame rate. Choose the lowest frame rate compatible with all your slides. Use 0.2 for a series of slides that are 5 seconds long, for example. If the slides have different durations, use the lowest frame rate that works, such as 1 (rounds frame durations to the nearest second). Note that a frame rate of 1 frame per second sends a copy of the image every second, even if it doesn't change. Some compressors do this very efficiently, however.

If you don't want to recompress the images or set a fixed frame rate, you can either keep the images in separate tracks or reimport them into a single track from the original sources using Open Image Sequence. Generally speaking, there's no compelling reason to consolidate your video tracks.

Note Most movie-editing programs let you visually lay out tracks on a timeline so you can add or rearrange images without creating new tracks. Not all programs provide the option of saving as a QuickTime movie without recompressing the images and setting a fixed frame rate, however. That's one advantage of using QuickTime Player.

Putting It on the Page

Add your slideshow to a Web page using the <EMBED> tag. Position it on the page just as you would a JPEG or a GIF, but use the <EMBED> tag instead of the <IMG> tag.

Here's the HTML for a slideshow that plays like an animated GIF, starting automatically and looping endlessly without a controller:

```
<EMBED SRC="SlideShow.mov" HEIGHT="240" WIDTH="320"
  AUTOPLAY="True" LOOP="True" CONTROLLER="False">
```

Set the SRC, HEIGHT, and WIDTH parameters to your movie's actual filename, height, and width. To add a controller that lets the viewer start, stop, and skip around, delete the CONTROLLER="False" parameter and add 16 to the HEIGHT.

Here's the HTML for a slideshow that plays once automatically and has a controller:

```
<EMBED SRC="SlideShow.mov" HEIGHT="256" WIDTH="320"
   AUTOPLAY="True">
```

Like any QuickTime movie, a slideshow can be opened from a poster movie, targeted to a frame or QuickTime Player (which can open it in full-screen mode), or used in a group of alternate movies. Slideshows make particularly good fallback movies for viewers with slow Internet connections. See Chapter 5, "Special Delivery: QuickTime + HTML," and Chapter 8, "Alternate Realities: Language, Speed, and Connections," for details.

▶ Adding a Still Image as a Movie Background

You can use a still image as a background in a movie, and there are good reasons for doing so. You can send the background image to the viewer just once, instead of once for each video frame; QuickTime composites the rest of the movie over the background as the movie plays, using no additional bandwidth.

A background image also adds a nice touch when the credits are rolling. Or it can tie together the different elements of a multimedia presentation. It can also be used to create a larger canvas for your other images. It really gives you a lot of bang for the bandwidth.

Adding a background image is easy:

1. Open the image you want to add as a background using QuickTime Player. Select All. Copy. Close. (Don't save.)

2. Open the movie you want to add the background to. Select the part of the movie timeline you want a background for—the credits, for example, or the whole movie.

3. Choose Add Scaled from the Edit menu. This adds the image as a new video track. It has the duration of whatever part of the movie you selected. The image initially appears superimposed on the movie, aligned in the upper-left corner. If the image is taller or wider than the movie's display area, the display area grows to accommodate it.

4. Choose Get Movie Properties from the Movie menu. Choose the new video track from the left pop-up menu (it will be the last video track on the list), and choose Layer from the right pop-up menu:

5. Increment the layer number until the image is in the background.

6. If you want to scale the image, rotate it, skew it, or move it around in the movie's display area, choose Size in the right pop-up menu, click Adjust, and mess with it until you're happy.

7. To reposition the other movie elements on top of the background, choose the track you want to reposition (using the left pop-up menu), choose Size in the right pop-up menu, click Adjust, and drag it where you want it.

8. Save the result as a self-contained movie.

If you export the movie, rather than saving it, QuickTime composites all the visual elements of the movie into a single video track. This typically results in a much higher data rate for the background image because it becomes part of every frame. If the video track is compressed, which it normally is, this can also blur the compositing of background and foreground. For best results, add the background image as a separate track *after* performing any necessary export, so that the image is sent only once and the compositing is done at runtime on the viewer's computer.

You can make the tracks on top of your background image translucent or partly transparent, as described in "Transparency and Alpha Channels" (page 271).

Two examples of movies with background images can be found on the CD in the Images folder:

- `Backtext.mov` contains scrolling text over a background image. Because the image is sent only once, and the text is rendered and composited by the viewer's computer, the data rate for this movie is only a few hundred *bits* per second. It plays in real time over a 9600 baud modem!

- `Widget.mov` uses a single background image to tie together a series of slides with a talking-head movie, as shown in the following illustration.

Adding a Logo to a Movie

You've probably noticed the network logos superimposed on the corner of your television screen. Aren't they annoying? Now *you* can create the same effect! You can brand QuickTime movies with your personal logo. Here's how:

1. Make a digital image of your logo that's approximately the right size. Somewhat too big is better than too small. Suitable image formats include PICT, GIF, Photoshop, and Flash.

Note If you want part of the image to be transparent or translucent, you may want to create the image with an alpha channel or with a single color used only for the transparent parts. You can also use a GIF with transparent areas. See "Transparency and Alpha Channels" (page 271).

2. Open the logo image in QuickTime Player. Select All. Copy. Close.

3. Open the movie you want to brand with your logo. Select the part of your movie timeline where you want your logo to appear.

4. Choose Add Scaled. This adds a video track with your logo to the upper left corner of the movie for the duration of the selection.

5. Choose Get Movie Properties from the Movie menu. Choose the new video track from the left pop-up menu, and choose Size in the right pop-up menu. Click Adjust. Red handles will appear on your logo.

6. Click any part of your logo except the red handles. If your logo is so small the handles overlap, choose Double Size or Fill Screen in the Movie menu to make the image larger. Drag the logo to the lower right corner of the display area, or wherever you want it. You can move it in one-pixel increments using the arrow keys.

7. Drag the red handles in the corners to stretch or shrink your logo if you need to. You can rotate or skew it this way if you like.

8. Click Done.

9. If you want part of the image to be transparent or translucent, choose Graphics Mode from the right pop-up menu. You'll see a list of graphics modes available. See "Transparency and Alpha Channels" (page 271) for an explanation of the graphic modes.

10. Save as a self-contained movie.

You probably don't want people who watch your movie to be able to remove your logo. There are three ways to prevent this.

If you disallow saving the movie using Plug-in Helper, no one can edit it. Even if they manage to copy the file, it will always have your logo. You might also want to add a Track URL to the logo's video track using Plug-in Helper, so clicking on your logo always takes the viewer to the website of your choosing.

If you export your movie using Movie to QuickTime Movie, all the video tracks are composited together, making your logo an inextricable part of the image rather than a separate track that could potentially be deleted. This usually increases the movie's bandwidth requirements, however, and may reduce the image quality as well.

If you put your movie on a streaming server, rather than a Web server, people can watch your movie but can't download it or edit it. You can either make your logo part of the video stream, which has the advantages and disadvantages of blending the video and logo into a single track, or you can deliver the logo as part of a Fast Start movie, composited over the video stream at runtime, as described in Chapter 17, "Mixing It Up: Streaming and Nonstreaming."

If you use the pro version of the Sorenson 3 codec to compress your streamed video, you can also use Sorenson's watermark feature to add a logo—this effectively allows you to send the logo as a separate video track while delivering the whole movie from a streaming server.

Transparency and Alpha Channels

When one visual track overlaps another in a QuickTime movie, they can interact in different ways. The default behavior is for the image on top to cover the image underneath, with the most recently added track on top. This is a fine way to add a Picture In Picture (PIP) effect, as long as the image on top is smaller than the image underneath.

You can change which track is on top by changing the track's layer number. Open the QuickTime Player movie properties window, choose the track from the left pop-up menu, and choose Layer from the right pop-up menu. The smallest layer number goes on top; negative numbers are fine.

You can also change the way the images are composited, so that the image on top is partly transparent or translucent. You control this behavior by setting the graphics mode of the track on top. To change a track's graphics mode, choose the track from the left pop-up menu, and choose Graphics Mode from the right pop-up menu.

Graphics Modes

QuickTime supports several different graphic modes: copy, dither copy, transparent, blend, and four alpha channel modes (straight, blend, premul white, and premul black). Here's a rundown of each mode and what it's good for.

Copy and Dither Copy

The copy and dither copy modes have no transparency or translucence. The image on top just covers the image underneath.

Important Transparent GIFs are an exception. If your image is a GIF, any transparent areas remain transparent in copy and dither copy modes.

The dither copy mode adjusts the color of adjacent pixels so they approximate the image color when the display is set to a lower bit depth, typically when an image with millions of colors is viewed on a 256-color display. This is normally the mode you want. To use higher-quality error-diffusion dithering (better, but slower), use dither copy mode and enable high quality (choose High Quality from the right pop-up menu and click the High Quality Enabled checkbox).

For line art or areas of solid color, you might prefer a less accurate color to the mottled look that dithering can create. In that case, choose copy mode instead of dither copy.

Blend

With blend mode you can control the degree of transparency for each color channel, but it applies to the whole image.

Blend mode makes the whole image partially transparent, or translucent. It can apply a separate degree of transparency to each color channel (R, G, B), giving a tint to the image. You control both the degree of transparency and any tint by choosing a control color. A darker control color makes the image more transparent, while a lighter color makes it more opaque—black makes your image invisible, white makes it solid. To apply transparency to all color channels evenly, use any shade of gray (equal values for R, G, B) as the control color.

If you set the control color using HSV values, the Hue and Saturation settings control the color of the tint while the Value or brightness setting controls the transparency. To make the image translucent without applying a tint, set the Hue Angle and Saturation both to zero to select a shade of gray.

Transparent

With transparent mode you can control what part of the image is transparent but not the degree of transparency.

Transparent mode makes one color in the track transparent. Any areas of that exact color become completely transparent. This works well for images on a solid color background, as long as the background color is used *only* for the background. If your image is a GIF with transparent areas, you don't need to use transparent graphics mode; copy or dither copy works fine. You can use transparent mode to make one of the GIF's *other* colors transparent, however.

This mode is less useful for JPEGs or images with smoothly changing or dithered colors.

If your image includes text, and you want the text or its background to be transparent, you get better results if you don't anti-alias the text. Anti-aliasing blends the color of the text and the background to make the text appear smoother, so some parts of the text and background are no longer the original color and are not transparent.

Tip If your image is just text, in a QuickTime text track, don't use transparent mode. Use dither copy, and set the text track to Keyed Text. For details, see Chapter 13, "Text! Text! Text!"

Alpha

The four alpha modes allow you to set the degree of transparency for each pixel in the image independently, but the image must already have an alpha channel.

If your image has an alpha channel, you can use it to control the areas and degree of transparency. Use a graphics program such as Photoshop or After Effects to mask out the areas you want transparent, create an alpha channel, and set the degree of transparency for each pixel.

Use straight alpha mode for most images. Use premul white alpha or premul black alpha for images created on a white or black background with a premultiplied alpha channel value. A common method of adding an alpha channel to an image is to feather a selection on a white background in Photoshop—this results in an image that works best with premul white graphics mode.

The straight alpha blend mode mixes the effect of the straight alpha and blend modes. The alpha channel creates areas and degrees of transparency, the entire image has an additional translucence controlled by the Value or Lightness of the control color, and the Hue and Saturation of the control color are applied to the image as a tint.

QuickTime can import images that include alpha channels in three different formats: Photoshop, PNG, and TIFF. Alpha channels in JPEGs are not supported.

If you compress the video track, the alpha channel is preserved *only* if you use a compressor that supports millions+ colors (32-bit color). Millions+ means millions of colors (24-bit) plus an alpha channel. Currently, the QuickTime compressors that support millions+ colors are Animation, None, Planar RGB, PNG, TGA, and TIFF.

What Exactly Is an Alpha Channel?

This won't be on the test, so feel free to skip ahead.

Images and Channels

Images are commonly stored as an array of pixels. Each pixel has a value. If the image uses an RGB color model, separate values are stored for the red, green, and blue in each pixel; 24-bit color usually means 8 bits of red, 8 bits of green, and 8 bits of blue.

For some operations, such as printing color separations, it's convenient to treat each color value independently. Many graphics programs allow you to break out the red, green, and blue values as three independent channels, often called the R channel, G channel, and B channel. For 32-bit color, a fourth 8-bit channel is added that defines transparency. It's called an alpha channel.

If you look at it by itself, an alpha channel is an 8-bit grayscale image that acts as a mask. This mask is applied to the image defined by the RGB channels. Where the alpha channel is black, the image is transparent. Where the alpha channel is white, the image is opaque. Where the alpha channel is gray, the image is translucent.

Compositing with Alpha Channels

Transparency makes sense only in the context of a background—something that shows through the transparent parts. An image with an alpha channel is meant to be composited over a background.

Consequently, the alpha channel is applied to the image to determine how much to leave out and is also applied to the background to determine how much shows through. The two are then added together to create a composite image.

The Math

The alpha channel defines the degree of transparency. Think of transparency as having a value from 0 to 1, with 0 being completely transparent and 1 being completely opaque. Think of the alpha channel values as ranging from 0/255, or 0, to 255/255, or 1.

If you multiply the RGB values by the alpha channel values, completely transparent areas are multiplied by 0 (become 0), completely opaque areas are multiplied by 1 (are unchanged), and partly transparent areas are multiplied by a fraction (are attenuated).

To determine how much of the background to use, the RGB values of the background are multiplied by (1 – alpha). This leaves the background unchanged where the image is transparent, reduces the background value to 0 where the image is opaque, and attenuates the background proportionally in partially opaque areas.

The composite image is created by multiplying the top image by alpha, multiplying the bottom image by (1 – alpha), and adding the two together:

$rgbComposite = (alpha * rgbImage) + ((1 – alpha) * rgbBackground)$

Premultiplied Alpha

Since we know we're going to composite the image by multiplying the RGB values times the alpha values, we could save some time by doing that calculation in advance. We could then modify the original image by replacing the RGB values with the RGB values *premultiplied* by the alpha values. Compositing then gets simpler:

$rgbComposite = premulImage + ((1 - alpha) * rgbBackground)$

It's faster to composite premultiplied alpha images because you don't have to perform the multiplication at runtime. The disadvantage is that the image's RGB information has been changed, so if it's *not* composited over a background, the transparent areas become black.

There's another reason to use premultiplied alpha. You can use one alpha value to premultiply the original image, then modify the alpha channel so that different values are used to composite the background. You might do this to capture the highlight on a sheet of glass, for example: Almost all of the background comes through (transparent alpha), but a lot of the original image is superimposed (opaque alpha). This particular trick is performed by some ray-tracing software.

Premul White and Premul Black

Graphics programs that create premultiplied alpha images, such as Adobe After Effects, usually perform anti-aliasing as well. Anti-aliasing smoothes the outlines of an image by mixing some of the background color into the edges. If you use an alpha channel to make the background transparent, some of the original background color remains, mixed into the edges of the image. If you then composite the image onto a different background, it has a vague halo of the original background color.

If you're creating an image in a program that uses premultiplied alpha, use a black background or a white background and set the QuickTime graphics mode to premul white alpha or premul black alpha to compensate. This eliminates the halo.

▶ Color and Gamma

Images are brighter on Macintosh computers than on Windows machines. In addition, some people can see only 256 colors on their computers, while others can see thousands or millions. For that matter, plenty of people who *could* see millions of colors have never found the right control panel and are stuck at 256. When you put your images on the Web, they're seen by all these people.

As a consequence, you need to view your images on both a Mac and a Windows computer, or at least on a Mac with gamma correction On (Mac standard) and Off (Windows standard), and adjust your image brightness so it doesn't look horrible on either. You may be able to change your gamma correction using the Monitors control panel.

Similarly, you should view your images at 24 or 32 bits (millions of colors), 16 bits (thousands of colors), and 8 bits (256 colors), adjusting the color so it's at least bearable at 256.

Popular Image Formats

- **BMP**

  BMP is a format for bitmapped images on Windows computers. Images in BMP format may be compressed using a variety of compression algorithms. BMP images created by QuickTime are uncompressed.

  A BMP image can be grayscale or color. Color depths of 8, 16, and 24 bits are supported.

  Uncompressed BMP images are large compared to images in compressed format. Images created in BMP format by QuickTime are lossless because they are uncompressed.

  Most browsers require a plug-in to display BMP images.

  The BMP format is well-suited for transporting bitmapped images of all kinds, provided that file size and bandwidth are of no concern. The BMP format is often the lowest common denominator for image transfers on Windows.

- **GIF**

  Graphic Interchange Format is a ubiquitous Web graphics format developed by CompuServe. GIF is both a file format and a compression format.

  A GIF image can contain a maximum of 256 colors (8-bit color, also known as indexed color). The system color palette can be used, or the GIF can contain a custom palette of up to 256 colors.

  A GIF that uses less than 256 colors can sometimes be compressed using fewer bits per pixel. If the GIF uses 128 colors or less, for example, 7-bit color can be used. A GIF with 64 colors or less can use 6-bit color, and so on. The most efficient packing is achieved when the number of colors used is a power of two and is exactly represented by 8-bit, 4-bit, 2-bit, or 1-bit color.

In addition to colored pixels, a GIF can contain transparent pixels. Contrary to popular belief, one color is not "designated" as transparent; transparent pixels have a noncolor value inside the GIF. Some graphics editors allow the user to change pixels with a particular color value into transparent pixels.

GIF files may contain multiple images, each with an assigned duration. These are called animated GIFs. Subsequent images can be further compressed by reusing areas from previous images in the same file.

Browsers can typically display GIFs without using a plug-in. Most browsers support animated GIFs, but cannot animate a GIF used as a background image.

GIFs are compressed using the LZW compression algorithm. This is a lossless compressor; the image after compression and decompression is identical to the original. The image can be compressed and decompressed multiple times without degrading quality.

If an image contains more than 256 colors, it must be converted to 256 colors before it can be made into a GIF. In Photoshop, for example, an image in RGB color must be converted to indexed color before it can be saved as a GIF. This conversion can severely degrade image quality, so in this sense GIF compression is not always lossless. Once the initial conversion to 256 colors is made, however, GIF compression does not cause any further loss.

GIF compression is most efficient with large areas of uniform color. If an image is captured using a scanner, what appear to be areas of uniform color may actually be subtly different shades of color, or a dithered pattern. For optimal GIF compression, use a graphics editor to select these areas and fill them with a single color.

GIF compression preserves sharp edges. It is well suited to images that contain text and graphics and use less than 256 colors. GIF compression is poorly suited to photographic images that contain continuous color gradients or more than 256 colors.

The owners of the patent on LZW compressions used in GIF have requested license fees for using their algorithm. Consequently, GIF is becoming less popular and will probably be replaced by the PNG format over time. QuickTime can read and display GIF images, convert

GIF images to other formats, and save already-compressed GIF images as part of QuickTime movies, but it does not export to GIF from other formats.

- **JPEG**

  Joint Photographic Experts Group images are also a ubiquitous Web format. The JPEG format is both a file format and a compression format.

  JPEG images can use 16-bit color (thousands of colors) or 24-bit color (millions of colors). They can also include an alpha channel, but this is not used by QuickTime.

  Two variants are progressive JPEG, which provides a low-resolution preview while the main image downloads, and lossless JPEG (JPEG-LS). QuickTime can display progressive JPEGs, but not lossless JPEGs.

  Browsers can typically display JPEGs without using a plug-in.

  JPEG compression is not lossless. It preserves the general color tone, but blurs edges and smears areas of similar color. Compressing images in JPEG format, decompressing them, then recompressing them, degrades quality sharply.

  JPEG compression is well suited to photographic images with smooth color gradients and thousands or millions of colors.

- **JPEG2000**

  JPEG2000 is a new standard that is just now being completed. It produces more accurate images at lower sizes than JPEG, using a form of wavelet compression. It has a number of new features, including the following:

  - Progressive download sends a low-resolution copy of the image that becomes progressively more detailed.
  - For low-bit-rate connections or low-resolution displays, the download can be terminated at the desired data size or image resolution.
  - Nonlinear access to parts of the image file allow you to examine part of the image in greater detail without downloading the whole image at that resolution.
  - Improves on JPEG's handling of sharp edges, solid colors, and text, yielding sharper imagery at lower data rates than JPEG or GIF.
  - Supports multiple compression schemes, including lossless compression.
  - Supports multiple color depths and color spaces (including RGB and CMYK).

- Supports descriptive tags with metadata inside the file for rapid searching and indexing.

QuickTime 6 can open and display JPEG2000 files on Mac OS X. It does not currently provide access to the metadata tags. This is very much a work in progress.

- **PDF**

  Adobe's Portable Document Format (PDF) is widely used on the Web and elsewhere to distribute electronic copies of documents. Adobe provides free PDF readers for Windows, Macintosh, and other operating systems.

  PDF provides very accurate representation of printed material and incorporates text, including embedded fonts, and images in EPS format. It is largely based on PostScript.

  Mac OS X includes PostScript rendering as a service to all applications, including QuickTime. QuickTime 6 and later for Mac OS X include the ability to read and write PDF files. Each page in a PDF document is treated as a video frame with PDF compression. This is currently a Mac-only feature.

Note Because PDF creation and rendering is available to QuickTime for "free," as a system service of Mac OS X, it is less likely that PDF import and playback will soon become available in QuickTime for Windows.

- **PICT**

  PICT files are widespread on Macintosh computers. Any computer with QuickTime, and any Macintosh computer, can display images from PICT files. PICT files can contain bitmap images, vector graphics, text and font information, or a combination of these data types. PICT is a file format that supports multiple compression formats.

  Bitmapped images may be in black-and-white, grayscale, or color. Color depths from 2 to 24 bits are supported. Alpha channels (32-bit color) are also supported. Bitmapped images can be compressed using a wide variety of codecs, including any of the standard QuickTime codecs.

  Vector graphics are stored as QuickDraw instructions. QuickDraw is the native graphics engine for Macintosh computers. QuickTime for Windows includes the QuickDraw graphics engine. This storage format is compact, lossless, and scalable. Vector graphics include such objects as lines, circles, area fills, and patterns.

Text and font information are stored as ordinary text, along with descriptor tags that specify fonts, type sizes, and type styles such as bold and italic. This format is compact and lossless. If the specified font is not present on the viewer's computer, a similar font is substituted. This can cause major changes in the appearance of images, so careful font selection is important when using PICT format. Recommended cross-platform fonts are Times, Courier, and Helvetica (Arial may be substituted for Helvetica).

Browsers generally require a plug-in such as QuickTime to display PICT images.

PICT images are well suited for bitmapped images of all kinds, as they can be compressed with a variety of lossless or lossy codecs, and an optimal codec for the source material can usually be applied. PICT images are very well suited for line art and vector graphics because the compression is efficient, lossless, and scalable. PICT format is well suited to images that include text because text compression is lossless and requires very little data, but the selected fonts must be installed on the viewer's computer or the results are hard to predict.

■ **PNG**

The Portable Network Graphics format is increasingly common on the Web. It was created as a replacement for the GIF format that could be used without license fees. PNG is a file format that includes a compression specification.

PNG images can use 1-bit, 2-bit, 4-bit, and 8-bit color palettes (indexed color), just like GIF. PNG also supports 1-bit, 2-bit, 4-bit, 8-bit, and 16-bit grayscale images. Unlike GIF, 24-bit RGB color is also supported, as is 48-bit RGB colors (16 bits each for red, green, and blue). Alpha channels are supported, in both 8-bit and 16-bit depths. An efficient "palette-alpha" mode, effectively transforming the normal RGB palette into an RGBA palette, is also supported.

PNG images can include gamma correction information for cross-platform brightness control, and color correction for cross-platform precision color.

PNG does not include animated images, but a closely related format, MNG, does.

Most current browsers can display PNG images without a plug-in, including Internet Explorer and all Netscape browsers, versions 4.0 and later.

PNG compression is lossless and is typically from 5% to 50% more efficient than GIF compression for images with 256 or fewer colors. It is also lossless and efficient at compressing images with thousands or millions of colors, including images with alpha channels.

The PNG format is well suited to images with sharp edges, text, and large areas of solid color. It provides less compression than JPEG for most photographic images, but it is far more accurate. PNG is unusual in having a lossless compressor for alpha channels. PNG is well suited to images that are intended for the Web because it supports gamma correction.

- **TIFF**

  Tagged Image File Format is a common format for transferring bitmapped images from scanners to graphics editors, or between graphics application programs. TIFF is a file format that supports a few different compressors.

  TIFF images can use various color models, including grayscale and RGB color, with a variety of bit depths per color. Alpha channels are supported. Common image formats include 8-bit grayscale, 24-bit color, and 32-bit color (24-bit color plus an 8-bit alpha channel). TIFF was recently revised to include an efficient representation of fax images.

  Most TIFF images are either uncompressed or compressed using a lossless algorithm, such as RLE or LZW compression. The newer fax formats use a variety of bilevel compressions. QuickTime can currently import TIFF images in most of the common formats. QuickTime can export images to TIFF either uncompressed or using RLE compression.

  Most browsers require a plug-in to display TIFF images.

  Compressed TIFF images are well suited to fax images and graphics that contain large areas of continuous color or mixed text and graphics. TIFF format preserves photographic images accurately but usually does not compress them very much.

Just Like in the Movies

The most obvious way to use QuickTime on the Web is to put traditional movies—motion video and sound—on a Web page. It's easy to do, but it's hard to do well. In the first place, it's hard to make good movies. Hollywood spends millions of dollars on every production, focusing the efforts of hordes of people, and it creates expectations that are hard to meet. Meeting those expectations on the bandwidth budget of a 56K modem is, well, *really* hard.

That said, importing a movie into QuickTime, compressing it for delivery at a given speed, and putting it on a Web page are all pretty easy. The hardest part is creating a good movie in the first place. The second-hardest part is choosing the compressor settings that will look and sound the best. We'll cover the easy parts first, then give you some help with the hard parts.

This chapter describes

- importing movies from other formats
- putting movies on a Web page
- making movies for the Web
- digitizing and editing movies
- QuickTime effects
- video codecs and settings
- secrets of the Apple compressionist
- tools for capturing, editing, compositing, and compressing
- other popular video formats

▶ Importing Movies

Getting an existing movie into QuickTime format is dead easy. Just open it with QuickTime Player, choose Save As from the File menu, and save it as a self-contained movie with the .mov file extension.

This doesn't change the size, frame rate, or compression of the movie. To change some or all of these characteristics, see "Compressing Your Movie" (page 317).

There are a couple of caveats. If you open a movie compressed with a particular codec, that movie can play only on computers equipped with that codec. If it isn't available as a QuickTime codec, you need to recompress the movie so people with QuickTime can view it. And of course you need to have that codec on your own computer to see the movie.

There are roughly three categories of QuickTime codec:

- codecs Apple includes in the QuickTime download, such as Sorenson 3
- codecs from third parties that are available from Apple's servers, and that QuickTime will automatically offer to download when needed, such as Pulse 3D and Zoomify
- codecs the user must download from a third party without help from QuickTime, such as DivX

For example, if you open an AVI movie compressed with Cinepak, it just works. If you open an AVI movie compressed with On2 or ZyGoVideo, QuickTime offers to get the codec for you (if it isn't already installed). But if you try to open an AVI movie compressed using DivX, QuickTime just warns you that it can't play the movie (unless, of course, you've installed the DivX codec for QuickTime).

Most QuickTime components are in the same category for everyone, but there are exceptions. The Indeo codecs, for example, are common on Windows computers but not widespread in the Mac world, even though they're available for download. To open an .avi movie compressed with an Indeo codec, you may need to install the Indeo codec on your computer, but in some cases it will already be there.

Similarly, if your computer has a video capture card, it may have a special codec that uses that card's hardware. Computers that don't have that brand of card may not have that codec, or may have a software-only version of the codec that can't play movies nearly as well. For example, users without Avid cards probably don't have the Avid codec, and users without any graphics accelerator card have software-only Motion-JPEG codecs. If you digitize a movie using a video capture card, it's normally saved using the card's codec by default. You need to recompress the movie using a standard codec before it can be played smoothly, or at all, by everyone with QuickTime. The standard QuickTime codecs are listed in "Compressing Your Movie" (page 317).

In addition, QuickTime has limited support for MPEG-1 movies (.mpg). QuickTime can play MPEG-1 audio and video, but you can't copy, cut, or paste from or into MPEG-1 video (you can add additional tracks, but not modify the video sequence). In addition, if the movie has multiplexed MPEG-1 video and audio (layer 1 or layer 2), QuickTime saves only the video portion when you recompress. Currently, you need to demultiplex the MPEG-1 audio and video using a demux program, such as mgptx from sourceforge.net, before QuickTime Player can export them. Alternatively, you can export the audio to an AIFF or WAV file using a tool such as Proteron's Drop Decoder.

If your existing movie is in a format that QuickTime Player just can't open, you need to open it using another application and export it to a format that QuickTime can work with. For example, you can open movies in Microsoft ASF or WMV format using Discreet's Cleaner 5, then export them as QuickTime movies.

Note QuickTime can open, play, edit, and export movies compressed using the MPEG-4 video codec if the movies are in MPEG-4 file format (.mp4) or QuickTime File Format (.mov). QuickTime cannot open or play .wmv or .asf files using Microsoft's "MPEG4" codec.

▶ Putting Movies on the Web

In this section, we'll look at putting full-motion video movies on your website (as compared to slideshows or animated graphics). We'll focus on Fast Start movies in particular; the techniques for streaming movies are a little different, and we'll look at them in Chapter 14, "Gently down the Stream."

■ In General

The techniques for embedding a QuickTime movie in a Web page are covered in Chapter 4, "Basic Training: Putting QuickTime in a Web Page," and Chapter 5, "Special Delivery: QuickTime + HTML."

The basic HTML is simple:

```
<EMBED SRC="MyMovie.mov" HEIGHT="240" WIDTH="320">
```

Set SRC to your movie's name, plus any path. Set WIDTH to your movie's width, and set HEIGHT to your movie's height plus 16.

Add your favorite parameters for the browser and the plug-in, or target QuickTime Player in full-screen mode, or optionally wrap the <EMBED> tag in an <OBJECT> tagset, as described in Chapters 4 and 5.

- **Size Considerations**

Movies with motion video are usually large files. Uncompressed 640 x 480 video at 30 frames per second uses 27 *MB* per second. QuickTime movies for the Web are compressed, but they're still large. Make sure you have enough space on your Web server to hold all the movies you want to use. If your website is going on a CD-ROM, remember that 650 MB is all one disk can hold.

Large files take a long time to load, so you might want to put a poster movie on your Web page and download the movie only if the user requests it.

Poster movies and how to use them are described in "Using a Poster Movie" (page 53) and "Making a Poster Movie with Plug-in Helper" (page 92).

If you're planning to put multiple video movies on a single Web page, *always* use poster movies, or use one of the other techniques discussed in "Putting Multiple Movies on a Page" (page 109).

- **Bandwidth Considerations**

It's impossible to make large, high-quality, full-motion movies that can play in real time over a 56K modem. You really have three options:

- You can sacrifice image size, quality, and frame rate to get the data rate down to 56K.
- You can use whatever data rate you need to get good quality, and let people with slower connections wait.
- You can compress different versions of your movies, optimized for different bandwidth connections, and automatically send people the best version that can play as it downloads over their connection.

Compressing multiple versions of a movie takes time, and posting multiple versions uses disk space. But it makes a better experience for your audience. For details, see Chapter 8, "Alternate Realities: Language, Speed, and Connections."

If you use alternate movies, it's nice to include a way for people to download the high-bandwidth version, regardless of their connection speed. Some people are willing to wait to get your best. Why disappoint them?

For example, let's say you have a reference movie named `Master.mov` that points to three versions of your movie: `56k.mov`, `ISDN.mov`, and `T1.mov`. You can create one link to `Master.mov` and another link directly to `T1.mov`. If you use poster movies, your HTML might look something like this:

```
<TABLE>
   <TR>
      <TD> <-- link to alternate movie \-->
        Click below to see the movie that plays best
        over your Internet connection...<BR>
      <EMBED SRC="Poster1.mov" HEIGHT="240" WIDTH="320"
        CONTROLLER="False" HREF="Master.mov"
        TARGET="myself">
      </TD>
      <TD> <-- link to best movie \-->
        Click below to see the highest quality
        movie available (24 MBytes)...<BR>
      <EMBED SRC="Poster2.mov" HEIGHT="240" WIDTH="320"
        CONTROLLER="False" HREF="T1.mov" TARGET="myself">
      </TD>
   </TR>
</TABLE>
```

For an example, see `Choice.htm` in the Movies folder of the CD:

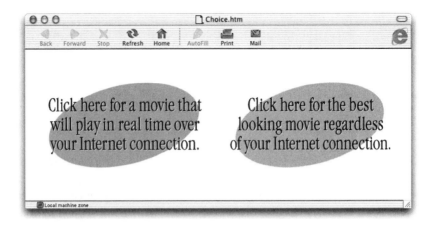

If you change the connection speed setting in your QuickTime Settings control panel, you see a different movie when you click the poster on the left. The poster on the right always loads the highest-bandwidth movie.

- **The Big Picture**

Putting full-motion video on the Web means serious compression, typically with the Sorenson 3 or MPEG-4 Video codec. In the process of compressing the movie, you usually end up with an image that's smaller than you'd like. Fortunately, images compressed with Sorenson 3 and other new-generation compressors, such as MPEG-4, scale up pretty nicely.

If your movie is playing in the plug-in, try adding SCALE=2 to the <EMBED> tag. Change the HEIGHT and WIDTH settings to twice your movie's height and width, adding 16 to the height for the movie controller.

If your movie is targeted to QuickTime Player, open it in QuickTime Player before you upload it to your Web server, choose Double Size from the Movie menu, and save. It plays back at double size, even over the Web.

Because this kind of scaling is done on the viewer's computer, it allows you to send an image of given pixel dimensions at one-quarter the data rate of an unscaled image with the same dimensions.

Tip If doubling the size makes the image blurry or pixelated, try setting SCALE=1.5 or SCALE=1.25. For QuickTime Player, drag the movie to a larger size and set to full-screen mode at Current Size. For details, see "Full-Screen Movies" (page 106).

- **Using the Whole Screen**

For the maximum cinematic experience, you want your movie to play on a black background with no browser, no movie controller, and no other distractions. To see what this looks like, open your movie in QuickTime Player and choose Present Movie from the Movie menu. You can watch your movie at its normal size, current size, half size, double size, or scaled to fill the screen. Press the Esc key if you want to get back to your desktop before the movie ends.

You can play full-screen movies over the Internet by targeting QuickTime Player from your Web page and setting full-screen mode. You can accomplish this in a number of ways—by setting full-screen mode in the movie itself, by adding a sprite with a full-screen action, or by wrapping the URL of any movie in a SMIL presentation or a three-line XML file. All this is discussed in detail in "Full-Screen Movies" (page 106).

You don't ordinarily want to take over the viewer's whole screen unexpectedly though, especially with no visible user interface. If you launch a movie in full-screen mode, open it from a poster movie and include a warning on your Web page. For an example, see Present.htm in the Movies folder of the CD.

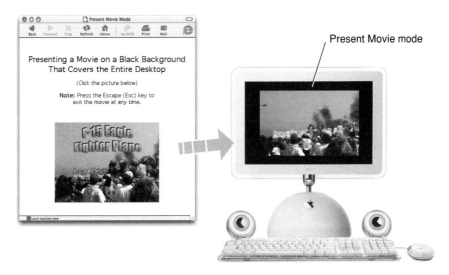

Clicking the poster movie plays the actual movie, which was saved in Present Movie mode.

Making Movies for the Web

A complete tutorial on making motion pictures is *way* outside the scope of this book, but here are some tips on creating movies specifically for the Web.

Note This section is aimed at people who are trying to put professional-quality video on the Web. If you want to put up a video of your kids, wedding, or vacation for friends and relatives to enjoy, reading this section will give you some valuable tips—but you don't need to take them all that seriously. Your mom is going to love it anyway.

■ **Start with the Best Stuff**

Many people think that movies shot for the Web don't need high production values, since they're going to get squashed anyway. Many people are dead wrong. Squashing movies for the Web lowers quality rapidly, so you need to start with a level of quality that's very high, or you'll impact the zero-quality barrier long before your movie is ready for the Web.

Use the best camera, best lighting, and best sound equipment you can afford. Seriously consider having your movie shot by professionals, then editing and compressing it yourself. If you do it all yourself, get help or advice from people experienced in lighting and sound. You won't regret it.

- **Plan**

  It's amazing how many people decide to start a video shoot by setting up a camera or hiring a video crew. As a rule, this becomes an expensive lesson in what not to do.

  Write a script and do a storyboard before you start shooting. If you don't know what a storyboard is, find out.

  Decide how you're delivering the movie: Fast Start for the Web, streaming, CD, DVD, or some combination. Let that final destination guide your decision making.

  Pick your delivery tool: a browser and plug-in, QuickTime Player, Macromedia Director, Tribeworks iShell, or some combination.

  Do a trial run. Shoot a minute of video that approximates your content. Digitize or transfer it to your computer. Run it through your editing tool. Compress it. Embed it in your delivery medium, such as a Web page or a Director project. Put it on a Web server or a CD-R and watch it on the slowest computer with the slowest CD or modem that you intend to support.

  If it doesn't meet your expectations, go back in the process and change things until it works. You may end up changing the lighting, moving the camera closer to the subject, using a different editor or compressor, or changing your mind about the delivery medium or the minimum system requirements. I guarantee that you'll learn important lessons at a relatively low cost.

- **Shoot High**

  If you can afford it, hire professionals to do your first few video shoots and carefully observe them. In any event, use the best equipment you can lay your hands on.

  The camera is important. If you shoot with an analog camera, you'll have to digitize the results. That costs money or reduces quality, usually both. A DigiBeta, DV, or Digital-8 camera captures digitally, so you can transfer the output directly to your computer. If you use a DV or Digital-8 camera, get one with a FireWire port (also known as Sony iLink or IEEE 1394).

The best results come from the best cameras:

- BetaSP, D1, or studio broadcast equipment gives the best results.
- Second best is a professional DV camera, one that shoots DVC-Pro or DV-Cam format. These cameras typically have three CCDs, one each for red, green, and blue. This gives you better color fidelity than the single CCD in a consumer camera.

Tip If you plan to shoot against a blue or green backdrop and matte in a background later, you need to use one of these high-end cameras to capture accurate-enough color information. You may want to hire a pro crew or rent the equipment; it's tricky.

- Consumer DV cameras shoot in mini-DV format, which is fine for anything except blue-screen or green-screen work.

Tip If your DV camera has an option for progressive or interlaced, use progressive.

- Digital-8 cameras typically have lower-resolution optics than mini-DV, but store the images digitally and produce the same format DV streams. Image quality is usually closer to Hi-8 than to mini-DV, but copying or transferring to a computer does not degrade quality.
- Consumer analog cameras produce inferior results, but are more affordable. Hi-8 is the least bad, S-VHS is not as good, and VHS is the worst. Copying or digitizing will degrade quality even further.
- USB cameras generally produce poor video quality. Avoid them if you have a choice. Direct-to-FireWire Webcams come in a broader range of quality, and some produce a good-enough image for streaming.

Good lighting is critical. Aim for balanced lighting and moderate contrast. Dim light is worse than overexposure for desktop video; compressors don't work well with murky scenes.

- **Think Compression**

  Shoot from a tripod. The fluid handheld camera look can be nice, but it compresses poorly. By the time it's compressed to the desktop, it's blocky and jerky.

  Minimize motion. Avoid panning and tracking shots. Talking heads look great on the desktop; panning images of rippling wheat look like noise.

- **Get Blurry**

  Use a slow shutter speed, about half your frame rate: shoot 24 fps film at a shutter speed of 1/48 second, and shoot 30 fps video at a shutter speed of 1/60 second. Adjust your lighting so this doesn't overexpose your footage.

  A slow shutter speed causes moving objects to blur slightly, but leaves unmoving objects sharp. Scenes shot this way are easier to compress. Films generally have more motion blur than video, so you may find this actually increases the perceived quality of your movie. It also lowers the movie's final data rate, and that *does* increase the quality you can deliver.

- **Background Check**

  Use a simple background with moderate contrast to your subject. Avoid bright colors, stripes, and checks. A plain wall is better than a bookcase or a window. It's generally best if the subject is lighter than the background.

  Especially avoid trees or foliage with moving leaves; they compress horribly, even at high data rates.

  If you have the equipment and the expertise, shoot against a green screen or a blue screen and use QuickTime's transparent video mode to make it transparent, as described in "Transparency and Alpha Channels" (page 271). Paste a single Photo-JPEG compressed image into the background for a scene or a whole movie, as described in "Adding a Still Image as a Movie Background" (page 267).

  This improves image quality while greatly reducing the movie data rate. It takes a good camera and very careful lighting to shoot green screen or blue screen; if you haven't done it before, get help.

- **Details, Details**

  Details compress poorly, so dress your subjects in solid colors. Be especially careful to avoid high-contrast stripes or checks. Compression can create bizarre artifacts from such patterns. White clothes can also create problems; a light color is generally better.

- **Listen Carefully**

  Use wireless remote microphones on your subjects or boom microphones handled by sound experts. Record to DAT if you can. Recording to the sound input of a camcorder can produce acceptable results, particularly with a DV camera. But don't use the camera's built-in microphone—connect the sound input to a real microphone.

⏵ Capturing and Digitizing Movies

Once you have a movie on tape, you need to get it into your computer in digital format. If the tape is in DV (or Digital-8) format, it's already digitized, but you still need to capture the movie onto your hard disk. If the tape is in analog format, you need to digitize it as well as capture it.

By far the most popular way to capture video is to compress it using the DV codec and transfer it to your computer over FireWire (also known as Sony iLink or IEEE 1394). This is a good and inexpensive format to work in for most purposes.

If you buy a FireWire card, it should come bundled with software to capture DV audio and video. If you have a Mac, you can use iMovie for this. If you have Windows XP, you can use Microsoft's Movie Maker 2. In either case, you can purchase additional editing software that includes DV capture over FireWire, such as Final Cut Pro or Final Cut Express, Adobe Premiere, or Avid Express.

You don't need a super-fast Ultra SCSI AV hard drive for capturing DV video. It's already compressed to about 5 MB/sec, so an ordinary 7200 rpm ATA or EIDE hard drive will work fine in most cases. You may drop frames if your disk is fragmented, however, and you will need lots of free space (about a gigabyte for every 5 minutes of video).

Tip It's a good idea to capture your video to a drive that's used only for that purpose. If there's room in your computer for another drive, throw one in there—they're cheap. Use it just to capture video, and erase the whole thing before each project. If there's no room inside, add an external FireWire drive. They're not so cheap, but the prices are dropping.

If you have a FireWire port and you're shooting with some kind of DV camera (such as mini-DV, Digital-8, or DVC-Pro), you're ready to go. If you need to, you can add a DV card to most computers for under $100.

If your video is in an analog format, such as VHS, the simplest thing to do is convert it to DV. There are three ways to do this: you can use a digital video camera, an external media converter, or a PCI card.

A mini-DV or Digital-8 camera with a video input can convert analog video to DV and put it on FireWire for you. If you already have a DV camera with a video input, this is the cheapest way to go (and it works just fine).

Note   In Europe, this feature is frequently disabled in the camera software for legal reasons. If this affects you, and you find it irritating, by all means write to your elected representatives and let them know.

Media converters, such as the Dazzle Hollywood DV Bridge, Pyro AV Link, Formac DV Studio A/D Converter, or Datavideo DAC 100, are external boxes that have composite, S-video, and stereo sound inputs and outputs, and one or two FireWire ports. They sell for around $200–300 currently, and they all work as advertised. The Formac media converter includes a television tuner for direct capture from on-air broadcast to DV on your FireWire port.

Tip   If you plan to include broadcast video captured off the air (or cable, or satellite), capture to DV is a good choice; there's very little quality loss, it's reasonably compact, and the captured data is ready for editing in almost any editor. This is much better than capturing to MPEG-2 if you plan to edit the captured video and/or recompress it.

An interesting variation is the Datavideo DAC2, which also has component input (YUV, or Betacam). This allows you to convert component or Betacam video to DV and capture it on your PC or Mac. You take a small but visible quality hit going from Betacam to DV format, but it generally looks better than mini-DV source, and much better than S-video or composite source.

Tip   Don't confuse component with composite—component has three inputs, one for each component of the signal, making it very clean; composite has a single input, a composite of all the signal parts, making it noisy and blurry. S-video separates the signal into two parts, chroma and luma—cleaner than composite's single input, but not as sharp as component's three. If you have a choice, use the best one available.

All these products capture 720 x 480 DV video at 29.97 fps. Some also do PAL encoding (720 x 525 at 25 fps), while others have separate PAL and NTSC versions.

This is a huge change from just a few years ago, when a card that would capture 720 x 480 video at 30 frames a second was a rare and expensive beast that required a top-of-the-line computer and dedicated RAID (multiple hard drives, striped to act as a single disk for maximum speed).

DV is a good format for video capture for another reason. There are tons of editing packages that work in DV format—iMovie, Final Cut Pro, Avid Express, DV Creator, Movie Maker 2; the list goes on and on. All Macs, all media converters, and most FireWire add-in cards include editing software that works with DV video.

There are a number of more expensive cards available that are bundled with high-powered editing and special-effect software (3D transitions, 3D text, and so on). Those around $500, such as the Matrox and Pinnacle cards, include real-time effect rendering.

Note That's not the same thing as QuickTime effects—these cards can render effects into DV video in real time for the author; QuickTime renders effects in real time to display on the viewer's screen, not to a DV file on the author's disk.

Still more expensive cards, in the $1000 range, such as the Canopus DV Storm, include the ability to composite multiple video inputs in real time (such as a blend between two cameras), color correction in real time, and fast MPEG-2 compression for DVD authoring.

Important Recently a number of cards and external boxes have come out that convert analog video directly into MPEG-2 format. Some have USB interfaces; others use FireWire or write directly to CD or DVD. These are *not* good choices for capturing video that you intend to edit or compress for the Web.

Some compressors provide high quality but little compression. These are sometimes called *transfer codecs,* and they're the ones you want to use for capturing video. Examples are Animation (set to Best quality and millions of colors), Component Video, DV, and Motion-JPEG. Other codecs, such as Cinepak and Sorenson, give high compression but sacrifice quality. These are called *delivery codecs.* Use them to compress your movie after you edit it; don't use them when capturing or editing video.

MPEG-2 is a good codec for final delivery of a movie at very high bandwidth (4–9 Mbits/sec). But you don't want to edit MPEG-2 video and recompress it. You really, really don't.

At the very high end, cards for capturing uncompressed video (or video compressed with little or no loss) from BetaSP and D1 source, cost, ahem, *over* $1000. These cards are primarily for broadcast professionals, and they do require dedicated RAID hardware and very fast computers (by today's standards). These bad boys use 10–30 MB of disk space per second. If you can afford this stuff, by all means use it. The rest of us will have to get along with DV.

Regardless of your source, capture directly from the master tapes if possible, not from a copy. Specifically, don't dub a "rough cut" edit to tape and digitize that; use the original. Analog copies smear, and digital tape, especially mini-DV tape, suffers flaking and digital dropouts with repeated playback—get it while it's fresh.

If the original material is on film, transfer it to the highest-quality video format you can capture: D1, BetaSP, DV (pro format), mini-DV (consumer format), Hi-8, S-VHS, or VHS, in decreasing order of preference. If the film is shot with a wider aspect ratio than the video standard of 4:3, transfer to video in letterbox format. QuickTime can crop out the black bars later and present the movie in its original aspect ratio.

Once your source video is digitized and captured, you're ready to deinterlace it or do an inverse telecine to remove the 2:3 pull-down.

What, you may ask, do "deinterlace" and "inverse telecine" mean? And what in heaven is a 2:3 pull-down?

I'm so glad you asked.

Interlaced Video and Telecine

You can divide a video frame into horizontal stripes 1 pixel tall. These stripes are called scan lines, and NTSC video has 480 of them. You can group these scan lines into two fields. Each field contains either the even or odd scan lines, so each field has a copy of the frame as seen through venetian blinds. An NTSC video frame consists of two fields, broadcast separately, so 30-frame-per-second broadcast video sends 60 fields per second. On a television set, each field persists on the screen while the next one is being drawn, and the two blend together smoothly.

If both fields are shot at the same instant, they're just the even and odd scan lines of a picture—this is called progressive scan, and it's how film is generally stored on a video DVD. It makes sharp still images. It also requires a camera that can capture at full-screen resolution.

If the two fields are shot 1/60th of a second apart, the even and odd scan lines are really from two different pictures, unless the camera and the subject are perfectly still. This is called interlaced video, and it's what you see on TV. It allows a camera with half the vertical resolution to do the shooting. It also causes "motion blur" when anything moves, and this can make the image look especially bad when the movie is paused. This is one reason video imagery is not as crisp as film.

When film is transferred to video, the frames are broken into odd and even fields and interlaced. When the video plays, some of the video frames can contain odd and even fields from two adjacent movie frames. To fix this, you need to deinterlace the video. This ensures that every frame contains odd and even fields from the same original image, not from two successive images. You can do this using programs such as Adobe Premiere or Discreet Cleaner 5.

Your capture software may also include a deinterlace option, and some of the better DV cameras have a "progressive" option that captures in deinterlaced format. This can make a real difference.

As for inverse telecine, film is shot at 24 frames per second, and North American video (NTSC) is shot at 29.97 (call it 30 for this discussion). When film is transferred to video, extra frames are inserted to make up the difference. This is called telecine, or 2:3 pull-down.

If you have the appropriate software, you should do an inverse telecine for desktop video; the movie will look better and use less bandwidth if you restore it to 24 fps by deleting the duplicated frames. This is tricky. You need a program such as Premiere or Cleaner for this. You need to perform this step *before* you edit the video, or it may be impossible to determine which frames are duplicates.

European video (PAL) is shot at 25 fps. When film is transferred to PAL video, it plays a little speeded up (1 second shorter for every 24 seconds of film). Don't do inverse telecine on PAL video taken from film! Just set the frame rate back to 24 fps after you've digitized the video.

▶ Editing

After you capture your movie to disk, and before you compress it for delivery, you generally need to edit it. Editing involves rearranging your material, throwing away the unwanted parts, and sometimes adding material such as music.

Some editors also allow you to add transition effects and titles, and to composite material together using masks, overlays, and matte backgrounds. Most editors provide some of these features and leave the rest to specialized effects software such as Adobe After Effects or Boris FX.

We'll look at basic editing first and examine effects, titles, and compositing separately.

The pro version of QuickTime Player provides basic editing capability, but if you're doing a lot of editing you should get more sophisticated editing software as well. Actually, for most editing purposes, whatever software came with your computer or FireWire card (iMovie, for example) is more sophisticated than QuickTime Player. Many editors work only with a fixed aspect ratio or a fixed compression scheme, however—for example, iMovie works only with DV compression at 720 x 480 or 720 x 525. Similarly, video-oriented editors may not allow you to add QuickTime text,

MIDI, or effects tracks. Most video editors work at fixed frame rates as well.

Nevertheless, you probably want to do your primary video editing using a dedicated video editing program, especially if your footage is already in DV format. This section goes over the important steps of editing a Quick-Time movie for the Web and shows you how to accomplish them using QuickTime Player. But decide for yourself whether it makes more sense to perform a given step using QuickTime Player or another editor.

Tip If you're a Windows XP user, you can do DV editing in Movie Maker 2, then export to DV. This creates an AVI file with DV compression, which you can open using QuickTime Player. Once it's in QuickTime, you can do pretty much anything with it. (Well, anything in this book, at least. But that's a fair bit.)

QuickTime Player is like a Swiss army knife; it does a lot of different things, and sometimes it's the best tool for the job, but using QuickTime Player as your *only* tool is a little like building a house using only a Swiss army knife—interesting, but not the most productive use of your time.

Still, basic editing with QuickTime Player is pretty simple. Select the parts you don't want, hit the Delete key, and they're gone. To rearrange the order of things, select the part you want to move, choose Cut from the Edit menu, click the frame in the movie where you want to insert it, and choose Paste. The sound and video tracks are cut and pasted as a unit and stay synchronized.

Adding a sound effect or a music track is also fairly simple. Open the music or sound effect file using QuickTime Player, select as much as you want, choose Copy, click in the movie where you want the new sound to start, and choose Add. The sound is added as a new track.

Moving things in one track relative to another is harder. If you want to move the sound effect by a few frames, you need to delete its track, select the new starting point, and add it back in; you can't just slide it on a time-line the way you can in LiveStage, GoLive, or Final Cut Pro.

Some things are very hard in QuickTime Player. Suppose you add a sound track, then want to rearrange the video so the cuts come on the musical beats. You can't cut and paste just the video and dialog tracks, while leaving the music alone; the Cut and Paste commands affect all the tracks in a selected time segment. You have to delete the music track, cut sections from the rest, then add the sections to the music. You can synchronize the cuts to the music this way, but it's tedious. This kind of manipulation is difficult even with the right tool—don't do it with Quick-Time Player unless you're desperate.

When editing with QuickTime Player, save intermediate copies of your work as you go, using the Save command, or use Save As and allow dependencies. This consumes very little space and provides an extra level of undo, as well as cheap insurance against sudden power loss (Oops—sorry, man, did I unplug you?).

Cropping

When your basic editing is complete, and before you add any compositing, titles, or effects, you should crop your movie.

If your source material was film and you transferred to video in letterbox format, you want to crop off the black bars and return the movie to its original aspect ratio. This gives a more cinematic effect, and it lowers the movie's data rate as well. Television has a fixed aspect ratio, but QuickTime video doesn't. Why send millions of black bars over the Internet?

All video sources include overscan, and most add video noise to the bottom or left edge of the frame. Television screens don't display the full NTSC or PAL image size, so video includes material intended to bleed off the edges, and video noise on the edges doesn't show. Desktop video shows the whole image, and video compressors interpret noise as fine detail in constant motion. It not only looks bad, it soaks up a lot of bandwidth. Crop it off.

Your goal in cropping the video is twofold. You want to get rid of noise and unnecessary material, and you want to create a favorable height and width for compression. You can generally see what needs to be trimmed off, but it's a good idea to trim by about 5% to eliminate video noise you might not see—nearly identical colors look the same to us, but not to a compressor. Keep trimming until the height and width are both divisible by four. If you can, use a height and width divisible by 16; this is especially important if you plan to use the H.261 or H.263 compressor.

A good editing program or media preparation program, such as Adobe Premiere, Final Cut Pro, or Discreet Cleaner, includes an easy-to-use cropping function that lets you visually crop out the noise and black bars, while monitoring the exact height and width of the image.

Cropping a video using QuickTime Player isn't a user-friendly experience, but it's not rocket science either. You have to create a black-and-white image, then add it to the video track as a mask. Here's how:

1. Open your movie in QuickTime Player. Choose Get Movie Properties from the Movie menu. Choose the video track you want to crop using the left pop-up menu, then choose Mask from the right pop-up menu:

2. Launch a graphics application such as Photoshop. Create a black rectangle with the same pixel dimensions as your video track. Make a white border along the edges where you want to crop the video. The video will be cropped out wherever the image is white:

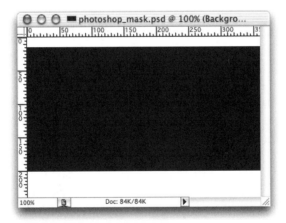

Tip Make sure your black is *black,* RGB or HSV 0-0-0, or 8-bit 0, and that your white is *white,* RGB or HSV 255-255-255, or 8-bit 255. Using almost-black or almost-white causes problems.

Tip You can click a video image in QuickTime Player, choose Copy, and paste the image into Photoshop. Create a new layer for your mask image, and you can use the pasted graphic as a guide for creating the mask. Delete the layer with the pasted graphic before saving.

3. Save the image in a format that QuickTime can open, such as GIF or Photoshop format. Click the Set button in QuickTime Player's Properties window and select the image using the dialog box that appears:

Your video should now appear cropped wherever the mask image is white. If you need to adjust the mask image to make the cropped area larger or smaller, click the Clear button in the Info window, change the mask image and save it, then click the Set button and select it again.

Like I said, not user-friendly, but not rocket science.

At this point, the video is not actually cropped; it's all still there, but part of it is being masked out when the movie is played. The mask image and the undisplayed video will be deleted, doing the actual cropping, when you export the movie.

You'll export the movie later, as part of the mix-down process (see page 315) or when you compress the movie for delivery. If you do it now, you'll degrade the image unnecessarily by compressing it twice.

▶ Compositing and Effects

Once editing and cropping are done, you're ready to do any necessary compositing (combining visual elements) and add any effects or transitions. This generally involves track-level editing.

In the examples that follow, we'll show you how to cut or copy material from a single video track and add it as a new track that can be overlapped with other material. Bear in mind that the Cut and Copy commands act on all tracks that occupy the selected time period. This is handy when you want to keep synchronized material together, but for compositing and effects you may want to work on the video tracks without altering the audio.

Use the Extract Tracks command (in the Edit menu) if you need to cut or copy from one track without affecting others. This copies a track into a new movie. Cut and paste the new movie, then copy it and add it back into the original movie, deleting the old version of the track you just edited. It sounds complicated because it is, but you'll get the hang of it.

Compositing

Compositing consists of blending different visual elements together, generally with some form of transparency. If you've shot footage against a blue screen or green screen, for example, you can make the blue or green parts transparent and overlay the footage on a different background.

For visual elements to be composited, they have to overlap in time and space. The mechanics of arranging the tracks depends on what software you're using. If you're compositing in QuickTime Player, you need to put the elements in separate tracks before you can arrange them.

You put footage in a separate track by copying or cutting it, clicking a frame in the movie at the desired starting point, and choosing Add (or Add Scaled) from the Edit menu. The footage can be copied or cut from another movie or from elsewhere in the same movie. In either case, the new track overlaps any existing track, beginning at its insertion point.

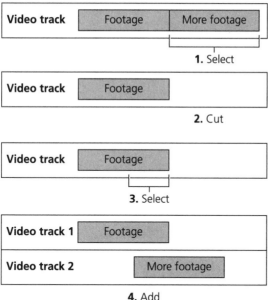

Video track | Footage | More footage

1. Select

Video track | Footage

2. Cut

Video track | Footage

3. Select

Video track 1 | Footage

Video track 2 | More footage

4. Add

The Add command sets the start time for the new track without changing the duration of the footage, as shown in the illustration.

The Add Scaled command sets the start time for the new track and scales its duration to match the current selection. Use this technique to composite a still image onto an image sequence, as described in "Adding a Still Image as a Movie Background" (page 267).

The new track overlaps any existing track in space as well as time. The new track appears on top of the existing track, aligned with the upper left corner of the display area. If the tracks have the same height and width, or the new track is larger, the existing track is completely covered. If the new track is smaller, some of the existing track is still visible.

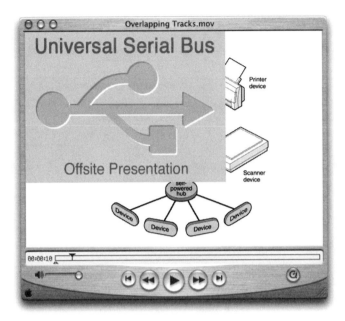

To put the new track beneath the existing track, rather than on top of it, use the Movie Properties window to increment its layer number (choose the track in the left pop-up menu, then choose Layer in the right).

To make one of the tracks visually larger or smaller, or to position it elsewhere in the frame, use the Movie Properties window to change its size and position (choose Size from the right pop-up menu, then click Adjust, to change size *or* position). You might do this to create a picture-in-a-picture effect, for example, or to add a logo as described in "Adding a Logo to a Movie" (page 270).

To make one of the tracks partly transparent or translucent, use the Movie Properties window to change its graphics mode, as described in "Transparency and Alpha Channels" (page 271). For a track with a blue screen or green screen, set the graphics mode to transparent, and select as your transparent color the green or blue that exactly matches the screen color.

Another way to make a track partly transparent is to add a mask. A mask is a black-and-white (not grayscale) image. The mask acts like a cookie-cutter. Where the mask is black, the track is visible. Where the mask is white, the track is transparent. Here's how to add a mask to a track:

1. Use a graphics program to create a black-and-white image. It should have the same pixel dimensions as the video track. Save it in a format that QuickTime can open, such as Photoshop or GIF.

2. Open your movie in QuickTime Player, choose Get Movie Properties from the Movie menu, choose the track you want from the left pop-up menu, and choose Mask from the right pop-up menu.

3. Click the Set button and select your mask image using the dialog box that appears.

Adding a mask or changing the graphics mode affects the whole track. If you want to apply a mask or a graphics mode to part of a track, cut the part you want to apply the change to and add it back as a separate track.

For example, suppose you have two image sequences, sequence A and sequence B, and you want to composite the sequences with a half-second overlap, using the blend graphics mode only for the overlapping part.

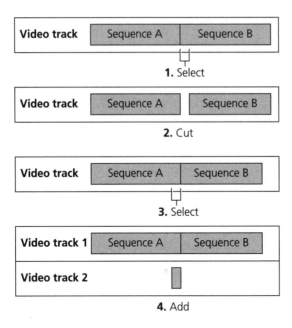

Video track	Sequence A	Sequence B

1. Select

Video track	Sequence A	Sequence B

2. Cut

Video track	Sequence A	Sequence B

3. Select

Video track 1	Sequence A	Sequence B
Video track 2		

4. Add

1. Select the first half-second of sequence B.

2. Choose Cut from the Edit menu.

3. Position the insertion point at the last half-second of sequence A.

4. Choose Add.

The overlapping part of sequence B is now in its own video track, on top of sequence A. Use the Movie Properties window to set its graphics mode to blend.

You may also want to composite a title or credits over a background image or over part of your movie. This is fairly easy. Use a text editor to create the text, then import it into a text track with QuickTime Player. In Windows or Mac OS 8 or 9, the import process allows you to select the font, size, alignment, style, and color, as shown in the following illustration.

Note This feature is not currently available in Mac OS X—you need to set these text characteristics after importing the text file, as described in "Setting Text Attributes" (page 365).

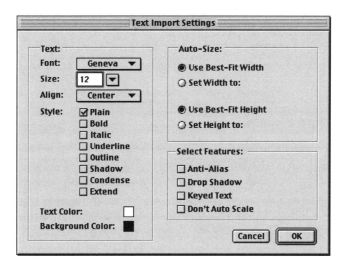

To composite the text track over a background track, select Keyed Text when you import the text, then add the tracks so the background is behind the text. For details, see Chapter 13, "Text! Text! Text!"

Tip Never use transparent graphics mode for a scrolling text overlay. It will be jerky. Use keyed text instead.

Effects and Transitions

You may want to add transition effects, such as dissolves or wipes, between visual sequences. There are two fundamentally different ways to do this: the traditional method and the QuickTime way.

Traditional Effects

The traditional way to add transition effects is to create a visual transition at the time you edit the movie, rendering each frame of the effect into the movie and saving it as part of the video track.

There are a number of tools you can use to create effects this way, including most video editors, such as Adobe Premiere, Edit DV, Final Cut Pro, and iMovie. There are also specialized software applications just for creating effects, such as Adobe After Effects. Which effects are available, and how you embed them, depend on what software you're using.

As a rule, traditional effects compress poorly. Adding a lot of dissolves, wipes, and cross-fades can drive up the movie's data rate dramatically. By the time you compress the movie enough to deliver it over a modem, the smooth transitions may become very jerky.

Tip Most transition effects need to be rendered into video at a frame rate of 12 fps or faster to look decent.

QuickTime Effects

The QuickTime effects architecture is a new thing under the sun. You specify the type of effect, its duration, and which tracks to use as source material, and this information is stored as part of the movie. The effect is rendered by the viewer's computer each time the movie is played.

This preserves maximum quality at minimum bandwidth by sending a *description* of the effect and harnessing the power of the user's computer to create the output.

Of course, if the viewer's computer doesn't have any power, there's nothing to harness. Older and slower computers render fewer frames, making the effect less smooth. On a very slow computer, the transition becomes a straight cut.

With Web-based video, however, the limiting factor is usually bandwidth rather than the speed of the user's computer. You may have to render your video at 6 or 10 frames per second in order to deliver it over the Web, while the viewer's computer is capable of displaying image data at three times that rate.

If you pre-render the effect as part of the video, the effect gets choppy as the frame rate goes down. If you send a description of the effect, the viewer's computer renders it at the highest frame rate it can, independent of the movie frame rate. On fast computers, this results in much smoother transitions than you could possibly deliver over the Web as pre-rendered video.

As usual, QuickTime gives you a choice. If you export a movie that contains QuickTime effects, the effects are rendered as part of the export process, which turns them into traditional effects. So you're free to go either way.

If you want your effects to be rendered on the viewer's computer at display time, add them *after* you've compressed the movie for delivery.

If you want to render the effects in advance and deliver them as video, add the effects before you compress.

QuickTime effects are applied to whole tracks. If you want a half-second transition from sequence A to sequence B, you need to cut a half-second from the end of sequence A, cut a half-second from the start of sequence B, put the clips from A and B into separate tracks that overlap, and apply the transition effect to both tracks.

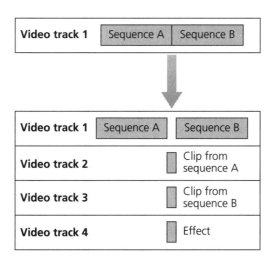

There are several programs that currently allow you to add QuickTime effects to movies. Among them are MovieWorks, LiveStage Pro, LiveSlide-Show, and Adobe GoLive (version 4 and later). There's also a little program called MakeEffectMovie in the Tools folder of the CD. It's a bit cumbersome to use, but it does let you add QuickTime effects to movies. And hey, it's free.

Note Most video editing programs, including Final Cut Pro, Final Cut Express, and iMovie, do not add QuickTime effects to movies. They add traditional rendered video effects, intended for video or DVD output. Web-savvy QuickTime editors, such as GoLive and LiveStage, can add genuine QuickTime effects.

Adding Effects with MakeEffectMovie

The MakeEffectMovie program uses whole movies as source material. To create a transition effect between sequence A and sequence B, you need to cut a section from the end of sequence A, save it as a new movie, cut a section from the start of sequence B, and save that as another movie. These are called source movies. Then you tell MakeEffectMovie to create a transition effect from the two source movies. The effect is saved as a third movie, containing three tracks that you can paste back into your original movie. Confusing? You bet. But not really hard.

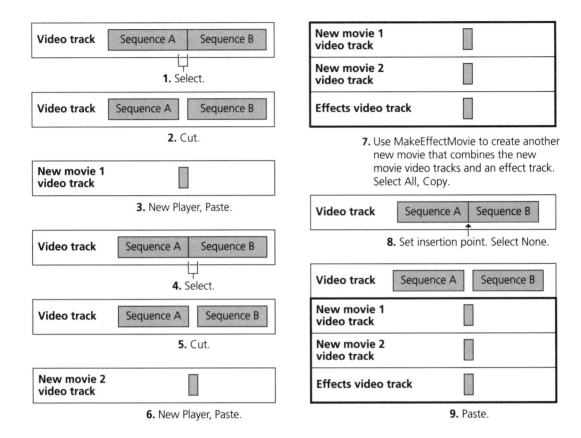

1. Select.

2. Cut.

3. New Player, Paste.

4. Select.

5. Cut.

6. New Player, Paste.

7. Use MakeEffectMovie to create another new movie that combines the new movie video tracks and an effect track. Select All, Copy.

8. Set insertion point. Select None.

9. Paste.

When you launch MakeEffectMovie, it prompts you for a source movie twice. It creates a transition from the first movie you specify to the second movie, so select them in the order you want them to appear.

Once you've specified the source movies, you're prompted to pick an effect.

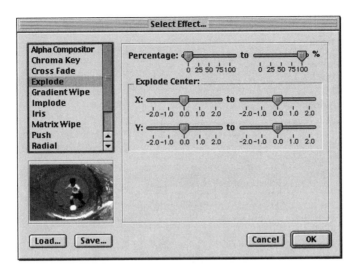

If the effect has adjustable parameters, the appropriate controls are displayed. A preview of the effect runs constantly in the lower left corner, so you can see what changing the parameters does.

When you have the effect and parameters you want, click OK. MakeEffectMovie creates a small movie (not self-contained) of the transition effect.

The effect movie has three video tracks: the first source, the second source, and the effect. Open this movie in QuickTime Player, choose Select All, choose Copy, and paste the selection into your destination movie just before the next frame of sequence B.

1. Select All, Copy.

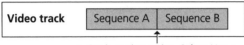

2. Set insertion point. Select None.

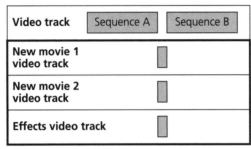

3. Paste.

Tips

- If the source movies have different heights or widths, the smaller image is scaled up to match the larger image.

- The effect duration is the length of the shortest source movie. If the movies aren't exactly the same length, make sure the second movie is the longest, so that it's on the screen when the transition effect ends.

- If one of the source movies is a still image, the effect duration is the length of the other movie.

- If both source movies are still images, the effect duration is two seconds.

To render an effect when the movie is playing, QuickTime has to decompress images from both sources and composite them together. If you plan to compress the movie with a demanding video codec such as Sorenson, there may not be enough horsepower on the viewer's computer to decompress two images and composite the results without dropping frames. To get around this, you can compress the source movies separately, using a less demanding codec such as Cinepak, before you build the effect. The momentarily lower visual quality of the individual frames won't generally be noticed during a cross-fade or other transition.

To add a transition between two sequences, without making a movie's duration longer or shorter, *cut* a section from one sequence, *copy* a single frame from the other sequence, and use the clip and the image as sources for the effect. MakeEffectMovie creates a transition the exact duration of the sequence that you cut, so you can paste the effect back into the movie without changing the movie's length. This kind of transition also tends to display more smoothly because the viewer's computer can use the same image as one source for every frame of the effect, rather than decompressing two new images for each frame.

When you create a transition using a motion video clip and a still image, you have a choice. You can create a transition from a clip at the end of one sequence to the first frame of the following sequence, or from the last frame of one sequence to a clip at the start of the following sequence.

For example, to create a transition effect blending the last two seconds of sequence A into the first frame of sequence B, do this:

1. Select the last two seconds of sequence A.

2. Choose Cut from the Edit menu.

3. Choose New, then Paste to create a new movie from the clip. Save.

4. Click the first frame of sequence B and choose Copy.

5. Choose New, then Paste to create a new movie from the image. Save.

6. Open MakeEffectMovie. Use the movie of the clip as the first source and the movie of the image as the second source. Choose the Cross Fade effect and Save. This creates a movie of the transition effect. Open this movie, Select All, Copy, close (don't save).

7. Set the insertion point at the first frame of sequence B in your original movie.

8. Paste. Save As (self contained).

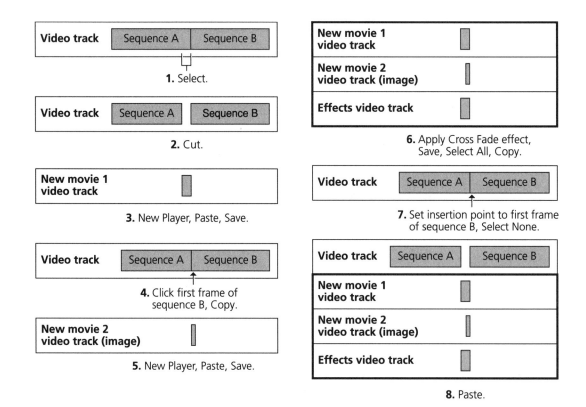

Video track	Sequence A	Sequence B

1. Select.

Video track	Sequence A	Sequence B

2. Cut.

New movie 1 video track	

3. New Player, Paste, Save.

Video track	Sequence A	Sequence B

4. Click first frame of sequence B, Copy.

New movie 2 video track (image)	

5. New Player, Paste, Save.

New movie 1 video track	
New movie 2 video track (image)	
Effects video track	

6. Apply Cross Fade effect, Save, Select All, Copy.

Video track	Sequence A	Sequence B

7. Set insertion point to first frame of sequence B, Select None.

Video track	Sequence A	Sequence B
New movie 1 video track	
New movie 2 video track (image)	
Effects video track	

8. Paste.

To create a transition from the last frame of sequence A into the first two seconds of sequence B, do this:

1. Click the last frame of sequence A and choose Copy from the Edit menu.

2. Paste the image into a new movie (New Player, Paste, Save).

3. Select the first two seconds of sequence B.

4. Choose Cut from the Edit menu.

5. Paste the clip into a new movie (New Player, Paste, Save).

6. Use the still image and the motion clip, *in that order,* as sources for MakeEffectMovie. Select the Cross Fade effect and save. Open the new effect movie, choose Select All, choose Copy, and close.

7. Set the insertion point to the first frame of sequence B in your original movie and Select None.

8. Paste the effect into the movie. Save As (self-contained).

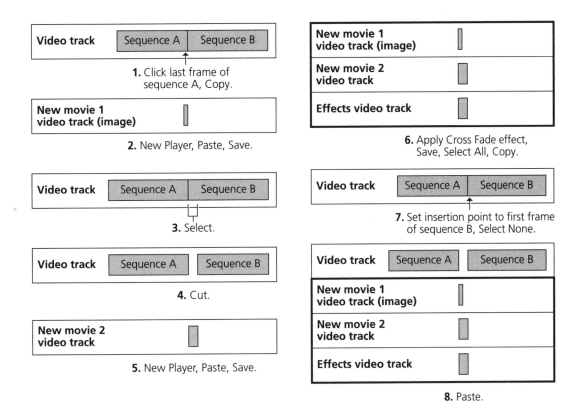

1. Click last frame of sequence A, Copy.

2. New Player, Paste, Save.

3. Select.

4. Cut.

5. New Player, Paste, Save.

6. Apply Cross Fade effect, Save, Select All, Copy.

7. Set insertion point to first frame of sequence B, Select None.

8. Paste.

▶ Mixing Down

When you're finally done editing your movie, and you've added your titles and transition effects, you may have created several tracks, including multiple sound tracks or multiple video tracks, as well as text and effects tracks.

Extra tracks use very little bandwidth, but each track makes extra demands on the viewer's computer. Multiple unnecessary tracks can sometimes prevent smooth playback. Consequently, you may want to mix down multiple tracks into single tracks. Most video editors, including QuickTime Player, do a mix-down as part of the final compression, but you may want to do a selective mix-down earlier.

The easiest way to do a mix-down in QuickTime Player is to choose Export Movie from the File menu, then choose Movie to QuickTime Movie from the pop-up menu. This combines all the visual tracks into a single video track with a single compression scheme. It combines all the sound tracks into a single sound track, also with a single compression scheme.

If your movie contains only video tracks and sound tracks using the same compressors, this is exactly what you want.

If your movie contains music tracks, text tracks, QuickTime effects, or still images, however, an export operation has consequences you may or may not want.

- Text tracks are rendered as video. This ensures a consistent appearance on computers that don't have the specified fonts, but it increases the required bandwidth.

- QuickTime effects tracks are also rendered as video. This provides a consistent appearance on computers that can't render the effects at runtime, but it also increases the required bandwidth and limits the maximum frame rate for the effect.

- Music tracks (MIDI music) are deleted. Probably not what you want.

- If a still image is being used as a background or a logo, it is "burned" into the surrounding video and compressed with the motion video codec. This generally lowers its visual quality and increases the movie's data rate.

Consequently, you may want to mix down only selected tracks.

To mix down selected tracks, extract the selected tracks into a new movie by choosing Extract Tracks from the Edit menu. You can extract multiple tracks by Shift-clicking in the Extract Tracks dialog box. This creates a new movie containing only the selected tracks. You can then export the new movie, which mixes down the selected tracks into one audio and one video track.

To replace the original tracks with the mixed-down tracks, open the exported movie, choose Select All, then Copy. Back in the original movie, choose Add. Delete the original tracks using Delete Tracks in the Edit menu.

We've described the sequence of events as editing, cropping, compositing, adding titles and effects, and mixing down. But if you plan to keep your titles and logo in separate tracks, you should probably mix down right after editing, then add the logo and text tracks afterwards. Music tracks should always be added after mix-down.

Compositing a still image into the background is a special case. If you want to keep the background as a separate track consisting of a single high-quality image, you should mix down selected tracks *after* compositing. That way the mix-down leaves the right parts of the video track transparent, and you can add the background image behind it.

When you do the mix-down, you also select the audio and video compression and settings. Use the same compression and settings as your source movie, so there's no recompression or loss of quality.

▶ Compressing Your Movie

The final step in preparing your movie is compressing it for delivery. This is where you choose the final size, frame rate, and compressors. Some compressors allow you to set additional characteristics, such as the target data rate, color depth, image quality, or frequency of key frames.

You can compress movies using QuickTime Player or any video editor that creates QuickTime movies. You can also use software that specializes in video preparation and compression, such as Sorenson Squeeze, Discreet Cleaner, or Totally Hip's HipFlics. These software packages typically include features that QuickTime Player doesn't have, such as batch processing and enhanced compressors. Squeeze is primarily an enhanced compressor for Sorenson 3 video. HipFlics is more powerful and flexible, allows cropping, and supports all QuickTime compressors. Cleaner is the mother ship; it does cropping, black restore, white restore, batch compression, export to QuickTime, Real, and Windows Media, and much more. As you might have guessed, Squeeze is economical, HipFlics is inexpensive, and Cleaner isn't.

We've included demo versions of Cleaner and HipFlics for both Windows and Macintosh in the Demos folder of the CD. Documentation is included. Check 'em out.

To compress your movie using QuickTime Player, choose Export from the File menu, then choose Movie to QuickTime Movie from the pop-up menu. Click the Options button to choose a compressor and adjust its settings.

An export operation also performs a mix-down to a single video track and a single sound track, as described in "Mixing Down" (page 315). As a consequence, you may want to export only selected tracks, or you may want to add text, effects, and music tracks after the movie is compressed.

Compression Guidelines

Uncompressed video uses a lot of bandwidth. At full-screen 720 x 480 resolution and broadcast quality (30 frames per second), it needs around 30 MB per second. That would saturate 20 T1 lines. Most computers can't get that kind of throughput from their hard drives.

There are lots of ways to reduce the bandwidth needed for video. You can make the video smaller than full screen. You can use fewer frames per second. You can use fewer colors per pixel. For example, if you send 1/8-screen video (160 x 120) at 10 frames per second, using 8-bit color, it needs only 192,000 bytes per second. Only. It still takes more than a T1 line to transport in real time, but you can play it from a hard drive or a CD-ROM. The problem is, it's tiny, jerky, and generally awful looking.

The solution is image compression. If you can compress the video by 4:1, you can make it four times larger without increasing the bandwidth. Compress it another 3:1 and you can use 24-bit color instead of 8-bit color. Another 1.5:1 and you can go from 10 frames per second to 15. In other words, with 18:1 image compression, you can deliver quarter-screen video at 15 frames per second, in millions of colors, using no more bandwidth than a jerky, pixelated, postage stamp—but looking a whole lot better.

To put video on the desktop, you have to compress it. To put video on the Web, you have to compress it hard. In most cases, you still need to reduce the image size and frame rate to something lower than television standards, but if you work at it, you'll end up with something that looks pretty good.

Pick a Target

The first thing to do is pick a delivery medium: hard drive, DVD, 4x-speed CD-ROM drive, LAN, T1, 56K modem, 28.8K modem, smoke signals . . .

If you have more than one target, you should compress your movie more than once. The alternative is to optimize compression for one delivery medium at the expense of the others; you can compress for delivery over a 56K modem, for example, with lower quality than you could provide to people with faster connections, and let people with slower connections wait a bit longer to see the movie.

If you compress for more than one target, you can also choose how much granularity to provide: a T1 version and a 28.8K version, for example, or a 28.8K version, a 56K version, a T1 version, and a hard drive version.

Each delivery medium has a maximum bandwidth. There are usually things that prevent you from getting the full rated bandwidth, so your target bandwidth should be lower. For a summary of reasonable data rates for various Web connections, see "Bandwidth" (page 210).

If you're delivering Fast Start movies, you can exceed the target bandwidth a little; it just causes a small delay before the movie starts. If you're going to stream the movies in real time, bandwidth is a hard limit; you *must* keep the data rate of the movie below the available bandwidth, or the movie won't get through.

Note   Starting with QuickTime 5 and Streaming Server 3, this is less of a hard limit. QuickTime will buffer a few extra seconds of video when the data rate is low, and read from the buffer if the data rate momentarily exceeds the available bandwidth. But if the data rate consistently exceeds the bandwidth, the movie still breaks up and does not play.

You also need to pick a target computer. Will the movie be played only on Windows computers, only on Macintosh, or both? Can you require 256 MB of RAM, or do you need to support computers with less? Can you require QuickTime 5 or QuickTime 6.1, or do you need to support QuickTime 4?

Because some codecs are better at delivering low-bandwidth video, some are only available on a particular operating system, and some require a minimum version of QuickTime, you need to know what your target is before you can choose a compressor.

Pick a Codec

Once you know what your target is, you can pick a video compressor and decompressor (codec). There are a number of considerations.

There are fundamentally two kinds of video codecs: low-loss transfer codecs and high-loss delivery codecs. Transfer codecs guarantee high quality along with fast compression and decompression. They usually require very high data rates and may require specialized hardware. They're suitable for capturing and editing video on a hard disk. Some transfer codecs are lossless; the image is not changed or degraded, no matter how many times it is compressed with a lossless codec.

Delivery codecs compress video for delivery at lower bit rates, such as DVD, CD-ROM, the Web, or cell phones. This usually involves a loss of quality, but that's the price you pay. Compress video for delivery only once; multiple compression with delivery codecs will ruin the image.

Codecs can compress image data in two different ways: spatially and temporally.

Spatial compression defines areas of similar color, repeating patterns, or smooth gradients and sends a description of those areas and their contents. Complex patterns, graphic detail, and noise are difficult to compress spatially. Some codecs work best with areas of flat color; others work best with smooth color gradients and slightly blurred images. Most codecs provide some spatial compression.

Temporal compression defines images in terms of how they have changed from previous images. Rapid motion, frequent cuts, and zooms are difficult to compress temporally. The less change there is from one frame to the next, the better video compresses temporally. Some codecs can obtain perfect temporal compression from still images, using the same amount of bandwidth no matter how long the image persists. Most codecs provide some temporal compression.

Note A variation on standard temporal compression is to describe a frame by its difference from a subsequent frame. This makes sense when you think of a cross-fade between two images. At first, frames are best described by their differences from the initial image. Near the end of the cross-fade, it's more efficient to describe a frame in terms of its difference from the final image. But how can the decompressor know what the subsequent image looks like before it arrives? It cheats. The subsequent frame is sent ahead, out of sequence, and marked as special. This kind of temporal compression is often described as using "B" frames.

There are standard QuickTime codecs that everyone who installs QuickTime gets free. These are normally the ones you want to use. In some cases only the decompressor is standard, and a compressor must be purchased separately. In other cases, both a compressor and a decompressor are standard, but an enhanced version of the compressor is also available for purchase.

Starting with QuickTime 5, there is a new class of component-download codecs. These codecs are registered with Apple, after careful testing, and can be downloaded automatically from Apple's Internet file servers. You can use these codecs freely in movies that play over the Internet—if a viewer plays the movie and doesn't have the codec, QuickTime will offer to download and install it automatically. If you're distributing movies on disk and aren't sure your viewers will be on the Internet, you should contact the codec vendor about including a copy on your disk.

Other codecs must be purchased or downloaded from a third party or require special hardware. You may want to use one of these codecs if you have control over the playback computer, as you might in a computer lab or kiosk, or if you're distributing your movies on a disk and can include the codec.

Some codecs are available only for Macintosh or only for Windows. Some require a PowerPC or a Pentium processor. Others will run on museum pieces.

Additional codecs are added with new versions of QuickTime, so some codecs require a minimum version of QuickTime for playback.

Some delivery codecs are "symmetrical," meaning they compress and decompress equally quickly. You need this for videoconferencing or live streaming, where you have to compress and decompress in real time.

Other codecs are sharply "asymmetric," meaning they take a long time to compress a file but can decompress it quickly. Codecs that offer high quality at low bit rates usually take a long time to compress.

Some codecs require LAN or CD-ROM data rates to deliver high quality, while others can deliver high-quality video at lower data rates.

For a complete listing of QuickTime codecs and their characteristics, see "Video Codecs and Settings" (page 323).

It's worth mentioning that you can use only one video and one audio compressor when you export a movie, but you can use multiple compression schemes in your final QuickTime movie by adding other tracks later. This is especially useful for compositing motion video over, say, a JPEG-compressed background image, or under a logo compressed using Planar RGB (Photoshop format) with an alpha channel.

Common Settings

Different codecs allow you to adjust different settings. If you leave a particular setting blank, the codec generally uses a sensible default based on your other settings. Here are some common settings and what they mean.

- **Size**

  The height and width of your video, in pixels. A smaller size uses less bandwidth. The movie can be scaled up for playback, so the size you set here can be smaller than the final display size. Video compressed with some codecs looks quite good when played back at double size. For best-looking results, use your actual height and width, or scale down by 1/2 or 1/4. Many codecs work best with a height and width that are both divisible by four. A few are optimized for multiples of 16, or for two or three specific sizes.

- **Data Rate**

  The number of kilobytes per second required to deliver your video. Choose a data rate that makes sense for your delivery medium, as described in "Bandwidth" (page 210). Remember, the data rate is expressed in kilobytes (1024 **bytes**), but modems are rated in kilobits (1000 **bits**), and it takes more than 8 bits to transport a byte over TCP/IP. The difference is roughly 10:1. If you set a data rate, this usually overrides any other codec settings, such as quality. The codec may exceed the specified data rate at times, so be conservative.

Tip   This data rate is just for the video track. Leave some bits in the budget for sound!

- **Variable Bit Rate (VBR)**

  Using a variable bit rate allows you to work more flexibly. You can either lower the required bandwidth by sending less data during the parts of the movie that compress well, or raise the quality by sending extra data for those hard-to-compress scenes. Most newer compressors offer a VBR option that can be set to emphasize quality or low data rate. In some cases, turning VBR on also enables the use of "B" frames, as described in the note in "Pick a Codec" (page 319).

  VBR with "B" frames is a relatively new feature of video codecs. There have been some teething problems (and the occasional hard-to-reproduce bug) using VBR compression in QuickTime movies, particularly with Sorenson 3 VBR video and QuickTime 5. Hopefully this is behind us now, but it probably bears watching.

- **Frame Rate**

  The number of images per second in your video. Higher frame rates make smoother motion but use more bandwidth. Use a simple division of your current frame rate, such as 1/2, 1/3, 1/4, 1/5, and so on. If your current frame rate is 30, for example, use 15, 10, 7.5, or 6. Fractional frame rates like 7.5 are no problem. Reducing the frame rate by 2/3, on the other hand, results in uneven motion. In other words, if your original frame rate is 30, don't compress to 20; go to 15 instead. It will look better.

- **Key Frames**

  Most codecs create key frames and difference frames. A key frame has all the information needed to create an image. A difference frame describes how the current image differs from a previous image. This saves a lot of bandwidth. Over time, errors build up and you need to insert another key frame. If there's a lot of motion, you need key frames more often. Random access is faster and smoother in a movie with frequent key frames. Some codecs need a lot fewer key frames than others. Set this field to a large number, such as 99, or select Natural key frames to let the codec do what it does best.

- **Quality**

  A subjective setting that generally trades visual quality for bandwidth. A preview thumbnail shows what the image will look like at the current setting. Keep turning the quality setting down until you don't like what you see, then bring it back up a little. If you enter fixed values for all the other settings, the compressor may not be able to deliver the requested quality.

- **Colors**

  Different codecs offer radically different choices for this setting. Use grayscale for black-and-white footage if it's available. You should generally use at least thousands of colors for photographic images. For graphics and animations, 256 colors may be plenty. Fewer colors means lower bandwidth, but less realistic rendering of photos. If your video contains an alpha channel, you need to use a codec that supports the setting "Millions of colors+."

Video Codecs and Settings

A video codec specifies how image data is compressed. To compress a movie using a particular codec, open the movie in QuickTime Player and choose Export from the File Menu.

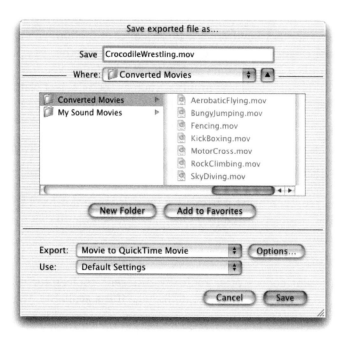

Choose Movie to QuickTime Movie from the pop-up menu and click the Options button.

This brings up the Movie Settings dialog box, shown in the following illustration:

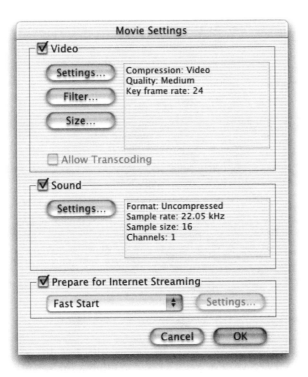

You can specify a number of movie settings in addition to choosing a video codec.

- To set the height and width of the video track, click the Size button in the Video section.
- To choose an audio codec and adjust its settings, click the Settings button in the Sound section of the dialog box.
- Use the pop-up menu at the bottom of the dialog box to choose Fast Start or Streaming.

When you're ready to choose a video codec, click the Settings button in the Video area. This brings up the video Compression Settings dialog box.

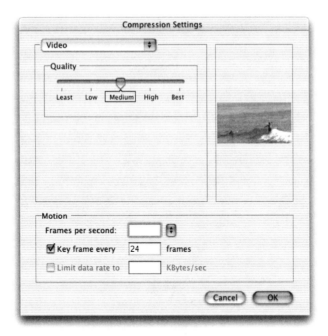

The current compressor and settings are displayed.

The pop-up menu at the top of the dialog box lists all the compressors available to you, as shown in the next illustration. This list includes the standard QuickTime compressors, any additional compressors you may have purchased or downloaded, and any compressors installed along with video capture cards, editing programs, or other software.

Don't assume that everyone else has the same codecs as are installed on your computer. Unless you know that your target audience has a particular codec installed on their machines, use one of the standard QuickTime codecs listed in the next section, or one of the component-download codecs, such as Streambox ACT-L2 or ZyGoVideo. For a current list of component-download codecs, see

www.apple.com/quicktime/products/qt/components.html

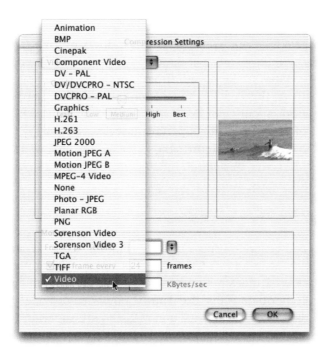

QuickTime Codecs

Animation

This compressor works best with graphics images, particularly if they have large areas of flat color. It can provide very high visual quality at DVD or hard disk data rates. It provides good temporal compression, so the data rate drops sharply with still images.

At the Best quality setting, this codec is lossless, making it a good editing codec. At lower-quality settings, it can be used for CD-ROM delivery. It can achieve Web data rates only for slideshows.

Compression time is short, and decompression is undemanding.

It supports all color depths, including millions+ (24-bit color plus alpha channel), so it's suitable for video with an alpha channel.

One key frame per second is recommended for moving images. For slideshows, leave the key frame setting blank.

You can't specify a data rate limit for this codec.

BMP

This compressor creates a series of Windows bitmap (.bmp) images. It works best with large areas of flat color. It provides no temporal compression, so the data rate increases directly with the frame rate. Even at low-quality settings, this codec is suitable only for DVD or hard disk delivery.

BMP supports four color depths: millions, 256, 16, and black and white. At depths of 256 and 16, it supports grayscale.

A movie created by importing a series of .bmp images into QuickTime uses the BMP codec by default, but you will probably never need to export a QuickTime movie using this codec.

Cinepak

This is a good general-purpose codec for motion video. It can provide good image quality at 1x and 2x CD-ROM data rates, and slightly better quality at higher rates. It does not provide good quality at Web data rates, however. For higher data rates, the Animation codec provides better quality; for lower data rates, Sorenson 3 and MPEG-4 are superior.

Cinepak compresses slowly, but playback is very fast, making this codec a good choice for old computers, such as 486 machines.

This is an old codec, and it's very widespread. QuickTime video compressed with Cinepak can play on Windows Media Player (versions prior to 6.0), any version of QuickTime on any platform, and a number of UNIX and Linux movie players.

Cinepak supports millions of colors, 256 colors, and 256-level grayscale. Quality tends to be poor in the 8-bit modes.

You generally want a key frame once a second for motion video. For still images, use the Animation, Graphics, or Photo JPEG codec instead.

You can specify a data rate limit, and that tends to give the best results. This can override the quality and key frame settings. Cinepak always gives at least 10:1 compression, so setting a data rate limit above the point needed for this won't increase quality or the actual data rate.

You can get better quality than Cinepak offers at a lower data rate using the Sorenson codec, but Sorenson requires a faster minimum computer for playback and takes longer to compress. Use Cinepak for slow computers or maximum backward compatibility at CD-ROM data rates.

Component Video

Component video provides 3:2 compression with almost no loss of quality. It uses YUV color space, rather than RGB, so instead of using 24-bit color

(8-bit red, 8-bit green, 8-bit blue), it uses 8-bit luma and 16-bit chroma. Component video does a 2:1 compression on the chroma, so a pixel can be represented using 16 bits. It compresses at very high speed, making it useful as a capture codec on computers that don't have hardware compression. It also decompresses very quickly.

This is a high-quality codec for capture and storage, but it creates files that use a lot of disk space. It does not provide any temporal compression.

Most computer hard drives lack the bandwidth to play full-screen 30 fps video at component video data rates, making it unsuitable as a delivery codec.

Component video supports 24-bit color only. The only adjustable parameter for this compressor is the frame rate. Every frame is a key frame.

This can be a good capture codec for digitizing live video from an analog source for a streaming broadcast. It requires very little time or computation, so your computer has the maximum resources free to decompress the images, recompress them using a streaming codec, create a stream, and broadcast it in real time. Since the component video frames are discarded immediately by the broadcaster, file size is not an issue. (When you archive a live broadcast, you make a copy of the stream *after* it has been recompressed by the broadcaster, typically in H.263 format.)

DV

The DV codec is used by digital camcorders. QuickTime supports both the North American (NTSC) and European (PAL) versions. The DV codec provides about 10:1 compression with very high quality, making it an excellent transfer codec. Both compression and decompression are processor-intensive, making this a poor capture codec and a poor delivery codec, unless you're capturing from DV tape or a DV camera or delivering material on DV tape or hard disk.

Improvements in the QuickTime DV codec introduced in QuickTime 5 make it suitable for capturing live broadcasts from a DV camera.

You can use the DV compressor to convert your movies to DV streams, which can then be transferred to an editing program, such as iMovie or Final Cut Pro, that works with DV streams. Your movie can then be sent to a digital camcorder via FireWire for archive or distribution on tape.

DV is also a good format for editing prior to delivery on DVD. The dimensions and characteristics of DV-encoded video allow it to be recompressed as MPEG-2 with very little loss of quality, using a DVD authoring application such as iDVD or DVD Studio Pro.

Note The DV codec is not the codec used for DVD movies. DVD uses MPEG-2.

Graphics

The Graphics codec creates 8-bit images using a compression technique similar to animated GIFs. It has good temporal compression and typically requires about half the bandwidth of the Animation codec. It decompresses more slowly than the Animation codec, so playback may not be quite as smooth, but this is still an undemanding codec on current hardware.

The Graphics codec supports only 8-bit color or 8-bit grayscale. If your image source uses less than 256 colors, this can be a good codec. Otherwise, converting your image to 8-bit color makes a poor impression. Some software, such as Discreet Cleaner, allows you to attach a custom palette; as with GIFs, this can improve the appearance in many cases.

Use this as an alternative to the Animation codec for 8-bit images. It's well suited to hard disk or CD-ROM delivery. It can achieve Web data rates only for slideshows or very small movies. Movies compressed with this codec are a reasonable alternative to animated GIFs.

H.261

This is an older codec designed for videoconferencing. It creates relatively low-quality images and blocky motion. It breaks each image into a grid, so it tolerates lost packets well—instead of throwing away a whole frame, it can throw away just one square from the grid. It provides good temporal compression, so it works best when there isn't much motion.

This codec provides very low data rates and compresses in real time. Decompression is CPU-intensive, so it may not play smoothly on older machines. It works reasonably well over a LAN, but not over modems.

H.261 requires QuickTime 3 or later, or Apple videoconferencing software, for playback.

H.261 is an international standard, so there are H.261 codecs available on several platforms.

H.261 uses a YUV color model with 2:1 chroma compression (24-bit color with 3:2 compression built in).

A key frame every 2 or 3 seconds helps keep the image from breaking up if there is packet loss.

You can specify a data rate for this compressor, and for best results you should.

This is a useful codec for sending live video streams over an ISDN connection, but in most cases you should use the newer H.263 codec instead.

H.263

This codec is a recent upgrade to the H.261 standard. It provides substantially better image quality at the same data rate. It was designed for real-time streaming and videoconferencing. It breaks images into a grid for transmission, so it tolerates lost packets well. The grid consists of 16 x 16 blocks, so the dimensions of the source image should be multiples of 16. It offers good temporal compression. This is a good codec for streaming video, particularly if the subject matter has a lot of motion.

H.263 provides good image quality at low data rates and compresses in real time. Decompression is CPU-intensive (though less so than Sorenson). It's not an optimum codec for data rates faster than 64,000 bits per second (single ISDN).

H.263 requires QuickTime 4 or later for playback.

H.263 is an international standard; H.263 codecs are available on many platforms.

H.263 uses a YUV color model with 2:1 chroma compression (24-bit color with 3:2 compression built in).

This codec works best at a standard image size of 176 x 144 pixels or 352 x 288 pixels. It deals with other image sizes by cropping or scaling to a standard size.

It's best to let the H.263 codec pick its own key frame rate by setting the user-selected key frame rate to a high value, such as 99.

Use the Cycle Intra Macroblocks option in the compression settings panel to prevent the image from breaking up due to packet loss in streaming movies. For Fast Start movies, turn this option off—it just repeats data that's guaranteed to get through anyway.

You can specify a data rate, and for best results you should.

This is the standard codec for live streaming.

Indeo (formerly Intel Indeo)

There are currently three versions of the Indeo codec for QuickTime: versions 3, 4, and 5. Some earlier versions of QuickTime shipped with a version of the Intel Indeo codec. In June 2000, the Indeo technology was acquired by ligos. You can download the Indeo Video 3.2, 4.5, and 5.11 codecs from the ligos website. The download page is currently located at

```
www.ligos.com/index.phtml?&n1=products&n2=indeo&n3=download
```

Indeo 3.2 was included in QuickTime 4 for the Macintosh. It provides good image quality at CD-ROM data rates and is similar to Cinepak. It compresses a little faster and can provide slightly better compression for low-motion video, such as talking heads. It has some color artifacting problems, however, and it doesn't work with video that is taller than it is wide. QuickTime for Windows did not include the Indeo 3.2 codec. Images compressed with Indeo 3.2 cannot be decompressed by later Indeo codecs. You should generally use Cinepak rather than Indeo 3.2.

Indeo 4.4 was included in QuickTime 4 for Windows. It provides high-quality images at CD-ROM data rates and good image quality at Web data rates. Image quality is generally inferior to the Sorenson codec at a given data rate. Compression is slow. This is a better choice than Cinepak if your target audience has exclusively Windows computers. It is not recommended for cross-platform projects.

Indeo 5 is the most recent version of this codec. Performance is improved on MMX-equipped processors, compared with Indeo 4.4. Indeo 5 can play movies compressed with Indeo 4.4. Most QuickTime users do not have the Indeo 5 codec, which limits its usefulness for Web delivery.

The Indeo codecs use YUV9 color space (24-bit color with 4:1 chroma compression). You can specify the frame rate, key frame rate, and maximum data rate. For Indeo 3.2, you should set a key frame every four frames, regardless of frame rate. Indeo 4.4 and Indeo 5 work best with one key frame per second.

Motion-JPEG

Motion-JPEG comes in two variants: M-JPEG A and M-JPEG B. They differ only by the placement of certain markers in the files. They are functionally identical. Both provide very high image quality at hard disk data rates. They are primarily used to capture video from analog sources. Most video digitizer cards provide M-JPEG compression in hardware. Some use M-JPEG A and some use M-JPEG B. It's a question of which one is chosen by a particular hardware vendor. QuickTime will translate between them on the fly if a movie is compressed in one variant and the graphics card on the playback computer uses the other.

M-JPEG uses the exact same compression algorithm as Photo JPEG.

M-JPEG provides no temporal compression; the data rate goes up in direct proportion to the frame rate.

M-JPEG supports 24-bit color or 8-bit grayscale.

Every frame is a key frame. You cannot specify a maximum data rate.

QuickTime includes software versions of the M-JPEG codecs. Compression is slow unless you have M-JPEG acceleration in hardware, in which case it's very fast, typically in real time.

Software playback is demanding, particularly at full screen and high data rates, making this generally unsuitable as a delivery codec unless viewers have graphics accelerators installed that support M-JPEG. This has become quite common in the last few years, however, so going forward this may be a good codec for broadband delivery.

It can also be used to deliver single frame video (320 x 240) at 30 fps in kiosk applications without hardware acceleration. It can be used successfully at lower data rates as well, and from single ISDN to DSL data rates it can provide better image quality than Cinepak.

Cinepak remains a better choice for CD-ROM. Sorenson or MPEG-4 is a better choice for motion video at dialup data rates. For slideshows or low-motion video, Photo-JPEG is a better choice.

MPEG-1, -2, and -4

There are several flavors of MPEG, specifying video and audio compression formats, stream and file formats, and multimedia presentation formats. Because the codecs and file format specifications are intertwined, they're primarily discussed in the "Other Movie Formats" section, under "MPEG" (page 349).

Here is a brief summary of MPEG video codecs and QuickTime:

- MPEG-1 video provides near-VHS quality at CD-ROM data rates. QuickTime plays MPEG-1 video but does not allow cut and paste editing from or into an MPEG-1 video sequence. QuickTime does not include an MPEG-1 video compressor. MPEG-1 compression for Quick-Time is available from companies such as Hueris and Roxio.

- MPEG-2 video provides DVD quality at DVD data rates. MPEG-2 playback and editing can be added to QuickTime as a download from the Apple Store ($20). QuickTime does not include an MPEG-2 video compressor, but you can export QuickTime video to a DV stream using QuickTime Player. You can export the DV stream to MPEG-2 video, or even directly to DVD or super VCD, using software such as iDVD, DVD Studio Pro, Roxio Toast, or DVD Creator.

- MPEG-4 video provides near-DVD quality at DSL data rates, near-VHS quality at dialup modem data rates, and near-miracle quality over cellular phones (hey, at that data rate *anything* is amazing). For the Web, MPEG-4 is comparable to Sorenson 3 video. QuickTime 6 includes MPEG-4 video playback, editing, and compression. QuickTime can create native MPEG-4 files (.mp4) as well as QuickTime movies with video tracks using MPEG-4 compression.

None

You can create a QuickTime movie with no compression whatsoever by choosing the None codec. As a rule, personal computers lack the internal bandwidth to capture or play uncompressed full-screen images at 30 frames per second, even using a fast hard disk. If you have the bandwidth and a huge high-speed disk array, or your image size and frame rate are low enough, this can be a useful capture or storage option. It is not useful for delivery over the Internet or on CD.

All color depths are supported, including millions+ (24-bit color plus an alpha channel).

Every frame is a key frame. The only adjustable parameter is the frame rate.

The None codec is useful for capturing video from a live analog source for a streaming broadcast. No CPU time is spent compressing or decompressing the image during the capture process, leaving the maximum real time free to compress the image for streaming and to send it. Since the broadcaster does not store the uncompressed images, disk space is not an issue for this application. The bandwidth requirements may overwhelm the broadcasting computer, however. If that happens, try capturing in single frame or half resolution mode, or using the Component Video codec; it's almost as fast as no compression, and it uses half the bandwidth.

Photo-JPEG

This codec uses JPEG compression. It uses a YUV color space, which often allows it to take advantage of hardware acceleration. It provides very high image quality at high data rates or low frame rates, and a smooth decrease in quality at progressively lower data rates. It has no temporal compression—the data rate goes up linearly with the frame rate—but it can achieve high image quality at Web data rates when used in slideshows because of the low frame rate.

Compression is slow, and playback is somewhat demanding, especially at high data rates. CPU loading is higher than Cinepak, but lower than Sorenson, at a given data rate.

Photo-JPEG supports 24-bit color or 8-bit grayscale.

You can't set the key frame rate or specify a maximum data rate for this compressor.

This makes a good delivery codec, at any data rate, for slideshows, still images used as background, or superimposed logos. It can be a better choice than M-JPEG for low-motion talking-head videos at ISDN to CD-ROM data rates.

The Graphics codec may be a better choice for 8-bit color images. Sorenson is a better choice for motion video at Web data rates, and Cinepak and Animation are generally better for motion video at higher data rates.

Planar RGB

This is the format used for Photoshop images. It's not really a compressor—it just stores the R, G, and B color values in separate tables. This can accelerate compositing, especially with multiprocessor, MMX, and Velocity Engine computers, and it works well with certain graphics accelerators.

It provides extremely high quality at equally high data rates. It's lossless, so this can be a useful transfer codec. No temporal compression is provided, so the data rate goes up with the frame rate.

Compression is fast, and decompression is also fairly fast, but the large file sizes produced with this kind of "compression" can bog down even a fast machine. This is not a useful delivery codec.

Planar RGB supports 8-bit grayscale, 8-bit color, 24-bit color, and 24-bit color plus an alpha channel.

Every frame is a key frame. The only adjustable parameter for this compressor is the frame rate.

This is the default codec for movies created by importing a sequence of Photoshop images.

PNG

This codec compresses images using the same algorithm as Portable Network Graphics files; see "PNG" (page 281). It does not provide temporal compression. It delivers high image quality at high data rates. It can be lossless, making it a useful transfer codec. It can achieve Web data rates only for slideshows with very low frame rates.

PNG supports 1-bit black-and-white; 2-bit, 4-bit, and 8-bit grayscale; 2-bit, 4-bit, 8-bit, and 24-bit color; and 24-bit color plus an alpha channel.

This can be a useful codec for static alpha channel overlays, such as a logo with transparent or translucent areas.

Every frame is a key frame. You can't specify a maximum data rate.

This is the default codec for movies created by importing a sequence of PNG images. It can be used as a delivery codec for such a movie to avoid recompression. It requires low frame rates to achieve low data rates. You will probably never have cause to export a whole movie using this codec, except to mix down a PNG slideshow that has multiple tracks.

Sorenson Video

This is the one of the best general-purpose codecs for motion video. It can provide very high image quality, even at low data rates. At higher data rates, image quality is stunning. This is arguably the best codec for Web video. For CD-ROM applications, it can allow you to put a lot more video on the disk than other codecs, without sacrificing quality.

Sorenson compresses very slowly, and playback requires a fair amount of processor time. Processor load goes up at higher data rates, but even a lowly 160 MHz CPU can manage smooth playback at CD-ROM or Web data rates.

The Sorenson codec was introduced in QuickTime 3. It was replaced by the Sorenson 2 codec as part of QuickTime 4. The new Sorenson 3 codec was added in QuickTime 5.0.2.

Sorenson uses a YUV color space.

This codec works best if the height and width of the video are both divisible by 4.

You generally want a key frame once every 10 seconds for motion video, or about 1/10 as many key frames as other codecs, such as Cinepak, for the same material. Additional key frames are inserted automatically as needed.

You can specify a data rate limit, and you should. Sorenson may exceed this limit at times, so be conservative, especially for streaming movies.

Only relatively recent machines can decompress Sorenson video at data rates above 200 Kbytes/sec without dropping frames, so be wary of high data rates with older computers. Sorenson video at 100 Kbytes/sec provides better image quality than Cinepak at 300, so you can probably use a lower data rate than you might anticipate.

Sorenson video scales up nicely, so it's often best to compress at half the height and width you want, then double the size for playback. This can be a good way to keep the data rate down for full-screen movies.

Tip Increase the data rate by about 10% to create video that stays sharp when it's scaled up.

The most common mistake that people make with Sorenson compression is setting the key frame rate too high. For CD-ROM and higher bandwidth delivery, another common mistake is setting the data rate too high. Either can prevent smooth playback without adding value.

If you click the Options button in the Compression Settings dialog box with Sorenson Video chosen for the compressor, it brings up additional settings:

QuickTime includes only the basic edition of the Sorenson compressor, so these settings are read-only unless you add the Developer Edition. You can buy the Developer Edition directly from Sorenson, or as part of a software bundle with Media Cleaner from Media 100.

If you add the Developer Edition of the Sorenson compressor, we suggest the following settings:

- B-Frames should be turned off, especially if you might need to edit the movie after compression.

- Playback scalability should be turned on for high data rate movies; it automatically allows slower computers to play the video at a lower frame rate. This provides smoother playback than dropping frames at irregular intervals.

- Image smoothing should always be turned on—smooth images are good!

- The Sorenson compressor may exceed your specified data rate limit for demanding parts of the video. Data rate tracking should normally be tight to minimize this, but if you want to make the highest-quality Fast Start movies, and you don't mind going a little over budget on bandwidth, you might want to loosen it up a little.

- Automatic key frame sensitivity should normally be around 70%, but you can adjust it for the degree of motion in the video. For very slow panning video, sensitivity of 50% can lower the data rate without creating problems. For a movie trailer that's all action sequences and cuts, a setting of 90% may be necessary to prevent artifacts.

The Developer Edition compresses faster than the basic edition. Versions 2.1 and later are accelerated for the G4 Velocity Engine (AltiVec) and for MMX, speeding compression even more. Version 3 delivers sharper colors, faster compression, and provides a given level of quality at a 30% lower data rate, compared with version 2.

If you use Cleaner, Squeeze, or HipFlics, the Sorenson video compressor can be set for two-pass variable bit rate (VBR) compression. For Fast Start movies, this is highly recommended.

This codec is capable of really beautiful output, but it takes a little skill and experience to get the most out of it. Looking for a shortcut? See "Secrets of the Apple Compressionist" (page 342).

TGA

This codec compresses images using the same algorithm as TGA files. It delivers high image quality at very high data rates. It includes some temporal compression.

TGA supports 8-bit grayscale; 8-bit, 16-bit, and 24-bit color; and 24-bit color plus an alpha channel.

You can set the key frame rate, but you can't specify a maximum data rate.

This is the default codec for movies created by importing a sequence of Targa images. Some 3D graphics programs export a series of TGA images, so this can be a useful transport codec. It can be used as a delivery codec for this kind of movie to avoid recompression, but only at high data rates. You will probably never have cause to export a movie using this codec.

TIFF

This codec compresses images using the same algorithm as Tagged Image File Format files; see "TIFF" (page 282). It does not provide temporal compression. It delivers high image quality at extremely high data rates.

TIFF supports 1-bit black-and-white; 2-bit, 4-bit, and 8-bit grayscale; 2-bit, 4-bit, 8-bit, and 24-bit color; and 24-bit color plus an alpha channel.

Every frame is a key frame. You can't specify a maximum data rate.

This is the default codec for movies created by importing a sequence of TIFF images. It can be used as a delivery codec for such a movie to avoid recompression, but only at high data rates. You will probably never have cause to export a movie using this codec.

Video (Apple Video)

This codec provides moderate quality at CD-ROM data rates and good quality at higher data rates. It provides both spatial and temporal compression. It yields quality slightly inferior to Cinepak at low data rates, but compresses much faster.

Compression is very fast. Decompression is even less demanding than Cinepak. The Video codec does not have a minimum 10:1 compression as Cinepak does, so it may provide superior image quality at 4x CD-ROM data rates and above, when the source may be compressed by 5:1 or less.

The Video codec supports 16-bit color only.

You can set a key frame rate; one per second is recommended for motion video. You cannot specify a maximum data rate using this compressor from QuickTime Player, but it can be set using Discreet Cleaner.

This codec is generally used to preview what video will look like after compression; it's much faster than Cinepak and it produces similar, though usually slightly inferior, results. It can be a good codec for motion video on very old machines at higher data rates, such as hard disk delivery on a 486 computer.

QuickTime-Compatible Codecs

There are some very nice video compressors that are available as Quick-Time components, even though they are not part of the QuickTime download or CD installation. You can add these compressors to QuickTime by purchasing and/or downloading them from a third party.

In some cases, the decompressor is available as part of the QuickTime Component Download program. QuickTime will offer to automatically install the decompressor when someone plays a movie that uses one of these compressors. In this case, only the authoring component (the compressor) needs to be purchased or downloaded from a third party.

In other cases, the decompressor must be downloaded or installed by a third party in order for people to see your movie. This limits the audience for such movies, but some compression formats, such as DivX, have an energetic, Web-savvy following who are happy to download the decompressor.

Component Download Compressors

You need to download these compressors from a third party to use them in QuickTime movies, but the movies they create can be viewed by just about anyone with QuickTime. If someone tries to play your movie and needs the decompressor, QuickTime will offer to download it for them. In most cases, this takes less than a minute and requires your audience to do little more than click OK.

ZyGoVideo

This is an exciting new wavelet-based compressor that compares favorably to Sorenson 3 and MPEG-4 as a video codec for the Web. It does particularly well with text and similar material, compared with most low-bit-rate compressors, and produces unusually smooth video at dialup data rates. The basic compressor is a free download from ZyGoVideo (www.zygovideo .com). The pro compressor gives more complete control for optimum output and is available for under $100. It is frequently bundled with Hip-Flics—a capable QuickTime editor and compression program that includes enhanced Sorenson 3 compression—for $129. The compressor is available for Windows and Mac OS 9 and OS X.

Streambox ACT-L2

The ACT-L2 video codec from Streambox provides broadcast-quality video at T1, DSL, and cable modem rates. It can deliver near-DVD quality at much lower data rates than MPEG-2 or MPEG-4. It can be used for high-bandwidth video on demand (300 Kbits/sec or greater), for transmission between video professionals over IP networks, or for highest-quality QuickTime movies on CD-ROM, DVD-ROM, or kiosk applications.

The encoder is available for Windows and Mac OS X as part of the Action editing and compression suite for $199 from Streambox (www.streambox.com). A free trial version is available for download from the same site.

A live encoder version of the compressor is available for sending near–TV-quality streams over dialup connections, as well as broadcast quality over broadband (quarter-screen QCIF at 50–100 Kbits/sec, half-screen CIF at 200–600 Kbits, 1/2 D1 at 350–800 Kbits, and D1 at 700–1200 Kbits). The live encoder is compatible with Channel Storm's Live Channel and QuickTime Broadcaster. The live encoder is included with the Action software and is also available bundled with Live Channel (www.channelstorm.com).

VP3 (formerly On2)

Provides full-screen, full-motion, TV-quality video. Comparable to, and arguably better than, Sorenson 3 or MPEG-4 at data rates from dialup to DSL. This compressor is no longer available from On2 or its successor site, vp3.com. If you have a VP3 compressor, you can use it and Apple will offer to install the decompressor for your viewers as needed. Development of this codec is now an open source project named Theora (www.theora.org), hosted by the Xiph organization (www.xiph.org), the same fine people who bring you the Ogg Vorbis audio codec and IceCast streaming. At the time of writing, an enhanced version of the compressor and decompressor were expected soon, according to Xiph.

Other QuickTime-Compatible Compressors

There are a number of other video compressors you can use with Quick-Time, some new or experimental, some old or little-used. These include various flavors of Indeo codec, Eidos Escape, and TrueMotion, plus hardware-specific compressors included with various capture cards, such as Avid and Radius. Most of these are of interest only to small groups, although some have the potential to become important. Of these, the most significant is DivX.

DivX

While the name "DivX" is an inside joke about a failed scheme for marketing self-destructing DVDs, the DivX codec is a solid piece of work based on the MPEG-4 standard. It's very popular on the Web as a means of passing around video files, much like MP3 for audio. The DivX decompressor for QuickTime is available as a free download from www.divx.com. Unfortunately, it is available for Mac OS only, the rationale being that Windows users will use the .avi format. A compressor for Mac OS is promised, but currently you need to compress DivX content on a Windows computer. Most applications that are compatible with the DivX compressor create .avi files. You can open an .avi with DivX-compressed video in Quick-Time Player on Mac OS and Save As (self-contained) to create a QuickTime movie that uses DivX video compression.

There are some additional DivX decompressor components floating around on the Web, some of which claim they allow QuickTime to open, play, edit, and export from MS-MPEG4 encoded .avi and .wmv files. Interesting, eh?

⏵ Secrets of the Apple Compressionist

The Apple website contains some of the best desktop video in the world. If you haven't seen it yet, definitely check it out (go to www.apple.com /trailers/). This is where the major studios go to post previews of their gazillion-dollar movies. The trailer for George Lucas's *Star Wars: Episode One* alone has been downloaded over 25 million times. The *Lord of the Rings* trailer was downloaded 1.7 million times in 24 hours. That's a lotta pixels. The reason this stuff is so popular is the quality of the QuickTime movies.

So the first question people ask is, "How do you do that?" Well, actually, the first question they ask is, "What compression settings do you use?" And the first answer is, "It's not that simple."

Here's the whole story of how we do it. No endorsement of a particular product should be implied; this is just a description of what we use internally.

The first secret is that there *is* an Apple Compressionist: one talented person who is dedicated to capturing and compressing movies for the Web. It's that important to get it right.

The source material is all the highest possible quality. We start with film trailers, music videos, or television commercials. It's all shot by professional filmmakers or videographers who employ specialists in lighting and sound. Special effects and titles are done on incredibly expensive workstations. If it's shot on film, it's transferred to video in letterbox format using a special deck that converts from 24 fps to 29.87 fps. It usually comes to Apple on DigiBeta (preferred) or BetaSP.

We capture it on either a high-end Power Mac G4 with 1 GB of RAM and 72 GB of striped Wide Ultra SCSI hard drives, or on a standard-configuration XServe. We capture using Digital Voodoo SDI cards, using their ten-bit uncompressed Video codec at full-screen size (768 x 486), 29.97 frames per second, interlaced.

We sometimes get source material on DV tape. We capture it using FinalCut Pro and save it as an uncompressed QuickTime movie.

We then process and compress the movie using Discreet Cleaner 5, Cleaner 6, or Sorenson's Squeeze.

If the source is film, we do an inverse telecine, converting it back to the original 24 frames per second. We also crop the black bars off the top and bottom to restore the original aspect ratio. This makes the file smaller and easier to compress, while giving the viewer a more cinematic experience.

In all cases, we crop off the video overscan and any video noise around the edges of the image. Again, this makes the file smaller and easier to compress, and it creates a more aesthetic presentation. We also deinterlace the video.

We set up an array of compression settings for various bandwidths, usually a T1/LAN broadband version, an ISDN or low-band xDSL version, and a 56 Kbit version. We tend toward the high end of the allowable bandwidth for each version; in our experience, people are willing to wait for higher quality. We tinker with the compression settings, then create the alternate movies and use AppleScript to annotate the movie, adding the title and copyright information and create a reference movie.

Tinker, you say? Yes, every video requires slightly different compression settings for the best results. We start with some basic settings that we adjust from, and sometimes no adjustment is needed, but usually there's room for improvement.

We use the Sorenson Video codec for the most part—the Developer Edition, version 3 (we are transitioning to MPEG-4). For audio we use either the QDesign 2 Music Codec, Professional Edition, or IMA 4:1. We use IMA only rarely, if the target is CD-ROM or the target data rate isn't an issue. We are transitioning to the AAC audio codec.

We choose a size that's a clean step down from the captured size after cropping, typically 1/2 the height and width. Sometimes the high-bandwidth version is 3/4 scale, and the low-bandwidth version is 3/8 scale. We always use a height and width that are divisible by 4.

We typically create three versions. One version is 320 pixels wide, and one version is 240 pixels wide. For studio blockbusters, we also create a high-end version 480 pixels wide. The heights depend on the aspect ratio. If we have to, we round the size down so both height and width are divisible by 4.

We don't normally set the movie to display at double its actual size. But if we expect viewers to play the movie at double size, we specify a little higher data rate during compression. That way it looks sharper when it's scaled larger.

We select a frame rate that's a simple submultiple of the original frame rate: 1/2, 1/3, or 1/4. For film (24 fps) we use 12 or 8 frames per second. For video (~30 fps), we use 29.97, 15, 10, or 7.5. For PAL video (25 fps), we use 12.5 or 6.25. We use higher frame rates if there's a lot of fast motion or cuts. We normally use a lower frame rate for the low-bandwidth versions.

We normally select black restore and white restore. Our default settings are 25 for black and 10 for white. This enhances the contrast, improves titles and credits, undoes some of the damage created by using videotape, and makes the image easier to compress.

Often we enhance the contrast and brightness; it depends on the source material. We generally add +10 to +14 gamma for good cross-platform viewing. Contrast starts at +6 to +10.

We set key frames at the frame rate times 10 (key frame every 10 seconds). That means a movie playing at 12 frames per second would have a key frame setting of 120. Natural key frames are set at 55% sensitivity, with higher sensitivity (up to 90%) for footage with a lot of motion.

For the high-end audio, we use a sample rate of 44.1 kHz, 16-bit samples, in stereo. We set the data rate to 8–10 Kbytes/sec and put the quality sliders at 100%. For the low end, we drop to 22 kHz, mono, and a data rate of 3.5–5 Kbytes/sec, with the quality sliders at 50%.

Those are the basic settings. We set a target bandwidth for each version, push the button, and see what happens. Then we start tinkering.

Usually, there are some parts of the movie that don't compress well in each version. We make a clip of the part that looks the worst, including about 5–10 seconds before and 5–10 seconds after the problem area, taking the clip from the uncompressed version. We recompress this section as many times as necessary, adjusting the settings each time until we get it right. Sometimes we have to go to a higher data rate. When the clip of the worst part looks right, we recompress the whole movie with those settings.

When it's all done, we update the annotations using QuickTime Player. We do it as a batch process using the same AppleScript scripts that you can find in the AppleScript folder on the CD.

We use half a dozen computers at a time for tinkering, each one with slightly different settings. That saves a lot of time, but it's not free. We keep our default settings on one server, so they don't get overwritten, and share them with the others over the network.

There's a four-part equation that trades time, money, bandwidth, and quality. If you have infinite time, money, or bandwidth, you can easily solve the equation for any desired quality. For the rest of us, it's a series of trade-offs. Buy as many of the fastest computers as you can, add hardware compression accelerators if you can afford it, and keep working until you run out of time or are satisfied with your output; you'll end up with the best possible quality for your circumstances. You can get the same results with less expensive hardware; it just takes more time.

And those are the secrets of the Apple Compressionist.

▶ Tools

There are a number of tools available to help you create and edit QuickTime movies. Following is a list of some useful tools, a quick summary of what they do, and contact information for the manufacturer, publisher, or distributor. This isn't a complete list by any means, and we apologize to anyone we left out. No endorsement of one product over another is intended.

For an up-to-date list of such tools, check this page on the Apple website:

www.apple.com/quicktime/products/tools/

Capture

These tools are useful for capturing movies onto your hard drive. Some include hardware to digitize analog audio and video; others are software packages that allow you to use existing hardware, such as a FireWire port.

- Reel-Eyes software, various hardware (www.irez.com/)
- iMovie (store.apple.com/) Click Apple Software link.
- Final Cut Pro (www.apple.com/finalcutpro/)
- Final Cut Express (www.apple.com/)
- CineStream (www.discreet.com/)
- XLR8 InterView with Strata VideoShop (www.xlr8.com/)
- MyCapture II with Strata VideoShop (www.eskapelabs.com/)
- ADS Technologies (www.adstech.com/)
- canopus (www.canopus.com/)
- Digital Voodoo (www.digitalvoodoo.net/)
- Avid (www.avid.com/)
- Movie Maker 2 (www.microsoft.com/windowsxp/moviemaker/)

Editing and Compositing

These tools are useful for editing QuickTime movies.

- Adobe Premiere (www.adobe.com/)
- Avid Express (www.avid.com/)
- CineStream (www.discreet.com/)
- eZedia MX (www.ezedia.com/)
- Final Cut Express (www.apple.com/finalcutpro/)

- Final Cut Pro (www.apple.com/finalcutpro/)
- GoLive (www.adobe.com/)
- Hip Flics (www.totallyhip.com/)
- iMovie (www.apple.com/software/)
- LiveStage Pro (www.totallyhip.com)
- Movie Maker 2 (www.microsoft.com/windowsxp/moviemaker/)

Compression and Format Conversion

These tools are useful for a variety of purposes. Some are codecs that extend QuickTime's ability to create or play back media in compressed formats such as MPEG. Some are useful for converting QuickTime movies into other formats, such as DVD Video, or importing data from formats such as Real Media into QuickTime movies. Some are general-purpose tools for modifying and compressing QuickTime movies.

- **DVD Studio Pro**

  MPEG-2 compression and DVD mastering and recording.

  www.apple.com/dvdstudiopro/

- **Heuris MPEG**

  QuickTime-compatible MPEG-1 and MPEG-2 compression and decompression.

  www.heuris.com/

- **Roxio Toast**

  QuickTime-compatible MPEG-1 and MPEG-2 compression, export to DVD or VCD.

  www.heuris.com/

- **DVD Fusion**

  MPEG-2 compression and DVD mastering software.

  www.sonic.com/

- **Sorenson Squeeze**

  Professional Edition Sorenson video encoding.

  www.sorenson.com/

- **Discreet Cleaner**

  Multipurpose tool for cropping, enhancing, and compressing Quick-Time movies. Converts from Real Media and Microsoft NetShow formats into QuickTime. Includes an MP3 encoder, and optionally includes enhanced versions of the QDesign and Sorenson codecs.

  www.discreet.com/

- **Hip Flics**

  Multipurpose tool for editing, cropping, enhancing, and compressing QuickTime movies. Includes enhanced control of the MPEG-4 and Sorenson 3 codecs. Compatible with all QuickTime codecs, including Streambox ACT-L2.

  www.discreet.com/

- **Spike**

  Utility program that analyzes movies and reports on the actual data rate, including any spikes. A lite version is available in the Demos folder on the CD. Macintosh only.

  www.yav.com/Spike.html

Other Movie Formats

A codec isn't the same thing as a file format, but they're related. File formats specify how the data in a file is arranged, and that includes the image data. The codec specifies how the image data is compressed. Some file formats support only one kind of video codec; an MPEG-1 movie is always compressed with the MPEG-1 video codec. Other file formats, such as AVI and QuickTime movies, can use a variety of codecs. If you import an AVI movie into QuickTime, for example, then save it as a self-contained movie, you've changed the file format from .avi to .mov, but you haven't necessarily changed the video codec. Similarly, while QuickTime can read the AVI file format, a particular AVI file may contain video compressed with a codec that isn't available to QuickTime. This section describes some of the common movie formats and how they relate to QuickTime.

Windows Media

Windows Media is a proprietary format used by Microsoft's Windows Media Player. Windows media files (.wmv) can be streamed from a Web server using HTTP, or by a Windows Media Services server using proprietary methods.

Windows Media supports a growing list of audio and video codecs, media types, and interactive features. Windows Media files are common on the Web, and several MP3 players can play audio in .wmv format as well. At least one of these players calls itself an "MP4 player," but it does not actually play files in MPEG-4 format (.mp4).

Note   Windows Media Player has claimed to have MPEG-4 video for some time, but as of this writing it can neither play nor create .mp4 files. It can compress video using MS-MPEG4 compression, a proprietary implementation based on MPEG-4, but it is not interoperable with actual MPEG-4 players. It cannot play MPEG-4 files, and the files it creates do not play on ISO-compliant MPEG-4 players.

On the Web, .wmv files are often embedded in HTML indirectly using an .asx file (a text file that contains the URL of the .wmv file). It works much like a QuickTime .qtl file and depends on the video/ms-asf MIME type being associated with the .asf and .asx file extensions, and on Windows Media Player being registered with the browser as the helper application for that MIME type. Of course, if the browser and Web server come from the same company that owns the media format, that's pretty much a given.

QuickTime does not import or export Windows Media. There are several software applications available, such as Discreet Cleaner, that can output to either QuickTime or Windows Media from the same source. Most of these programs accept QuickTime movies as source material, so they can also convert from QuickTime to ASF, usually with some quality loss. If the QuickTime movie is already highly compressed, the loss can be severe.

Tip   If you've edited your movie on Windows XP using Microsoft Movie Maker 2, you're not stuck with exporting to Windows Media; you can also export to DV. This creates an .avi file with DV compression that you can open with QuickTime Player and export to any format you like. Be aware that DV files are big—3–5 MB/sec.

AVI

Audio Video Interleave format was introduced as part of Microsoft's Video for Windows project, a technology that has since languished. AVI files are still fairly common on Windows computers and the Web, however, and most can be played by Windows Media Player.

An AVI file can contain exactly one video track and one audio track. This format supports a variety of codecs, including some common Quick-Time codecs such as Cinepak. AVI files compressed using Indeo codecs are common and can be played by QuickTime if the QuickTime version of that Indeo codec is installed on the playback machine. The Indeo codecs are currently available by download from www.ligos.com.

AVI files do not fast start over the Internet—they must download completely before they can play.

QuickTime can play AVI movies, as long as the audio and video are compressed using a codec that QuickTime understands, and that codec is installed on the viewer's computer. For example, adding the DivX decompressor for QuickTime allows Macintosh computers to play DivX or MS-MPEG4 AVI files in QuickTime Player.

QuickTime can export movies to AVI format, mixing down all tracks to one sound track and one video track. Some track types, such as MIDI music and sprites, are not exported.

DV

Digital Video is the format used by digital camcorders and DV editing programs such as iMovie, Final Cut Pro, and CineStream. Data in this format is sometimes referred to as a DV stream. The DV file format supports only DV video compression. There are actually two DV formats: DV-25, which is used in consumer camcorders, and a higher-resolution format known as DVC-Pro 50, or sometimes DV-50. QuickTime has supported DV-25 for some time. Starting with QuickTime 6.1, QuickTime supports DVC-Pro 50 as well.

DV streams are normally transferred between a computer and a camcorder over a FireWire connection (also known as Sony iLink or IEEE 1394). Special software is needed to transfer DV streams between tape and disk. This software is included in DV editing programs. QuickTime Player can open and play DV streams once they are on disk as files, but cannot import them directly from a camcorder via FireWire.

QuickTime Player can export both QuickTime movies using the DV codec and true DV streams. Both movies and streams can be opened by most DV editing software, which can transfer the movies to DV camcorders or decks. Some editing programs can open DV streams, but not QuickTime movies with DV-encoded video.

MPEG

The Motion Picture Experts Group defines standards for motion image compression. They have completed three standards; MPEG-1 and MPEG-2 are several years old now. The MPEG-3 standard was abandoned before completion. The file, video, and audio portions of the MPEG-4 standard have been completed more recently; work on the MPEG-4 standard is ongoing.

Note   MP3 audio is not MPEG-3. It is an extension of the MPEG-1 standard—it stands for MPEG-1, layer 3 audio.

QuickTime has full support for the MPEG-4 file system and currently has encoders and decoders for Profile 1 video and audio. The full MPEG-4 specification includes standards for interactivity, text, and more.

MPEG-1

MPEG-1, often simply called MPEG, is fairly common on the Web and CD-ROMs, typically with the .mpg file extension. MPEG-1 supports one kind of video compression and a few types of audio compression. The content of an MPEG file is one or more MPEG streams. Elementary audio and video streams can be multiplexed into a combined stream.

MPEG-1 was designed to provide VHS-quality video at T1 data rates (single speed, or 1x, CD-ROM). It is the basis for the video CD standard, which was little used in the United States or Europe until recently. Most commercial DVD players can play video CDs, and the rapid spread of CD-R burners and DVD players is fueling the popularity of this format, particularly among college-age people.

QuickTime can open and play MPEG-1 video on both Windows and Macintosh (requires QuickTime 5 or later for Windows). It can then export the video to other formats using any of the QuickTime compressors. Currently, QuickTime treats the entire MPEG-1 stream as a single sample, so you cannot cut or copy part of an MPEG-1 video unless you convert it to a different compression format first.

QuickTime Player 5.02 and later allows you to add other QuickTime media to MPEG-1 video, which allows you to do things like adding a background image, logo, or QuickTime sound track, but you cannot cut from or paste into the MPEG-1 video sequence.

MPEG-1 files can also contain audio. The audio can be compressed in two different formats: layer 2 (often called MPEG-1 audio) and layer 3 (known as MP3). Layer 2 audio can be multiplexed with video in the same stream.

QuickTime can play layer 2 audio, either alone or multiplexed with video. If the audio is multiplexed with MPEG-1 video, however, Quick-

Time cannot currently edit or export the audio. The current workaround is to demultiplex the MPEG stream using other software, such as bbDeMux, and convert the demultiplexed audio into AIFF format. Alternatively, you can play the multiplexed movie while running recording software, such as Total Recorder 3+, that captures the computer's audio digitally, before it gets to the analog output.

QuickTime plays MP3 audio without difficulty, including streaming MP3 such as ShoutCast.

QuickTime Player does not export to MPEG-1 streams, nor does it compress audio or video using MPEG-1 compression. MPEG-1 compression can be added to QuickTime with products such as the Heuris MPEG codec (www.heuris.com/) or Roxio Toast (www.roxio.com/).

MPEG-2

MPEG-2 was designed to provide broadcast-quality digital video at data rates appropriate for cable TV, satellite, and DVD. MPEG-2 compression is the basis for DVD video. MPEG-2 files are rarely found outside of broadcast studios and DVDs.

MPEG-2 is both a file format and a compression format. Decompression is extremely demanding. Most current computers require hardware acceleration to play back MPEG-2 streams in real time.

You can download a QuickTime MPEG-2 decompressor component from Apple. This component is licensed from the MPEG group and costs $19.99. It enables MPEG-2 playback, export, and editing.

This does not mean that you can open MPEG-2 video files from commercial DVDs using QuickTime Player and edit or save them, however. MPEG-2 video on DVD is generally wrapped in a VOB file and encrypted using CSS encryption. DVD video players are shipped under a license agreement that prohibits them from allowing encrypted data to be copied.

You can open and play nonencrypted MPEG-2 files in QuickTime Player once the MPEG-2 extension is installed. You can also edit MPEG-2 files and save them as QuickTime movies with video compressed in MPEG-2 format, or export the audio or video using other QuickTime codecs.

MPEG-2 compression can currently be added to QuickTime by means of the Heuris MPEG encoder, Apple's DVD Studio Pro software, Discreet Cleaner, Roxio Toast, or Apple's iDVD. The MPEG-2 encoding capability of iDVD is limited to creating DVDs, however. Other software enables MPEG-2 compression for QuickTime applications generally, including QuickTime Player. This allows you to create QuickTime movies with MPEG-2 compression. Roxio Toast supports the creation of Super Video CDs (S-VCD), which are CDs that use the DVD format and MPEG-2 compression. Obviously, a 650 MB CD holds less data than a 5 or 9 GB DVD, but for short films it's often enough. Many commercial DVD players can play S-VCDs as well.

MPEG-4

The MPEG-4 standard was recently completed. It outlines file conventions and compression formats not only for audio and video, but for text and multimedia integration. The MPEG-4 file format is based on the Quick-Time file format, with minor modifications, and MPEG-4 files are potentially as diverse in content as QuickTime movies. This is a rich and complex specification, parts of which are still under development.

Software and hardware vendors are implementing the MPEG-4 specification in stages. For example, Apple currently supports MPEG-4 audio (AAC simple encoder) and MPEG-4 video (both Basic and Improved). The parts of the specification that are implemented by a given MPEG-4 player are called a player profile.

The MPEG-4 video codec focuses on low-bandwidth video for Internet delivery, with the goal of delivering near-television quality over DSL and cable modems, and reasonable quality over dialup modems.

QuickTime can create and play true MPEG-4 files using the MPEG-4 file format and the .mp4 file extension. These files should also play on any MPEG-4 compliant player. These are not QuickTime movies, however. They must have the .mp4 file extension, not the .mov file extension.

QuickTime can also create and play QuickTime movies containing audio and video compressed in MPEG-4 format. These are QuickTime movies and should have the .mov file extension. They must not have the .mp4 file extension.

Important You cannot rename an .mp4 file with the .mov file extension—if you do, QuickTime will be unable to play it. Similarly, you cannot take a QuickTime movie compressed using the MPEG-4 codec and give it the .mp4 file extension—it will be unplayable by any .mp4 player, including QuickTime.

Real Media

Real Media is made up of a variety of proprietary file and compression formats created by Real Networks. It is very common on the Web, typically with the .ra or .ram file extension. Often these files contain URLs of other files or real-time streams (also in proprietary format).

Real Media requires the Real Media player or plug-in. It delivers moderate-to-good quality audio and video at Web data rates.

QuickTime does not import or export Real Media format. There are several software applications available, such as Discreet Cleaner, that can output to either QuickTime or Real Media from the same source. Most of these programs accept QuickTime movies as source material, so they can also convert from QuickTime to Real Media, usually with some quality loss. If the movie is already highly compressed, the loss can be severe.

Real Networks strongly discourages anyone from converting media from their format to anyone else's, so there is no good way to do it. Since Real Media is already highly compressed, in most cases it wouldn't be worthwhile to convert and recompress it anyway (it would look pretty bad). If you must do this, perhaps because you lost your original file after converting it to Real format, there are freeware applications such as TINRA (This Is Not Real Anymore) floating around that can capture audio and video from a computer's output buffers and store the results in an AVI file.

Note Real has announced support for .mp4 files in RealPlayer. This should enable RealPlayer to play content created in QuickTime and exported to the MPEG-4 file format, as well as .mp4 content from other sources.

Text! Text! Text!

Text can add a lot to your movies without taking up much bandwidth. QuickTime has the ability to embed text, such as titles, credits, and subtitles, in a movie *as text*. It's rendered on the screen by the viewer's computer only when the movie is played. Text is marvelously compact; a character can be encoded in just 8 bits. Even last decade's modems can pull 28,800 bits a second, or 3600 characters. That's a lot of text.

An 8-bit text character, rendered on the screen in 18-point type, might cover 200 pixels, each using 24 bits. That's 4800 bits to represent the same character. Sending it as text instead of pixels gives 600:1 compression, and because it's rendered by the viewer's computer, its appearance is razor sharp—no video compression artifacts.

QuickTime text is a flexible media type. You can specify the font, text color, size, and styles such as bold, outline, or italic. Text can have drop shadows or be highlighted at specific moments. Text can automatically scroll across the screen. Text can be overlaid on moving video or a still image as the movie is playing.

Text tracks can also add interactive chapter lists and clickable hypertext links to a movie, or autoloading URLs that display live Web pages synchronized to your audio and video. To make things even nicer, text tracks are easy to create and modify using a simple text editor. And text can be streamed in real time. This chapter covers

- importing text into a QuickTime movie
- exporting a text track and modifying it with a text editor
- setting fonts, styles, scrolling, karaoke, and other characteristics
- adding titles and credits to a movie

- adding subtitles and closed captions to a movie
- adding an interactive chapter list to a movie
- adding a hypertext reference (HREF) track
- choosing fonts for cross-platform movies
- "burning" text into a video track
- searching a text track using QuickTime Player Pro

▶ QuickTime Text Tools

There are now several tools that can build and format QuickTime text tracks for you, handling all the font, color, and style issues. There are also tools to add hypertext links, create chapter lists, HREF tracks, and subtitle and closed-caption tracks. They're all incredible time savers, and some are inexpensive, cheap, or even free. The more expensive ones do a lot of other useful things in addition to text.

Here are some of the tools available:

- **FinalChapter**

  Possibly the easiest and most convenient tool for making chapter lists.

  Mac OS 8 (runs in Classic)
  $10 (Free 30-day trial)
  www.acutabovesw.com/finalchapter.html

- **GoLive**

  Large software package designed for creating Web pages and managing websites. It includes a wysiwyg Web page editor and an HTML generator that automatically creates correct <EMBED> and <OBJECT> tags for Quick-Time movies (just drag them onto the page). It also has an exceptionally powerful QuickTime editor that supports audio, video, sprite, and text tracks—including chapter lists and HREF tracks. You can assign simple actions to sprites in GoLive to create buttons and movie controllers.

  Windows, Mac OS 9, Mac OS X
  $399
  www.adobe.com

- **LiveStage Pro**

  Premiere tool for creating interactive QuickTime. It unleashes the full capabilities of QuickTime wired actions and scripting, including support for editable text, XML list exchange with remote databases, and loading child movies (movie-in-a-movie). It supports all QuickTime media types and features, including VR, MPEG-4, and Flash 5. Most interactive QuickTime professionals find it indispensable.

Windows, Mac OS X
$899 ($100 discount coupon in this book; demo on the CD)
www.totallyhip.com

- **MacAW**

Primarily for creating subtitles and closed captions. This software lets you easily synchronize text samples with a movie, preview the results, add styles, and more. Includes a widget that enables/disables text tracks interactively.

Mac OS 9 (runs in Classic)
Free!
whitanderson.com/macaw/index.html

- **Textation**

Easy-to-use tool for creating chapter lists, subtitles, closed-caption tracks, HREF tracks, and styled text tracks.

Mac OS X
$23 (free demo—can't save)
home.netvigator.com/~feelorium/feelorium/products.html

- **TitleLAB**

Imports .srt, .ssa, and .sub files into QuickTime, sets font and size, and helps you synchronize subtitles to your movie. Read the excellent one-page tutorial that comes with the software; you'll be lost without it (but have no trouble if you read it).

Mac OS X
Free!
Azinesoftware.com (also available from www.versiontracker.com)

▶ Creating Text Tracks

You normally create a text track for a QuickTime movie in four steps:

1. Write the text using a text editor or word processor, saving as plain text.

2. Import the text using QuickTime Player and set the attributes for the track as a whole (font, point size, color, transparency, and so on).

Sometimes that's all you need to do. More often, you want to make certain text bold, alter the timing and appearance of some frames, or set special attributes such as scrolling or highlighting. If so,

3. Export the text track as Text with Descriptors. This creates a text file with properly formatted descriptor tags and time stamps.
4. Edit the exported file with a text editor and reimport.

This puts the text, edited to your taste, in a movie containing only a text track. You can then cut or copy the text track and add (or add scaled) to your destination movie.

If you know exactly what you're doing, you can write a finished text track, complete with descriptors and time stamps, using a text editor, and then just import it. It's fairly easy to mess this up, so I recommend the four steps of importing, exporting, editing, and reimporting, using QuickTime to generate a block of well-formatted descriptors that you can edit. As you gain experience, you can take shortcuts.

Tip There are several tools that will build and format QuickTime text tracks for you, handling all the font, color, and style issues, as well as hypertext links and chapter lists. They include eZedia QTI, VideoClix, and Textation. See "QuickTime Text Tools" (page 356) for details.

Creating Text for a Text Track

Write the text that you want in your movie using a text editor, or write it with a word processor and save it as plain text with a .txt file extension.

The text will be rendered on the screen in a series of visual frames, one paragraph at a time. Put text that you want on the screen at the same time in the same paragraph. Terminate each paragraph with a carriage return. Don't use any carriage returns within the paragraph.

Don't worry about formatting yet; just enter the text in blocks.

Importing Text into QuickTime

QuickTime can import plain text files created with a text editor such as Text Edit or BBEdit, or files created with a word processor such as Word-Perfect, Microsoft Word, or Word Pad and saved as text.

Using QuickTime Player, choose Import from the File menu, select a text file using the dialog box, and click Import.

Importing in Windows, Mac OS 8, or Mac OS 9

In Windows, Mac OS 8, or Mac OS 9, you'll be prompted to give the new movie a filename.

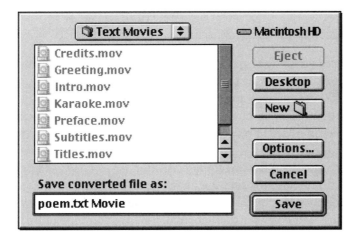

If you click Save, the text is imported with the default settings. To select different settings, click Options instead. This opens a dialog box showing the current text attributes and the available choices.

Note This feature is not currently available in Mac OS X. The Mac OS X dialog does not contain an Options button.

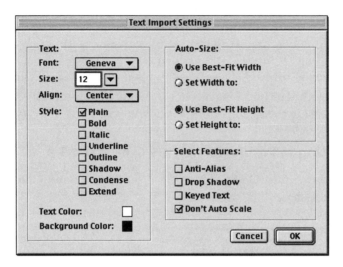

You can display text using any font installed on your computer. You may want to choose a font that's also installed on your target audience's computers. Good choices are Times, Courier, and Helvetica.

Text size can be chosen from 9 to 24 points, which may be further reduced or enlarged by scaling. You can specify other point sizes simply by typing them in.

Alignment can be left, right, or center.

The font styles include the usual variations, such as Bold and Italic, plus two you may not be familiar with, Condense and Extend, which make the text narrower or wider than normal. You can combine more than one style.

Tip For light-colored Helvetica or Arial text on a dark background, bold text makes easier reading.

Clicking the Text Color or Background Color box brings up a color-picker dialog box. You can select any color text and any color background.

The Auto-Size box allows you to specify a height and width for the text track, or to allow QuickTime to set an appropriate size based on the most text that will appear on the screen in any frame.

You can also select any of these features:

- **Anti-Alias**—softens the edges of the text by mixing in some of the background color. This makes text appear less jagged, but slightly out of focus.

- **Drop Shadow**—adds a translucent drop shadow to the text.

- **Keyed Text**—puts the text on a transparent background. Use this feature for text that will be displayed over other images.
- **Don't Auto Scale**—prevents the text from getting larger or smaller if the movie or the text track is resized.

The attributes you select are applied to the whole text track. You can apply different settings to selected text later.

Click OK to return to the dialog box where you specify a name and location for the text movie. Click Save.

Importing in Mac OS X

In Mac OS X, choose Import from the File menu, navigate to the text file, and click Open. Alternatively, just drag the text file onto QuickTime Player.

That's it.

Note You can't currently set the text size, color, style, and so on as part of the Import dialog, as you can in Windows or older versions of the Mac OS. Don't despair. You can set these characteristics as described in the following sections.

Modifying Text after Import

QuickTime creates one video frame from each paragraph of text (a paragraph is terminated by a carriage return). The text in any frame may wrap onto multiple lines on the screen, depending on the size of the text box. Each frame has a duration of two seconds. A text file containing

```
Movie without a title
written and directed by Alan Smithee
```

becomes the movie shown in the following illustration.

At this point, you see the results of your import settings. You may need to close the new movie and reimport the text file using different settings to get the effect you want.

You can create different text styles using a word processor or a text editor that supports styles (such as SimpleText) and drag the style onto the text track's Properties window to see how it looks. Here's how:

1. Open the Movie Properties window, choose the text track from the left pop-up menu, and choose Text Replace from the right one.

2. Create a word of styled text in another program, select it, and drag the selection onto the words "Drop Style Here." This copies the font, size, and text styles such as bold or italic onto your text track.

3. When you get the effect you want, close the Properties box and save the movie.

Bear in mind that this changes the style of the whole text track.

You'll also see an area labeled Drop Text Here in the Properties window, and it can be quite useful. Select any portion of the movie timeline using the QuickTime Player selection tools, select any amount of text in a text editor that allows drag and drop, and drag the text selection into the area labeled Drop Text Here. This adds the selected text to the text track as a single sample with the same timing and duration as your selection in the movie timeline. It's great for synchronizing a subtitle or closed caption with a selection of video footage.

You can change the duration of a text sample, or a sequence of samples, by using the Add Scaled command, as described in "Creating Titles and Scrolling Credits" (page 378). You can also change the duration of a text sample using a text editor.

To set special characteristics, such as scrolling or highlighting, or to change the style of selected text, you need to use a text editor.

Modifying Text Tracks with a Text Editor

Importing text creates a very simple text track. It has one frame every two seconds. All the text is the same size, color, and style. You can't directly control the way the text wraps, except by adjusting the text size and the frame size.

Sometimes that's all you need, but more often you'll want to do some fine-tuning. It's fairly easy to get your hands under the hood to make changes. Just choose Export from the File menu. Choose Text to Text, and Text with Descriptors, from the pop-up menus:

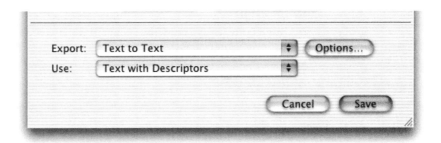

Click the Options button to set the format for the text descriptors. The default is Show Text, Descriptors, and Time, which is what you want:

The exported file is going to have a time stamp at the beginning and end of each text frame. This can be an absolute time stamp, showing when in the movie the text appears, or a relative time stamp, showing how long each frame is displayed. If you're going to synchronize the text with another movie's timeline, click Movie; if you just want to specify how long each text sample is on the screen, click Sample.

The time stamp will be in the format [00:00:00.000], showing Hours:Minutes:Seconds.Fractions. The fractional part is displayed using the track's timeScale units, which might be 1/10th of a second or 1/10000th. For convenience in synchronizing your text with a movie's timeline, set the timeStamps fractions to 1/30 or 1/300.

Why 1/30 or 1/300? Because the time displayed in a movie's Info or Properties window always displays fractions as thirtieths of a second. (At 30 frames a second, each fractional unit is 1 frame.) A setting of 1/30 for your time stamps lets you directly copy the time display from a movie's Info window into your text track. A setting of 1/300 creates a finer granularity when QuickTime is synchronizing multiple tracks, and it's easy to do the conversion by adding a zero.

Click OK, then click Save. Open the exported file using a text editor. If your original text file was

```
Movie without a title
written and directed by Alan Smithee
```

the exported file looks something like this:

```
{QTtext}{font:Geneva}{bold}{size:12}{textColor: 65535, 65535,
65535}{backColor: 0, 0, 0}{justify:center}
{timeScale:300}
{width:160}{height:48}{timeStamps:absolute}
{language:0}{textEncoding:0}
[00:00:00.000]
Movie without a title
[00:00:02.000]
written and directed by Alan Smithee
[00:00:04.000]
```

The first paragraph is a block of text descriptors, starting with {QTtext}. This block is followed by a series of time stamps and text paragraphs. The file ends with a time stamp indicating the end of the last text frame, followed by a carriage return.

You can change the start and end times for a text frame by editing the time stamps before and after it. If time stamps are relative, you can change a frame's duration just by editing its ending time stamp. If time stamps are absolute, all the subsequent time stamps must be changed as well.

For example, to hold the title on screen for four seconds, we would edit the earlier file to

```
[00:00:00.000]
Movie without a title
[00:00:04.000]
written and directed by Alan Smithee
[00:00:06.000]
```

Important   Absolute time stamps *must* be larger for each sequential sample, or the file will not import properly.

The fractional part of `timeStamps` is in `timeScale` units. The time scale is part of the descriptor block at the top of the file. If the time scale is 300, for example, the fractional part of `timeScale` is in 1/300ths of a second.

You can edit the text in any frame, inserting line breaks where you want the text to wrap. For example:

```
[00:00:00.000]
Movie without a title
[00:00:04.000]
written by Alan Smithee
directed by Alan Smithee
produced by Alan Smithee
[00:00:06.000]
```

When you import an ordinary text file into QuickTime, each paragraph becomes a text frame. When you import a file with descriptors, frames are divided by time stamps, so you can create frames with multiple paragraphs or line breaks.

If all you need to do is change the text, line breaks, and timing, you don't need to edit the descriptor tags; you can now save the text file and reimport it into QuickTime.

Setting Text Attributes

Text attributes are controlled by descriptor tags. A descriptor tag has the format {keyWord:setting}, for example: {timeScale:300}. The curly brackets tell QuickTime that this is a descriptor.

Important   You cannot use the { character in a file that will be imported into a QuickTime text track unless it is part of a descriptor tag. Sorry.

The keyword describes the attribute being set, such as font, size, or textColor. The keyword is case sensitive.

The setting can be a string, such as {font:helvetica}. The setting can also be a number, such as {size:12}, or a series of numbers separated by commas, such as {textColor:0,0,0}. Some descriptors don't require a setting; {bold}, for example, is a complete descriptor by itself.

The file must start with the {QTtext} tag, followed by a block of descriptors that define the settings for the track as a whole. There are required descriptors:

```
{font: }
{size: }
{textColor: , , }
{backColor: , , }
{justify: }
{timeScale: }
{width: }
{height: }
{timeStamps: }
{language: }
{textEncoding: }
```

There may be optional descriptors as well, such as {bold}. The descriptors must all be in a single paragraph (no carriage returns).

Tip The best way to create a valid descriptor block is to import some plain text into Quick-Time Player, then export it as Text with Descriptors.

The text attributes set in the initial block remain in effect unless other descriptors are inserted later in the file. New descriptors can generally be inserted at any point in the text, allowing you to change the attributes of frames, words, or even single characters. The new descriptors remain in effect unless there are subsequent descriptors. For example:

```
[00:00:00]
Written by: Alan Smithee
A Big {bold}{size:14}N{plain}{size:12} Production
[00:00:04]
```

This makes the "N" character bold and sets it in 14-point type, generating something that looks like this:

Some attributes, such as language, can only be applied to a whole text track. To switch from English to Japanese, for example, you need to make two separate text tracks. Other attributes, such as justification, can be applied only to whole frames.

Complete List of Text Attributes

Here's a complete list of text attributes and their tags. Use them cautiously. Typographic errors can prevent the text track from importing completely or cause unpredictable results.

General

These are required tags that cannot be changed within a text track.

- {QTtext} Required at the beginning of any text file that contains descriptors and time stamps.
- {language:} Specifies the language of the text track. The language is specified by a number. For example, {language:0} specifies English, while {language:11} specifies Japanese. Text is automatically rendered in the appropriate script for the specified language; Roman script for English or French, for example, Cyrillic script for Russian, or Kanji script for Japanese. Some common {language:} codes are shown in the following table:

Language	Code	Language	Code
Arabic	12	Hindi	21
Chinese (simplified)	33	Icelandic	15
Chinese (traditional)	19	Italian	3
Croatian	18	Japanese	11
Danish	7	Korean	23
Dutch	4	Norwegian	9
English	0	Portuguese	8
Farsi	31	Russian	32
Finnish	13	Spanish	6
French	1	Swedish	5
German	2	Thai	22
Greek	14	Turkish	17
Hebrew	10	Urdu	20

- {textEncoding:} Text is stored in computers as a series of 8-bit or 16-bit numbers. Each number represents one character, such as a letter or an ideogram. The {textEncoding:} descriptor specifies the mapping between numbers and characters. This allows QuickTime to convert a series of numbers into a visual representation of writing.

For example, {textEncoding:0} specifies the Roman script. Each character is represented by an 8-bit number, and the number 65 represents the character "A". As another example, {textEncoding:256} specifies the Unicode script. Each character is represented by a 16-bit number, and there are special characters for most non-Roman writing systems, such as Arabic or Katakana.

Roman script is the default, and Unicode is an all-purpose alternative, but QuickTime also supports language-specific scripts. Here's a list of some common text encoding values and the associated scripts:

Text encoding	Script	Text encoding	Script
0	Roman	20	Cambodian
1	Japanese	21	Thai
2	Chinese (traditional)	22	Laotian
3	Korean	23	Georgian
4	Arabic	24	Armenian
5	Hebrew	25	Chinese (simplified)
6	Greek	30	Vietnamese
7	Russian	256	Unicode

QuickTime can only display character sets that are installed on the user's system. Not all computers have all scripts installed. A Macintosh has at least Roman and an appropriate script for the user's system language.

Unless you are using Unicode, you can generally just specify the language, using the {language:} descriptor, and QuickTime will choose the appropriate text encoding for you. If no language is specified, QuickTime will set the text encoding appropriately based on the font.

QuickTime will automatically detect a Unicode text file during the import process if the file begins with the 2-byte Unicode header (either FEFF for big-endian Unicode, or FFEF for little-endian).

If you export Unicode text as Text with Descriptors, you will find that the text descriptors and time stamps are ASCII encoded, while the text samples remain in Unicode. You can edit the text descriptors using any text editor that tolerates Unicode, such as BBEdit, or using a programmer's Hex/ASCII editor.

If you're creating a text file with descriptors programmatically, and you want to include Unicode text, encode the text descriptors and time stamps as ASCII characters, and include the Unicode header at the beginning of your first sample.

- {timeStamps:} Specifies whether time stamps are absolute or relative. If time stamps are absolute, the time stamps for each sample are its starting and ending time in the movie. If time stamps are relative, the time stamp following a sample is how long that sample is onscreen. Possible values are absolute and relative. For example, {timestamps:absolute}.

- {timeScale:} Specifies the time scale for the text track, in units per second. This time scale is used to calculate the fractional part of a time stamp. For example, if {timeScale:300} is specified, the time stamp

[00:00:07.150] would be interpreted as 7.5 seconds because the fractional part is 150/300. If the time scale were 30, the equivalent time stamp would be [00:00:07.15]. The maximum value for this parameter is {timeScale:10000}, or 1/10th of a millisecond. The default value is 600.

Note   The fractional part of the time displayed in QuickTime Player's Info box is always expressed in 1/30ths of a second, regardless of the time scale. If you set the time scale to 30, your time stamps correspond to this display; otherwise, you need to do a conversion in order to synchronize timeStamps with the time display.

Text Display

These tags specify the text display for the track. They cannot be changed within a track.

- {height:} Specifies the height of the text track in pixels. For example, {height:50} sets the text track height to 50 pixels. The special setting {height:0} tells QuickTime to select an appropriate height.

- {width:} Specifies the width of the text track in pixels. For example, {width:150} sets the text track width to 150 pixels. The special setting {width:0} tells QuickTime to select an appropriate width.

- {doNotAutoScale:} Specifies whether to automatically scale the text if the track or movie is resized. Possible values are on and off. Automatic scaling is enabled unless you disable it by specifying {doNot-AutoScale:on}. Use this descriptor to lock the point size of your text regardless of the movie's display size.

Text Justification

Justification can be specified for the track as a whole or on a frame-by-frame basis.

- {justify:} Specifies the alignment of the text in the text box. Possible values are left, right, and center. For example, {justify:left} aligns text on the left. This value can be changed for each text sample (the text between consecutive time stamps is a sample), but can't be changed within a sample.

Text Styles

These tags describe the appearance of the text. They can be changed at any time on a word-by-word or even character-by-character basis.

- {font:} Specifies the name of the font. For example, {font:Courier} sets the font to Courier.
- {size:} Specifies the point size of the text. For example, {size:18} sets the text size to 18 points.
- {plain} Resets the text style. This text descriptor cancels any of the text styles below:
  - {bold} Specifies bold text.
  - {italic} Specifies italic text.
  - {underline} Specifies underlined text.
  - {outline} Specifies outlined text.
  - {shadow} Adds a drop shadow to text.
  - {condense} Specifies condensed (narrow) text.
  - {extend} Specifies extended (wide) text.

The bulleted text styles can be applied in any combination, except the {plain} tag, which deselects all the others.

Drawing Text

These descriptors control how text is drawn.

- {doNotDisplay:} Specifies whether to display the text. Possible values are on and off; the default value is off. For example, {doNotDisplay:on} causes the text not to be displayed. Use this to add invisible comments.
- {anti-alias:} Specifies whether text should be displayed using anti-aliasing. Anti-aliasing smooths the edges of the text by blending the edge colors of the text and background. Possible values are on and off; the default value is off.

Note Anti-aliasing is CPU-intensive, especially when combined with keyed text or scrolling text. If your text is not scrolling smoothly, try turning anti-aliasing off.

- {textBox:} Specifies the dimensions of a text display area, or text box, within the text track. By default, the text box is the whole text track. This descriptor takes four parameters: top, left, bottom, and right. For example, if you specify {textBox:0, 0, 80, 320}, the text box originates at the track's upper left corner and is 80 pixels high and 320 pixels wide. The dimensions of the text box must fall within the text track.

Important Text and the background color for the text track can be restricted to the text box independently, using {shrinkTextBox:} and {clipToTextBox:}. Setting the text box boundaries has *no effect* unless one or both of these descriptors is also used.

- {shrinkTextBox:} Specifies whether to restrict text display to the text box specified by the {textBox:} descriptor. Possible values are on and off; the default value is off.

- {clipToTextBox:} Specifies whether to display the text background color over the entire area of the text track box, or to clip the background to the text box. Possible values are on and off; the default value is off.

- {textColor:} Specifies the color of the text. This descriptor takes three parameters: red, green, and blue color values. Each parameter can be between 0 and 65535. For example, {textColor:32000,0,0} sets the text color to a medium shade of red.

- {keyedText:} Specifies whether the text background should be transparent. This is also known as masked text. Possible values are on and off; the default value is off. Use this descriptor to superimpose text on other visuals, such as a still image or motion video.

- {backColor:} Specifies the background color of the text track. This descriptor takes three parameters: red, green, and blue color values. Each parameter can be between 0 and 65535. For example, the text descriptor {backColor:0,45000,0} sets the background color to a shade of green. This descriptor has no effect when using keyed text, as the background is then transparent. If {clipToTextBox:on} is specified, the background color is limited to the region specified by the {textBox:} descriptor.

- {hilite:} Specifies characters to be highlighted in a text sample. This descriptor takes two parameters: the number of characters in the sample that precede the first character to highlight, and the number of characters to be highlighted. For example, {hilite: 0,3} highlights the first three characters in the sample. By default, the highlight is displayed using inverse video; you can change this by setting {textColorHilite:} and {hiliteColor:}.

Example [00:00:00]
{hilite: 10, 4}This is a text track
[00:00:02]

This example highlights the word "text." Remember: Spaces are characters.

- {inverseHilite:} Specifies to highlight text by using inverse video. Possible values are on or off; the default value is on.
- {textColorHilite:} Specifies text should be highlighted by changing the color of the text instead of using inverse video. Possible values are on and off; the default value is off. You should also specify the highlight color. This descriptor overrides the default inverse video highlight.
- {hiliteColor:} Specifies the color to be used for highlighted text. This descriptor takes three parameters: red, green, and blue color values. Each parameter can be between 0 and 65535. For example, {hiliteColor:0, 0, 65535} sets the highlight color to bright blue.
- {dropShadow:} Specifies whether to draw text with drop shadows. Possible values are on and off; the default value is off.
- {dropShadowOffset:} Specifies an offset for the drop shadow. This descriptor takes two parameters, an offset to the right and an offset down. For example, {dropShadowOffset: 3, 4} offsets the drop shadow 3 pixels to the right and 4 pixels down from the text. The default is {dropShadowOffset: 6, 6}. Drop shadows must be enabled for this descriptor to take effect.
- {dropShadowTransparency:} Specifies the transparency of the drop shadow. This descriptor takes one parameter, a value between 0 and 255, with 0 being completely transparent and 255 being completely opaque. The default value is 127, or 50% translucent. Drop shadows must be enabled for this descriptor to take effect.

Scrolling

These descriptors control text scrolling. The default, if none of these descriptors is present, is nonscrolling text. For examples of scrolling text, see Scroll.htm in the Text folder of the CD.

- {scrollIn:} Specifies whether text should scroll into the frame until the last of the text is in view. Possible values are on and off. The default value is off. Text begins to scroll in at the sample's start time, plus any specified scroll delay. (See Scroll1.mov in the Text folder of the CD.)

■ {scrollOut:} Specifies whether text should be scrolled out of the frame until the last of the text is out of view. Possible values are on and off. The default value is off. Text scrolls at the necessary speed to take the text off screen by the end of the sample's allotted time. (See Scroll2.mov in the Text folder of the CD.)

You can combine {scrollIn:} and {scrollOut:}. (See Scroll3.mov in the Text folder of the CD.)

■ {scrollDelay:} Specifies a delay before the text sample starts scrolling. If {scrollIn:on} is specified, the delay precedes the appearance of the text. If {scrollOut:on} is specified, but not {scrollIn:on}, the text is displayed in place during the delay, then begins to scroll out. The delay is specified in the text track's timeScale units. For example, if the time scale is 300, the text descriptor {scrollDelay:300} causes a one-second delay.

■ {continuousScroll:} Specifies whether previous samples should be "pushed out" as new samples are scrolling in. This is different from setting {scrollOut:on}, which scrolls the old sample out before a new sample appears. Possible values are on and off. The default value is off. In order for this text descriptor to take effect, {scrollIn:on} must also be set. (See Scroll4.mov in the Text folder of the CD.)

Tip For smooth continuous scrolling, set {scrollIn:on}, {continuousScroll:on}, and {scrollOut:on}, and make all the text a single sample with line breaks and a long duration. (See Scroll5.mov in the Text folder of the CD.)

■ {horizontalScroll:} Specifies whether to scroll text as a single line horizontally across the screen. This is sometimes called "Times' Square" or "marquee" scrolling. Possible values are on and off. The default value is off. If you do not specify this descriptor, scrolling is vertical. You normally want to set {scrollIn:on} and {scrollOut:on} when you choose horizontal scrolling. (See Scroll6.mov in the Text folder of the CD.)

■ {reverseScroll:} Specifies whether to reverse the direction of scrolling. Possible values are on and off. The default value is off. For vertical scrolling, the default direction is from bottom to top. For horizontal scrolling, the default direction is from right to left. This descriptor is used to make text scroll down, or from left to right.

- {flowHorizontal:} Horizontal scrolling text normally scrolls across the screen on a single line. If {flowHorizontal:on} is set, long text samples will flow in a serpentine pattern filling the entire text box before scrolling off screen. Possible values are on and off. The default value is off.

Hypertext Links

These descriptors allow you to add clickable hypertext links to text.

- {HREF: } Specifies a URL that will be opened when someone clicks the text between this descriptor and the following {endHREF} descriptor. Any valid URL can be used. The URL can be absolute or relative to the movie. All text between the {HREF: } and {endHREF} descriptors is underlined and drawn in blue, as it might be in a browser.

Example   Visit {HREF:http://www.apple.com/}Apple {endHREF}today.

This example loads the Apple website in the default browser window when someone clicks the word "Apple." You can target an existing browser frame or browser window, a new browser window, QuickTime Player, or the QuickTime plug-in, by adding a T<*target*> parameter, as shown in the following example.

Example   Click {HREF:http://www.apple.com/ T<fr1>}here{endHREF}.

This example loads the Apple website in the browser window or frame named fr1 if such a window or frame already exists; otherwise it creates a new window, names it fr1, and loads the URL in the new window. To target QuickTime Player, use T<quicktimeplayer>. To target the QuickTime plug-in, use T<myself>.

The syntax is subtly different from other QuickTime URL specifications, so be alert. The URL must follow the colon in {HREF: } immediately, with no quotes, spaces, or angle brackets. If a target is specified, it is separated from the URL by a space and takes the form T<*target*>—preceded by a capital "T" and surrounded by angle brackets.

Note   Currently, {HREF: } links do not work in scrolling text.

- {endHREF} Closes the previous {HREF: } descriptor.

Karaoke Text

These descriptors turn highlighting on and off for strings of characters at fixed times. You can use this to help synchronize text with other media. An example would be highlighting the text of a language lesson as the words are read aloud in a sound track. Of course, if the text highlights are synchronized to music, you have Internet karaoke—feel free to sing along.

Tip You can use other software to create standard karaoke files (.kar) and import them into QuickTime. This creates a movie that has a music track and a text track (with karaoke highlights).

- {karaoke:} Highlights groups of characters in a text sample at specified times. This descriptor can have a lot of parameters, and they can get pretty confusing. Don't be dismayed if it takes more than one reading to get it.

    - The first parameter specifies the number of highlight events in the sample and is followed by a semicolon. Use 0; to turn off karaoke.

      This is followed by three numbers for each highlight event, in the form timeOffset, startingOffset, endingOffset. The three numbers are separated by commas, and sets of three are separated by semicolons.

    - The timeOffset specifies when the highlight event *ends.* The first highlight event starts when the sample begins. Subsequent highlight events start when the preceding event ends. Each event ends at its specified time offset.

    - The time offset is specified in timeScale units relative to the text sample's start time. If the absolute starting time for the sample was [00:00:01] and the time offset was 03, the highlight event would end at [00:00:01.03]. (The time scale is specified in the descriptor block at the start of the track.)

    - The startingOffset is the number of characters in the sample, including spaces and punctuation, before the first character that should be highlighted. To highlight text starting with the first character, the starting offset is 0. For the tenth character, the starting offset is 9.

    - The endingOffset is the position of the last character in the sample to highlight. To highlight just the first character, the ending offset is 1. For a string ending with the tenth character, the ending offset is 10.

      In other words, the starting offset is one less than the position of the first character, and the ending offset is the position of the last character. If the sample consisted of "Happy birthday," for example, you would highlight "Happy" with starting offset 0, ending offset 5, and highlight "birth" with starting offset 6, ending offset 11.

- To turn highlighting off for a period of time, specify a highlight event with the same starting offset and ending offset, such as 0,0.

For each highlight event, the text from the starting offset to the ending offset is highlighted until the specified time.

Example
```
{timescale:300}
[00:00:00.000]
{karaoke: 5; 150,0,5; 300,6,14; 400,15,17; 570,18,21; 600,0,0;}
Happy birthday to you...
[00:00:02.000]
```

This example has five highlight events. It highlights "Happy" for 150 time units, "birthday" for another 150, "to" for 100, "you" for 170, then turns highlighting off for the rest of the sample (600 time units = 2 seconds).

Important If the last highlight event ends before the sample ends, there may be unpredictable highlighting at the end of the sample. Make sure the last highlight event extends in time to the end of the sample. You can use a null highlight event (starting and ending offset both zero) for this purpose.

The specified highlight sequence automatically repeats for all subsequent text samples unless another {karaoke:} descriptor is encountered. To turn highlighting off, use {karaoke: 0;}. This will disable highlighting for subsequent samples.

Example
```
{timescale:300}
[00:00:00.000]
{karaoke: 2; 300,0,9; 600,10,12;}Highlight on...
[00:00:02.000]
Highlight on (repeat)
[00:00:04.000]
{karaoke: 0;}Highlight off!
[00:00:06.000]
Highlight stays off...
[00:00:06.000]
```

- {continuousKaraoke:} Specifies whether karaoke should ignore the starting offset and highlight all text from the beginning of the sample to the ending offset. Possible values are on and off; the default value is off. In order for this descriptor to take effect, the {karaoke:} descriptor must also be in effect.

Those are all the text descriptors that you can modify. Now let's look at some examples of what you can do with them.

Creating Titles and Scrolling Credits

It's easy to add titles and scrolling credits to a movie using text tracks, and it's a good idea. Credits or subtitles can be zipped across the Internet in a few milliseconds as text, then rendered onto video by the viewer's computer. A QuickTime text track 8 Kbytes in size can stand in nicely for a 6 MB title animation created by special-effects software.

Titles and credits can be presented on a solid background color of your choice, or overlaid on still images or moving video with almost equal ease.

Note   Anti-aliasing, scrolling, and keyed text each add to the CPU load for rendering. Combining all three may overtax older computers. Combining all three and overlaying the text on motion video that uses a demanding codec, or on a QuickTime effect, requires a fast computer for smooth playback.

Creating Titles

Adding a title to a movie is simple:

1. Type the title using a text editor or word processor and save as plain text.

2. Import the text file into QuickTime Player. In Mac OS X, you're done.

3. In Windows, Mac OS 8, or Mac OS 9, you'll be prompted for a filename (the familiar Save As dialog box). Click Options instead. You'll see the Text Import Settings dialog box (showing default settings):

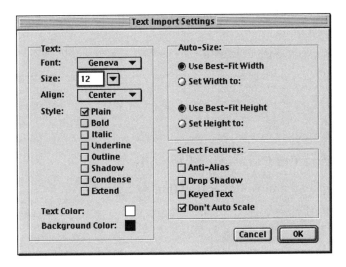

- Choose an attractive font.
- Choose a large size, such as 24 or 36 points.
- Choose Center alignment.
- Select a text color. If you want the title on a solid background, pick a background color as well. The default is white text on a black background.
- Enter the height and width of the movie you're titling.
- Select Anti-Alias.
- Add a drop shadow if you like.
- If you're going to overlay the title on video or on a still image, select Keyed Text (transparent background).

4. Click OK.

5. In Mac OS X, export the movie as Text with Descriptors, set the font, size, alignment, color, anti-alias, and keyed text properties using a text editor, then open the exported and modified file in QuickTime Player.

6. Give your new movie a name and click Save. Your title appears in its own movie. The title movie has a default duration of two seconds.

Overlay Title on an Existing Movie (Keyed Text)

1. Select All in the title movie, Copy.

2. Open the destination movie. Select the part you want the title overlaid on.

3. Add Scaled. This overlays the title on the video for the duration of your selection.

4. Save as a self-contained movie.

Tip You can use essentially the same technique to add background music to the title. Just open the music in QuickTime Player, Select All, and add the title to the music using Add Scaled.

Change the Duration of the Title

1. Export the movie as Text with Descriptors.

2. Edit the exported text file, changing the ending time stamp so the title is onscreen for as long as you like. Save as plain text.

3. Reimport the edited file into QuickTime Player (don't click Options this time).

Add a Still Image as Title Background

1. Open the still image in QuickTime Player. Select All. Copy.

2. Open the title movie. Select All.

3. Add Scaled. This adds the image to the title, but with the image on top of the title.

4. Choose Get Movie Properties from the Movie menu. Choose the video track from the left pop-up and choose Layer from the right pop-up. Increment the layer until the text appears over the image.

5. Save as a self-contained movie.

Insert Title and Any Background at Beginning of Movie

1. Open the title movie. Select All. Copy.

2. Open the destination movie. Click on the first frame.

3. Paste.

4. Save as a self-contained movie.

If you use a decorative font that viewers may not have, consider delivering the title as a video image. See "Burning Text into a Video Track" (page 403).

Adding Credits to a Movie

Scrolling credits are an especially good use of text tracks. As a video image, scrolling text is a bandwidth hog; it's very difficult to get readable text at a reasonable bandwidth. QuickTime text makes sharper credits than you'll see on most DVD movies; VHS tapes don't even come close. But the QuickTime credits play in real time at dialup data rates. Score one for desktop video.

For an example of a movie with scrolling credits in a text track, see Credits.htm in the Text folder on the CD.

Create Scrolling Credits

1. Type the first line of the credits using a text editor or word processor. Save as plain text.

2. Import the text file into QuickTime Player.

3. In Windows, Mac OS 8, or Mac OS 9, you'll be prompted for a filename. Click Options instead. You'll see the Text Import Settings dialog box (showing default settings):

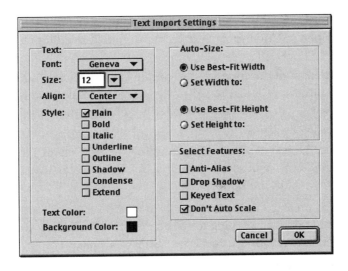

- Choose a common font, such as Times or Helvetica; use a monospace font such as Courier if you need to create justified text like

```
Key Grip..............Big Tim
Best Boy...........Little Tim
```

- Choose an appropriate size, such as 14 points.

- Choose an alignment. Center often works best.
- Choose any combination of styles. Bold is often a good choice.
- Select a text color. If you want the credits on a solid background, pick a background color as well.
- Enter the height and width of the movie you're adding credits to.
- Select Anti-Alias.
- Add a drop shadow if you like.
- If you're going to overlay the credits on imagery, select Keyed Text (transparent background).

4. Click OK.

5. Give your new movie a name and save it. The first line in your credits appears in its own frame for two seconds.

6. Export the movie as Text with Descriptors, as described in "Modifying Text Tracks with a Text Editor" (page 363).

7. Add the following descriptors to the first sample using the text editor:

   {scrollIn:on}{continuousScroll:on}{scrollOut:on}

Note In Mac OS X, this is where to set the font, style, alignment, and so on, as described in "Modifying Text Tracks with a Text Editor" (page 363).

8. The default duration for the sample is two seconds. Edit the closing time stamp from [00:00:02.00] to the length of time you want your credits on screen. For 30 seconds of credits, change the closing time stamp to [00:00:30.0].

9. Add the rest of your credits between the time stamps, so they are all one sample that will scroll smoothly. You can use carriage returns and blank lines within the sample.

   This creates credits that scroll onto the screen smoothly from the bottom and keep scrolling until the credits roll off the top of the screen. For alternate scrolling effects, see "Scrolling" (page 373).

10. Reimport the edited file into QuickTime Player (don't click Options this time).

11. Play the movie. If the credits scroll too fast, close the movie, add more time to the last time stamp in the text file, and reimport. If the scrolling is too slow, make the closing time stamp smaller.

Overlay Credits on an Existing Movie (Keyed Text)

1. Select All in the credits movie. Copy.

2. Open the destination movie. Select the part you want the credits overlaid on.

3. Add Scaled. This overlays the credits on the video for the duration of your selection. The scroll speed will increase or decrease as necessary.

4. Save as a self-contained movie.

   You can also use this technique to add background music to the credits. Just open the music in QuickTime Player, Select All, and add the credits to the music using Add Scaled. The credits will scroll exactly as long as the music plays.

Add a Still Image as Credits Background (Keyed Text)

1. Open the still image in QuickTime Player. Select All. Copy.

2. Open the credits movie. Select All.

3. Add Scaled. This adds the image for the duration of the credits, but with the image on top.

4. Choose Get Movie Properties from the Movie menu. Choose the video track from the left pop-up and choose Layer from the right pop-up. Increment the layer until the text appears over the image.

5. Save as a self-contained movie.

Add Credits and Background to End of Movie

1. Open the credits movie. Select All. Copy.

2. Open the destination movie. Click on the last frame.

3. Paste.

4. Save as a self-contained movie.

Adding Subtitles or Closed Captions to a Movie

Subtitles are simply text that transcribes movie dialog, usually into another language. Closed captions are similar, but are intended to assist the hearing impaired, so they are typically in the same language as the movie and include important cues that audience members normally get from the sound track, such as an off-screen telephone ringing, dog barking, car honking, or kettle whistling. For simplicity, we'll refer to both subtitles and closed captions as subtitles in this section, unless we are calling out a feature specific to closed captions. While they serve different purposes, there is little technical difference between them.

Tip You can purchase professional-looking QuickTime widgets (interactive buttons you can add to any movie) to toggle closed captioning on and off for about $15 from www.qtilities.com. There are also tools to help you create subtitles and closed captions and to import .srt, .ssa, and .sub files. See "QuickTime Text Tools" (page 356).

Believe it or not, subtitles you add to a movie using QuickTime text often look better than the subtitles that come out of the best studios. For one thing, the text is exceptionally sharp and clear because it's rendered at runtime on the viewer's computer. For another thing, studios can't alter the aspect ratio of the film or video by adding a text track at the bottom of the screen; they either have to cut off the bottom of the movie to make room for the text, or they have to superimpose the text on the movie, making it hard to read when the screen changes between light and dark. You have no such constraints.

It's easy to create a text track containing subtitles with sharp white text on a black background (or whatever color combination you prefer), and it's easy to add it to the bottom of a QuickTime movie, extending the height of the movie frame to accommodate it.

Editing the time stamps to synchronize the subtitles with the dialog is somewhat tedious and painstaking, but it's not difficult or complicated.

As a bonus, once you've created a synchronized text track in one language, its very easy to add identical text tracks in different languages (well, it's easy if you know the languages). QuickTime can automatically display the correct subtitles based on the language setting of the viewer's computer, downloading only the needed text track from a set of alternates.

To Create a Subtitle Track

1. Type the subtitles using a text editor or word processor. Type any words that you want to appear on the screen together as part of the same paragraph. Use carriage returns only at the end of paragraphs. Save as plain text.

2. Launch QuickTime Player, choose Import from the File menu, select the file with the subtitles, and click Convert (or Open in Mac OS X). In Mac OS X, skip to step 5.

3. In Windows, Mac OS 8, or Mac OS 9, you'll be prompted for a filename. Click Options instead. You'll see the Text Import Settings dialog box (showing default settings):

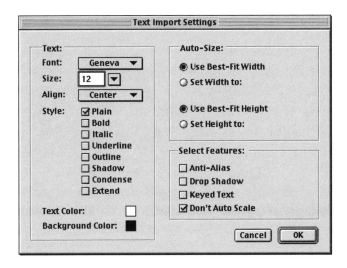

- Choose a common easy-to-read font, such as Helvetica.
- Choose an appropriate size, such as 12 or 14 points.
- Choose Center or Left alignment.
- Bold text is often easier to read, particularly for white Helvetica or Arial on a black background.
- Select a text color and a background color, or keep the default: white text on a black background.
- Enter the width of the movie you're adding subtitles to.
- Enter a height tall enough to accommodate your largest subtitle. If all your subtitles fit on one line, the point size plus ten is a good guess. If your guess is wrong, you'll have an opportunity to correct it later.
- Anti-aliased text looks better, but it's harder to read, especially at small font sizes. You're probably better off without it for subtitles—easy readability is more important than beauty in this case.

- Drop shadows also make text harder to read; not recommended for subtitles.

- Don't select Keyed Text unless you're going to overlay the subtitles on the movie image (not recommended).

4. Click OK.

5. Give your new movie a name and save it.

Each subtitle appears on screen for exactly two seconds, so you'll need to change the timing later. For now, make sure the font is large enough, clear enough, and that it fits in the frame. If there's a problem, Windows, Mac OS 8, or Mac OS 9 users should close the movie and reimport using a different font, font size, or track height. Mac OS X users should export as text with descriptors and modify these characteristics as described in "Modifying Text Tracks with a Text Editor" (page 363).

Repeat until you like what you see. If you need to add line breaks to a subtitle, do it now.

Synchronizing the Subtitles with the Dialog

This requires patience, so take a deep breath and prepare yourself.

Tip If you have a Macintosh, there's a free program called MacAW (www.whitanderson .com) that will do this part for you (and a bit more). See "QuickTime Text Tools" (page 356).

1. Export the subtitle movie as Text with Descriptors: choose Export from the File menu. Choose Text to Text, and Text with Descriptors, from the pop-up menus.

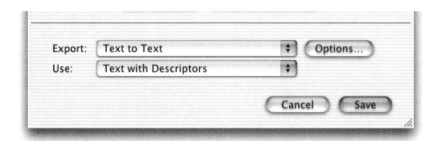

Click the Options button to set the format for the text descriptors.

Select "Show Text, Descriptors, and Time," "Show time relative to start of: **Movie,**" and change default to "Show fractions of seconds as: 1/**30**."

2. Click OK, then Save.

3. Open the exported file in a text editor.

4. Open the movie you're adding subtitles to. Choose Get Movie Properties from the Movie menu, then choose Time from the right pop-up menu.

5. Try to arrange the windows on your desk so you can see the movie, the Properties window, and a few lines in your text editor. (This could be the excuse you need to go out and buy a larger monitor.)

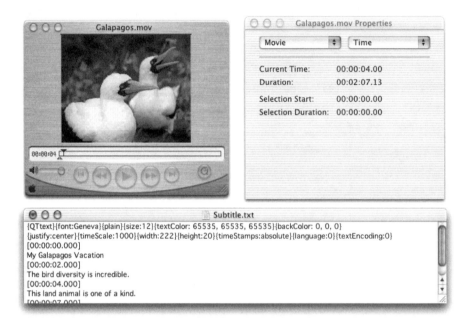

6. Play the movie, pausing or stepping frame by frame as needed (use the arrow keys to step frame by frame). Use the time display in the Properties window to determine when each subtitle should begin.

7. Modify the time stamp preceding each subtitle so it matches the time displayed in the Info window. For example, if the first dialog begins at time 00:01:17.03, set the first time stamp in the text file to [00:01:17.03].

8. If you need to insert blank subtitles for periods without dialog, enter a new time stamp and a blank line between existing subtitles using the text editor.

9. Continue until all the time stamps have been synchronized to the dialog. You'll probably want to insert a blank subtitle after the last bit of dialog.

10. The file should end with a time stamp and a carriage return.

11. Edit the last time stamp to match the duration of the movie.

12. Import the modified subtitle file into QuickTime Player. Select All. Copy.

13. Click the movie. Select All. Add Scaled. This adds the subtitles to the movie and cleans up any minor errors in time stamps.

14. Select the Text Track in the Properties window's left pop-up menu, then select Size in the right pop-up.

15. Click Adjust. Click anywhere in the subtitle area except on the red handles. Hold down the Shift key and drag the subtitle down until it just disappears off the bottom edge of the movie.

16. Let go of the mouse. The movie frame will grow to accommodate the subtitle as a bar across the bottom. Click Done in the Properties window.

 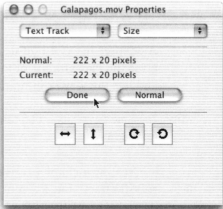

17. Play the movie to verify that the timing is right for the subtitles. If not, delete the text track, adjust the time stamps in the text file as needed, reimport, add, and resize.

18. When it's right, save it. If you're just adding subtitles in one language, save as a self-contained movie. If you'll be adding others, allow dependencies.

Whew! Are we having fun yet?

An alternative method is to play the movie in QuickTime Player with the Movie Properties window open, the text track selected in the left pop-up menu, and Text Replace selected in the right pop-up. As you play the movie, select the part of the movie's timeline where a bit of dialog appears, and drag the subtitle for that scene onto the area marked "Drag Text Here." This is a much simpler technique for adding a few subtitles, or for correcting a typo in a hurry, but it's harder to keep things organized and tends to be more error-prone for large projects.

To add alternate subtitle tracks in other languages, open the text version of your subtitles with a text editor, do a Save As with a new filename, and replace each subtitle with its equivalent. Don't mess with the time stamps. Import each alternate subtitle track into its own movie and put all the alternates in one folder.

Once you've assembled all your alternates, follow the directions for assigning alternate language tracks in Chapter 8, "Alternate Realities: Language, Speed, and Connections," "Alternate Tracks" (page 159) to create a movie that automatically downloads and plays the right subtitles for the viewer's language.

▶ Adding a Chapter List to a Movie

A chapter list is a pop-up menu integrated into the movie controller. It gives the viewer a list of topics, each corresponding to a part of the movie, and lets the viewer jump directly to any topic. It's also a text track.

Tip There are several tools that can add a chapter list for you. See "QuickTime Text Tools" (page 356).

Creating a chapter list is fairly straightforward. It's similar to creating a subtitle track, but it's much easier because you typically have less than a dozen topics, rather than hundreds of subtitles. It works like this:

1. Using a text editor or a word processor, type a list of topics or a list of descriptive entry points into your movie. Make the descriptions very short—no more than two or three words, preferably one word—and terminate each topic with a carriage return. Save the list as plain text.

2. Import the list into QuickTime Player, then export as Text with Descriptors.

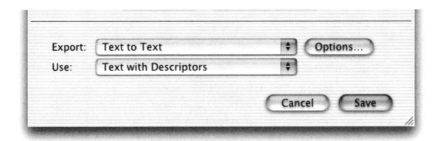

Click the Options button to set the format for the text descriptors.

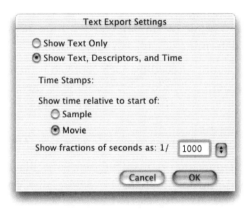

Select "Show Text, Descriptors, and Time," "Show time relative to start of: **Movie**," and change default to "Show fractions of seconds as: 1/**30**."

3. Click OK, then Save.

4. Open the exported list in a text editor.

5. Open the movie that you're adding the chapter list to in QuickTime Player. Choose Get Movie Properties from the Movie menu, then choose Time from the right pop-up menu. Try to arrange the windows on your desk so you can see the movie, the Properties window, and a few lines in your text editor.

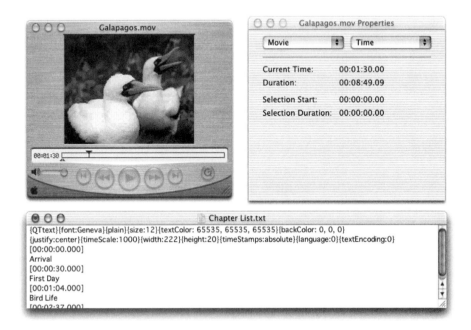

6. Play the movie, pausing or stepping frame by frame as needed (use the arrow keys to step frame by frame). Use the time display in the Properties window to determine when each topic begins.

7. Modify the time stamp preceding each topic so it matches the time displayed in the Properties window. For example, if the second topic begins at time 00:02:30.01, set the second time stamp in the text file to [00:02:30.01].

8. Modify the last time stamp to match the duration of the movie.

9. Save the text file and import it into QuickTime Player. This creates a new movie containing only a text track. Select All. Copy. Close.

10. Click in the main movie. Select All. Add Scaled. This adds the text track to your movie, making sure they are the exact same length.

11. Choose the new text track from the left pop-up menu in the Properties window, then choose Make Chapter from the right pop-up. Choose the main audio or video track as the chapter owner. If you have a movie with alternate subtitle or sound tracks, you can create multiple chapter lists in different languages; set the appropriate subtitle or sound track as the owner of each chapter list, and the chapter list will change to match the selected language.

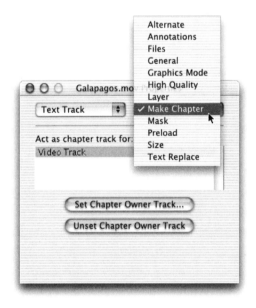

12. Choose Preload from the right pop-up menu and click the Preload checkbox, so the chapter list loads first.

13. Choose Enable Tracks from the Edit menu and disable the new text track, so it isn't displayed on top of your video. It still works as a chapter list.

14. Save as a self-contained movie.

As you play the movie, you should see the current topic displayed in the movie controller. You can use the mouse to jump to the next topic or previous topic.

QuickTime Player

QuickTime Plug-in

Important If the movie is not wide enough for the controller to accommodate the words of the chapter list entries, the chapter list is not displayed. QuickTime Player normally has a minimum width, but the controller for the plug-in is only as wide as the movie, and a movie with a media skin can modify the width of the player window. Make your chapter names short, or make your movie wide, or the chapters won't show.

One way to widen a movie to make room for a chapter list is to create a black GIF as tall as your movie and as wide as necessary, then add it as movie background using the Add Scaled command. See "Adding a Still Image as a Movie Background" (page 267).

For an example of a movie with a chapter list, see `Chaplist.htm` and `Chaplist.mov` in the Text folder of the CD.

By the way, you can also create chapter lists using LiveStage Pro, GoLive, Cleaner, Textation, Final Chapter, or CineStream. It's very easy.

Note Chapter lists work very well in local movies or streaming movies as the viewer can jump to any chapter at any time. Fast Start movies can jump ahead only as far as the movie has downloaded already, making chapter lists useful only for reviewing earlier material, and not useful at all for skipping ahead.

▶ HREF Tracks

An HREF track is a wonderful thing. Like other text tracks, it contains a series of text samples and time stamps. But these text samples are URLs and their targets. They can specify movies that replace the current movie, load in another frame, or load in QuickTime Player. They can also specify JavaScript functions or Web pages, and can direct any Web page to a specific browser frame or window.

Tip There are now several tools that can build HREF tracks for you. See "QuickTime Text Tools" (page 356).

The URLs can be interactive or automatic. Interactive URLs load when someone clicks in the movie's display area, much like a hypertext link in a Web page. Automatic URLs load at a particular time in the movie, allowing you to create a narrated tour of your website, or to use Web pages as slides in a presentation.

An HREF track is very different from a text track that includes URLs using the {HREF: } and {endHREF} descriptor tags. An ordinary text track contains text that's meant to be displayed, and the {HREF: } descriptor tag turns some of that text into a clickable link. An HREF *track,* on the other hand, is just a list of URLs and targets; it isn't meant to be displayed as text, and you don't click any text to activate the links.

The URLs in an HREF track can load automatically when the movie that contains them is played, with no clicking at all, or they can turn the whole display area of the movie into a clickable link, not just some of the text.

HREF tracks work when a movie is played in the QuickTime plug-in, or when a streaming movie is played in QuickTime Player. Currently, when a local or Fast Start movie is played in QuickTime Player, it treats an HREF track as an ordinary text track. This may change in the future.

HREF Syntax

Each sample in an HREF track is preceded and followed by a time stamp. The specified URL is active during the interval between the two time stamps. The URL is active even if the movie is paused or stopped.

The syntax for an HREF track text sample is

A<*URL*> T<*frame*>

A<*URL*> specifies the URL. The "A" stands for automatic. If the "A" is omitted, the viewer must click in the movie's display area during the period when the URL is active to load the URL. If the "A" is present, the URL loads automatically when the movie is played.

The URL can be absolute or relative to the movie.

Important   A relative URL is relative to the *movie,* not the Web page that contains the movie. If the movie and its parent Web page are in the same directory, this is the same thing, but if the movie and the Web page are in different directories, the difference is crucial.

The URL can include an internal anchor name as well as a path and a filename (for example, <../HTML/Page1.htm#StepOne>). However, some versions of Internet Explorer behave very oddly when a link from outside a given frame or window points to a name in an already-open file—it should scroll the file to that named point, but it frequently doesn't. This isn't something QuickTime can change—the browser acts the same way when you type the URL in the Location window.

The URL can be the name of a JavaScript function in the current HTML page. "Loading" the URL executes the function. You can also pass parameters or actual JavaScript code as part of the URL string. Here are two examples:

```
<javascript:openQTwin('MyMovie.mov')>
A<Javascript:alert("Hello World");>
```

Note   A bug in Internet Explorer 4.5 caused it to ignore URLs in javascript: format. This bug is not present in earlier or later versions. A workaround is to use a frame-loaded JavaScript function embedded in a small HTML page, as described in "HREF Tracks and JavaScript" (page 400).

The URL can be a blank sample (a carriage return). Clicking inside the movie when a blank sample is active has no effect. Use a blank sample to deactivate the previous URL without activating a new one. You might want to do this at the end of a movie; otherwise the last specified URL remains active after the movie has stopped playing.

T<*frame*> is an optional parameter. It specifies a target frame or target window. If a target is specified, the URL is loaded in the specified frame or window. If there is no frame or window with that name, a new browser window of that name will be created.

You can combine the T<*frame*> parameter with the "A" in the URL to cause a movie playing in one frame to automatically load a series of URLs in other frames at specified points in the movie.

If no target is specified, the URL loads in the default browser window or browser frame. If the movie is playing in a browser window, the movie and any Web page containing the movie are replaced by the specified URL.

If the special target T<myself> is specified, the URL is opened directly by the QuickTime plug-in or QuickTime Player, whichever is playing the movie. The specified URL replaces the currently playing movie. This will work properly only if the URL points to a file that QuickTime can handle directly, such as a QuickTime movie or an AIFF audio file.

You can use the T<myself> parameter to link a series of QuickTime movies into a single virtual movie over the Web or to cause a movie to morph back into a poster when it's done playing.

The special target T<quicktimeplayer> causes QuickTime Player to open the URL. If the movie is playing in a browser window, this launches QuickTime Player. If QuickTime Player is already active, the URL may open in a new player window or replace the existing player window, depending on the viewer's QuickTime settings. Again, for this to work properly the URL needs to specify something that QuickTime can play.

Tip Don't use an automatic URL at time zero [00:00:00.000], particularly if you're creating a frameset and opening a movie at the same time. Give the browser 1 or 2 seconds to load the initial pages for the frameset before you start sending it URLs. Otherwise the browser may become confused or even irritable, and no one wants that.

Examples

If someone clicks in the movie's display area in the first five seconds of the movie, load the main Apple website in the default browser window:

```
[00:00:00.00]
<www.apple.com>
[00:00:05.00]
```

Five seconds into the movie, automatically load the QuickTime website into an adjacent frame. One minute later, load the QuickTime hot picks page into the same frame:

```
[00:00:05.00]
A<www.apple.com/quicktime/> T<frame2>
[00:01:05.00]
A<www.apple.com/quicktime/hotpicks/> T<frame2>
```

Adding an HREF Track to a Movie

You can add an HREF track to a movie using a QuickTime editor, such as LiveStage Pro, GoLive, Discreet Cleaner, or CineStream, using a text tool such as those listed in "QuickTime Text Tools" (page 356) or using Quick-Time Player and a text editor.

Adding an HREF track to a movie using QuickTime Player is very similar to adding a chapter list. You type a list of URLs, import the text into QuickTime Player and export it as Text with Descriptors, edit the time stamps and reimport, then use the Properties window to make the text track into an HREF track. Here are the steps in detail:

1. Using a text editor or a word processor, type a list of URLs. Use the syntax A<*Url*> T<*Target*>, as described in "HREF Syntax" (page 395). Terminate each URL with a carriage return. Save the list as plain text.

2. Import the list into QuickTime Player, then export as Text with Descriptors.

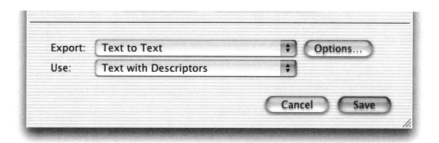

Click the Options button to set the format for the text descriptors.

Select "Show Text, Descriptors, and Time," "Show time relative to start of: **Movie**," and change default to "Show fractions of seconds as: 1/**30**."

3. Click OK, then Save.

4. Open the exported list in a text editor.

5. Open the movie you're adding the HREF track to. Choose Get Movie Properties from the Movie menu, then choose Time from the right pop-up menu. Try to arrange the windows on your desk so you can see the movie, the Info window, and a few lines in your text editor, as shown in the next illustration.

6. Play the movie, pausing or stepping frame by frame as needed. Use the time display in the Properties window to determine when each URL should load or become active.

7. Modify the time stamp preceding each URL so it matches the time displayed in the Info window.

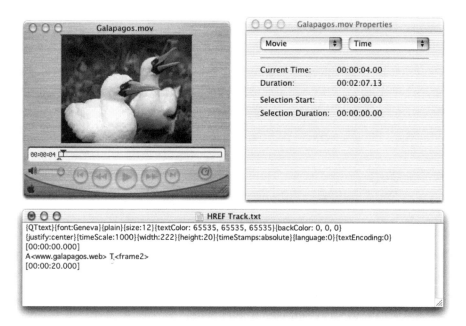

Important QuickTime can skip short media segments to maintain movie timing when the viewer's computer gets behind. If you're using a text sample to automatically load a URL, give the sample a duration of at least half a second, so there's little danger of it being skipped.

8. Modify the last time stamp to match the duration of the movie. The last URL remains active after the movie has stopped playing. If it's a clickable link to your home page, this may be exactly what you want. If not, you may want to add a blank URL so that clicking the movie after it stops doesn't load a URL.

9. Save the text file and import it into QuickTime Player. This creates a new movie containing only a text track. Select All. Copy. Close.

10. Click in the main movie. Select All. Add Scaled. This adds the text track to your movie, making sure they are the exact same length.

11. Choose the new text track from the left pop-up menu in the Properties window, then choose General from the right pop-up. Click Change Name and rename the track HREFTrack. Use capitalization as shown, with no space between HREF and Track.

12. Choose Enable Tracks from the Edit menu and disable the new text track, so it isn't displayed on top of your video. It still works as an HREF track.

13. Save as a self-contained movie.

For examples of movies that use HREF tracks, see HREF.htm in the Text folder of the CD.

Tip If you need to export an HREF track to modify it with a text editor, you have to re-enable it first. QuickTime Player doesn't export disabled tracks.

By the way, you can use an HREF track in a streaming movie. Just export Movie to Hinted Movie from QuickTime Player, and the HREF track is hinted for streaming. To add an HREF track to a live broadcast, use LiveChannel. There's a demo version on the CD.

HREF Tracks and JavaScript

You can specify a JavaScript function instead of a URL in an HREF track sample. You can also include parameters or actual JavaScript code. If the user clicks the movie when the HREF is active, the specified JavaScript function is executed. The text sample looks like this:

```
<javascript:FunctionName:parameters>
```

Here are two examples:

```
<javascript:openQTwin('MyMovie.mov')>
<javascript:alert("Hello World");>
```

The T*<Target>* parameter can be used with JavaScript functions, but the target must be an existing frame, an existing browser window, or a new browser window; the special targets `quicktimeplayer` and `myself` cannot be used.

You can use the optional A*<URL>* to activate a JavaScript function automatically, instead of in response to a mouse click, but for reasons having to do with message-passing between plug-ins and browsers, this is not always reliable.

Note A bug in Internet Explorer 4.5 causes it to ignore URLs in `javascript:` format. This bug is not present in earlier or later versions.

A foolproof way to automatically execute a JavaScript function from an HREF track is

1. Create a hidden frame in your main HTML document, such as a one-pixel-tall frame at the bottom of the page.

2. Put the JavaScript function in its own small HTML page and set it to activate on load.

3. Set the HREF track sample to automatically load the small page in the hidden frame. For example:

```
A<Javapage.htm> T<HiddenFrame>
```

Tip Give the HREF track sample a duration of at least half a second, so it won't be skipped if the viewer's computer gets behind during playback.

▶ Fonts and Cross-Platform Movies

Text is rendered by the viewer's computer when a movie is played. If the specified font isn't installed on the viewer's computer, QuickTime substitutes a similar font. If there is no genuinely similar font, the substitution may not be what you had in mind. Windows and Macintosh systems typically have different fonts, so you need to choose carefully for cross-platform movies.

For best results, we recommend using Times, Courier, or Helvetica.

This is Times: a proportional serif font.

This is Helvetica: a proportional sans-serif font.

This is Courier: a monospaced serif font.

All of these fonts tend to create a very similar display on Macintosh and Windows computers. There are versions of Times and Courier installed on almost all Windows and Macintosh systems. Nearly all Macintosh computers also have Helvetica; Windows computers typically have Arial, which is very similar. If you specify Helvetica, QuickTime will use Arial as its first choice for a substitute.

For credits or subtitles, one of these three fonts will usually do nicely. Bear in mind that you can use any type size, drop shadows, and a variety of styles, including bold, italic, outline, extended, and condensed, to create the look you want.

Important Keep in mind the fact that text of a given point size is generally displayed onscreen as larger on a Macintosh than on a Windows computer.

We recommend viewing your movie on both a Macintosh and a Windows computer, to make sure the layout and alignment are satisfactory on both, before you put a movie with a text track on the Web. This often involves a compromise, in which the bounding box is a little larger than necessary on Windows screens, and a little tighter than you'd like on Mac screens.

Tip The Verdana font is installed on most Windows and Macintosh computers and renders in nearly the same size on both platforms. Give it a try.

Alternatively, you can use XMLtoRefMovie to make a QuickTime movie that detects Intel-compatible CPUs and loads one movie for Windows and another for Macintosh, each with a text track tailored to fit. For details, see "Using XMLtoRefMovie" (page 157).

If you want your text to have an identical appearance on all computers, you can prevent font substitution by burning the image of the text into video, as described in the following section.

QuickTime also supports Flash text, which can be represented as vectors instead of characters. This takes a lot more bandwidth, but it is an option. For details, see Chapter 16, "Getting Interactive."

▶ Burning Text into a Video Track

Sometimes it's better to render text on your own computer and deliver it to the viewer as part of the video track, instead of as a text track. There are a couple of reasons for doing this.

A QuickTime text track uses very little bandwidth, but it makes demands on the viewer's computer, which has to render the text while the movie is playing, perhaps compositing the text over moving video. On slower computers this can affect smooth playback, especially for keyed and anti-aliased text.

If the viewer doesn't have a specified font installed, a different one is substituted. This can affect the appearance and layout of the text in ways that are hard to predict. This generally works fine for credits and subtitles (just leave a little extra room in case the substitute font is larger), but it can be a problem with titles. If you're using a decorative font that most people don't have, such as an elaborate Old English font for a movie title, font substitution may not be acceptable.

The solution is to "burn" the text into the movie's video track. This is similar to creating a GIF image for decorative text items in a Web page. It's very straightforward:

1. Set up your movie using text tracks, as described earlier in this chapter, until it all looks right on *your* computer.

2. Do a mix-down of your visual tracks by choosing Export from the File menu, then selecting Movie to QuickTime Movie from the pop-up menu.

3. Click the Options button, then the Settings button in the Video area, to select a video compressor.

When you export the movie, all the visual tracks are combined into a single video track. The text is rendered as a visual image and compressed as part of the video.

Text has a lot of detail and sharp edges, so it's hard to compress efficiently as part of the video. You may need to increase the data rate or the text size to get readable results. You may also want to use a simple sans-serif font and a plain or bold text style. Drop shadows and italics are especially difficult to compress readably.

Static text compresses far more efficiently than scrolling text. If you use static text on a solid color background or on a still image, you may want to compress it as a still image using a high-quality codec such as Photo-JPEG or Graphics—the Graphics compressor works well for text on a colored background. You can get some of your bandwidth back by leaving it on the screen for several seconds.

If you need to compress the portion of the movie that contains text using different compression settings than the rest of the video, you can do a selective mix-down by extracting some tracks, exporting them, then adding the exported tracks back into your movie. This is described in more detail in "Mixing Down" (page 315). Or you can just cut the portion of the movie that has the title, compress it separately, and paste it back.

Starting with QuickTime 5, you have the option of using Flash text in your movies. This vector-based text media is not as compact as a QuickTime text track, but it's far more efficient than sending text as bitmapped video, and it looks the same on Windows and Macintosh screens. For details, see "Shocking Behavior with Flash Tracks" (page 522).

Searching a Text Track

Text tracks are searchable using the pro version of QuickTime Player. It couldn't be much easier—choose Find in the Edit menu, type in some text, and click the Find button.

If a text track contains matching text, the movie jumps to the point in the timeline where the text first appears—whether the text is visible or not, whether the text track is enabled or not, and whether the text appears in credits, subtitles, or a chapter list. If the text is visible and the text track is enabled, the matching text is highlighted.

If the movie contains multiple text tracks, they are all searched, so a movie with multiple subtitle tracks can be searched in any language the movie supports.

There are radio buttons in the Find box to search forward or backward through the movie timeline. There is also a Find Again command in the Edit menu to search for the next occurrence of the specified text.

▶ QuickTime Text in Director

A bug in Macromedia Director can cause problems when displaying QuickTime text tracks that are created on Windows computers. When QuickTime creates a text track on Windows, it stores a copy of the original text inside the movie, in addition to the QuickTime-formatted text.

If you plan to play your QuickTime movie in a Director project, and it includes a QuickTime text track, import your text into QuickTime using a Macintosh. Once the text is in QuickTime format, you can composite it with other media on a Windows computer without worry. Only the initial import needs to be done on a Mac.

Gently down the Stream

So far, we've looked at movies with digital sound, MIDI music, still images, motion video, and text. By a happy coincidence, movies made with all these media types can be streamed in real time.

You already know how to deliver movies from local disk and using Fast Start. Now let's look at delivering them as real-time streams. We'll look at two kinds of streaming: video on demand (VOD) and live streaming (broadcasting). While we're on the subject, we'll show you how to set up a streaming server (it's easy) and how to do a live broadcast (it's fun!).

This chapter covers

- alternatives to do-it-yourself streaming
- making movies that will stream
- hinting movies and MPEG-4 for streaming
- staging and testing streaming movies on a server
- embedding streaming VOD movies in a Web page
- setting up a streaming server
- streaming MP3 playlists
- how live streaming works
- choosing and setting up a broadcaster
- embedding live streams in a Web page

⊙ Do-It-Yourself Streaming (or Not)

This chapter mainly covers do-it-yourself streaming in QuickTime—setting up a server, planning, preparing, and staging movies for streaming. But before we get started, I'd like to address a pair of frequently voiced concerns.

- Making streaming movies is more demanding than making Fast Start movies. Is there any way to make it simpler?
- For Fast Start movies, QuickTime kicks butt; but for streaming, Quick-Time, Real, and Windows Media each offer certain advantages. How can I reach the broadest possible audience?

If you want to stream with the least possible fuss and reach the broadest possible audience, here are some possibilities to consider.

Software packages such as Discreet Cleaner can take ordinary Quick-Time movies as input and generate all three streaming formats as output. They can compress a QuickTime movie for streaming at multiple data rates as QuickTime, Real, and Windows Media streams, all from a single batch command. To support this, there are streaming servers that also handle multiple streaming formats, including QuickTime, Real, Windows Media, and MPEG-4. The Helix streaming server from Real Networks is one example. The IBM Video Charger is another.

One alternative is letting someone else do it for you. Services such as Generic Media (www.genericmedia.com/) are available to do the grunt work of streaming. This lets you create and archive your movies using Quick-Time and have the service compress the movies for various bandwidths, prepare them for streaming, and automatically deliver them in Quick-Time, Real, or Windows Media format (whichever a viewer prefers).

Another simplifying alternative is to simply stream in MPEG-4 format. It provides audio and video quality comparable with just about anything else, from dialup to DVD data rates. QuickTime exports movies to streaming MPEG-4 and the QuickTime Streaming Server can deliver them. It's much simpler and cheaper than doing all three formats, but it reaches a broader audience than any of the other streaming formats alone. Quick-Time Player works with MPEG-4, iTunes and other applications work with MP4 audio, and Real has announced that Real Player will play MPEG-4 as well. Envivo has announced an MPEG-4 plug-in for Windows Media Player, and SourceForge (www.sourceforge.net) has an MPEG-4 player for Linux. That's three out of three, plus extras. And there's a groundswell building; the audience you can reach using MPEG-4 gets bigger every day.

All that said, there are plenty of reasons to stream in QuickTime format, and it's really not that difficult to do it yourself. This chapter will show you how.

Making Streaming Movies

There are a few things that are different about streaming movies: the data rate limit, the types of media you can deliver, the optimum codecs, and something called "hinting." None of it is very complicated, but it's all important.

Data Rate Limiting

The main difference between making streaming movies and making Fast Start movies is the bandwidth limit. For streaming movies, keeping your data rate lower than the connection speed isn't just a good idea; it's the law.

When you deliver a Fast Start movie, you're transferring a file. It takes however long it takes, and the viewer can play however much has arrived. If the transfer speed is faster than the movie's data rate, the viewer can start the movie immediately, and all the data will arrive before it's needed. If the transfer speed is slower than the movie's data rate, the viewer can do something else while the movie downloads and watch it later.

When a movie is delivered using real-time streams, the data is sent at a constant rate: a one-minute movie is transmitted in exactly one minute. A faster connection doesn't speed things up—it takes a minute, no matter how fast your connection is. If the connection is not fast enough to carry all the data in one minute, some data gets lost. If more than about 10% gets lost, the movie becomes unplayable.

In other words, if the data rate is higher than the connection speed, you can't watch the movie. Since no file is transferred, you can't stream it now and watch it later. If you want to see it later, you have to ask for the stream again. There's no way around it: you *must* make your movie's data rate lower than the viewer's connection speed.

So how do you get the data rate low enough?

Plan

Make your movies with a low data rate in mind. Use low-motion video or still images, small image sizes, and low frame rates. Take advantage of low-bandwidth media like MIDI and text.

Compress

Always use a compressor that allows you to specify a data rate. Make sure that the data rates of all the tracks together are less than your target data rate. Be conservative; leave some room for overhead and congestion.

Note   Compression is the most time-consuming and CPU-intensive part of making and delivering streaming movies. One server can send 4000 simultaneous streams, but for a busy site you may need several computers working simultaneously to compress the movies for that server to send. You compress each movie only once for each data rate, so it depends on how often you put up new movies.

Test

Check the movie's data rate using the Properties window (choose Streaming Track in the left pop-up, Data Rate in the right, while the stream is playing), but remember: that's an *average* data rate. If you have any doubts, check for data spikes with a product such as Spike (there's a lite version of Spike in the Demos folder of the CD). Don't quit halfway; put the movie on a server and watch it yourself over the slowest type of connection it's intended for.

Use Alternates

Not everyone has the same connection speed. You could compress your movie for the slowest possible connection, but you don't have to settle for that. You can create multiple versions of your movie that stream at different rates. For example:

- Compress one version of your movie at 2 Kbytes/sec for 28.8K dialups, so everyone can see it.
- Compress another version at 4 Kbytes/sec for typical 56K dialups, so most people get something twice as good.
- Compress one really nice-looking version at whatever speed it takes; the people you most want to impress can probably afford fast connections.

Or you might skip the 28.8K version and do an ISDN/cable version and a LAN version. Whatever your bandwidth choices, combine the versions using a reference movie that automatically sends the best movie the viewer can handle, as described in "Making a Fast Start Reference Movie" (page 423) and Chapter 8, "Alternate Realities: Language, Speed, and Connections."

Media Types

You need to pay special attention to media types when you're making a streaming movie. All the media types we've looked at so far can be streamed in real time, but there are other media types that can't be.

Remember that streams are different from movie files. A file plays from beginning to end, so an image at the start of the file is always available. People can start a streaming movie in the middle or join a live stream in progress, so they don't have access to anything that came earlier. So if you use a still image as a movie background, for example, you need to send a copy of the image periodically for people who tune in late.

Unlike a file, a real-time stream has no persistence. All the data is time-stamped, and when its time has expired, it's thrown away. So you can stream the image of a rotating cube, but you can't stream persistent data *about* a cube that the audience can then rotate interactively.

Unlike file transfer, streaming usually involves data loss, so it works best when there's a lot of redundancy in the data. If video drops a frame, it's no big deal—there are several frames every second. Similarly, an image with a missing block of pixels still shows what you need. But if a packet of text gets lost, your written instructions may become meaningless, or worse (all that got lost were the words "Do NOT" . . .). So you typically want to send multiple copies of media types like text or MIDI, even though they do stream.

You need to use special techniques to mix streaming media with non-streaming media, and you need to know which is which. Here's what you *can* stream:

- You can stream digital sound. Speech compresses better than music, but they both stream.

- You can stream MIDI music. MIDI uses a lot less bandwidth than digitally sampled sound, but it doesn't tolerate packet loss very well.

- You can stream still images. They often have a very spiky data rate—high when the image is first sent, then very low while it remains on screen—so the average data rate doesn't tell the whole story here. Also, you may need to retransmit the images periodically to compensate for packet loss (and for people who join the stream later, after the image has been sent).

- You can stream motion video. This is bandwidth-intensive stuff, so don't expect to deliver full-screen action movies over dialup modems. Think smaller images without too much movement, or think fast connections.

- You can stream text, including HREF tracks, and it hardly uses any bandwidth at all. It's very sensitive to packet loss, and usually stays on screen for quite a while, so you need to retransmit your message periodically. You can't stream chapter lists, even though they're text; they need to be persistent, so they need to be sent another way.

- You can stream .mp4 files and .mp3 playlists. You must prepare them for streaming, however, as described in "Hinting" (page 414) and "Playlists" (page 442).

Other media types, such as Flash and VR (and chapter lists), must be delivered locally or in Fast Start movies. You *can* mix streaming media with local or Fast Start media in the same movie, and that's a very powerful technique; for details, see Chapter 17, "Mixing It Up: Streaming and Nonstreaming."

Streaming Codecs

Some codecs are particularly useful for streaming. The main features you need are high compression, good quality at low bit rates, and the ability to recover gracefully when data gets lost in transmission.

Note   Many of the best streaming codecs for video-on-demand require 2–5 times the movie's duration to perform compression, so they can't be used for streaming live events. For live streams, you need a codec that can compress in real time.

Voice

- Qualcomm PureVoice provides the maximum compression for audio, and it handles loss well. It delivers much better quality for speech than for music, but it can deliver music at extraordinarily low bit rates. It can compress in real time (160 milliseconds encoding delay) for live streaming.

Music

- QDesign Music provides the highest-quality audio at Web data rates. It's ingeniously designed to deal well with data loss in real-time streaming. It can compress in real time—though at reduced quality—for live streaming, but is more suitable for video-on-demand (VOD) sound tracks. There is about a 6-second encoding delay.

- AAC (advanced audio codec), part of the MPEG-4 specification, provides higher quality at lower bit rates than MP3, but still requires a relatively high bit rate (> 100 Kbits/sec) for high-fidelity music. Capable of 5.1 surround sound at higher bit rates (no live encoder for 5.1 at this time). QuickTime streaming server can stream MPEG-4 audio (AAC) either in hinted .mp4 files or as AAC-encoded audio in hinted Quick-Time movies.

- MP3 gives good quality at high data rates and fair quality at lower data rates. You can deliver FM-quality MP3 at about 128 Kbits/sec. You can deliver MP3-compressed audio in streaming QuickTime movies, or you can deliver MP3 streams using IceCast-compatible playlists (.m3u or .pls), compatible with QuickTime Player, iTunes, WinAmp, and others. For details, see "Playlists" (page 442).

Video

- MPEG-4 is a very high-quality codec for streaming video at dialup to DSL data rates. It can encode in real time for live broadcasts. Quick-Time Streaming Server can stream MPEG-4 files (.mp4) as well as QuickTime movies (.mov) that use MPEG-4 video compression.

- H.263 video offers moderate to very good quality, and it is extraordinarily resilient to data loss. This is a good codec for unreliable data connections and is sometimes preferable to Sorenson for high-motion source material. It encodes in real time, making it useful for live streaming. It only encodes at a few set heights and widths, though.

Tip H.263 works *much* better if you don't force key frames. Set the key frame rate to 99; the codec will create key frames as needed.

- Sorenson Video compression generally provides the highest-quality motion video at Web data rates for video-on-demand. It can encode in real time for live streaming, but with reduced quality.

- Motion-JPEG compression gives very high-quality motion video, but only at very high data rates (LAN). It compresses readily in real time if you have a graphics card that supports it. Perfect for LAN broadcasts.

Still Images

- Photo-JPEG compression provides high-quality still images. (If you're running Mac OS 9, the PictureViewer application in your QuickTime folder can compress an image to the data size you specify.) Scale an image to the desired duration, then export as video with a frame rate of 1/20 to 1/5 (0.05 to 0.2) per second to repair any data loss and for people who tune in late.

Hinting

There's an extra step in preparing QuickTime movies for streaming. It's called *hinting*. It creates a hint track for every streamable media track in the movie. The streaming server uses the hint track to turn the media into real-time streams.

If you've already compressed the movie, and you want to add hint tracks so it can be streamed, open the movie in QuickTime Player and export it using the Movie to Hinted Movie option. The export dialog is shown in the following illustration.

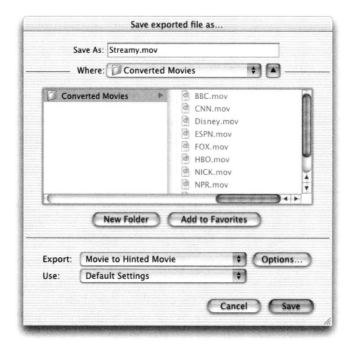

This kind of export doesn't mix down tracks or recompress them the way a Movie to QuickTime Movie export does. It just adds the hint tracks. Click Save and your movie is ready to stream. There's an AppleScript script on the CD that you can use to automate this procedure, making it even simpler.

Click Save to use the default hint settings (usually what you want), or click Options to modify the hint settings. See "Hint Exporter Settings" (page 417) for details.

Hinting for MPEG

QuickTime can stream MPEG audio and video in different ways: as MPEG-compressed media in a QuickTime movie, or as various kinds of MPEG streams. For QuickTime movies with MPEG media, use the procedure just described: open the movie in QuickTime Player and Export choosing Movie to Hinted Movie.

QuickTime can stream MP3—also known as MPEG-1, layer 3 audio—as IceCast-compatible streams (.m3u or .pls). For details, see "Playlists" (page 442).

QuickTime can stream MPEG-4 movies in native MPEG format, which can be played by any ISO-compliant player. To stream files in MPEG-4 format, open an .mp4 file—or a QuickTime movie you want to convert to .mp4 format—in QuickTime Player, then Export, choosing Movie to MPEG-4. This brings up the MPEG-4 export dialog. Click the Streaming tab and choose basic streaming from the pop-up menu. For details, see "Hinting an MPEG-4 (.mp4) File for Streaming" (page 419).

QuickTime streams MPEG-1 video (or MPEG-1 layer, 1 or 2 audio) and MPEG-2 audio and video, but only as media inside QuickTime movies, not as MPEG streams.

Compressing and Hinting in One Step

If your movie isn't already compressed, and you don't need to preserve text or MIDI tracks, you can compress and hint in one step. Open your movie in QuickTime Player, choose Export from the File menu, and Movie to QuickTime Movie from the pop-up menu, then choose your compression settings.

If your movie is sound only (no video), the lower pop-up menu, shown in the following illustration, is the easiest way to choose the compression settings.

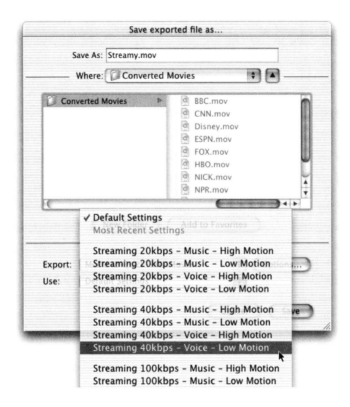

As you can see, there are settings for 20, 40, and 100 Kbits/sec. The Music selections use the QDesign compressor, while the Voice selections use Qualcomm compression.

If your movie contains video, or you want finer control than the pop-up menu provides, choose your compression settings by clicking Options. This brings up the Movie Settings dialog box:

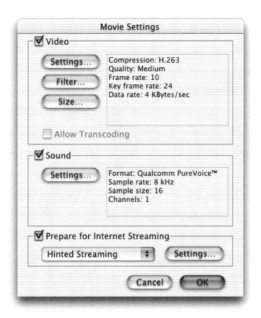

Choose the video size and compressor settings using the buttons in the Video section. For details, see "Video Codecs and Settings" (page 323).

Choose the sound compressor settings by clicking Settings in the Sound section. For details, see "Making It Fit" (page 212).

Check the Prepare for Internet Streaming box and choose Hinted Streaming from the pop-up menu. You can access some additional settings by clicking Settings.

Click OK and your movie is compressed, hinted, and ready to stream. If you want to tweak the hint settings (you normally won't), click the Settings button.

Hint Exporter Settings

The default settings for hinting are generally what you want, but if you're a networking guru, you can modify the hint track settings. For example, if you know the maximum packet size your network allows, you can set that as the streaming packet size. Or if you're streaming MIDI or text, you might adjust the repeat data rate.

Note MIDI and text are very sensitive to data loss, but they don't use much bandwidth, so QuickTime sends all text and MIDI data twice by default. If you're streaming on a LAN, you might not need the redundancy. If it's critical to get the data through over the Internet, you might want to send the data three times as extra insurance.

The hint exporter dialog looks like this:

If you check the Optimize Hints For Server box, the media data for the movie is copied into the hint track, so your streaming server may run just a little faster—but it makes the movie file twice as large. Don't bother.

Important Optimizing the hint track is no longer recommended. It was a way to make things run faster for Streaming Server v.1, but not a really efficient way. The streaming server is much faster now, and this step is no longer necessary, or even particularly useful.

You can access more settings by clicking Track Hinter Settings. This brings up the RTP Track Settings dialog box:

Native RTP payload encoding allows the codec to execute its own error recovery, which can improve playback when packets are lost. This is almost always what you want. QuickTime encoding provides a generic alternative that normally uses more bandwidth and less robust error handling, but in rare cases when a bug turns up in a native payload encoding component, QuickTime encoding provides a fallback until the problem is fixed. If you suspect a problem in the native encoder, you can use the QuickTime encoder as a test.

You can also set the packet size and packet duration limits. The packet size should be no larger than the largest packet used on any network between the streaming server and the viewer. The duration affects audio tracks only; it limits the maximum amount of audio, in milliseconds, in any packet, which limits the audio dropout created by the loss of a packet.

If you really, really want to, you can access yet another setting by clicking Options. This brings up the QuickTime Settings dialog box, shown in the following illustration.

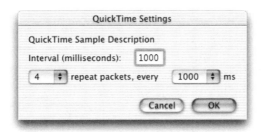

This setting affects only streams that use QuickTime packing instead of native RTP encoding and is particularly important when viewers may be jumping into a stream in progress. They won't be able to decode any audio or video until they receive a sample description. Making the interval smaller than once a second can significantly increase the movie's data rate. Making the interval larger than once a second decreases the data rate only slightly, while making the movie less accessible. In other words, it does the right thing by default; just leave it alone.

When you've specified all the settings you like, click OK in each box until you get back to the screen with the Save button, then click Save. If you change your mind about some of the settings, but don't remember what they were originally, just click Cancel instead of OK.

Hinting an MPEG-4 (.mp4) File for Streaming

An MPEG-4 file is very similar to a QuickTime movie file, but there are subtle differences. The QuickTime and Darwin streaming servers can stream both MPEG-4 movies and QuickTime movies, and the QuickTime Player plug-in can play both MPEG-4 and QuickTime movies, but they need to know which one they're dealing with.

⇲Warning Never change the file extension of a QuickTime movie from .mov to .mp4, and never change the file extension of an MPEG-4 file from .mp4 to .mov. QuickTime can play both, but only if they are properly labeled. Mislabeling will confuse other MPEG-4 players as well.

There are two ways to hint an MPEG-4 file for streaming using Quick-Time Player. In either case, open the MPEG-4 file and choose Export. Then choose either Movie to Hinted Movie or Movie to MPEG-4.

The difference is in the file format. If you export to Hinted Movie, the MPEG-4 audio and video are part of a hinted QuickTime movie (.mov file). If you export to MPEG-4, you create an actual .mp4 file.

Note You can also create a streaming .mp4 by opening a QuickTime movie and choosing Export and Movie to MPEG-4. The steps are the same.

To make an MPEG-4 (.mp4) file into a streaming MPEG-4 file, open it in QuickTime Player, choose Export from the File menu, and choose Movie to MPEG-4 in the pop-up menu. Press the Options button. This brings up the MPEG-4 export dialog box. Click the Streaming tab. Your screen should look something like the following illustration:

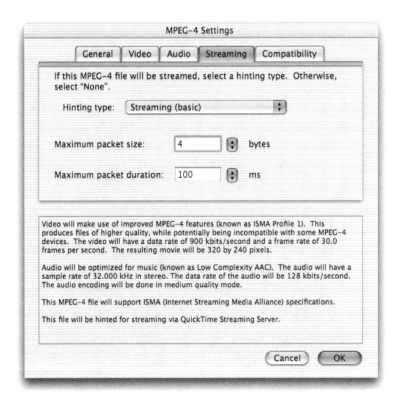

In the Hinting type pop-up menu, choose Streaming (basic). You can set the packet size and packet duration limits if you like.

Note The packet size should be no larger than the largest packet used on any network between the streaming server and the viewer. For audio-only streams, the optimum packet size may be quite small. The duration affects audio tracks only; it limits the maximum amount of audio, in milliseconds, in any packet, which limits the audio dropout created by the loss of a packet.

Unless you know what you're doing, accept the default packet settings—just click OK and you're done. When QuickTime exports the file, it won't recompress or alter an MPEG-4 file, except to add a hint track for each MPEG-4 audio and video track, making it streamable.

Note If you're exporting a QuickTime movie to streaming .mp4, and the media is not already compressed in MPEG-4 format, use the audio and video tabs to specify the data rate and compressor settings. Your movie will be compressed and hinted at the same time.

You can put the exported .mp4 file on any MPEG-4 streaming server, including the QuickTime streaming server or the Darwin streaming server.

Important Always save your MPEG-4 files with the .mp4 file extension, *not* .mov. MPEG-4 files are not QuickTime movies, but they're close enough to confuse QuickTime if you misname them.

Uploading Your Movies to a Streaming Server

Once you've compressed and hinted your movies, you need to upload them to a streaming server. This is a straightforward FTP upload or a drag-and-drop operation, depending on your connection to the server. It's the same as uploading your HTML pages and Fast Start movies to a Web server.

This can be either your own streaming server or one belonging to a streaming host or content-delivery service, such as ABHost or Akamai. A streaming host provides space on a streaming server, just as a Web hosting service does on a Web server. A content-delivery network hosts your streaming movies on multiple geographically distributed servers for reliable stream delivery to distant viewers.

Tip If most of your clients are within a relatively small area, such as, say, Holland, a service with a smaller network may be just as good for your purposes.

Just as Web pages generally go into a Web folder on the server, streaming movies go into a Movies folder on the streaming server. When the server gets a request for a movie, it looks for the movie in that folder. On the QuickTime Streaming Server for Mac OS X Server, this folder is normally

`./Local/Library/QuickTimeStreaming/Movies/`.

The location of the streaming movies folder can be changed by using the Streaming Admin interface, so it may be a different folder on your server.

Like a Web folder, the streaming movies folder can have many subdirectories. The webmaster can set up password access to particular subdirectories for individuals and groups, and can set up domain name service (DNS) entries, so for example your access to

`./Local/Library/QuickTimeStreaming/Movies/YourSubFolder`

might be through `ftp://YourDomain.com/anything/`.

By default, only the system administrator has write access to the Movies folder itself. Movie authors have their own folders and gain access to the Movies folder indirectly. To allow access to someone who needs to upload movies, the administrator opens the Movies folder and adds a symbolic link to the author's folder. For details, see "Setting Up a Streaming Server" (page 431).

After you've uploaded a movie to the streaming server, you should test it to make sure everything works, then create a Fast Start reference movie, as described in the next two sections.

▶ Testing

To test your movie after you've uploaded it to the streaming server, launch QuickTime Player, choose Open URL from the File menu, and type in the URL of your movie.

If your movie is in the main Movies folder on the streaming server, the URL is `rtsp://xxx.xxx.xxx/YourMovie.mov`, where *xxx.xxx.xxx* is the IP address of your server, and *YourMovie*.mov is the filename of your movie. You can use a domain name instead of an IP address. No path or directory needs to be specified.

If the movie is in a *subfolder* of the Movies folder, include the path from the Movies folder to your subfolder in the URL:

`rtsp://IPAddr_or_DomainName/Subfolder/YourMovie.mov`

Note If there is a symbolic link to your folder inside the main movies folder, it appears in the path just as if it were in the Movies folder.

Once you enter the URL in QuickTime Player, you should see a series of progress messages: "Contacting," "Negotiating," "Requesting Data," "Buffering." Then the movie should start to play. If you have a fast connection, this may happen too quickly to see, particularly if the server has QuickTime Streaming Server 4.12 or later, with Instant-On technology.

Four common error messages are "Connection Failed," "Not Enough Bandwidth," "404: File Not Found," and "415: Media Not Supported."

"Connection Failed" occurs when you can't contact the streaming server. Check the URL of the streaming server, try using the server's IP address instead of a domain name, and verify that the QuickTime streaming process is running on the server.

"Not Enough Bandwidth" generally means either that the movie requires more bandwidth than the server is configured to use for streaming or that all the allowable bandwidth is already in use by other streaming clients. The webmaster can increase the allowable bandwidth by adjusting the Server Settings. See "Setting Up a Streaming Server" (page 431), or you can recompress the movie so it uses less bandwidth. If it's a case of too many clients, you may need to add real bandwidth—allowing the server to use more than you actually have doesn't help much.

"404: File Not Found" generally means that the user is behind a firewall and has requested the streaming movie over HTTP on port 80, and Web server software running on your server has intercepted the request. You need to disable the Web server software, so it doesn't intercept requests sent to port 80, or else assign separate IP addresses to your Web server software and your streaming server software. Of course, you also get this message if you mistype the URL, so it doesn't hurt to check your spelling.

"415: Media Not Supported" generally means that the requested movie doesn't have a hint track. This typically happens when someone puts a Fast Start movie on a streaming server without hinting it first. Open the movie in QuickTime Player and export it, choosing Movie to Hinted Movie.

If you successfully contact the server and negotiate a streaming session, but the movie doesn't play (gets no further than "Requesting Data"), it's likely that you have HTTP access to the server, but RTP packets are being blocked; you may be behind a firewall, proxy server, or NAT. See "Firewalls, NAT, and Streaming on Port 80" (page 459).

Making a Fast Start Reference Movie

A Fast Start reference movie is a small Fast Start movie that points to your streaming movie. When someone plays a Fast Start reference movie,

QuickTime automatically connects to your streaming server and plays the streaming movie.

A Fast Start reference movie is like any Fast Start movie; you can double-click it, embed it in a Web page, or put it on a disk and mail it to a friend. It lets people play your streaming movie the way they play other movies, without typing a URL into QuickTime Player.

To make a Fast Start reference movie, open your streaming movie in QuickTime Player as described in "Testing" (page 422), press the Pause button, slide the Current Position indicator to the very start of the movie, and choose Save from the File menu. That's it. This technique also works with streaming MPEG-4 files, but the reference movie is a .mov, not an .mp4. It will play just fine in QuickTime, but other .mp4 players may not know what it is.

If you need to use Plug-in Helper to add something to a streaming movie, such as SCALE=2 or CONTROLLER=True, add it to the Fast Start reference movie instead—the parts of the file that Plug-in Helper uses to store that kind of information aren't streamed.

If you're creating alternate versions of your movie to stream at different data rates, you can make a Fast Start reference movie for each version, drag the Fast Start movies into a folder, and combine them using MakeRef-Movie, as described in "Alternate Movies" (page 151).

Tip The current version of MakeRefMovie allows you to create a single Fast Start reference movie using the URLs of the alternate streaming movies. This saves you from having to create a Fast Start reference movie for each alternate (unless you need to modify the alternates themselves, by adding nonstreaming media or by using Plug-in Helper).

▶ Embedding Streaming Movies in a Web Page

Unlike Fast Start movies, you can't reliably embed a streaming movie in a Web page by passing its URL in the SRC parameter of an <EMBED> tag. Here are four good ways to embed a streaming movie in a Web page:

- You can use the QTSRC parameter to specify a streaming URL.
- You can create a text file that points to a streaming URL.
- You can embed a Fast Start movie that points to a streaming movie.
- You can use the HREF parameter in the <EMBED> tag to specify a streaming URL and target QuickTime Player.

Important It's not currently a good idea to embed a streaming movie directly in a Web page by putting its URL in the SRC parameter of an <EMBED> tag. The URL of a streaming movie starts with an `rtsp:` protocol identifier, and many browsers don't yet understand RTSP. Use one of the methods described in this section instead.

It's okay to use the URL of a streaming .mp4 file in the SRC parameter of an <EMBED> tag, but only if you want it to be played by any available .mp4 player, regardless of whether the viewer has QuickTime. Of course, you're taking potluck, hoping the browser will do the right thing, and that whatever player or plug-in it loads does a good job. (Not always a safe assumption.) If you do this, and you wrap your <EMBED> tag in an <OBJECT> tagset, don't specify a `ClassID` or `Codebase`.

If you want the MPEG-4 streams to play in QuickTime, you can use the techniques described in this section with streaming MPEG-4 files. All of them force the browser to open the streams in QuickTime. Any differences when streaming native MPEG-4 files are noted.

You can also embed streaming movies in Web pages using Synchronized Multimedia Integration Language (SMIL), as described in Chapter 18, "SMIL for the Camera."

Streaming and QTSRC

If you're embedding a streaming movie at a single data rate, it's generally best to use the QTSRC parameter. This puts the URL of the streaming movie in your HTML. Since it's plain text, you can easily change it using a text editor or generate it from a script, allowing you to automatically create a page with a movie of the day, for example.

The HTML for embedding a streaming movie using QTSRC looks like this:

```
<EMBED SRC="UNeedQT.pntg" TYPE="image/x-macpaint"
  HEIGHT=240 WIDTH=320 BGCOLOR="#000000"
  QTSRC="rtsp://Server.Domain.com/Streaming.mov">
```

Note For streaming MPEG-4 files, the URL in the QTSRC parameter ends in `.qt4`, not `.mov`.

If the streaming movie is in the main Movies folder on the streaming server, the movie's URL is the domain name of the server plus the filename of the movie; no path or directory name is required.

If the streaming movie is in a subfolder of the Movies folder, include the relative path from the main folder as part of the URL:

```
QTSRC="rtsp://Server.Domain.com/Subfolder/Streaming.mov"
```

You might want to specify a fallback movie in the SRC parameter for people with earlier versions of QuickTime (streaming requires QuickTime 4 or later). The fallback can be a Fast Start movie or an image telling viewers they need a new version of QuickTime.

Remember, the file specified in the SRC parameter is what the browser looks at to determine which plug-in to use, so specify an existing .mov, .qti, or .pntg file.

The browser downloads the movie pointed to by the SRC parameter, even when QuickTime doesn't display it, so make this a small file to avoid wasting bandwidth. A single frame that says, "You need QuickTime 4 or later to see this movie," with an HREF to www.apple.com/quicktime/download/ is optimal. Feel free to use UNeedQT.pntg, in the Tools folder of the CD.

Important   If you use a .qti, .qtif, or .pntg file in the SRC parameter, make sure your Web server is configured to associate the file extension with the correct MIME type. For details, see Chapter 6, "What Webmasters Need to Know."

Set the HEIGHT and WIDTH parameters to the size of your streaming movie, adding 16 to the height for a controller.

All the usual <EMBED> parameters, such as AUTOPLAY, SCALE, and HREF, work normally when embedding a streaming movie using QTSRC.

The main disadvantage of using the QTSRC parameter is that QuickTime has only the URL of the streaming movie initially; it doesn't know the movie's characteristics, such as the actual movie size or whether this is a sound-only movie, until it gets that information from the streaming server.

As a consequence, QuickTime creates a default window of 160 x 120 pixels to display the initial progress messages, then resizes the window to fit the actual movie once it knows how big it is. If your actual movie is larger than 160 x 120, the smaller initial window may detract from your page layout. If your actual movie is smaller than 160 x 120 or contains only audio, the initial window is clipped to the height and width you allocate in the <EMBED> tag, which may keep the viewer from seeing progress or error messages.

So, when you use the QTSRC parameter for a movie smaller than 160 x 120, allocate at least 160 x 120 pixels to the plug-in, so the progress messages are visible.

If your movie is smaller *or* larger than 160 x 120, specify a background color to fill the space around your movie, or the space around the initial window, in an attractive way.

For streaming audio, consider adding a still image to the movie. A still image doesn't require much bandwidth. It can be an image of the artist or the CD cover, or any image that complements the music, and it can contain a clickable HREF to a page where the listener can buy the CD, read the lyrics, or get more information about the composer. It's a nice thing all around.

Streaming from a Text File

Another approach that you can take is to embed the URL of a streaming movie in a text file and pass the text file to QuickTime. There are two different formats you can use for this: RTSPtext or a QuickTime Media Link (XML).

RTSPtext

It doesn't get much simpler than this—use a text editor to create a one-line text file in the format

```
RTSPtextRTSP://server.com/path/filename
```

In other words, type the eight characters "RTSPtext" (case is important), followed immediately by the URL of your streaming movie.

Note If your streaming movie is an MPEG-4 file, the filename ends in .qt4, not .mov.

Save as plain text, *but with the .mov file extension*. If your operating system helpfully adds the .txt file extension, remove it manually. This text file should be treated as a movie file by all concerned. Embed it in the page as if it were an ordinary QuickTime movie. For example, if your text file is named rtspURL.mov:

```
<EMBED SRC="rtspURL.mov" HEIGHT=yy WIDTH=xx >
```

Name the text file using the .mov extension, even if it's pointing to an .mp4 file.

All the usual <EMBED> parameters apply normally.

QuickTime Media Link (XML)

You can create a text file that automatically launches QuickTime Player and includes the URL of a streaming movie. It's called a QuickTime Media Link, or .qtl file. You can create the file by exporting your streaming movie from QuickTime Player (export as Movie to QuickTime Media Link)

or by typing three lines of text (or having a script generate them). The first two lines are always the same:

```
<?xml version="1.0"?>
<?quicktime type="application/x-quicktime-media-link"?>
```

The third line contains the URL of your streaming movie:

```
<embed src="rtsp://www.server.com/MyStreaming.mov" />
```

If your streaming movie is an MPEG-4 file, it's name ends in .mp4, not .mov, but everything else is the same.

Important Don't leave out the /> at the end of the third line! This is XML, not HTML.

You can also set playback characteristics for your streaming movie in the.qtl file, such as autoplay, looping, or full-screen modes. You don't embed a .qtl file; you link to it as if it were a .PDF or a .doc file. For more about creating and using .qtl files, see "Launching QuickTime Player from a Text Link" (page 100) and "Making a QuickTime Media Link (.qtl) File" (page 102).

Streaming from a Fast Start Reference Movie

When you open a streaming movie in QuickTime Player and choose Save, it creates a Fast Start movie that points to the streaming movie. You can embed this Fast Start movie in a Web page. When the viewer plays the Fast Start movie, QuickTime connects to the streaming server and gets the streams. This works with MPEG-4 files or any file type that QuickTime can open and play.

The HTML is the same as for any Fast Start movie:

```
<EMBED SRC="PointsToStreaming.mov" HEIGHT=320 WIDTH=240>
```

All the usual <EMBED> parameters, such as AUTOPLAY and HREF, work normally.

The nice thing about this approach is that you can manipulate the Fast Start movie in all the usual ways, such as modifying it with Plug-in Helper or setting it to play at double size in QuickTime Player.

An additional feature of a Fast Start reference movie is that it contains the characteristics of the streaming movie, such as its height and width, duration, and whether this is a sound-only movie. Instead of opening a default window and resizing it to fit the movie, QuickTime opens the right-sized window initially.

There are some drawbacks to this approach as well. You need to create a new Fast Start reference movie each time you create or modify a streaming movie, which adds a step to your workload. The Web page depends on two external files, the Fast Start movie *and* the streaming movie, so there's twice as much that can go wrong. If you update the streaming movie, but not the Fast Start reference movie, the movie characteristics may be wrong initially, which could confuse QuickTime.

Still, this is a popular and versatile way to add a streaming movie to a Web page.

Streaming with HREF and QuickTime Player

You can use a poster movie to launch a streaming movie in QuickTime Player by putting the streaming movie's URL in the HREF parameter of the <EMBED> tag and targeting QuickTime Player.

The HTML looks like this:

```
<EMBED SRC="Poster.mov"
  HEIGHT=320 WIDTH=240 CONTROLLER="False"
  HREF="rtsp://server.domain.com/Streaming.mov"
  TARGET="quicktimeplayer" >
```

The HREF can also point to a streaming MPEG-4 file, in which case the URL ends in .mp4, not .mov. When the viewer clicks the poster movie, QuickTime Player launches and plays the streaming movie or .mp4. The poster movie itself is always a movie (.mov) file.

Important   This technique works only if you target QuickTime Player. If you target a browser window or a browser frame, the rtsp:// protocol identifier in the URL can confuse the browser. (When you target QuickTime Player, movie access is handled directly by QuickTime without troubling the browser.)

If the streaming movie is in the main Movies folder on the streaming server, its URL is the name of the server plus the filename of the movie or .mp4 file; no path or directory name is needed. For example:

```
HREF="rtsp://server.domain.com/Streaming.mov"
```

If the streaming movie or .mp4 file is in a subfolder of the main Movies folder, include the relative path from the main folder. For example:

```
HREF="rtsp://server.domain.com/subfolder/Streaming.mp4"
```

Note The subfolder may also be a symbolic link to a folder elsewhere on the server. This allows the system administrator to give read/write access for a user's personal Movies folder, without giving access to the main Movies folder.

This method of embedding streaming movies has a couple of advantages. Like the QTSRC parameter, the HREF parameter puts the URL of the streaming movie in your Web page as plain text. It's easy to modify with a text editor, and it's easy to generate from a script. Because the movie is launched in QuickTime Player, any resizing of the display area has a minimal aesthetic impact, and any progress or error messages are guaranteed to be visible.

This method has all the usual benefits of using QuickTime Player instead of the browser plug-in: you're not constrained by the size of the browser window, the viewer can add your movie to the Favorites list, and you can use full-screen mode or media skins.

One thing that's cool about playing streaming movies in QuickTime Player is that HREF tracks work. HREF tracks in a local or Fast Start movie work only in the plug-in, not in QuickTime Player. But HREF tracks in streaming movies *do* work in QuickTime Player.

Note It's likely that at some point in the future, HREF tracks will work the same way in Quick-Time Player as they now work in the plug-in. Check the QuickTime website for updates.

If you want to launch a streaming movie in QuickTime Player without asking the viewer to click a poster, just add the AUTOHREF parameter. The HTML looks like this:

```
<EMBED SRC="Decoration.mov"
  HEIGHT=320 WIDTH=240 CONTROLLER="False"
  HREF="rtsp://server.domain.com/Streaming.mov" AUTOHREF=True
  TARGET="quicktimeplayer" >
```

In this example, Streaming.mov automatically plays in QuickTime Player as soon as the <EMBED> tag loads in the browser.

Decoration.mov loads and displays in the plug-in—if you have enough bandwidth, memory, and CPU speed, you can make this a real movie that plays at the same time as your streaming movie by setting `AUTOPLAY=True` and/or `CONTROLLER=True`. Conversely, you could make it a 2-pixel-by-2-pixel dot disguised as the period at the end of a sentence. Its main job is to get the browser to load the QuickTime plug-in, which will execute the `HREF` automatically. What you do with this movie after that is entirely up to you.

Set `HEIGHT` and `WIDTH` to the dimensions of `Decoration.mov`. Any other parameters set in the `<EMBED>` tag also apply to `Decoration.mov`, not to your streaming movie.

Setting Up a Streaming Server

To deliver streaming movies, you need access to a streaming server. You can either arrange to have your streaming movies hosted by a commercial service provider, such as PlayStream, Akamai, Generic Media, ABHost, or AnyStream, or you can set up your own streaming server.

Apple provides streaming server software in three flavors. They all stream QuickTime, MPEG-4, and MP3 (IceCast-compatible playlists), and they're all free. That's right, free. No, *really* free—no fee for the software, no fee for licenses, no fee for 10,000 streams, no fees. Free. The three flavors are QTSS, DSS, and DSS source code:

- **QTSS**—If you purchase Apple's XServe hardware, or Mac OS X Server software, QuickTime Streaming Server (QTSS) is included free.

  `www.apple.com/products/xserve/`

- **DSS**—For Windows 2000, Windows NT, Mac OS X, Solaris, or Linux, you can download the Darwin Streaming Server (DSS) from Apple. Just install it and go. It's free.

  `www.apple.com/quicktime/products/qtss/`

- **DSS source code**—If you want to run your streaming server on other operating systems, or want to modify the streaming server software, you can download the Darwin Streaming Server source code (open source) and compile it yourself. Free, of course.

  `www.publicsource.apple.com/projects/streaming/`

Note   If you have **Mac OS X Server**, you have **QTSS**.
If you have **Mac OS X**, you need to download **DSS**.
If you have **Windows NT** or **2000**, download **DSS**.

You can also obtain streaming server software for QuickTime from other sources, many of which stream not only QuickTime, but Real, Windows Media, and other formats as well. Here are a few.

- **IBM VideoCharger**(Windows NT, AIX)

  www.software.ibm.com/data/videocharger/

  www.software.ibm.com/data/videocharger/quicktime.html
- **Helix Universal Server** (Windows, Sun Solaris, IBM AIX, HP UX)

  www.realnetworks.com/

  Helix DNA Open Source: www.helixcommunity.org/
- **SGI Kasenna MediaBase** (IRIX)

  www.sgi.com/software/mediabase/

This section shows you how to set up the QTSS and DSS streaming servers.

Streaming Server Administrator's Guide

There is a copy of the *QuickTime Streaming Server Administrator's Guide,* in PDF format, in the Streaming folder of the CD. The latest version is really good, and it covers most of the material in the rest of this section ("Setting Up a Streaming Server") in a different organizational format. Check there if you need more information, or just want a different or better explanation.

Hardware Requirements

The requirements for QTSS and DSS are different.

DSS

DSS runs on a variety of Windows, Linux, and Mac hardware platforms, and can be recompiled for other operating systems. It doesn't require a particularly fast processor by current standards—average will do. You do want plenty of RAM, though. It should run fine on 256 MB or even less, but I recommend 512 MB. A large, fast hard drive is a must for heavy use, but for light duty, a typical hard drive is fine. Minimum free space is 1 GB, but 40 GB is better. Just make sure there's room for all the movies. At least one ethernet port is necessary. I recommend two or more 100Base-T or Gigabit Ethernet ports.

QTSS

QTSS runs on any Macintosh that runs Mac OS X Server (basically any G3 or G4 Macintosh with FireWire). I recommend a G4 with 512 MB of RAM and a large hard disk. A second Ethernet port is recommended. An XServe is ideal and comes with QTSS preinstalled (along with mail server, Web server, and more). You can buy Mac OS X Server for your Mac for $499 (including QTSS). A new XServe with 500 MB of RAM and a pair of Gigabit Ethernet ports costs less than $2999, software preinstalled.

Number of Servers

The number of servers you need depends on the maximum number of simultaneous client connections and the bandwidth of each stream. It also depends on the speed of your hardware.

For QTSS running on a base model XServe, you need roughly one server for every 4000 simultaneous 28-Kbit streams (or 2000 simultaneous 56-Kbit streams, or 100 Mbits/sec of output).

Performance of DSS is the same, on similar hardware. Obviously, you'll run out of steam sooner running DSS on a 400 MHz iMac or a 500 MHz Pavillion, but just about any modern desktop should be able to manage 1000 streams, and a fast, well-designed machine can reliably serve 4000.

If you're not streaming a lot of content, you don't have to dedicate even one computer to acting as a streaming server (heck, I have DSS running on my desktop machine). Smallish websites can use Web server software on the same computer as the streaming server (if you have Mac OS X Server, Apache Web server software is included).

Note The streaming server isn't usually what takes the most CPU power when it comes to streaming movies. Compressing a movie can take many hours, and compressing each movie for several data rates multiplies things proportionately. If you have lots of new movies coming in regularly, as you might with movie trailers or music videos, expect to spend more on compression hardware than on streaming hardware. A lot more.

Network Connections

It may come as a surprise to you that the streaming server itself is rarely the limiting factor for streaming over the Internet: it's bandwidth. A single XServe running QTSS can deliver 2000 simultaneous streams at 56 Kbits each, an aggregate of over 100 Mbits/sec. That's enough to saturate *80* T1 connections to the Internet, or completely swamp a 100Base-T Ethernet LAN.

If you're streaming primarily over a campus or corporate intranet or LAN, this won't affect you greatly, but if you're delivering a lot of streaming content over the Internet, telecommunications bandwidth is going to be the major expense. Leasing costs for your high-bandwidth digital lines will cost more per week than your server and software cost per year, even if you upgrade your servers annually.

Of course, you don't need dozens of T1 connections to deliver streaming movies. You need only enough bandwidth to carry the maximum number of simultaneous streams you'll be sending. A single T1 carries 1.5 Mbits/sec, or enough streams for 25 simultaneous viewers using 56K modems, or 50 simultaneous streams of 20-Kbit audio. If you're streaming low-bandwidth video to a few viewers at any moment, a single relatively inexpensive cable or sDSL modem connection may be plenty (that's **sDSL**, not **aDSL**), depending on your upstream speed.

Tip Consumers generally get asymmetric DSL, or aDSL, which limits you to 128 Kbits "upstream" (from you to the world). For a little more, you can often get symmetric DSL (sDSL), which is typically 720 Kbits in both directions. For streaming, aDSL isn't much better than a dialup modem, whereas sDSL can carry half a dozen streams at a time.

Think about how much bandwidth you need, or how much you can afford, and plan accordingly. There's no sense buying multiple servers if you have only a few T1 connections to carry the traffic; one server will do nicely. If you do need multiple servers to deliver your content to the world, be sure to lay in enough pipe to carry the load to the Internet.

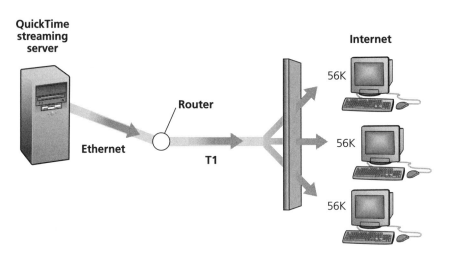

One T1 connection for every 25 viewers at 56 Kbits (1.5 Mbits/sec)
One 100Base-T Ethernet connection for every 15 T1 lines (25 Mbits/sec)
One server for every four Ethernet connections (100 Mbits/sec)

Your digital Internet connections are typically hooked internally to a router (or multiple routers), and each router is connected to your server by Ethernet. You want Gigabit Ethernet, rather than 100Base-T, if you plan to send more than 12 Mbits/sec of throughput.

Important If you're going to administer the server remotely, it's a good idea to use separate Ethernet ports for streaming and administration, with the admin port securely behind your firewall.

Size Considerations

If you're sending a few or a few hundred streams at any given moment, it's not all that complicated. One server, one Ethernet connection to a router, and as much telecom pipe as it takes, from an sDSL line to a few T1s. Whatever you need and can afford.

For large enterprises, it often makes sense to have your own streaming server for in-house streaming and use a content delivery service for large-scale Internet streaming.

Apple has streamed all of the largest Internet events to date, some with over 10,000 simultaneous viewers. In our first large webcasts, even with plenty of bandwidth at our end, we found that people in remote areas (Australia and Philadelphia, for example) were getting poor reception— there were just too many choke points between us and them. For us, the solution was Akamai networks. They're one of a few large content delivery services with servers around the world. We send them one stream, they replicate it to their "edge" servers, and it gets streamed to now-happy Aussies and Philadelphians from a local source. This works.

But it's still expensive. You pay for total and peak bandwidth usage. If your content is pay-per-view or has sufficient ad revenue to pay for its bandwidth, that's okay.

But if it costs more to send a stream than you generate from it, budget accordingly. Some news agencies were shocked to see their bandwidth bill for the day the World Trade Center towers were attacked was over $1 million. They had unexpectedly spent more than a year's budget in a single day.

Happily, your streams probably won't be *that* popular.

Of course, bandwidth will get cheaper, and practical business models for streaming are going to emerge—there will be a lot more streaming done in the future than there is today. It's worth something to be genuinely involved in this technology, even if it isn't yet profitable. It's likely to go fast when it takes off. Just try not to overextend until then.

Load Sharing

If you have multiple streaming servers, you can spread the load in a couple of different ways. You can put different movies on different servers, or you can use round-robin DNS.

Putting different movies on different servers makes efficient use of disk space. This works well for a movie library with many popular titles. It doesn't work well when more people than a single server can support all want to watch the same movie at the same time.

Round-robin DNS requires a Domain Name Server configured to route requests for a domain name to a series of IP addresses, one after another. This can also be accomplished using router/proxy software and NAT—in the latter case, the DNS for your streaming server resolves to the IP address of the router, which acts as an RTSP proxy, forwarding requests to a group of servers in serial fashion.

Tip The cheap/easy way to do this is to put a small 100Base-T router/switch (in the $99–199 range—the kind you might use to share a DSL modem) between your servers and the Internet. Plug the Internet side into your router's WAN port, set the router to provide DHCP (default for most routers), and plug the servers into the router's other ports. Use the router's setup utility to give it the IP address your streaming servers will "share." Set your servers to DHCP using their network or TCP/IP control panels. Then use the streaming server admin program to restart your streaming servers.

In either case, this spreads the load equally among all your servers, even when you get multiple requests for the same URL. It requires that each server be a mirror of all the others, though, so the same content is on every server. This works well if you're serving a live stream, which uses very little disk space, but can be in high demand at a particular instant. If you have a large movie library, round-robin DNS requires enough disk space to hold multiple copies of each movie.

Setting Up the Software

Setting up the streaming server software is surprisingly easy. The QTSS Admin program is browser-based software that runs from the desktop on Mac OS X Server, or by typing an address in a browser window for everyone else.

To run QTSS Admin from the server itself, just open a browser and type http://localhost:1220 in the address bar (then press Enter or Return).

To run QTSS Admin from a different computer, open a browser and type `http://hostname or IP address:1220` in the address bar (then press Enter or Return).

Setup Assistant

The first time you run QTSS Admin, it will load the Setup Assistant to get you started. The Setup Assistant application steps you through a series of screens.

1. The first time you run it, you'll need to provide a name and password. Needless to say, *do not forget your password*. Ahem. This name and password will be required to administer the streaming server from now on.

2. Next you'll be asked to provide an MP3 broadcast password. This password will be needed to create or modify MP3 playlists.

3. You'll then be asked if you want to use secure, encrypted SSL for remote administration of your server. *Do not check this box*—not unless you have a valid SSL certificate in hand and know what you're doing.

   This setting is used when you access your computer over IP to administer the server. If you do this on a LAN, you really shouldn't need SSL encryption (unless you're being hacked from the next cubicle).

   If you plan to administer the server over the Internet, however, SSL is a good idea. But it's also a big hassle. Do it later. See the *QTSS Admin Guide* (in the Streaming folder on the CD) for details.

Tip If you want security and *don't* know what you're doing, it's simple: don't enable port 1220 through your firewall. Use the keyboard for administration—it can't be hacked over the Internet—and lock your office door when you're away from the keyboard.

4. You'll be shown the location of the streaming media folder. This is where all your streaming media goes. You can set it to anything you like. The defaults are different for each operating system, but yours is shown. See the *QTSS Admin Guide* (on the CD) for the others.

5. Next you'll see a checkbox for streaming on port 80. This allows you to stream through firewalls. That's a good thing. Check it, unless you're also running a Web server on the same machine. Web servers use port 80 for HTTP.

   If you want to run a Web server from this machine *and* be able to stream on port 80, I suggest you use a separate Ethernet card for the Web server and give the Web server its own IP address.

That should do it. You should now see the main QTSS Admin screen, and the streaming server should be up and running. How easy was that?

QTSS Admin Main Screen

From this screen you can see the server status and other interesting stats, such as the number of current connections, bandwidth usage, and CPU load. You can access a number of other screens from this one:

- If you have a broadcaster running on the same machine, you can administer it from the Broadcast screen to start, stop, or modify a broadcast. See "Live Streaming" (page 445).
- The Connected Users screen gives you instant reports on the details of each computer currently receiving your streams (IP address, bit rate, packet loss, and so on).
- The Relay Status screen gives you instant reports on any relay servers that are relaying your streams.
- The General Settings screen lets you
  - change the media directory
  - enable SSL for remote admin (but don't, unless you know what you're doing)
  - set the maximum number of simultaneous connections allowed
  - set the maximum outgoing bit rate for all streams combined
  - set the default authentication mode (use Digest)
  - choose whether to restart the server automatically on reboot
  - change the admin, movie broadcast, or MP3 broadcast password
- The Port Settings screen lets you toggle streaming on port 80.
- The Relay Settings screen lets you determine how to handle relay requests. See "Server, Reflector, and Relay" (page 440).
- The Log Settings screen allows you to control error logging and access logging.
- The Playlists screen lets you create, edit, and delete playlists. See "Playlists" (page 442).
- The Error Log screen lets you read and reset the error log.
- The Access Log screen provides streaming history. It lets you see when and how often each movie has been accessed (streamed), and who it was streamed to. Access errors are also reported in this log. You can set

this log to reset periodically, or when it reaches a maximum size. See the *QTSS Admin Guide* (on the CD) for details.

Sanity Test

At this point the server should be up and running. Before we go into too much detail on how to modify and customize its behavior, it might be a good idea to check and see if it's actually working as advertised.

You can test your setup using the sample movies in the Movies folder. Launch QuickTime Player on a computer with an IP connection to your server (over a LAN or the Internet). Choose Open URL in QuickTime Player and enter `rtsp://xxx.xxx.xxx/sample_300kbit.mov`, where *xxx.xxx.xxx* is your server's IP address. Don't include any path or directory name. Your streaming server should stream the movie to QuickTime Player (if you're on a dialup connection, you might want to use a lower-bandwidth sample movie).

If you see the sample movie, your streaming server is indeed up and running. If you need to change your software setup, you can access the QTSS Admin utility through a browser by logging on to the server at port 1220 (or, on Mac OS X Server, from the dock).

Access to the Media Folder

The media folder holds your streaming movies and the ancillary files the streaming server needs to play them, such as playlists.

It also holds Session Description Protocol (`.sdp`) files for every streaming movie. For video-on-demand movies, the streaming server creates `.sdp` files automatically. When it's relaying a live stream, the streaming server gets an `.sdp` file from the broadcaster. In any case, don't be alarmed at their appearance or let anything bad happen to them.

Only the system administrator has read/write access to the media folder. You'll probably want to create folders that other people can put movies into. That way individual users or groups can have their own secure folders for their movies. And you want these folders to be inside the media folder, so their movies are streamable without your intervention.

The problem is, you don't want to give everyone access to the media folder, so you can't just create subfolders for people.

Note Ordinarily, UNIX-type access permissions follow a top-down model: the deeper into a file system you go, the more restrictions are added. If you have access to a folder, you automatically have access to all the enclosing folders.

The solution is to give users their own folders with read/write access somewhere else, and create symbolic links to those folders in the media folder. For streaming purposes, they become subfolders—the streaming server can search them for a requested movie as if they were really there. For instructions on creating symbolic links, and creating access lists for user folders, see the *QTSS Admin Guide* (in the Streaming folder on the CD).

That takes care of direct file access. You can restrict streaming access to content in your media folder, or any subfolder, by putting an Access file—containing the user names and passwords of authorized users—inside the restricted folder. The restrictions also apply to any folders contained within the restricted folder, unless they have Access files of their own.

When someone asks for a movie from the streaming server, the server checks for an Access file in the same folder, or any higher folder, until it either gets to the media folder or finds an Access file. If it finds an Access file, it prompts the viewer for a user name and password. Only authorized viewers can watch the movie. If no Access file is found, the movie is streamed without prompting for a password.

Server, Reflector, and Relay

The main function of a streaming server is to act as a server: wait for RTSP requests and create streams in response. In that mode, it acts like a big tape deck, but it can also perform other functions to support large-scale streaming networks and transmission of live streams.

Note If you don't have a large network with multiple servers, and you're only serving video-on-demand (no live broadcasts), you don't really need to read this section. It will help you understand what some of the streaming server settings are for, however.

When the streaming server gets an RTSP request, it looks in the media folder for a matching session description file (an .sdp file). This is a small file that describes the streams. If it finds an .sdp file, it tries to send the stream. In its server role, it creates the stream from a hinted file in the media folder.

But the .sdp file can specify a stream originating elsewhere on the network, in which case the server requests the stream from its source and then reflects it to the viewer. If someone else requests the same stream, the server doesn't request a second copy from the source; it reflects a copy of the stream that already exists, also called a live stream. The streaming server acts as a reflector: it reflects a stream that originates elsewhere.

A single stream can be reflected to many people this way. Because they share a single source stream, people who request a reflected stream are tuning into a broadcast—everyone sees the same thing. This is called live streaming because the server is reflecting a live stream, not creating a stream from a hinted file.

Note This is called live streaming, but the *source* of the stream may not be live. The stream is a live signal, a transmission in progress. The contents of the transmission, the source material, can be anything. Just like a radio broadcast—the signal is live, but the music is prerecorded. The streaming server is reflecting a live stream—the source of the stream can be live, prerecorded, or a mixture.

Normally, a live stream is originated by something called a broadcaster. It creates the stream and sends an .sdp file to the server. When the server gets a request for the stream, it finds the matching .sdp file, requests the stream if it hasn't already done so, and reflects that stream to as many people as request it.

For this to happen, the broadcaster needs limited write access to the media folder, so it can drop the .sdp file there, overwriting any older one, and delete the .sdp file when the broadcast terminates.

Rather than give every broadcaster full access rights to the media folder, the streaming server provides a list of names and passwords for people who have the right to initiate and terminate broadcasts by inserting, deleting, and modifying .sdp files for live streams.

The broadcaster sends a single stream to the server, which can reflect it to as many as 4000 viewers at dialup bandwidth, or 500 viewers of high-bandwidth DSL or cable streams. But what if that isn't enough?

In theory, the broadcaster could send streams to multiple servers, with each server acting as a reflector. But that would be impractical for large networks—the broadcaster would have to send .sdp files and streams all over the network and have password access to all the servers. Adding or removing servers would be complicated. Every server would have to know about every broadcaster, and vice versa.

Instead, the server has the ability to act as a relay. When it gets an .sdp file and a relay request, it passes a modified copy of the .sdp file to another server or group of servers. When these servers get a request for the stream, they get a copy of it from the relay server. They then act as reflectors, each one able to serve hundreds or thousands of people from that one relayed stream.

One relay server can spread the broadcast to thousands of servers, each of which can reflect to thousands of viewers, allowing a broadcaster to reach millions of viewers with a single stream, having password access to a single media folder. New servers can be added to the network simply by putting them on the list of a single relay server.

There are a couple of neat twists on this. The relay server can be set up to hold the .sdp file until it gets an announcement that the stream has started, then relay it to the list. This lets you cue the network to start when the conductor raises the baton, without wasting any bandwidth beforehand.

The relay server can also be set up to request the stream from the source when it gets a relay request. That's how a live stream normally gets to the relay server in the first place. But this can also be used to trigger the relay server to request a stored movie, triggering a prerecorded broadcast.

For *really* large networks, it's possible to have one relay server forward the relay request to others. Since each relay server can serve tens of thousands or millions of people through reflectors, this scales up very nicely.

For smaller networks, the functions of server, reflector, and/or relay can be performed by the same streaming server without conflict. No need to dedicate a second computer just to add live streams or a relay.

Playlists

The streaming server can also send a series of movies, MPEG-4 streams, or MP3 audio files from a playlist. This allows you to simulate a live broadcast—the streaming server creates a stream from the playlist and sends the stream to itself. It then acts as a reflector, so when people ask for the stream they get a copy of the existing stream in progress (sometimes called a live stream). Like a broadcast, all the viewers see the same thing at the same time.

A playlist is a list of files to play, in sequence or out of order, once through or continuously. It's all presented as a continuous stream, so the files in the playlist need to have the same streaming characteristics (the same .sdp file would describe any of them). A playlist can contain hinted movies, hinted MPEG-4 files, or ordinary MP3 files, but it can't mix these file types. In fact, all files in the playlist need to have the same compression, audio sample rate, number of tracks, and so on. If one file has Sorenson 3 video at 320 × 240, for example, all the files must have 320 × 240 Sorenson 3 video.

Once you have your files assembled in a single folder, either in the media folder itself, or in a folder represented by a symbolic link in the media folder, creating a playlist is a snap.

Fire up the QTSS Admin utility on port 1220 and click Playlists, then click New MP3 Playlist or New Movie Playlist.

Note Movie playlists and MPEG-4 playlists behave exactly the same and are both called movie playlists. (But you can't mix movies and MPEG-4 files in the same list.)

A nice list of available media appears. Drag the items you want, in the order you want them, from the list of available items into the playlist window.

The repetition and playmode settings are self-explanatory, as is the name field (every playlist needs a unique name).

The "Mount Point:" requires a little explanation. A mount point is a name for your playlist that people can link to over a network. Unlike the name field, this needs to follow Internet filename syntax—no spaces, quotes, colons, slashes, and so on. (Be kind to yourself; just use letters.)

The mount point is used a little differently for movie playlists and MP3 playlists because they use different protocols—RTSP/RTP for movies, and the icy:// variant of HTTP for MP3 files (IceCast protocol). Here are the details.

For a movie or MPEG-4 playlist, the mount point is the name of the .sdp file for the playlist; you can either link directly to the .sdp file (leaving off the .sdp file extension) or create a reference movie that points to it. For example, if the mount point is in the media folder itself, and named MyPlayList.sdp, your HTML can look like this:

```
<embed src=UNeedQT.mov
  qtsrc=rtsp://myserver.com/MyPlayList
  height=yy+16 width=xx autoplay=true />
```

Use the qtsrc parameter because a browser might misdirect an RTSP URL to some other client. Since the playlist is in the media folder itself, no path beyond the server name is required. When you link to an .sdp file, the syntax is such that you don't include the .sdp file extension.

To create a reference movie, launch QuickTime Player, choose Open URL from the File menu, and type rtsp://myserver.com/MyPlayList. When the movie opens, choose Save, with the .mov file extension, as always.

For an MP3 playlist, the mount point is a symbolic name for the path to the playlist. The streaming server takes care of the actual path, so you just have to provide a unique name that follows Internet filename conventions (no spaces, slashes, and so on).

Important Unlike a movie playlist's mount point, the mount point of an MP3 file is not an `.sdp` file (so don't give it the `.sdp` file extension). It's a symbolic name, not a filename, so it doesn't have a file extension.

For example, if your mount point is named `MyMP3PlayList`, you can link to it by creating an M3U playlist file that looks like this:

```
http://myserver.com:8000/MyMP3PlayList
```

MP3 playlists use modified HTTP format and a port in the 8000 neighborhood (the streaming server uses port 8000). Specify the playlist by its mount point. If you're unfamiliar with M3U playlists, they're one-line text files with the .m3u file extension. Link to them using normal hyperlinks:

```
<A HREF=http://some.m3u> Radio Free Code Monkey </a>
```

A browser will open the link using an MP3 player such as iTunes or WinAmp. If you want the playlist to open in the QuickTime plug-in, use a reference movie (add an `HREF` to open the movie in QuickTime Player).

To create a reference movie to an MP3 playlist, open the playlist *as an IceCast stream*, using `icy://` protocol. For example:

```
icy://myserver.com:8000/MyMP3PlayList
```

Just substitute `icy://` for `http://` in the URL. When the audio begins to play, choose Save, using the .mov file extension as always.

The streaming server also supports PLS playlists, which are formatted differently than M3U playlists and carry more information. The details of PLS format fall outside the scope of this book, but here's an example of a PLS playlist for a streaming server with mount point `MyMP3PlayList`.

```
[playlistname]
File1=http://myserver.com:8000/MyMP3PlayList
Title1=Playlist Title
Length1=-1
NumberOfEntries=1
Version=2
```

Note Hmm. Maybe the mount point field required more than a little explanation . . .

Anyway, after you specify the mount point for your playlist, and all the settings are the way you want them, press the Enter or Return key (oddly, there's no Done, Save, or OK button). If you return to the main screen by clicking a link, without pressing Return or Enter, the playlist is not saved. Yikes!

You can start and stop playlists, create them and delete them, or edit them by clicking Playlists from the main QTSS Admin screen. Always stop a playlist before you edit it.

▶ Live Streaming

So far, we've looked at ways to stream from hinted movies and other files, but you can also create streams from live sources, such as a microphone or video camera. Like live television or radio, you can use live streams to send things over the Internet as they happen.

This radically compresses the whole process we've been looking at in this book: capturing audio and/or video, resizing or resampling it, compressing it for the Web, putting it on a streaming server, sending it out to people over a network, perhaps going over the Internet, and maybe through a browser. But instead of spending hours or days, getting it all done in a few seconds. Right now.

You'll need a special piece of software to help you with this. It's called a *broadcaster.*

Introduction to Broadcasters

A broadcaster is an application program that takes input from real-time sources—such as a video camera, a live audio feed, or the audio output of a CD player—and creates real-time streams from them.

Note A broadcaster produces a single stream from each input and sends it to a single IP address. Software that sends multiple streams from the same input is acting as a streaming server as well as a broadcaster.

This is much more demanding than creating a stream from a hinted movie. A hinted movie is already compressed for streaming at the desired bandwidth, and its hint tracks contain precise instructions for packing the compressed data into real-time packets.

A broadcaster takes video and/or audio input, decompresses it if necessary—video from a mini-DV camera, for example, must be decompressed—resizes the video or resamples the audio as needed, compresses the audio and video for transmission, stores a copy on the local hard drive if asked, and sends the audio and video out over an IP network, packetized as real-time streams. It does all this simultaneously—the input and output are both continuous real-time events.

Consequently, a computer acting as a broadcaster can't do much else at the same time. Specifically, it can't act as a streaming server and expect to handle 4000 simultaneous streams. More like 400 on a current-generation machine (less, if you're also using it to check your email or play video games).

In addition, you may want to broadcast something happening at a remote site, such as a breaking news story, concert, or other live event. If your broadcaster is running on the same computer as your streaming server, this means you need to either pipe the audio and video from the event to your broadcaster/server (expensive), or supply a lot of Internet bandwidth to the remote site and drag your broadcaster/server out there with you (expensive and painful).

So, why not put the broadcaster on a separate computer—a laptop, maybe? Then you could take it out to remote events and leave your server and fat Internet pipes at home—all you need is enough bandwidth to send a single stream from the broadcaster to the server. The broadcaster can send a single stream of audio and/or video to the streaming server, which relays the signal to as many people as you like.

But that takes two computers. What if you just want to put your radio station on the Internet, or send video of your goldfish bowl to the larger universe, and don't expect more than a few hundred in the audience at a given time? Do you need two computers?

Not at all. Your computer can do double duty, acting as a broadcaster and a streaming server. There are two ways to do this. You can either buy integrated broadcaster/server software, or you can run a stand-alone broadcaster and an ordinary streaming server on the same computer. The server and broadcaster don't even need to know about each other. When you tell the broadcaster to send its streams to a server, just use your own IP address as the server address. (I'm such a geek I think this is cool.)

In fact, if you're broadcasting over a LAN, as opposed to the Internet, you may be able to deliver streams to as many viewers as you like without using a streaming server at all, just the broadcaster. Bear in mind that a broadcaster creates an audio stream, or a video stream, or both, and sends out one copy of each stream to an IP address.

Now, if that IP address is one of a special group of addresses reserved for broadcasts or multicasts, anyone on the LAN can tune in. Way cool. We'll look at that more closely in "Broadcasting on a Campus or Corporate LAN" (page 448).

Broadcasting to a Streaming Server

To send a live transmission to thousands of people over the Internet, you need both a broadcaster and a streaming server. The broadcaster creates an audio stream, a video stream, or both, and sends them to a streaming server. The streaming server sends copies of the streams over the Internet in response to viewer requests.

The broadcaster doesn't need to be connected to a streaming server over a LAN; it just needs to be able to reach the streaming server over IP. It's quite possible to stream live events from a remote location over a dialup Internet connection. In fact, this is typical for event coverage. The connection needs just enough bandwidth for one copy of each stream. Your streaming server then replicates the live streams to the world over its faster connections.

With a portable computer, a microphone, and a DV camera, you can send Internet webcasts of virtually anything from virtually anywhere. It's a virtual mobile TV studio. And did I mention it's virtual?

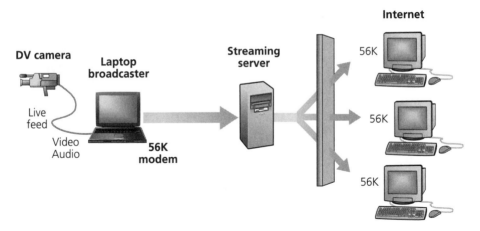

(Up to 4000 streams per server)

Starting with Streaming Server 3, a broadcaster can send its stream to a server using TCP/IP, instead of the usual RTP. This is better, as it prevents packet loss, so the server always has the whole stream to work with. RTP is more efficient, which matters a lot when you're sending thousands of streams, but less so when you're sending one or two.

Tip   The only time you should broadcast to the server using RTP instead of TCP/IP is if your stream won't quite fit over your connection because of the extra overhead. If you're pushing a 50 Kbit stream down a 56 Kbit connection, for example, you might have to fall back to RTP instead.

Broadcasting on a Campus or Corporate LAN

Even though we've been tossing around the word "broadcast," everything we've looked at so far is, technically, unicast. That is, each stream is a one-to-one transmission. Either the broadcaster sends a copy of the stream to each client, or the broadcaster sends a copy of the stream to a server, and the server sends one copy to each client.

That's not very efficient. Instead of being like radio or TV, it's more like a postal system, where you send an addressed copy of the message to each recipient. On a LAN, it's especially wasteful, since you all live on the same block and share the same postman—sending a private message to each of you just clogs the street and makes the postman grumpy.

On the Internet, you currently have no choice. There's no "magic IP address" on the Internet that translates to "everybody." You have to send a stream to each member of the audience.

But on a LAN there are a few magic IP addresses, if your router supports them (most do). These are called multicast addresses. When you send a stream to a multicast IP address, it's more like sending a postcard—anyone can read it, not just the person it's addressed to.

This is a tremendous bandwidth saver. You can have a thousand people watching your presentation over a LAN, and only send one copy of the stream (or one copy for each LAN segment where people are watching the presentation). That's much better than sending a thousand streams!

Implementing this is usually simple:

1. Tell your broadcaster to set up for a multicast instead of a broadcast or unicast.

2. Ask your broadcaster to generate an .sdp file or a QuickTime reference movie.

3. Put the .sdp file or movie in a shared folder, or on an internal Web page, or send copies as email attachments (usually less than 1 Kbyte).

4. Start your broadcast. Anyone who has QuickTime Player can use it to open the .sdp file or movie and press Play.

Your broadcaster sends one stream of audio and/or one of video to the multicast IP address. Everyone on your LAN segment or small LAN can play them. If someone from another LAN segment plays the movie, your router sends a copy to them. If more people from that LAN segment tune in, they all see the same copy.

Frankly, large-scale streaming over the Internet tends to be impractical today, because large amounts of bandwidth are expensive, advertising revenue for streams is low, and people are reluctant to pay for Internet content. All these factors are subject to sudden change without warning, but that's how it is today.

LANs, on the other hand, are a perfect medium for streaming to moderately large audiences. Bandwidth is essentially free (or rather, already paid for), the pipe is large enough for high-quality video and sound, there's little or no packet loss, and everyone on a LAN segment can share a single stream.

If your broadcaster software is any good, you shouldn't need to know the actual IP multicast addresses, but in case you do, here they are:

```
Class D (multicast) addresses
Range from 224.0.0.0 through 239.255.255.255

Well known addresses designated by IANA:
Reserved use: 224.0.0.0 through 224.0.0.255
224.0.0.1—all multicast systems on subnet
224.0.0.2—all routers on subnet

Transient addresses, assigned and reclaimed dynamically
Global scope: 224.0.1.0 - 238.255.255.255
Limited scope: 239.0.0.0 - 239.255.255.255
Site-local scope: 239.253.0.0 - 239.253.0.16
Organization-local scope: 239.192.0.0 - 239.192.0.14
```

Generally speaking, you should use transient addresses with global scope, with your audio on port 5432 and your video on port 5434.

You should be able to just select "multicast," however, and watch as your broadcaster has a chat with the local router, finds an available multicast IP address, and claims it.

Setting Up a Broadcaster

Enough generalities. Let's actually set up a broadcaster and send some live data (or at least go over the actual steps).

We'll use QuickTime Broadcaster as an example because it's a free download (Mac OS X only), but the steps are similar for any broadcaster. Windows users should probably follow along using the demo version of Abstract Plane's Uplink. There's a copy in the Demos folder of the CD. Mac users, hit the Web and get the current version of QuickTime Broadcaster: `www.apple.com/products/broadcaster/`.

We'll do this in stages. First we'll set up the broadcaster to do an audio broadcast to itself, then to another computer over a network, then to do a local multicast. Then we'll set it up to broadcast to a streaming server and onto the Internet.

Using the Broadcaster Alone (No Streaming Server)

One step at a time. Let's get something that we can stream.

Audio and Video Sources

Once you have broadcaster software installed, you need to lay your hands on an audio or video source that's compatible with your computer and broadcaster.

The number and type of supported input devices varies considerably depending on your choice of broadcaster software. Check the software publisher's website for a current list. QuickTime Broadcaster accepts video from DV cameras or media converters (such as Formac or Holly-wood converters) over FireWire, and some video capture cards. Audio can come in over FireWire, USB, or built-in audio input (if available on your model).

A mini-DV camera is usually the best way to go for both audio and video if your computer has FireWire. Otherwise, just connect the line-level or headphone output of a CD player, MP3 player, or radio to the audio input of your computer or sound card, so you have some kind of source.

Don't use an MP3 player except as a test signal. Decompressing MP3, then recompressing it for a live broadcast, will pretty much wreck the sound. If you want to stream MP3, you can use playlists (a server feature, not a broadcaster feature). See "Playlists" (page 442).

Note An audio CD in the internal drive is no longer supported as a sound source for Mac OS X. You can play a CD on an external drive and capture the audio output, though.

Launch your broadcaster and open the audio configuration panel. For QuickTime Broadcaster, click the Audio tab (click the Show Details button if there's no Audio tab showing).

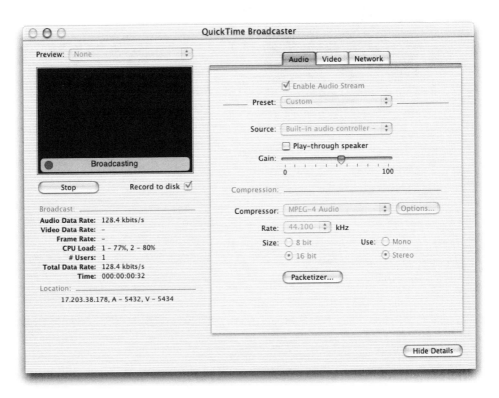

Important If your audio source is FireWire or USB, make sure the source is plugged in and turned on before trying to configure your broadcaster's audio settings.

Enable audio streaming and set the audio source to your audio input. If your audio input is not available as a choice, open your operating system's Sound control panel and select it. If your system's Sound panel can't find your audio, you have a problem I can't solve from here.

Choose a compressor. For most live audio, the MPEG-4 compressor is the best choice. Use the Options button to select high quality and set the data rate. Choose 100 Kbits/sec or higher for high fidelity.

Now go to your network settings. On QuickTime Broadcaster, click the Network tab.

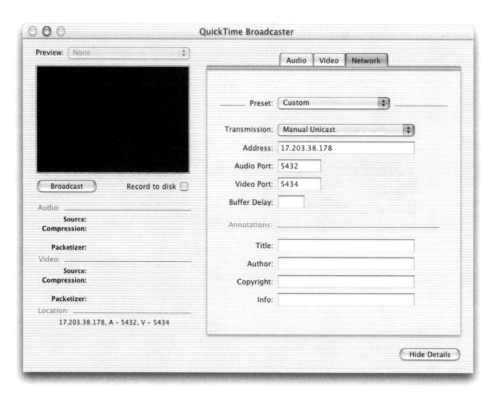

Quick Loop Test

We'll start with a simple unicast to test things (Manual Unicast in Quick-Time Broadcaster). Enter your own IP address as the destination. Accept your broadcaster's default port addresses.

Tip   If you're not connected to a network, enter the magic IP address for "me" (127.0.0.1).

Okay, you've configured your audio and network settings. You should be able to go live. Create an announcement file for your broadcast (sometimes called a reference movie or an SDP file). In QuickTime Broadcaster, choose Export from the File menu—movie or SDP file, either will do fine.

Your system can probably create an archive of your broadcast, if you ask it nicely. In QuickTime Broadcaster it's a checkbox marked "Record to disk," and by default it stores your broadcast as mymovie.mov in your Movies folder. Turn this feature on to help with debugging.

Okay, all systems are go. Push the Broadcast button (or equivalent).

Hmmm. Not too dramatic, is it? Okay, go find that announcement file and open it using QuickTime Player. Open the Properties window, choose the streaming track, and choose Bit Rate. Are you getting data? Does the player connect and open a movie? Can you hear your stream? Hooray.

No? If you get a bit rate but no sound, choose Volume in the Properties window. It should look something like the following illustration.

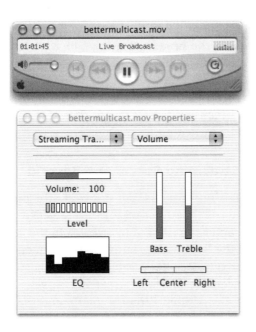

If there's nothing showing in the level gauges, turn up the audio volume of your input source, or in your sound input panel, or your broadcaster. In QuickTime Broadcaster's Audio panel, there's a Gain slider for this. If the levels look good but there's still no sound, unmute your speakers, or turn them up.

Point to Point Test

When that works, try the same trick with two computers. Quit QuickTime Player, stop the broadcast, go to the network settings, and type in the IP address of another computer. Generate a new announcement file and email it to the other computer or put it in a shared folder.

Hit the Broadcast button. Go to the second computer and open the announcement file in QuickTime Player. It should open as an audio movie whether it's a .mov file or an .sdp file.

Multicast Test

If you're on a LAN, the third thing to try is multicast. In QuickTime Broadcaster, just choose Multicast transmission in the Network panel and click the Generate IP Address button. If you get an IP address, you should be good to go. Generate a new announcement file, press the Broadcast button, and email the announcement file to various people on your LAN. They should all be able to hear the broadcast using QuickTime, but your LAN administrator should see the same network load as when you sent a single stream to a second computer.

That's all there is to it. If your LAN doesn't support multicast, it may be that it's been disabled because it wasn't in use. Talk to your LAN administrator and see if it can be turned back on. Odds are, it can.

Broadcasting to a Streaming Server and Beyond

The broadcaster creates live streams, but it's your streaming server that actually sends them out over the Internet to your audience.

To get a streaming server to reflect your streams to the world, you need to put a description of the live streams in the server's media folder. You do this by telling the broadcaster to create an announcement file, then uploading the announcement file to a streaming server. The announcement file uses Session Description Protocol (SDP), and the filename ends with the .sdp extension.

The server responds to requests for the announcement file by sending a copy of the live streams that you send to the server.

But how do you get the .sdp file to the streaming server?

In QuickTime Broadcaster, the whole process is automatic—just set the Transmission type to Automatic Unicast (Announce). Put the URL or IP address of the server in the Host Name field, give your SDP file a name (leave off the .sdp extension), and provide a valid user name and password for broadcasting from that server. In most cases, check the box for broadcast over TCP. For details, see "Broadcasting to a Streaming Server" (page 447). Hit the Broadcast button and you're live, from Bangor to Bangkok.

Other broadcasters may require more manual intervention. Here are the steps:

1. Set up a live broadcast using your broadcaster.

2. Create an SDP file. The details vary depending on your software.

   In Live Channel, for example, use the Announce menu to create the SDP file (if you are streaming directly from the broadcaster to the Internet, Live Channel will create a Fast Start reference movie instead, so you can skip steps 3-6).

3. Upload the SDP file to the streaming server's Movies folder. By default, the path is `./Local/Library/QuickTimeStreaming/Movies/`.

4. Start the broadcast.

At this point, your broadcast should be available from the streaming server. To deliver it over the Internet, embed the URL of your SDP file—without the `.sdp` file extension—in a Web page. You can do that by using QTSRC to point to the URL, or by creating a Fast Start reference movie.

If your `.sdp` file is `MyStream.sdp`, the HTML using QTSRC looks like this:

```
<embed src=UNeedQT.mov
  width=xx height=yy+16
  qtsrc=rtsp://streaming.server.com/MyStream />
```

Note The path to the default Movies directory is implied, and the `.sdp` file extension is omitted.

Alternatively, you can create a one-line text file that starts with `RTSPtext`, followed immediately by the SDP file's URL. Save the file as plain text, but with the `.mov` file extension. For example, if the SDP file is named `Stream1.sdp`, and it is in the default `Movies` directory of `www.YourServer.com`, the text file is

```
RTSPtextRTSP://www.YourServer.com/Stream1
```

Embed the text file just as if it were a QuickTime movie.

To make live streams play in QuickTime Player from your Web page, use a poster movie.

If there are multiple versions of the transmission available at different data rates, create an SDP file for each version and upload it to the streaming server. Then create a multiple data rate movie using MakeRefMovie and the URLs of the `.sdp` files (minus the `.sdp` extension), as described in "Alternate Movies" (page 151), and embed the multiple data rate movie in your Web page.

Making a Copy of Your Transmission

You can tell most broadcasters to save a copy of the streaming transmission as a hinted movie. After the event, you can upload the movie to a streaming server for people who missed the live version.

The saved copy is a hinted QuickTime movie or a hinted MP4, compressed using the settings you chose for the broadcast. It's essentially a copy of the live transmission.

Note A bug in early versions of Broadcaster sometimes truncated saved files of long broadcasts. Upgrade to version 1.01 or later to prevent this.

You can get higher-quality audio and video after the fact by capturing a less-compressed movie (using hardware Motion-JPEG or DV compression, for example), and compressing it for your target data rate offline. Live streaming has to compress the data in real time, whereas optimized encoding may take several times longer to compress than it takes to play.

If you want to deliver higher-quality versions of your transmission later, rather than repeating the live version, split your input feeds and send one copy to a DV camera or a computer that just captures at the highest possible quality, and another copy to the broadcaster for real-time encoding and transmission. Compress the high-quality version later and deliver it as a hinted movie or a Fast Start movie. If you're using Live Channel, you can deliver a high-resolution composite of your actual output to a video recorder or other device, and compress from that later.

Transmitting at Multiple Data Rates

It's basically all a computer can do to encode audio and video at a given data rate in real time. If you want to transmit live streams of the same material at different data rates, you need to use multiple computers, each running a broadcaster and compressing the input at one of the desired rates. You can use a mixer or splitter to send the same analog input to multiple broadcasters. They can all broadcast their streams to the same IP address. Create a reference movie to autoselect the correct data rate for each audience member.

This limitation applies only to broadcasting live streams. Sending prerecorded QuickTime movies at multiple data rates simultaneously from a single computer is no problem.

Some content distribution services offer real-time encoding using hardware solutions, in which case you can send a single high-resolution stream to the service, and they can encode and deliver it at multiple data rates simultaneously.

Choosing a Broadcaster

There are a small number of broadcaster applications available for both the Mac OS and Windows, ranging from simple general-purpose tools to full-blown systems for radio or television. Most broadcast software runs on Mac OS X. If you're standardized on Windows or UNIX, and worried about supporting Macs, rest easy. A broadcaster can be a completely separate entity, such as a laptop. All it needs is a dialup or Ethernet connection to the IP network. No special network software required. No need to reconfigure anything. You can assign the Mac an IP address or let it get one using DHCP.

Here's a current list of QuickTime broadcasters.

QuickTime Broadcaster for Mac OS X

This is a free download from Apple (Mac OS X required). It can send audio and/or video as either QuickTime streams or ISO-compliant MPEG-4 streams. It supports a variety of audio and video compressors when sending QuickTime streams—not the full set of QuickTime codecs, but those that can do real-time compression and streaming (including third-party codecs such as ACT-L2).

Download from

`www.apple.com/quicktime/download/broadcaster`

or

`www.apple.com/products/broadcaster/`

It downloads as a disk image (`.dmg`) file. Double-click it to mount the virtual disk, which contains the broadcaster package (`.pkg`) file. Double-click that and follow the prompts to install QuickTime Broadcaster, then eject the virtual disk (Command-E) and trash the `.dmg` file.

QuickTime Broadcaster works with most DV cameras, and this is the easiest way to input video and sound. USB audio is also accepted, but most USB audio interfaces are relatively low fidelity—there are exceptions, though; see "USB Audio" (page 228). If a DV camera is out of the question, consider an inexpensive FireWire Web camera (under $200) or a media converter ($250–300).

The broadcaster can be controlled using AppleScript to automate production. The program is easy to set up and use. Possibly the most attractive feature, besides the price, is its ability to send genuine MPEG-4 streams. This means your audience can include not only anyone with QuickTime, but anyone with an ISO-compatible streaming player.

Uplink for Windows and Mac OS X

Abstract Plane's Uplink (www.abstractplane.com.au) runs on Windows 98/2000/NT/ME or Mac OS X, and streams audio and video in several compression formats. It has a clean, easy-to-use interface, is compatible with most DV, USB, and PCI audio and video sources, streams most audio and video media formats supported by QuickTime, is designed to be part of a larger broadcast environment, supports remote control and monitoring, and is designed to interoperate with many standard "back end" streaming server solutions. It currently sells for about $650 Australian dollars (say, $425 US, at today's exchange rates, but that will vary).

Sorenson Broadcaster for Windows and Mac OS

Sorenson Broadcaster was the original broadcast application for QuickTime. It has mysteriously disappeared from the Sorenson website recently, with no comment or forwarding address. Is it dead, just sleeping, or undergoing metamorphosis into something new and wonderful?

We live in interesting times . . .

Live Channel for Mac OS X

Channel Storm's Live Channel (www.channelstorm.com) is far more than a broadcaster—it's a complete television studio in software. It accepts any number of simultaneous audio and video inputs, and allows you to switch between them using real-time effects.

Queue up your next source in a live preview window. Composite video with titles and overlay graphics in real time, including layered video and picture-in-picture. Cut between live and prerecorded material using effects and transitions. Did I mention the audio mixer? Live and prerecorded sound, live mixing and fading, with independent volume, bass, treble, midrange, and reverb for each source.

Live Channel takes full advantage of QuickTime, letting you stream a mix of live and recorded audio and video, graphics, still images, and text. It even includes a live text feed!

Version 2.0 delivers not only live streams, but real-time video output, ready for broadcast or video recording, with no special added equipment. You can stream live to Internet viewers, and simultaneously broadcast to video projectors or monitors, local TV networks, and videotape.

Oh yeah, it also acts as a streaming server. Simultaneously. It supports unicast and multicast, and can stream to a hundred simultaneous clients while broadcasting. It's frankly amazing, and it keeps getting better.

The full-blown version is currently $999—which is practically free, considering what you get. This is really a $250,000 portable live television studio. They also offer educational discounts. There's even a fully functional version you can download over the Web that is, in fact, actually free.

Did I mention that there's a copy of it in the Demos folder of the CD? Fire it up! (Hey, go out and get a Mac if you have to—it's worth it, just for this.) I'd tell you how much fun it is to use, but I don't want to distract you from how powerful it is.

BackBone Internet Radio for Mac OS X or Mac OS 9

This audio-only broadcaster is a lot more than an audio digitizer with streaming output. It's a full radio station software suite. It includes production, live and automated programming, on-the-fly playlist management, storage, streaming, and—get this—full DMCA logging and reporting, compliant with the Small Webcaster Settlement Act (SWSA). Yup. It's legal.

The basic version combines broadcasting and streaming on a single Mac and can send up to 250 unicast streams, plus unlimited listeners via multicast on a campus LAN. The Pro and Pro Plus versions add Linux servers running Darwin Streaming Server, for an additional 800 streams per Linux box. Sweet. It also streams MP3 and MPEG-4 audio.

These people understand radio.

Check out the demo version. Free, of course: www.backbone.com.

MegaSeg for Mac OS X

Attention, DJs. Live mixing of QuickTime and/or MP3. Set up in and out points and segue without dead air. Music mixing (cross-fade and beat matching) and more: song rotation, timed playlist events, and instant playback of drop-in clips and sound effects. Prioritization of playback by song or genre, music management (same artist or same song are never played too close together). All for $169. Runs on an iBook (is that an Internet radio station in your tote bag?). Free demo version: www.megaseg.com.

▶ Firewalls, NAT, and Streaming on Port 80

I'm happy to report that the early problems people had with streaming content have almost disappeared. Most Network Address Translation software works with streams now. Most firewalls permit streaming audio and video, and QuickTime can detect most firewalls that don't and ask for the streams over an open port.

Streaming on Port 80

If you are setting up a streaming server and you think some of your clients are behind Internet firewalls that allow only Web traffic, enable streaming on port 80 of your streaming server. This lets the server accept connections on port 80, the default port for Web traffic.

QuickTime clients will be able to connect to your streaming server even if they are behind a Web-only firewall.

Important   If you enable streaming on port 80, make sure you disable any Web server on the same computer, or bind the Web server and streaming server to different IP addresses.

Firewalls and NAT

The streaming server normally sends data using User Datagram Protocol (UDP). Firewalls designed to protect information on a network often block UDP packets. Client computers located behind a firewall that blocks UDP packets can't receive streamed media, even though they can often connect to the server. The stream sets up, but no data comes through.

Note   This is because the setup takes place using RTSP protocol, which uses the same TCP/IP transport scheme as HTTP. But the movie data is sent using RTP protocol, which uses lower-level UDP transport over different port addresses, which the firewall blocks.

Fortunately, the QuickTime streaming server can also stream over HTTP connections, which allows streamed media to get through even very tightly configured firewalls. QuickTime 5 and later should automatically detect this condition and request the streams over HTTP. This works only if you have enabled your server to stream over port 80.

Some client computers sharing an Internet connection that uses Network Address Translation (NAT) may also be unable to receive UDP packets. Again the answer is to stream over HTTP on port 80, and it should happen automatically.

If users have problems viewing media through a firewall or via a network that uses address translation, they should upgrade their NAT software or ask the network administrator to allow their firewall to permit RTP and RTSP throughput.

Opening Ports

The simplest solution is to open necessary ports for RTP and RTSP traffic. This should cause no increased security risk. You need to open ports 554 and 555 for outbound traffic and allow incoming traffic on ports 6970 and 6999 in response to outgoing traffic on these "trigger" ports. For a typical Linksys DSL router, set the Application Name to QuickTime, the Trigger Port Range to 554 and 555, and the Incoming Port Range to 6970 and 6999. If it's a company firewall we're talking about, your network administrator may or may not go along with this, however—network administrators are paid to be paranoid (and with pretty good reason). It's worth a try; if it doesn't work, use HTTP.

Proxy Servers

Firewalls can be equipped with proxy servers for RTP and RTSP. Apple maintains a website with proxy server information at

`www.apple.com/quicktime/resources/qt4/us/proxy/`

The QuickTime Settings control panel has a Proxy Servers menu item that allows viewers to tell QuickTime what proxy server they're using. Viewers need to talk to their network administrator to find out what settings they should specify. See "Streaming Proxy (Mac OS 8 and Mac OS 9 Only)" (page 710).

NAT Software Updates

NAT software works fine with RTP and RTSP if it's written with real-time streams in mind. People can often obtain an update to their NAT software from the manufacturer over the Web, and that typically solves the problem.

NAT software that currently works with QuickTime streams includes the software from Vicom, IpNetRouter, Flowport, and the Apple Airport base station. The NAT software built into Linksys routers is also compatible with QuickTime streams, though you may need to open the ports using a Web browser—see "Opening Ports" (page 461).

Customer Service

If a customer calls with a problem receiving streaming media on the company LAN, or from a shared Internet connection, have them open the

QuickTime Settings control panel, choose the Connection tab, and click Transport Setup...

This brings up the Transport Setup Screen. Have the customer click the Auto Configure button first; that usually solves the problem.

If the viewer's network allows RTSP only on a specific port, and they know what the port number is, tell them to enter it here.

If all else fails, have them click the Use HTTP button (have them use port 80 unless they know otherwise). This allows real-time streams to get through almost any firewall or NAT software.

All should now be sunshine and bunny rabbits.

An Animated Approach

Animation lets you use still images—drawings, photographs, CGI—to create motion video. Using art as the source of your images frees you from real-world constraints; your talent and imagination are the only limits. Using a computer to generate images can remove a lot of the tedious work involved in traditional animation, and QuickTime can help you reduce the bandwidth needed to deliver animation over the Web.

QuickTime supports three kinds of animation: traditional cel-based animation, vector images, and sprite animation. As you've come to expect with QuickTime, you can mix and match, using vector graphics in a cel animation or as sprites, or superimposing sprites over a background of cel animation.

And of course, you can mix animated video tracks with other Quick-Time tracks—music, narration, text, live streams from Uzbekistan, the works. You can even use recorded video or live streams *as* animated sprites. Sprites are a particularly wonderful media type because you can "wire" them to trigger actions, interactively or automatically.

This chapter covers

- traditional cel-based animation, including animated GIFs
- vector graphics, including the Flash media type
- basic sprite animation, including Flash tracks

Wired sprites (and wired Flash) are described further in Chapter 16, "Getting Interactive."

▶ Cel-Based Animation

Cel-based animation happens when you create a series of still images and display them in rapid succession, using a flip-book, a film projector, video-tape, or a computer screen. In the early days of animation, the images were painted on celluloid film and individual images were called cels. And, well, a lot has changed, but they're still called cels. Go figure.

There are basically three ways to create cel-based QuickTime animations:

- You can create a series of images in a graphics program and import them as an image sequence.
- You can use animation software to create a FLIC or animated GIF file and import the animation into QuickTime.
- You can use animation software that creates QuickTime movies directly.

Importing Image Sequences

You can use virtually any graphics or drawing program to create a series of still images, then import the image sequence into QuickTime as a movie. The process is very similar to importing an image sequence to create a slideshow.

QuickTime can open still images in most formats: Windows bitmap (.bmp), FlashPix, GIF, JPEG, MacPaint, Photoshop, TIFF, PICS, PICT, and PNG. You can create images with any graphics program that can export to one of these formats. You can use a program such as GraphicConverter or DeBabelizer to convert more esoteric image files into a format that Quick-Time can work with.

Start by creating a series of images (all the same height and width) using your favorite graphics program, then import the images into QuickTime using QuickTime Player. The import process is pretty straightforward:

1. Give the images a common root name followed by a sequence number, such as Image1.png, Image2.png, Image3.png, or Anim01.gif, Anim02.gif, Anim03.gif.

Important   The sequence number must be the *only* number in the filename. Don't use filenames like July1st01.tif. The extra number in the filename confuses the sequence importer.

2. Create a folder and drag in all the images you want to use.

3. Choose Open Image Sequence from the File menu in QuickTime Player.

4. Select the first image in the sequence using the Open File dialog box.

5. A Frame Rate dialog box appears. Use the pop-up menu to choose a frame rate for the movie.

A cel-based animation is basically a slideshow with a rapid frame rate. Smooth animation generally requires a frame rate of 8 to 15 fps. Higher frame rates can give smoother motion, but they drive the data rate up, and of course you have to draw more pictures.

Tip Traditional animators do something called a pencil test: they draw one or two images per second of animation in a sketch book and flip the pages to see how it looks. To do a pencil test in QuickTime, sketch the key images in your graphics program and import them into QuickTime with a frame rate of 1 to 2 fps. Voilà—electric pencil test.

Animation created by importing an image sequence has no temporal compression—every frame is a key frame—so it uses a lot of bandwidth. Unlike a slideshow, you don't get the bandwidth back by leaving each image up for several seconds; animation has to keep moving. Consequently, animation created by importing an image sequence is better suited to CD-ROM or hard disk delivery than it is to the Internet.

Of course, you can reduce bandwidth by using smaller image sizes, fewer colors, or fewer frames per second, with corresponding loss of quality.

You can also compress an animation by exporting the video (Export command—Movie to QuickTime Movie) and applying a video compressor. Unfortunately, most video compressors don't do well with animation, partly because they tend to blur sharp outlines. The compressors that do work well with animation—Video, Animation, and Graphics—generally produce large files that still need a lot of bandwidth.

You should definitely try some of the standard video compressors, such as Sorenson 3 and MPEG-4, or some of the new compressors, such as ZyGoVideo or Streambox ACT-L2. One of them may work quite well with your material.

Your most reliable tack for getting a low-bandwidth cel animation with decent quality, starting with an image sequence, is to do this:

1. Start with images of 256 or fewer colors, all with the same background color, in GIF or PNG format.

2. Make sure the background is a solid color, not a dithered pattern.

3. Import the images into QuickTime and export the video using the Graphics compressor.

The background should compress temporally, and the remainder of each frame will use one byte per pixel at most. Obviously, minimizing the image size and frame rate are also important.

In traditional animation, only the foreground figures are painted on celluloid. The celluloid is transparent, so the foreground can be filmed in front of a background using a rotoscope. The QuickTime equivalent is to use a transparent graphics mode and composite the foreground images over a background image or video track. By a transparent graphics mode, I mean either the graphics mode named "transparent" or one of the four alpha modes.

Using an alpha channel for transparency requires 32-bit color images. For animation, it's more efficient to use 8-bit color with a solid background, then designate the background color as transparent using the transparent graphics mode. For details, see "Transparency and Alpha Channels" (page 271).

The transparent graphics mode can allow you to use a far more complex or photo-realistic background without paying a high price in bandwidth. The background can be a track with a much lower frame rate than the foreground. It can even be a still image. QuickTime composites the foreground and background together on the viewer's computer when the movie is played, so you send the background image over the Web only when it changes. For details, see "Adding a Still Image as a Movie Background" (page 267).

Importing FLICs

A common output format for 2D animation programs is a FLIC, FLC, or CEL file. They're essentially the same thing. The format was originated by Autodesk Animator (which became Animator Pro, then Animator Studio). Some 3D modeling programs also have the ability to output a visual rendering to a FLIC file. QuickTime can import these files directly.

The FLIC format uses some temporal compression, but FLIC files still tend to be large and require a lot of bandwidth; they're better suited to delivery from disk than over a dialup modem.

As with imported image sequences, the best way to reduce bandwidth is by reducing the image size and frame rate, using an 8-bit or even a 4-bit palette, using a solid-color background, and exporting the video using the Graphics compressor.

Importing Animated GIFs

The animated GIF is a ubiquitous art form on the Web. Consequently, a lot of work has been done to create tools that make animated GIFs more bandwidth-efficient. You can take advantage of this by creating animated GIFs using specialized software, then importing the finished product into QuickTime.

Creating animated GIFs is usually a two-step process:

1. Create a series of images using a graphics program such as Adobe Illustrator, FreeHand, Adobe Photoshop, or CorelDRAW, or from a 2D or 3D animation program such as Animator Studio or Infini-D.

2. Turn the images into an optimized animated GIF using a program such as Adobe ImageReady, GIF Wizard, GIFBuilder, GIFmation, GIF-Cruncher, or GIF Animator.

Alternatively, you can use an integrated program such as Fireworks, WebPainter, or e-Picture that has the ability both to create a series of images and also to export them as animated GIFs.

An animated GIF can be optimized to reduce its data rate in several ways. If less than 128 colors are used, the palette can be reduced to less than 8 bits. A 16-color animation can use a 4-bit color palette, which reduces the file size by 50%.

GIFs use LZW compression, which can compress patterns in rows of pixels. Some programs can do LZW optimization on images, adding a few pixels to some rows so they complete a repeating pattern, which can further reduce file size by 2% to 5%, depending on the material.

Some programs can modify images to make them more compressible by rearranging existing pixels into repeating patterns. This is called LZW preprocessing, and it alters the image, but it can reduce file size by an additional 5% to 40% depending on the material (and on how much alteration you're willing to tolerate).

The animated GIF format can also use temporal compression, so each frame stores only the data that's changed from the previous frame. For an animation with a foreground character moving over an unchanging background, this can reduce file size by 75% or more.

Tip There are different algorithms for determining what's changed in a frame; software that uses a frame-differencing method typically provides better bandwidth reduction than software that uses a minimum-bounding-rectangle method.

For Mac users, the standard optimization tool is a freeware program called GIFBuilder. It uses a minimum-bounding-rectangle algorithm with no bells or whistles. There are more powerful programs available, but you can't beat the price.

Here are four particularly good optimization tools available for both Windows and Mac OS:

- GIFmation is easy to use and includes LZW optimization.
- ImageReady (bundled with Photoshop 5.5) combines excellent frame differencing with a quality slider for LZW preprocessing. It can produce genuinely tiny image files (but preprocessing does cause distortion).
- WebPainter combines frame differencing and LZW optimization with drawing tools, as well as image manipulation tools similar to Photoshop's. Bundled with LiveStage Pro, it can produce QuickTime vector graphics as well as bitmapped images. It produces very small animated GIFs without LZW preprocessing.
- Fireworks offers image creation, easy LZW optimization, frame differencing, and unique always-editable graphics that combine vector paths and bitmapped images (the final output is bitmapped).
- BeatWare's e-Picture Pro 2 has a very similar feature set to Fireworks, plus the ability to export directly to QuickTime video, Flash, Real, and Windows Media. It's available for both Mac OS and Windows. Version 2 is recommended over version 3, which is available only for Windows and does not create QuickTime or Real output.

For Windows users, another option is Ulead's SmartSaver, which comes in a freeware and a paid version. Both versions include frame differencing. Neither does LZW optimization. The paid version lets you remove comments, which produces slightly smaller files.

Important   All these programs let you set the duration of each frame, usually in hundredths of a second, with the option to set a duration of zero (as fast as possible). Some browsers play zero-duration frames at 18 fps. QuickTime plays them at 100 fps, skipping frames if necessary (you *said* as fast as possible). If you want 18 to 20 fps, set the duration to 5 or 6 hundredths of a second, and it should work the same everywhere. In any case, *never* use 0—you might be taken literally.

When you import an animated GIF into QuickTime, it creates a video track that retains the compression and timing of the original file. This generally produces the best low-bandwidth cel animation available.

Of course, if you just want to display an animated GIF in a Web page, you don't need QuickTime. But if you want to add sound, MIDI, text, or other goodies, you should import the animated GIF into QuickTime and take advantage of the facilities.

And if you need to add an animated video track to a QuickTime movie, you can get good low-bandwidth results by creating an animated GIF and importing it.

Tip   For the artistically challenged, and for people who love free stuff, there are several websites with vast collections of animated GIFs. Many may be freely copied and distributed, so help yourself. You may need to edit them to replace zero-length frame durations, and you can often improve optimization as well, but neither requires much effort.

The Direct Approach

Many applications programs offer the ability to output graphics directly as QuickTime movies. This includes Web graphics programs such as e-Picture Pro 2 and WebPainter, animation studio software such as Toon Boom Studio, character-animation programs such as HASH Animation Master, 3D modeling programs such as Infini-D, Pulse, and Axel, screen-capture utilities such as CameraMan and Snapz Pro, as well as scientific and educational software such as Starry Night.

Most of these programs use QuickTime's API for exporting movies, so you have access to the same compression settings and dialog boxes as in QuickTime Player.

The output files tend to be large and bandwidth-intensive, but good-looking and easy to produce. They're well suited for use as instructional aids on a CD or a LAN, of for some broadband Internet applications.

Tip   Many 3D modeling programs can render a fly-by as a QuickTime animated movie. Often, a better alternative is to either use a program that can generate interactive 3D QuickTime media, such as Pulse 3D or Axel, or to render a series of images and use them to create a QuickTime VR object movie (for 3D models) or a QuickTime VR panorama (for 3D landscapes). For details, see Chapter 9, "Let's Get Virtual" (page 613).

There is an example Web page in the Animation folder of the CD named Eclipse.htm. It uses movies created with Starry Night—an astronomy program—that show an eclipse of the sun as viewed from the Earth, the moon, and the sun. The movies would have taken a lot of time and talent to create using a graphics program; generating them as QuickTime output from an application program was dead easy.

A program worth noting in this regard is WebPainter, a graphics and animation program for Windows and Macintosh from Totally Hip. This program can directly open most QuickTime movies, creating separate graphic layers from each QuickTime track, and separate cels from each frame. It also uses QTIF as its internal file format, allowing WebPainter files to be opened as movies directly by QuickTime Player.

Another notable program is Adobe LiveMotion. It exports bitmap graphics directly into QuickTime as video but also exports vectors and sprites as .swf files that QuickTime can open.

Vector Graphics

Vector graphics are fundamentally different from bitmapped images. Bitmapped images describe arrays of pixels, while vector graphics describe shapes such as lines, circles, polygons, area fills, and patterns.

Vector graphics are particularly well suited to line art and illustrations, while bitmaps tend to be better for complex textures. Vector graphics are stored in a format that is compact, lossless, and scalable—vectors scale very cleanly compared to bitmaps. When you scale up a bitmapped image, it becomes jagged and pixelated because the source image contains fewer pixels than the magnified image, and the computer has to guess what the new pixels should look like. When you scale up a vector graphic, on the other hand, the computer redraws it quite smoothly because it can use the equation for a circle or a line to generate any number of pixels, right where they belong.

Vector graphics deliver high-quality content using very little bandwidth by leveraging the power of the viewer's computer. Just as MIDI music tracks contain instructions for creating music, and text tracks contain instructions for rendering text, vector graphics contain instructions for drawing graphic images.

For low-bandwidth animations delivered over the Web, vector graphics are generally superior to bitmaps.

Graphics programs that create vector graphics are usually referred to as drawing programs or illustration programs, whereas programs that create bitmapped images are generally called painting programs. Graphics programs that can create both bitmaps and vectors usually have a drawing mode and a painting mode.

Image manipulation programs such as Photoshop typically work with bitmaps; they must rasterize vector images before they can work with them.

QuickTime includes a media type called QuickTime Vectors, but it isn't widely used by other applications, with a few notable exceptions: Web-Painter, Lightning Draw, and Electrifier Pro can export images as Quick-Time vectors. You can open the images in QuickTime Player as still images or as image sequences. Either method creates a QuickTime video track that uses the curve codec (QuickTime vectors).

The most popular software for creating QuickTime vector graphics is WebPainter, which is available for Windows and Mac OS (classic).

Most of the graphics programs that create output directly as Quick-Time vectors run on the Macintosh platform. Of course, QuickTime movies containing these vector images can be edited or played equally well on Windows.

Fortunately, QuickTime can play other vector formats as well. The most widespread vector type on the Web is Flash media, usually found in .swf files. QuickTime can read and play Flash, and can import .swf files created by Flash, LiveMotion, and others, as QuickTime tracks, allowing you to combine and composite Flash with every other QuickTime media type. Still other vector formats, such as Pulse 3D and Axel, which combine vectors, 3D modeling, and interactivity, also play in QuickTime, using media handlers provided by the companies that created these formats.

Many drawing programs, such as Illustrator and Freehand, use vector graphics internally, but can't export to QuickTime vectors; you need to export your work into one of the many formats that QuickTime understands, such as Photoshop, JPEG, TIFF, or .swf, to use it in QuickTime movies.

Exporting to most of these formats converts vectors into bitmapped images, which is usually not what you want. To keep images in vector format, export to Flash or .swf, unless your application supports QuickTime vectors or has its own QuickTime media handler.

If your graphics program doesn't export to QuickTime or Flash, or lacks a QuickTime media handler, there may be a utility program that converts your program's output to a vector format QuickTime can use—you can use Flash itself to convert Illustrator or AutoCAD files to Flash, for example, or use Electrifier Pro to convert Illustrator files to QuickTime vector format.

Flash Vectors

Flash is the name of a graphics animation program from Macromedia, available on both Macintosh and Windows computers. Flash is also a file format, also known as ShockWave Flash (.swf). Flash format can include both vector graphics and bitmaps.

The `.swf` file format is used as an interexchange medium by other software, such as LiveMotion, AfterEffects, and swf3D. A `.swf` file created by one of these programs can also be imported into QuickTime.

Images created in Flash itself are always vectors. Vector images created in other programs, such as Adobe Illustrator and FreeHand, can be converted into Flash format. Bitmapped images can also be imported into Flash, but they remain in bitmap format. Alternatively, you can convert bitmapped images into Flash vectors by using Flash's Trace command.

When a Flash file is imported into QuickTime, a Flash track is created. Media in a Flash track retains its native format—Flash vector images are not converted into QuickTime vectors. For most practical purposes, the characteristics of Flash vectors are the same as QuickTime vectors: they are compact, scalable, and lossless. And they work fine in QuickTime. Bitmapped graphics in a Flash file remain bitmapped when imported into QuickTime.

The Flash graphics program can import vector graphics from Illustrator, FreeHand, and AutoCAD (release 10, 2D ASCII DXF format). This converts them to Flash vector format, allowing them to be used in QuickTime movies.

Flash can save files in several formats, including `.fla`, `.exe`, and `.swf`.

Flash files saved in Shockwave Flash format (`.swf`) can be opened and played by QuickTime Player or the QuickTime plug-in. If you open a `.swf` file in QuickTime Player and save it as a self-contained movie, this creates a QuickTime movie with a Flash track. Flash tracks can be mixed and composited with other QuickTime tracks in all the usual ways (and a few unusual ways, as well).

The Flash graphics program can export images directly to QuickTime movies in two different ways: as a QuickTime Flash track or as a QuickTime video track.

Exporting to a QuickTime movie with a Flash track is similar to saving the file as an `.swf` file, opening it with QuickTime Player, and saving it as a self-contained movie, but it saves some steps.

Flash files exported as QuickTime *video* are converted to bitmaps and exported as cel animations. These files are typically much larger than they would be in Flash format. QuickTime 3 or later can play Flash animation exported as video; QuickTime 4 or later is required to play a movie with a Flash track.

One excellent cel-based animation program that exports to Flash or QuickTime is Toon Boom Studio (`www.toonboom.com`). Be sure you export to

Flash, then import the .swf into QuickTime; direct export to QuickTime renders the nice compact vectors into big messy pixels.

LiveMotion (www.adobe.com) creates both cel and vector animations, and exports either to QuickTime (as video) or .swf (preserving vector animation as well as cel animation).

AfterEffects (www.adobe.com) is a well-known special-effects package that can also export to QuickTime video or QuickTime-compatible .swf.

Flash is generally used to create animated sprite sequences rather than single images. This is discussed in the next section, "Sprite Animation."

▶ Sprite Animation

Sprite animation takes full advantage of your computer. It's radically different from cel-based animation. In a cel animation of a bouncing ball, for example, each frame contains the whole image of the ball and the background. With temporal compression, each key frame contains the whole image, while the intermediate frames describe the differences from frame to frame using an algorithm. An animated GIF, for example, can send just the image of the ball in a new position and the part of the background revealed by the ball's movement.

In a sprite animation, on the other hand, you typically send just one image of the background and one of the ball; the first frame contains the image data, and each subsequent frame contains a reference to the ball image with different x and y coordinates. The viewer's computer composites the ball over the background as the movie plays.

This is powerful for at least three reasons. Obviously, you send one image for the whole movie instead of sending 10 or 15 images per second over the Internet, so you have a lot more bandwidth.

Less obviously, since the image isn't composited until the movie is actually playing, the ball doesn't have to follow the same path every time the movie plays.

Perhaps even less obviously, the frame rate of a sprite animation doesn't have to be a fixed rate. You can specify a path and the time it takes for a sprite to travel the path, and let the viewer's computer render as many frames per seconds as its hardware can manage. Imagine that—your animation actually gets better over the years, as hardware improves.

What's more, sprites are automatically cropped when parts of them fall outside the track's display area, so your animated sprites can walk smoothly onstage and offstage with no special effort on your part.

And that's just the tip of the iceberg. Each frame in a sprite animation contains the sprite's properties at that moment, and a sprite can have many different properties.

For example, a sprite has a transformation matrix property—nine numbers that specify the sprite's position, scale, and rotation. So a sprite can not only move, it can rotate, skew, shrink, or enlarge as the movie plays, by changing just nine numbers per frame. Now that's low-bandwidth animation.

Note   For *way* too much information on the transformation matrix, see "Transformation Matrix" (page 550).

Another sprite property is depth. You can have multiple sprites in a sprite track, and they can pass in front of or behind each other. The viewer's computer automatically composites them according to their depth property. And their depth relative to each other can change as part of the animation.

I'm just getting started here—yet another sprite property is its image source. The image source can be a bitmap, a vector image, a video track, a live stream, or just about anything that QuickTime can display. The image source can even be specified by a URL, allowing you to treat images on the Internet as sprites.

But wait, there's more! You can specify an array of images for a sprite. The image source is just one of a sprite's properties, so a sprite can use a different image in different frames. A sprite animation of a walking figure, for example, can use several images of the figure in different postures; each frame specifies which image to use, and the images can be recycled repeatedly as the figure walks across the screen.

Naturally, these properties can be combined. A video track can bounce, spin, and skew when used as the image source for a sprite, or a walking figure can weave through other sprites, getting larger or smaller as it gets nearer or further away, or skewing in perspective as it walks toward the horizon, all by changing the values of a few sprite properties over time.

These features alone would make sprite animation a powerful way to create low-bandwidth animation and special effects. But learning about QuickTime sprites is like walking into gradually deeper water. It just keeps getting more interesting.

Take a deep breath. It's about to get *very* interesting.

Tweens and Modifier Tracks

Most of a sprite's properties are represented as numbers, and computers are great at generating numbers. If you specify a starting value, an ending value, and a period of time, it's child's play for a computer to generate a series of numbers that go smoothly from start to finish over that period.

QuickTime includes a media type that's never displayed. It's called a modifier track, and its data is used only to modify other tracks. A modifier track could be a series of numbers that specify a sprite's location, for example.

The most common type of modifier track is a tween track, which generates a series of values from a specified starting point to a specified ending point over a given period of time.

You can tell a sprite to get the values for its properties from a tween. In effect, you can tell a sprite to go from *here* to *there* in *this many* seconds.

For example, if it takes 5 seconds for a sprite to cross the screen, and you want to render the sprite at 15 frames a second, you could use 75 sprite samples, each with a different position property and a duration of 1/15 second. That's a big improvement over using 75 image samples, but you can do better—lots better.

You can set the start position, end position, and duration, and tell the sprite to get its position property from a tween track. You have a single sprite sample and a single tween for the whole animation; the tween's value keeps changing, and that changes the sprite.

And the data rate? The data rate for a tween animation is zero. Zip. Nada. You already downloaded the reference images and the tweens; now they're just generating data inside the viewer's computer.

Tweens can be used to control things like the position, rotation, size, and depth of a sprite, and the index into an array of source images.

Animating sprites with tweens is incredibly efficient. A few initial images, a single sprite sample, and three tweens—one each for matrix, depth, and index—can send a sprite moving, tumbling, dodging around other sprites, and wagging its tail, for as long as you like, at as many frames per second as the viewer's computer can render, with a data rate that quickly drops to *zero* bits per second.

A sprite animation that takes advantage of tweens can produce spectacular effects at the lowest possible bandwidth.

And tweens don't have to generate point-to-point transitions. A tween can count repeatedly from 1 to 10, for example, to animate a sprite's image index as the sprite moves. Or a tween can oscillate smoothly up and down like a sine wave or generate a series of points along a curving Bezier path. There are lots of different tween types.

Tweens aren't useful just for animating sprites, either; they're also useful for things like smoothly fading video in or out (by setting the blend value of a video track), smoothly panning the audio balance from left to right in a sound track, or fading the audio volume.

Some sprite animation programs, such as LiveStage Pro, allow you to create tweens and apply them to movie or track properties, as well as to sprites.

The example FlashyIntro.mov, in the Animation folder of the CD, uses tweens to spin and zoom a sprite whose image source is a QuickTime effect. It uses another tween to make the vector image of a logo fade in gradually. The movie was created by Michael Shaff (www.smallhands.com).

This would be a multimegabyte file if it were created in After Effects or Commotion. It would be hundreds of kilobytes as an animated GIF. As a sprite animation created in LiveStage Pro? 40 Kbytes (and 26 Kbytes of that is the sound track!).

But there's more to sprites than properties and tweens. Are you ready for more?

Actions and Events

A sprite can carry out actions in response to events. A typical sprite action is to move and bounce: to change its own x and y coordinates by a fixed amount, check to see if it's reached the edge of the window, and bounce—trigger a sound and reverse directions, as if the window edge were a wall.

A typical event would be a mouse click, which might activate a button sprite. A less obvious event type is the idle event, which tells the sprite that time has passed. Idle events occur even when the movie is paused, allowing sprites to animate themselves or take other actions as time passes in the real world, even though movie time has paused. The difference between real time and movie time can be difficult to get your head around, especially if you've been working in a frames-per-second model of animation. Here are some examples that may help.

The example movie ball1.mov, in the Animation folder of the CD, is a single-frame movie with a bouncing ball. The ball is a sprite that moves and bounces. Even though the movie is a single frame with a duration of 1/15 second, the animation goes on forever—because the sprite keeps getting idle events and acting on them. Let's see, a 3 Kbyte movie that goes on forever has a data rate of, uhm, let's see, 3 divided by infinity, carry the 2 . . . .

A second example movie, ball2.mov, shows how real time and movie time can overlap. The same sprite ball is composited over a video track. The movie is set to loop back and forth, so the background video cycles endlessly as the ball bounces. If you pause the movie, the background video stops—but the ball keeps bouncing.

In both examples, the sprite track contains a single sample whose duration is the whole movie, so it's unaffected by the passage of movie time. The sprite has an idle event handler, so it *is* affected by the passage of real time.

You make a sprite respond to movie time by creating multiple samples, each with a fixed duration in movie time, and each having its own properties. The example movie ball3.mov has two sprite samples, each with a duration of half a second, with different image properties—one is a red ball, one is a blue ball. The ball changes color while the movie plays. It's a loop, so the ball is red, blue, red, blue, and so on. If you pause the movie, the ball stops changing color.

As you would expect, a sprite can respond to movie time and real time both—ball4.mov has two sprite samples, each with a different image. The ball is red in the first half of the movie and blue in the second half. Both sprite samples have an idle event action that makes them move and bounce. Again, the movie is looping back and forth, so the ball keeps bouncing and changing colors. If you pause the movie, the ball stops changing color, just like ball3.mov. But it keeps bouncing. It moves in response to the passage of real time. It changes color at fixed points in the movie timeline.

These are very simple examples. With a little imagination you can use these techniques to do some amazing things.

A different kind of event is the frame-loaded event, which occurs at a fixed point in the movie timeline. This is another way to make a sprite respond to movie time. If you want to trigger an event at some point in the movie, you can create a sprite sample at that point in movie time and trigger an action on the frame-loaded event. If you're just using it as an event trigger, the sprite can even be invisible.

Tip QuickTime drops frames if the viewer's computer gets behind, so either set the movie to play every frame (which also mutes the audio) or make sure that any sample with a frame-loaded action has a long enough duration that it won't be skipped (half a second is usually adequate).

Other events include mouse-over, mouse-exit, button-down, and button-up, which tell the sprite that the mouse cursor is over it, or that the cursor has moved off, or that the mouse button is pressed or released (left mouse button for Windows). These events allow a sprite to respond to user input.

Actions aren't limited to modifying the sprite's own properties. A sprite action can modify the properties of other sprites, other tracks, the whole movie, or even other movies. That's right. A sprite can enable or disable other tracks, or change their audio volume or graphics mode. A sprite action can start or stop the movie, make it play backward or in slow motion, or jump to any point in movie time. A sprite in one movie can also perform these actions on other movies loaded in the same browser window (or in QuickTime Player).

Actions that control a movie are commonly linked to mouse events. Like the idle event, mouse events can take place even when the movie is paused. This allows you to create your own movie controller using sprites, which is a popular way to use them.

The example control.mov, in the Animation folder of the CD, has four sprite buttons that control the rest of the movie: Play, Stop, Play Backward, and Fast Forward. Check it out.

Sprite actions are controlled by adding properties to a sprite sample.

You can create sprite images using any graphics program.

You can add simple actions using a number of tools, including LiveMotion, GoLive, and Flash. If you use LiveStage Pro, you can also add complex actions called *behaviors* or even invent your own actions using QScript. VRHotwires also supports scripting of complex actions. Here's how to add actions to sprites using three popular tools:

- In Flash, use the Action tab to assign an action to a button or key frame. Pick an action from the list.

- In GoLive, open a QuickTime movie with a sprite track and open the Timeline window. Click a sprite key frame in the Timeline window, then click the Actions tab in the Properties inspector. Choose an event from the list, such as a mouse click, and click the + button to attach an action.

- In LiveStage, click the Tracks tab in the Project window, then double-click a sprite sample to open the Properties window. Click the Script Editor, choose an event handler from the list, such as Mouse Click, and either drag in an existing script or behavior, or type the name and parameters of the action or actions.

Using a Video Track as a Sprite

Wouldn't it be great if you could apply sprite animation techniques to a video track, using low-bandwidth tweens to make it skew, shrink and zoom, twist, fly around, and pass in front of and behind things? Well you can. What's more, it's pretty easy.

Begin by creating the sprite animation using your favorite sprite authoring tool. Use a simple placeholder graphic for the sprite image, such as a one-color GIF with the same dimensions as your video track.

Next, create a movie that contains both the sprite animation and a video track. You can do this in some sprite authoring tools just by dragging a video track onto the timeline. Alternatively, you can open the sprite animation in QuickTime Player and use Add or Add Scaled to add it to a movie with a video track. Or you can extract a video track from a movie in QuickTime Player and add it to the sprite animation. Use any method you like, as long as the video track and the sprite animation end up in the same movie.

Once you have a sprite animation and a video track in the same movie, follow these steps:

1. Open the Info window, choose the video track in the left pop-up menu, and move it into the background by adjusting its layer number (choose Layer from the right pop-up menu and increment it until the video drops into the background).

2. Choose the sprite track in the left pop-up menu, and choose Image Override in the right pop-up menu.

3. Click the name of the sprite image, then click Select Override Track.

4. Choose the video track from the list of tracks in the ensuing dialog box.

5. Save as a self-contained movie.

Your animated sprite should have a new face. The sprite animation is now a video track animation.

Note The video track is now a modifier track—instead of displaying its output, the video track sends its images to the sprite track, which uses them as the image source for a sprite.

Since the video track is now invisible, you'll probably want to add an image (or a new video track) as a background for your sprite track.

To see an example of a sprite that uses a video track as its image source, play Bouncetv.mov, in the Animation folder of the CD.

You can use the image override technique to replace a sprite's image with any kind of visual media from another track, including Flash, VR, and text.

You can also use a streaming track (even a live video stream) as the source for a sprite. For details on mixing streams and sprites in the same movie, see Chapter 17, "Mixing It Up: Streaming and Nonstreaming."

We'll look at more amazing stuff you can do with wired sprites in Chapter 16, "Getting Interactive." Now let's look at sprite animation using Flash.

Flash Sprites

Flash animation is similar to QuickTime sprite animation. As previously mentioned, Flash is the name of a graphics animation program from Macromedia, available on both Macintosh and Windows computers, and Flash is also a file format. The file format is also usually just called Flash, but the file extension is .swf and the MIME type is x-shockwave-flash. If you've been confused by this, you're not alone.

The Flash animation program can also create files that are stand-alone applications, called projectors (.exe files in Windows), and files that play only in the Flash authoring environment (.fla). When *we* refer to Flash files, however, we mean .swf files.

Flash is an excellent way to create sprite animations for use in Quick-Time movies. While somewhat more limited than QuickTime sprites, Flash sprites possess most of the same important features:

- A Flash sprite can be animated by modifying its properties; you don't need to store a copy of the image for each frame.

- Flash sprite properties include position, rotation, scale, and depth relative to other sprites.

- A Flash sprite's properties include its image source, so you can create a series of images and assign them to a sprite on a per-frame basis as part of the animation.

- Flash sprite properties can be set by tweens; you can specify a starting value, an ending value, and a duration, and Flash will generate the intermediate values. Path tweens are also supported—you can specify a set of points joined by curves or line segments, and the sprite will follow the path.

- Flash sprites can take actions in response to events. Possible actions include starting or stopping the movie, and possible events include mouse clicks that can occur when the movie is paused, making it possible to create a custom movie controller in Flash.

There are some differences between Flash sprites and QuickTime sprites that you should also be aware of:

- You cannot use a video track, streaming track, or URL as the source of a Flash sprite image; it must be a vector or bitmapped image within the Flash track.

- Even though Flash can manipulate both vector graphics and bitmaps, it is far more efficient when using vectors as sprites; bitmaps are best used as static elements.

- Flash animations have a fixed frame rate, and Flash sprites are updated by tweens on a per-frame basis. A higher frame rate increases bandwidth requirements. This is very different from QuickTime sprites.

- By default, a Flash sprite's position and center of rotation are the coordinates of its center; a QuickTime sprite uses its upper left corner by default. (You can modify the default of either sprite type by changing its registration point.)

- Flash can contain special tracks—which they call movies—with their own time base. These tracks can start, stop, and loop independently of the rest of the movie.

- Flash has fewer tween types, fewer event types, and fewer possible actions than QuickTime.

There is no equivalent of the idle event in Flash. Animation while the movie is paused is generally limited to simple loops, unless there is a mouse event.

Flash actions are similar in scope and complexity to QuickTime actions, but Flash's ActionScript language doesn't know about QuickTime tracks or media. There are a few Flash actions that apply directly to movies, such as play, stop, and goto time, but no actions to enable or disable a QuickTime track, for example.

Note You can open a Flash track in LiveStage Pro and add any QuickTime sprite actions to Flash sprites. This is discussed further in Chapter 16, "Getting Interactive."

- QuickTime sprite images are usually stored at the beginning of the track; once they download, the sprite track data rate drops to little or nothing. Flash images are usually stored where they are first used, so each new sprite creates a data spike for the frame where it first appears.

Note To make Flash sprites behave more like QuickTime sprites, put all the images in the library as symbols, and make each sprite an instance of a symbol.

In addition to animated sprites, Flash files can contain text, embedded fonts, and digitally sampled sound. If you import a .swf file into Quick-Time, these media types are included in the Flash track.

You can export a Flash animation directly to QuickTime from within the Flash application. If the Flash file contains sound, you have the option of saving the audio as a QuickTime sound track rather than part of the Flash track.

To optimize a Flash animation for the Web, use these guidelines:

- Use symbols for any image that you use more than once.
- Use tweens rather than specifying properties frame by frame.
- Use solid lines and colors rather than dashed lines and gradients.
- Use bitmaps sparingly or not at all—use vectors for all sprites.
- Keep static elements in a separate layer from animations.
- Make the animation a single scene.
- Use the Simplify Curves option before saving.

Additional tips can be found in the Flash user's guide.

Because QuickTime and Flash are made by different companies, their feature sets tend to play leapfrog. QuickTime 6 can import Flash files that are Flash 5 compatible. You can—and probably should—use the current version of Flash to create content for QuickTime; just don't include any elements that require a later version than Flash 5 to play back.

New versions of QuickTime generally support the existing version of Flash. Flash 4 features, such as editable text fields, require QuickTime 5 or later. If you need backward compatibility with QuickTime 4, use only the Flash 3 feature set.

Flash gives you the option of importing QuickTime into your Flash files. That's nice, but it requires the viewer to have both QuickTime and Flash installed for playback, and it locks you into the more rigid Flash framework. I recommend you do this only if you need to use the very latest Flash features.

In general, the more powerful approach is to embed Flash media in QuickTime. The viewer doesn't need to have Flash to play the movie, only QuickTime. You can target either the player or the plug-in, and you can use special features of QuickTime Player, such as media skins and full-screen mode.

You can also use Flash to create vector graphic images for QuickTime sprites. Just create a Flash image, such as a button, as a single frame, and save it as a .swf file. Open it in QuickTime Player and add it to your movie (Copy the Flash image, Select All in your movie, Add Scaled). You can change the layer of the Flash image to make it invisible. Now choose any

QuickTime sprite and use the Image Override feature, described in "Using a Video Track as a Sprite" (page 479). The Flash track is now the image source for a QuickTime sprite.

Another powerful approach is to use tools that work with Flash to create QuickTime media. For example, an animation program such as Toon Boom Studio lets you easily create complex animations, using Flash characters that move along 3D paths while the point of view swoops, pans, and zooms like a camera on a track. It can be a stunning effect. Just save your work as a .swf file and open in it QuickTime. Now you can add a sound track, video, or a floating logo and have it play in full-screen mode from a browser.

Or you could add wired actions. Oh, yeah. Let's talk about that.

16

Getting
Interactive

We've looked at a lot of things you can do with QuickTime movies, but the surprising fact is that we've just scratched the surface. So far, we've looked at movies that are essentially passive—just media that gets presented; the viewer watches or listens, but doesn't really interact.

Now we're going to look at QuickTime movies that interact—with the viewer, with a browser, with streaming servers and Web servers, with other movies, with XML files, and with remote databases.

We'll look at movies that are control panels, musical instruments, guided tours of websites, scientific calculators, games, puzzles—things that will amaze and delight you.

This chapter covers

- an overview of QuickTime interactivity and tools
- interactivity using text tracks
- interactivity and more with wired sprites
- intermovie communication
- interactivity using Flash tracks
- adding a media skin to a movie
- controlling QuickTime with JavaScript, and vice versa

QuickTime Interactivity

You can control the degree of interactivity in a QuickTime movie several ways. You're already familiar with some:

- **No controller**—You can prevent any interaction with the user at all by setting the parameters CONTROLLER="False", AUTOPLAY="True", and KIOSK MODE="True". The user can't stop the movie, rewind it, or save it.

- **Movie controller**—You can provide the normal QuickTime plug-in controller by setting the parameter CONTROLLER="True" (the default setting, except for VR movies). The user can start and stop the movie, jump to any point in the movie's timeline using the slider, control the sound volume, and save the movie to disk (if allowed).

- **Player controls**—You can target QuickTime Player, giving the user the additional abilities to add the movie to the Favorites list, step through the movie frame by frame, play the movie at different screen sizes, and adjust the video (brightness, color, contrast) and audio (bass, treble, and balance).

- **Hotspots**—You can use Plug-in Helper to make the movie or any of its video tracks into clickable links that load Web pages or QuickTime movies.

Now we'll look at ways to extend interactivity beyond the basics. First we'll touch briefly on the different methods and what they have to offer, then we'll get into specifics.

Text Tracks

Text tracks can add five distinct kinds of interactivity to a movie:

- Individual words and phrases in a text track can be made into hyperlinks.

- A text track can be made into a chapter list, giving the viewer a pop-up menu of named entry points into the movie. The pop-up menu is added to the movie controller (the control bar at the bottom of the movie).

- A text track can be made into an HREF track, which adds two different kinds of functionality (both can be present at the same time):
  - An HREF track can make the movie's display area into a clickable link that points to different URLs at different times in the movie.
  - An HREF track can cause Web pages or other movies to automatically load as the movie plays.

- You can add wired actions to a text track, giving it essentially the same capabilities as a sprite track (see the next section for details).

- You can create editable text fields. These fields can be modified by the person watching the movie. The text field's contents can be read, modified, and acted on by wired actions, or sent to an external program such as a database, either as XML or as text appended to a URL.

Wired Sprites

You can add an astonishing degree of interactivity by putting a sprite track in a movie and attaching actions to the sprites. The actions can be triggered by different kinds of events—mouse movements, mouse clicks, keystrokes, a frame loading in the movie, the passage of real time, even events generated by other sprites.

There are over 100 wired sprite actions. They include

- starting and stopping movies
- going to full-screen mode
- enabling and disabling tracks dynamically
- changing VR field of view or pan angle
- triggering sounds
- performing calculations
- sending messages to a Web server
- exchanging XML lists with a database
- loading a URL in the browser, the QuickTime plug-in, or QuickTime Player

This is just a tiny sampling from the list. You can combine multiple actions to create complex behaviors that include IF-ELSE-THEN tests, loops, and branches. You can actually create small cross-platform application programs, just using wired sprites.

Flash Tracks

Flash 5 supports interactive sound and animation, a large set of actions called ActionScript, drop-in controls including buttons and sliders, simple rendering of HTML text, XML data exchange, and editable text fields. Starting with QuickTime 6, you can bring all these features into QuickTime just by adding a Flash track to a QuickTime movie. QuickTime 6 supports Flash 3, 4, and 5.

Note QuickTime 5 supports Flash 3 and 4. QuickTime 4 supports Flash 3.

Some Flash actions work on the QuickTime movie containing a Flash track, such as starting and stopping a movie or jumping to a point in the movie timeline, so you can create a custom movie controller in Flash and import it directly into QuickTime without modification. There are other Flash actions, such as loading a URL, that serve much the same function as the equivalent QuickTime wired actions. You cannot, however, directly manipulate QuickTime at the track level (disabling or enabling a text track, for example) using Flash actions—most actions, such as triggering a sound or animation, take place within the Flash track.

With LiveStage Pro, however, you can add QuickTime's wired sprite actions to Flash tracks, combining the full interactive feature set of wired sprites with low-bandwidth Flash animation and editable text. It's a powerful combination.

Media Skins

You can now exercise total control over how your movie looks and acts when played in QuickTime Player. Adding a media skin to a movie causes QuickTime Player to hide its normal interface and play the movie using the interface you specify.

You control the size and shape of the playback window, what part of the skin is draggable, the look and placement of any controls, and the shape and texture of the player. The player's skin can be made of anything QuickTime can display—still images, motion video, QuickTime effects, text, VR, anything at all.

It's like creating a customized player application and bundling it with your movie. Only there's no programming required.

JavaScript

You can execute JavaScript code from QuickTime, or control QuickTime from JavaScript. Starting with QuickTime 6, you can script the QuickTime ActiveX control using JavaScript in Internet Explorer for Windows.

You can target JavaScript functions in any JavaScript-enabled browser using any of QuickTime's URL-generating mechanisms, including clickable HREFs, HREF tracks, sprite actions, and VR hotspots.

You can control QuickTime using JavaScript methods. You can use JavaScript to play audio movies in response to rollovers, for example, or put a

JavaScript movie controller in your Web page. Most wired sprite actions are available as JavaScript methods, so you can use JavaScript to change movies dynamically—to modify a track's transparency, for example, or enable subtitles or closed captions.

Media-Specific Interactivity

QuickTime wired actions are supported in sprite, text, and Flash tracks, and most actions are available as JavaScript methods as well. But you can also add media-specific interactivity to QuickTime. For example:

- QuickTime VR is a special media type that allows you to click and drag in the movie to look around in a 3D photograph, or to examine a 3D object from different angles. Panning, tilting, and zooming are supported by keystrokes. Hotspots can trigger URLs or wired actions.
- Pulse 3D media lets you turn, rotate, pan, and zoom 3D models. Very compact and responsive.
- BeHere media lets you tilt and pan around in a 360° motion picture as it plays. No 3D glasses required.
- Zoomify media lets you pan and zoom seamlessly into progressively higher-resolution versions of an image (without downloading the parts you don't look at). Extremely Web-friendly.
- Axel media lets you change things in texture-mapped, ray-trace rendered, 3D model worlds that include light and physics, and react accordingly. It's almost too cool to describe.

To learn more about QuickTime VR, see Chapter 19, "Let's Get Virtual." To learn more about Pulse, BeHere, Zoomify, and Axel, visit the Quick-Time Component Download page and click through to their sites: www.apple.com/quicktime/products/qt/components/

Note You can add new media types to QuickTime by creating QuickTime components.

Interactive Tools Galore

There's been a lot of activity in this area recently, and there are several new tools to help you create interactive QuickTime movies—everything from thousand-dollar Web creation suites to freeware utilities, with all stops in between. Here's a partial list:

- Cleaner XL/Cleaner 6

  This is the big gun of movie compression suites for the Web. Compresses to QuickTime, MPEG-1, -2, -4, Windows Media, Real, and Kinoma (Palm OS). Creates multiple-data-rate alternates. Interactivity is called Event Streams, and includes HREF track, chapter list, subtitle and closed-caption editor, and a few sprite actions (start, stop, goto time) in QuickTime.

  Windows (Cleaner XL), Mac OS 9, Mac OS X (Cleaner 6)
  $599, free trial version
  www.discreet.com/products/

- eZedia qti

  Simple drag-and-drop creation of frame-based multimedia. Add any QuickTime-supported media into presentations as linked scenes. Add buttons to change scenes, trigger a URL, hide/show a graphic, play a movie or sound. Saves as a QuickTime movie file.

  Windows, Mac OS X
  $99, free trial
  www.ezedia.com

- FinalChapter

  Possibly the easiest and most convenient tool for making chapter lists.

  Shareware, Mac OS 8 (runs in Classic), $10
  www.acutabovesw.com/finalchapter.html

- Flash MX

  Primarily used to create and edit vector-based animations, with text and some sound and video capability (one video codec), Flash has a rich set of interactive actions. Some can be applied directly to QuickTime movies (mainly movie controller actions—play, stop, goto time), but most affect other aspects of the Flash animation. The complete Flash animation, including actions, can be imported into a QuickTime movie as a Flash track. QuickTime wired actions can be added to a Flash track using a script editor such as LiveStage Pro or VR Hotwires.

  Windows, Mac OS, Mac OS X
  $499 (upgrade for $199), free trial
  www.macromedia.com

- GoLive

  This is a large software package designed for creating Web pages and managing websites. It includes a WYSIWYG Web page editor and an

HTML generator that automatically creates correct <EMBED> and <OBJECT> tags for QuickTime movies (just drag them onto the page). It also has an exceptionally powerful QuickTime editor that supports audio, video, sprite, and text tracks—including chapter lists and HREF tracks. You can assign simple actions to sprites in GoLive to create buttons and movie controllers.

Windows, Mac OS 9, Mac OS X
$399
www.adobe.com

- Live Channel

  A live broadcaster that's also a streaming server and a complete portable television studio, with ready-for-broadcast audio/video output and ready-for-webcast Internet/Ethernet output simultaneously. Includes the ability to insert HREFs into a live stream to bring up relevant URLs in the audience's browser.

  Mac OS X
  $999 ($699 for educators), demo on CD
  www.channelstorm.com

- LiveMotion

  This is a very similar product to Flash MX, including vector graphics creation and Flash actions, editable text, and export to QuickTime video or QuickTime-compatible .swf file. LiveMotion does a better job of exporting animations to QuickTime video, has better text handling, and has a richer feature set, but a more difficult user interface to master.

  Windows, Mac OS 9, Mac OS X
  $399
  www.adobe.com

- LiveStage Pro

  This is the premiere tool for creating interactive QuickTime. It unleashes the full capabilities of QuickTime wired actions and scripting, including support for editable text, XML list exchange with remote databases, and loading child movies (movie-in-a-movie). It supports all QuickTime media types and features, including VR, MPEG-4, and Flash 5. Most interactive QuickTime professionals find it indispensable.

  Windows, Mac OS X
  $899 ($100 discount coupon in this book), demo on the CD
  Promotional price, Spring 2003: $449 ($349 for educators)
  www.totallyhip.com

- MacAW

  Primarily for creating subtitles and closed captions, this software lets you easily synchronize text samples with a movie, preview the results, add styles, and more. Includes a widget that enables/disables the text track interactively.

  Mac OS 9 (runs in Classic)
  Free
  whitanderson.com/macaw/index.html

- Movie Works Deluxe 6

  Scene-based multimedia authoring software that exports to QuickTime movies. Contains editors for multiple QuickTime-compatible media. Includes simple tools for audio record/editor, video capture/edit, graphics paint/edit, text, and animation. QuickTime effects. Supports interactivity through QuickTime VR and simple button actions (go to scene, activate object).

  Windows, Mac OS, Mac OS X
  $99 ($39 upgrade), free 15-day trial.
  www.movieworks.com

- Qtilities

  These guys make widgets and utilities for QuickTime, mainly using interactive sprites you can add to your movies without purchasing a sprite authoring package. Widgets include a QuickTime detector and redirector, a remote movie controller for your Web page, a working closed-caption button, and a movie controller with extra features (fade audio in/out, go full screen, slow motion, and so on). Cool stuff.

  Any OS with QuickTime 5 or later
  Most widgets cost around $15.
  www.qtilities.com

- Tattoo

  Simplifies creation of skinned players, includes prebuilt controls for Play, Stop, Go to Beginning, Go to End, Step Forward, Step Backward, Mute, Half Volume, Full Volume, Close Window, Go to URL. Add buttons for 25 different wired actions. Inexpensive source of prebuilt buttons and simple actions for skinned movies.

  Mac OS X
  $23 (or bundled with Textation, both for $35), free demo (can't save)
  home.netvigator.com/~feelorium/feelorium/products.html

- Textation

  Easy-to-use tool for creating chapter lists, subtitles, closed-caption tracks, HREF tracks, and styled text tracks.

  Mac OS X
  $23 (or bundled with Tattoo, both for $35), free demo (can't save)
  home.netvigator.com/~feelorium/feelorium/products.html

- VideoClix

  Specializing in hotspots and automatic HREFs in motion video. Hotspots can track objects and characters in full-motion video. Product placements become click-throughs to catalog shopping. Historical video is annotated for students. Actors are linked to names and bios. Fun stuff. Couldn't be much easier to use, either.

  Mac OS, Mac OS X
  $399 (currently $50 if purchased with Live Channel), free trial.
  www.videoclix.com

- VRHotWires

  Primarily oriented toward QuickTime VR, this application lets you add wired actions to VR hotspots, and also create sprite tracks in any Quick-Time movie. This is currently the only program besides LiveStage Pro to support the complete set of QuickTime wired actions. This is a particularly good program for mixing VR with other QuickTime media and wired actions. Oriented toward people with a programming background and/or aptitude, but many features are easy for anyone to use. Some rough edges, but a lot of great stuff.

  Mac OS, Mac OS X (check for Windows version)
  $199
  www.vrhotwires.com

Well, that's the big picture on QuickTime Interactivity. Let's see how you actually do this stuff.

Getting Interactive with Text Tracks

There are several different ways to add interactivity to a QuickTime movie using text tracks. Three of them can be authored using very simple tools, such as a text editor and QuickTime Player.

- Use the {href: } text descriptor.
- Create a chapter list.
- Create an HREF track.

Two newer ways to interact with text tracks were introduced in QuickTime 5. Currently, you can create them using LiveStage Pro, version 3 or later.

- Create an editable text field.
- Add wired actions and event handlers to your text.

Note   LiveStage Pro is currently the only authoring software that helps you create editable QuickTime text fields. You can create editable Flash text fields using Flash authoring software and import it into QuickTime as part of a Flash track, if you don't need to work with the text in QuickTime and can manage entirely using Flash actions.

Link Up with {href:}

You can make any word or phrase in a text track into a clickable link. The text is automatically rendered in blue and underlined, just like a typical link in a Web page. You can target the URL to load in an existing browser frame or window, a new window, QuickTime Player, or the QuickTime plug-in.

To add a clickable link to a text track, add the {HREF: *url*} and {endHREF} descriptor tags around the words that should act as links, as described in "Hypertext Links" (page 375).

To learn how to create text tracks and add descriptor tags, see "Creating Text Tracks" (page 357) and "Setting Text Attributes" (page 365).

Skipping Along with Chapter Lists

One of the easiest ways to enhance the interactivity of a QuickTime movie is to include a chapter list. A chapter list adds a pop-up menu to the movie controller. Each item in the pop-up menu corresponds to a point in the movie's timeline; when the viewer chooses an item from the list, the movie jumps to that point in its timeline.

A chapter list acts like the table of contents for a book: It provides a list of topics, shows what order they're presented in, and lets the viewer jump directly to any topic. In addition, it displays the name of the current chapter while the movie is playing, and it lets the viewer jump forward or backward to any chapter from anywhere in the movie.

Chapter lists are particularly useful for long movies that contain instructional material. Viewers can get a quick overview of what's being presented and can easily jump to the information they need or the section they want to review.

Chapter lists work well in local movies; the viewer can jump immediately to any chapter.

Chapter lists are terrific for streaming movies. A streaming server can start sending a movie from any point in its timeline, so the viewer can jump ahead or jump back without downloading the intervening material. Chapter lists really let you take advantage of this feature.

Chapter lists are considerably less useful in long Fast Start movies. The chapter list can only give access to the parts of the movie that have already downloaded. The viewer can't jump ahead in a movie until the movie has downloaded to that point, and this can be confusing or even frustrating.

A chapter list is a special kind of text track. You can easily create one with a text editor or word processor and add it to a movie using QuickTime Player. For details, see "Adding a Chapter List to a Movie" (page 390) or "Adding a Chapter List to a Streaming Movie" (page 553).

Creating Web Tours with HREF Tracks

An HREF track is a special kind of text track. Its text isn't normally displayed on the screen—it's used internally by QuickTime as a source of hypertext references, or links.

This section describes what you can do with HREF tracks and provides some examples. For a detailed explanation of how to create HREF tracks, see "HREF Tracks" (page 394) in Chapter 13, "Text! Text! Text!"

HREF tracks work in local, Fast Start, and streaming movies (like other track types, HREF tracks need to be hinted before you can stream them).

Important HREF tracks in *streaming* movies can be played using *either* QuickTime Player or the QuickTime plug-in, but HREF tracks in local or Fast Start movies work *only* with the plug-in.

An HREF track can contain two different kinds of references: clickable links and autoloading links. Both kinds of links are defined by text samples in the HREF track.

Clickable Links

Clickable links make the entire display area of the movie into a link for the duration of the text sample, so you can create time-based links for what's displayed on the screen.

To see an example, point your browser at Slidelink.htm, in the Interactive folder of the CD. It contains a movie that consists of a slideshow and an HREF track—clicking any slide in the movie opens a browser window and loads the Web page associated with that slide. The URL of each Web page is a text sample synchronized with a slide.

Autoloading Links

Autoloading links load a specified URL as soon as the text sample loads, so you can synchronize Web-based content or local HTML pages with the rest of your QuickTime movie.

For an example, see tour.htm, in the Interactive folder of the CD. It gives a narrated tour of the Web pages on the CD. To accomplish this, it creates a frameset with a QuickTime movie in the lower frame. The movie, tour.mov, consists of an audio description of the CD's contents and an HREF track. The HREF track contains autoloading links that open HTML pages from the CD and display them in the upper frame as the narration describes them.

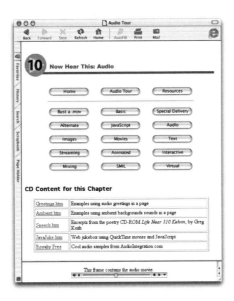

A powerful feature of this kind of presentation is that it isn't just a canned slideshow—the upper frame contains live HTML. You can pause the movie in the lower frame at any time and follow links in the upper frame, exploring the CD and even the links from the CD to the World Wide Web. When you're ready to continue, press the Play button in the narration movie and the tour picks up where it left off.

This can be a great way to provide website navigation help. It lets your users roam at will, but makes it easy for them to continue with a structured tour if they get lost. Or use an HREF track for distance learning—build your lecture slides in HTML, or link to existing sites on the Web and have QuickTime synchronously load the URLs in your students' browsers during the lecture. This is very powerful when combined with live streaming, using a broadcaster such as Live Channel.

The key to making this kind of presentation work properly is allowing enough time for things to load in the viewer's browser—you don't want the narration to get ahead of the HTML content. Estimating the download time isn't hard for CD or LAN-based movies, but it's more challenging for Web-based presentations that have to accommodate different connection speeds.

One answer for recorded presentations is to remind your viewers that they can pause the movie to let Web pages load. A more sophisticated approach is to use a wired sprite to pause the movie automatically—tell your viewers to push the Play button or choose a destination from the chapter list when they're ready to continue.

Tip There's a StopMovie sprite (and quite a few other useful sprites) in the Widgets folder of the CD. They're free, so knock yourself out.

For live presentations, you may want to implement a simultaneous chat session, so participants can type a message to you if they're falling behind. It also allows someone to "raise their hand" with a question. There's actually a small chat application, in the form of a QuickTime movie, in the Interactive folder on the CD. It's written by Michael Shaff (www.smallhands.com), it's called Chatter.mov, and it's way cool.

Note There are now several tools that can add URL hotspots to your movie, or set the movie to load a URL at any point in the movie timeline, using HREF tracks or sprites. These include VideoClix, CineStream, GoLive, LiveStage Pro, Tattoo, Cleaner, and Textation. Most of these products can also create chapter lists.

Seriously Wired Text

A picture may be worth a thousand words, but text still has its place. Accessing a remote database, for example, generally calls for a lot of text, flowing in both directions. Using the new text features of QuickTime 5, you can create movies that serve as small, graphical, cross-platform front ends for databases—movies that can be installed over the Internet or included in a Web page.

The new features are editable text fields, wired text, XML, and lists.

QuickTime 5 and later allow you to include editable text fields in a QuickTime movie. The person watching the movie can click a text field and enter, change, or delete information.

Because the contents of a text field can change while the movie plays, you can also modify the text using wired actions. This means you can change the information you display based on user action. It also means you can update the field with current information obtained from disk or over the Internet, while the movie is playing.

Wired text means that you can trigger actions based on what a user types into a text field. It also means that the text field itself can respond to mouse actions, timeouts, and frame load events, without having to create a parallel sprite track as an event handler.

Lists combine with these other elements in a powerful way. Lists allow you to create hierarchical databases in QuickTime. You can attach them to movies or to individual tracks. You can access the contents of lists in a structured way, and display any part of them in an editable text field. You can also store the input from an editable text field in a list—it's a two-way street for data storage and retrieval inside a QuickTime movie.

QuickTime can export lists in XML format, sending them to a CGI or PHP program on a Web server, for example. In other words, data entered by the viewer in a text field can be stored in a local database and uploaded in a structured manner to a remote server. Data can be passed in XML format for exchange with a database or as key-value pairs formatted for delivery in URLs, such as

```
http://server.com/your.php?userID=xx99?product=800GB-FWHD
```

And again, the street runs in both directions. QuickTime can query a server or read an XML file from disk or over the Internet to update the contents of its local databases. In other words, a movie can obtain structured information from a remote server, store it in a local database, and act on it or display it in an organized way.

A movie can contain multiple lists—one for the movie as whole, and another for each track. You can add sprite tracks to act as list containers if needed.

New in QuickTime 6, you can set the contents of the movie list (as opposed to one of the track lists) directly from your HTML using XML syntax:

```
<Embed src=my.mov height=yy width=xx MovieQTList=
  "<myDataBase>
    <myRecord>
      <lastname>Bailey</lastname>
      <firstname>Bill</firstname>
      <phone>555-1212</phone>
    </myRecord>
  </myDataBase>"
/>
```

Note that there is no XML header, just the data. It's important to enclose the entire list in quotes, so browsers realize it is all a parameter value. Older browsers may have trouble with this syntax anyway, and close the embed tag when they encounter the first "`>`" character. You can prevent this by writing out the list using JavaScript:

```
<script language="JavaScript">
embedTag = ' <embed'
+ ' src=\"my.mov\"'
+ ' height=yy width=xx'
+ ' MovieQTList='
+ ' \"<myDataBase>'
+ ' <myRecord>'
+ ' <lastname>Bailey</' + 'lastname>'
+ ' <firstname>Bill</' + 'firstname>'
+ ' <phone>555-1212</' + 'phone>'
+ ' </' + 'myRecord>'
+ ' </' + 'myDataBase>\"'
+ ' /' + '>';
document.writeln(embedTag);
</script>
```

These are relatively new features of QuickTime, so it will take time for most movie authoring tools to add support for them. As of this writing, the only authoring software that lets you create movies with editable text fields, lists, XML data exchange, and wired text is LiveStage Pro (version 3 or later). VR Hotwires also supports the wired actions used to control these features, but doesn't yet have much documentation on using them.

Pushing Buttons with Wired Sprites

The most powerful way to add interactivity to a QuickTime movie is to use wired sprites. A sprite, as you'll remember, is a compact data structure that contains properties such as location on the screen, rotation, scale, and an image source. A *wired* sprite is a sprite that takes action in response to events. If you haven't read about sprites, actions, and events yet, skip back to "Sprite Animation" (page 473) and check it out.

One of the most significant features of sprites is that a sprite can be animated by changing its properties without retransmitting its image—you can toggle a sprite's image source between a picture of a raised button and a picture of a pressed button, for example, and no matter how many times you toggle it, the sprite uses the same sample data for the two images.

Like a still background image, a single sprite can have the same duration as a whole movie. Unlike a still background image, a sprite can be wired to change in response to user input or other events. Consequently, sprites make great buttons.

You can use wired sprite buttons in a number of ways—as customized graphics for a basic movie controller, for example, or to add controls for things like playback speed, graphics mode, and language; as a navigation bar in a Web page; or as presets for tuning in broadcast streams.

Widgets, Actions, and Scripting

A lot has changed in the world of wired sprites since the first edition of this book. There are over a dozen more tools on the market that can help you create sprites and/or wire them to do exciting things. What's more, a cottage industry is growing in wired sprites themselves—people create them and sell them, trade them, or give them away. You can now add wired sprites to your movies in three distinct ways: with widgets, actions, and scripts.

A Crash Course in Widgets

A widget is a wired sprite that's created to just work, without modification, in different movies. You don't need to draw anything, animate anything, or know anything about wired actions. Just add the widget to your movie and voilà! You're wired.

For example, if you want your movie to pause when it gets to a certain point, requiring the viewer to press Play to continue, just open the movie in QuickTime Player, drag the playhead to where you want the movie to pause, and add a StopSprite. There are several fun widgets that you're welcome to use in the Widgets folder of the CD. Check 'em out.

Widgets are usually stand-alone QuickTime movies—you can add them to your own movies using QuickTime Player or any other general-purpose QuickTime editor. The technique varies slightly with the type of widget.

In general, to add widgets to your own movies, do this:

1. Open the widget movie in QuickTime Player, Select All, Copy, Close (don't save).

2. Open your own movie. (If it's a VR movie, choose Get Movie Properties and set the controller to Movie Controller.)

3. Add the widget in one of the two following ways:

   For control widgets, Select All and Add Scaled.

   For widgets that do something at a certain point in the movie timeline, such as load a URL, position the playhead at the desired point in your movie and choose Add. You can add several copies of such sprites; just reposition the playhead and choose Add again, as many times as you need.

   Either way, this adds a sprite track to your movie. If it's a visible sprite, such as a button, and you need to change the sprite's size or location, use the Movie Properties window (choose Sprite Track from the left pop-up menu, Size from the right pop-up menu, then click Adjust).

4. If your movie is a VR movie, set the controller back to VR Controller.

Commercial widgets are likely to come with an application program, or even an interactive movie, that acts as a specialized widget factory. For example, you can get a free widget to autorotate your VR panorama in the Widgets folder, but you can't program it to go faster, or slower, or, well, anything else; but for $15 you can buy a copy of RevolVR from Squamish Media Group (www.smgvr.com) and crank out autorotate sprites to your heart's content, each with its own customized settings.

There are widgets that add sound to VR panoramas, widgets that detect QuickTime and redirect people to different pages based on their Quick-Time version, widgets that act as movie controllers, widgets that toggle closed captions on and off—the list of off-the-shelf wired sprites is constantly growing.

Currently the two premiere vendors of commercial widgets are Squamish Media Group (www.smgvr.com) and Qtilities (www.qtilities.com), with a smattering available from Feelorium (home.netvigator.com/~feelorium/feelorium/).

Free widgets are available on the CD, on the author's home page, and through the kindness of various QuickTime developers, including Matthew Peterson (www.matthewpeterson.net) and various members of the LiveStage Developers Network (www.totallyhip.com/lsdn/).

Sprite Actions

The actions of a widget can be arbitrarily complex. It's the authoring part that's simple. You just add it to your movie. At the next level of authoring complexity are sprite actions. Actions are simple things a sprite can do without author programming, such as start or stop a movie, jump to a point in the movie timeline, change the audio volume, or open a URL.

To move to the next level, you need to be able to create a sprite and assign an action to it. Unfortunately, you can't do that using QuickTime Player. You need some kind authoring software. See "Interactive Tools Galore" (page 489) for a list of authoring programs; they all have a free trial or demo version that you can download, and where possible I've included the demo or trial version in the Demos folder on the CD—have a look. In fact, try a few. They're surprisingly different in the way they present things and the kind of wired movies they create. See what works for you.

You can do a lot using simple sprite actions in QuickTime. The following table shows a sampling of the simple wired actions available with no programming required:

General actions	Movie actions	Track actions	Sprite actions
GotoURL	SetVolume	SetEnabled	SetImageIndex
AddFavorite	SetRate	SetLayer	SetVisible
RemoveFavorite	Start	SetGraphicsMode	SetLayer
SetCursor	Stop	PlayNote	SetGraphicsMode
SetStatusString	SetLooping	SetVolume	MoveTo
EnterFullScreen	GoToTime	SetBalance	MoveBy
ExecuteJavaScript	GoToBeginning	LoadChildMovie	Scale
ExecuteLingoScript	GoToEnd	GoToFrameNamed	Rotate
	StepForward	SetPanAngle	Stretch
	StepBackward	SetTiltAngle	ExecuteEvent
	SetSelection	SetFOV	
	PlaySelection	GoToNode	
	SetLanguage		

No matter what authoring software you use, when you attach an action to a sprite (or text, Flash, or a VR hotspot), you need to specify two things: the action and the event that triggers the action. Sometimes you need to specify a third thing: the target.

For example, a StopMovie action might be triggered by a mouse click on a sprite, or by a frame-loaded event (when the movie gets to a specific point in the timeline). You need to specify which event triggers the action. Similarly, if the action were to enable or disable a track, you would have to specify both the trigger event and the target: which track to enable or disable.

Some software will shield you from these choices, often simply by limiting actions to the ones that don't need a specific target (play, stop, goto time, open URL), or by treating the same action as different objects—either a button or a timeline event, for example, depending on whether it's triggered by a mouse click or a frame load. As another example, in VideoClix you can designate an object or character in a motion video as a click-through to a website. VideoClix doesn't tell you it needs to create an invisible sprite that tracks the object's movement and responds to mouse-click events with a GoToURL action—it just does it.

Among the most flexible tools for adding simple sprites and sprite actions is Adobe GoLive. Open or create a QuickTime movie (Open Special or Make Special), open the timeline, drag a penguin from the object palette (okay, maybe it's not so straightforward—the penguin represents a sprite track), then add a sprite and set its properties using the Properties Inspector. There's a short pop-up menu of actions to choose from, with associated pop-up menus for trigger events and, where appropriate, targets.

Flash and LiveMotion are two programs that also allow you to create sprites and assign actions from a pop-up list. Actions that control the movie or open a URL work when the sprite is added to a QuickTime movie as a Flash track. Flash is a great way to make custom movie controls. Most Flash actions are targeted at other items within the Flash track, however, so you can't use Flash actions to do things like toggle a QuickTime text track on and off. Still, you can bring a lot of interactivity into QuickTime in a Flash track.

Most of these programs do create sprites with a lot of internal logic, but it's in the sprite already, just waiting for you to supply an action. A button, for example, may come preprogrammed to respond to a mouse-over and a mouse click by changing its image to highlighted and then pressed. You just specify an action for the button to take. These sprites require some scripting to implement, but it's done for you.

In the so-inexpensive-it's-almost-free category, Tattoo allows you to create visible or invisible buttons (hotspots), add them to your movie, and assign one of 25 different actions to them. A lot of power for a little program.

You can also add simple actions using more powerful applications that permit scripting.

Scripting Sprites

The jump from adding a sprite action to scripting a sprite can be a hard one. But it doesn't really have to be. Part of the problem is that you may find you need different authoring software to do scripting. This means learning a new program. And programs that offer scripting for wired sprites typically do a lot of other things as well, which can be confusing at first. But there are ways to ease the pain.

When you start to think about making an interactive movie that goes beyond what simple sprite actions can do, download a free trial version of an authoring package that supports scripting. Start by learning to do the same things you already do using simple actions. As you see how a button is implemented, or how a GoToURL action is constructed, you'll gain insight into the things you're familiar with, while becoming comfortable with a new toolset. You'll break into scripting naturally when, either purposefully or by accident, you change a value and your familiar control acts in a new way.

Then you can register your software or buy the boxed set with a sense of confidence, and dig into scripting with some direction and purpose. Small steps are easier than big jumps.

Scripts allow sprites to do more than react to an event with an action. They permit a sprite to use logic and make choices, triggering one or more actions from a larger set of possibilities. They also allow sprites to communicate with other sprites, scripts, and servers, and to work together as part of a larger design.

Scripts put the full power of wired sprites into your hands. And like most power tools, you need to spend a little time learning how to use them effectively (and yes, aptitude for programming is very helpful at this level).

Flash MX and LiveMotion allow you to script sprites using ActionScript, which is roughly comparable to QuickTime's wired actions. You can author in Flash MX or LiveMotion, export to .swf, and open in QuickTime Player. This creates a Flash track with all of the interactivity intact. The only shortcoming is that you have limited ability to manipulate the QuickTime movie's other tracks from within a Flash track. However, you can add QuickTime wired actions to Flash, and read and write Flash variables, using any authoring tool that supports the appropriate QuickTime actions.

There are currently two applications that support full scripting of wired actions in QuickTime: LiveStage Pro (for Mac OS X and Windows) and VRHotWires (Mac OS and Mac OS X). LiveStage Pro is a full-featured QuickTime authoring suite that you can use to take full advantage of QuickTime. It has a large number of prebuilt behaviors, a slick new interface, tons of documentation, and a lively developer community. VRHot-Wires is more programmer-oriented and has some rough edges, but it implements the entire QuickTime wired action set, has some great VR features no one else has, and costs a fifth as much. If you can afford it, get them both; otherwise, choose the one that best suits your budget and abilities.

Applied Button-ology

Okay, so you know how to make cool-looking sprite buttons. Now, what can you do with them, besides making your own movie controllers?

I'm glad you asked. Here's a sampling of uses for wired sprite buttons.

Website Navigation

You can use wired sprite buttons to provide website navigation. This is mainly accomplished by using the GoToURL action that nearly all authoring tools support. If you use a more advanced tool, the buttons can have graphic rollover actions, pop-up windows that describe what they do, and separate sound effects triggered by rollover and clicking. The Web page at the top level of the CD, Start.htm, contains an example of this kind of movie. The navigation movie itself is Nav.mov. There are two versions of Nav.mov—one for the top-level page on the CD and another for the chapter-level pages.

Language Selection

Wired sprite buttons can be used to select a movie's language by using the SetLanguage action. You create alternate language tracks for your movies, as described in Chapter 8, "Alternate Realities: Language, Speed, and Connections," then use a wired sprite action to control which language is presented.

You can have more than one movie playing simultaneously, and different buttons can control the language for different movies, allowing you to do things like setting the audio and the subtitles to two different languages. This is a popular feature when people are learning a language—they can read and listen in a foreign language, which strengthens both skills, or they can have a written or audible translation.

An example of this kind of multiple-language, multiple-movie presentation can be found at www.totallyhip.com/show_lsp.

Definitely check it out.

Web Radio or TV Tuner

A button in your movie can enable one streaming track and simultaneously disable others, using the SetEnabled and ToggleEnabled actions. If your movie contains multiple streaming tracks, a series of such buttons are like the presets on a car stereo—each one activates a particular Web-based radio or TV broadcast. For an example, see WebRadio.mov, in the Interactive folder of the CD.

Lots More

You can attach any wired sprite action to a button. QuickTime currently provides over 100 actions and over 20 operators.

Here's a list of some wired sprite actions, just to give you an idea:

General actions	Movie actions	Track actions	Sprite actions
GotoURL	SetVolume	SetEnabled	SetImageIndex
DebugString	SetRate	SetLayer	SetVisible
AddFavorite	Start	SetGraphicsMode	SetLayer
RemoveFavorite	Stop	RotateMatrix	SetGraphicsMode
SetCursor	SetLooping	FindText	MoveTo
SetString	GoToTime	ReplaceText	MoveBy
AppendString	GoToBeginning	PlayNote	Scale
SetStatusString	GoToEnd	SetVolume	Rotate
EnterFullScreen	StepForward	SetBalance	Stretch
ExecuteJavaScript	StepBackward	LoadChildMovie	ExecuteEvent
ExecuteLingoScript	SetSelection	LoadListFromXML	
LoadComponent	PlaySelection	MakeNewSprite	
	SetLanguage	GoToFrameNamed	
	GetVariable	SetFlashVariable	
	SetVariable	SetPanAngle	
	GetMovieURL	GoToNode	

In addition, you can make buttons perform complex actions that read properties, perform calculations, and perform sets of actions based on the outcome of IF-THEN-ELSE statements, branches, and loops.

Here's a sampling of some wired sprite operators and logic elements:

Operators	Comparators	Logic
+ (addition)	=	IF
− (subtraction)	<	ELSE
* (multiplication)	>	ELSEIF
/ (division)	<=	SWITCH-CASE
Sqr, Log, Exp	>=	WHILE
Sin, Cos, Tan, ArcTan	!= (not equal)	FOR-NEXT
OR (logical OR)		
AND (logical AND)		

Wired sprites can also read properties of QuickTime (such as the current version), movies (such as the current play rate or the amount of the movie that has downloaded), tracks (such as a track's enabled/disabled status), sprites (such as a sprite's location or its image index), text fields, Flash variables, the mouse and keyboard, and the system clock (such as current time and date).

QuickTime 6 introduces these additional wired actions:

- Load new sprite images dynamically from URLs
- Jump to a chapter by name or chapter number
- Turn hit-testing on or off for particular sprites
- Test for a key-up event
- Set a new, random seed for the pseudo-random number generator
- Toggle the view state of a VR object (normally determined by the mouse button's up/down state)
- Scale a target movie (set the scale to 2 to display a movie at double size, for example, or to 0.5 to display at half size)
- Read movie annotations (copyright and so on) and other user data
- Read status and progress messages for streaming movies

What can you do with all these features? Well, what *can't* you do?

QuickTime Can Do That?

The following illustration is a picture worth a thousand words.

As you can see, it's a scientific calculator. As you can also see, it's a QuickTime movie. Astonishingly, it's a working scientific calculator that's *just* a QuickTime movie. It runs on Windows (including NT) and Macintosh computers. You can embed it in a Web page, plop it into a PDF file or a Word document (to name a couple of ploppable formats), put it on a removable disk, or send it as an email attachment. Its file size is 13 Kbytes.

This calculator was created without any C or Java programming. It's a normal wired sprite movie made in LiveStage Pro. It's in the Interactive folder of the CD as QTCalc2E.mov. The calculator was created by Matthew Peterson of UC Berkeley (matthew@matthewpeterson.net), an astoundingly bright guy who created this calculator *before* the higher math functions were added to QuickTime (they can be derived geometrically, if you have the talent). Try examining the contents of the folder Matthew's Behaviors using your trial copy of LiveStage Pro (both in the Demos folder). Nice, nice, *very* nice.

As this movie demonstrates, you can use wired sprites to create compact and portable applications programs with graphical user interfaces. They're small, they run on Windows and Mac OS, they work over the Internet, you can embed them in Web pages or any kind of document that can contain QuickTime movies, and they require no C or Java programming—just some scripting.

Come back here—I'm not done yet. QuickTime sprites can not only be wired to perform complex functions within a movie, they can send data out to other programs. That's right, a CGI or PHP script running on your Web server can get information from a QuickTime movie running in a viewer's browser.

The Web page named DrawPDF.htm in the Interactive folder of the CD contains an embedded QuickTime movie, DrawPDF.mov (you need to be connected to the Internet to really use it). Open it in your favorite browser.

You can use your mouse to draw colored lines in the movie's display area. Nice, but no big deal, right?

Now click the PDF icon in the movie—a wired sprite action sends data describing the lines you just drew to a CGI script running on a Web server. The CGI script creates a PDF version of your drawing and sends it back to you.

Think about what's happening here. You can create graphical applications that are QuickTime movies. The movies can generate data through interaction with the user, including graphic data. You can send that data back to your Web server and feed it to a CGI script. The CGI script can do *anything*, including creating files and sending them back to the viewer. The possibilities are endless.

The methodology is fairly straightforward. You can store data in variables or in the properties of sprites (visible or invisible). Wired sprite actions include the ability to read those variables and properties. The GoToURL action sends a string to the browser, which can take the form

```
http://server.filename?Data,data,data.
```

The data can be generated dynamically by user interaction with the movie, and a CGI script can use the data to generate a file named `filename`, which is then returned to the browser. And of course, it can be targeted to an adjacent frame or window.

In other words, it's a general-purpose I/O mechanism for communications between the viewer and a script running on your server, and that's the stuff dreams are made of.

QuickTime now has the ability to store and structure information in database format, import and export databases over the Internet in XML format or as key-value pairs, and display information and collect user input in editable text fields. Hey, this is getting serious!

Games People Play

But enough about serious applications. Let's talk about fun. In fact, let's have some. By adding behaviors and logic to your sprites, you can create all manner of games and puzzles.

Refrigerator Magnets

Simply by creating sprites from graphic images of text and making the sprites draggable (a prebuilt behavior in LiveStage Pro), you can recreate the venerable refrigerator magnet poetry corner on your website. Point your browser at Refrigerator.mov, in the Interactive folder of the CD, to see what I mean.

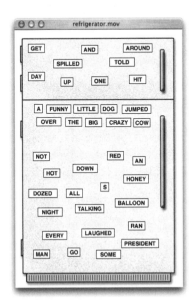

This version is very simple, but it wouldn't be hard to add a button that would send the sprite positions to a CGI script as part of a URL, so visitors to your website could submit their entries and have them added to your Web pages.

Puzzle Me This

With a little more logic, you can make puzzle games like Cruiseline.mov, also in the Interactive folder of the CD.

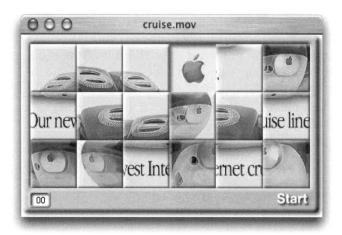

In addition to seeing the completed picture, a puzzle game can give a reward of a movie or sound effect, or load a Web page that the user couldn't get to otherwise (just include a password and user name in the GoToURL action).

Puzzles in Motion

Here's a jigsaw puzzle whose pieces are segments of a moving video. Is it a new art form? I don't know, but I like it.

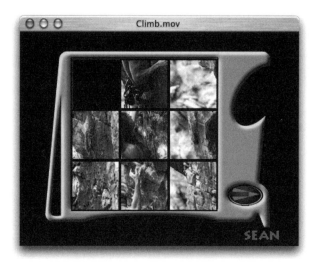

You can find this as `Climb.mov` in the Interactive folder of the CD. You can create the puzzle pieces by masking different parts of a video track and exporting them, as described in "Cropping" (page 299), then creating a sprite movie with sliding pieces, then adding the exported video tracks and assigning them as sprite images, as described in "Using a Video Track as a Sprite" (page 479).

Speak and Spell

You want cute? We got cute. Check out `Katy.mov`, in the Interactive folder of the CD.

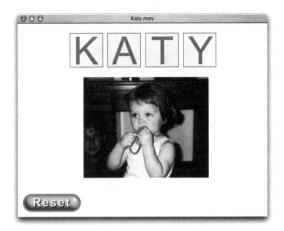

The tiles are graphically simple. They have the prebuilt bounce behavior from LiveStage Pro. They respond to a mouse-click event by playing a note on a custom MIDI instrument, moving to a preassigned position on the screen, and not bouncing anymore. When the last tile is in place, it triggers another custom MIDI note. The custom MIDI notes are recordings of someone speaking.

Awww . . . . Little kids *love* this game. It was contributed by Ken Loge. Check out some of his other fine work at `www.ori.org/~ken1/`.

Intermovie Communication

You can use wired sprites in one movie to control another movie, as long as both movies are embedded in the same Web page, the same SMIL presentation, or both movies are open in QuickTime Player at the same time. Any wired sprite action can be targeted to another movie. Currently, this feature is supported only by LiveStage Pro among the wired sprite authoring tools.

For an example of intermovie communication, see Readout.htm, in the Interactive folder of the CD.

This Web page contains four movies—a large VR panorama movie and three tiny text movies. As you drag in the panorama, a wired sprite inside the panorama movie reads the current pan angle, tilt angle, and field of view, then uses these values to control the text movies. The text movie that displays the current pan angle, for example, has 360 frames, each consisting of a readout in degrees—0°, 1°, 2°, and so on. The wired sprite in the panorama movie reads the current pan angle, then performs a GoToTime action on the text movie. Since each degree of pan angle corresponds to a time in the text movie, this creates a live text readout of the pan angle.

Readout.htm was contributed by Steven M. Cox, Ph.D., of Interval Communications LLC (http://virtualthink.com/).

Another example of intermovie communication can be found in Playme.htm in the Interactive folder of the CD. It contains two movies—a large movie framed by curtains like an old movie theater and a small controller movie at the bottom of the page. Pressing buttons on the controller starts and stops the other movie.

There are two parts to making a wired sprite in one movie control another movie: The wired sprite action must be targeted to a particular movie, and the target movie must be assigned a movie name or a movie ID. You can assign a name or ID using the MOVIENAME or MOVIEID parameters, either as part of the <EMBED> tag in your HTML or embedded directly in the target movie by Plug-in Helper.

The <EMBED> tag for the target movie in Playme.htm looks like this:

```
<EMBED SRC="Sample.mov" HEIGHT="240" WIDTH="160"
  CONTROLLER="False" MOVIENAME="Remotely-controlled" >
```

The controller movie, Remotecontrol.mov, contains a wired sprite that targets its actions at a movie named Remotely-controlled. Because the movie name is assigned in the HTML, you can modify Playme.htm by changing the SRC, HEIGHT, and WIDTH parameters to point to another movie instead of Sample.mov. The controls at the bottom of the page play whatever movie is named in the <EMBED> tag.

To use targeted wired sprite actions between movies that are open in QuickTime Player, assign a target name or ID using Plug-in Helper. For example, to use Remotecontrol.mov on another movie outside of a browser, open a target movie in Plug-in Helper and enter MOVIENAME="Remotely-controlled" in the Plug-in Settings pane. Open the target movie and the controller movie in two QuickTime Player windows, and you can use one movie to control the other.

Tip To disable the normal controller of a target movie in QuickTime Player, set the movie's controller to None using QuickTime Player's Properties window. To hide the controller, but leave the keyboard controls enabled, give the movie a media skin instead.

The MOVIEID parameter works like the MOVIENAME parameter, but it takes a number as a value instead of a name. This allows you to target one movie out of a selection of possible targets based on a calculation, or simply to use a number to identify a movie rather than a name.

Internet Communication

For another nifty example of a small QuickTime movie acting as a cross-platform Internet application, fire up Michael Shaff's Chatter.mov, in the Interactive folder on the CD. Yup, real-time chat, over the Internet, can be a feature of your QuickTime movies.

Last Blast

For a fine example of a wired sprite controller for multiple movies, look at Visit.htm in the Interactive folder of the CD. It's a VR tour with a selection of sound tracks, contributed by Erik Fohlin, Barsark AB (www.barsark.com/), and it's *hot*.

The controls in Visit.htm are labeled in the following illustration.

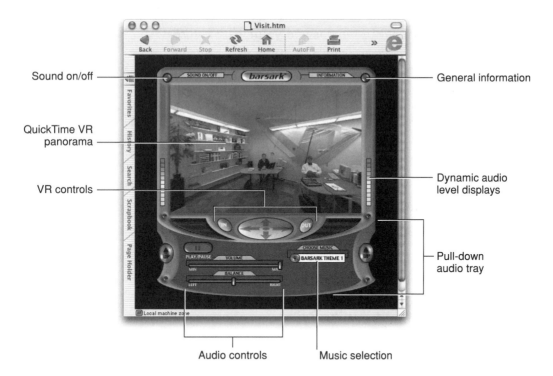

Sound on/off

QuickTime VR panorama

VR controls

General information

Dynamic audio level displays

Pull-down audio tray

Audio controls   Music selection

Ready for something really mind-blowing? This was state-of-the-art for *QuickTime 4*. For a look at something along the same lines, but combining streaming MPEG-4, wired sprites, QuickTime media skins, and cubic VR, search the Web for Superfluid's Nightfall at the Crashsite (Google: super-fluid nightfall).

How Can I Learn to Do This Stuff?

The creator of some of the more amazing QuickTime interactive movies ever made is Matthew Peterson. He's written a book, *Interactive Quick-Time—Authoring Wired Media* (Morgan Kaufmann Publishers), that will take you through it, step by step. And blow your mind in the process.

Interactive Audio

Interactive audio can take many forms—sprite-based sound controls for volume and balance, a sound effect when the cursor rolls over an object, a noise when a sprite bounces, a musical fanfare when someone completes a puzzle, even a mixing board that allows the user to enable and disable tracks, change tempos and volumes, and create audio loops. All these things can be accomplished using wired sprites.

There are four ways to create interactive audio with wired sprites:

- You can use sprites to enable, disable, and set the volume of audio tracks.
- You can use intermovie communication to control audio movies.
- You can use audio movie tracks with independent time bases.
- You can use the QuickTime Music Architecture to play MIDI notes and digital samples.

Note You can also create interactive audio using Flash, as described in "Shocking Behavior with Flash Tracks" (page 522), or by using JavaScript, as described in "QuickTime and JavaScript" (page 534).

Controlling Audio Tracks

You can get some interactive audio effects by controlling a movie's audio tracks using wired sprites.

You adjust the sound volume for a movie, or turn the sound on and off, using the SetVolume action, and you adjust the volume and balance of individual audio tracks, and turn them on or off, using the SetVolume, Set-Balance, and SetEnabled actions. For an example of a movie with wired sprite audio controls, point your browser at Wiredaudio.mov, in the Interactive folder of the CD.

The problem with creating interactive audio this way is that audio tracks are synchronized to the movie time base, so while you can fade the sound up or down, or toggle it off and on, you can't start it at a particular point except by going to that point in the movie timeline. Since all the tracks in the movie share the same timeline, they all jump to that point.

Sometimes that's not an important limitation; if you're just adding some audio controls to a movie, it's fine. But if you want to play a "boink" sound when a sprite bounces, or play a note when someone clicks a sprite-based keyboard, or play looping audio track that you can trigger interactively, you need to use another technique.

Using Intermovie Communication

Creating interactive audio using intermovie communication is very powerful and fairly straightforward:

1. Put each sound effect, piece of music, digital sample, or loop in a separate movie.

2. Assign each movie a name or an ID, either as part of the <EMBED> tag, part of a SMIL media tag, or using Plug-in Helper. For details, see "Intermovie Communication" (page 513).

3. Create a wired sprite movie that controls the audio movies using actions such as Start, Stop, GoToTime, SetRate, SetVolume, SetLooping, and PlaySelection, targeting the actions to particular movies using movie names or IDs.

4. Embed the audio movies and the wired sprite movie in the same Web page (the audio movies can be hidden or in another frame).

That's it. You can wire a sprite to trigger on a mouse-over or mouse click, an event such as a bounce or completion of a puzzle, or the position and state of sprite-based controls such as sliders and knobs.

Because the sounds are in separate movies, they each have their own time base. They can be started, stopped, looped, or sent to the beginning independently. By setting each movie's playback rate, you can even adjust their tempos independently. The audio movies can be pretty much any kind of audio: MIDI, MP3, QDesign or Qualcomm compressed sound—you name it.

For examples of Web pages with multiple audio movies, drop by Mouse-Jam (www.mousejam.com).

The main limitation of this approach to interactive audio is that it involves multiple files, which is an ongoing housekeeping chore. One of the nice things about it is that it decouples the audio from the sprites—it's easy to modify your controller movie to use different audio movies, and it's easy to use the controller movie in another Web page.

Getting multiple movies to open simultaneously in a browser window is no problem, and the audio movies can be hidden so they're transparent to the viewer.

To open multiple movies simultaneously in QuickTime Player, on the other hand, is not so easy. The user selects whether new movies are opened in a new window (hence, multiple movies) or in the current window (one movie open at any time). You need to enlist the viewer's cooperation to display multiple movies, and this tends to be clumsy. A better solution, in most cases, is to use movie tracks with independent time bases.

Movie Tracks with Independent Time Bases

In the movies we've looked at so far, all the nonstreaming tracks are synchronized to a common timeline. To make an audio track loop, you have to loop the whole movie. Starting with QuickTime 4, a movie can contain something called movie tracks. A movie track is basically a reference to another movie, but you can set its start time, duration, and visual layer with respect to the other tracks in the parent movie.

This is often called Movie-in-a-Movie. The child movie can be slaved to the parent movie's timeline, so that pausing or jumping ahead in the parent movie acts on the child as well, or it can have an independent timeline, allowing it to start, stop, or loop independently.

You can add wired sprite actions to the parent movie to control a child movie. The techniques are the same as for intermovie communication, as described in "Intermovie Communication" (page 513), but the syntax is slightly different because you're targeting a track in the same movie.

This lets you create looping background music or sounds that play in response to events. For example, your movie could be a still image of a mixer, with sliders and buttons made using wired sprites to control a series of audio-only movie tracks—starting and stopping them, controlling their volume and balance, or setting them to loop.

You can also load a new child movie into a movie track as a wired action. This lets you dynamically select a sound track or a video, for example, downloading only what the user wants, while providing a continuous player environment of your own design, which can continue to play other media while the new movie downloads.

Like intermovie communication, this involves extra housekeeping—you have to keep track of multiple movies and either point to them using absolute URLs or move them all together as a group. LiveStage Pro will let you embed small child movies into a parent movie file, but these child movies are loaded into RAM as part of the movie header, so this isn't usually a good idea—it's OK for text or MIDI, but you could easily run out of memory loading an MP3.

Unlike intermovie communication, movie-in-a-movie gives you a single parent movie that will play in QuickTime Player, or any other QuickTime-aware application, such as Acrobat or PowerPoint. It also uses a single <EMBED> tag in your HTML.

To create a movie track with an independent time base in LiveStage Pro, select Movie Track from the Track menu and uncheck the Time checkbox under the "Take from parent:" heading, then enter the URL of a movie in the Movies box as your default child movie.

Using QuickTime Music Architecture

Another way to create interactive audio in a wired sprite movie is to use the QuickTime Music Architecture, which is basically a superset of MIDI. QuickTime comes with dozens of built-in musical instrument sounds, including drums, woodwinds, brass, strings, piano, electric guitar, whole ensembles, and sound effects like gunshots and applause.

You can assign any of these instruments to play a note, or a series of notes, using the QuickTime Music Architecture. You can specify the pitch, duration, and volume of each note.

You can also assign a MIDI-style control, or multiple controls, to an instrument to give it pitch bend, reverb, and other characteristics.

You accomplish these things by attaching the PlayNote and SetController actions to wired sprites. This requires almost no bandwidth—the instruments and controls are built into QuickTime; your wired sprites just provide the score.

And you aren't limited to the built-in musical instruments and sound effects, versatile as they are. You can add digital audio samples as custom instruments. This currently has some tight limitations: The samples can't be larger than 256 Kbytes, they can't be compressed, and they must be in .sfil format (you can open any audio in QuickTime Player and export it as an uncompressed System 7 Sound File). They're great for short bits of recorded speech or textured sound, though. The movie Katy.mov (see page 513) uses this technique. And because the sound samples are instruments, you can modify them by using different pitches, durations, reverb, and so on.

Adding a lot of custom instruments can rapidly swell the file size of your movie, so you need to use them sparingly, at least over the Internet. You can also create new instruments by adding a Sound Forge or DLS2 sound font to your QuickTime Extensions folder as described in "Getting the Most Out of MIDI" (page 195). This won't swell the file size because it isn't embedded in the movie. That's a mixed blessing because it means your listener needs to have the same sound font installed in order to hear the music as you do.

For examples of movies that use QuickTime Music Architecture and custom instruments, see mousejamqt4.mov (in the Interactive folder of the CD). It's wild.

It was created by James Bisset of Mediachrome (www.mediachrome.com), for Mouse Jam (www.mousejam.com), and contributed by Clifford P. Walker.

Other examples include Katy.mov, Cruiseline.mov, and Nav.mov, all in the Interactive folder of the CD.

More Wired Sprite Examples

We haven't shown you a tenth of the things you can do with wired sprites, but I hope it's at least fired your imagination.

For more wired sprite example movies and projects, drop by the Live-Stage site at www.totallyhip.com.

Definitely check it out.

▶ Shocking Behavior with Flash Tracks

Flash and QuickTime make a powerful combination. Flash is a cross-platform authoring tool that creates low-bandwidth vector animations. For an introduction to Flash animation and QuickTime, see "Flash Vectors" (page 471) and "Flash Sprites" (page 481) in Chapter 15, "An Animated Approach."

Note You can also create QuickTime-compatible Flash .swf files using authoring programs such as LiveMotion (which also supports Flash actions and ActionScript).

QuickTime 6 and later supports the full Flash 5 feature set, including editable text fields, XML data exchange, a greatly expanded set of actions, and simple rendering of HTML text. You can bring all these features into QuickTime by importing a Flash track.

Mouse Capture Property

One thing to keep in mind when adding layers of interactive media is that layers on top can block access to layers below. In general, events such as a mouse click are sent down through a cascade of possible receivers; most ignore the event or act on it and pass it along. Others act on it and mark it as processed—no one further down the cascade sees the event.

Flash 5 and later can contain actions and scripts that use the mouse position and mouse-click events without passing them on. Most of these actions take place only if the mouse is over an active element in the Flash track, so no harm is done, but some Flash actions use up mouse events that are over any part of the Flash track, which prevents the mouse events from passing through transparent areas to reach underlying media.

Flash tracks have a new Properties menu choice in the Movie Properties window of QuickTime Player. You can set or unset the Mouse Capture property to obtain the best behavior for your movie. In some cases, you may need to change the size of the Flash track and/or move other interactive elements so the two do not overlap.

Interactive Audio and Video

Flash offers another way to add interactive audio and animations to Quick-Time. You can create what Flash calls a "movie" inside a Flash animation—basically a track with its own time base. Flash sprites can be programmed to respond to mouse clicks by playing these movie tracks, which can contain animation or sound. You can bring these behaviors into QuickTime by importing the Flash file. Here's how:

1. Save your Flash file as a Flash 5 .swf file.

Note   Flash and QuickTime are built by separate companies on independent schedules, so Flash 6 supports the QuickTime 5 feature set, and QuickTime 6 supports the Flash 5 file format. Presumably, they will continue to develop in a complementary fashion.

2. Open the .swf file in QuickTime Player. This creates a QuickTime movie with a Flash track.

3. By default, QuickTime opens .swf files in Play All Frames mode. You need to uncheck the Play All Frames command in the Movie menu to hear the audio.

4. By default, QuickTime also opens .swf files with no movie controller. If you want to composite the Flash track with other QuickTime tracks, you need to give the movie a controller—open the Movie Properties window, choose Controller from the right pop-up menu, and select the Movie Controller.

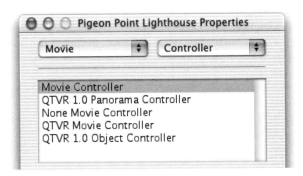

5. You can now add and composite other QuickTime tracks in the normal manner. If you don't want the movie to have a controller, use the Properties window to select None Movie Controller when you're done editing.

6. Save as a self-contained movie with the .mov file extension.

The movie can now be played using QuickTime Player or the QuickTime plug-in.

If you're coming to QuickTime from a Flash background, there are a few things it might help to keep in mind when mixing the two formats. Flash has a fixed frame rate and does things in terms of frames. At 15 fps, the 16th frame is synonymous with time 00:01. QuickTime has samples instead of frames, and every sample can have a different duration, so time and frame count are independent. If you want to go to time 00:01, you go to a time, not a frame.

When you add a Flash track to a movie, your frames are imported as samples, each with the same duration. If you use Add Scaled, you have the same number of frames, but each frame's duration is scaled to its portion of the new track duration.

Flash Movie Controllers

Flash sprites can trigger actions that affect the whole movie in response to mouse clicks. These actions include the basic movie controller functions: Start, Stop, GoToBeginning, GoToEnd, and GoToTime.

You can create a Flash file with sprites that trigger these actions, import the file into QuickTime as a Flash track, and use the Flash track to control the movie. The steps are essentially the same as for importing any Flash track into QuickTime, but you normally use the Add Scaled command in QuickTime Player to give the controls the same duration as the rest of the movie, and you typically set the Flash track's graphics mode to Transparent or Straight Alpha so it overlays your other video tracks. For more about setting graphics modes, see "Transparency and Alpha Channels" (page 271).

Flash Text

Flash text is similar in many ways to a QuickTime text track. Text is stored as text, with font information, and is rendered to video when the movie is played, not when it's created. This has the drawback of not rendering as expected if the viewer doesn't have the chosen font installed.

Flash 5 has the ability to embed fonts in the file—that works well across platforms, but not perfectly. And of course it adds to the file size.

Unlike QuickTime, Flash doesn't offer the option of pre-rendering the text and sending it as video. Instead, you have the option of "breaking up" the text into vectors and sending it as a drawing. Like rendering to video, this eats up file space and bandwidth, but in many cases using vectors is more efficient than rendering to video. And vectors invariably look sharper and scale better than video text. In addition, vector text can be easily manipulated by rotation, skewing, and using a Bezier curve for a baseline. You can get some nifty effects. These features can be a compelling reason to use Flash text in a QuickTime movie.

Flash also has editable text fields. Starting with QuickTime 5, these can be imported into QuickTime movies, where they work as expected.

Another nice feature of Flash tracks is that Flash 5 supports simple rendering of HTML text. This allows you to display simple Web pages inside QuickTime movies, simply by adding a Flash track.

Extending Flash Interactivity

Currently, only a handful of Flash actions act directly on QuickTime when imported. The rest can be used only to modify the Flash track itself. This is because there is currently no way to "target" QuickTime media from a Flash action (except for the "Movie" target). You can either make use of the sprite actions available directly in Flash, add QuickTime wired actions to Flash using LiveStage Pro, or combine the two.

There's a trial version of LiveStage Pro, including tutorials and PDF documentation, in the Demos folder of the CD. You can import Flash files into LiveStage Pro and wire them using hundreds of prebuilt actions and behaviors, or create custom behaviors using QScript. It's really sweet. You can also use the LiveStage Pro editor to composite the Flash media with other QuickTime media types, including live streams.

▶ Skinning the Cat (But in a Good Way)

You can completely customize the appearance and user interface of a movie in QuickTime Player by adding a media skin. A media skin specifies the size and shape of the window that your movie is displayed in, and it specifies what parts of your movie are visible. It also specifies which parts of the window can be used to drag the window around on the desktop.

This is radically different from the kind of skins you've seen on other media players, and from the point of view of someone distributing movies over the Web, it's much better. A conventional skin is something the end-user puts on a player, and it usually just pastes a different image over the existing window and controls. It's fun for users, but your movie may look ridiculous in a leopard-print player application with zebra-head buttons . . . well okay, it *will* look ridiculous.

QuickTime media skins are part of the movie. *You* decide what the player application should look like when it plays your movie. The player window can be any size or shape you like. It can look like anything you want—sure, it can look like a space-age plastic appliance, but it can also look like a shimmering disc, a flaming pillar, a column of scrolling text, a translucent sheet of glass, or nothing at all.

It can look like anything that QuickTime can display. Because the media skin just defines the shape of the window—the visible "player" is actually part of your movie!

QuickTime Player becomes invisible when a media skin is applied. No controls are displayed. The keyboard equivalents still work—the Space bar starts and stops a movie, the Shift and Control keys zoom a VR panorama. But there are no visible controls, except the ones you add using Flash or wired sprites. (There are some wired controllers in the Demos folder of the CD, for VR and regular movies, that you're free to use.) If you prefer, your movie can autoplay with no controls at all.

You can use a media skin to mask the rectangular nature of your movie, giving it rounded corners, or even making it completely circular.

Any part of your movie can be designated as the "frame" that lets you drag the movie window around—it doesn't have to be an actual frame around your video. In fact, the window doesn't have to be draggable at all, or you can let viewers use any part of the movie to drag the window. It's up to you.

Normally, you'll want to make the window draggable for the viewer's convenience, and you'll want to make it visually obvious what parts can be used to drag. You'll also want to mark the interactive parts of your movie—such as VR panoramas and sprite buttons—as *not* draggable, so clicking a button or dragging a panorama does what it should, instead of moving the window.

For a silly but instructive example, take a look at FireOval.mov in the Interactive folder of the CD. Its window is made of two disconnected ovals—one containing motion video and the other a bowl of fire. The fire is draggable. There are no visible controls. This isn't a practical movie player

—it's just there to allay any preconceptions you might have about what a "skin" is. This is really something different.

For an example that's more beautiful and practical, see Hardrock Casino.mov in the Interactive folder of the CD. (Credit where it's due: HardRockCasino was created by Michael Shaff, Janie Fitzgerald, and Robert West using Totally Hip Software's LiveStage Pro 3.)

As you can see, media skins give you a powerful ability to brand your movies. The more often people copy a movie in a branded media skin, the happier the brand's owner is.

Creating Media Skins

There are three main steps in making a movie with a media skin:

- create a movie with the desired elements placed where you want them
- create the window masks
- import the masks into your movie as a media skin

Let's step through the whole process in detail.

Your movie might have no visible frame, or the frame might be motion video, a special effect, or any QuickTime media. For this example, though, we'll use a conventional still image.

Create Your Movie (Skin and All)

1. Create an image of your new player application (the visible "skin") using a graphics program, or perhaps scan in a photo of an actual device. Save in the compression format you want to use over the Web, such as JPEG.

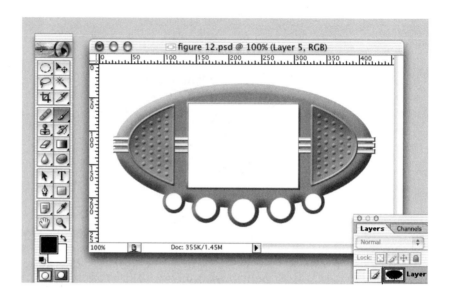

2. Open this image in QuickTime Player and add it to an existing movie as a background:

   ■ Select All. Copy. Close (don't save).

   ■ Click existing movie. Select All. Add Scaled.

   ■ Get Movie Properties. Choose last Video track.

   ■ Move to background using Layer menu.

   ■ Reposition elements using Size menu.

   ■ Make areas transparent or translucent using Graphics Mode menu.

   The new player image is now positioned with respect to your other movie content.

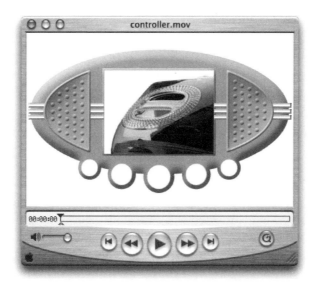

Note   If your movie is a VR panorama, you need to change the movie's controller from the VR Controller to the Movie Controller in order to add a background. For details, see Chapter 19, "Let's Get Virtual."

3. Add any Flash or wired sprite controls, just as you added the background image (but without putting the controls in a background layer).

Your movie should now look and act pretty much the way you want except that it's playing inside of QuickTime Player. Next you need to create masks to hide the QuickTime Player interface (and the areas of your movie that you don't want to display).

Draw the Masks

4. Create a white image the size and shape of your movie rectangle, with black areas in the size, shape, and position of your desired window. The image should be black where you want your window, and white elsewhere. The image can be a BMP, GIF, PICT, or any other format that QuickTime understands. Let's call this WinMask.pct. The black areas don't have to be connected—you can mask out any part of your movie by painting it white.

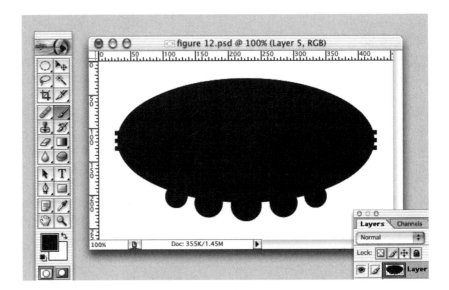

Tip To make things easier, click in the display area of your movie, Select None, and Copy. In Photoshop, select New—Photoshop will create the right-sized image by default. Paste. You now have a pixel-perfect drawing of your movie in Photoshop. Create a new layer and cover the parts of your movie that you want to show in black. When you're done, select the rest of the layer and fill it with white. Flatten the image and save, or save the mask layer alone.

5. Create a second mask image the size and shape of the draggable part of your window. Usually, this is the same as your first mask, with white areas where your video and controls go. Again, this should be saved as a

black-and-white image in a format that QuickTime can display. Let's call this `DragMask.pct`.

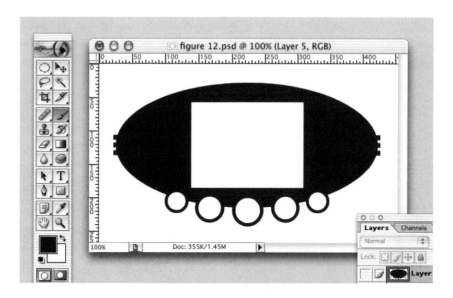

Tip Any part of your movie can be made into a draggable region. However, tracks that respond to mouse events, such as VR panoramas or wired sprites, should not be covered by a drag mask—the drag behavior prevents mouse events from reaching underlying tracks.

Now you're ready to add the media skin to your movie. You can do this using LiveStage Pro 3, AppleScript, or a text editor and QuickTime Player.

Important Media skins can't currently be edited after they're added to a movie, so do all your compression and prep work first. Add a media skin as the last step.

Importing the Masks (Puttin' on the Skin)

One way to skin your movie is to use a text editor and QuickTime Player.

6. Using a text editor, create a seven-line text file that looks like this:

```
<?xml version="1.0"?>
<?quicktime type="application/x-qtskin"?>
<skin>
    <movie src="Framed.mov"/>
    <contentregion src="WinMask.pct"/>
    <dragregion src="DragMask.pct"/>
</skin>
```

The first three lines, and the last line, are always the same. Modify the middle three to point to your movie. Put the name of your movie file in the src parameter, the name of your window mask in the contentregion parameter, and the name of the drag mask in the dragregion parameter.

7. Save as plain text, *but with the* .mov *file extension.* This text is a special kind of movie that QuickTime's XML importer understands. Call it Skin.mov.

8. Open Skin.mov using QuickTime Player. Your movie should open on the desktop in a custom window. Save as a self-contained movie. Let's call it Finished.mov.

Important Be sure to *save as a self-contained movie*, and distribute the self-contained version, *not* the XML text file. The XML text file is dependent on external files—it won't run locally unless the source movie and masks travel with it, and a link to its URL will not fast start over the Internet. The self-contained version will fast start.

Misalignment Problems

You may find that the mask is offset from the rest of your movie, cutting part of the movie off and creating a gray border on the opposite side.

⬇Warning Dragging the window with a misaligned skin may cause QuickTime Player to crash under some circumstances. Don't do it.

You can correct the misalignment, as I'll explain in a moment, but you can also prevent it if you understand why it happens. It's like this.

When you add a track to your movie, it's aligned with the upper left corner of the original movie, also known as the 0,0 point. If you use the Size function in the Movie Properties window to move or stretch a track up or to the left, beyond the 0,0 point, the upper left corner of the bounding box moves to match, but the 0,0 point does *not* move, and any new track will be added aligned with the *old* upper left corner, not the new one.

Similarly, moving *all* the visual tracks down or to the right causes the upper left corner to follow—again, the bounding box of the movie changes, but not the 0,0 point.

When you apply the skin masks to your movie, they are added like any other tracks—at the 0,0 point. Unlike other tracks, however, you can't use the Size function to move a skin track—it must remain aligned with the 0,0 point. You can still fix the problem using the Size function—you just have to move all the other tracks instead.

That can be a pain, so it's best not to get in this situation in the first place. When building a movie, leave the upper leftmost element anchored at the 0,0 point—stretch it from the lower right corner if it needs to be larger or smaller, and move any other elements down or to the right, relative to the anchor, as needed.

Tip Clicking the Normal button in the Size panel aligns a track with the 0,0 point instantly. If the Normal button is grayed out, the track is already aligned.

Distributing Your Skinned Movie

You can now put your finished movie on a CD, email it to a friend, or embed a link to it in a Web page. If you use a Web page, you need to target QuickTime Player, not the plug-in. You can target a link to open your movie in QuickTime Player using the <EMBED> tag. For example:

```
<EMBED SRC="poster.qtif" TYPE="image/x-quicktime" HEIGHT=120 WIDTH=160
  HREF="Finished.mov" TARGET=
  "quicktimeplayer" >
```

This tag embeds a QuickTime image file named poster.qtif in a Web page. If the viewer clicks the poster, QuickTime launches Finished.mov using the QuickTime Player application.

To launch Finished.mov automatically, without the viewer clicking anything, just add AUTOHREF="true" to the <EMBED> tag.

Here's an example with AUTOHREF turned on, wrapped in an <OBJECT> tag-set that specifies the QuickTime ActiveX control:

```
<OBJECT HEIGHT="120" WIDTH="160"
  CLASSID="clsid:02BF25D5-8C17-4B23-BC80-D3488ABDDC6B"
  CODEBASE="http://www.apple.com/qtactivex/qtplugin.cab">
```

```
<PARAM NAME="src" VALUE="poster.qtif">
<PARAM NAME="href" VALUE="Finished.mov">
<PARAM NAME="target" VALUE="quicktimeplayer">
<PARAM NAME="autohref" VALUE="true">

<EMBED HEIGHT=120 WIDTH=160
  SRC="poster.qtif" TYPE="image/x-quicktime"
  HREF="Finished.mov" TARGET="quicktimeplayer"
  AUTOHREF="True">
</EMBED>
</OBJECT>
```

Limitations

Versions of QuickTime prior to 5.01 cannot play movies that have media skins. This includes QuickTime 5.0, which originally shipped with Mac OS X, and QuickTime 5 RT, which shipped with some real-time effects boards for the Macintosh (all versions of QuickTime 5 or later for Windows support media skins).

The QuickTime plug-in can play a movie that has a media skin, but does not currently use the masks—the movie looks just as it did before the masks were applied. At this writing, most other QuickTime-aware applications behave similarly—they can play skinned movies but don't mask the movie or hide the controls.

Currently, a movie can have only one skin track. You cannot dynamically enable or disable skin tracks. The skin track's masks are stored in the movie file as PICTs with 1-bit pixel depth and cannot be changed. You cannot add new tracks to a movie once a media skin has been applied. The visible skin can be animated, but the actual shape of the window cannot change as the movie plays.

▶ QuickTime and JavaScript

QuickTime and JavaScript can communicate in both directions. You can wire a QuickTime movie to execute JavaScript functions—either automatically or in response to user actions—and you can use JavaScript to control and modify QuickTime movies.

Executing JavaScript Functions from Movies

You can execute a JavaScript function from QuickTime by passing a function name—rather than a URL—in the HREF or QTNEXT parameters, or as part of an HREF track, a VR hotspot, a wired sprite GoToURL action, or almost anywhere that QuickTime generates a URL (the exception is the QTSRC parameter in the <EMBED> tag, which must be something that QuickTime can play).

For example, you can execute a JavaScript function in response to a mouse click in a QuickTime movie by using the HREF parameter. Define the JavaScript function in the <HEAD> section of your HTML, and pass the function name in the HREF parameter of the <EMBED> tag:

```
<EMBED SRC="my.mov" WIDTH=320 HEIGHT=256
  HREF="FunctionName(parameters)">
```

When someone clicks in the display area of the movie, the QuickTime plug-in passes the function name and parameters to the browser for execution, just as it would pass a URL.

You can use the optional TARGET parameter in a QuickTime URL, but the special targets quicktimeplayer and myself cannot be used. The target must be a frame or a window. For example:

```
<EMBED SRC="my.mov" WIDTH=320 HEIGHT=256
  HREF="LoadMovieScript('NewMovie.mov')" TARGET="_parent">
```

You can also execute JavaScript code from a QuickTime URL by preceding it with "Javascript:". For example:

```
<EMBED SRC="my.mov" WIDTH=320 HEIGHT=256
  HREF="Javascript:alert('Hello World');" >
```

Note A bug in Internet Explorer 4.5 for the Mac caused it to ignore Javascript: URLs. This was fixed in version 5.

You can automatically execute JavaScript functions while a movie plays by putting them in an HREF track. The syntax is

```
A<Javascript:Function(parameters)> T<target>
```

For details, see "HREF Tracks" (page 394).

You can also execute JavaScript functions as the result of user actions and calculations, by using a wired sprite URL function and a Javascript: URL—the exact syntax varies, depending on what authoring tool you use. Here are the three most common:

In Flash, use the Action tab to assign a GetURL function to a button or key frame, and set the target attribute by setting the Window parameter.

In GoLive, click a sprite key frame in the Timeline window, then click the Actions tab in the Properties inspector, choose an event from the list, such as a mouse click, and click the + button to attach an action—in this case GoToURL.

In LiveStage, click the Tracks tab in the Project window, then double-click a sprite sample to open the Properties window. Click the Script Editor, choose an event handler from the list, such as Mouse Click, and type

```
GoToURL("<javascript:Function(paramaters)>T<target>")
```

Browser Support for JavaScript Control of QuickTime

The QuickTime plug-in has been scriptable since QuickTime 4, but was limited to Netscape browsers and those that used the Netscape methods of communicating between JavaScript and plug-ins, such as OmniWeb and Mozilla. Starting with QuickTime 6, you can control the QuickTime ActiveX control using JavaScript in Internet Explorer for Windows as well.

This means that QuickTime can be controlled by JavaScript from any common Windows browser, as well as Netscape, OmniWeb, and most other Mac OS browsers.

There are two notable exceptions. The public beta version Apple's Safari browser does not yet support JavaScript control of QuickTime. This is expected to change in the near future, probably by the time you read this book. Internet Explorer for Mac OS, on the other hand, doesn't allow Java-Script to communicate with plug-ins at all. This is *not* expected to change in the near future.

Note Technically, you can control QuickTime using JavaScript from any browser that supports any of the COM, XPCOM, or LiveScript interfaces.

You can detect Internet Explorer for the Mac as a special case, and either implement a workaround, go to an alternate page, or suggest that the visitor come back using a browser that supports JavaScript control of plug-ins.

Workaround for Internet Explorer for the Mac

There is a workaround that you can use to at least play and stop movies using JavaScript in Internet Explorer for the Mac. The workaround is to embed each QuickTime movie in its own HTML page (with AUTOPLAY=True) and use JavaScript to play movies simply by loading the appropriate page.

You can use a frameset and have JavaScript load the page in a dedicated QuickTime frame. Alternately, you can have JavaScript open the page in a new window (or an existing window). Either way, the page can load in a nearly invisible 2-pixel-by-2-pixel dot (useful for hidden audio movies), or in its own display area.

For examples of playing QuickTime movies this way, see "Targeting a Frame or a Window" (page 116) and "Creating a Window with JavaScript" (page 120).

The HTML page for each movie can be quite small—just the head, title, body, and embed tags, if you like. Here's an example:

```
<html>
  <head>
  <title>Audio Movie</title>
  </head>

  <body>
    <EMBED SRC=bullet1.mov HEIGHT=2 WIDTH=2
      HIDDEN=True AUTOPLAY=True >
  </body>
</html>
```

To play the movie, have your JavaScript load the HTML page.

To stop the movie, load another HTML page in the same frame or window (it can be a blank page), or close the window.

This technique causes the movie to load each time it is played, but you can make it more responsive by loading the movie in the browser cache ahead of time. To load the movie into the browser cache, load a version of the HTML page with AUTOPLAY=False in the <EMBED> tag.

Playing a new movie automatically stops the old one if you target the same frame or window.

Controlling Movies from JavaScript

There are a lot of ways to control QuickTime movies from JavaScript. This section will give you a quick overview, then show you how to set things up and provide some examples. A complete reference for QuickTime's Java-Script methods follows.

Overview

You can use JavaScript functions to dynamically control most things that can be set by parameters in the <EMBED> tag, such as LOOP and AUTOPLAY. You can also use JavaScript to perform most of the actions that wired sprites can perform, such as enabling tracks or changing the properties of a sprite. In addition, you can use JavaScript to get information about movies, tracks, sprites, and QuickTime itself (the version of QuickTime on the viewer's computer, for example).

Unlike <EMBED> tag parameters, JavaScript control is dynamic. Instead of simply setting AUTOPLAY="True" or AUTOPLAY="False," for example, you can play a movie in response to a rollover event. Similarly, you can use Java-Script to turn a movie's sound volume up, down, or off, make a movie loop, or replace it with another movie.

You can use JavaScript to modify a movie in ways that might otherwise require an editing session with QuickTime Player; you can enable and disable tracks, change the movie's language, or change a video track's size, position, and rotation. And again, you can do these things dynamically as the movie plays.

You can even reach inside a movie with JavaScript and change it in ways that are impossible with QuickTime Player. You can set the movie playing backward in slow motion, for example, or set a sprite's appearance or behavior.

You can use JavaScript to get quite a bit of information from QuickTime, such as how long a movie is, how much of it has been downloaded, whether it's playing, whether it's finished, how many tracks it has, or what version of the plug-in is installed.

To get the *most* out of JavaScript and QuickTime, you need to be a pretty accomplished JavaScript programmer. But don't despair if you're not; you can do a lot with a few simple JavaScript functions.

We'll show you how to do some obvious and some not-so-obvious things with cut-and-paste examples. We'll also list the full set of JavaScript methods you can use to control and communicate with QuickTime.

Setting Up

There are a few things you need to do any time you want to control a QuickTime movie from JavaScript.

The first thing you need to do is add the ENABLEJAVASCRIPT parameter to the movie's <EMBED> command. You should also assign a name to the movie (using the NAME parameter, *not* the MOVIENAME parameter):

```
<EMBED SRC="my.mov" HEIGHT="256" WIDTH="320"
   ENABLEJAVASCRIPT="True" NAME="Movie1" >
```

Note Many JavaScript methods for controlling QuickTime use the same values as parameters that can be passed in the <EMBED> tag. If an equivalent <EMBED> tag parameter is listed, you can get more details from the "Complete List of QuickTime Plug-in Parameters" (page 69).

Example: Playing and Stopping QuickTime Movies

This example shows three different techniques for playing and stopping QuickTime movies from JavaScript. You can use these techniques to invoke any QuickTime JavaScript method on a given movie.

The example Web page opens two QuickTime movies and accesses their Play() and Stop() methods three different ways:

- by passing the movie object, referenced by the NAME parameter of the <EMBED> tag, to a JavaScript function in the same Web page
- by calling the movie directly and invoking a method on it, again identifying the movie by referring to its NAME parameter
- by calling the movie directly, this time identifying it as an element in an array (JavaScript maintains an array of all objects embedded in a Web page)

```
<html>
<head>
   <title>Very Simple QT Movie test</title>
</head>

<script language ="JavaScript">
<!--
   function PlayIt(anObj)
   { anObj.Play(); }

   function StopIt(anObj)
   { anObj.Stop(); }
//-->
</script>
```

```
<body bgcolor="#ffffff">

<P>
This movie is named "movie1":
    <EMBED NAME="movie1" SRC="First.mov" WIDTH="180"
    HEIGHT="160"
    AUTOPLAY="False" ENABLEJAVASCRIPT="True">
<P>
This movie is named "movie2":
    <EMBED NAME="movie2" SRC="Second.mov" WIDTH="180"
    HEIGHT="160"
    AUTOPLAY="False" ENABLEJAVASCRIPT="True">
<P>
Calling a JavaScript function that takes an object referenced by
  name<br>
    <a href="javascript:PlayIt(document.movie1);">Play 1</a><br>
    <a href="javascript:StopIt(document.movie1);">Stop 1</a><br>
    <a href="javascript:PlayIt(document.movie2);">Play 2</a><br>
    <a href="javascript:StopIt(document.movie2);">Stop 2</a><br>
<P>
Calling an object method directly (referenced by name)<br>
    <a href="javascript:document.movie1.Play();">Play 1</a><br>
    <a href="javascript:document.movie1.Stop();">Stop 1</a><br>
    <a href="javascript:document.movie2.Play();">Play 2</a><br>
    <a href="javascript:document.movie2.Stop();">Stop 2</a><br>
<P>
Calling an object directly (by index in the document.
  embeds array)<br>
    <a href="javascript:document.embeds[0].Play();">Play 1</a><br>
    <a href="javascript:document.embeds[0].Stop();">Stop 1</a><br>
    <a href="javascript:document.embeds[1].Play();">Play 2</a><br>
    <a href="javascript:document.embeds[1].Stop();">Stop 2</a><br>
<P>
Calling an object directly (in the document.embeds array by name)<br>
    <a href="javascript:document.embeds['movie1'].Play();">Play 1
    </a><br>
    <a href="javascript:document.embeds['movie1'].Stop();">
    Stop 1</a><br>
    <a href="javascript:document.embeds['movie2'].Play();">
    Play 2</a><br>
    <a href="javascript:document.embeds['movie2'].Stop();">
```

```
    Stop 2</a><br>
</body>
</html>
```

QuickTime JavaScript Methods

This section contains a summary of all the JavaScript methods that you can invoke on a QuickTime movie object.

QuickTime Properties

- `string GetQuickTimeVersion()`

  Returns the version of QuickTime.

- `string GetQuickTimeLanguage()`

  Returns the user's QuickTime language (set with the plug-in's Set Language dialog box).

- `int GetQuickTimeConnectionSpeed()`

  Returns the connection speed setting from the user's QuickTime preferences.

- `boolean GetIsQuickTimeRegistered()`

  Returns `true` if the user has the pro version of QuickTime, `false` otherwise.

- `string GetComponentVersion(string type, string subType, string manufacturer)`

  Returns the version of a specific QuickTime component. The component is specified using a four-character string for the type, subtype, and manufacturer. For example, to check the version of Apple's JPEG graphics importer call

  `GetComponentVersion('grip','JPEG','appl')`

  The value 0 is a wildcard for any field. If the component is not available, 0.0 is returned.

Plug-in Properties

- `string GetPluginVersion()`

  Returns the version of the QuickTime plug-in.

- `string GetPluginStatus()`

  Returns a string with the status of the current movie. Possible states are

  - `Waiting`— waiting for the movie data stream to begin
  - `Loading`—data stream has begun, not able to play the movie yet
  - `Playable`—movie is playable, but not all data has been downloaded
  - `Complete`— all data has been downloaded
  - `Error:nnnn`—the movie failed with the specified error number

- `boolean GetResetPropertiesOnReload()`
  `void SetResetPropertiesOnReload(boolean reset)`

  Get and set the reset property, which determines whether plug-in parameters, such as `CONTROLLER`, `AUTOPLAY`, and `VOLUME`, return to their default values when a new movie is loaded. By default, plug-in parameters are reset when a new movie is loaded. Use the set function to make parameters persistent across movies.

Movie Commands

- `void Play()`

  Plays a movie, starting at the current movie time.

- `void Stop()`

  Stops a movie.

- `void Rewind()`

  Sets a movie's current time to its start time and pauses the movie.

- `void Step(int count)`

  Steps a movie forward or backward the specified number of frames and pauses the movie.

Movie Properties

- `boolean GetAutoPlay()`
  `void SetAutoPlay(boolean autoPlay)`

  Get and set whether a movie automatically starts playing as soon as it can. This is equivalent to the `AUTOPLAY` parameter in the `<EMBED>` tag, but the `@HH:MM:SS:FF` feature is not yet supported in JavaScript.

- `boolean GetControllerVisible()`
  `void SetControllerVisible(boolean visible)`

Get and set whether a movie has a visible controller. This is equivalent to the `CONTROLLER` parameter in the `<EMBED>` tag.

- `float GetRate()`
  `void SetRate(float rate)`

Get and set the playback rate of the movie. A rate of 1 is the normal playback rate. A paused movie has a rate of 0. Fractional values are slow motion, and values greater than one are fast-forward. Negative values indicate that the movie is playing backward. Setting the rate of a paused movie to a nonzero value starts the movie playing.

- `int GetTime()`
  `void SetTime(int time)`

Get and set the current time of a movie. Setting this property causes a movie to go to that time in the movie and stop.

- `int GetVolume()`
  `void SetVolume(int volume)`

Get and set the audio volume of the movie. A negative value mutes the movie. This is equivalent to the `VOLUME` parameter in the `<EMBED>` tag.

- `boolean GetMute()`
  `void SetMute(boolean mute)`

Get and set the audio mute of a movie while maintaining the magnitude of the volume, so turning mute off restores the volume.

- `string GetMovieName()`
  `void SetMovieName(string movieName)`

Get and set a name that can be used by a wired sprite when targeting an external movie. This is equivalent to the `MOVIENAME` parameter in the `<EMBED>` tag.

- `int GetMovieID()`
  `void SetMovieID(int movieID)`

Get and set an ID that can be used by a wired sprite when targeting an external movie. This is equivalent to the `MOVIEID` parameter in the `<EMBED>` tag.

- `int GetStartTime()`
  `void SetStartTime(int time)`

Get and set the time at which a movie begins to play and the time at which it stops or loops when playing in reverse. Initially, the start time of a movie is set to 0 unless specified in the `STARTTIME` parameter in the

<EMBED> tag. The start time cannot be set to a time greater than the end time. This is equivalent to the STARTTIME parameter in the <EMBED> tag.

- int GetEndTime()
  void SetEndTime(int time)

  Get and set the time at which a movie stops playing or loops. The end time of a movie is initially set to its duration, unless specified in the ENDTIME parameter in the <EMBED> tag. The end time cannot be set to a time greater than the movie's duration. This is equivalent to the ENDTIME parameter in the <EMBED> tag.

- string GetBgColor()
  void SetBgColor(string color)

  Get and set the color used to fill any space allotted to the plug-in by the <EMBED> tag and not covered by the movie. This is equivalent to the BGCOLOR parameter in the <EMBED> tag and takes the same values. Regardless of how the color is specified, GetBgColor() always returns the color number—for example, if the background color is set to Navy, GetBgColor() returns #000080.

- boolean GetIsLooping()
  void SetIsLooping(boolean loop)

  Get and set whether a movie loops when it reaches its end. A movie can loop in either reverse or forward play. This is equivalent to setting the LOOP parameter to true or false in the <EMBED> tag.

- boolean GetLoopIsPalindrome()
  void SetLoopIsPalindrome(boolean loop)

  Get and set whether a looping movie reverses direction when it loops, alternately playing backward and forward. The loop property must be true for this to have any effect. This is equivalent to setting the LOOP= "Palindrome" parameter in the <EMBED> tag.

- boolean GetPlayEveryFrame()
  void SetPlayEveryFrame(boolean playAll)

  Get and set whether QuickTime should play every frame in a movie even if it gets behind (playing in slow motion rather than dropping frames). The sound is muted when playAll is true. This is equivalent to the PLAYEVERYFRAME parameter in the <EMBED> tag.

- string GetHREF()
  void SetHREF(string url)

  Get and set the URL that is invoked by a mouse click in a movie's display area. The URL can be a Web page, a QuickTime movie, a live streaming session, or a JavaScript function name. This is equivalent to the HREF parameter in the <EMBED> tag.

- string GetTarget()
  void SetTarget(string target)

  Get and set the target for a movie's HREF. The target can be an existing frame or browser window, a new browser window, myself (the Quick-Time plug-in), or quicktimeplayer. This is equivalent to the TARGET parameter in the <EMBED> tag.

- string GetQTNEXTUrl(int index)
  void SetQTNEXTUrl(int index, string url)

  Get and set the URL and target for a specified item in a sequence. The URL of the first item in the sequence is invoked when the currently selected movie finishes. If the URL specifies a QuickTime movie and the special target myself, the next specified URL in the sequence is invoked when that movie finishes, and so on. This is equivalent to setting the QTNEXTn parameter in the <EMBED> tag.

- string GetURL()

  Returns a movie's full URL.

- void SetURL(string url)

  Replaces a movie with another movie specified by the URL.

- boolean GetKioskMode()
  void SetKioskMode(boolean kioskMode)

  Set and get whether kiosk mode is currently set. In kiosk mode, the QuickTime plug-in does not allow the viewer to save a movie to disk. Setting kioskMode to true is equivalent to setting the KIOSKMODE parameter in the <EMBED> tag.

- int GetTimeScale()

  Returns the number of units of time per second in a movie's time scale.

- int GetDuration()

  Returns the length of the movie (in the movie's time scale).

- int GetMaxTimeLoaded()

  Returns the amount of the movie that has been downloaded (in the movie's time scale).

- int GetMovieSize()

  Returns the size of the movie in bytes.

- `int GetMaxBytesLoaded()`

  Returns the number of bytes of the movie that have been downloaded.

- `int GetTrackCount()`

  Returns the number of tracks in the movie.

- `string GetMatrix()`
  `void SetMatrix(string matrix)`

  Get and set a movie's transformation matrix. QuickTime uses a 3 x 3 transformation matrix, represented in JavaScript by three lines of three numbers separated by commas:

  ```
  a, b, u
  c, d, v
  h, k, w
  ```

  You can use a movie's transformation matrix to scale, translate, and rotate the movie image. For the scary details, see "Transformation Matrix" (page 550).

- `string GetRectangle()`
  `void SetRectangle(string rect)`

  Get and set the location and dimensions of the movie within the embed area.

Note   Normally, the QuickTime Plug-in keeps the movie centered within the embed area, even if the embed area changes. Once a movie's location is changed with `SetRect` or `Set-Matrix`, the movie's absolute location within the embed area is maintained rather than centering it.

- `string GetLanguage()`
  `void SetLanguage(string language)`

  Get and set the movie's current language.

  Setting the language causes any tracks associated with that language to be enabled and tracks associated with other languages to be disabled. If no tracks are associated with the specified language, the movie's language is not changed.

Supported language names are shown in the table below.

Language	Script system
English	Roman script
French	Roman script
German	Roman script
Italian	Roman script
Dutch	Roman script
Swedish	Roman script
Spanish	Roman script
Danish	Roman script
Portuguese	Roman script
Norwegian	Roman script
Hebrew	Hebrew script
Japanese	Japanese script
Arabic	Arabic script
Finnish	Roman script
Greek	Greek script using Roman script code
Icelandic	variant Roman script
Maltese	variant Roman script
Turkish	variant Roman script
Croatian	Serbo-Croatian in variant Roman script
TradChinese	Chinese (Mandarin) in traditional characters
Urdu	Arabic script

- `string GetMIMEType()`

Returns the movie's MIME type.

- `string GetUserData(string type)`

Returns the movie user data text with the specified tag. The tag is specified with a four-character string; for example, `'©cpy'` returns a movie's copyright string. The following table contains a complete list of user data tags.

String	Data
'© nam'	Movie's name
'© cpy'	Copyright statement
'© day'	Date the movie content was created
'© dir'	Name of movie's director
'© ed1' to '© ed9'	Edit dates and descriptions
'© fmt'	Indication of movie format (computer-generated, digitized, and so on)
'© inf'	Information about the movie
'© prd'	Name of movie's producer
'© prf'	Names of performers
'© req'	Special hardware and software requirements
'© src'	Credits for those who provided movie source content
'© wrt'	Name of movie's writer

Track Properties

- `string GetTrackName(int index)`

  Returns the name of the specified track.

- `string GetTrackType(int index)`

  Returns the type of the specified track, such as video, sound, text, music, sprite, 3D, VR, streaming, movie, Flash, or tween.

- `boolean GetTrackEnabled(int index)`
  `void SetTrackEnabled(int index, boolean enabled)`

  Get and set the enabled state of a track.

Sprite Track Properties

- `string GetSpriteTrackVariable(int trackIndex,`
  `int variableIndex)`
  `void SetSpriteTrackVariable(int trackIndex,`
  `int variableIndex, string value)`

  Get and set the specified sprite track variable in the specified track.

QuickTime VR Movie Properties

- `boolean GetIsVRMovie()`

  Returns true if the movie is a QuickTime VR movie, `false` otherwise.

- `void ShowDefaultView()`

  Displays a QuickTime VR movie's default node, using the default pan angle, tilt angle, and field of view as set by the movie's author.

- `void GoPreviousNode()`

  Returns to the previous node in a QuickTime VR movie (equivalent to clicking the Back button on the VR movie controller).

- `string GetHotspotUrl(int hotspotID)`
  `void SetHotspotUrl(int hotspotID, string url)`

  Get and set the URL associated with a specified VR movie hotspot. This is equivalent to the HOTSPOT*nn* parameter in the <EMBED> tag.

- `string GetHotspotTarget(int hotspotID)`
  `void SetHotspotTarget(int hotspotID, string target)`

  Get and set the target for a specified VR movie hotspot. This is equivalent to the TARGET*nn* parameter in the <EMBED> tag.

- `float GetPanAngle()`
  `void SetPanAngle(float angle)`

  Get and set the QuickTime VR movie's pan angle (in degrees). This is equivalent to the PAN parameter in the <EMBED> tag.

- `float GetTiltAngle()`
  `void SetTiltAngle(float angle)`

  Get and set the QuickTime VR movie's tilt angle (in degrees). This is equivalent to the TILT parameter in the <EMBED> tag.

- `float GetFieldOfView()`
  `void SetFieldOfView(float fov)`

  Get and set the QuickTime VR movie's field of view (in degrees). This is equivalent to the FOV parameter in the <EMBED> tag.

- `int GetNodeCount()`
  Returns the number of nodes in a QuickTime VR movie.

- `int GetNodeID()`

  Returns the ID of the current node in a QuickTime VR movie.

- `void SetNodeID(int id)`

  Sets the current node (by ID) in a QuickTime VR movie (the movie goes to the node with the specified ID).

Transformation Matrix

QuickTime movies contain compact data structures called transformation matrixes. A transformation matrix is used to scale, translate, and rotate a movie's visual image.

When you scale a movie to make it larger or smaller, or use the Size command in QuickTime Player's Info window to move or rotate a video track, QuickTime changes one or two numbers in a transformation matrix.

When the movie is played, the proper position of each pixel is determined by running the source pixel's x and y coordinates through the transformation matrix. There are transformation matrixes for movies, tracks, and individual sprites, so one pixel can undergo multiple transformations.

Ordinarily this "just works" and you don't have to worry about it. If you use JavaScript or wired sprites to modify a transformation matrix, on the other hand, you need to understand how it works. If you're curious, or you need to know, read on. For everyone else, class is dismissed; skip to the next section.

A transformation matrix consists of nine numbers, represented by a grid:

```
a   b   u
c   d   v
h   k   w
```

These numbers are used to scale, translate (move), and rotate an image along the x, y, and z axes.

The left column (a, c, h) changes a pixel's x coordinate. The middle column (b, d, k) changes a pixel's y coordinate. The right column (u, v, w) would be used for depth information in 3D.

The diagonal from top-left to bottom-right (a, d, w) controls scaling; a scale of 1 is normal (no transformation). The other numbers control translation and rotation, so for them a 0 is normal (no transformation).

Here's the quick-and-dirty way to use a matrix without doing much math:

- To leave an image unchanged, use the identity matrix: the diagonal a, d, and w set to 1, all other values set to 0.

```
a   b   u          1   0   0
c   d   v          0   1   0
h   k   w          0   0   1
```

- Scale images using a and d. a makes things wider or narrower, d makes things taller or shorter, so use a to scale the width (xS) and use d to scale the height (yS). 1 is normal size, 2 is twice as big, 0.5 is half as big. Don't use negative numbers.

a	b	u		xS	0	0
c	d	v		0	yS	0
h	k	w		0	0	1

- Translate images using h and k. h moves the image right by h pixels; a negative value moves it left. k moves the image down by k pixels; a negative value moves it up.

a	b	u		1	0	0
c	d	v		0	1	0
h	k	w		xT	yT	1

- Rotation requires a little math. To rotate an image counterclockwise by P degrees, set a $= \cos P$, b $= \sin P$, c $= (-\sin) P$, d $= \cos P$.

a	b	u		cos	sin	0
c	d	v		−sin	cos	0
h	k	w		0	0	1

You can also combine matrixes. To scale and translate, for example, set a and d to the scalar values and set h and k to the pixel offsets. To translate and rotate, set h and k to the pixel offsets and set a, b, c, and d to the rotation values.

Mathematically, you combine two matrixes using matrix multiplication. Which is, ahem, solidly outside the scope of this book.

The transformation starts with a point X, Y and creates a new point X_1, Y_1 using the matrix

a	b	u
c	d	v
h	k	w

and the formulas

$$X_1 = aX + cY + h$$
$$Y_1 = bX + dY + k$$

The rest, as they say, is just arithmetic.

Mixing It Up: Streaming and Nonstreaming

So far we've looked at streaming movies, local movies, and Fast Start movies as separate things. Now we'll look at ways to combine streams with local and Web-based media, all in the same Fast Start movie.

This lets you add things that can't be streamed, such as chapter lists, sprites, skins, and Flash, to your streaming audio and video.

It also lets you add things that must be streamed, such as live webcasts, to a QuickTime presentation on a CD-ROM or a Web server.

This chapter covers

- adding chapter lists to streaming movies

- adding streaming content to local or Fast Start movies

- allocating bandwidth for a mixture of streaming and Fast Start media

- adding wired sprites and Flash animation to streaming movies

- creating a skinned player for your streaming audio or video

In addition to the techniques presented here, you can mix streaming and nonstreaming movies using Synchronized Multimedia Integration Language, as described in Chapter 18, "SMIL for the Camera." SMIL provides an easy way to add live streams, stored streams, and other kinds of media to the same presentation.

Adding a Chapter List to a Streaming Movie

Streaming is a great way to deliver long movies; they don't take up any space on the viewer's hard disk, and the viewer can jump to any point in the movie without downloading the intervening material. Streaming delivery is especially nice for lectures or tutorials—material that invites the viewer to jump to a particular point in the presentation or to review certain segments multiple times.

Chapter lists are great for these kinds of movies. They provide a pop-up list of topics or segments, allowing the viewer to jump directly to the beginning of any segment without having to hunt for it.

This is especially convenient in streaming movies because they're awkward to hunt around in.

Note QuickTime 6 and Streaming Server 4 have greatly improved the responsiveness of the player when scrubbing through a long movie by making use of the Instant On feature, which presents the current frame immediately, instead of waiting for the buffer to fill. It's still a bit less responsive than scrubbing through a local movie, but it's much better.

When you move the current position indicator in a local movie, Quick-Time displays the corresponding image as the slider moves, so you can see what's playing at that point. When you move the current position indicator in a streaming movie, QuickTime repeatedly asks the server to start streaming from the new point. This can take a second, making it tedious to find a particular point in a long movie.

A chapter list fixes that quite nicely. Just click and go. Unfortunately, chapter lists don't stream. They have to be delivered in a local or Fast Start movie.

Fortunately, you can wrap a streaming movie in a local or Fast Start movie with a chapter list.

Of course, we're talking about on-demand streams here—hinted movies stored on a streaming server—not live streams. It's hard to put chapter markers in a live stream for some reason; something about time travel, I guess.

Anyway, here's how to add a chapter list to a streaming movie:

1. Open the streaming movie using the Open URL command in Quick-Time Player. Save as a self-contained movie. This creates a tiny Fast Start movie with a streaming track (just a pointer to the streaming movie, really).

Tip Once you have a Fast Start movie, you can add a chapter list using one of several tools. See "Adding a Chapter List to a Movie" (page 390).

The remaining steps are the same ones you would use to add a chapter list to any QuickTime movie (as described in Chapter 13).

2. Using a text editor or a word processor, type a list of topics, one line per entry. Make each entry short—no more than two or three words—and terminate each topic with a carriage return. Save the list as plain text.

3. Import the text into QuickTime Player and then export it, choosing Text to Text and Text with Descriptors from the pop-up menus. This will add descriptors and time stamps to your list.

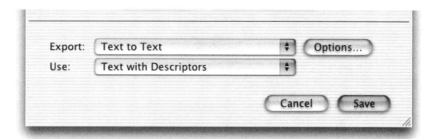

4. Click the Options button to set the format for the text descriptors. Select Show Text, Descriptors, and Time. Under Time Stamps, select "Show time relative to start of: **Movie**" and set "Show fractions of seconds as: 1/**30**" by choosing 30 in the pop-up menu.

5. Click OK, then Save. This exports the chapter list as a text file with time stamps and text descriptor tags.

6. Open the exported list in a text editor.

7. Open the movie with the streaming track that you created in step 1. Choose Get Movie Properties from the Movie menu, then choose Time from the right pop-up menu. Try to arrange the windows on your desk so you can see the movie, the Properties window, and a few lines in your text editor.

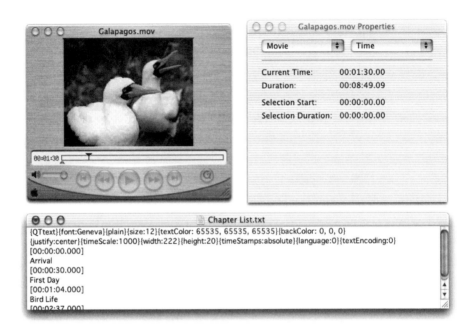

8. Play the movie, pausing as needed. Use the time display in the Properties window to determine when each topic begins. The first topic should begin at [00:00:00.00].

9. Modify the time stamp preceding each topic in your list so it matches the time displayed in the Properties window. For example, if the second topic begins at time 00:02:30.01, set the second time stamp in the text file to [00:02:30.01].

10. Modify the last time stamp to match the duration of the movie.

11. Save the text file and import it into QuickTime Player. This creates a new movie containing only a text track. Select All. Copy. Close.

12. Click in the movie with the streaming track. Move the Current Position indicator to the start of the movie (make sure the time in the Properties window is 00:00:00.00). Select All. Choose Add Scaled from the Edit

menu. This adds your list to the movie as a text track, precisely matching the duration of the stream.

13. Choose the new text track from the left pop-up menu in the Properties window, then choose Make Chapter from the right pop-up menu. Choose the streaming track as the chapter owner.

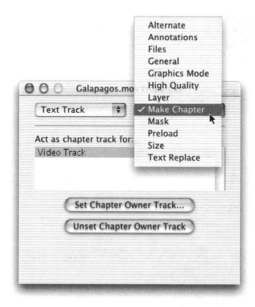

14. Choose Preload from the right pop-up menu and click the Preload checkbox, so the chapter list loads right away.

15. Choose Enable Tracks from the Edit menu and disable the new text track, so it isn't displayed on top of your streaming video. It still works as a chapter list.

16. Save as a self-contained movie. It should be very small (1–2 Kbytes).

Note   Sixteen steps seem like too many? Use a chapter list tool and reduce it to four. See "Adding a Chapter List to a Movie" (page 390).

As you play the movie, you should see the current topic displayed in the movie controller. Clicking the current topic creates a pop-up menu, allowing you to see the complete list of available topics and jump directly to the start of any one. The functionality is the same in QuickTime Player or the QuickTime plug-in, even though the two have slightly different controls.

QuickTime Player   **QuickTime Plug-in**

Important   If the movie is not wide enough for the controller to accommodate the chapter list entries, the chapter list is not displayed.

If your list is not displayed, you need to either make your topic entries shorter or make your movie wider.

One way to widen a movie is to create a black GIF as tall as your movie and as wide as necessary, then add it as a background. See "Adding a Still Image as a Movie Background" (page 267). Alternatively, you can set the movie to play back at double size, which is often a good idea for streaming movies anyway.

For an example of a streaming movie with a chapter list and a black GIF background image, see Keynote.htm and Keynote.mov in the Mixing folder of the CD.

You can embed your new movie in a Web page like any Fast Start movie. When your movie is played over the Web, QuickTime loads the chapter list and any background image immediately via HTTP. It attempts to get the stream from the server only when the movie is played or the viewer selects an entry point using the chapter list.

Tip   It's a good idea to set AUTOPLAY=true when you embed a streaming movie with a chapter list. Otherwise the viewer sees the QuickTime logo instead of the first frame of the movie.

▶ Adding Streaming Content to a Local Movie

You can add streaming content to local or Fast Start movies using Quick-Time Player, whether the streams are live webcasts or streamed from a movie stored on a server. The technique varies slightly for live streams.

Adding Stored Streaming Content

Adding content from a movie on a streaming server to a local or Fast Start movie is pretty easy. It's just a matter of opening the streaming movie in QuickTime Player, selecting the part you want to add, saving it—which creates a tiny movie with a streaming track—then adding the streaming track to another movie. You add streaming tracks the same way you add any QuickTime track.

Here are the steps for adding stored streaming content to a local or Fast Start movie:

1. Open the streaming movie in QuickTime Player by choosing Open URL from the File menu and typing in the movie's URL. It should look something like this:

   `rtsp://your.server.com/streaming.mov`

2. The streaming movie should open and start playing. Stop the movie and move the Current Position indicator to the beginning. If you want to use the whole streaming movie in your local or Fast Start movie, skip to step 4.

3. Use the Time slider and the QuickTime Player selection tools to select as much of the movie as you like. Choose Copy from the Edit menu, New Player from the File menu, then Paste from the Edit menu. This creates a new movie that points to the part of the streaming movie that you selected.

4. Choose Save As from the File menu and save as a self-contained movie with the .mov file extension. This creates a Fast Start movie with a streaming track.

Note The streaming track consists mainly of the URL of the streaming movie. If you saved a clip from the movie, the streaming track contains the beginning and ending time of the clip as well.

5. Open the movie you just created and verify that it plays as much of the streaming movie as you want. Choose Select All from the Edit menu, then choose Copy.

6. Open a local or Fast Start movie. Move the Current Position indicator to the time in the movie where you want the streaming content to appear.

7. If you want to *insert* the streaming content—before or after the local content or between two segments—choose Paste. If you want to *composite* the streaming content with local content, choose Add (*not* Add Scaled).

8. If you're compositing, open the Properties window, choose the streaming track from the left pop-up menu, and use the Size and Layer items in the right pop-up menu to position the streaming track where you want it in the display area and to set its layer. Use the Graphics Mode item to make it partly transparent or translucent if you like.

9. Save as a self-contained movie with the .mov file extension.

That's it. You've added a streaming track to your movie. You can double-click your new movie or embed it in a Web page. When the movie is played, the file you just created downloads to the viewer's computer and the streaming content is sent from the server when needed.

You may need to do some bandwidth allocation for the movie to play smoothly over the Internet; see "Allocating Bandwidth" (page 564) for details.

Adding a Live Stream to a Movie

Adding a live stream to other media using QuickTime Player is a little tricky, primarily because live streams have an unknown duration. Quick-Time Player displays live streams with no Time slider in the control bar, and without a Time slider, QuickTime Player's main editing commands are disabled—no Copy, Cut, Add, or Paste commands are available.

There's a simple workaround for this, however. If you disable the streaming track—using the Enable Tracks item in the Edit menu—the editing features are available again. When you're done editing, simply re-enable the track. You still have to deal with the fact that part of your movie has an indefinite duration, but that can be dealt with separately.

You can also add live streams to local or Fast Start movies using Live-Stage Pro, GoLive, or SMIL. We'll go over using QuickTime Player in detail, then look briefly at the other methods.

Adding a Live Stream Using QuickTime Player

Here are the steps for adding a live stream to a local or Fast Start movie using QuickTime Player:

1. Open the live stream in QuickTime Player by choosing Open URL from the File menu and typing the URL of the stream's SDP file, without the .sdp file extension. For details, see Chapter 14, "Gently down the Stream."

   If the SDP file is called stream1.sdp, the URL should look something like this:

   rtsp://your.server.com/stream1

2. The stream should open and start playing. Stop the movie, choose Save As from the File menu, and save as a self-contained movie with the .mov file extension. This creates a Fast Start movie with a streaming track.

3. Open the movie you just created and choose Enable Tracks from the Edit menu. Turn the streaming track OFF and click OK. The Time slider should now be visible in an otherwise empty player window.

4. Open a local or Fast Start movie. Select All. Copy. Close (don't save). Click the streaming movie.

5. Now you have a choice. You can either insert your movie before the stream, or composite the stream with the rest of the movie.

   ▪ To precede the stream with your movie, as you might for an advertisement, choose Paste.

   ▪ To add your movie for the length of the stream, as you might a station logo for an Internet radio broadcast, choose Select All, then Add Scaled.

6. Choose Enable Tracks again and turn the streaming track ON.

7. If you're compositing a visual stream, open the Properties window, choose the streaming track from the left pop-up menu, and use the Size and Layer items in the right pop-up menu to position the streaming track where you want it in the display area and to set its layer. Use the Graphics Mode item to make it partly transparent or translucent.

8. Save as a self-contained movie with the .mov file extension.

That's it. You've added a live stream to your movie. You can double-click your new movie or embed it in a Web page. When the movie is played, the file you just created downloads to the viewer's computer and the live stream is requested from the server.

Adding a Live Stream with Other QuickTime Editors

Two programs you can use to add live streams to a QuickTime movie are LiveStage Pro and Adobe GoLive. LiveStage Pro is generally used for creating wired sprites, and GoLive is generally used as a site management tool, but both programs include powerful general-purpose QuickTime editors.

Here's what you do:

1. Open a live stream in QuickTime Player using the Open URL command.

2. Save as a self-contained movie.

3. Open LiveStage Pro and drag the movie you just created onto the stage, or drag the movie onto GoLive (or choose Open Special in GoLive).

This adds a streaming track to your LiveStage project or opens the movie in GoLive's editor. The live stream has an unknown duration, so it can do odd things to the movie timeline—it appears as a track with a *very* long duration.

You can create other tracks directly in LiveStage Pro or in GoLive, and you can drag other QuickTime movies onto the timeline in either program to add tracks to your project.

Both QuickTime editors allow you to modify the tracks in various ways, such as setting the layer, time offset, and position of each track. When you're ready, save your work as a self-contained QuickTime movie. This creates a Fast Start movie that contains a live streaming track.

Now, the odd thing about this movie is that all the tracks have a fixed duration except the live track. If your movie is a drawing of a radio, for example, and the live stream is a webcast from a radio station, playing the movie causes an undesirable effect—eventually the track with the radio's image ends, and the live audio stream plays on in an empty player window!

You can fix this by scaling the nonstreaming tracks to match the duration of the streaming track. Now that you have a mixture of live streams and media with a fixed duration, you can do this in QuickTime Player. Here's how:

1. Open the movie in QuickTime Player.

2. Extract the nonstreaming tracks into a new movie (you can select multiple tracks in the Extract Tracks dialog box by Shift-clicking).

3. Choose Select All in the new movie, then Copy.

4. In the original movie, use the Enable Tracks command to disable the nonstreaming tracks, then choose Select All. This selects the live streaming track.

5. Choose Add Scaled (press Shift-Ctrl-Alt or Shift-Option while opening the Edit menu). This adds new copies of the nonstreaming tracks scaled to match the live stream's duration.

6. Use the Delete Tracks command to delete the original copies of the nonstreaming tracks.

7. Save as a self-contained movie.

Now you have a self-contained Fast Start movie whose duration is indefinite, containing a mixture of live streams and other media. To see an example, play MyWGBH.mov (located in the Mixing folder of the CD). It's an animated image of a television set with a live stream from station WGBH superimposed on the screen. Also check out Webradio.htm (located in the Interactive folder of the CD)—it's a sprite radio that plays live webcasts.

Using a Live Stream as a Sprite Image

Creating a sprite whose image is a live stream is a multistep process. You begin by creating a movie that contains a live streaming track and a sprite track, as we just described in "Adding a Live Stream with Other Quick-Time Editors" (page 562).

Then you use QuickTime Player to set the sprite's image source to the live stream, as described in "Using a Video Track as a Sprite" (page 479).

You can set the rest of the sprite's properties as you normally would to position the sprite, scale it, rotate it, and so on.

When the movie plays, the sprite gets its image data from the live stream. For an example of this, see Watchtv.mov in the Mixing folder on the CD. The TV set bounces around the screen while playing a live stream from WGBH. It bounces even when the movie is paused, but the live stream updates only when the movie is playing.

The TV set is a cartoon created in Flash and imported into LiveStage Pro. It has the bounce behavior in its idle event handler. The stream from WGBH is the image assigned to a second sprite, which gets its position from the TV set sprite, so they move together.

You can open the file Watchtv.lsp (also in the Mixing folder of the CD) using the demo version of LiveStage Pro (in the Demos folder) to see how it's put together.

Adding a Live Stream with SMIL

Mixing live streams with local or Fast Start content in SMIL is really easy—just specify a live stream as one of the SMIL media elements. All the media elements in SMIL are specified by URL anyway; the URL for a live stream just starts with rtsp://.

You can create SMIL presentations using a text editor. For details, see Chapter 18, "SMIL for the Camera." For an example of a SMIL presentation that combines a local movie and a live stream, see page 596.

▶ Allocating Bandwidth

When you deliver a mixture of streaming and Fast Start content, you need to pay attention to how the viewer's bandwidth is used.

Streaming content uses a fixed bandwidth—it requires a certain amount of bandwidth to work at all, and it won't use any more than that. Fast Start content is more variable—it gets there eventually, even over the slowest connection, but it uses all the available bandwidth while it downloads.

If you just mix streaming and Fast Start content together, the Fast Start content uses all the available bandwidth while it downloads, preventing the streaming media from getting through intact. This is not usually what you want.

There are two ways to get around this problem: reserve some bandwidth for the streaming media, so the Fast Start content doesn't use it all, or delay starting the streams until after the Fast Start media has downloaded.

For a long, low-bandwidth Fast Start movie with a streaming track—where you're essentially streaming part of the movie using HTTP and part using RTP—you need to reserve bandwidth for the RTP streams. For a streaming movie with a media skin, or a Flash or wired sprite controller, you're usually better off delaying the stream until the Fast Start parts have downloaded.

Note If you're just adding a chapter list to a streaming movie, don't worry about it. A few hundred bytes of text can load in a fraction of a second—the download will be complete before the streaming content has finished buffering.

Reserving Bandwidth with QTSRCCHOKESPEED

A movie that contains both Fast Start and streaming content delivers some of its media using HTTP and some of its media using RTP. The nature of RTP is that it sends packets at regular intervals, using a fixed amount of bandwidth. By default, HTTP uses all the available bandwidth to transfer data as quickly as possible.

Consequently, media being delivered over HTTP tends to fill the data pipe completely, leaving no room for streaming media. Another aspect of RTP is that lost or delayed packets aren't retransmitted—they're just lost. So when streaming media gets shoved aside by Fast Start media, the stream breaks up and doesn't play.

You can tell QuickTime to limit the bandwidth used for HTTP transfer by specifying a choke speed. The parameter for setting the choke speed is QTSRCCHOKESPEED and, as the name implies, it sets the choke speed for the URL specified in the QTSRC parameter. The HTML looks like this:

```
<EMBED SRC="Dummy.mov" HEIGHT="256" WIDTH="320"
  QTSRC="http://domain.com/Actual.mov"
  QTSRCCHOKESPEED="30000" />
```

This example limits the bandwidth used to download the file `Actual.mov` to 30,000 bits per second.

The choke speed applies only to the download of the file `Actual.mov`—external media pointed to by `Actual.mov`, including streaming media, are treated separately. If `Actual.mov` contains a streaming track with 9600 bit-per-second audio, the movie should play over a 56K dialup connection with no problem: the Fast Start movie file downloads using about 3 Kbytes/sec of bandwidth, and the stream occupies about another 1 Kbyte/sec.

Important The choke speed limits *only* the bandwidth used by the file specified in the QTSRC parameter, so the Fast Start parts of the movie must be self-contained for this technique to be effective. Media in external files (such as streaming media) are not affected by QTSRCCHOKESPEED. If the movie points to *nonstreaming* media in external files, they use all available bandwidth while they download.

Tip The browser also downloads the file specified in the SRC parameter as fast as it can, even though it isn't displayed, so make Dummy.mov as small as practical—ideally less than 2 Kbytes.

Set the choke speed to the combined data rate of all the *nonstreaming* media, plus 10–20% for overhead. Whatever bandwidth remains is available for streaming.

Alternatively, you can calculate the appropriate choke speed by subtracting the bandwidth needed for streaming from the minimum connection speed you intend to support. For example, if the streaming media needs 10,000 bits per second (roughly 1 Kbyte), and the movie is designed to play over a 20 Kbit connection, subtract 10,000 bits from 20 Kbits and set QTSRCCHOKESPEED="10000".

Either way, the data rate of the *whole* movie—streaming and nonstreaming—must be less than the bandwidth of the connection for things to work properly. For the streams to play, there must be enough RTP bandwidth available; for the rest of the movie to play smoothly as the Fast Start parts download, there must be enough HTTP bandwidth for the nonstreaming tracks.

Tip It's a good idea to offset the streaming tracks a few seconds into the movie so the streams can set up and begin buffering data while the movie is getting started.

Delaying the Streams

If the nonstreaming part of your movie is basically a container for the streams—a frame, controller, and animated background, for example—then you don't want to divide the bandwidth between them; you want the non-streaming parts to download as quickly as possible, then give all the bandwidth to the streams.

You can delay the streams simply by adding any streaming tracks to your movie later in the movie's timeline. For example, if you set the insertion point 15 seconds into the movie when you add the streaming tracks, you effectively reserve 15 seconds for the nonstreaming tracks to download before the streams begin.

Starting with QuickTime 5, you can specify that the movie should autoplay after it has downloaded to a specified point in the movie timeline. The syntax is

```
<EMBED SRC="sample.mov" WIDTH="190" HEIGHT="256"
  AUTOPLAY="@00:02:20.0" >
```

By default, earlier versions of QuickTime will not autoplay if the AUTOPLAY parameter is set to a time. If you prefer, you can set AUTOPLAY=True for older versions, then override that setting with a delay time for QuickTime 5 and later. The HTML looks like this:

```
<EMBED SRC="sample.mov" WIDTH="190" HEIGHT="256"
  AUTOPLAY="true"
  ALLOWEMBEDTAGOVERRIDES="true"
  AUTOPLAY="@00:02:20.0"
  ALLOWEMBEDTAGOVERRIDES="false" >
```

For details on using the AUTOPLAY parameter, see "Stuttering" (page 206).

Alternatively, you can use wired sprites or Flash actions to automatically pause the movie or show a short animated loop until enough has downloaded to play the rest of the movie smoothly. This is described in the next two sections.

Adding Wired Sprites to a Streaming Movie

Wired sprites add so many possibilities to QuickTime that it's natural to want to combine them with streaming content. It isn't hard to do, but it requires some thought and planning. The wired sprites can't be delivered over RTP, so you need to deliver some of the movie locally or via HTTP.

You generally want to design your movie so that the sprites all download at the beginning and the streams start afterward. This lets you take advantage of the fact that the data rate of sprite animation drops rapidly to almost nothing.

It's also a good idea to put a wired sprite at the very beginning of the movie that monitors the download and starts the movie when enough has arrived to play smoothly.

As a rule, your movie won't work properly until most of the sprite track has loaded, partly because that's how sprites are, and partly because the download uses all the available bandwidth, which keeps the streams from playing properly until it's done.

To prevent the viewer from jumping ahead in the movie timeline prematurely, you can have the movie play without a standard controller. Of course, that means you need to provide your own wired sprite controller for the movie, but that's a fun thing to do with wired sprites anyway.

Let's say you want to use wired sprites to create an animated frame and graphic controls for some streaming content, perhaps with a JPEG backdrop. Here's how you'd go about it using LiveStage Pro and Quick-Time Player:

1. Create an image to start your movie that says something like "Downloading movie—please wait."

Tip A text prologue that takes 15 seconds to read makes an excellent distraction while you're stuffing rabbits into your hat.

2. Open LiveStage Pro and create a sprite track. Add a sprite and make the image you created in step 1 its source image. Give it a duration of 1 second.

3. Add the sprites for the controls and animation immediately after the first sprite on the timeline—include wired sprite buttons that act as a movie controller.

4. If there are sprites that you need to introduce later during the movie, create them at this point in the timeline but make them invisible until you need them.

5. Add the background JPEG at this point in the timeline as well.

6. Add an action to the first sprite. Have it respond to the idle event by checking the current download status using MaxTimeLoadedInMovie. If the JPEG and the rest of the sprites have downloaded, have it set the movie's rate to 1 (start playing); otherwise, have it set the rate to 0 (keep waiting). This pauses the movie at the first frame until it's ready to go.

7. To add streams, open a streaming movie in QuickTime Player, using the Open URL command, and save it as a self-contained movie. This creates a small movie with a streaming track. Drag this movie into LiveStage Pro to add the streaming track to your wired sprite movie.

8. Position the streaming track in the timeline so it begins after all the sprites.

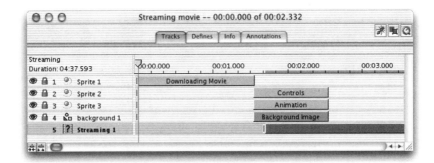

Note   You can't click and drag a live streaming track the way you can other track types in LiveStage Pro—double-click the streaming track icon and set the Time Offset field to position the stream.

9. Export as a wired movie and open the movie in QuickTime Player.

10. If you're using a live stream, scale the duration of all the sprites—except the initial "Downloading movie" sprite—to match the indefinite duration of the live stream, as described in "Adding a Live Stream to a Movie" (page 560).

11. Disable the movie controller so the user can't start the movie prematurely (open the Properties window, choose Controller in the right pop-up menu, and select None Movie Controller). Then enable the autoplay feature so the first sprite is activated automatically in QuickTime Player (choose Auto Play in the right pop-up menu and click the checkbox).

12. Save as a self-contained movie.

13. Embed the movie in your Web page with `CONTROLLER="False"` and `AUTOPLAY="True"`, so the first sprite is activated automatically and the user can't jump ahead prematurely when the movie is played in the QuickTime plug-in.

14. Take a break. You've earned it.

To see an example of this kind of movie, point your browser at `Sprite Stream.htm` (in the Mixing folder of the CD).

For this movie, a cloud effect was added to the downloading frame. You can look more closely into the structure of the movie by opening the `SpriteStream.lsp` file (also in the Mixing folder) using the trial version of LiveStage Pro in the Demos folder.

`Spritestream.mov` was contributed by Michael Shaff of SmallHands (`www .smallhands.com`).

An alternate approach to positioning the live stream later in the movie is to start the movie with the streaming track disabled, then enable the streaming track with a wired sprite action when you're ready to go. This is also the technique you would use to select one live stream from a set—to make an Internet radio tuner with preset buttons, for example. For an example, see `Webradio.mov`.

▶ Adding Flash to a Streaming Movie

Flash is a great way to add low-bandwidth vector graphics and interactivity to a QuickTime movie. You can't stream Flash over RTP, but with a little planning, you can mix Flash content and streaming content in the same movie, delivering part of the movie over RTP and part locally or via HTTP. Here's how:

1. Create a short Flash animation to start your movie that includes a message like "Downloading movie—please wait."

2. Create your main Flash content and place it in the timeline after the short animation—include buttons that act as a movie controller in your main Flash content.

3. Add an action to the last frame of the short animation that checks to see if the last key frame of your main Flash content has loaded. If your short animation is three frames long, for example, and the last key frame in your main Flash content is frame 30, you would add this action to frame 3:

```
If (_frameloaded) (30) Goto 4 and Play
Else Goto 1 and Play
Endif
```

4. Save everything as a Flash 4 .swf file and import it into QuickTime Player.

5. Open a streaming movie in QuickTime Player using the Open URL command. This creates a movie with a streaming track. Stop the movie, move the Current Position indicator to the beginning, choose Select All, then Copy.

Note This works only with streams from movies stored on a streaming server; to add *live* streams, see "Adding a Live Stream to a Movie" (page 560).

6. Add the streaming track to the movie at a point after the short animation.

7. Open the movie in QuickTime Player and use the Properties window to do the following:

   ▪ Assign the None Movie Controller, so the user can't jump ahead in the movie prematurely.

   ▪ Click the Auto Play checkbox, so the movie starts automatically in QuickTime Player.

   ▪ Position the streaming track in the display area, and set its layer and graphics modes, so it composites with your Flash content the way you want.

8. Embed the movie in your Web page with AUTOPLAY="True" and CONTROLLER="False" so the movie starts automatically and viewers can't jump ahead prematurely when the movie is played in the QuickTime plug-in.

9. Howl with delight.

To see an example of this kind of movie, check out `FlashStream.htm` (in the Mixing folder of the CD).

To examine the movie more closely, open `FlashStream.mov` in QuickTime Player. If you have Flash, you might also want to open `FlashStream.fla` to look more closely at how the Flash content is structured.

`Flashstream.mov` was contributed by Michael Shaff of SmallHands (`www.smallhands.com`).

▶ Adding a Media Skin to Your Streams

There are a lot of great things about streaming: you can put your radio station on the Internet, you can share music and videos without giving away downloaded copies—the list goes on. One of the less-nice features is that your work is displayed in a streaming player application. Let's face it; most of them look dorky. Some of them run ads or flashing banners. None of them have anything to do with your content, and most of them make it easy for the audience to be drawn away to some other attraction through the player's interface.

What you want is to have your own customized player application that looks and acts exactly the way you want it to. If you're streaming your radio station, you don't want the player to have a tuner listing 500 other radio stations—you want it to have your call letters and logo, the look that goes with your format, and you want it locked to your station, with a click-through to your website. If you're putting your music or video on the Internet, you want a player that visually complements it, or actively enhances it, or stays out of the way.

With QuickTime (and only in QuickTime) you can have exactly that. No programming required. Here are four profoundly different examples of what you can do:

You and what army? Well, how about the U.S. Army? Soldiers' Radio (www.army.mil/srtv/soldiersradio/) is a 24/7/365 broadcast for U.S. soldiers around the world. They need a rugged, all-weather, camouflaged player that does the job and stays out of the way.

Wire on fire? Tune into Radio WireOnFire (www.wireonfire.com). Naturally, they want a player that shows what they're currently playing, has a click-through to buy the CD, includes a crawl where they can talk about their current promo, and is, at all times, on fire.

Ed Harcourt's streaming music and video are exceptionally well framed by this custom player made from crumpled note paper, which includes a click-through to his website (www.edharcourt.com), multi-data-rate movies, and a full-screen button (but no brushed metal or neon plastic).

Obviously, the hard part of this is coming up with a good-looking player. The rest is actually a snap. It's really no different than adding a media skin to any other movie. It's just that you have to apply the skin as the last step. And of course you need to add the stream and the static movie together beforehand.

This draws on the skills covered in Chapter 16, adding wired sprites or Flash to a movie and creating a media skin, and skills from earlier in this chapter: adding streams to Fast Start movies.

It's a simple sequence:

1. Create the graphics for your player.

2. Add wired sprite or flash controls.

3. Save As (self-contained). You now have a Fast Start movie.

4. Add your stream to the Fast Start movie in one of two ways: either as described in "Adding a Live Stream to a Movie" (page 560), or as described in "Adding Stored Streaming Content" (page 559).

5. Save As (self-contained). Now you have a Fast Start movie that looks and acts right, but plays inside the QuickTime Player's normal interface. This corresponds to the illustration at the end of step 3 in "Creating Media Skins" (page 527).

6. Now you need to create a black-and-white image to mask out your player's custom shape and define which parts are draggable and where the controls poke through. Proceed with steps 4, 5, and 6, of "Creating Media Skins," beginning at "Draw the Masks" (page 530).

Congratulations. You're done.

18

SMIL for
the Camera

SMIL (pronounced "smile") stands for Synchronized Multimedia Integration Language, and it's a World Wide Web Consortium standard for describing multimedia presentations.

QuickTime 4.1 and later can play SMIL presentations as if they were QuickTime movies, so you can use SMIL to create multimedia presentations that play from the desktop or over the Web using the QuickTime plug-in or QuickTime Player.

This chapter includes

- an introduction to SMIL and QuickTime

- a short SMIL tutorial

- how to create QuickTime-friendly SMIL presentations

- a list of QuickTime-specific SMIL extensions

- how to embed SMIL in Web pages for QuickTime

Introduction to SMIL and QuickTime

A SMIL presentation is a lot like a QuickTime movie—it can display images, text, audio, and video; it can position visual elements on the screen at specified locations; and media elements can be sequenced and synchronized in time.

SMIL presentations are described by SMIL documents—text files that specify what media elements to present, and where and when to present them.

Media elements in a SMIL document are specified by URLs. Media elements can be files—such as text files, JPEG images, and QuickTime movies—or live streams. The URLs that specify the media elements can use any of the common protocols—HTTP, FTP, RTSP, local file access, and so on.

You can import SMIL documents into QuickTime and play them using the QuickTime browser plug-in or QuickTime Player, provided that their individual media elements are all things that QuickTime can play.

When you import a SMIL presentation into QuickTime, the SMIL media elements become QuickTime movie tracks, and the SMIL document describes how the tracks are arranged and overlaid in time and space.

SMIL can be a good way to combine streaming movies with local or Fast Start movies without having to edit or combine them in QuickTime Player. Just use a text editor to list the movie URLs and describe where on the screen and in what order to play the movies.

Because SMIL documents are text files, SMIL also gives you a way to automatically generate customized QuickTime movies using a script, such as an AppleScript, PERL, or CGI script—anything that can generate text output can create a SMIL document. If you have a script that inserts banner ads into your Web pages, for example, you could use the same script to insert the ads into a SMIL document along with a streaming QuickTime movie.

By stitching together media elements using text and SMIL syntax, you can build customized presentations from existing media—movies, slides, text, and audio recordings—and play them using QuickTime. This gives you a simple way to author QuickTime movies with a text editor.

Ready to start stitching?

SMIL Tutorial

This tutorial will give you a brief overview of SMIL, then show you

- how to create a basic layout
- how to define display regions
- how to create a timeline with sequential and parallel media elements
- how to specify media elements and set their durations
- how to make an element into a clickable link
- how to show different elements to different viewers using a switch

Overview

SMIL presentations are described by text files. You can create or edit a SMIL presentation using a text editor, and you can automatically generate a SMIL document using any script language that creates text files. A SMIL document specifies what media elements to present, and where and when to present them.

Each media element is specified by a URL.

Your SMIL presentation can use any media elements that QuickTime can play, including still images, audio, text, QuickTime movies, sprite animations, live streams, VR panoramas, and VR object movies.

The URL of a media element can point to local or remote media, using any format that QuickTime supports, including local file access, HTTP, and RTSP.

Like the tracks in a QuickTime movie, the media elements in a SMIL presentation can be sequenced, overlapped, or offset in time and space.

In addition, SMIL lets you select from a set of elements based on things like the user's language or Internet connection speed.

In other words, a SMIL presentation is a lot like a QuickTime movie that depends on external media files.

Although a SMIL presentation is similar to a QuickTime movie in its function, the two are very different in structure. SMIL is a lot like HTML in structure.

SMIL Structure

SMIL is based on XML, so it's more rigidly structured than HTML, but it uses the same familiar <tag> and </tag> syntax.

SMIL is different from HTML in that all the tags are case-sensitive (always lowercase) and all tags have to be explicitly ended—either there are a pair of tags that enclose other elements (<tag> *elements* </tag>) or a tag is self-contained and ends with "/>" (<tag *parameters* />).

SMIL also differs from HTML because HTML routinely mixes structure and content together in the same document, whereas SMIL normally does not. Where an HTML document contains text to be displayed, a SMIL document would contain the URL of a text file instead.

Like HTML, a SMIL document has a head and a body. The structure of a SMIL file is shown below.

```
<smil>
  <head>
    <layout>
      <!-- layout tags -->
    </layout>
  </head>

  <body>
    <!-- body tags -->
  </body>
</smil>
```

All the layout information is specified in the head. The media elements are listed in the body.

Layout

The layout specifies the whole display area for the presentation, then defines regions where individual media elements can be displayed.

Root Layout

A SMIL layout always starts with a <root-layout /> tag that gives the dimensions of the display area in pixels and assigns a background color.

```
<layout>
  <root-layout id="main" width="320" height="240"
  background-color="red" />
</layout>
```

The id parameter gives the presentation a name; it can be anything you like. The height and width parameters define the display area for the presentation in pixels. You can specify the background color using hexadecimal values ("#FF0000") or names ("red"). Here's a very simple SMIL document—it's just a red rectangle, but you can play it using QuickTime Player:

```
<smil>
  <head>
    <layout>
      <root-layout id="main" width="320" height="240"
```

```
                background-color="red" />
        </layout>
    </head>
    <body> </body>
</smil>
```

Regions

The layout also defines regions within the display area. Regions themselves are invisible, but they define areas where visual media elements can be displayed. Regions can be positioned anywhere in the display area and can overlap.

Here's a layout that specifies a root layout and two regions:

```
<head>
    <layout>
        <root-layout id="main" width="320" height="240"
            background-color="red"/>

        <region id="r1" width="160" height="120" />
        <region id="r2" width="50%" height="100%"
            left="100" top="0" />
    </layout>
</head>
```

The first region is named r1 and is 160 x 120 pixels, extending from the top-left corner of the display area (the default position for a region).

The second region, r2, is half as wide as the display area (width="50%") and fills it from top to bottom (height="100%"). Region r2 is offset 100 pixels from the left edge of the display area (left="100"). Since the first region is 160 pixels wide, the two regions overlap by 60 pixels.

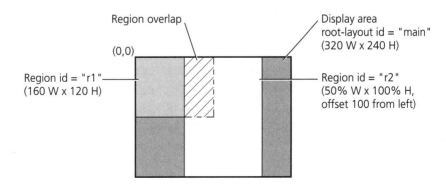

The <region /> tag accepts the following parameters:

- id—gives each region a name, much like an HTML frame name.
- height and width—define the size of the region, either in pixels or as a percentage of the display area.
- top and left (optional)—specify the position of the region within the display area, either in pixels or as a percentage of the display area.

Important If you want to set the top or left parameter, you must specify *both* top and left as a pair, even if one of them is zero.

By default, a region extends from the top-left corner of the display area. You can change this by specifying a top and left offset. For example, top="50%" left="100" creates a region whose top-left corner is halfway down and 100 pixels from the left edge of the display area.

- z-index (optional)—specifies the layering order when regions overlap.

When regions overlap, one lies on top of the other. By default, a region defined later in the layout is on top of any regions defined earlier. You can set the layering explicitly using the z-index parameter. The layer with the highest z-index value is on top. For example, the following layout defines three regions.

```
<region id="r1" width="160" height="120" z-index="3" />
<region id="r2" width="160" height="120" z-index="2" />
<region id="r3" width="160" height="120" z-index="1" />
```

The three regions overlap completely, with r1 on top, r2 in the middle, and r3 at the bottom of the pile. If no z-index values had been specified, the layering would be reversed, with the last-defined region on top.

- fit (optional)—defines how media elements are cropped or scaled if they don't have the same pixel dimensions as the region they're displayed in. There are four possible values for this parameter:
  - fit="hidden" (default)—images are not scaled. If an image is larger than the region, it is cropped. If an image is smaller than a region, part of the region is left empty.
  - fit="fill"—images are scaled to match the height and width of the region, so an image always fills the region completely. The image's aspect ratio may be distorted to make it fit.
  - fit="meet"—images are scaled to meet the region's boundaries while preserving each image's aspect ratio, without cropping. An image

may not fill the region completely, but always fills either the whole width or the whole height. The image is not cropped or distorted.

- `fit="slice"`—images are scaled to fill the region completely while preserving each image's aspect ratio, cropping if necessary. If the aspect ratio of an image differs from the region, the image is cropped by taking a slice from the edge or bottom where it would extend beyond the region.

See the following illustration for examples.

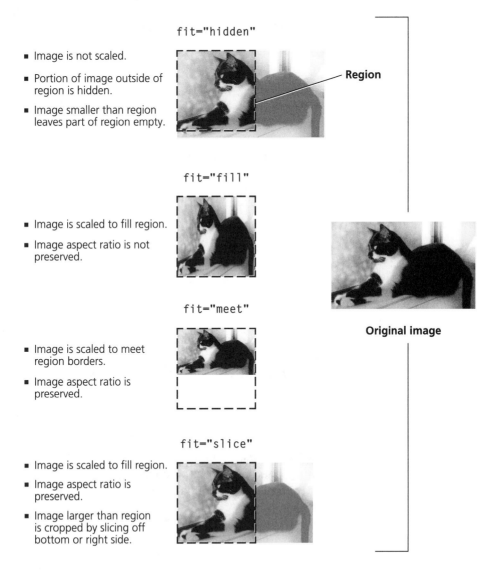

The top-left corner of a media element is always aligned with the top-left corner of the region it is displayed in. If you need to position an image somewhere else, just create another region at a different position—you can have as many regions as you like, and each one uses only a few bytes.

Note QuickTime does not currently support the background-color attribute for regions—it is supported only for the root layout.

Here's a SMIL document with two overlapping regions. It looks like a red rectangle when you play it using QuickTime Player because regions are invisible—they just define areas where media elements can be displayed.

```
<smil>
  <head>
    <layout>
      <root-layout id="main" width="320" height="240"
        background-color="red"/>

      <region id="r1" width="160" height="120" />
      <region id="r2" width="50%" height=
        "100%" left="100"
        top="0" fit="fill" />
    </layout>
  </head>
  <body> </body>
</smil>
```

The Body

The body of a SMIL document specifies what media elements to present, which regions to display the visual elements in, and a timeline for the presentation. We'll look at the timeline first.

Timeline

The timeline groups media elements in two ways: things that happen in sequence and things that happen in parallel. If you don't specify whether elements should be played sequentially or in parallel, QuickTime plays them in sequence.

Sequences

Sequences are surrounded by the <seq> and </seq> tags. Media elements in a sequence are presented one after the other—each element is presented after the previous element ends. There are different ways to determine when an element should end.

Media elements such as audio and video have an inherent duration, so they end when you would expect them to. For example:

```
<seq>
    <audio src="audio1.mp3" />
    <audio src="audio2.aiff" />
    <audio src="audio3.wav" />
</seq>
```

This sequence plays three audio files in a row. Each element ends when the audio has played all the way through. As soon as one element ends, the next begins.

Media elements such as still images and text have no inherent duration, so they're usually assigned explicit durations:

```
<seq>
    <img src="image1.jpg" region="r1" dur="5 sec" />
    <img src="image2.gif" region="r1" dur="7 sec" />
</seq>
```

In this example, the first image ends after being displayed for 5 seconds, then the second image appears and is displayed for 7 seconds.

If you specify an explicit duration for an element that has its own inherent duration, it either ends when it normally would or after the duration you specify, whichever comes first.

Parallel Groups

Media elements that are displayed at the same time are surrounded by the <par> and </par> tags.

Parallel elements are presented starting at the same time, but they don't necessarily end at the same time. For example:

```
<par>
    <audio src="themesong.mp3" />
    <img src="poster.jpg" region="r1" dur="30 sec" />
    <text src="lyrics.txt" region="r2" dur="30 sec" />
</par>
```

This example plays an MP3 audio file while simultaneously displaying a JPEG image in one region and some text in another. The image and the text are displayed for 30 seconds; the audio element ends when the MP3 finishes playing.

QuickTime does not support the endsync attribute, but you can make elements end at the same time using the <end> attribute. For details, see "Begin and End" (page 590).

Combining Sequences and Parallel Groups

You can put a group of parallel elements into a sequence. The parallel group is treated as a single element in the sequence. All the elements in the parallel group start together at the appropriate point in the sequence. When the last element in the parallel group ends, the sequence continues.

Here's an example:

```
<seq>
    <video src="Intro.mov" region="r1" />
    <par>
      <audio src="narration.aiff" />
      <video src="slides.mov" region="r1" />
    </par>
    <text src="credits.txt" dur="20 sec" region="r1" />
</seq>
```

In this example, Intro.mov plays first. The narration and the slides start together as soon as Intro.mov ends. When both the narration and the slides have ended, the credits are displayed.

Similarly, you can include a sequence inside a parallel group. The first element in the sequence begins when the parallel group begins and the sequence executes normally. The sequence is treated as a single element within the group, so the whole sequence must end for the parallel group to complete.

Here's an example:

```
<par>
    <audio src="bgmusic.mov" id="music" />
    <seq>
      <img src="slide1.jpg" region="r1" dur="5 sec" />
      <img src="slide2.jpg" region="r1" dur="5 sec" />
      <img src="slide3.jpg" region="r1" dur="5 sec" />
      <video src="lastslide.jpg" region="r1" end
        ="id(music) (end)" />
```

```
      </seq>
      <text src="copyright.txt" region="r2"
        end="id(music) (end)" />
</par>
```

In this example, the music, the first slide, and the copyright text all come up simultaneously. The first three slides have durations of 5 seconds each. The last slide and the copyright text don't have durations. They have end attributes instead. When the music ends, it generates an end event, which ends the display of the text and the last slide.

Nesting

You can nest parallel groups and sequences inside of each other to an arbitrary and even insane level. It's all part of the fun.

SMIL Media Elements

SMIL media elements are classified by type and specified by URL. Each visual media element is assigned to a region defined in the layout. The media type, the URL, and the region for visual media *must* be specified. All other parameters are optional.

Media Types

There are currently six defined media types:

- `<audio />`
- `<video />`
- `<img />`
- `<text />`
- `<textstream />`
- `<animation />`

Use the media type that most closely describes a given media element. For a sound-only QuickTime movie, for example, use the `<audio />` media type. SMIL isn't terribly strict about this, so you can specify a FLIC animation file, for example, using `<animation />` or `<video />`.

URL

Each media element is specified by an `src` parameter whose value is a URL. The URL can be absolute or relative and can use any protocol that QuickTime understands, including HTTP and RTSP.

Here are some example media types and URLs:

- `<audio src="http://www.myserver.com/path/myaudio.mp3" />`
- `<video src="rtsp://streamserver.com/VideoOnDemand.mov"/>`
- `<img src="slides/slide01.jpg" />`
- `<text src="subtitles.txt" />`
- `<textstream src="rtsp://streamserver.com/streamtext.mov" />`
- `<animation "http://www.myserver.com/myanim.flc" />`

Note Relative URLs were not fully implemented in QuickTime Player prior to QuickTime 5. Remember: relative URLs are relative to the currently loaded movie (the SMIL file).

One URL protocol you may not be familiar with is `data:`, which lets you embed a media element inside your SMIL document. It's normally used to embed small amounts of text that would otherwise require a separate file. Here's an example of a `data:` URL:

```
<text region="aregion" dur="1:30"
  src="data:text/plain,Copyright Apple Computer, 2000" />
```

Note The `data:` protocol identifier is followed immediately by the data format and a comma, then the actual data. Images can be embedded using the Base64 data format.

Important You can get too clever with the `data:` protocol if you're not careful. Remember that relative URLs are relative to the currently loaded movie—when you load a movie using the `data:` protocol, it doesn't *have* a URL. The next URL QuickTime encounters had better not be relative . . . .

Region

Every visual media element needs to be assigned to a display region defined in the layout. Only one element can be displayed in a region at any time (but you can have multiple regions covering the same screen area).

If a media element contains an image that is larger or smaller than its assigned display region, the image can be scaled, clipped, or both scaled and clipped, depending on the `fit` parameter for that region.

Note Clipping and scaling are attributes of a *region*, not a media element. To use different scaling or cropping guidelines for different images, create multiple regions covering the same area but with different `fit` parameters.

Here's a SMIL document that displays a series of JPEG images:

```
<smil>
<head>
  <layout>
     <root-layout id="slideshow" width="320" height="240"
        background-color="black"/>
     <region id="r1" width="100%" height="100%"
        fit="meet" />
  </layout>
</head>

<body>
  <seq>
  <img src="http://www.myserver.com/ourlogo.jpg"
     region="r1" dur="5sec" />
  <img src="slide1.jpg" region="r1" dur="5sec" />
  <img src="slide2.jpg" region="r1" dur="5sec" />
  </seq>
</body>
</smil>
```

This example displays a sequence of three JPEG images. All the images are displayed in the same region. Images are automatically scaled to fill the region as completely as possible without clipping or changing their aspect ratios. Each image has a duration of 5 seconds.

Duration

Some media elements, such as audio and video, have inherent duration. Text and still images, however, have no inherent duration. The easiest way to assign a duration is with the dur parameter. For example:

```
<img src="slide1.jpg" region="r1" dur="30sec" />
```

You can assign an explicit duration to override an element's inherent duration. For example, if you specify

```
<audio src="sound1.wav" dur="1:05" />
```

the audio file sound1.wav ends after 1 minute 5 seconds, or when the audio finishes naturally, whichever comes first.

Duration is specified in Hours:Minutes:Seconds.DecimalFractions. You can leave off the hours, or the hours and minutes, or the fractions. You can add the "sec" identifier to make things more readable. These are all equivalent:

```
dur="00:00:05.000"
dur="00:05.000"
dur="05.000"
dur="05"
dur="5 Sec"
```

Another way to explicitly set an element's duration is to specify an end time or an end event. An element ends when its duration is exceeded, its end time or end event occurs, or it reaches its inherent end, whichever comes first. We'll look at setting begin and end parameters next.

Begin and End

You can specify an explicit start time and end time, or an event that triggers an element's start or end, using the begin and end parameters. The time value that you specify is relative to when the element would normally begin.

For example, when you specify

```
<img src="slide1.jpg" region="r1" begin="5sec"/>
```

you get this timing:

- If the element is part of a <seq> </seq> sequence, it begins 5 seconds after the preceding element ends.

- If the element is part of a <par> </par> group, it begins 5 seconds after the parallel group as a whole begins.

If you specify an end time, the element ends that amount of time after it would naturally *begin*. For example:

```
<img src="slide1.jpg" region="r1" begin="5sec"
  end="35sec" />
```

In this example, the image begins 5 seconds after its natural start time, and it ends 35 seconds after its natural start time, giving it a duration of 30 seconds. The element's duration is equal to its end time minus its start time. If no begin value is specified, an end value is the equivalent of a dur value.

Alternatively, you can specify that an element should begin or end when another element begins, ends, or reaches a specified duration. Instead of using a time as the value of the begin or end parameter, use the string

```
"id(idname)(event)"
```

where *idname* is the id value of another element, and *event* is either begin, end, or a time value. For example:

```
<par>
    <audio src="themesong.mp3" id="x" />
    <img src="poster.jpg" region="r1" end="id(x)(end)" />
    <text src="lyrics.txt" region="r2" end="id(x)(end)" />
</par>
```

This example assigns an id of x to the audio and sets the end of the image and text elements to synchronize with the end of element x.

Here's another example:

```
<par>
    <audio src="Sound1.aif" id="master" />
    <audio src="Sound2.aif" begin="id(master)(5sec)" />
    <audio src="Sound3.aif" end="id(master)(end)" />
</par>
```

In this example, the element Sound1.aif begins normally and has the id of "master". Sound2.aif begins 5 seconds after master begins. Sound3.aif begins normally, but ends when master ends.

Playing Clips

You can specify a clip from a media element using the begin-clip and end-clip attributes. This lets you play a selection from a longer file or stream. Clips work most efficiently with local content or streams—files delivered by HTTP will download in their entirety, even if only a small clip is actually played, and the file must download to the begin-clip point before it can play.

Tip Don't confuse begin-clip and end-clip with begin and end.

Clickable Links

You can make any visual media element in a SMIL document into a clickable link using the <a> </a> tags. You can direct the URL to load in a browser window or to replace the current SMIL presentation.

To make a visual element into a link:

- precede the element with the <a> tag
- put the URL of the link in the href parameter
- set the show parameter to "new" or "replace"
- follow the element with the </a> tag

The end result looks like this:

```
<a href="http://www.apple.com/" show="new" >
   <img src="poster.jpg" region="r1" dur="00:05" />
</a>
```

In this example, if the user clicks in region r1 while poster.jpg is being displayed there, the Apple website loads in the default browser window.

The show parameter can have two possible values:

- show="replace"—replaces the current SMIL presentation in the plug-in or QuickTime Player (whichever is active). The URL must specify something that QuickTime can play.
- show="new"—opens the URL in the default browser window. The URL can specify a Web page or anything the browser or one of its plug-ins can display.

You can use show="new" to target a specific browser frame, specific browser window, or QuickTime Player, using the target SMIL extension. See "QuickTime SMIL Extensions," beginning on page 602.

QuickTime doesn't currently allow you to jump to named points in SMIL presentations using the href parameter—you can't use URLs of the form href=filename.smi#name or href=#name.

Note Even though you can't use href parameters to jump around in the current presentation, you can still give users a way to navigate the SMIL timeline. If you use the chapter SMIL extension, it creates a chapter list in the movie controller, allowing the viewer to jump to named points in the presentation using a pop-up menu. See "QuickTime SMIL Extensions," beginning on page 602.

Throwing a Switch

You can automatically present different elements to different viewers using the <switch> </switch> tags.

SMIL supports a set of user attributes, such as screen resolution, color depth, maximum data rate, and language. Groups of elements can be listed between <switch> and </switch> tags. QuickTime selects one element from the list based on user attributes, much like QuickTime's alternate track and alternate movie mechanism.

This can be used to select an audio track based on language, for example:

```
<switch>
    <audio src="french.aif" system-language="fr"/>
    <audio src="german.aif" system-language="de"/>
    <audio src="english.aif" system-language="en"/>
</switch>
```

This example selects french.aif for French speakers, german.aif for German speakers, and english.aif for English speakers.

The <switch> element selects the first item in the list that matches the user's system attributes. If you're selecting an item based on connection speed, list the elements from highest speed to lowest speed—QuickTime loads the first element the viewer's connection speed can handle:

```
<switch>
    <audio src="192k.mp3" system-bitrate="192000"/>
    <audio src="128k.mp3" system-bitrate="128000"/>
    <audio src="qdesign.mov" system-bitrate="28800"/>
</switch>
```

This example plays 192k.mp3 for people with high-speed connections, 128k.mp3 for people with connections slower than 192 Kbits/sec, but as fast or faster than 128 Kbits/sec, and qdesign.mov for people with connections slower than 128 Kbits/sec, but at least 28.8 Kbits/sec.

To provide a default, make the default the last item in the list and don't specify any required attributes. For example:

```
<switch>
    <audio src="french.aif" system-language="fr"/>
    <audio src="german.aif" system-language="de"/>
    <audio src="english.aif"/>
</switch>
```

This example selects french.aif for French speakers, german.aif for German speakers, and english.aif for all others. It's almost always a good idea to include a default.

QuickTime supports the following user attributes:

- system-bitrate—corresponds to the user's connection speed in the QuickTime Settings control panel. For example: 14400, 33600, 56000, 128000.

- system-language—corresponds to the user's system language setting. The language is specified by a two-character code matching the ISO 639 language code specification, such as these:

Language	Code	Language	Code
Arabic	AR	Japanese	JA
Chinese	ZH	Korean	KO
Danish	DA	Persian (Farsi)	FA
Dutch	NL	Polish	PL
English	EN	Portuguese	PT
French	FR	Russian	RU
German	DE	Spanish	ES
Greek	EL	Swahili	SW
Italian	IT	Swedish	SV

For additional language codes, see

www.oasis-open.org/cover/iso639a.html

- system-screen-size—the minimum required screen resolution in pixels. The resolution is specified by *HeightxWidth*. Note that this is contrary to common usage—a 640 x 480 minimum screen resolution is specified by system-screen-size="480x640".

- system-screen-depth—the minimum required color depth, in bits. Common values are 8 (256 colors), 16 (thousands of colors), and 24 (millions of colors).

Tip For selections based on bit rate, screen size, or screen depth, always list the elements from most demanding to least demanding, and always include a default element with no required attributes as the last item in the list.

That's it for the tutorial on SMIL. For the full SMIL specification, check the W3C website: www.w3.org/ (be forewarned—the spec is not for the faint of heart). QuickTime doesn't currently support all the features described in the spec, however—only the features described in this chapter.

There's also a good SMIL tutorial on the Web at

www.helio.org/products/smil/tutorial/

Now let's look at using SMIL in QuickTime.

QuickTime and SMIL

SMIL presentations make a nice addition to QuickTime. You can create standard SMIL documents and play them from the desktop or in a browser as if they were QuickTime movies. There are also QuickTime-specific extensions to SMIL that you can use to enhance your presentations.

Creating QuickTime-Friendly SMIL Documents

There are three primary things you should do to make your SMIL presentations QuickTime-friendly:

- Use media elements QuickTime can play.
- Minimize the number of structural elements.
- Use only the parts of SMIL that QuickTime supports.

First, for QuickTime to play a SMIL presentation, the presentation must be made up of media elements that QuickTime can play individually. This includes QuickTime movies, real-time streams in QuickTime format, AIFF and MP3 sound files, JPEG and GIF images, FLIC animations, text files, and MIDI music files. It doesn't include .rm, .ram, or .asm files.

Tip If you can use a URL in the QTSRC parameter of an <EMBED> tag, and the QuickTime plug-in can play it successfully, you can use that URL as a media element in a SMIL document for QuickTime.

Second, QuickTime must parse every <seq> and <par> element in a presentation and turn it into a movie structure before the movie can play. If you have a hundred such elements, it will take several seconds to start the presentation—a viewer may think the computer has hung. For optimum performance, arrange your structure to minimize the number of required elements.

For example, suppose you have two display areas, and you want to display a series of images in each region, synchronized to play together. You could make a parallel group for each pair of images and have a sequence of parallel groups. If you had 20 pairs of images, this would create 20 <par> elements. Alternately, you could treat the two regions as each having a sequence of images, with the two sequences running in parallel. This would require only one <par> and two <seq> elements, no matter how many slides you used.

Third, QuickTime doesn't currently support the whole SMIL specification—you can use all the SMIL tags and parameters described in the chapter, but if you're working from the W3C specification, note the following exceptions:

- Regions can't have scroll bars (don't use fit="scroll" in the <region> tag).

- The repeat attribute is not supported.

- Only the basic layout is supported (no CSS-based layout).

- The <switch> tag can't be used to specify a root layout from a list.

- Hyperlinks can't be used to pause the current SMIL presentation, load another one, then resume the current presentation (don't use show="pause" in the <a> tag).

- You can't jump to a named point in a SMIL presentation—don't use links of the form <a href="fname.smil#anchor" > or <a href= "#anchor" >.

- The attribute value fill="freeze" is not supported for media elements.

- The background-color attribute is not supported for regions, only for the root layout.

- The endsync attribute is not supported.

Examples

A common use of SMIL is to specify an advertisement that should play when the viewer requests a live stream. Here's a simple SMIL document that does just that. It defines a display area and a background color, then specifies two display regions—one for the ad and one for the live stream. It plays an ad—a QuickTime movie from the CD—that includes a click-through link to www.apple.com. When the ad is done, the SMIL document opens a live stream.

```
<smil>
   <head>
   <layout>
   <root-layout id="rl" width="320" height="240"
      background-color="red"/>

   <region id="ad" width="200" height="240" left="60" top="0" />
   <region id="bbc" width="100%" height="100%" fit="fill"/>
   </layout>
   </head>

   <body>
   <seq>
      <!-- ad -->
      <a href="http://www.apple.com"show="new">
         <video src="sample.mov" region="ad" />
      </a>
      <!-- live stream -->
      <video src="rtsp://a628.q.kamai.net/7/628/52/935780134/
      qtv.akamai.com/bbc/bbc100" region="bbc" />
   </seq>
   </body>
</smil>
```

Note that the ad is centered by specifying a top and left offset for the ad region. Note also that you must specify both top and left as a pair, even though the top offset is 0. The live stream's region is set to 100% of the available display area, and the stream's visual area is scaled up to fill the region by specifying fit="fill".

This example can be found as ad.smil in the SMIL folder of the CD.

As another example, here's a way to create a narrated slideshow using SMIL:

1. Step through your slides using any tool, such as PowerPoint, JPEGView, or QuickTime Player (Present Movie—Slideshow mode).

2. Record a narration as you go, using recording software or recording to tape and capturing to disk later.

3. Open your narration in QuickTime Player, choose Get Movie Properties, and display the movie time as you listen to your narration.

4. Write down the appropriate time to begin displaying each slide.

5. Write a SMIL document like the one below, substituting the URLs of your slides and narration, and changing the slide durations as appropriate.

```
<smil>
  <head>
  <layout>
     <root-layout id="rl" width="320" height="240"
        background-color="black" />

     <region id="slides" width="320" height="240" />
  </layout>
  </head>
  <body>
  <par>
  <audio src="narration.aif" />
  <seq>
     <img src="slide1.jpg" region="slides" dur="5S" />
     <img src="slide2.jpg" region="slides" dur="15S" />
     <img src="slide3.jpg" region="slides" dur="10S" />
  </seq>
  </par>
  </body>
</smil>
```

This creates a slideshow that starts the audio narration and the first slide in parallel, then displays the slides in sequence, giving each slide the specified duration.

This example is in the SMIL folder of the CD as slides.smil. Feel free to open it with a text editor and use it as a template.

Special Media Types

Text files, QuickTime VR panoramas and object movies, and HTML pages can all be specified as media elements in SMIL documents for QuickTime, but they deserve special mention.

Text

You normally specify a text file as a media element using the <text> tag:

```
<text src="http://my.server.com/some.txt" region="rl" dur="5" />
```

Other SMIL players may present the whole text file as a block of text. QuickTime displays the text as it would any text file imported into QuickTime Player. You can see how the text will be displayed by importing it into QuickTime Player using the default import settings.

To modify the way the text is presented, import the text into QuickTime Player using any settings you like, export it as Text with Descriptors, and edit the descriptors in the exported file as needed. This process is described in "Creating Text Tracks" (page 357). You can also generate a text file that includes QuickTime text descriptor tags using a CGI script or other software.

You can use a text file with QuickTime text descriptors in it as a SMIL media element. All the descriptors are supported, including scrolling, keyed text, and hyperlinks.

SMIL considers text as not having an inherent duration, but importing a text file into QuickTime creates a movie with a duration of 2 seconds for each paragraph of text, or the duration specified by the last time stamp in the file.

If you specify a duration for a text element that's less than the duration of the text movie that QuickTime creates, the display of the text movie is truncated.

You can get around this by specifying the text file using the <video> tag:

```
<video src="http://www.server.com/some.txt"
  region="aregion" />
```

This causes the text to be displayed for the duration of the text movie that QuickTime creates.

VR

Specify a QuickTime VR panorama or object movie using the <video> tag:

```
<video src="http://www.myserver.com/vr.mov"
  region="aregion" />
```

You can use VR panoramas and object movies, including multinode panoramas and VR movies that have been enhanced using wired sprites, soundsaVR, or revolVR.

However, VR movies inside SMIL presentations don't have a VR controller attached. Viewers can navigate the VR movie in QuickTime Player by using the mouse to drag left, right, up, and down, and to click from node to node, but they can't zoom in or zoom out. You can add zoom controls by adding a wired sprite controller to the VR movie, as described in Chapter 19 in "Adding a Wired Sprite Controller to a VR Panorama" (page 656).

You'll find a wired sprite controller that you can use for this, vrcontrol.mov, in the Virtual folder of the CD.

If a VR movie inside a SMIL presentation is played using the QuickTime browser plug-in, rather than QuickTime Player, a bug currently prevents mouse-button-down events from reaching the VR movie. If you need to play your VR movie in a SMIL document, it's better to target QuickTime Player.

If you must use the plug-in to play VR inside of SMIL, the user will be unable to drag in the movie to navigate—you need to provide wired sprite controls that work while the mouse is over them, instead of when the mouse button is pressed. There's a controller that does exactly what you need in the VR folder of the CD. It's named hovrcontrol.mov.

HTML

You can't display HTML pages inside QuickTime Player or the QuickTime plug-in. It's possible to use SMIL to display media *from* a Web page in QuickTime Player or the QuickTime plug-in, however. This capability is currently very limited, but it may be sufficient for your needs.

Suppose you want QuickTime to display an animated GIF, for example, but you don't have a URL for the GIF itself, just the URL of a Web page that uses the GIF as a banner ad.

Note This is fairly common if you have a script that generates Web pages and inserts banner ads according to an algorithm, and you want to take advantage of this script to put the same ad in a SMIL presentation.

Use the SMIL <img> tag to set up the presentation for the GIF, but use the URL of the Web page that contains the GIF in the SRC parameter. For this to work, you need to explicitly set the MIME type to HTML in the element tag:

```
type="text/x-html-insertion"
```

The SMIL element looks like this:

```
<img src="http://www.myserver.com/index.html"
    type="text/x-html-insertion" region="aregion" dur="time" />
```

QuickTime opens the HTML document specified in the URL and scans it for any playable media specified by a SRC parameter in the HTML. QuickTime follows a particular logic in scanning a document for a playable element:

- First it looks for an `<A HREF>` tag that uses an image for an anchor, such as `<A HREF="www.sponsor.com"><IMG SRC="adbanner.gif"></A>`.
- If no `<A HREF>` tag with an image source is found, QuickTime looks for an `<EMBED>` tag with a playable source, such as `<EMBED SRC="playable.mov">`.
- If no `<EMBED>` tag with a playable source is found, QuickTime looks for an `<IMG>` tag, such as `<IMG SRC="displaythis.jpg">`.

QuickTime takes the first source that it finds using this logic and attempts to use it as the media element specified in the SMIL document. For this to work, the first source QuickTime finds needs to match the specified element type, such as audio, video, or image.

Here's an example of a Web page with a banner ad, and a SMIL document that uses the banner ad from the Web page as a clickable link over a streaming movie:

```
<HTML>
    <HEAD> <TITLE>Welcome to XYZ Corp</TITLE></HEAD>

    <BODY>
        <A HREF="sponsor.htm"><IMG SRC="adbanner.gif"></A>
        ...
    </BODY>
</HTML>

<smil>
    <head>
        <layout>
            <root-layout height="290" width="512"
                background-color="black" />
            <region id="ad" height="50" width="512" />
```

```
            <region id="movie" height="240" width="320"
                 top="50" left="98" />
         </layout>
      </head>

      <body>
         <par>
         <a href="sponsor.htm" show="new">
            <img src="welcometoxyz.html"
                 type="text/x-html-insertion"
                 region="ad" end="id(x)(end)" />
         </a>
         <video src="rtsp://server/stream.mov"
              region="movie" id="x" />
         </par>
      </body>
</smil>
```

QuickTime SMIL Extensions

SMIL is an extensible standard, and QuickTime provides several SMIL extensions. This allows you to add QuickTime-specific attributes to your SMIL presentation, such as autoplay="true".

To use QuickTime extensions in your SMIL document, include the xmlns: parameter and the URL of the QuickTime extensions as part of the initial <smil> tag:

```
<smil
xmlns:qt="http://www.apple.com/quicktime/resources/
  smilextensions">
```

QuickTime doesn't actually access the URL; it's used only to uniquely identify the QuickTime SMIL extensions.

You can include QuickTime extensions within the <smil> tag, along with the URL. For example, to create a SMIL presentation that starts automatically:

```
<smil
xmlns:qt="http://www.apple.com/quicktime/resources/
  smilextensions"
qt:autoplay="true">
```

In the examples that follow, the `xmlns:` parameter and the URL have been omitted for readability, but they are a required part of the `<smil>` tag when any QuickTime extensions are used in a SMIL presentation. These are the current QuickTime SMIL extensions:

- **autoplay**
  Specifies whether the presentation should play automatically. Legal values are `true` or `false`. The default is `false`.

Example   `<smil qt:autoplay="true">`

- **bitrate**
  Specifies the bandwidth a media object needs in order to play back in real time. This is used to give QuickTime enough information to decide how far in advance to begin loading a media element to provide seamless playback. Possible values are positive integers, in bits per second. See also `preroll`.

Example   `<video src="stream56k.mov" qt:bitrate="56000" />`

Important   Don't confuse `qt:bitrate` with `system-bitrate`. Use `system-bitrate` to select a media element based on the user's connection speed. Use `qt:bitrate` to help QuickTime determine when to start downloading a media element.

- **chapter**
  Specifies a chapter name for a media element. Valid values are any character string. This creates a QuickTime chapter list—a pop-up menu in the movie controller with the name of each chapter. Choosing a chapter name from the menu causes the SMIL presentation to jump to the appropriate point in its timeline.

Example   `<video src="some.mov" qt:chapter="chap1" region="r1" />`

- **chapter-mode**
  Specifies whether the Time slider represents the duration of the whole presentation or the duration of the current chapter. Legal values are `all` and `clip`. Specify `all` for the whole presentation, `clip` for chapter-at-a-time.

Example   `<smil qt:chapter-mode="clip"/>`

- **composite-mode**

  Specifies the graphics mode of a media element. This is used to create partial or complete transparency. See "Transparency and Alpha Channels" (page 271). Possible modes are

  - **copy**
    none
    direct

    These modes all specify no transparency, which is the default for most image formats.

  - **blend;***percent*

    Specifies a blend between the image and the background, with a required *percent* integer value (for example, 50%) specifying the blend weight—0% means complete transparency, 100% complete opacity.

  - **transparent-color;***color*

    Specifies that all pixels of a particular color within the image should be treated as transparent. It accepts a second parameter, *color*, that specifies the color to be rendered as transparent. The color parameter may be any valid color specification supported by Cascading Style Sheets, level 2.

  - **alpha**
    straight-alpha
    premultiplied-white-alpha
    premultiplied-black-alpha

    Specify that the image has an internal alpha channel that should be used when compositing. The `alpha` and `straight-alpha` modes refer to a separate alpha component; the `premultiplied` modes refer to an image that has been premultiplied with the alpha against a white or black background, respectively.

  - **straight-alpha-blend;***percent*

    Specifies that the image has an internal alpha channel as a separate component, and that an additional level of transparency should be applied to the whole image.

Example   `<img src="test.png" qt:composite-mode="alpha" />`

- **full-screen**

  Tells QuickTime Player to use the whole screen when displaying the SMIL presentation. Any part of the screen not used in the presentation is cleared to black. The presentation plays automatically until it ends, then exits full-screen mode. No controller is displayed (the viewer must press the Esc key in order to exit full-screen mode before the presentation ends). Legal values are `false` (default), `normal`, `half`, `double`, `current`, or `full`.

Example `<smil qt:fullscreen="double">`

- **immediate-instantiation**
  When used in the `<smil>` tag, specifies whether all the media elements in the presentation should be downloaded (or streamed) immediately or whether this should be deferred until each element is about to be played. Legal values are `true` and `false`. Default is `false`. Opening all the media elements at the beginning of the presentation can take considerable time and memory, so we recommend that it be done only for simple presentations with a few small media elements.

  When used in an element tag, specifies that this particular element should be downloaded or streamed as soon as the presentation is opened. You might use this to preload an element to be sure it is already in memory when it needs to play.

Example `<smil qt:immediate-instantiation="true">`

Example `<img src="bgimg.png" qt:immediate-instantiation="true"/>`

- **next**
  Specifies a presentation to play when this presentation finishes. Legal value is the URL of something QuickTime can play: a media file, a movie, a stream, or a SMIL presentation. This is similar to the QuickTime plug-in's `QTNEXT` parameter.

Example `<smil qt:next="nextpresentation.smil">`

- **preroll**
  Tells QuickTime to start loading a media element a certain number of seconds before it is scheduled to play. For example, if you know it takes 30 seconds to load a large image over the user's Internet connection, you might set preroll to 30. The default preroll is 15 seconds when this is not specified (unless `qt:immediate-instantiation` is specified, in which case the media element is loaded "immediately").

Example `<img src="http://isp.com/giant.jpg" qt:preroll="30">`

- **system-mime-type-supported**
  Specifies the MIME type that needs to be supported in order to play a media element. This is normally used in conjunction with the `<switch>` tag to allow the player software to choose a media element that it can handle. Possible values are character strings matching a valid MIME type.

Example
```
<switch>
<img src="qt.mov"
qt:system-mime-type-supported="video/quicktime"/>
<img src="someotherformat.suffix"
qt:system-mime-type-supported= "other/mime-type"/>
</switch>
```

- **target**
  Specifies a target for a presentation specified by the `href` parameter in the anchor tag. Possible targets are an existing browser window, a browser frame, or `quicktimeplayer`. If the target string is none of these, a new browser window is created. Used in conjunction with `show="new"`.

Example
```
<a href="http://www.server.com/another.smil" show="new"
qt:target="quicktimeplayer">
<img src="OpenNewSMIL.gif" region="r2" dur="5:00" />
</a>
```

- **time-slider**
  Specifies whether the movie controller should include a Time slider. During a SMIL presentation, QuickTime dynamically loads media elements as required, so the known duration of the overall presentation can change as a movie is played or navigated. When the known duration changes, the scale of the Time slider changes to reflect that. This can be confusing to the viewer. Because of this, QuickTime movies created from SMIL documents do not normally display a Time slider. Legal values are `true` and `false`. Default is `false`.

Example
```
<smil qt:time-slider="true">
```

Note If you want to import a SMIL presentation into QuickTime and edit it using QuickTime Player's editing features, you must set `time-slider="true"`. QuickTime Player's editing features rely on the Time slider.

Embedding SMIL Documents in a Web Page

There are four ways to embed a SMIL document in a Web page so that it plays in QuickTime Player or the QuickTime plug-in:

- Use the QTSRC parameter.
- Save the SMIL document as a .mov file.
- Make a Fast Start reference movie.
- Target the SMIL document to QuickTime Player.

Important Other applications, such as RealPlayer and Windows Media Player, also use SMIL, but support a different set of media elements. The viewer's browser may be configured to use any of these for .smil files. To be sure that QuickTime handles your SMIL document, use one of the techniques described in this section.

It's also worthwhile to have your webmaster configure your Web server to associate the .sml and .smil file extensions with the MIME type application/smil. Otherwise, the browser may treat the SMIL document as a text file. This is a fairly common problem because SMIL documents *are* text files.

Using QTSRC

The <EMBED> tag's QTSRC parameter is the ideal way to pass a SMIL document to QuickTime. The SRC parameter should point to a small image that says, "You need QuickTime 4.1 or later to see this movie." Feel free to use UNeedQT41.qti, in the SMIL folder of the CD.

The HTML looks like this:

```
<EMBED SRC="UNeedQT41.qti" TYPE="image/x-quicktime"
  HEIGHT=256 WIDTH=320 QTSRC="smil1.smil">
```

Set the height and width to the dimensions of your SMIL presentation, adding 16 to the height for the movie controller. The usual plug-in parameters, such as AUTOSTART="True" and CONTROLLER="False", work normally.

Remember, the movie controller won't have a Time slider unless you specify one using qt:time-slider="true" in the SMIL presentation. See "QuickTime SMIL Extensions," beginning on page 602, for details.

If your SMIL presentation is a different height or width from the image specified in the SRC parameter, use the larger dimensions as your height and width, and set a background color using the BGCOLOR parameter to fill any gaps.

As long as the viewer has QuickTime 4 or later installed, the QuickTime plug-in is called when a .qti file is specified in the SRC parameter. If the viewer has QuickTime 4.1 or later, QuickTime plays the SMIL presentation specified in the QTSRC parameter. Viewers with QuickTime 4 see the single image instead. If you want people with QuickTime 3 to see a "You need QuickTime 4.1" image, use a .pntg image in the SRC parameter instead of a .qti image. See "Adding the <OBJECT> Tag" (page 48) for details.

Saving a SMIL Document as a .mov File

A SMIL document is really a text file. Saving it with the .smil file extension is a way to let the Web server and the browser know that it describes a SMIL presentation. Saving or renaming the same file with the .mov file extension normally causes the browser to use the QuickTime plug-in to handle the file. Add the eight-character string SMILtext to the beginning of the file so QuickTime knows what it is when it opens it.

Important The first eight characters of the file *must* be SMILtext in order for QuickTime to successfully import a SMIL file saved with the .mov file extension: <smil> becomes SMILtext <smil>.

The HTML looks like this:

```
<EMBED SRC="smil1.mov" HEIGHT=256 WIDTH=320>
```

Set the height and width to the dimensions of your SMIL presentation, adding 16 to the height for the movie controller. All the optional parameters work normally.

The main disadvantage to this technique is that there's no fallback movie if the viewer doesn't have QuickTime 4.1 or later installed, or has Windows Media Player configured to handle .mov files.

Make sure your Web page has a Get QuickTime button if you use this method, and this shouldn't be too much of a problem.

Making a Fast Start Reference Movie

You can open a SMIL document in QuickTime Player and save it as a self-contained movie. This creates a Fast Start movie that you can double-click from the desktop or embed in a Web page.

A Fast Start movie created this way typically has several tracks. The display area defined in the SMIL document's root-layout element becomes a video track with the specified background color, and each media element in the SMIL document becomes a movie track with a URL data reference. The tracks are arranged in time and space as the SMIL document describes.

The media elements are not copied into the Fast Start movie, only their URLs. If your SMIL document uses relative URLs, you need to maintain the same relative path between the Fast Start movie and its media elements as existed between the original SMIL document and the media elements.

When the Fast Start movie is played in the QuickTime plug-in or Quick-Time Player, each URL is resolved as needed. Embed it in a Web page as you would any Fast Start movie:

```
<EMBED SRC="smil1.mov" HEIGHT=256 WIDTH=320>
```

Set the height and width to the dimensions of the movie, adding 16 to the height for the movie controller. All the optional parameters work normally.

The main advantage to this technique is that you can manipulate the SMIL presentation as a QuickTime movie in all the usual ways; set it to autoplay or play at double size in QuickTime Player, add locally stored tracks, or use Plug-in Helper to copy-protect the movie. In addition, the URLs of your media elements are concealed from the casual observer (it's possible to ferret them out by doing an ASCII dump of the movie file, but they're no longer in plain text).

Note If you want to edit the movie using QuickTime Player's editing features—to add a chapter list for example—you must set qt:time-slider="true" in the SMIL document before importing it. QuickTime Player's editing features rely on the Time slider.

You can pass a .mov file made from a SMIL presentation in the QTSRC parameter and provide a fallback image in the SRC parameter, for people with older versions of QuickTime and to prevent MIME-type hijacking.

You can also include a SMIL movie as an alternate in a reference movie, with a fallback movie for people who don't have QuickTime 4.1 or later.

You can use a Fast Start reference movie of the SMIL presentation with MakeRefMovie or use the SMIL file's URL with XMLtoRefMovie—both are described in Chapter 8, "Alternate Realities: Language, Speed, and Connections."

The main disadvantage of using a Fast Start movie is that you can't edit or create it using a text editor or the text output of a script. You need to edit or create the SMIL document, import it into QuickTime Player, and save it. It's an extra step.

Targeting QuickTime Player

You can specify a QuickTime image in the SRC parameter and link it to a SMIL document using the HREF or QTNEXT parameter, with the target set to QuickTime Player.

The main advantage to this approach is that the SMIL presentation takes place outside the browser, so you're not constrained by the size or appearance of the browser window. You can even use full-screen mode.

If you want a mouse click to launch the SMIL presentation, the HTML looks like this:

```
<EMBED SRC="poster.qti" TYPE="image/x-quicktime"
  HEIGHT=160 WIDTH=120
  AUTOSTART="False" CONTROLLER="False"
  HREF="smil1.smil" TARGET="quicktimeplayer">
```

Set the height and width to the dimensions of the poster. When someone clicks the poster, the SMIL document loads in QuickTime Player as a movie. Playing the movie causes QuickTime Player to fetch the media elements as needed.

If you want to launch a SMIL presentation in QuickTime Player without making the viewer click a poster, add the AUTOHREF parameter. The HTML looks like this:

```
<EMBED SRC="poster.qti" TYPE="image/x-quicktime"
  HEIGHT=160 WIDTH=120 AUTOHREF="True"
  AUTOSTART="False" CONTROLLER="False"
  HREF="smil1.smil" TARGET="quicktimeplayer">
```

Set the height and width to the dimensions of poster.qti, which can optionally be hidden (HIDDEN="True"). The SMIL presentation launches immediately in QuickTime Player.

If you want to launch a SMIL presentation in QuickTime Player after playing an introductory movie in the plug-in, use the QTNEXT parameter. The HTML looks like this:

```
<EMBED SRC="intro.mov" TYPE="video/quicktime"
  HEIGHT=160 WIDTH=120
  AUTOSTART="True" CONTROLLER="False"
  QTNEXT1="smil1.smil" TARGET1="quicktimeplayer">
```

Set the height and width to the dimensions of intro.mov, which can optionally be hidden for an audio fanfare (HIDDEN="True"). The SMIL presentation launches in QuickTime Player when intro.mov finishes playing.

19

Let's Get Virtual

Sometimes a picture is worth a lot more than a thousand words. For travel, architecture, real estate, fine arts, or anatomy, there is just no substitute for a picture. In fact, one picture may not be enough. You may need several pictures, or even a physical model.

But a single picture is often your only opportunity to engage the browsing reader's interest, convincing them to stop and look inside. So what can you do when a picture needs to be worth a million words?

QuickTime Virtual Reality (QTVR) is a picture worth a thousand pictures. It's a picture of a landscape that invites your viewers to explore, to stick their heads inside the frame and look around, to crane their necks up and down, zoom in and read the brushstrokes on the canvas. It's a picture of an object that invites the reader to pick it up and turn it over, to look at it from every angle. QTVR is photorealistic and interactive. It grabs people's attention like nothing else. It's magic.

QuickTime VR landscapes are called panoramas (they aren't just landscapes; they can display the interior of a building, an automobile, or an art studio). QuickTime VR models are called object movies. QTVR can be cylindrical (a landscape where you can turn around, or an object you can rotate on one axis) or cubic (a panorama where you can also look up and down, or an object you can rotate on any axis).

This chapter covers

- an overview of QuickTime VR
- creating QTVR panoramas, both cylinders and cubes
- creating QTVR object movies
- compositing QTVR tracks with other QuickTime media
- embedding QTVR movies in a Web page

▶ QuickTime VR Overview

QuickTime Virtual Reality (QTVR for short) delivers a photorealistic virtual reality experience. This is different from model-based virtual reality formats such as VRML, which usually offer much lower visual quality in exchange for a faster download. QuickTime VR can offer extremely high visual quality, but it usually requires a large image download.

Note You can provide a low-res preview that downloads quickly and is gradually replaced by a high-res image, or use the new Zoomify component to download higher-resolution tiles as needed to give the viewer staggering resolution without a staggering download. For details, see "Zoomify It?" (page 638).

QuickTime VR comes in two distinct flavors—panoramas and object movies. They're both pretty tasty.

Pan-O-Rama

A QTVR panorama let's you stand in a virtual place and look around. It generally provides a full 360° panorama and the ability to tilt up and down about 120°, but the actual horizontal and vertical range is determined by the panorama itself—you can create a panorama that allows you to view 360° in all directions, including up and down, or restrict it to a narrow field in one plane. You look around by dragging with the mouse or using the arrow keys. You can make a panorama auto-rotate by adding a sprite.

Panoramas typically offer the viewer the ability to zoom in and out as well; the amount of zoom available usually depends on the resolution of the image—there's no sense letting the viewer zoom in until a single pixel fills the screen.

For an example of a simple QTVR panorama, see `Pigeonpoint.mov`, in the Virtual folder of the CD.

Panoramas can be created from actual photographs or from images rendered by 3D software. You can create panoramas from architectural rendering software, such as ArchiCAD, or virtual landscape software, such as MetaCreations' Bryce or Pandromeda's MojoWorld. Some 3D software can render directly to QuickTime VR panoramas; other software renders a series of views that can be stitched together like photographs.

A panorama can consist of the view from a single place or a linked set of views from a number of places. Each viewpoint is called a node, and a series of linked viewpoints is called a multinode panorama, or scene. The viewer can move from node to node by clicking hotspots. Hotspots can also be linked to URLs or wired sprite actions.

A typical multinode panorama might feature the view of a building from the outside, linked to an interior view by clicking a hotspot on the building's front door. Other interior views might be reached by clicking hotspots on interior doorways or staircases, allowing the viewer to "walk through" a building.

If you search the World Wide Web, you'll find QTVR panoramas of Mayan temples, the Louvre museum, New York tenements, Greek islands, Hawaiian bed and breakfasts, and countless real-estate sites. It's not quite as good as being there yourself, but it can save you a trek through the jungle, a trip halfway around the world, or a drive across town—or perhaps inspire you to actually make the journey.

A QTVR panorama is typically a series of photographs or computer renderings, stitched together and projected mathematically onto a cylinder or a cube, then displayed through a window on a computer (I know, it does sound romantic when you describe it that way).

Most people have been tempted at one time or another to take a series of pictures, turning in a circle to get the full view of some spectacular place, then lay the pictures out side by side in a photo album.

That's pretty much what a cylindrical QTVR panorama is, only you digitize the pictures, use software tools to lay them out side by side, and instead of a photo album, you put them on a CD or the World Wide Web.

Because of the mathematical stitching and projection, it's possible for QuickTime to pan smoothly through the images as the viewer drags left or right, rather than clicking from one image to the next, so the viewer sees one continuous image (a cylinder) rather than a series of views (a polygon).

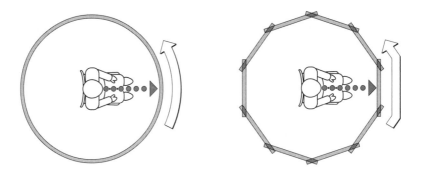

QuickTime allows the viewer to see one continuous image rather than a series of views.

QuickTime not only smooths the transition between images, it blends them into a single image, correcting for changes in perspective in real time as you look around. There are a number of JavaScript viewers available that allow you to pan around in a QuickTime VR without installing Quick-

Time, but to date none of them perform this perspective correction. The difference is like night and day.

Starting with QuickTime 5, it's possible to make a panorama that lets you look in *any* direction—a full 360° left or right, 180° up or down. This would be like going into a room with images projected on all four walls, the ceiling, and the floor. The image is mathematically corrected as you look around, so again you see a continuous image, rather than the faces of a cube. For the person watching, it's like floating in a glass bubble. This new type of panorama is called cubic VR, or a cube, and the original type is now called a cylindrical panorama, or cylinder. Of course, when you say something like "drag with the mouse to look around in a VR panorama," it applies equally to both types.

Object Oriented

A QTVR object movie is usually a series of still images showing an object from several angles. It typically shows an object in full rotation, often tilted at several angles as well. The images are arranged so that when the viewer drags using the mouse, the object seems to tilt and rotate.

Unlike a VR panorama, an object movie jumps from one discrete image to the next—there is no stitching, blending, or projection. The illusion of motion is created by the persistence of vision and by using images that vary only slightly from frame to frame, exactly like a motion picture.

In fact, if you put an object on a turntable and film it as it makes one rotation, you can use the footage as either a normal QuickTime movie or a simple QTVR object movie (the viewer can rotate the object but not tilt it). To see an example of this, open Objects.htm, in the Virtual folder of the CD. It uses the same series of images as a normal, or "linear," QuickTime movie and as a QTVR object movie.

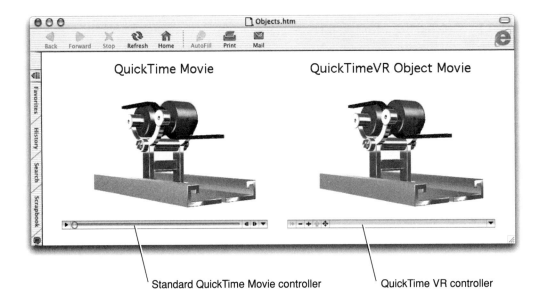

QuickTime Movie   QuickTimeVR Object Movie

Standard QuickTime Movie controller   QuickTime VR controller

As you can see, the main difference is the user interface. With the linear movie controller, the viewer can play the movie or pause it; with the object movie controller, the viewer can drag the image to rotate it. Dragging the indicator in the Time slider in the linear movie's control bar has much the same effect as dragging the object in the object movie; the main difference is that the slider has a beginning and an end, whereas you can keep spinning the object until your arm gets tired.

But suppose you filmed a rotating object from several angles by tilting the camera a little for each rotation. You would have images of the object from several tilt angles at each point in its rotation.

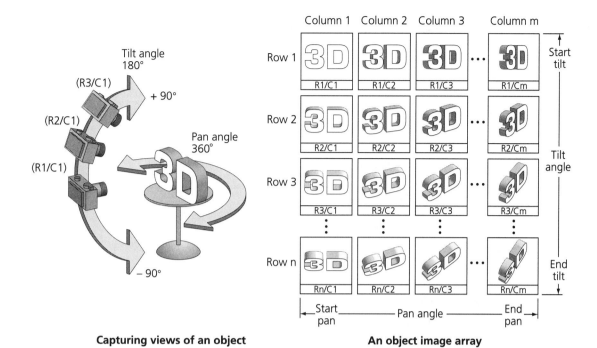

Capturing views of an object   **An object image array**

If you arrange the images in a grid, you can not only see the image rotate by panning left or right through the pictures, you can see the object tilt at any point in its rotation by panning up and down.

This is called a multirow object movie, and it allows the viewer to tilt and rotate the viewed object. For an example, see iBookQTVR.mov (in the Virtual folder on the CD).

You don't have to provide full rotation of an object—you can film, photograph, or render the object through as many or as few degrees of rotation as you like. Similarly, an object movie can have a single row, and no tilt control, or multiple rows (up to 256), providing views from straight overhead to directly underneath.

A typical object movie uses an image for every 10° of rotation or tilt. To make the apparent motion smoother, use more images separated by fewer degrees. To make the object movie smaller, either use fewer images with more degrees between them, or show less than 360° of rotation and 180° of tilt.

An object movie doesn't have to be a rotational view of an object. You can use any array of images you like. As an example, see ObjectLetters.mov (in the Virtual folder of the CD).

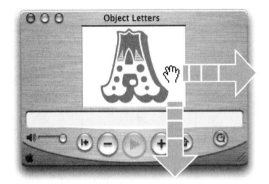

Drag to the right to see additional letters of the same font style

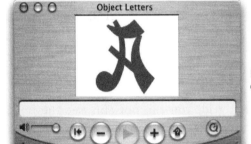

Drag downward to see letters of different font styles

An object movie doesn't have to be a series of still images, either. Each view of the object can be a video clip or an animation. You can mix and match, using animations for some views and still images for others (but each view has to have the same duration). You can set the object movie to autoplay the clip or animation whenever the user drags to a new view; you can also set the object movie to loop any clips or animations continuously. For an example of an object movie with animated views, see Laptopobj.mov (in the Virtual folder of the CD).

The images for an object movie can be digitized from photographs or video, or they can be rendered from a 3D-modeling program such as Infini-D.

Now let's look at how you actually create panoramas and object movies.

▶ Creating QTVR Panoramas

This section describes the equipment you need and the steps you need to take to create VR panoramas, both cylindrical and cubic. Of course, the equipment and the steps vary somewhat, depending on your circumstances and goals.

If you're rendering images using 3D software, for example, you don't need a camera. If you're using a film camera, you need to scan or digitize the images (with a digital camera, the images are already digitized). Regardless of your camera type, if you're shooting with a fish-eye lens you need to correct the distortion before you can stitch the images. Some tools work only with cylinders, while others work with cylinders or cubes, and some work with cubes only.

And of course, it takes more effort and better equipment to achieve museum-quality results than it does to show a house or share your vacation pictures over the Web.

Cranky Old Man Says...

When I was a boy, making QuickTime VR was *hard*. You had to work with a film camera on a tripod, fuss with the exposure, print the film, tape your prints to a flatbed scanner *just right*, scan them in and clean up the scans in Photoshop, give them sequential names, spend hours waiting for MPW, then later QTVR Studio, to work mathemagic on them, then touch them up again, then wait again for more mathemagic. When it finally came out of the oven, it was too big to download! And the average computer barely had the horsepower to display it in a tiny window. But it was so *cool* . . .

I don't how they managed back in the twentieth century, I really don't.

Anyway, here in the future it's all different. Shoot a series of overlapping pictures as you turn in a circle. (A tripod is good, an attachment that puts the point of rotation precisely under the camera lens is better, but you know—whatever.) Plug your camera into the computer, drag the images you want onto your favorite VR software, maybe drag the edges a little to line them up better, and click OK. A minute later you've got a VR panorama that anyone can play in full-screen mode. It works fine over the Internet. Still a little bulky for dialup, I guess, but what isn't? If it's really too big, just Zoomify it. Sheesh. Hmm, might as well add an AAC sound track and some sprites . . .

You kids today.

Equipment

Unless you're rendering panoramas directly from 3D-modeling software, you need a camera. You'll get much better results with a tripod. For professional work, you need some lenses, a sturdy tripod, a bubble level, and a special pano head for the tripod. If you're using a film camera, you probably need a film scanner as well. The quality of your panoramas will mainly depend on your skill as a photographer and the quality of your equipment.

Camera

You can use any point-and-shoot camera or any video camera that takes stills, if you like. The Pigeon Point panorama on the disk was shot with a video camera. But a better camera will give you a sharper, more detailed image, and you'll have more control with a camera that allows manual adjustment for exposure, white balance, and focus. A good camera can make a world of difference.

Tip You'll be shooting almost exclusively from a tripod, so make sure your camera has a stable and convenient mounting mechanism. Some cameras have to be removed from the tripod in order to change film or memory—avoid them, or face frustration when the camera runs out of film or memory in mid-shoot.

Film or Digital

Until very recently, most professionals shot panoramas using 35 mm single lens reflex (SLR) cameras. Now everyone uses digital cameras, unless they need exceptionally high resolution (large format film for print work, for example) or they've been in the business so long the 35 mm SLR has become an extension of their hand and eyes.

When it comes to shooting VR, it's hard to overstate how completely a digital camera changes things. Hours of tedious work are literally transformed into minutes of creative play. If that were the only factor, it would be a no-brainer, but of course it isn't.

Inexpensive digital cameras currently have lower resolution and less exposure range (fewer f-stops) than most film cameras. And most digital cameras do not allow you to change lenses—there are wide-angle adapters available for most of the better cameras, but they tend to introduce barrel distortion. Only the most expensive digital cameras (digital SLRs) use high-quality optics and allow you to change lenses, attach professional flash equipment, and so on.

For the amateur or semi-pro, digital is the way to go. Period. For the professional photographer, there are still trade-offs. Digital cameras continue to get better and cheaper, however, and the remaining advantages of film cameras for VR photography are gradually disappearing.

Important   If you go digital, be sure to include a high-capacity rechargeable battery and a large memory card in your budget. They're absolutely critical.

Lenses and Field of View

Photographers tend to use lens length, field of view, and magnification as interchangeable ways of describing the same thing. If you're a little vague on how field of view relates to lens length and film size, you're not alone. A true understanding requires a short course in optics and a willingness to do real math, but here's the fuzzy version: Your field of view is dependent on the focal length of the lens, and also on the imaging area (exposed area of the film). Using a longer lens, or exposing a smaller area of film, makes the field of view smaller, as illustrated in the misleadingly simplistic drawing that follows (this is just a conceptual aid—not to be construed as actual physics).

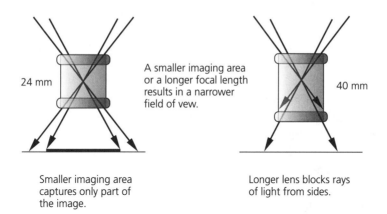

24 mm

A smaller imaging area or a longer focal length results in a narrower field of vew.

40 mm

Smaller imaging area captures only part of the image.

Longer lens blocks rays of light from sides.

A 35 mm film camera has an image capture area of about 35 mm x 26 mm for each photograph. Most digital cameras use an image-capture chip with a smaller area, about the same size as APS film. This results in a smaller field of view, cropping the image about as much as a 1.6x magnification.

This means that if you need to be ten feet from something to get it all in the frame using a 35 mm film camera, you need to be sixteen feet from it to get the same framing with a typical digital camera, using the same lens.

Most 35 mm film cameras have a 24–28 mm lens available as a standard feature, which gives a fairly wide field of view. Because of their smaller image capture area, most digital cameras have a much narrower maximum field, equivalent to a 38 or 40 mm lens. This can be a handicap when shooting panoramas, particularly indoors, where you want a tall field of view.

To make things more interesting, different digital cameras use differently sized chips. Comparison charts of digital cameras typically list the difference as a magnification factor compared to 35 mm film. A 1.6x factor is standard, while a 1x factor means the camera's chip has the same exposure area as 35 mm film.

Somewhere in its documentation, a digital camera should give the size of the CCD (or CMOS imaging chip, or whatever) or the magnification, or the equivalent lens focal lengths—for a 35 mm camera. You will need to know the field of view and equivalent lens length for a 35 mm camera to use some VR software, including QTVR Authoring Studio and PT Tools. There's a handy calculator that will give you the field of view for any lens length and "film" size at www.worldserver.com/turk/quicktimevr/authoring.html.

Field of View and Panoramas

A narrower field of view means you need to take more pictures to capture the same panorama, and for cylinders, a narrower field of view creates a panorama with less vertical dimension; stitching together a strip of side-by-side pictures can produce 360° of horizontal view, but the whole strip is still just 1 exposure tall.

This isn't always important for outdoor panoramas, where the horizon is far away and the incentive to look up at the sky or down at the ground is low, but for interior spaces it can be a critical limitation. Unless the room is large, you may be unable to see from floor to ceiling without a wide-angle adapter.

For an example, see Annapano.html in the Virtual folder on the CD, shot with a Coolpix 770 (2 megapixels, widest field of view equivalent to 40 mm lens). The image detail is good, but you simply cannot see from floor to ceiling, even with the camera in portrait mode at the center of the room.

Resolution

Resolution is a measure of how much detail you can see. If your computer monitor has 768 lines of resolution, for example, you could theoretically make out up to 768 alternating black-and-white lines (*sure* you could). In fact, the light from adjacent lines blurs together, so you actually see less detail than that, but the number of lines defines the maximum *possible* resolution, optics and eyesight permitting. The screen can't display 769 alternating lines; it doesn't have the resolution.

Similarly, digital cameras are rated in (mega)pixels of resolution. Back when pixels were counted in thousands, this was all you needed to know—a cheap plastic lens gave about the same result as precision-ground glass when the pixel count was that low. But today the pixel count measures only one constraint on resolution. A 6-megapixel camera with a cheap lens produces a lot of blurry pixels. A 4-megapixel camera with a good lens produces a sharp image.

Note Panorama resolution also is usually given in pixels. If you're talking about the width of a 360° panorama, that's fine. But when you start to talk about the vertical resolution, or the horizontal resolution of panoramas that are less than 360°, you need to express it in pixels per degree for the number to be very meaningful.

You can photograph a panorama at almost any horizontal resolution just by taking more pictures with a narrower field of view, bearing in mind that a narrower field of view results in a shorter cylinder.

A higher-resolution camera allows you to capture higher-resolution images (more pixels) using a given field of view. Correspondingly, it allows you to get the same image resolution using a wider field of view, which requires fewer pictures and creates a taller cylinder.

You can shoot professional-quality panoramas using a middle-of-the-road 2-megapixel camera, but you need to shoot 18 to 24 images to get enough detail.

Note A 2-megapixel camera with a 38 mm (equivalent) lens has a horizontal field of view of about 30° in portrait mode—12 exposures with no overlap (18 to 24 with 30% to 50% overlap). Given a 1600 x 1200 pixel image, that's 14,400 pixels of horizontal resolution.

A 6-megapixel camera with a professional wide-angle lens will capture just as much horizontal detail using six photos and give you a much taller vertical field of view. *If* you can get a wide-angle lens for your 6-megapixel camera.

Most digital cameras have a nonremovable zoom lens, so you'll need a wide-angle adapter to get a shorter lens than 38 or 40 mm. They're not available for all cameras, so ask before you buy.

Tip Nikon is very good about providing wide-angle adapters for all their digital cameras, and the Minolta Dimage series features some cameras with unusually wide-angle lenses built in. The Dimage 7i, for example, comes with a 28–200 mm zoom lens.

Alternative Camera Systems

An expensive but intriguing alternative is a camera that automatically takes full panoramas, such as the cameras from PanoScan or BeHere. These are extremely high-resolution cameras that automatically take a series of photos to create a cylindrical panorama with up to 65,000 pixels of horizontal resolution. They cost several thousand dollars, but if you're going to shoot panoramas for a living, they're worth looking into.

Also intriguing, and considerably less expensive, are panorama lens attachments, such as the Kaidan OneShot or the 0-360.com 1-Click. These are generally based on a curved mirror that lets you shoot a complete cylinder with one exposure, using almost any camera. Of course, this means that you have only the resolution of a single exposure, spread over 360°, so unless you use a high-resolution digital or film camera, your image will tend to be either small or blurred (or both). These attachments cost from $500 to $999. With a 6-megapixel camera, you can shoot a cylinder with about 3000 pixels of horizontal resolution.

The attachment is unlikely to be optically perfect, however, so expect some image degradation in addition to spreading your pixels a bit thin. The advantage here is convenience—a single exposure and you're done. This also allows you to capture a busy scene with minimum motion blur.

There are also two companies that provide convenient one-shot or two-shot panorama systems with a twist. The Ipix system creates a spherical VR from two fish-eye exposures, and the Sunpak SurroundPhoto system creates a cylindrical VR from a single exposure using a reflective plate. They share the unusual business model of charging you on a per-image basis, in addition to your initial equipment cost. In effect, the images do not belong to you; you license the right to display them. These systems are most commonly used for quick-and-dirty commercial real-estate work because of their convenience, somewhat limited image quality, and restrictive terms of use. But they do have their place.

Lenses

Ideally, you want rectilinear camera lenses (nondistorting). There are tools that correct for fish-eye or barrel distortion, but it's an extra hassle. Shorter lenses give a wider field of view, which allows you to make a panorama using fewer shots and with more overlap. Taking fewer shots is more convenient, and more overlap is better for reasons we'll get into later.

A shorter lens also gives you a taller field of view, which can be important for interior scenes, especially for cylindrical panoramas, which are only one exposure tall. You probably want a 24 or 26 mm lens for outdoor work and a 15 mm lens for indoor work (lens length for 35 mm film).

It's difficult to get rectilinear lenses shorter than about 15 mm, and the shorter the lens, the more expensive a nondistorting one is—if you want to shoot with a 9 mm, you'll be looking through a fish-eye for sure.

Tripod

If you're going to be shooting panoramas professionally, you need a tripod. If you have steady hands, you can shoot exterior panoramas by hand—Pigeonpoint.mov was shot without a tripod, for example—but the results are usually less than professional (the key is to hold the camera level and rotate around the axis of the camera). To shoot indoor panoramas or scenes with nearby objects, a tripod is pretty much essential. (If you have steady hands and a fish-eye lens, a monopod can also be made to work.)

A bubble level is a must-have item for your tripod, unless you want your panorama to look like it was shot from a roller coaster.

You *can* tilt the tripod deliberately, to frame a panorama that looks down a cliff on one side and up a mountainside on the other, for example, but it tends to make people queasy.

You want the sturdiest tripod you're willing to lug around, so it doesn't shift when you rotate it or when you touch the camera (to press the shutter, change focus, advance the film, or change memory cards, for example).

Tip The more you diddle with the camera during a shoot, the more likely you are to shift the tripod—a shutter-release cable and automatic film advance are extras worth having, along with a large memory module and a high-capacity battery for digital cameras.

Pano Heads

You should have a disk, calibrated in degrees, that mounts under the camera, so you can divide the panorama into equal sections for each shot. You can make one yourself using acetate and a marking pen, but you're better off buying a commercial pano head.

Pano heads are made by companies like Kaidan (www.kaidan.com), Peace River (www.peaceriverstudios.com), BLS Designs (www.blsdesigns.com), and Jasper Engineering (www.stereoscopy.com/jasper) specifically for shooting VR panoramas. They range in price from around $100 to over $1000. The main features a pano head offers are a calibrated disk, detents that let you easily click to a specified angle, and a slider that lets you mount the camera on the tripod so that it *rotates around its optical nodal point* (the point inside the lens where the light rays "cross").

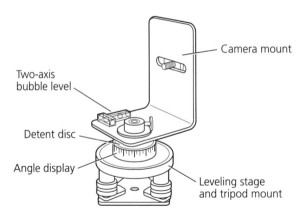

Two-axis bubble level

Camera mount

Detent disc

Angle display

Leveling stage and tripod mount

Panoramic tripod head

A tripod normally rotates a camera around a point in the camera body, well behind or to one side of the optical focal point. This results in a parallax effect, so that nearby objects appear to move relative to distant objects when you pan the camera. This makes it difficult for software to stitch the images together properly and results in blurry panoramas.

If you're shooting an outdoor panorama with no near objects, the effects are less noticeable and less important. For interior shots, or panoramas with both near-field and distant elements, it matters a lot.

A pano head also allows you to mount the camera vertically (portrait mode) on the tripod, so the widest field of view is up and down, and this is usually how you'll shoot, at least for cylindrical panoramas.

To shoot high-quality *cubic* panoramas, you really need a pano head that can point 45° up and down, as well as traverse a 360° circle in the horizontal plane, all around a common nodal point. Yikes! Cubic VR pano heads like this are currently available, starting at around $500.

The alternative of shooting a cubic panorama with two or three images, using a monopod and a fish-eye lens, has its adherents, but again you want to mount the camera on the monopod so the nodal point of the lens lines up with the center of rotation.

Software

You need software to do some or all of the following things:

- touch up or edit digital photographs
- stitch multiple photographs into panoramic images

- convert one or more panoramic images into a QuickTime VR movie

- add interactive hotspots to your VR movie

- optimize your movie for Web or CD delivery

- perform utility functions, such as converting cylinders to cubes or extracting images from VR movies

Many applications do more than one of these functions, but as far as I know, no single program does them all. In addition, some programs work only with cylinders or only with cubes.

There's a lot of activity in the VR software market right now. I mean a *lot* of activity. So check the Web and ask questions on the QuickTime VR mailing list (http://lists.apple.com) to supplement the information presented here.

Note For great panoramic pictures of your vacation, just drag the photos from your camera into your favorite VR software. Your friends will be amazed. Artists and/or professionals should choose a set of tools that suit their workflow.

Image Editor

You need some kind of image editing software to touch up your photos, correct exposure problems, erase your feet, and so on. The most common choice is Adobe Photoshop, but there are alternatives, some of them quite a bit easier and/or less expensive, including Photoshop Elements ($99 for Windows, Mac OS 9, Mac OS X). A Google search on "alternative photoshop" will lead you to several lists. At the high-end, PanoPost (www.kaidan.com) is designed especially for postproduction editing of panoramic images (cylinders, cubes, and spheres).

Stitcher

You need software that can stitch your scanned or digital photos into panoramic images. For cylinders, this means stitching a row of images into a single cylindrical image. For cubes, it means stitching either multiple rows of images or a few fish-eye images into a suitable format, typically a single equirectangular cubic projection (photosphere) or six equirectangular cube faces (and try saying *that* with a mouthful of flan).

These packages do stitching. Most also create VR panoramas from the stitched images. Many also do touch-up and add hotspots.

- Apple's QuickTime VR Authoring Studio (www.apple.com/quicktime/qtvr/) does a bang-up job of stitching cylinders. Mac OS (Classic) only.

- PTMac (www.kekus.com/ptmac/) is based on Helmut Dersch's Panorama Tools, with a friendly graphical user interface. Stitches cylinders, cubes, and more. Mac OS, Mac OS X.

- VRPanoWorx (www.vrtoolbox.com) also stitches cylinders. It's more up-to-date than Authoring Studio and runs on Mac OS, Mac OS X, or Windows.

- Realviz's Stitcher (www.realviz.com) does cylinders or cubes, and does a particularly nice job of creating cube faces from multiple rows. It also creates hotspots, does cropping, and more. (Also available: Stitcher EZ.) Mac OS, Mac OS X, Windows.

- PanoramaMaker (www.arcsoft.com) can stitch a series of digital photos into a single wide-angle or tiled image or a QuickTime VR cylindrical panorama. It couldn't be much easier to use. Mac OS 8, Windows.

- PanoWeaver (www.panoweaver.com) can stitch two or three fish-eye images into a cubic or spherical VR panorama. Includes numerous editing and touch-up tools.

Converter

Once you've stitched together a panoramic image or six, you probably want to do some touch-up using an image editor. Then you need to convert the image into a QuickTime VR movie.

For cylinders, this step usually involves breaking the image into one or more tiles. For cubes, this may involve breaking a photosphere into six cubic faces. The tiles or faces are compressed at this point, and a .mov file is generated. The window size, default view, and pan-and-zoom constraints are also set by the converter software. This software may allow you to add interactive hotspots or a preview image as well.

- **QTVRAS**—conversion and tiling for cylinders, generates hotspots. Mac OS (Classic) only.

- **Panoworx**—conversion and tiling for cylinders, hotspots, preview.

- **ClickHere Design's Cubic Converter** (www.clickheredesign.com.au/products/)—conversion for cubes (photosphere or faces), hotspots, preview. Mac only.

- **MakeCubic**—conversion for cubes (photosphere or faces), hotspots.

- **GoCubic**—conversion for cubes (photosphere or faces), Windows only.

- **Zoomify**—converts a panoramic image into a cylindrical VR panorama, compressed, tiled, and optimized for Web delivery at multiple resolutions (only what the viewer looks at is actually downloaded).

Utilities

Utility software allows you to convert multinode scenes into individual panoramas or vice versa, add or change preview images, extract images from panoramas, turn cylinders into cubes, add hotspots to existing panoramas, and similar good things.

- **Cubic Connector** (www.clickheredesign.com.au/products/)—links individual cubic VRs into multinode scenes, or breaks multinode scenes into separate panoramas linked via HTML.
- **SwingTime**—extracts a series of images from a VR. Mac OS, Windows.
- **DeliVRator** (www.vrtools.com/)—handy utility for optimizing VR for Web delivery, editing default pan, tilt, zoom, and so on, including low-level things you should leave strictly alone (unless you know what you're doing, of course). Also allows you to set the movie so that Quick-Time will not allow the movie to be saved or edited. Free. Mac OS only.

Planning

If you're shooting a multinode panorama, lay out the center point for each node, making sure you have a clear view of a distinct entry point for each adjacent node. It helps orient the viewer if you begin a node facing the same direction you would have traveled from the previous node (you can specify a different initial viewing angle when entering a node from other nodes).

You can't shoot a 360° panorama with the sun behind you—the low light angle that looks so good in one direction will shine directly into the camera when you turn around. High overhead light is generally best—and a little overcast can be a godsend—so plan your shoot accordingly. Naturally, the problem is more pronounced when shooting cubic VR outdoors—at some point, you must aim the camera at the sun. It can help enormously to have a tree between you and the sun's disc.

Tip If you're getting lens flare, take two exposures—use a piece of cardboard to block the sun in one of them—and composite them together later using a graphic editor such as Photoshop.

It's generally a bad idea to have people or cars whizzing through your panorama, so plan to shoot at a time when your site is uncrowded—for the financial district, Sunday afternoon is a good bet; for the beach, a weekday before lunch. If you can't eliminate moving objects, try to shoot when objects are moving toward you or away from you, not across your field of vision. Alternatively, invest in a curved pano mirror and shoot the whole panorama in a single exposure.

Shooting

Pick a good spot. A panorama with some near-field elements is generally more interesting than one where everything is the same distance away.

Set up and level your tripod. Height matters—a low panorama can look strikingly different than a high panorama of the same scene.

Check the lighting in all directions, preferably with a light meter.

Make sure the camera has enough film (or memory and battery charge).

Important A cylinder is typically a single row of photographs stitched side-to-side, so the cylinder gets more pixels horizontally as you add more pictures, but it's only as tall as a single image. By shooting with the camera in portrait mode, you give the viewer the maximum vertical view.

Pick your lens, if you can. For cylinders, you need a wider-angle lens to photograph the interior of a small space, or the vertical field of view will not capture it from top to bottom. A 15 mm lens is the standard, but you'll have a hard time finding an equivalent lens for a digital camera. For exterior shots, 24 mm is a common choice. Maximize the vertical field of view by shooting with the camera on its side, if your equipment allows.

For cubic panoramas, a good choice is a 15 mm lens, indoors or out—but it isn't easy to get that with a digital camera (a 14 mm lens on a typical digital has the same field of view as a 110 mm lens on 35 mm film). Whatever lens you use, you're going to end up either with six images, each with a field of view exactly 90° in both dimensions, or a photosphere. You can crop a wide angle down to 90°, or you can stitch overlapping images together into cube sides or a sphere. A 15 mm lens, focusing on 35 mm film, has a 97.5° x 74.5° field of view, so you can stitch each face of a cube from two overlapping images. A 14 mm lens on a digital camera will require 24 to 36 exposures around the circumference, and a similar number tilted at 45° up and down, to capture everything in detail.

Adjust the camera on the pano head so that the focal point of the lens (sometimes called the nodal point) is exactly centered over the tripod's axis of rotation—this is critical to avoid parallax problems if there are objects in the near field.

Decide how many shots you'll take, at what increment of degrees, based on your horizontal field of view. You need a minimum of 10% overlap for any stitching software to work with, and some software requires 30%. Apple's QuickTime VR Authoring Studio (QTVRAS) works best with 50% overlap, especially if the lighting is uneven. More overlap (up to 70%) is better, provided you have sufficient time and film. It's common to shoot a panorama as a sequence of 12 images at intervals of 30°—if your horizontal field of view is 60°, this allows a 50% overlap between images.

If you can set detents for a certain number of degrees on your pano head, do it now, so you can click, click, click your way around the circle.

For cubes, point the camera up at a 45° angle, then shoot in whatever degree increments (rotating to the right) to complete one circuit, repeat with no tilt (parallel to the ground), then repeat a third time tilted 45° down. Finally, pick up the tripod, hold it parallel to the ground with the camera pointing straight down, step back and photograph the ground under the camera site (you'll need a shutter release cable—or arms like an orangutan).

For cylinders, just click through one circuit with no tilt at all.

The number of exposures per row, and the degrees of rotation between shots, depends on your lens and the amount of overlap you choose. Using 35 mm film with a 15 mm lens and approximately 50% overlap, you'll shoot 8 exposures per row.

A panorama is a single row, and a cube is three rows and a bottom shot, so 8 shots total for a cylinder, 25 for a cube—rotating 45° for each exposure. Using a digital camera with a typical 40-mm-equivalent fixed lens, also with 50% overlap, you'll shoot 24 pictures per row—24 total for a cylinder, 73 for a cube—rotating 15° per shot.

If you have any doubt about the exposure, use a gray card. It's not a bad idea to shoot two exposures from each position, one with a gray card in the frame. If you don't know what a gray card is, go down to your local camera store and find out—your photography will improve dramatically.

If the lighting is uneven, there are several ways you can compensate. If you're stitching with QuickTime VR Authoring Studio, you can shoot with automatic exposure and a 50% overlap—the stitching software will create a smooth blend from frame to frame to compensate for changes in brightness. If you're using a fixed exposure for all frames, you can bracket the exposure, shooting two or three pictures from each position. You can cut and paste from different exposures using a graphics editing program afterward.

Probably the best approach—particularly for cubes—is to find the average exposure for the entire panorama, set the shutter speed accordingly, and lock it down.

If you decide to bracket the exposure, you have a tough decision to make—changing the exposure multiple times for each shot makes it more likely that you'll make a mistake or nudge the tripod; shooting the whole panorama multiple times, each with a different exposure, makes it more likely that the registration or the light will change between two shots of the "same" scene. There's no right answer, so do whatever works best for you.

If you can't get the perfect exposure, underexpose slide film and overexpose negative film. This results in a darker slide or a darker negative. You can get additional detail out of a dark area by pushing more light through it when scanning or printing, but a transparent area has no information that can be recovered.

If you have people in the panorama, make sure they hold completely still while you shoot all the frames they appear in. If you're shooting with a 30% overlap or less, you may be able to center them in a frame so they appear in only one image. You can do this by centering the first frame on your human subjects, or by positioning the subjects at the center of a subsequent frame—it's generally a bad idea to adjust the center point of any frame after the first, as it makes the stitching awkward.

Once you start shooting, work in a rhythm—shoot, rotate, shoot (or gray card, shoot, film advance, shoot, film advance, rotate, repeat). Stay focused. It's repetitive, and it's very easy to find yourself in the middle of a panorama wondering whether to shoot or rotate. When in doubt, shoot another exposure; it's easier to discard a duplicate than to go back and reshoot the whole thing because an image is missing. With practice, you can often shoot a whole cylinder in under a minute, a cube in less than five.

An alternative approach, for cubes or cylinders, is to shoot two images with a fish-eye lens, rotating 180° so the two images line up back-to-back. This simplifies the shooting process greatly, but it results in distorted images that have to be corrected later, though there are now user-friendly tools to do that for you.

It also creates an image whose whole resolution is constrained by the pixel dimensions of two images, which is considerably lower than eight or a few dozen overlapping images.

Worse still, someone has a patent that they believe covers the process of dewarping fish-eye images to create spherical VR panoramas. The patent holder is asking a royalty payment for each image and has threatened legal action against people who provide dewarping tools.

Shooting three wide-angle images at 120° intervals alleviates some, and perhaps all, of these problems, but doesn't completely eliminate any of them.

Image Preparation

If you're shooting film, it needs to be developed and digitized. You can get good-quality results in a convenient format by having a photo lab print directly to CD. Otherwise you need to scan the prints, slides, or negatives after developing. With care and a good scanner, you can often get better results yourself than a commercial photo lab typically delivers.

It's normal for the print maker or CD scanner to optimize each image for color and brightness using a scene-balancing algorithm (SBA). You generally want this feature turned *off* for a panorama because you're going to stitch them all into a single image, and you don't want different parts of the image processed differently.

Work in the highest resolution you can when scanning film or prints. Even if your work will end up at 72 dpi and JPEG-compressed, scan it in at 1200 dpi or higher from a print or 2400 dpi or higher from a slide or negative. You can get excellent results scanning prints at 2400 dpi and slides at 4800 dpi.

Tip   Make it a rule to throw information away as late in the game as possible—you'll never regret it.

Give your images nice sequential filenames, like `Pigeonpoint01`, `Pigeonpoint02`, and so on. Use a leading zero for numbers below 10. If your pano contains more than 99 images, use two leading zeroes for numbers below 10 (001, 002, . . .) and one leading zero for numbers below 100 (010, 011, . . .). This makes it easier for stitching software to process the images later.

If you're making a cubic VR, number the images in this order: upper row, middle row, lower row, bottom shot.

If the images weren't shot with a rectilinear lens, you need to correct the distortion. Two useful tools for this are DeFish (in the Tools folder on the CD) for the Macintosh, and Panorama Tools, available for download at no cost from Helmut Dersch (`www.fh-furtwangen.de/~dersch/`), as Photoshop plug-ins for both Macintosh and Windows. Most cubic VR software now does this for you.

Tip URLs are ephemeral. If the link above has gone bad, search the Web for "Pano Tools" or "Helmut's tools." They're around.

You may want to modify your images to adjust for exposure and lighting. If you bracketed your exposures, you may want to do some cutting and pasting to replace dark or washed-out areas of an image with better versions from an alternate exposure. This is also a good time to remove stray cats, errant pigeons, or your feet using the Rubber Stamp tool.

Don't adjust the sharpness, punch up the contrast and saturation, or apply compression yet—that comes after the stitching.

Stitching

The process of stitching creates single images from sequences of overlapping images. The overlapping portions of the images are blended together, and the final image is warped onto a cylinder or the faces of a cube. The following illustration shows a series of still images and a composite image after stitching.

A cylindrical panorama will use a single image stitched together from all of your exposures. A cubic panorama can be created either from six faces of a cube, each face stitched from two or more exposures, or from a single equirectangular projection, stitched together from all of your exposures.

The process of stitching typically involves putting your images into a folder and pointing your VR software at it, or dragging your photos into your VR software's stitching window. Some software will allow you to manually line up the images to align the overlapping parts—this is especially useful for handheld panoramas, where the overlap varies from shot to shot.

The software may ask you to supply the lens length, horizontal field of view, and overlap for the images. QuickTime VR Authoring Studio is particularly fussy about this and will abort with error messages about there being "too many" images or "more than 360°" if you give it the wrong lens size.

Tip If you're using QuickTime VR Authoring Studio with a digital camera, you may have to define a 38 or 40 mm portrait lens with a 54° by 40° field of view. An incorrect lens specification will result in an error message that suggests you may have more than 360° in your panorama.

Most software will also tile the stitched image, create a VR movie, add previews and hotspots, and optimize for Web delivery.

Even if your chosen tool can take you directly to Web-ready output, you may very well want to export the stitched image as a PICT file and touch it up with a graphics editor before continuing.

Note Prior to QuickTime 5, the stitched image was also rotated 90° counterclockwise. This was done because the image is typically very wide and, historically, the PICT image format had a width limit but no height limit. Since the PICT format no longer has such a limit, this transformation is no longer necessary. Cubes are stored in QuickTime as six square images and are not rotated.

Making Panoramas with 3D Software

If you use 3D software to generate your panoramas, you can generally bypass most of the steps we've discussed so far.

For cubic VR, render six images: four with the x and z axis at 0°, rotating through 0°, 90°, 180°, and –90° on the y axis, then two with the y and z axis at 0°, and the x axis at 90° and –90°. All the images should be square, with a field of view of 90°. Turn them into a cubic VR by dropping them on MakeCubic (in the Tools folder of the CD) or by opening Make-Cubic, selecting the settings you want, clicking the File button, and Shift-clicking to select all six images.

For cylindrical VR, you can usually just tell your software to generate a panorama image in PICT format. 3D modeling packages that generate panorama images directly include Infini-D, Strata 3D, form•Z, and Bryce.

If your 3D software doesn't generate cylindrical panorama images, create a set of overlapping images instead, then stitch them together as if they were photographs. To create the images, select a viewpoint for your virtual camera and render a series of images, rotating the "camera" by a fixed number of degrees each time.

For example, if you set your field of view at 120° and rotate the virtual camera by 60° for each image, you can render a series of six images with 50% overlap that can be used to create a panorama—0–120°, 60–180°, 120–240°, 180–300°, 240–360°, and 300–60°.

Treat the rendered images as you would a series of overlapping photographs—see "Stitching" (page 636).

Touch-up

Once you have a single stitched or rendered panorama image, or a set of six cubic faces, you generally want to open it in a graphics program such as Photoshop to optimize its appearance. This typically involves sharpening (using the paradoxically named Unsharp Mask operation), enhancing contrast, boosting color levels, and performing gamma correction.

You can't compress the images yet—that comes later—but you could shrink the image file size by reducing the pixel dimensions. You can sometimes shrink an image by scaling at 70% without significant loss of detail. This is generally not recommended. You get much higher quality at the same file size by compressing more aggressively later than by shrinking the image now.

Important The pixel dimensions of a cylindrical image file should be evenly divisible by 96 in the long dimension and evenly divisible by 4 in the narrow dimension. This is important for tiling. Crop or scale as needed to make this happen.

Depending on how your image was created, it may have been rotated 90° by the stitching software. If so, you may want to rotate the image so it looks more natural while you're working on it. Just remember to rotate it back when you're done.

Zoomify It?

If you're making a cylindrical panorama, either photographically or using 3D software, once you have a stitched image, you can Zoomify it (if your 3D software generates VR panorama's directly, extract the stitched image using a utility). You can use this technique to deliver extremely high resolution panoramas over the Internet.

Zoomifyer Pro is required to create Zoomified QTVR movies, but they will play back using the free QuickTime Zoomify component. If a viewer doesn't have the component, QuickTime will offer to download and install it automatically.

Zoomifier takes your high-resolution image and creates a cascade of lower-resolution versions. It then breaks all but the lowest-resolution image into tiles. When a viewer opens your QTVR over the Internet, the smallest, lowest-resolution image downloads, giving the viewer an almost immediate image that can be panned, zoomed, and tilted. Tiles from a higher-resolution image load whenever the viewer pauses to look at something. If the viewer zooms in, tiles from a still higher-resolution image load, until the viewer is looking at tiles from your original image (optionally with additional compression).

The upsides are impressive—immediate viewing and navigation of the movie, high-detail zooming without waiting for a large image download, and the efficiency of downloading only what the audience actually looks at.

The downside is that there is a noticeable lag between panning to a new view and seeing it clearly. An impatient viewer may glance around and conclude that you have a blurry VR that isn't worth watching. It is a little disconcerting to constantly see new things appear out of focus, then suddenly sharpen, but it's also kind of cool.

For disk-based material, the trade-offs tend to weigh against Zoomify except for very large images (>20 MB). For the Web, it's clearly the best solution for delivering large, high-resolution VR over any kind of connection.

If you Zoomify, you can skip the "Tiling, Compressing, and Optimizing" section.

Tiling, Compressing, and Optimizing

When your image looks the way you want, it's time to take the final steps to get it ready for Web delivery. The image needs to be diced into tiles, compressed, and optimized for Web delivery. You may want to create a low-resolution preview image as well.

In most cases, this means reimporting the image into the tool you used for stitching, and performing the tiling, compression, and preview operations. In other cases, it means using separate tiling and compression tools, such as QTVR Authoring Studio (or Make Panorama 2, in the Tools folder of the CD), and a separate preview generator, such as QuickTime Player.

The free MakeCubic application on the CD does tiling, compression, and preview creation for cubic VR. To use the default settings, just drag an equirectangular image, or six cubic face images, onto the application. To adjust the tiling, compression, or preview parameters, launch the application by double-clicking it. Adjust the settings as you like, then use the File button to select the image or images (Shift-click to select multiple images).

Tiling

Tiling breaks the panorama into pieces so it can be played back without loading the whole image into memory. This reduces system requirements, especially for large panoramas. It also allows people to begin viewing and navigating the panorama while it downloads. There is, however, a small but perceptible hesitation as each tile loads and decompresses.

As you rotate through a panorama, each tile is loaded into memory. If QuickTime has enough RAM available, it will eventually load the entire panorama into memory, and panning will be very smooth; if not, it will unload one or more offscreen tiles, reloading them as needed.

If your software gives a choice of tile sizes, use fewer tiles for disk-based presentations and more tiles to make a panorama more responsive during Web download.

Tip For a fast computer and a disk-based presentation, tell your software to put the whole panorama in a single tile (Tiles: 1). This results in the smoothest panning. But make sure the whole panorama will fit in memory!

You generally want a single row of tiles for a cylindrical panorama, but if it's tall enough that the default field of view is only 1/2 or 1/3 the full height, you might use three or four rows of tiles for Web delivery—viewers can navigate the default view while the rest of the panorama downloads.

Each tile is compressed separately, which is why you shouldn't compress the image prior to tiling—the image would have to be decompressed, tiled, and recompressed, which would degrade it badly.

Compression

Compression reduces the image size, which is critical for Web panoramas and usually necessary for good performance even from disk. It also reduces image quality, particularly sharpness.

JPEG compression usually gives the highest quality for the bandwidth, though it does get blurry if you compress aggressively. Cinepak compression gives more responsive playback—especially on older computers—because it's easier to decompress. But Cinepak quality is lower at a given file size. Sorenson compression isn't nearly as efficient with still images as it is with motion video, but it scales up well. JPEG images generally look good scaled up to 1.25—for more aggressive scaling, try Sorenson instead.

There is a set of panoramas in the Virtual folder on the CD that are made from the same image, JPEG-compressed at 100% quality (uncompressed), 70%, 60%, 50%, and 40%. The file sizes range from 27 MB to 700 Kbytes. Interestingly, there is very little drop-off in quality at 70% or even 60%, but the file size drops dramatically. Take a look and judge for yourself. See how far you can zoom in before it starts to pixelate or look fuzzy.

Optimization

Once you're done with tiling and compression, you should optimize Web-based panoramas for download. Panoramas are usually pretty large—300 Kbytes to 3 MB—so you don't want to leave your viewers drumming their fingers the whole time. There are two parts to optimizing for download—setting a preview and reordering the tiles.

In most of the tools, you can set the preview using the same software that does the tiling and compression. If you created your panorama using QuickTime VR Authoring Studio or Spin Panorama, on the other hand, you need to use another tool, such as DeliVRator or QuickTime Player, to set the preview. If you have a Mac, DeliVRator is highly recommended. It's free, and the current version lets you copy-protect your VR movie. (www.vrtools.com).

Starting with QuickTime 5, the ability to create previews is built into QuickTime Player. Earlier versions of QuickTime required you to install the VR Flattener extension manually—if you have such an extension installed, you can throw it away now.

Here's how to set the preview using QuickTime Player (the process is similar for other tools):

1. Open the panorama in QuickTime Player.
2. Choose Export from the File menu, then choose Movie to Fast Start QuickTime VR Movie from the pop-up menu.

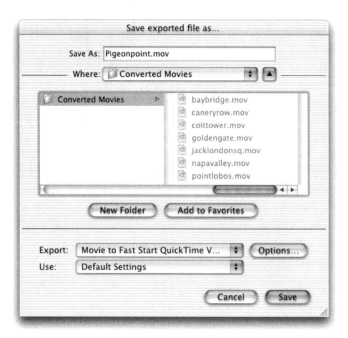

3. Click the Options button to bring up the preview dialog box. The settings in this dialog box determine what the viewer sees while the panorama is downloading:

- If you don't select Create Preview, the viewer sees a black grid with yellow lines (similar to the holodeck grid in Star Trek). The grid is filled in as each tile downloads.

- If you click the Create Preview box, a small low-resolution preview image is downloaded ahead of the panorama tiles. The viewer can pan, tilt, and click hotspots almost immediately and has at least a vague sense of what the panorama looks like. The resolution of the image improves one area at a time as each tile downloads.

- You normally want a low-quality JPEG preview, but you can choose any QuickTime compression settings you like. A low-quality JPEG is typically 1/8 the file size of a high-quality JPEG.

- A quarter-sized preview is 1/16 the file size of a full panorama at the same quality setting; a half-sized preview is 1/4 the file size. Multiply the file size reduction by the compression reduction (low quality vs. high quality) to see how long it will take the preview to download compared with the panorama.

- The preview is scaled up to fill the view window—you can choose to have it blurred or pixelated, whichever you prefer.

- If you prefer, you can use another program to create the preview image. If so, click the Import Preview Image box. You are prompted for a filename when you click OK.

4. Select the kind of preview you want and click OK, then click Save.

Your panorama now has a preview image or a preview grid that the viewer can pan around in during the download.

As a final step in optimization for Web delivery, you may want to run your panorama through DeliVRator (www.vrtools.com). This program rearranges the tiles so that the default view downloads first, then the tiles to the left and right, then the next pair of tiles to the left and right, and so on around the circle. If there are multiple rows of tiles, the center or default row loads first, then the rows above or below.

Hotspots and Multinode Panoramas

Hotspots are areas in a panorama that link to another node in the same scene, or to a URL—or they may simply tell QuickTime that a particular hotspot has been clicked and let it decide what to do. A node can be another panorama or an object movie. Multinode panoramas are created by linking individual panoramas with hotspots, but hotspots can also be used as general-purpose links from a panorama to any URL.

There are several tools that you can use to add hotspots to panoramas, such as QuickTime VR Authoring Studio, PanoWorx, and a nice freeware tool called VRL that you can download from www.marink.com. You can add hotspots to cubic VR using MakeCubic.

Note Hotspots are implemented as an 8-bit image map that parallels the panorama image. Each pixel has one of 256 possible values—255 possible hotspots and a background color. The color value and the hotspot number are the same. If your software offers compression options for your hotspot image, be sure to use a lossless 8-bit nondithering compressor, such as GIF or PNG.

There are three kinds of hotspots—node, URL, and blob.

- A node hotspot links to another panorama or object movie within a multinode QTVR movie file.
- A URL hotspot links to a URL—often another panorama in a separate file, or a Web page with an embedded panorama.
- A blob hotspot just tells the application playing the panorama that a particular hotspot has been clicked. If your VR is playing in the QuickTime plug-in, this links to the URL specified in the corresponding HOTSPOT*n* parameter in the movie's <EMBED> tag.

Tip You can program wired sprites to perform actions in response to hotspot events using a program such as LiveStage Pro or VR Hotwires.

For CD-based panoramas, it's often more convenient to use node hotspots and put all the panorama nodes in a single file. For Web-based panoramas, it's generally best to use blob hotspots and keep each node of a multinode panorama in a separate file; you can link a blob hotspot to a particular destination using the HOTSPOT*n* parameter in the <EMBED> tag of your HTML, or you can embed it in a movie using Plug-in Helper.

Note Blob hotspots can also be interpreted by other software that can contain QuickTime VR movies, such as Macromedia Director or Tribeworks' iShell.

You can link a blob hotspot to another panorama, any QuickTime movie, any media that QuickTime can play, or any URL that the viewer's browser can handle. You can use the TARGET*n* parameter, as part of the <EMBED> tag or through Plug-in Helper, to target a hotspot's action to the QuickTime plug-in, QuickTime Player, a particular browser frame, a particular browser window, or the default browser window.

You can link a blob hotspot to a QuickTime movie that has a QTNEXT to another panorama (the QTNEXT can be in the HTML or embedded in the movie using Plug-in Helper). This is one way to put transition movies between VR nodes.

You can have as many as 255 hotspots in a given panorama. They can be any size and any shape.

Note   There was an "off by one" error in the QuickTime plug-in for QuickTime 4.1, which caused HOTSPOT*n* to activate the link specified for HOTSPOT*n+1*. The workaround was to limit the hotspots in any node to 127, not to use consecutive hotspot numbers in the same node, and to use two HOTSPOT parameters (both *n* and *n+1*) in your HTML to specify the link. The problem was fixed in QuickTime 4.1.1.

For examples of using QTVR hotspots, see "Embedding QTVR in a Web Page" (page 667).

▶ Creating QTVR Object Movies

You create a QTVR object movie by taking and digitizing a series of photographs (or rendering a series of computer-generated images) that show an object from multiple perspectives, typically by rotating the object on a pedestal or turntable. Once you have a series of digital images, you generally need to retouch them with a graphic editor to remove the pedestal and background. You then assemble the images into an object movie using authoring software such as QuickTime VR Authoring Studio, Widgetizer, or PanoWorx.

Equipment

Unless you're generating your images directly from software, you need a camera, lights, a backdrop, a turntable or pedestal to rotate the object, a hot glue gun (this is really essential), and probably an object VR rig that allows you to swing the camera through a vertical arc.

You generally don't need as flexible or as high-resolution a camera for object movies as you do for panoramas. You're photographing a fixed object under controlled lighting with a shallow depth of field, so you have a lot fewer variables to deal with.

A 35 mm SLR camera with a telephoto or macro zoom lens is the standard for museum-quality work, but a good digital camera can produce comparable quality, especially for Web delivery, and is vastly more convenient. A digital video (DV) camera that can take still frames and has a FireWire connector is ideal for this kind of work, provided you don't need higher resolution than DV can offer (for the Web, you generally won't).

You typically take a lot of shots for object movies—36 exposures for a rotation, and up to 18 rotations to cover an object from top to bottom. That's 648 exposures. Unless you enjoy changing film, a digital camera that can download images to your computer in mid-shoot is the way to go, and the faster the better.

In addition, your camera may be swinging on a rig several feet in the air, making it difficult to change film, look through the viewfinder, or work the shutter. A film camera with a lot of film, a shutter release cable, and a motor drive can be made to work (though you may need a ladder to look through the viewfinder), but a digital camera that can use a video monitor as a viewfinder, has a remote control, and downloads over FireWire makes life a lot easier.

You need a set of lights to illuminate your object and a backdrop to shoot against. A black backdrop usually works best, but you can also use a white backdrop effectively—especially if you're shooting a black object.

Tip Use low light with a black backdrop and hot lighting with a white backdrop, so the background is completely black or white. It makes it easier to composite the background out later.

You generally want to rotate your object on a pedestal or turntable that's stable and easy to rotate in increments of 5–10°. For a single-row object movie, a lazy susan can be made to work. If you plan to shoot the object from below, you also need a pedestal, preferably thin and black. The hot glue gun allows you to pose a shoe on its toe or a raygun upright on its handle.

There are some very nice motorized turntables available from companies like Kaidan (www.kaidan.com) and Peace River (www.peaceriverstudios.com) that are designed for this kind of work. Some of them include a rig for vertically aligning your camera and remote-control software that works directly with QuickTime VR Authoring Studio or Widgetizer.

And yes, you can get a really big turntable that you can use to rotate a car—it's made by Emery Manufacturing and Equipment (www.emerymfg .com), and it costs as much as you would expect. Unless you expect to use it a lot, consider using someone else's. Studios like eVox Production (www.evox.com) are happy to power up the big turntable so you can spin a sport utility vehicle.

If you're shooting a single-row object movie, you can position your camera using a tripod. Get a really sturdy one—you won't be carrying it around, and it's critical that the camera not jiggle around during the shoot.

For multirow object movies, you need a rig that can swing the camera through a precise arc. I've seen people make their own camera rigs from a microphone boom, counterweighted with a plastic water jug. I've also seen people balance chairs on their noses. You're welcome to try it if you like—let me know how it works out.

For the rest of us, a commercial object VR rig is the way to go. They range from moderately pricey manual models to really expensive motorized jobs with turntables and remote-control software. The main manufacturers are Kaidan and Peace River, and the better models can shoot an entire object movie, top to bottom and round-and-round, under automated control from QuickTime VR Authoring Studio or Widgetizer, while you have lunch. Awesome stuff.

Shooting

You're going to shoot a series of exposures, keeping your camera at precisely the same alignment with your object, while you rotate the object around its center.

If you're shooting a multirow object movie, you're going to repeat the shoot with the camera at different vertical positions, but otherwise with the exact same alignment, rotating the object to exactly the same positions.

This can be extremely finicky and painstaking work, or it can be a walk in the park, depending entirely on your equipment.

You may need to use a hot glue gun to get your object stable and positioned properly, especially if you're shooting it from underneath. Don't be stingy with the glue—you don't want the object to sag in the middle of your shoot.

You generally want to shoot against a black backdrop, but you may need to use a different color, particularly if your object is black and you plan to matte in a different background later.

It's a good idea to include a small marker object in the frame (but not on the turntable) in case you need to precisely align your images later. This is particularly important if you're shooting film and scanning it, or you're working with inexpensive equipment that isn't rock solid. You'll crop or edit the marker object out after the images are digitized.

You normally want to shoot an exposure every 10° of rotation for a total of 36 images. You can save film and make the movie smaller by shooting 24 exposures 15° apart, but the motion of the object will be jerky. Of course, you don't have to shoot the object from every angle—maybe the back isn't interesting—and four exposures 90° apart provide a complete view, just not smooth animation.

For a multirow movie, you typically want to shoot at 10° vertical increments as well. A full top-to-bottom shoot requires 18 rows, but people rarely shoot from more than 10° to 30° degrees underneath.

Shooting from directly underneath is almost impossible—you can do it with a glass turntable or by suspending the object, but matching the rotation angles and camera registration with the rest of the shoot is hard, hard, hard. Expect to spend many hours with Photoshop trying to get it just right afterward. Of course, if you've been hired by a shoe company, that may be what you're getting paid for—just don't underestimate the effort.

Do a dry run, looking at the object from every angle and rotation. Set up your lighting so you don't get glare or lens flare and the object is well lit at every angle. It's important not to change the lighting, exposure, or focus during the shoot. Be sure to set your camera for fixed exposure, not auto-exposure.

Now you're ready to take some pictures. With the right camera and rig, you can automate the whole shoot and capture your images directly into QuickTime VR Authoring Studio, Widgetizer, or VR PanoWorx. Otherwise, you have a lot of clicking and rotating to do.

Generating 3D Imagery

If you're generating images directly from a 3D modeling program, your task is much simpler. Generate a series of images of your chosen object at 10° intervals of rotation, rendered with your favorite texture maps and lighting effects.

If you're doing a multirow movie, start from the highest point—normally 0° or directly overhead—do a row, drop 10° and do another, until you're as low as you need to be.

Save the images with sequential filenames, using a leading zero for numbers below 10—for example, Row01shot01, Row01shot02, . . . , Row01shot36, Row02shot01, and so on to Row18Shot36.

You may be rendering as many as 648 images, so allow plenty of time and disk space. It may literally require days to render. You might want to render a series of images at 45° (45 images) or 90° (12 images) to make sure you're happy with your settings before you commit to a full series of 648.

Image Preparation

The amount and type of image preparation you need to do depends on how you created your images.

If you shot with film, you need either to develop to CD or to scan prints, slides, or negatives. See "Image Preparation" (page 635) in the section on panoramas for some tips on digitizing. This process is likely to introduce some jitter from frame to frame, so shoot your images with a marker object in the frame and use it to precisely align and crop your images.

If you used a camera of any kind to generate your images (as opposed to using 3D modeling software), you probably need to retouch every image using Photoshop or a similar program.

You generally need to delete the pedestal or supports from each image by hand.

You should probably select the entire background and erase it to a single color in every image (it may all *look* black, but it probably isn't all #000000 *black* black). A solid color compresses better, and you can easily make a solid color transparent. If you're going to make the background color transparent, you probably want to turn anti-aliasing off when you select the background prior to filling it with a solid color. Otherwise, some of the background color will "stick" to the edges of your object.

Tip People commonly matte a background image into each frame at this point. You can save yourself a lot of work, and a lot of bandwidth, by making the background transparent and compositing a single background image into the whole movie later.

You have the option of compressing the images now or when you create the object movie. You can probably get finer control of the compression for each image by doing it now, but you can take advantage of the similarity between adjacent images, resulting in a smaller file, if you compress the whole movie at once. If you compress the images now, be sure to use the same compressor for all the images—don't use JPEG compression on one and GIF compression on another, for example.

Making the Object Movie

You need special software to create an object movie. Some software that does the job includes QuickTime VR Authoring Studio, VR PanoWorx, and Widgetizer.

The exact procedure for making an object movie depends on the tool you choose. You generally specify the number of rows, the degrees of rotation and number of images per row, the initial view, and the folder that contains the images, and then the software creates the movie.

You also choose a compressor at this point. Photo-JPEG compression usually yields the sharpest images, but it tends to create large files.

Cinepak compression takes advantage of the similarity between images, resulting in much smaller files, but it provides only moderate quality at low bandwidths. Sorenson is probably the best compressor for Web delivery, as it gives high quality at low bandwidths, taking good advantage of image similarities. You may want to create key frames a little more often than normal so the movie is more responsive to random access. For more information on image compressors and settings, see "Compressing Your Movie" (page 317).

Some software documentation recommends that you save your object movie with the .obj file extension. Do nothing of the kind—use the .mov extension.

You make several choices when creating the object movie, such as pan and tilt limits, autoplay, and whether to animate views. If you need to modify these settings later, you can do so using QTVR Edit Object, in the Tools folder of the CD.

Compositing QTVR with Other Media

You can mix QTVR with any other kind of QuickTime media, including still images, motion video, music and sound, text, wired sprites, and live streams. The techniques for compositing with panoramas and object movies are somewhat different, however.

Note You can composite other media with VR, including cubic VR and VR object movies, quite easily using LiveStage Pro 3.

Compositing with VR Panoramas

A cylindrical panorama is basically a still image that the viewer can pan around in, so a single-node panorama is a movie with a single video frame. Consequently, no time passes in the movie timeline, no matter what parts of the panorama are displayed and no matter how much time passes in the real world. The movie is essentially paused at the same frame.

A multinode panorama has one video frame per node, so the movie advances by one frame in its timeline, or jumps to a particular frame, when the viewer changes nodes. Once it gets to its new node, the movie is again paused.

A cubic panorama has six video frames, one for each face. They progress clockwise through a circle, followed by the top and bottom.

Like any still images in QuickTime, VR panoramas can be given an extended duration. The techniques for compositing a VR panorama with other media are similar to those for adding a still background image—copy the panorama, select the media you want to add the panorama to, and choose Add Scaled.

Let's look at some examples—adding a picture frame, a sound track, and a wired sprite controller to a VR panorama. We'll show you how to do the editing using QuickTime Player, but you can do essentially the same things using any QuickTime editor that understands panoramas, such as the one in LiveStage Pro.

Adding an Autorotate Sprite to a VR Panorama

One of the few drawbacks of VR panoramas is that until you start to click, drag, and zoom them, they look like static images. It's not unusual for someone to mistake a VR panorama in a Web page for a JPEG and never find out what they're missing.

One simple solution is to add a sprite that autorotates the panorama when no one is using it. Viewers who think they're looking at a JPEG will do a double-take, if not a triple-take. Of course, it helps to tell your audience how to manipulate the VR on your page. Many will discover panning and tilting, but never realize they can zoom in and out unless you tell them.

An autorotate sprite is a wired sprite, so it can be programmed to spin the VR in any direction, at any speed, along any path, with any amount of zooming in or out. It can be programmed to turn itself off when anyone starts to manipulate the VR with the mouse. It can also be programmed to turn itself back on if the VR is left idle for a period of time.

There's a free autorotate sprite widget in the Widgets folder on the CD. It spins the VR slowly counterclockwise until someone clicks the mouse on the VR. If no one clicks the mouse for 5 minutes, it starts again.

For $15, you can buy a flexible widget factory called RevolVR, from Squamish Media Group. It will let you set the spin rate, direction, and so forth.

Or you can purchase VRHotwires or LiveStage Pro, and program autorotate sprites that do whatever you like.

Here's how to add the autorotate widget to your pano:

1. Open the widget in QuickTime Player. Select All. Copy. Close.

2. Open your pano in QuickTime Player. Get Movie Properties.

3. Choose Controller in the right pop-up menu, then choose the Quick-Time Movie Controller.

4. Click in the movie to activate that window. Go to start. Select None. Choose Add from the Edit menu.

5. Reset the controller to the QTVR controller in the Properties window. The pano should start to spin. Close the Properties window.

6. Save As (self-contained).

Sit happily for hours, watching it spin.

Adding a Picture Frame to a VR Panorama

You can add any kind of visual frame to a VR panorama, and it's fairly easy to do. This can be the equivalent of a simple picture frame, an elaborate screen, a logo, or even a very large image—similar to a background image for a Web page. You can superimpose the panorama on the frame, or make part of the frame transparent and let the panorama show through it.

Here are the steps for adding a frame or a logo to a panorama:

1. Open the frame or logo image in QuickTime Player. Select All. Copy.

2. Open the panorama in QuickTime Player and choose Get Movie Properties from the Movie menu.

3. In the Properties window, select Movie Controller. This lets you edit your VR movie.

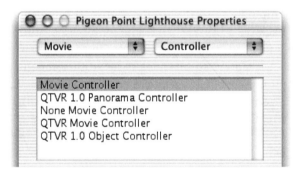

4. Choose Select All in the Edit menu, then Add Scaled. This adds the image on top of the panorama. Both the image and the panorama are aligned in the upper left corner of the display window. The image is on top of the panorama, which is what you want for a logo, but not for a frame.

5. For a frame, use the left pop-up menu in the Properties window to choose Video Track 2 (the image you just added). Choose Layer in the right pop-up menu and increment the layer number until the panorama is on top of the frame.

   If you want the panorama to show through the frame, rather than sitting on top of it, skip step 5. But remember that the panorama can look like it's showing through a hole in the frame, even when it's drawn on top of the frame.

6. Choose Video Track 2 in the left pop-up menu, choose Size in the right pop-up menu, click Adjust, and drag the image so the panorama is centered, or so the logo is where you want it. Click Done. Your panorama is now floating on a background image, or your logo is floating on the panorama.

7. For a logo (or a frame on top of a panorama), set the image graphics mode to transparent, blend, or alpha, as appropriate, by choosing Graphics Mode from the right pop-up menu. For more about graphic modes, see "Transparency and Alpha Channels" (page 271).

8. Reset the movie controller to the QTVR Controller and save as a self-contained movie.

The panorama is far more responsive to user input if it's floating on top of a frame image than if it's showing through a hole. This is particularly noticeable on slower computers. If you shade the edges of the frame image surrounding the panorama, you can still create the appearance of the panorama being under the frame. For an example, see `PigeonFrame.mov` (in the Virtual folder of the CD). It looks like the panorama is behind the frame. It's very effective.

Adding a Sound Track to a VR Panorama

Adding a sound track to a VR panorama is a little tricky because the sound track is time-based and the panorama is not. We can stretch the duration of the panorama to match the sound track using Add Scaled, but there is also the issue of the controller.

The VR controller provides no way to play the audio—the movie is always paused—but the standard movie controller doesn't allow the viewer to pan or zoom in the panorama.

Don't worry. These are all solvable problems. Here's how you do it:

1. Open the panorama in QuickTime Player and choose Get Movie Properties.

2. In the Properties window, select Movie Controller. This lets you edit the VR movie.

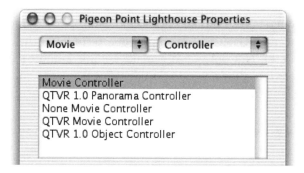

3. Choose Select All in the Edit menu, then Copy. Close (don't save).

4. Open a sound file—such as a WAV, MP3, or MIDI file—or a sound-only QuickTime movie in QuickTime Player. Choose Select All from the Edit menu, then Add Scaled. This adds the panorama to the sound track, scaled to have the same duration.

5. Open Playbutton.mov (in the Interactive folder of the CD) in QuickTime Player. Choose Select All, then Copy. Close (don't save).

6. Click anywhere in the panorama sound movie. Choose Select All in the Edit menu, then Add Scaled. This adds a Play button on top of the panorama. The button is aligned in the upper left corner of the panorama.

7. Use the left pop-up menu in the Properties window to choose Sprite Track. Choose Size in the right pop-up menu, click Adjust, and drag the button to the bottom of the frame (or wherever you prefer). Click Done.

8. Reset the movie controller to the QTVR Controller and save as a self-contained movie.

Your panorama now looks and acts like any VR panorama, but it has a Play button floating on it. Clicking the Play button plays any audio tracks. If the viewer is downloading the movie over the Web, clicking the Play button plays as much of the audio as has downloaded. This works equally well for cubic and cylindrical panoramas.

If you'd prefer to have your audio start as soon as the file is downloaded, use a wired sprite authoring tool to create an invisible sprite that automatically starts the movie. You can also use a sprite to set the movie looping for continuous audio.

If you want a more sophisticated audio controller, use a wired sprite authoring tool such as LiveStage Pro to create one.

Another nice tool for adding sound to a VR panorama is Squamish Media's soundsaVR. There's a demo version in the Demos folder of the CD—you can register it on the Web to unlock the full feature set (www.smgvr.com). Not only does it make adding sound to a panorama drag-and-drop easy, it allows you to add *directional* sound—sound that pans left or right and changes volume as you look toward or away from it. Way cool.

Adding a Wired Sprite Controller to a VR Panorama

You can use wired sprites to add your own controller to a VR panorama. You might want to do this for aesthetic reasons, or to create a custom controller that mixes panorama controls with other controls—such as a Play/Stop button or volume control—for movies that contain both panoramas and time-based media. If you're going to apply a media skin to a panorama, and you want visible controls, you need to add a wired controller to your movie.

In addition, if you use a VR panorama within a SMIL presentation, you need to add a wired controller to enable the user to zoom in or zoom out—panoramas do not have a VR controller attached to them when viewed as part of a SMIL presentation.

You can create a wired sprite VR controller—using an authoring tool such as LiveStage Pro or GoLive—by assigning actions such as SetPanAngle and SetFieldOfView to your Flash or sprite buttons.

You generally want the panorama to pan or zoom smoothly while activated, and there's a little trick to making that happen. It works like this:

1. Create a sprite variable and have your sprite set the variable to 1 in response to a mouse-down event or a mouse-enter event, whichever you want to activate the control.

2. Have the same sprite set the variable to 0 in response to a mouse-up or mouse-exit event.

3. Have the sprite read the variable in response to the *idle* event and change the pan angle or field of view only if the variable is true. You can control the speed of the pan or zoom by setting the idle event rate.

There are two wired sprite VR controllers that illustrate this behavior in the Interactive folder of the CD (VRsprite.mov and hoVRsprite.mov). Feel free to add one to your panoramas if you like.

Actually adding a wired sprite controller to a VR movie is straightforward:

1. Open the panorama in QuickTime Player and choose Get Movie Properties.

2. Use the Properties window to select Movie Controller.

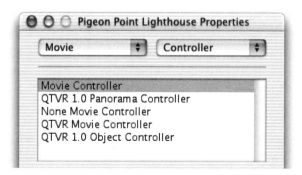

3. Open the movie that contains your wired sprite controller in QuickTime Player. Choose Select All, then Copy.

4. Click anywhere in the panorama movie. Choose Select All in the Edit menu, then Add Scaled. This adds the wired sprite controller on top of the panorama. The controller is aligned in the upper left corner of the panorama.

5. Use the left pop-up menu in the Properties window to choose Sprite Track. Choose Size in the right pop-up menu, click Adjust, and drag the controller to the bottom of the frame (or wherever you prefer). You can use the red handles to stretch or shrink the controller if you need to. Click Done.

Tip If you're trying to reposition a small sprite, you may find that the red handles overlap, leaving you nowhere to click and drag. Try choosing Double Size in the Movie menu; this will double the displayed size and create gaps between the handles. If it's still not big enough, go full-screen.

6. If you want the controller to have a transparent background, choose Graphics Mode in the right pop-up menu and set the graphics mode to transparent or to one of the alpha modes, as described in "Transparency and Alpha Channels" (page 271).

7. Reset the movie controller to the QTVR Controller and save as a self-contained movie.

For an example of a VR panorama with a sound track and a wired sprite controller, see Visit.htm (in the Virtual folder of the CD); this movie was kindly provided by Erik Fohlin of Barsark AB, Sweden (www.barsark.com).

Adding All Kinds of Stuff to Panoramas

Wouldn't it be cool if you could use QTVR to create seamless environments with smooth visual transitions between nodes, embedded objects, sound effects, and pretty much everything else? Well, you can.

One tool for the job is LiveStage Pro (www.totallyhip.com), which was used to create the tunnels.mov example (in the Virtual folder on the CD). It combines multiple panoramas, object movies, animated transitions, and wired sprites. You can examine the tunnels.lsp project (also in the Virtual folder) using LiveStage Pro to see how it's done.

For a breathtaking example of VR, Flash, sound, and wired sprites, check out archive.greenpeace.org/greatbear/, built by ici Media using LiveStage Pro. It's genuinely beautiful.

There is also some very cool software, Deep Forest Multimedia's VRHotWires (www.mountain-inter.net/~bmeikle/), that can link panoramas together using hotspots, transitional effects, video clips, and more. There are some great examples on Deep Forest's website. It's cheap, too.

You should also check out Squamish Media Group (www.smgvr.com). They make inexpensive and easy-to-use tools that add directional sound and wired sprite maps to panoramas, make panoramas autorotate, and other fun stuff.

Compositing with Object Movies

Object movies are a unique type of time-based media, so compositing them with other QuickTime media can be a little tricky. Here are the main things to remember:

- Each view in an object movie—whether it's a single image or an animation—has the same duration.

- There are the same number of views in any row.

- Consequently, dragging the mouse—left, right, up, or down—jumps in the movie timeline by a fixed amount of time to reach the next view.

- That fixed amount of time is not calculated when the movie plays—it is stored as a constant in the VR track of the movie when the movie is created.

- If you change the duration of any part of an object movie—by using Cut, Paste, or Delete, for example—dragging jumps by the wrong amount of time and navigation won't work properly anymore.

- You can add media to an object movie, without changing the object movie's duration, using the Add or Add Scaled command.

- An object movie can be set to play all the frames of a view when the user drags to a new view—it can be set to play them once or loop them continuously.

Note You can set these characteristics when you create an object movie using QuickTime VR Authoring Studio or modify them later using QTVR Edit Object (in the Tools folder of the CD).

- When the frames of a view are played, a portion of the movie timeline is being played—any media added to that part of the timeline also plays.

- To add media to an object movie, open the movie in QuickTime Player and use the Properties window to assign the Movie Controller—the QTVR Controller doesn't allow editing (you can restore the QTVR Controller when you're done editing).

With these, uh, *simple* guidelines in mind, you can composite a wide variety of media with VR object movies.

To do things that these guidelines simply don't allow—like adding continuous background music—put the media in separate movies and integrate them with the object movie using a QuickTime container such as SMIL, a Web page, LiveStage Movie Tracks, or Director. In fact, if you plan to do a lot of compositing with VR object movies, LiveStage Pro 3 is more or less indispensable.

Now let's look at some specific examples—adding still images, sound, motion video, and sprites.

Adding Still Images to an Object Movie

Adding a still image to an object movie is fairly easy—you copy the still image and add it to the object movie using the Add Scaled command. We'll look at three practical applications—adding a background, adding a frame, and adding a logo.

Many people who make object movies painstakingly matte a background image into every frame using Photoshop. You can save a lot of work and a lot of bandwidth by adding a background image to the whole object movie at once using QuickTime Player. And since you're downloading only a single background image for the whole movie, you can use a much higher-resolution image.

The trick to making this work is either to create the object movie images on a solid background color, so that color can be made transparent, or to add an alpha channel to the images.

Using an alpha channel creates a more visually seamless composition, but it's almost as much work to add an alpha channel to every image as it is to matte in a background image. Using an alpha channel also requires 32-bit color, which uses more bandwidth than 8-bit, 16-bit, or 24-bit color, and it restricts you to using a 32-bit color compressor—you can't use JPEG or Cinepak, for example.

Consequently, a solid background color is a more practical choice. Be sure to choose a background color that doesn't appear anywhere in your object, or those areas of your object will also become transparent (you can use this fact intentionally to create windows in your object).

Similarly, a frame or foreground image adds a lot of character to an object movie without using much bandwidth—and because it's a single image you can afford to use very high resolution.

The benefits of adding a logo are obvious—every copy of the movie is an advertisement for your company. The logo can also be a live link to your website. You generally want to create your logo on a solid color background or with an alpha channel, so it composites cleanly over the object movie. In this case, it's usually better to use an alpha channel than a solid color. Since it's a single small image, the extra effort and bandwidth required for an alpha channel are minimal (and well worth it for the improved visual quality).

Here are the steps to add a still image to an object movie:

1. Open the still image in QuickTime Player. Select All. Copy.

2. Open the object movie in QuickTime Player and choose Get Movie Properties.

3. In the Properties window, select Movie Controller.

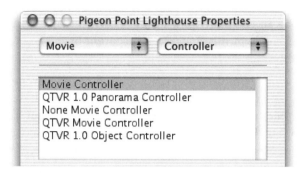

4. Choose Select All in the Edit menu to add a background, frame, or logo to the whole movie. Alternately, use the selection tools in the control bar to select a row or a view that you want to add the image to.

5. Choose Add Scaled. This adds the image on top of the object movie. The image is aligned in the upper left corner of the display window.

If your image is a logo, do this:

6. Choose Video Track 2 (your logo) in the left pop-up menu, then choose Size in the right pop-up menu and click Adjust.

7. Drag your logo where you want it. You can scale your logo by dragging the red handles. Click Done.

8. If you want your logo to be translucent or have a transparent background, choose Graphics Mode from the right pop-up menu and set the graphics mode to transparent, blend, or one of the alpha modes, as appropriate.

9. Reset the movie controller to the QTVR Controller and save as a self-contained movie.

If your image is a frame or a background, do this after step 5:

6. Use the left pop-up menu in the Info window to choose Video Track 1 (the object images). Choose Layer in the right pop-up menu and decrement the layer number until the object movie is on top of the frame or background.

7. Choose Size in the right pop-up menu, click Adjust, and drag the object to the center of the frame (or wherever in the frame you prefer). Click Done. Your object movie is now floating on a background image.

8. To composite the object movie over a background image, choose Graphics Mode in the right pop-up menu of the Info window and set the graphics mode of the object to transparent or to one of the alpha modes, as appropriate.

9. If you want the object movie to show through a frame, rather than sitting on top of it, increment the object's layer until it disappears, then set the graphics mode of the frame image to transparent, blend, or alpha, as appropriate, by choosing Video Track 2 from the left pop-up menu and Graphics Mode from the right pop-up menu.

10. Reset the movie controller to the QTVR Controller and save as a self-contained movie.

Note For more about graphic modes, see "Transparency and Alpha Channels" (page 271).

Adding Sound to an Object Movie

Adding sound to an object movie is tricky. The sound is played only when its part of the movie timeline is played, and an object movie jumps around in the movie timeline in a nonlinear way as the user drags the image.

You can easily add a narration or sound effect to a given view. If you set the object movie to play all frames in a view (Animate Views), the sound plays along. If you set the object movie to loop the frames until a new view is selected, the sound loops as well.

Adding music to a view is generally a bad idea—as the user jumps from view to view, the music jumps abruptly and the effect is disconcerting (like pushing buttons on a car radio).

Adding music to a row or the movie as a whole generally doesn't work either—as the user jumps from view to view or row to row, the music skips around as well.

The best way to add background music to an object movie being played in a browser is to embed an audio-only movie in the same Web page.

The best way to add music to an object movie being played in Quick-Time Player is to use SMIL. See Chapter 18, "SMIL for the Camera," for details.

The sound associated with a view cannot be longer than the view's duration (but it can be shorter).

When you initially create an object movie using a tool such as Quick-Time VR Authoring Studio, you can set the object movie to play all frames in a view, even if there is only one frame in each view, and you can make the duration of the views as long as you like (but they must all be the same).

Create your movie so the view duration is long enough for the longest audio segment that you want to attach to a view. If you need to make the views longer, recreate the movie using your authoring tool—don't modify its duration using QuickTime Player.

All that said, these are the steps for adding sound to a view:

1. Open the object movie in QuickTime Player and choose Get Movie Properties.

2. In the Properties window, select Movie Controller.

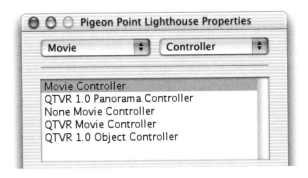

3. Open a sound file—such as a WAV, MP3, or MIDI file—or a sound-only QuickTime movie in QuickTime Player. Choose Select All from the Edit menu, then Copy.

4. Use the selection tools to select a particular view in the object movie, then choose Add. This adds the sound to the view.

5. Repeat steps 3 and 4 for as many sounds as you like. To add the same sound to multiple views, just repeat step 4.

6. Reset the movie controller to the QTVR Controller and save.

   ▪ If you've used a unique sound for each view, save as a self-contained movie.

   ▪ If you've used the same sound dozens or hundreds of times, consider saving the movie but allowing dependencies—this prevents Quick-Time from duplicating the sound data dozens or hundreds of times, but the sound files need to travel with the movie for it to play. (It can still play over the Web if the sound files are on the Web server.)

Your object movie should now play sound when you drag to a view.

If your object movie is set to play the frames for each view once, you might want to add a Play button to let the user hear the audio again without changing views. This is discussed in "Adding a Sprite Controller to an Object Movie" (page 665).

Adding Motion Video to an Object Movie

You can add motion video to a view, a row, or even a whole object movie. Just remember that the video jumps around as the user jumps from view to view and row to row. Motion video plays smoothly only for the duration of a particular view.

If you create an animation with the same number of frames as the object movie, so that the two are synchronized, this can work out very nicely. A video of your object rotating in a mirror would be one example; an animated character that watches your object in rapt fascination would be another.

If your logo is animated, as a different example, you might attach a copy to each view, so that the animation loops no matter which view is selected.

These are the steps to add motion video to an object movie:

1. Open the object movie in QuickTime Player and choose Get Movie Properties.

2. In the Properties window, select Movie Controller.

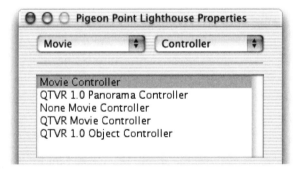

3. Open the motion video file in QuickTime Player. Choose Select All from the Edit menu, then Copy.

4. In the object movie, choose Select All, or use the selection tools to select a particular view or a particular row, then choose Add Scaled. This adds the motion video to the object movie, scaled in duration to match the movie, row, or view.

5. The video is aligned with the upper left corner of the display area. To move it or scale it, choose the last video track in the left pop-up menu of the Properties window, then choose Size in the right pop-up menu and click Adjust. You may also want to set the new video track's graphics mode by choosing Graphics Mode from the right pop-up menu.

6. Repeat steps 3, 4, and 5 for as many videos as you like. To add the same video to multiple views, repeat steps 4 and 5 only.

7. Reset the movie controller to the QTVR Controller and save.

In most cases, you should save as a self-contained movie.

If you've used the same video dozens or hundreds of times, consider saving the movie but allowing dependencies—this prevents QuickTime from duplicating the video data dozens or hundreds of times, but the video files need to travel with the movie for it to play. (It can still play over the Web if the video files are on the Web server.)

For an example of an object movie that includes motion video, see Laptopobj.mov (in the Virtual folder on the CD).

Adding a Sprite Controller to an Object Movie

You might want to add a sprite controller to an object movie for various reasons. You can create a controller that has a unique appearance, for example. If you added sound bites to the views, you might want to give the user a way to play them again without changing views (or a way to stop them).

If you're using an object movie in a SMIL presentation, you may want to add a zoom control so the user can zoom in or out.

You generally want to add a controller to a whole movie, rather than a row or a particular view. A sprite controller can often take actions that are local to the currently displayed view, even when a single control sprite persists through the whole movie.

For example, the PlayMovie action plays only the selection of the movie timeline associated with the current view. Similarly, the StopMovie action stops playing any time-based media only until the user changes views. To turn off sound completely, for example, you need to mute the movie's volume—stopping the movie only interrupts the sound until the user drags the image.

You can jump to a particular row or view using the GoToTime action. Since this action can take absolute or relative parameters, you can create a sprite controller that emulates dragging with the mouse by jumping ahead or back a fixed amount of time.

These are the steps for adding a sprite controller to an object movie:

1. Open the object movie in QuickTime Player and choose Get Movie Properties.

2. In the Properties window, select Movie Controller.

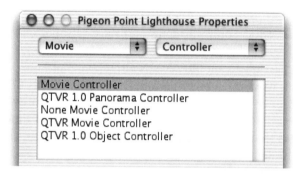

3. Open a sprite controller movie, such as `Playbutton.mov` (in the Virtual folder of the CD), in QuickTime Player. Choose Select All, then Copy.

4. Click anywhere in the object movie. Choose Select All in the Edit menu, then Add Scaled. This adds the sprite controller to the whole object movie. The controller is aligned in the upper left corner of the panorama.

5. Use the left pop-up menu in the Properties window to choose Sprite Track. Choose Size in the right pop-up menu, click Adjust, and drag the controller to the bottom of the frame (or wherever you prefer). Click Done.

6. Reset the movie controller to the QTVR Controller and save as a self-contained movie.

That's it. The mechanics of adding the controller are fairly simple, but understanding how some sprite actions affect object movies involves a certain amount of head scratching.

There's a reason why adding wired sprite controllers to a VR object movie is almost the last thing we discuss in this book—people who do it are pushing the envelope of what's possible.

Keep pushing. I'll go get you a bigger envelope.

 # Embedding QTVR in a Web Page

You can embed a QTVR movie in a Web page as you would any Quick-Time movie, but there are some special aspects to VR movies that are worth noting.

Basics

Size Matters

VR movies are almost always large—300 Kbytes is considered small in the VR world, and 3 MB is not unusual. Consequently, you should almost always use a poster movie to prevent large and unwanted downloads. See "Click Here, Play There (Poster Movies)" (page 63) and "Making a Poster Movie with Plug-in Helper" (page 92) for details.

Check Your References

Whenever possible, you should create multiple versions of your VR movies and point to them using a multiple-data-rate reference movie. For details, see Chapter 8, "Alternate Realities: Language, Speed, and Connections."

It's hard to create good VR movies at acceptably small sizes, so you might consider adding a direct link to your highest-resolution version, in addition to the reference movie. Sometimes people with slow modems are willing to wait to get the real goods—you might as well show them your best.

Note If you zoomify your movie, there's no reason to make multiple copies—it's done for you, and more. See "Zoomify It?" (page 638).

Intruder Alert

If another plug-in has taken over the QuickTime .mov file type, it won't be able to display a VR movie, so be sure to embed a "You need QuickTime" image as the default image in the reference movie, or use the `SRC="Dummy.pntg" QTSRC="QTVR.mov"` technique, as described in "Using QuickTime to Play Files in Other Formats" (page 30). You can also ensure that viewers running Internet Explorer for Windows use the QuickTime ActiveX control by wrapping your `<EMBED>` tag in an `<OBJECT>` tagset and specifying the QuickTime CLASSID, as described in Chapter 4, "Basic Training: Putting QuickTime in a Web Page."

Node Logic

When you embed a multiple-node panorama in a website, it's generally best to break up the download by putting each node in its own HTML page. Link the nodes by using blob hotspots and inserting HOTSPOT parameters into the <EMBED> tag. For details, see "Fun with QuickTime" (page 59).

Note There was an "off by one" error in the QuickTime plug-in for QuickTime 4.1, which caused HOTSPOT*n* to activate the link specified for HOTSPOT*n+1*. The workaround was to limit the hotspots in any panorama to 127, not to use consecutive hotspot numbers, and to use two HOTSPOT parameters (both *n* and *n+1*) to specify the link. The problem was fixed in QuickTime 4.1.1.

To preserve continuity when presenting multiple panoramas this way, it's best to use frames. If a panorama loads in a frame, you don't need to use the TARGET parameter to replace it with another panorama in the same frame—the current frame is the browser's default target.

Here's an example that shows the syntax for linking a VR panorama to other panoramas using "blob" hotspots. Load the page containing this HTML into a frame, so only that frame is replaced by the hotspot's URL. Each panorama must be embedded into its own HTML page with its own hotspots specified. Link each hotspot to the HTML page containing the desired panorama. This example includes redundant hotspots to prevent the "off by one" problem, and uses the <OBJECT> tag as well, just for completeness.

```
<OBJECT WIDTH="320" HEIGHT="256"
  CLASSID="clsid:02BF25D5-8C17-4B23-BC80-D3488ABDDC6B"
  CODEBASE="http://www.apple.com/qtactivex/qtplugin.cab">

<PARAM NAME="src" VALUE="Pano1.mov">
<PARAM NAME="HOTSPOT20" VALUE="Pano2.htm">
<PARAM NAME="HOTSPOT21" VALUE="Pano2.htm">
<PARAM NAME="HOTSPOT30" VALUE="Pano3.htm">
<PARAM NAME="HOTSPOT31" VALUE="Pano3.htm">
```

```
<EMBED WIDTH=320 HEIGHT=256
   SRC="UNeedQT.pntg" TYPE="image/x-macpaint"
   QTSRC="Pano1.mov"
   HOTSPOT20="Pano2.htm"  HOTSPOT21="Pano2.htm"
   HOTSPOT30="Pano3.htm"  HOTSPOT31="Pano3.htm"
   PLUGINSPAGE="http://www.apple.com/quicktime/download/">
</EMBED>

</OBJECT>
```

In addition, you should probably provide a map in an adjacent frame with hotspots that load the appropriate node's HTML page in the panorama frame. You can do this by creating a QuickTime movie with HREF links or by creating a simple client-side image map in HTML.

Note   Image maps are created using the IMG, AREA, and MAP tags. For an explanation of these tags, consult any HTML tutorial website.

For an example of a Web page that uses frames, blob hotspots, and an image map to display a series of linked panoramas, open Multinode.htm (in the Virtual folder of the CD) using your browser.

The Web page shown in the following illustration was created by converting a multinode panorama—created using QTVR Authoring Studio—into a series of single-node panoramas with blob hotspots. The conversion was done automatically using the NodeSaVR tool from Squamish Media Group (www.smgvr.com).

The NodeSaVR program generated the HTML for the hotspots, which was then modified by hand to fix any potential hotspot bug in the viewer's browser, simply by adding a HOTSPOT$n + 1$ for every HOTSPOTn. So for example,

```
HOTSPOT84="monolake4.html"
```

became

```
HOTSPOT84="monolake4.html" HOTSPOT85="monolake4.html".
```

The image map was created manually using a GIF and HTML. A nice tool for creating animated maps with wired sprite position indicators is mapsaVR, also from Squamish Media Group.

Appendix A

QuickTime Player Pro
Editing Features

The pro version of the QuickTime 6 Player application is a handy tool for working with QuickTime movies and media. You can use it to play, edit, composite, and save movies. You can also import media from other file types and export media to other file types. This appendix takes you on a quick tour of QuickTime Player's editing menus, dialog boxes, and panels. To get more information about its movie-playing controls, choose QuickTime Player Help in the player's Help menu.

Note If you are running Mac OS X or Windows, the CD in the back of this book will install QuickTime 6.2. If you are using an older version of the Mac OS, it will install version 6.03. There are minor differences between the Windows, Mac OS X, and Mac OS Classic versions of QuickTime Player, which are summarized at the end of this appendix.

By default, QuickTime Player is configured to play movies in a single window. Consequently, only one movie can be open at a time (opening a second movie replaces the existing movie in the window). You need to have more than one movie open sometimes, so the first thing you need to do is set the preferences to open movies in a new player window. Do this using the QuickTime Player > Preferences > Player Preferences menu choice.

▶ Editing

Now then. We'll start by looking at the most common editing operations, such as selecting part of a movie, copying, cutting, and pasting. Later on we'll talk about the Properties window, in which you can make deeper structural changes to a movie.

Basic Controls

The basic controls for QuickTime Player are similar to a VCR. You can play, pause, fast-forward, and rewind. You can also jump directly to the beginning or end and adjust the audio volume. There are often multiple ways to do the same thing, such as an onscreen button and a keyboard equivalent.

- The Play/Pause button starts and stops movie playing.

  Pressing the Space bar on your keyboard also starts and stops the movie.

  Clicking in the player's display area stops the movie, and double-clicking starts it playing.

Tip To play a movie backward, you can hold down the Macintosh Command key (Ctrl in Windows) and press the Left Arrow key, or you can hold down the Shift key and double-click the movie's image in the player window.

- The Go to Start button takes you to the beginning of the movie, and the Go to End button sends you to the end. The Fast Rewind and Fast Forward buttons let you race backward and forward through the movie.

- To adjust the sound volume, move the slider on the left side of the player or press the Up and Down Arrow keys on your keyboard. If you hold down the Ctrl or Alt key when you click the Play/Pause button, the movie's sound will be muted.

Selection Tools

Before you edit a movie using QuickTime Player, you need to know how to select the sections of the movie that you want to change or move around.

When you make a selection in a movie, you select all tracks in that movie for a range of time. You can then cut or copy this piece of cinematic experience and add or paste it into another movie, or elsewhere in the same movie. QuickTime Player's Time slider provides the controls you need to select a section of the movie.

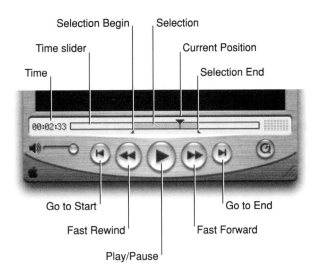

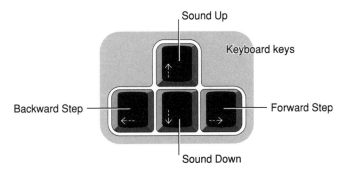

Note Some movies hide the controls or use a different set of controls, such as the VR controller. If the selection controls aren't visible, open the Movie Properties window and select the Movie Controller. For details, see "Movie Properties" (page 693), particularly "Controller" (page 696).

- The Selection Begin and Selection End indicators (triangles) mark the two ends of the current selection on the Time slider. The region between them is gray to show the selection. You can make a selection simply by dragging these indicators.

- The Current Position indicator marks the current point in the movie timeline. Click anywhere on the timeline to change the current position, or drag the indicator to the desired point. Choose Select None (or shift-click the Current Position indicator) to bring both selection triangles to the current position.

- As you move any of the indicators along the Time slider, QuickTime Player displays the image corresponding to that point in the movie timeline. When you release what you're dragging, the player reverts to the image for the current position. This can be disconcerting when you're nudging one of the selection indicators.

- The Right and Left Arrow keys on your keyboard move the indicator you touched last, one frame at a time. The screen briefly shows the movie at the indicator's point in the timeline, then returns to showing the current time.

- The Time indicator shows the instant in the movie timeline of the frame being displayed, in hours, minutes, and seconds. (The frame being displayed corresponds to the current time in the movie unless you are moving one of the selection indicators.)

Note To see these times more precisely (down to thirtieths of a second), choose Get Movie Properties from the Movie menu, then choose Time from the right pop-up menu. This displays the current movie time, duration, and the beginning, end, and duration of the current selection. You can leave this window open on your desktop to see continuously updated information.

- If you hold down the Shift key, moving the Current Position indicator extends the selection. This works whether you move the indicator by dragging, using the arrow keys, or by playing the movie.

Tip Holding down the Shift key while the movie plays is a good way to monitor what you're selecting. Use the arrow keys to fine-tune your selection frame-by-frame once you get it approximately right.

To review your selection, choose Play Selection Only from the Movie menu. You can use Loop, or Loop Back and Forth, to loop just the selection repeatedly. Press Play to play the selection.

What Gets Selected

When you make a selection, you're selecting a chunk of the movie timeline. Your selection has the same number and kind of tracks as the movie. It also has a starting point, an end point, and a duration.

To see the starting point, click and hold the Selection Begin indicator. If the movie contains visual tracks, you see the first frame of your selection.

You can adjust the starting point frame-by-frame using the keyboard's Left and Right Arrow keys.

Tip Be aware that each frame has an independent duration—all the frames in a video may have identical durations, but this is not necessarily the case. For narrated slideshows, for example, each frame typically has a *unique* duration of at least several seconds (however long the narration for that slide is).

Click and hold the Selection End indicator to see the first frame *after* your selection. To add that frame to your selection, use the Right Arrow key. (To remove the previous frame from your selection, use the Left Arrow key.) Adding the last frame of the movie to your selection does not change the display—it still shows the last frame.

To see the exact duration of your selection, open the Movie Properties window (Movie menu, Get Movie Properties) and choose Time from the right pop-up menu. All times are displayed in hours, minutes, seconds, and a fractional part in units of 1/30 of a second (for standard NTSC video, each fraction corresponds to one video frame). For example, 1:02:03.4 represents a duration of 1 hour, 2 minutes, 3 seconds, and 4/30ths of a second.

The duration of your selection is important, as it affects several editing commands. If nothing is selected (duration zero), the editing commands can do some unexpected things.

Important For some operations, no selection is the same as selecting the current frame. For other operations, no selection is the same as selecting the whole movie.

Cut, Copy, Clear (delete), and Trim treat no selection the same as selecting the currently displayed frame. In a sound-only movie, these commands are grayed out when there is no selection.

If your selection has a duration of zero, a Copy, Cut, or Clear (delete) operation will affect the current visual frame, whatever its duration, including all underlying tracks. This is typically a small fraction of a second, but a given frame can have *any* duration.

The Trim command deletes everything in the movie *except* your selection. If nothing is selected, only the current frame remains. The rest of your movie goes, well, wherever bits go when they're gone. (Yikes!)

Tip QuickTime Player has one level of Undo. If that's not enough, close without saving and start over. Always make a copy of irreplaceable movies, and work on the copy.

The Add Scaled and Replace commands treat no selection as selecting the whole movie. You can get the same result by choosing Select All prior to giving these commands.

If your selection has a duration of zero (nothing selected), the Add Scaled command adds the new material starting at the beginning of your movie, with the same duration as your movie.

A Replace command replaces your selection with whatever is on the clipboard (from your last Cut or Copy operation). If nothing is selected, your *entire movie* is replaced. Probably not what you had in mind. Undo.

In the next sections we'll describe the basic Edit menu operations that you can perform on a selection, and then we'll go into the more general ways you can use the File and Movie menus to move media around and create finished movies.

Edit Menu

QuickTime Player's Edit menu lets you copy and paste material from one movie to another (or from one part of a movie to another), select all the contents of a movie, and find text strings in text tracks. If you have used commands such as Open Movie and Import to create several single-track movies containing the sounds and images you want, you can use the Edit menu commands to merge your content into one movie.

Cut, Copy, Paste, Replace, and Clear

QuickTime Player's Cut, Copy, Paste, and Clear commands act as these commands usually do in a text or drawing program. To copy a chunk of a movie, just select it and choose Copy from the Edit menu. As explained in the previous section, however, your selection defines a range of movie time and may contain a portion of several tracks. If you want to copy a selection from just one track, you must extract the track into a temporary single-track movie and do your copying from that. Track extraction is explained on page 679.

When you paste one chunk of movie into another movie, the player inserts the chunk *just before* the frame that is currently showing. So move the Current Position indicator in the Time slider until you can see the first frame that you want to follow the insertion, then choose Paste from the Edit menu. You can use the Right Arrow and Left Arrow keys to move the Current Position indicator a frame at a time.

One exception to the foregoing is when you paste a chunk onto the end of a movie. When you move the Current Position indicator to the far right end of the Time slider, the player places the new material *after* the last frame.

Tip If you absolutely must paste something immediately before the last frame, you have to do a little dance: paste it at the end, select what used to be the last frame, cut, go to the end, paste.

If there is a current selection in the receiving movie, you can use Replace to replace it with the movie chunk you're moving. If there is no current selection, the Replace command will replace your entire movie. Oops. Fortunately, there is an Undo command in the Edit menu as well.

The Clear command removes the current selection from the current movie without putting anything in its place. You can accomplish the same action by pressing the Delete key on your keyboard. If there is no current selection, only the current frame is deleted. If the current movie is sound-only (thus has no frames) and there is no current selection, Clear is unavailable.

The Cut command combines Copy with Clear. It copies the current selection and removes the original at the same time.

You can paste a number of different kinds of media into a nonempty movie after having copied them out of other applications. If you're pasting a still graphic into a movie that already has a visual track, the graphic is resized to fit the movie's current dimensions and it is inserted as a new frame at the current position, with the same duration as the current frame. If the movie has no visual track, the graphic retains its size and becomes a 2-second frame in a new video track.

If you're pasting text from a word processor, it will appear as a new 2-second frame. The text is white on black and centered. Depending on the word processor, it may retain some or all of the original style and typography. To bring text into a movie with more control, use Import (page 683).

Drag-and-Drop Copying and Pasting

You can do quick Copy and Paste operations by using the drag-and-drop feature of QuickTime Player and many other applications. In the simplest case, it works like this:

1. Open a movie in QuickTime Player and select a part of it.
2. With the pointer in the player window, press and hold down the mouse button. Drag the image over to another movie that's open in another

player window. That window will display a barber-pole frame to show that it's ready to receive.

3. Release the mouse button to drop the selection into the other movie.

The drag-and-drop procedure does the same job as the Copy and Paste commands described in the last section. Step 2 performs the Copy and step 3 performs the Paste.

You can exchange media between movies and a variety of other applications, provided the applications are "drag-and-drop aware." A little experimentation will show you the possibilities. When you drag part of a movie onto the Macintosh desktop, it shows up as a movie clipping—a Quick-Time movie that is dependent on the source movie. When you drag part of a movie onto the Windows desktop it shows up as a still-image file in BMP format.

Add and Add Scaled

The Add command works like Paste, except that it adds the new chunk of movie in one or more new tracks—on top of what's already there—instead of inserting it. To do this, the player makes new tracks, running concurrently with the movie's existing tracks, and places them on top of the other tracks. You can change a new track's visibility relative to other tracks by using the Layer panel of the Properties window (page 699).

The Add Scaled command scales the chunk you are pasting in time (not in spatial dimensions). The chunk becomes stretched or compressed so that it plays for the same duration as the current selection in the receiving movie. (The result can be a slow-motion or fast-motion effect.) If there is no current selection, the new chunk is scaled to the duration of the whole movie.

Note   When QuickTime Player makes a new track for Add or Add Scaled, it may renumber the default names of existing tracks (Video Track 1, Video Track 2, and so on). To avoid confusion, you may want to use the General panel to give these tracks more meaningful names, as explained on page 698.

Add Scaled can help you scale a track to a specific duration. To do this, extract the track from its present movie, and use Add Scaled to add it to another movie in which the current selection has the duration you want. Then extract the track again, and use Add to add it back to the original movie.

Note Material is normally added by reference, without changing its compression or duplicating the actual sample data. On Macs only, if you hold down the Ctrl key while choosing Add or Add Scaled for certain visual tracks, the player may present the Compression Settings dialog box (see page 691). You can either accept the codec's default settings for the new track or you can change them. If it's a text track, you get the Text Settings dialog box, as you do with the Import command (page 683). If you use the Ctrl key, new copies of the sample data are made.

Trim

The Trim command deletes everything in the current movie *except* the current selection. If there is no current selection, it deletes everything except the current frame. If the current movie is sound-only and there is no current selection, Trim is unavailable.

Select All and Select None

These Edit menu commands help you select portions of a movie for other editing operations. Select All selects the whole movie; Select None creates an empty selection, as described in "What Gets Selected" (page 674).

Enable Tracks

The Enable Tracks command lets you enable or disable one or more tracks in a movie. It gives you a list of all the tracks in a movie and lets you click them on or off. This can help you remove clutter when you're editing, or it can let you hide tracks in a final movie. Here's a suggestion: A text track that's hidden is still searchable and can constitute an index for your movie. Be careful when exporting movies though—only enabled tracks are exported.

Tip Temporarily disabling a live streaming track lets you add other media to the movie timeline.

Extract Tracks

The Extract Tracks command lets you select one or more tracks from an existing movie and create a new movie that references them. (Be sure to save the result as a self-contained movie if you want to *copy* the tracks.)

For example, to copy a track from one multitrack movie into another, you can use Extract Tracks to create a new movie containing just the selected track, choose Select All and Copy in the new movie, then choose Paste or Add to insert the track into the destination movie.

When selecting tracks for this command and for the Delete Tracks command, you can hold down the Shift key to select a range in the track list. If you hold down the Command key on the Macintosh (Ctrl in Windows), you can make a discontinuous selection.

Delete Tracks

The Delete Tracks command lets you remove one or more tracks from a movie. If you save the movie as self-contained, you'll find that the movie file is smaller and the deleted tracks are gone.

Find and Find Again

These commands search all the text tracks in a movie, very much like the Find commands in a word processor. They find any occurrence of the string you type in, displaying that part of the movie with the text highlighted (if the text is visible). The search is not case-sensitive, and you can search forward or backward.

Opening, Playing, and Saving Files

QuickTime Player can open or import files in a variety of formats. It can also export movies or parts of movies to a variety of formats, and can save QuickTime movies either as self-contained files or as data structures that point to media data in other files. These capabilities are all accessed through the File menu.

QuickTime Player also has several options for playing a movie, such as looping, playing only the current selection, or using the full screen. Many of these presentation options can be saved along with the movie. These features are controlled through the Movie menu.

File Menu

QuickTime Player's File menu commands help you access QuickTime movies and get data into and out of them.

New Player

The New Player command creates an empty movie and opens it in the player. You can paste into it anything copied from another QuickTime movie, using the techniques described in "Cut, Copy, Paste, Replace, and Clear" (page 676). When you save the result, you can either save it as a self-contained movie, duplicating all the movie chunks you pasted, or save allowing dependencies, just storing references to data in other movies.

Open Movie and Open URL

These commands let you open a wide range of movie and still media files, both QuickTime and non-QuickTime. (For a list of all the media types that QuickTime handles, see Appendix E.) The Open Movie command presents an Open dialog box that lets you choose a local file; the Open URL command lets you enter the URL of a file (not a Web page) accessible over the Internet. The chosen movie or media opens in a player window.

The new movie will open either in a new window or in the current player window, depending on how you have set your preferences.

Here are some rules and tips about opening files:

■ Neither Open Movie nor Open URL can open a PICT or text file, and Open URL cannot open MIDI or karaoke files. Use the Import command instead.

■ Open URL can open files via HTTP, FTP, and RTSP.

■ A new movie can open either in a new player window or in the current player window. Select the behavior you prefer by choosing Preferences from the QuickTime Player menu, then choosing Player Preferences. There is a checkbox for opening movies in a new player window.

Important To follow the examples in this book, you must set your preferences to open movies in a new window.

■ Some media files must be converted to movie files before QuickTime Player can open them. These include Macintosh System 7 sound files, PICT files, and PICS files. Conversion of text, MIDI, and karaoke (.kar) files is optional; if you hold down the Command key (Macintosh) or Ctrl key (Windows) when clicking the Convert button, they open directly.

QuickTime Player opens various media in different ways, sometimes presenting an Options button. Clicking this button opens a dialog box that lets you enter settings appropriate to that media. Here are a few notes to remember:

- For a single image, the player creates a QuickTime movie containing one frame that plays for 1/15 second.

- When you open an MPEG-1 video or layer 2 audio file (but not an MP3 audio file), the player creates an MPEG track that contains any multiplexed sound along with the video. You cannot select and copy a portion of an MPEG track; the entire track is always copied. You cannot demultiplex MPEG-1, layer 2 audio into a separate sound track or export it to another format. MP3 files are converted into sound tracks in the usual way.

- After you open a DV movie file, you may need to improve the image by selecting High Quality (see page 698).

- You may encounter problems opening a Macintosh System 7 sound file using a Windows copy of QuickTime Player. Open it on a Macintosh instead and then open the resulting movie in Windows.

- When you open a Flash file, QuickTime Player creates a Flash track, not a video track. By default, the None controller is selected and Play All Frames is set. To enable the editing commands, use the Properties window to select the standard Movie controller. To hear any audio, deselect Play All Frames.

- You can create a movie with one 3D track in it by opening a 3DMF file (Macintosh QuickDraw 3D Metafile format) and clicking Convert.

Open Image Sequence

This command lets you convert a set of images into a QuickTime movie, with each image occupying one frame. When the Open dialog box appears, you choose any image file in a folder. The names of all the image files in the folder must contain serial numbers, as described in "Creating Slideshows Using QuickTime Player" (page 241). The player asks you for a frame rate (which determines how fast the images will run) and creates a new movie, taking the files in numerical order. The movie's video track has the dimensions of the first image—all subsequent images are scaled to fill the same dimensions, without regard for aspect ratio.

For a slideshow effect, you can specify a frame rate of 2 seconds or longer; for the illusion of motion, you should choose at least 6 fps.

You can use this command with all the still-image formats that Quick-Time can handle (including PICTs), and you can mix files of different formats. For a list of the QuickTime media formats, see Appendix E.

Save As and Save

These commands let you save whatever QuickTime Player is playing, storing it as a QuickTime movie file on your local disk.

The Save As command lets you choose how much information you want to put into a new movie file:

- **Save normally (allowing dependencies)** stores only the changes in the movie's data structure. Any media data that was already in the movie is unchanged—unused samples are not deleted, and there may be references to data stored in other files. This doesn't copy any media that the movie references into the new movie file, so it may depend on other files for its media.
- **Make movie self-contained** stores copies of all the media that the movie uses along with the movie structure and deletes any unused media data. A self-contained movie file can be huge, so the player warns you of the disk space it needs.

The ordinary Save command stores the current version of a movie, over-writing the file previously saved. If you have pasted new media into the movie, it is automatically saved with dependencies. If you have deleted material, it is not deleted from the file.

Important Movies saved using Save may not have the Fast Start feature. Movies saved using Save As always have the Fast Start feature. Movies saved with dependencies must not be separated from the files that contain their data or they will not play.

Import

This powerful command lets you bring almost any kind of media into QuickTime. (For a list of all the media types that QuickTime handles, see Appendix E.) You don't need to tell QuickTime Player the kind or format of the media you want to import—just choose a file using the dialog box and let QuickTime figure it out. The player creates a new movie that contains the imported media and asks you where to store it.

A checkbox in the Open dialog box lets you see a preview of each media file as you highlight it, before you decide to import it.

Most media files can be opened equally well using either the Open Movie or the Import command; in most cases it makes no difference. There are three special cases:

- QuickTime movies must be opened using the Open Movie or Open URL command—you cannot use Import.

- You must use the Import command to import PICT files—you cannot use Open.

- You must use the Import command to import text files—you cannot use Open.

With some media types, the Convert button in the file dialog box changes to Convert... and takes you to a dialog box that has an Options... button. You may need to choose compression settings or make other choices in the Options panel. The rules for the media that you can import are the same as those for Open Movie (see page 681). For a discussion of the Compression Settings dialog box, see page 691.

You can import text from a text-only file, in which case each paragraph is placed in a separate frame. For text, the dialog box that appears when you click Convert... includes an Options... button that takes you to a Text Import Settings panel. This panel lets you set the text's font, alignment, style, and color. If you select Best Fit Width and Height, you get a text track that's 160 pixels wide and high enough to display the longest paragraph. You can also select Keyed Text to make the background transparent (in subtitles, for example). Don't get too fancy with text because it can take a lot of machine cycles to render such niceties as drop shadows, anti-aliasing, and keyed text together.

For a wider variety of text features in a movie, including links to Web pages, you can mark up your original text file as described in Chapter 13, "Text! Text! Text!"

The import process for PICS and System 7 sound files sometimes encounters problems on Windows computers. If this happens, you can import the file on a Macintosh, save as a QuickTime movie, and then open the resulting movie in Windows.

On Macintosh computers you can use the Import command to digitize content from an audio CD and turn it into a movie sound track. You simply put the audio CD in your Mac CD-ROM drive and open an audio track like any other sound file. (Bear in mind that most audio CDs are copyrighted.)

Export

Once you have a movie open in QuickTime Player, you can export it (or some of its media) in a variety of formats. When you combine these export choices with the import choices just discussed, the result is a versatile format-to-format media converter.

For each export format, a second menu offers a choice of settings. In many cases, there is an Options button for still more choices. Here are the Export menu choices:

Exported format	*Setting choices presented in menu*
AVI	1x CD-ROM, 2x CD-ROM, or animation
BMP	256 or millions of colors
DV stream	NTSC or PAL; 32, 44.1, or 48 kHz
FLC	Mac OS, Windows; 12 or 30 fps
Hinted movie	Make movie self-contained, Optimize hints for server, Track Hinter Settings for each hintable track
Image sequence	BMP, JPEG, Picture, or Targa; 25 or 29.97 fps
MPEG-4	General: Video Track profile, Size, Audio Track contents Video: profile, data rate, fps, key frames Audio: audio content, data rate, channels, sample rate, quality Streaming: hinting type, packet size, packed duration Compatibility: ISMA or none, connection speed
QuickTime Media Link	URL, type, name ID, audio volume, full-screen mode, loop mode, autoplay, play every frame, kiosk mode, controller, quit when done, QT Next URL, HREF URL, defaults
Picture	Uncompressed, Photo-JPEG, or PNG
QuickTime movie	Streaming at 20, 40, or 100 Kbits/sec; high or low motion; music (mono or stereo) or voice; 1x or 2x CD-ROM; Sorenson or Cinepak video compression
Text	Show text only, Show text, descriptors, and time

Here are the ways you can export just the sound in a movie:

Exported format	Setting choices presented in menu
AIFF, System 7 sound, or WAV	Compression; 8 or 16 bits; mono or stereo; 11.025, 22.050, or 44.1 kHz
uLaw	8.0, 11.025, 22.050, or 44.1 kHz; mono or stereo

You can also export a music track to AIFF or Standard MIDI. Music tracks contain MIDI-like instructions for synthesizing sound. Exporting a music track to AIFF converts it into a digital recording. If there are multiple music tracks in a movie, QuickTime Player exports only the one that occurs first in the track list.

When you export sound from a movie, you get the Sound Settings dialog box. It lets you determine whether the resulting sound file is mono or stereo and set the sample rate and bit size. It won't do you any good to make these settings better than what's already there, but you can use them to reduce the sound quality and make the file smaller. All the sound tracks will be mixed together into the output file.

You can export the text in a movie to a text-only file, with or without its markups. This lets you suck the text out of a movie, edit it, and then import it back in.

When exporting anything, click the Options button to view a range of additional choices of compression and playing parameters. For information about the Compression Settings dialog box, see page 691.

An alternative to exporting images from a movie is to simply drag them into a graphics application, as explained in "Drag-and-Drop Copying and Pasting" (page 677). Sometimes this is simpler and more effective than using the Export command.

One of the Export choices is Movie to QuickTime Movie. This process alters your movie in several ways, compared to just saving it:

- It combines the movie's visual tracks (video, text, and 3D) into a single video track and combines its sound tracks into a single sound track.

- It deletes other track types, such as music, Flash, and sprite tracks.

- It lets you apply visual filters to the video track and set its final size. The filters produce a wide range of visual effects, and each one has its own panel of settings, which you can save.

- It compresses the resulting single video and sound tracks.
- It lets you prepare the output file for streaming over the Internet, including hinting it.

You specify your choices in this process by means of a series of Movie Settings dialog boxes that are self-explanatory.

Movie Menu

The Get Movie Properties command in the Movie menu brings up a window that provides information about the currently running movie and lets you change many details of its structure; for a full discussion of this command, see "Properties Window" (page 693).

Other Movie menu commands that are useful when playing and editing movies are described below.

Loop and Loop Back and Forth

These commands cause the movie either to loop endlessly or to play forward and backward repeatedly. Saving the movie with these characteristics affects playback in QuickTime Player, but not in the QuickTime plug-in.

Half Size, Normal Size, Double Size

These commands (with their handy keyboard equivalents) let you change the size of the current player. They can help you manage your screen real estate while you move clips from one movie to another. These settings are preserved if you save the movie.

Screen Sizes and Full-Screen Modes

Fill Screen and Full Screen

QuickTime 6.1 introduced Full Screen mode for Mac OS X, replacing the earlier Fill Screen mode. In 6.1.1, this was added to Windows as well. QuickTime 6.01 is the most current version of QuickTime for Mac OS 8 or Mac OS 9, so these systems retain the older Fill Screen command.

The older Fill Screen command is similar to the half, normal, and double size commands. It changes the movie size to fill the screen (to the limit of the aspect ratio, and leaving room for the controller).

The new Full Screen command is similar to Present Movie, in that it plays the movie in full-screen mode with no visible controller.

Present Movie

"Presenting" is a handsome way to display a movie, available only in the pro version of QuickTime Player for Mac OS X. The movie appears in the center of the screen, against a black background, and plays without a controller from its current location to the end. You can stop its playing by clicking anywhere, pressing the Esc key, or (on Macs only) pressing Command-period.

When you choose the Present Movie command, the player shows a dialog box that lets you set the movie's window size and decide whether it runs normally or as a slideshow.

You can't play a sound-only movie with Present Movie.

Differences between Full Screen and Present Movie

The Present Movie and Full Screen commands both display the movie in full-screen mode. Here are the differences:

- Present Movie will change the screen resolution to 640 x 480 if the movie has a similar aspect ratio. This helps older computers display movies in full-screen mode, but it can cause an initial delay, lower the resolution of the display, and rearrange desktop icons.

- Full Screen scales the movie to match the screen resolution, to the limit of the aspect ratio, using hardware graphics acceleration. This is both faster and better on current computers.

- Present Movie will exit full-screen mode if the movie is paused or stops for any reason (such as a transmission delay in a Fast Start movie).

- Full Screen allows the movie to be paused in full-screen mode.

- Present Movie has no movie controller; in its normal mode, pressing the Esc key is the only way to control the movie (the movie exits full-screen mode and stops).

- Full Screen hides the movie controller, but the controller is still active using keyboard equivalents and by clicking on the movie itself. You can stop and start the movie using the Space bar or by clicking/double-clicking the movie. The movie remains in full-screen mode. You can move forward or back a frame at a time using the arrow keys, and so on.

- Present Movie has an optional Slide Show mode, in which the arrow keys take you to the next or previous video frame. To accomplish this using Full Screen, simply pause the movie—the arrow keys are always active.

Show/Hide Sound Controls

When you choose this menu item, or click the graphic equalizer display on the right side of the player, the Time slider is replaced by a set of sound controls. They let you adjust the bass, treble, and stereo balance of the player's sound output:

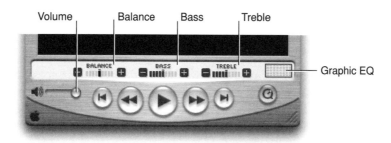

Show/Hide Video Controls

This menu item presents a transparent slider over the bottom of the player window. By clicking the diamond shape, you can choose to adjust the video image's color, brightness, contrast, and tint. These adjustments have roughly the same effect as they do on a television image:

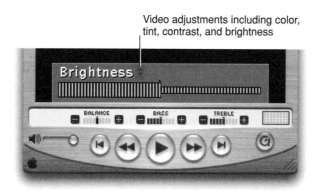

These video settings can be saved with the movie but may not produce the desired result when played on computers with dissimilar graphics cards.

As I mentioned earlier, the multifaceted Get Movie Properties command is discussed in its own section, starting on page 693.

Play Selection Only

The name says it all. When you click the Play button, only the selected part of the movie plays. You can combine this command with either of the Loop commands just described. It's often helpful to watch a selection loop, to make sure you've bracketed exactly the part you want. Saving the movie with this characteristic affects playback in QuickTime Player, but not in the QuickTime plug-in.

Play All Frames

If you're editing a movie that's intended for a faster computer than yours, you may discover that QuickTime drops frames in order to keep the playback up to normal speed. This command tells QuickTime to play every frame, even if that means slowing the movie down. Saving the movie with this characteristic set affects playback in QuickTime Player, but not in the QuickTime plug-in.

Important   Play All Frames mutes the audio.

You can see a movie's normal frame rate and the rate at which it is actually being played by accessing the Frame Rate panel through the Properties window (page 697).

Play/Stop All Movies

QuickTime Player should really be called QuickTime Cineplex because you can open several movies in different windows (limited only by the capacity of your system). This command lets you play or stop simultaneously all the movies that are currently open (assuming you have set "Open movies in new players" in the Preferences).

When you choose Play All Movies you can set any number of video windows running at the same time. Normally, the sound comes only from the window you last touched. If you want to hear sound mixed from all the movies, you need to set the Preferences. In Mac OS 9 or Windows, choose Preferences in the Edit menu, then choose General; in the dialog box, deselect Only Front Movie Plays Sound. In Mac OS X, the Preferences item is in the QuickTime Player menu, and the selection is labeled "Play Sound in frontmost player only."

Doing this can be very helpful in editing. If you have a video track and a sound track in two one-track movies, for example, you can check their synchronism by opening both movies and choosing Play All Movies. For best results, the player windows you are running should not overlap.

You can combine Play All Movies with the loop commands described earlier, setting a loop command separately for each player window.

Go To Poster Frame and Set Poster Frame

A poster is a still image that represents a movie. It's what appears in QuickTime Player's Favorites window or in the dialog box that you use to find a movie in the file system. By default, it is the first image in the movie. However, you can set it to be any visual frame you want.

To change a movie's poster, move the Current Position indicator in the Time slider so the image you want is showing and choose Set Poster Frame. To see a movie's poster, choose Go To Poster Frame.

Compression Settings Dialog Box

QuickTime Player can compress audio and video using a wide variety of compression formats, each of which has its own capabilities and limits. Whenever you export QuickTime data, either as a QuickTime movie or to another format, you have the opportunity to select the compression method. You control the process through the Compression Settings dialog box.

A display in the dialog box shows you a sample frame from the track and updates that frame to reflect any changes you make in the compression settings. You can zoom in to examine the frame more closely by clicking it while you hold down the Option key (Macintosh) or Ctrl-Alt (Windows). To zoom back out, hold down Shift-Option or Shift-Ctrl-Alt.

The Compression Settings dialog box looks like this:

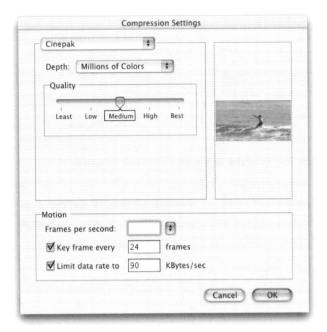

Here are some notes about the settings you can make:

- The top-left pop-up menu lets you make a choice from all the Quick-Time codecs that you have installed.

- If the codec offers a choice of color depth, you can set that in the pop-up menu just below.

- You can set the Quality slider to achieve the quality and quantity of data you want in the compressed output. For a discussion of compression trade-offs, see "Compressing Your Movie" (page 317).

- The "Frames per second" field selects the number of video frames per second. When reducing the frame rate, use a simple division, such as 1/2, 1/3, 1/4, or 1/5 of the source material's frame rate. Avoid ratios such as 2/3, as they result in uneven motion. In other words, if your source is 30 fps, use 15, 10, 7.5, or 6 fps, not 20 fps.

- The key frame setting determines how often key frames are inserted. Most codecs create key frames and difference frames. A key frame has all the information needed to create an image. A difference frame describes how the current image differs from a previous image. This saves a lot of bandwidth. Over time, errors build up and you need to insert another key frame. If there's a lot of motion, you need key frames more often. Random access is faster and smoother in a movie with frequent key frames. Some codecs need a lot fewer key frames than others. Cinepak works best with a key frame for every ten frames, for example, while Sorenson works well with a key frame every hundred frames.

- The data rate setting allows you to specify the maximum bandwidth for the video track in *bytes* per second. This setting is used as a guide—the actual data rate for the video track may exceed the setting value from time to time. Not all codecs allow a data rate to be specified.

- Some codecs show you an Options button in the lower left corner, which takes you to further choices in the compression process.

After you have finished compressing a video track, your choices are summarized in the Format panel of the Properties window, as described on page 697.

▶ Movie Properties

A QuickTime movie has a number of properties that you can inspect, such as its height, width, duration, what files it depends on, and the number and kind of tracks it contains. Each track also has a number of properties that you can inspect, and sometimes directly change, using the Get Movie Properties command in the Movie menu.

Properties Window

When you choose the Get Movie Properties command in QuickTime Player's Movie menu, you get a window that tells you a lot about the currently running movie. You can change quite a few of the movie's characteristics in the Properties window without using other menu commands.

At the top of the Properties window are two pop-up menus: the left one lists the movie itself and all its tracks, and the right one lists various attributes of the selected item. The left pop-up menu constitutes a handy table of contents for the entire movie.

Note QuickTime automatically gives tracks generic names with serial numbers, such as "Video Track 2." You can edit them to more meaningful names—like "Blue Explosion Overlay"—using the General panel (described on page 698).

The list of characteristics that appears in the right menu is different for the movie as a whole and for each kind of track (video, sound, sprite, or whatever). When you choose a track or the whole movie in the left pop-up menu, and choose a characteristic in the right one, the contents of the Properties window change to show whatever information you can view, add, or change.

Every track has a General panel, where you can find out what kind of track it is. The panels that you can access for each of the 14 different track types are listed in "Movie and Track Characteristics" (page 703). The next sections describe these panels, in alphabetical order, and tell you how you can use each one to analyze or change the structure of your movie.

Alternate

This panel lets you set up alternate language tracks as described in "Making Alternate Tracks with QuickTime Player" (page 160). You can enter the track's language from the following (very international) set of choices, and you can designate the base track for which this track is an alternate:

Albanian	Farsi	Irish	Portuguese
Arabic	Finnish	Italian	Russian
Chinese (Simplified)	Flemish	Japanese	Spanish
Chinese (Traditional)	French	Korean	Swedish
Croatian	German	Lappish	Thai
Danish	Greek	Latvian	Turkish
Dutch	Hebrew	Lithuanian	Urdu
English	Hindi	Maltese	
Estonian	Hungarian	Norwegian	
Faeroese	Icelandic	Polish	

For information about these languages, including the countries where they are used and the scripts in which they are written, see Apple Computer's *Guide to Macintosh Software Localization* (ISBN 0-201-60856-1).

Annotations

The set of annotations in a movie and all of its tracks is like a miniature database, in which each record has a property field and a data field. You can add or edit any of the following 39 properties, and enter up to 255 characters for the data of each one, in the whole movie and in each track separately:

Album	Genre	Track
Artist	Host Computer	Warning
Author	Information	Writer
Comment	Make	URL Link
Composer	Model	Edit Date 1
Copyright	Original Artist	Edit Date 2
Creation Date	Original Format	Edit Date 3
Description	Original Source	Edit Date 4
Director	Performers	Edit Date 5
Disclaimer	Producer	Edit Date 6
Display Source As	Product	Edit Date 7
Encoded By	Software	Edit Date 8
Full Name	Special Playback Requirements	Edit Date 9

When a user plays your movie through QuickTime Player, the text you put in the Full Name field for the whole movie appears as the movie's title at the top of the player window and as a menu item if you add the movie to the Favorites menu. The text in certain movie fields also appears as three centered lines in the window that appears when the user chooses Show Movie Info from the Window menu. The text for those three lines is copied (in order) from the first three nonempty fields found in this list:

Full Name (enclosed in quotation marks)
Copyright
Information
Artist
Author
Writer
Performers
Album
Director
Producer
Description
Comment

Make sure that the text displayed in the Movie Info window will fit—if a line is too long, the player truncates it with an ellipsis (...). On Macintosh systems the ellipsis is placed at the end of the line; on Windows systems, in the middle.

Users who have not upgraded QuickTime Player to the pro version can see only the first three fields in which you have entered text.

Auto Play

This panel lets you set the movie to play as soon as it is opened. This feature is active when the movie is played in QuickTime Player, but not in the QuickTime plug-in.

Bit Rate

With a streaming track, this panel tells you the current bit rate (in kilobits per second) of the incoming data. It also tells you how much data is being lost over the current RTSP or RTP connection.

Colors

This panel lets you import a color table from a still graphics file (such as a GIF) or from another movie. You may want to do this to get appropriate color rendering in movies with a low color depth, such as 256 colors.

Controller

This panel lets you set the controller that the movie requests when it is downloaded from a Web page or CD. Here are your choices:

Movie Controller
None Movie Controller
QTVR Movie Controller
QTVR 1.0 Panorama Controller
QTVR 1.0 Object Controller

If you want to edit a movie using QuickTime Player, you can use this panel to activate the Movie Controller, do your editing, and then switch back to the appropriate controller for that movie (such as the QTVR controller).

If you assign the None Movie Controller, the player window is reduced to a narrow frame, losing all of its brushed-aluminum grandeur. (But unless you've included Flash or wired sprite controls in the movie, it has no controls.)

QuickTime will not allow you to assign a VR controller to a non-VR movie.

Debug Messages

With a sprite track, this panel helps you debug your interactive wiring code. Checkboxes let you choose to show alerts on your screen and automatically invoke a low-level debugger. A text box displays the last debug message. If you insert wired sprite DebugStr messages in your movie, they are displayed here as the movie plays.

Files

This panel lets you see all the files that contain data used by a movie or any of its tracks. If the movie is self-contained, only the movie file itself is listed. Otherwise you see the file or files that contain data needed for this track or movie to play. You can double-click any filename to open that file.

Format

This panel tells you a track's data format, such as the codec used to compress it, and gives you some additional general information:

- With a video track, it tells you a track's width and height in pixels and its color depth.
- With a sound track, it tells you the sample rate and size and whether the track is mono or stereo.
- With a streaming track, it lists the media types that are being streamed (typically video and sound), tells you how they were compressed, and gives you information such as the video dimensions, sound sample rate, and whether the sound is mono or stereo.

Frame Rate

With a video or streaming track, this panel tells you its default frames per second and the actual frames per second being played. A track may not have a constant frame rate for its entire duration, so this may be an average value.

General

For a movie and all its tracks, this panel tells you its total data size and the rate at which it consumes data at the default play rate. For the movie as a whole, it also tells you the total number of tracks.

For each track, it tells you the track's media type and its start time and duration (in the movie's time scale).

A button in the General panel for any track takes you to a dialog box that lets you change the name of that track. Regardless of what name you give it, however, the media type remains the same (video, sound, sprite, and so on).

To make a text track into an active HREF track, you need to change its name to HREFTrack using this panel.

Graphics Mode

This panel lets you change the graphics mode of a video or text track to any one of the following:

Blend	Dither copy	Straight alpha
Composition (dither copy)	Premul black alpha	Straight alpha blend
Copy	Premul white alpha	Transparent

If you choose Blend or Straight alpha blend, a Color button lets you set the degree of translucency or colorization (or both) with a color picker.

If you choose Transparent, the Color button lets you select which color in the track will become transparent. With this feature, you can create a matte effect with layered tracks. To pick the background color in the matte exactly, Macintosh users can hold down the Option key while the color picker is open; the cursor turns into an eyedropper with which you can sample the actual color.

Graphics modes are discussed in "Transparency and Alpha Channels" (page 271).

High Quality

This panel lets you enable high quality for a visual track. The result has several improvements, such as increased video resolution and anti-aliased text. This is particularly noticeable with DV video. With a video track, you can also select single field video.

Enabling High Quality requires faster hardware for smooth playback.

Image Formats

With a sprite track, this panel gives you a scrolling list that shows all the images your sprites use. When you choose an image from the list, Quick-Time Player displays it and tells you its dimensions, color depth, data format, and registration point. Where images have groups of alternates, this panel tells you each image's group ID.

Image Overrides

Use this panel to override a sprite image with visual data from another track. This lets you superimpose the output of a video track or a text track onto a sprite, for example, effectively turning that track into a sprite.

With a sprite track, this panel gives you a scrolling window that lists all the override images that your sprites use. You can delete the override, restoring the sprite's normal image, or change the override to a different track.

Instruments

With a music track, this panel displays a scrolling list of all the instruments that the track uses to synthesize sound. When you double-click the name of an instrument, you get a complete instrument chooser panel. This panel lets you choose a synthesizer, select a sound category (piano, brass, sound effects, and so on), and choose a specific instrument.

For example, the brass choices include everything from a solo trombone to a complete brass section; the sound effects include ringing telephones, gunshots, and applause. There's even a keyboard image that lets you try out your choice of instrument at various pitches.

On Macintosh computers, you can make an instrument take its voice from a System 7 sound file. Just drag the file over the name of the instrument in the scrolling list and release the mouse button. The sound file becomes part of the movie and that instrument's voice. The file must be smaller than 256 Kbytes.

Layer

This panel lets you set the layer number of a visual track. Lower numbers are closer to the viewer, and layer numbers can be negative. Every time you add a new track to a movie it is placed in the topmost layer (it is given a layer number one less than the lowest existing layer). Track layering is discussed in "Transparency and Alpha Channels" (page 271).

Mask

This panel lets you mask a video, sprite, flash, 3D, or streaming track. After clicking Set, open a still image file that contains a black-and-white mask image. The video image is masked to the black part of the mask image; if you click Invert, it's masked to the white part.

Make sure that the mask image has the same pixel dimensions as the track being masked.

Preload

This panel lets you set whether or not a track is preloaded into memory (select Preload) and whether or not it should stay loaded for as long as possible after it plays (select Cache Hint). These techniques can improve the playing performance of tracks that loop or contain small amounts of data. It is also a good idea to preload chapter tracks in movies delivered over the Web, so the player's chapter list display is sized to the longest chapter name.

Preview

This panel lets you set the preview for a movie. If you have already selected the part of the movie that you want to be its preview, click Set Preview to Selection. If you want to look at the movie's existing preview, click Set Selection to Preview and then choose Play Selection Only from the Movie menu.

You can also use this panel to set a movie's preview to a selection from another movie. Simply open the other movie, make a selection in it, and drag the image over to the Preview panel; then release the mouse button to drop the image on the panel where it says Drop Preview Movie Here.

If you don't set your movie's preview, the default preview for Macintosh systems is the movie's poster; for Windows systems, it's the first 10 seconds of the movie.

Properties and Properties 2

With a sprite track, these panels let you set certain of its general properties. The Properties panel gives you a color picker from which you can set the track's background color; it also lets you decide whether the media used by sprites in the track should scale dynamically.

The Properties 2 panel lets you make the track visible or not, determine whether or not it can respond to user actions (assuming it's wired for interactivity), set its preferred color depth, and set the frequency at which

QuickTime sends idle messages to your sprites. You set the idle frequency in terms of *ticks,* each of which is 1/60 second.

Renderer

This panel lets you choose a renderer to be used with a 3D track. The standard choices are the QuickDraw 3D Interactive renderer (the default) and the QuickDraw 3D Wireframe renderer, but you can add other plug-in renderers.

Make Chapter

If you have imported a text track into your movie, you can use the Make Chapter panel to make it function as a chapter track. The text samples then become a pop-up menu in the movie controller—choosing an item in the menu takes the viewer to that sample's time in the movie. A chapter list has to have an owner track, so pick one of the other tracks and click Set Chapter Owner Track.

You can have multiple chapter tracks, each in a different language, by setting the chapter owner for each chapter track to an alternate language track.

For a discussion of chapter tracks, see "Adding a Chapter List to a Movie" (page 390).

Size

The Size panel lets you view the dimensions of a movie image and set the location and dimensions of any video, text, sprite, flash, 3D, or streaming track. For example, you can scale a track down to produce a picture-in-picture effect, or move a track to the right so that two video tracks play side by side.

The height figure for the movie as a whole does not include the standard controller, which is 16 pixels high.

With visual tracks, the Size panel also lets you flip the image horizontally or vertically, as well as rotate it in 90° increments.

If you click Adjust, handles appear on the movie image that let you resize, skew, and rotate it to your heart's content. If you hold down the Option key (Macintosh) or Ctrl-Alt (Windows) when you drag a corner handle inward, the image will go half-size to give you plenty of room.

You can position the track in the player window by dragging any part of the image outside the red handles, to move a logo to the lower edge of the screen, or to position one video track beside another, for example. If you drag the edge of a track outside the boundaries of the player window, the window will expand when you release the track.

Tip If you're trying to reposition something small, you may find that the red handles overlap, leaving you nowhere to press and drag. Try choosing Double Size in the Movie menu; this will double the image size and create gaps between the handles.

Note One gotcha with using the Adjust handles is that you have to click the movie window to activate it, then click the Properties window before you click Done.

Text Replace

The Text Replace panel lets you make drag-and-drop changes to text that's already in a movie. First you prepare the replacement text, using a text editor such as SimpleText or WordPad. Then you select the text in your movie that you want to change. If you drop the replacement text on Drop Text Here in the Text Replace panel, its content replaces the selected text. If you drop it on Drop Style Here, the replacement text's font, size, and style is applied to all the text in the track without changing the wording.

Texture Overrides

With a 3D track, this panel gives you a scrolling window that lists all the 3D objects in the track. For any textured object, you can select a visual track to be mapped onto its surface as an overriding texture.

Time

The Time panel lets you view (but not change) a movie's duration and current time, as well as the start time and duration of the current selection (if any). It presents time information in hours, minutes, seconds, and thirtieths of a second (which correspond to frames at 30 fps).

Volume

The Volume panel lets you make permanent changes to the default volume and stereo balance of any sound, music, or streaming track. You can also make temporary changes to its bass and treble response. This panel also lets you view graphic equalizer values as the track plays, so you get some feedback for your bass and treble changes.

If you hold down the Option key (Macintosh) or Ctrl-Alt (Windows), your adjustments in this panel will jump in preset increments instead of being continuous.

Movie and Track Characteristics

The previous section described the various panels that appear when you select a track (or the whole movie) in the left pop-up menu of the Properties window and a characteristic in the right pop-up menu.

The following lists give all the characteristics that apply to whole movies and to tracks of the 14 different format types (video, sound, and so on). Where characteristics are listed in *italic,* you can view them using Get Movie Properties, but you have to use other QuickTime Player commands to change them.

Whole movie	Video track	Sound track	Text track
Annotations	Alternate	Alternate	Alternate
Auto Play	Annotations	Annotations	Annotations
Colors	*Files*	*Files*	*Files*
Controller	*Format*	*Format*	General
Files	*Frame Rate*	General	Graphics Mode
General	General	High Quality	High Quality
Preview	Graphics Mode	Preload	Layer
Size	High Quality	Volume	Mask
Time	Layer		Preload
	Mask		Make Chapter
	Preload		Size
	Size		Text Replace

Streaming track	Sprite track	Flash or movie track	3D track
Alternate	Alternate	Alternate	Alternate
Annotations	Annotations	Annotations	Annotations
Bit Rate	Debug Messages	*Files*	*Files*
Chapters	*Files*	General	General
Files	General	Graphics Mode	Graphics Mode
Format	Graphics Mode	High Quality	High Quality
Frame Rate	High Quality	Layer	Layer
General	Image Formats	Mask	Mask
Graphics Mode	Image Overrides	Preload	Preload
High Quality	Layer	Size	Renderer
Layer	Mask	Volume	Size
Mask	Preload		Texture Overrides
Preload	Properties		
Size	Properties 2		
Volume	Size		

QuickTime VR or VR object track	VR panorama track	Music track	Tween or skin track
Annotations	Annotations	Alternate	Alternate
Files	*Files*	Annotations	Annotations
General	General	*Files*	*Files*
High Quality	High Quality	General	General
Preload	Layer	High Quality	High Quality
	Mask	Instruments	Preload
	Preload	Preload	
		Volume	

QuickTime Player Differences by Operating System

QuickTime Player is currently distributed for three operating systems: for Mac OS X, for Mac OS 8 or 9, and for Windows. Here are some notes on how the versions differ:

- In the Mac OS 8/9 and Windows versions, you access Preferences at the bottom of the Edit menu.

- Fill Screen in Mac OS 8/9 is replaced by Full Screen in Mac OS X and Windows.

- The Mac OS X version has additional controls in the Window menu to zoom the Player window, put it in the Dock, or bring it in front of other windows.

Appendix B

QuickTime Configuration

Sometimes you need to adjust the QuickTime settings or the QuickTime plug-in to get things working properly. This appendix shows you how.

▶ QuickTime Settings

Once QuickTime is installed, you should open the QuickTime Settings control panel (it's with the rest of your Windows or Mac OS control panels).

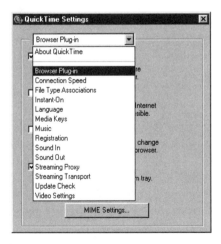

The illustration shows the Windows menu. On Mac OS 8 or Mac OS 9, there is also an AutoPlay item, while the File Type Associations, Sound In,

Sound Out, and Video Settings items do not appear. On Mac OS X, there are tabs for Plug-in, Connection, Music, Media Keys, and Update.

AutoPlay (Mac OS 8 and Mac OS 9 Only)

Click the appropriate checkboxes to enable audio CDs, and some CD ROMs, to start playing automatically when inserted.

Browser Plug-in and MIME Types

Choose the Browser Plug-in item (or the Plug-In tab). It brings up a panel with three checkboxes and a button; the appearance differs in Windows, Mac OS (classic), and Mac OS X, but the functionality is the same.

Click "Play movies automatically" to play movies embedded in Web pages without having to click the Play button.

Click "Save movies in disk cache" to save movies in the browser's disk cache when possible (there isn't always enough room).

Click "Enable kiosk mode" to disable the plug-in's ability to save movies or change the plug-in settings from within the plug-in. You might want to do this if you are setting up a computer as a public Internet kiosk.

Click the "MIME settings" button to select the media types you want the QuickTime plug-in to handle. The Macintosh list has a checkbox next to each file type. The Windows list has a " + " beside the selected file types. Click the checkbox on a Mac, or double-click the file type on a Windows machine, to toggle the selection. QuickTime updates the registry used by any browsers that use the plug-in.

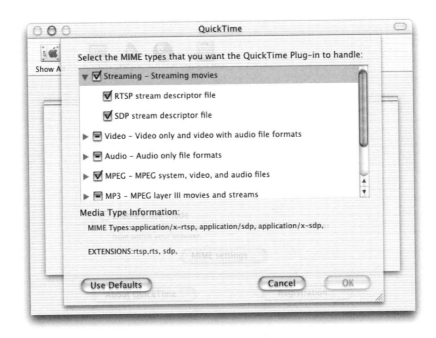

This is the simplest and most reliable way to configure your browser to use the QuickTime plug-in for the media types you want QuickTime to handle.

Note If you install an updated version of Windows, Internet Explorer, Real Player, or Windows Media Player after configuring QuickTime, you may find that your browser has been reconfigured to use Media Player or Real Player for some media types you have selected in QuickTime (how rude!). Use this panel to repair the damage.

Connection Speed

Choose the Connection Speed menu item or the Connection tab to tell QuickTime how fast your Internet connection is. Choose the setting closest to your actual connection speed. If your 56K modem habitually connects at 29K, for example, select 28.8K.

QuickTime looks at this setting when it plays a movie with alternate tracks over the Web. It plays the highest bandwidth version of the movie that can play over the connection selected here.

If you make a movie that plays different tracks depending on the user's connection speed, you can change the setting here to see them all on your machine.

The Mac OS X panel also has a Transport button to select the preferred streaming transport mode. See "Streaming Transport" (page 711).

File Type Associations (Windows Only)

Windows users can choose to have QuickTime handle files in three categories: "Windows files (.avi, .bmp, . . .)", "Macintosh files (.mov, .aiff, . . .)", and "Internet files (.gif, .jpg, . . .)". The installation default is to handle only Macintosh files.

Media Keys

QuickTime movies can be password-protected. Only people who have the key can play them. If you distribute a protected movie, tell your users to enter the key for it through this panel.

Music

This setting allows you to tell QuickTime to play MIDI music either through the QuickTime software synthesizer or through an alternate MIDI output device, if one is available.

Registration

This is where you enter your name, organization, and serial number to register QuickTime Pro. Entering a valid name and serial number unlocks the QuickTime Player's editing features, turning the free version of QuickTime into QuickTime Pro.

There is a piece of paper with a name and serial number that came with the CD in the back of this book. Actually, there are two names and two serial numbers: one for Macintosh and one for Windows. Use the one that's appropriate. Enter the name and serial number *exactly as shown* on the paper to unlock QuickTime Pro. You can enter whatever you like as your organization, but the name and serial number fields must be entered as a matched pair. There is also a URL on the paper where you can get help or upgrade information.

Important The serial numbers in this book unlock the editing features of **QuickTime 6**. The serial number may, or may not, be valid for QuickTime 7 or later. If not, you can either continue to use QuickTime 6 for editing and authoring or upgrade to a later version and purchase new serial numbers from Apple. Check the URL on the registration slip in the book to see if there is an alternative upgrade path.

Anyone can upgrade to QuickTime Pro by purchasing a serial number on the Apple website and entering it through this panel. The current price is $29.99. The URL is www.apple.com/quicktime/upgrade.

Tell your friends.

Sound In (Windows Only)

Windows users can use this panel to choose a source for making Quick-Time audio recordings, such as recording from a CD-ROM drive or a sound card's input jacks.

Sound Out (Windows Only)

Windows users can adjust QuickTime's sound output quality here. Playback quality can be set from 8 kHz, 8-bit, mono (telephone quality) to 48 kHz, 16-bit, stereo (better than CD quality). Higher-quality settings need a faster machine for smooth playback.

This panel can also be used if there are problems getting sound to play correctly on your system. Try the following steps *in sequence* to troubleshoot sound problems, going to the next step only if the problem is not solved:

1. Download the latest drivers for your sound card from the Web. You can find out what kind of sound card you have by running QTInfo.exe, selecting the System Info tab, and looking at the Audio information.

2. Make sure DirectSound is installed (Windows 95/98).

3. Make sure DirectSound is selected in QuickTime's Sound Out settings panel.

4. Click the Options button and double the fifo size in milliseconds. If this solves the problem, reduce the fifo size incrementally to the smallest value that works smoothly.

5. Choose WaveOut in the Sound Out panel instead of DirectSound.

6. Double the WaveOut buffer size in milliseconds. If this solves the problem, reduce the buffer size incrementally to the smallest value that works.

Streaming Proxy (Mac OS 8 and Mac OS 9 Only)

Use this panel if you have trouble receiving real-time streaming movies and the Streaming Transport screen doesn't help, your computer is behind a firewall, and your firewall uses a proxy server.

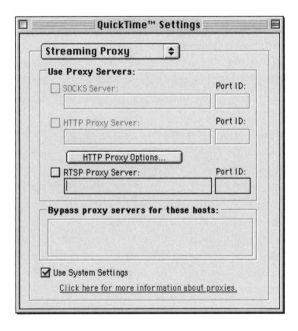

If there is no firewall between you and the Internet, click Use System Settings. Otherwise, ask your network administrator what proxy to use. Also, see the next section.

Streaming Transport

Use this panel if you can't receive real-time streams. Choose Streaming Transport from the pop-up settings menu or click the Connection tab (Mac OS X).

You have a choice between UDP streaming (default port 554) or HTTP streaming (default port 80). UDP streaming is more efficient and can deliver a higher-bandwidth stream over a given connection. HTTP streaming works when the viewer is behind a firewall or a router for a shared modem connection.

Click the Auto Configure button first. That almost always solves any problem.

If your network allows UDP and RTSP on a nonstandard port, and you know what the port number is, enter it here.

If all else fails, select HTTP (use port 80 unless you know otherwise). This allows real-time streams to get through almost any firewall or NAT router. It adds overhead to the streams, though, so you'll have less bandwidth than if you use UDP.

For HTTP transport to work, the streaming server must have version 2 or later software installed, with streaming on port 80 enabled. This is almost always the case.

Instant On

This menu choice was added in QuickTime 6 and appears as a button in the Transport panel for Mac OS X. Your choices are to disable Instant On (enabled by default) or to modify the length of a small prebuffer delay.

Instant On allows you to start playing streams without waiting for a 4–6 second buffer to fill, using only a tiny prebuffer (the main buffer fills as the stream plays, whenever bandwidth permits).

If your connection is marginal for a given stream, you may get better playback by allowing the main buffer to fill before starting the stream (disable Instant On).

You can also adjust the length of the prebuffer; if you have a very fast connection, choosing Immediate can make it easier to scrub through a streaming movie using the time slider in the movie control bar. If you experience choppy streaming, you might try lengthening the prebuffer delay before disabling Instant On altogether.

Update Check

This menu choice was added in QuickTime 5. Use it to check for updates manually or to control whether QuickTime should check for updates automatically and to control the type of update.

The "Update my existing QuickTime software only" radio button is selected by default. QuickTime will check only for updates to the software you have chosen to install—if you do a minimum install, QuickTime won't check for updates to authoring components.

The "Update and install additional QuickTime software" radio button tells QuickTime to get any new or updated QuickTime components that have become available.

Click the Update... button to make QuickTime check for updates right now.

The Check for Updates Automatically checkbox is set by default. It tells QuickTime to automatically check for the kind of updates you've selected when you run QuickTime with an active Internet connection.

Video Settings (Windows Only)

Windows users can troubleshoot video problems using this panel. Try the following steps in sequence to solve video problems, going to the next step only if the problem persists:

1. Download the latest drivers for your video card from the Web. You can find out what kind of video card you have by running QTInfo.exe, selecting the Video Settings tab, and looking at the Video information.

2. Make sure DirectX is installed for Windows 95/98, or Service Pack 3 for NT.

3. Make sure DirectDraw and DCI are selected in the Video panel.

4. Disable DirectDraw acceleration in the Video panel.

5. Disable DirectDraw in the Video panel.

6. Choose GDI in the Video panel.

Configuring the QuickTime Plug-in

You can tell the QuickTime plug-in which file types you want it to handle. This is done automatically when you install QuickTime, but you might want to change the default settings. You can tell the QuickTime plug-in that you don't want it to play `.avi` files, for example, or that you want it to handle `.swf` files.

Tip You can configure the plug-in using the QuickTime Settings control panel, as described in "Browser Plug-in and MIME Types" (page 706), and that's the easy way to do it.

You can't launch the plug-in directly. Your browser launches the plug-in, but only when the browser encounters a media type for which it is already configured to use the QuickTime plug-in. This can be a somewhat circular problem, which is why it's often easier to configure the plug-in from the QuickTime Settings control panel.

From the QuickTime plug-in, you can access the settings through the pop-up menu on the right side of the control bar.

Choose Plug-in Settings from the menu. This opens the Plug-in Settings dialog box. Click the MIME Settings button. This brings up a list of all the file types that the QuickTime plug-in can display.

The Macintosh list has a checkbox next to each file type. The Windows list has a " + " beside the selected file types. Click the checkbox on a Mac, or double-click the file type on a Windows machine, to toggle the selection. Enable all the file types that you want QuickTime to handle, and turn off any types that you don't want QuickTime to handle. When all the settings are the way you want them, click OK.

To exit the dialog box without changing your original settings, click Cancel.

You need to quit your browser and relaunch it for any changes to take effect.

▶ Configuring Browsers

The first step in configuring your browser is to install the QuickTime plug-in in the browser's plug-ins folder and restart the browser. The plug-in should be installed automatically when you install QuickTime.

If the plug-in is not installed in the correct folder, Macintosh owners should find the plug-in and drag it where it belongs (it's called "QuickTime plug-in," and it belongs in the Plug-ins folder of the browser you want to use).

Windows users should run the QuickTime installer again. When the installer indicates that it's about to install the plug-in, use the Browse button to point the installer to the right Plug-ins folder.

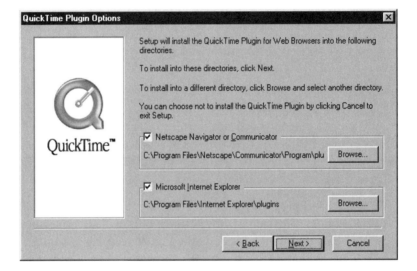

Alternatively, Windows users can copy all the QuickTime plug-in files from wherever they were installed to the browser's Plug-ins folder. In the Windows environment, the QuickTime plug-in consists of one or more files: npqtplugin1.dll, npqtplugin2.dll, and so on. The number of files varies, but their names all start with npqtplugin and end with .dll.

The plug-in files can usually be found in the C:\Program Files\QuickTime folder. All of the plug-in files need to be copied to the browser's Plug-ins folder.

By default, the Windows operating system does not display the .dll file extension, however (in fact, the default is not to list .dll files at all), so finding the files can be a challenge. Once found, they can be copied or moved to the desired location in the usual way.

If you copy the plug-in files manually on a Windows computer, you should also run the QuickTime control panel and choose Browser Plug-in to update the registry, as described on page 706.

Installing the plug-in and restarting the browser automatically makes QuickTime the default plug-in for all the media types that it handles, unless the browser is configured to use a different plug-in for that media type. In general, Netscape browsers use the first plug-in that was installed for a given file type, and Microsoft browsers use the most recent plug-in installed for that file type, unless you change the configuration manually.

Browsers are often configured to use plug-ins other than QuickTime for .aif and .wav audio files, .mpg and .mpeg files, and .avi movies. Internet Explorer for Windows may even be configured to use a different plug-in or helper application for .mov files (QuickTime movies).

The main thing is to make sure your browser is configured to use the QuickTime plug-in to play these file types:

- MIME type video/quicktime with extension .mov
- MIME type image/x-quicktime with extension .qti or .qtif
- MIME type image/x-macpaint with extension .pntg

In addition, the browser should be configured to play this file type using the QuickTime Player application:

- MIME type application/x-quicktimeplayer with extension .qtl

Having QuickTime play the other media types is optional because all of these media types can be delivered from your website as QuickTime movies or by using the QTSRC parameter.

The procedure for telling your browser to associate a MIME type with a plug-in is different for various versions of Netscape browsers and Internet Explorer on Windows and the Mac OS. (In fact, there *is* no way for the user to tell Internet Explorer for Windows which plug-in to use for which MIME type.)

Don't torture yourself. Open the QuickTime Settings control panel, choose Browser Plug-in, and click the "MIME settings" button. Click the media types you want the QuickTime plug-in to handle. QuickTime will update the registry for your browser. On a Windows computer, that should be all you need to do.

On a Macintosh, you may need to use your browser's Edit Preferences command (in the Edit menu) to add MIME types or to select the Quick-Time plug-in to handle them.

Appendix C
Contents of the CD

This appendix tells you what's on the CD that comes with this book. The CD is divided into these sections:

- a Software folder that contains the QuickTime 6 installer, which installs QuickTime, including QuickTime Player, on your hard drive
- a Tools folder, containing free tools and templates designed to help you with various multimedia tasks
- a Demos folder with lite or trial versions of some QuickTime development applications, to give you a feel for what these apps can do
- an Examples folder containing a series of folders named after the chapters in this book, with example Web pages, scripts, and movies for each chapter
- folders named MacRedistributable and WinRedistributable, containing files with HTML, JavaScript, and QuickTime movie content that you are free to redistribute (use them in your own projects to give away or sell)
- an HTML page, Start.htm, that provides structured access to all the material in the various chapter folders

The CD is designed to be an integral part of this book. Feel free to view the movies and Web pages, take them apart using QuickTime Player and the apps in the Demos folder, and copy their contents onto your own computer. These resources are here to help you. The easiest way to navigate the CD is to open the file Start.htm in your browser and run the audio tour.

Some of the files on the CD are copyrighted and are for your use only. The materials that you are legally allowed to use for profit or distribute to others are in the folders MacRedistributable and WinRedistributable. You'll find copies of all the HTML and JavaScript files that are used elsewhere on the CD, as well as some wired sprite controllers that you can drop into your own movies.

Software Folder

The Software folder contains the QuickTime installers: 6.2 for Mac OS X, 6.1 for Windows, and 6.03 for Mac OS 8 or 9. Run the QuickTime installer in the Software folder first. Use the registration number provided to unlock QuickTime Pro. This registration number is valid for all releases of QuickTime 6, including QuickTime 6.3 for Windows and Mac OS X, which have not been released at this writing. For additional instructions, see Chapter 2, "First Things First: Installing QuickTime."

Tools Folder

The Tools folder contains the following folders:

- AppleScript folder, containing documentation and scripts referred to in the book.
- Plug-in Helper folder, containing an application that helps you put plug-in parameters inside a movie. See "Plug-in Helper," beginning on page 87.
- MakeEffectMovie folder, containing an application that helps you to add QuickTime effects to movies.
- MakeEffectSlideShow folder, containing an application that helps you to add QuickTime effects to a series of still images.
- XMLtoRefMovie folder, containing an application that helps you make reference movies, as described in Chapter 8, "Alternate Realities: Language, Speed, and Connections."
- QTStreamSplicer, containing an application that allows you to add an image to an audio-only live stream or in front of a streaming track.
- Hint Track Profiler, containing an application that graphs a streaming movie's hinted packets over time.

- DeFish folder, containing an application you can use to correct the distortion of images that weren't shot with a rectilinear lens.

- QTVR Edit Object, containing an application that allows you to set many parameters for QTVR object movies, such as column and row settings, pan and tilt controls, autoplay, and animate settings.

- QTVR Make Panorama 2 (Macintosh only), containing an application that allows you to create QuickTime VR panoramas from stitched PICT images.

- Make Cubic (Macintosh only), containing an application that creates a cubic VR panorama from either an equirectangular image or six cubic faces.

- HackTV, containing a basic movie capture application that allows you to record audio and/or video.

▶ Demos Folder

The Demos folder contains lite or trial versions of the following applications:

- LiveStage Pro, an application for wired sprite creation, scriptable actions, and QuickTime effects. For information about getting the complete version, go to www.totallyhip.com/. You can save $99 by using the coupon in this book.

- WebPainter, an application for creating and editing vector and bit-mapped graphics and animation. You can get the full version at

  www.totallyhip.com/.

- Live SlideShow, an application for creating slideshows than can play over the Internet and can include sound and transition effects. For the full version, go to www.totallyhip.com/.

- HipFlics, an application for quick and easy movie compression, cropping, and resizing. For the full version, go to www.totallyhip.com/.

- Live Channel (Macintosh only), a streaming broadcaster, streaming server, and television studio program. You can buy the fully functional version at www.channelstorm.com/.

- soundsaVR, a tool that adds directional sound to VR panoramas. You can unlock the full feature set by registering the demo version at www.smgvr.com/.

- Spike, a program that analyzes movies and reports on their actual data rate, including any spikes. You can unlock the full feature set by registering the demo version at `www.yav.com/Spike.html`.

▶ Mac and Win Redistributable Folders

The files in these folders are free of use restriction. You can use them any way you like, including use of part or all of them in projects you are free to redistribute (give away or sell). Enjoy.

▶ Licensing Info Folder

This folder contains PDF files in several languages that tell you, in effect, that you can't redistribute any of the material on the CD *except* what's in the folders MacRedistributable and WinRedistributable.

▶ Chapter Folders

The chapter folders contain Web pages, QuickTime movies, and some JavaScript snippets and LiveStage project files. These files provide working examples to illustrate the ideas and techniques described in the book. You're welcome to cut and paste from the HTML and JavaScript.

The movies are copyrighted—you can play them, examine their structure using QuickTime Player or the other tools provided, and mess with them for personal use, but you can't redistribute them without written permission from the copyright holders.

Some of the movies contain noncopyrighted wired sprite controls that you are free to use in any way you like, including using them in projects that you redistribute (give away or sell). There are copies of these movies in the MacRedistributable and WinRedistributable folders.

The easiest way to access the chapter folders is by opening `Start.htm` in your favorite browser, but you're welcome to root around in them any way you please.

The chapter folders are (in chapter order):

- **Bustamov**—converting existing media files into QuickTime
- **Basic**—putting QuickTime movies on a Web page

- **SpecialDelivery**—controlling the QuickTime plug-in through HTML
- **Alternates**—making movies that show different things to different people
- **JavaScript**—some useful JavaScript
- **Audio**—making and using QuickTime audio
- **Images**—using still images; visual editing using QuickTime Player
- **Movies**—making, editing, and using motion video
- **Text**—making and using text tracks, chapter lists, and HREF tracks
- **Streaming**—delivering movies as real-time streams
- **Animation**—cel animation, vectors, sprites, and Flash
- **Interactive**—adding interactivity to QuickTime movies
- **Mixing**—mixing real-time streams with local or Web content
- **SMIL**—Synchronized Multimedia Integration Language
- **Virtual**—making and using QuickTime VR

Appendix D
Compatibility Issues

This appendix discusses QuickTime compatibility issues in the following areas:

- differences between Windows, Mac OS X, and older versions of the Mac OS
- browser issues
- issues involving CPU speed
- compatibility with older versions of QuickTime
- compatibility with other plug-ins

▶ Windows and the Mac OS

QuickTime is virtually the same on Windows and all Mac OS computers, and content created on one platform almost always plays without modification on both, so there are very few compatibility issues. There are a few exceptions that you should be aware of, however.

Fonts

Windows and the Mac OS come with different sets of fonts. If you use text tracks in a movie, a substitute font is used when the movie is played on a system that lacks the specified font. Depending on what fonts you use, the available substitute may be almost identical or strikingly different.

There are three Mac OS fonts that have almost-identical counterparts on Windows: Times (Times New Roman), Courier, and Helvetica (Arial).

Tip   The Verdana font is installed on most Windows and Mac OS systems and is rendered in almost exactly the same size on both platforms.

Text of a given point size is generally rendered at a larger screen size on Windows computers. Preview your text on a Windows computer to make sure there is enough space to display it properly. Preview text on a Macintosh to make sure the smaller text has acceptable line breaks. You may have to compromise to get good results on both platforms. For a complete discussion of cross-platform fonts, including numerous screen shots of fonts at specific sizes on Windows and Mac OS, see

`developer.apple.com/internet/fonts.html`

Alternately, you can include two text tracks in your movies—one optimized for Windows and one for Macintosh. Text tracks are generally quite small, so this is a practical approach. Unfortunately, QuickTime Player doesn't currently provide a way to mark tracks as alternates based on the viewer's operating system, so you need to use a wired sprite action to enable one track and disable the other based on the operating system. It's not terribly difficult, but you need LiveStage Pro to do it.

Another approach is to use alternate movies instead of alternate tracks. You don't need LiveStage for this—you can use the free XMLtoRefMovie tool to play one movie for viewers with Mac OS and another for viewers with Intel-compatible processors. For details, see "Using XMLtoRefMovie" (page 157).

You can get identical text appearance on all platforms by pre-rendering the text as video, as described in "Burning Text into a Video Track" (page 403). It generally takes more bandwidth to deliver text this way, but for rare or decorative fonts it may be the best alternative.

Starting with QuickTime 5, you can also use Flash text. If you tell Flash to "break apart" the text, it turns text into vectors that look the same on Mac OS and Windows. This makes the movie larger, however.

Is QuickTime Installed?

QuickTime is installed on all Macintosh computers at the factory and updated automatically when users update the Mac OS. QuickTime is common on Windows computers, but not as universal. You can test for QuickTime's presence—the steps vary slightly depending on the viewer's operating system and browser.

If the viewer has a Netscape or Mozilla browser for Windows or the Mac OS, or Internet Explorer for the Mac, you can use JavaScript to test for the QuickTime plug-in.

For Internet Explorer on Windows, you can use VBScript to test for the QuickTime ActiveX control. You can also use the <OBJECT> tag and the CLASSID parameter to have Internet Explorer automatically test for the QuickTime ActiveX control and offer to install it if it's not already there.

There's an example Web page that contains both JavaScript and VBScript to detect QuickTime in Chapter 9, "It's in the Script: Basic Java-Script."

In many ways the best and simplest solution is to use QuickTime itself to detect whether QuickTime is installed and configured, as described in "Detecting the QuickTime Plug-in" (page 121).

Browsers

The QuickTime plug-in works equally well inside Internet Explorer and Netscape browsers, but there are some ancillary functions that are different.

JavaScript

Internet Explorer for the Mac does not allow JavaScript to communicate with plug-ins; consequently you cannot use JavaScript to control Quick-Time or any other plug-in.

Explorer does allow JavaScript to detect and communicate with ActiveX controls on Windows computers, and you can detect the QuickTime ActiveX control this way. The QuickTime ActiveX control is scriptable in QuickTime 6 and later.

You can call JavaScript functions from within a QuickTime movie by passing a JavaScript function name and parameters in place of a URL—in an HREF parameter, for example. Some people have reported that even this functionality is unreliable in Internet Explorer, however, and recommend that you instead pass the URL of a Web page, perhaps targeted to a hidden frame, containing JavaScript code that executes on loading.

A bug in Internet Explorer 4.5 caused it to ignore JavaScript: URLs. This bug is fixed in later versions.

VR in Tables

An unpleasant flashing on the screen can occur when a QuickTime VR panorama or object movie is placed inside an HTML <TABLE> element in Internet Explorer. The flashing occurs when the mouse cursor is outside the display area of the QuickTime VR movie, but still inside the table cell that holds the movie.

If possible, you should avoid putting QTVR movies inside tables for this reason. If you must put a QTVR movie in a table, try to arrange things so that the movie exactly fills its cell—make sure there is no text in the same cell, not even a blank space between the <DATA> tags and the <EMBED> tag, and set the CELLPADDING and CELLMARGIN parameters to zero.

HTML

There are numerous small differences in the ways that different browsers interpret HTML. None of them are specific to QuickTime, but they can affect the appearance and behavior of Web pages used to display Quick-Time content. For example, using the Align parameter inside an <EMBED> tag can cause movies not to display.

Various versions of Netscape browsers and Internet Explorer support and interpret the <OBJECT> tag in a baffling variety of ways. We recommend using the <OBJECT> tag *only* with the CLASSID and CODEBASE parameters set to specify the QuickTime ActiveX component, and with an <EMBED> tag inside the <OBJECT> </OBJECT> tagset. Currently, all browsers except Internet Explorer for Windows ignore such an <OBJECT> tag and execute the nested <EMBED> tag instead, while IE for Windows reliably uses (or offers to install) the QuickTime ActiveX control specified in the CLASSID.

Tip Always view your Web pages on both Macintosh and Windows computers, using every version of every browser that you plan to support. It's worth the trouble.

ActiveX

You need the ActiveX control included with QuickTime 5.0.3 or later to play QuickTime movies in Internet Explorer for Windows, version 5.5, SP2 or later. Internet Explorer for Windows no longer works with Netscape-style plug-ins. Only ActiveX controls are supported.

The original ActiveX control supplied with QuickTime 4.1 cannot be used with the new versions of Internet Explorer; it was intended solely to allow scripts to detect QuickTime. The ActiveX control included in Quick-Time 5.0.3 and later is fully functional.

The ActiveX control can be downloaded separately and added to an existing version of QuickTime.

Internet Explorer for Windows will automatically offer to install the QuickTime ActiveX control (if it is not already installed) if a Web page includes an <OBJECT> tag with the following parameters:

```
CLASSID="clsid:02BF25D5-8C17-4B23-BC80-D3488ABDDC6B"
CODEBASE="http://www.apple.com/qtactivex/qtplugin.cab">
```

Users with QuickTime 3 or later can add the ActiveX control without downloading a new version of QuickTime. If a compatible version of QuickTime is not already installed on the user's computer, the ActiveX control will offer to download the current version of QuickTime whenever the browser encounters a page that includes QuickTime content.

It is not necessary to use the <OBJECT> tag to invoke the QuickTime ActiveX control. Once installed, the ActiveX control is called whenever Internet Explorer for Windows is asked to display QuickTime content, so the <EMBED> tag works fine.

▶ CPU Speed

QuickTime has a number of features that let you deliver high-quality content over low-bandwidth connections. This is generally accomplished by putting a compact description of the content inside the movie and using the viewer's computer to recreate it when the movie is played.

Text tracks, MIDI music, QuickTime effects, and advanced compressors such as Sorenson and QDesign all place a relatively high demand on the viewer's CPU in order to minimize bandwidth.

If you want your movies to play smoothly on older and slower computers, follow these guidelines (bear in mind that you may lose quality or increase bandwidth requirements by doing so):

- Don't overlay a video track with alpha layer compositing on another video track, especially if they are both with high-bandwidth video compressed with a demanding decompressor such as DV.

- Use MPEG-4 audio and video, rather than Sorenson video and QDesign audio compression; substitute Cinepak video and IMA 4:1 audio for very slow systems.

- Use a lower sampling rate for sound (22 kHz or 11 kHz), in mono.

- Don't use more than a single MIDI music track. Use as few voices as possible—preferably no more than four or five.

- If you use a text track (instead of mixing the text into the video), avoid scrolling, keyed text, and anti-aliased text. Certainly don't combine them.

- Mix all video, sound, text, and effects tracks into a single sound track and a single video track by opening the movie in QuickTime Player, choosing Export, then choosing Movie to QuickTime Movie from the pop-up menu.

You don't necessarily need to follow *all* these guidelines—play your movie on the slowest computer you plan to support and apply the guidelines one by one until it plays smoothly. It's often enough to reduce the audio sampling rate and turn off anti-aliasing, for example, or to simply combine multiple video and sound tracks.

▶ Versions of QuickTime

New features are added to QuickTime in every release. In general, you'll get the best results by using whatever features you need in your movies and including a Get QuickTime button on your site for people who need to upgrade. Still, in some cases you might consider leaving out an unnecessary feature, or deferring it until a little more time has passed, to reach the broadest possible audience.

QuickTime 2.1

This is the oldest version of QuickTime that you'll ever encounter. It's the last version of QuickTime available for Windows 3.1. All later versions of QuickTime for Windows require Windows 95 or later.

If you need to support this version of QuickTime, bear in mind that it's probably running on a slow '386 or '486 processor with an 8-bit or 16-bit graphics card and an obsolete operating system. Follow these guidelines for movies that need to play in QuickTime 2.1:

- Use QuickTime Player's Export command (Movie to QuickTime Movie) to reduce your movie to one sound track and one video track. Compress the video using Cinepak, set to thousands of colors. Compress the audio using IMA 4:1. Don't include any other track types.

- Consider using the <A HREF> tag instead of the <EMBED> tag, in case the browser is an older version of Internet Explorer. Don't use any of the QuickTime <EMBED> tag parameters—stick to the browser parameters.

- If you're delivering the movie on disk, use exclusively eight-dot-three filenames, such as maxlengt.htm—a maximum of eight characters, followed by a period and a three-letter file extension.

- If you're delivering the movie on CD-ROM, use ISO-9660 format (no Joliet extensions) and keep the data rate below 200 Kbytes/sec.

Obviously, restricting yourself to this kind of movie severely limits what you can do.

QuickTime 3

This is the oldest version of QuickTime you're remotely likely to encounter. It supports most QuickTime track types. It also supports QTVR, most simple wired sprite actions, and reference movies made using MakeRef-Movie, Cleaner, or XMLtoRefMovie. It is compatible with the new Quick-Time ActiveX control (but not scriptable using it).

If you need to be compatible with QuickTime 3, don't use the QTSRC parameter—use reference movies instead. Embed the image or movie that you would normally pass in the SRC parameter as the default movie.

You can't use Flash, real-time streams, SMIL, or MPEG-4 with Quick-Time 3.

QuickTime 3 can play media compressed using the original QDesign Music Codec and Sorenson Video codec, but not audio compressed using QDesign 2 or Sorenson 3.

QuickTime 3 can't play back MP3 audio.

You can't control QuickTime 3 using JavaScript, and you can't detect it using VBScript. QuickTime 3 does not have an ActiveX control. Adding the QuickTime 5 or later ActiveX control allows you to use QuickTime 3 and later with Internet Explorer 5.5 or later for Windows.

QuickTime 4

QuickTime 4 (including 4.1.2) is very rarely found. In addition to Quick-Time 3 media, it can play Flash 3, real-time streams, and MP3 audio.

QuickTime 4 supports most of the <EMBED> tag parameters, including the QTSRC parameter.

QuickTime 4.1

QuickTime 4.1 adds support for SMIL, variable-bit-rate (VBR) MP3 audio, and M3U playlists.

This is the oldest version of QuickTime that can be controlled using JavaScript and introduces the JavaScriptEnabled <EMBED> parameter. It cannot be controlled using JavaScript in Internet Explorer, however, only Netscape and similar browsers using the Live Script interface.

QuickTime 4.1 also adds the Browser Plug-in item to the QuickTime Settings control panel, allowing you to specify which MIME types QuickTime should handle.

There is a bug in QuickTime 4.1 that affects QTVR hotspots when played in the plug-in. The work-around is to double-reference any hotspots. For details, see "Hotspots and Multinode Panoramas" (page 643). This bug is corrected in 4.1.2.

QuickTime 4.1.2

This version fixed a number of bugs in 4.1, including the VR hotspot bug.

QuickTime 4.1.2 also added the ability to detect QuickTime using VBScript in Internet Explorer for Windows. This version of the ActiveX control is not scriptable, however.

Adding the QuickTime 6 or later ActiveX control to QuickTime 4.1.2 or later makes QuickTime scriptable in Internet Explorer for Windows using JavaScript. Use the <OBJECT> tag with the QuickTime ClassID and Codebase to trigger the ActiveX download.

QuickTime 5

QuickTime 5 is the oldest version of QuickTime still found in any significant numbers. Version 5.0.3 is the most common, as it is sometimes used by people who want QuickTime Pro and have a QuickTime 5 key, but not a QuickTime 6 key.

QuickTime 5.0

This version was released for OS X version 1.0 and for Mac OS 9 as a bundle with certain hardware graphics accelerators. There should be very few copies still in circulation, as they will automatically upgrade themselves as soon as they are attached to the Internet.

It shares the feature set of QuickTime 5.0.1, with the exception of media skins.

QuickTime 5.0.1

This was the first general release of QuickTime 5 for Mac OS 8, Mac OS 9, and Windows. It was not available for Mac OS X. It added a number of features:

- cubic VR
- media skins
- new MIME type (.qtl/application-quicktimeplayer) that launches QuickTime Player from an HTML text link
- XML importer that allows lightweight text files to stand in as QuickTime movies and to specify playback settings such as full-screen mode
- wired text, wired actions for VR, lists, XML data exchange
- support for SoundForge and DLS-2 sound fonts
- MPEG-1 playback on Windows
- improved DV codec efficiency, allowing DV cameras to be used by broadcasting applications
- support for Flash 4, including editable text fields
- SMIL support for clip-begin, clip-end, full-screen, and pre-roll attributes
- export from QuickTime Pro supports creation of Fast Start VR panoramas and object movies, splitting of multinode panoramas into multiple single-node panoramas with URL links
- automatic download of missing QuickTime components, including third-party components
- extended AppleScript support, including setting full-screen mode and quit when done from AppleScript
- full support for relative URLs in QuickTime Player
- URL extensions (E < >) that allow you to attach <EMBED> tag parameters to a URL
- AllowEmbedTagOverrides parameter for <EMBED> tags
- support for a start time as part of the AUTOPLAY parameter

- ability to jump between discontinuous chapter list entries in QuickTime Player

QuickTime 5.0.2

QuickTime 5.0.2 fixes some minor bugs and introduces a few new features.

Most notable are the Sorenson 3 codec and the ability to add other media types to MPEG-1 video and MPEG-1, layer 2 audio in QuickTime Player.

QuickTime 5.0.3

QuickTime 5.0.3 adds an ActiveX version of the QuickTime browser plug-in that works with Internet Explorer for Windows, version 5.5/SP2 and later.

The ActiveX control is downloaded automatically when needed if Internet Explorer encounters an <EMBED> tag that specifies the QuickTime ClassID and CodeBase.

The ActiveX control is compatible with QuickTime 3 and later.

QuickTime 6

QuickTime 6 introduced a number of new features, most notably MPEG-4 authoring and playback and a scriptable ActiveX control for Windows. There are several different versions, with (mostly) minor differences.

QuickTime 6.0, 6.01, and 6.02

QuickTime 6.0 introduces the ability to play Flash 5 media, including the greatly enhanced set of Flash actions and scripts.

QuickTime 6.0 and later can play and encode MPEG-2 software with an additional download from Apple or in conjunction with other software that encodes (such as DV Studio Pro or iDV) or decodes (DVD Player software).

QuickTime 6.0.1 adds the ability to create, play, and stream MPEG-4 files containing audio, video, or both. The MPEG-4 video and audio (AAC) codecs can also be used in QuickTime movies, together or individually, and mixed with other QuickTime media, such as Flash, VR, and skins.

QuickTime 6.01 was intended as the last release of QuickTime for Mac OS 8, Mac OS 9, or Windows 95. QuickTime 6.02 was later released as a security bug-fix for these operating systems, however. You should upgrade any 6.0x system to 6.02 or later to eliminate this security problem.

QuickTime 6.1 and 6.1.1

QuickTime 6.1 and 6.1.1 share essentially the same feature set. Quick-Time 6.1 was not released for Windows due to an installer problem (by the time it was fixed, version 6.1.1 was almost ready and the two were combined).

QuickTime 6.1 (and 6.1.1) are bug-fix releases with a few notable exceptions:

- An improved fullscreen mode was added that takes advantage of hardware acceleration and does not change screen resolution.
- The ActiveX control for QuickTime 6.1 and later is scriptable in Internet Explorer for Windows. This ActiveX control is compatible with QuickTime 3 and later and adds scriptability in Explorer for Windows to QuickTime 4.1 and later.
- The Mac OS X version includes support for PDF and JPEG2000 media, as well as DVC-50 (DVCPro) compression.

QuickTime 6.2 and 6.3

QuickTime 6.2 was released for Mac OS X only, largely to support new features of iTunes and the Apple music store. It also allows XML import of formatted unicode text, which was formerly quite difficult, and support for 8-bit unicode.

QuickTime 6.3 provides bug fixes for 6.2 and brings QuickTime Windows to parity with Windows for Mac OS X. It also adds support for third-generation digital telephone delivery (3GPP) of audio, video, and text, as well as import, export, and creation of 3GPP text. Support for 3GPP audio and text requires a separate download, much like the one for MPEG-2, for licensing reasons.

QuickTime 6.3 has not been officially released as of this writing, so its feature set could vary somewhat from the description just given.

▶ Other Plug-ins

There are two different compatibility issues concerning the QuickTime plug-in and other plug-ins: plug-ins that can play some QuickTime movies and media that can be played by multiple plug-ins (including QuickTime).

Plug-ins That Can Play QuickTime Movies

There are a few plug-ins available besides the QuickTime plug-in that can play some QuickTime movies. There are only two that you need to be concerned about: Windows Media Player and the open-source UNIX movie player.

QuickTime Player and the QuickTime plug-in are not directly available for UNIX (or Linux, or IRIX, or Solaris). However, Crossover software (www.codeweavers.com) allows UNIX and Linux users to play QuickTime movies using the QuickTime for Windows browser plug-in and ActiveX controls, and this seems to be a satisfactory solution for most people.

The OpenQuickTime movie player for UNIX is also under active development by the open source community (www.openquicktime.org), and can play most movies that are compatible with QuickTime 4 and earlier.

Windows Media Player is also able to play simple QuickTime movies that are compatible with QuickTime 2.1. There are two circumstances where you might want to make your QuickTime movies compatible with Windows Media Player.

One case is where you want to provide a movie that absolutely everyone can see. If you make your movies QuickTime 2.1 compatible—one Cinepak video track and one uncompressed or IMA 4:1 sound track—they can be played by the widest possible audience—anyone with Windows Media Player, any version of QuickTime, or the open-source movie player for UNIX.

Of course, this limits you to 1980s technology—long downloads, blurry postage-stamp video, and high-bandwidth audio. No text tracks, MIDI tracks, Flash, sprites, or MP3. No high-quality, low-bandwidth Sorenson video or QDesign audio. Least common denominator stuff—it's just sad.

The other circumstance arises because earlier versions of Windows Media Player had an unfortunate tendency to take over the QuickTime movie MIME type (.mov files—video/quicktime) without consulting the user, so if you embed QuickTime movies in your website using the SRC parameter, a few of your viewers might see only whatever an old version of Windows Media Player shows them (typically not much).

You can avoid this problem by passing a QuickTime image file in the SRC parameter (SRC="UNeedQT4.qtif") and passing your QuickTime movies in the QTSRC parameter, as described in "Using QuickTime to Play Files in Other Formats" (page 30).

Alternatively, you can pass a reference movie with an embedded default movie. People with versions of QuickTime prior to QuickTime 3, and people whose video/quicktime MIME type has been snatched by Windows

Media Player, see the embedded default movie, so it needs to be Quick-Time 2.1 compatible.

Make the default movie a Cinepak-compressed image that says something like this:

"You need QuickTime 3 or later to see this movie. Get it free at `www.apple.com/quicktime/download/`."

There's a movie that says exactly that, ready and waiting for you in the Basic folder of the CD—UNeedQT.mov. Feel free to use it on your website.

If the user is running Internet Explorer for Windows, you can invoke the QuickTime plug-in to play any media that QuickTime understands, regardless of MIME type, by using the `<OBJECT>` tag with `CLASSID` set to `clsid:02BF25D5-8C17-4B23-BC80-D3488ABDDC6B` and `CODEBASE` set to `http://www.apple.com/qtactivex/qtplugin.cab`.

Media Supported by Multiple Plug-ins

Some media types, such as WAV, AIFF, and MP3 audio, AVI movies, Flash (`.swf`) files, and MPEG-4 streams, can be played by various plug-ins, including QuickTime.

Who Gets It?

When you install QuickTime on a Mac, it selects the QuickTime plug-in to handle all these media types except Flash.

When you install QuickTime on Windows, it registers the QuickTime plug-in only for QuickTime movies (`.mov`), QuickTime images (`.qti`, `.qtif`), and System 7 and AIFF audio (`.snd` and `.aif`).

Other plug-ins may be selected to handle some or all of these media types, or the user may select QuickTime for all of them. There is no way for you to know which plug-in is selected for a given media type on a viewer's computer.

What to Do?

In some cases, such as AVI movies, you should probably just leave it to the viewer's discretion. Include the QuickTime `<EMBED>` parameters that you want, but realize that they may be ignored because the viewer is using a different plug-in.

In most cases, you get the best results by either converting the media into a QuickTime movie, as described in "Importing Media into Quick-Time" (page 28), or telling the browser to use the QuickTime plug-in by specifying a .qti file in the <EMBED> tag's SRC parameter and using the <OBJECT> tag, as described in "Using QuickTime to Play Files in Other Formats" (page 30).

Sounding Off

Audio files are a more ambiguous case. Netscape browsers and Internet Explorer each include a default plug-in that can handle uncompressed WAV and AIFF audio. If you're using uncompressed audio in WAV or AIFF format, you might not want to restrict your audience to those who have QuickTime.

If you use the right parameters, you can embed an audio file so it plays using QuickTime or either of the default browser plug-ins. There are a few tricks to making this work because you need to pass different parameters to accomplish the same thing in different plug-ins. Each plug-in ignores the parameters it doesn't understand, so you load your <EMBED> tag with parameters for all the possible plug-ins. No kidding, this actually works.

For background audio, the main thing is to use both the AUTOPLAY and AUTOSTART parameters. Here's the HTML to automatically play a sound in the background in a continuous loop:

```
<EMBED SRC="Sound.wav" HEIGHT="2" WIDTH="2" HIDDEN="True"
  AUTOPLAY="True" AUTOSTART="True" LOOP="True">
```

Internet Explorer's default audio plug-in uses the PLAYCOUNT parameter instead of the LOOP parameter, but it defaults to continuous looping when the HIDDEN parameter is true, so in this case it doesn't need to be specified.

- To loop continuously, set LOOP="True".

- To play once, set LOOP="False" PLAYCOUNT="1".

- To play *n* times, set LOOP="*n*" PLAYCOUNT="*n*".

To play a sound with a controller, you need to allot enough space for the plug-in with the largest controller and include both the CONTROLLER and CONTROLS parameters. You're allocating too large an area for the QuickTime controller, so set an appropriate background color to fill the gap.

Here's what the HTML looks like to play a sound with a controller:

```
<EMBED SRC="Sound.wav" HEIGHT="60" WIDTH="200"
  CONTROLLER="True" CONTROLS="console" BGCOLOR="#000000" >
```

To have the sound play automatically, you can set both AUTOPLAY="True" and AUTOSTART="True".

The Flash Factor

One of the most frequently asked questions regarding multiple plug-ins concerns Flash. A number of people would like to have .swf files play in the Flash player if it's available and in the QuickTime plug-in as a fall-back for people who have QuickTime but not Flash.

Sadly, this is not possible. Once QuickTime is selected to handle the Flash media type, it becomes the default player for Flash media even if the Flash player is installed. But QuickTime doesn't automatically select the QuickTime plug-in to handle .swf files—that kind of media hijacking is rude, to say the least. The user has to manually select the Flash MIME type in the QuickTime Settings panel.

You can force QuickTime to handle .swf files by using the QTSRC parameter, or by importing the .swf file into a Flash track in a QuickTime movie.

MPEG-4

One of the truly wonderful things about MPEG-4 is that it is a genuine standard. QuickTime can play it, RealPlayer can play it, Envivio can play it, and there are more players becoming available all the time.

Your obvious choice is whether to allow the user's browser to pick a player or to force the browser to use QuickTime. Unfortunately, neither the <EMBED> tag nor the <OBJECT> tag allows you to specify a preferred player or a list of fallbacks. You either specify a single player or take pot-luck. One gives you the broadest possible audience; the other allows you to take advantage of all the features QuickTime has to offer, and to exercise some control over how your media is presented.

Use the <OBJECT> tag with a ClassID and CodeBase, or the <EMBED> tag with the QTSRC parameter set to a .mov or .qti file, to force the browser to use QuickTime. Use just the <EMBED> tag with SRC=your.mp4 to take potluck.

Appendix E
QuickTime Media Types

This appendix gives you a quick survey of how QuickTime imports and exports the media types with which it is compatible.

▶ Digital Video

Besides its own movie format, QuickTime handles DV, MPEG, OpenDML, SDP, and AVI files, as listed below. Movies in all of these media types open in place.

Media type	Filename extensions	MIME types
QuickTime movie	.mov, .qt	video/quicktime
QuickTime media link	.qtl	application/x-quicktimeplayer
AVI (Video for Windows)	.avi	video/x-msvideo
DV (Digital Video)	.dv, .dif	video/x-dv
OpenDML	.avi	video/x-msvideo
MPEG-1 (Motion Picture Experts Group)	.mpeg, .mpg .mpa, .mp1a .mp3	video/mpeg audio/x-mpeg audio/xmpeg
MPEG-2 (Motion Picture Experts Group)	.mp2, .mp2v .mpa2, .mp2a	video/mpeg-2 audio/x-mpeg-2
MPEG-4 (Motion Picture Experts Group)	.mp4, .mp4v .mp4a, .m4a .m4p	video/mpeg-4 audio/x-mpeg-4 audio/x-mpeg-4-protected
SDP (Session Description Protocol)	.sdp	application/sdp

QuickTime's Movie Type

QuickTime movie files can contain any media type that QuickTime can play—audio, video, text, URLs of live streams, Flash, VR, and so on. The specification for the QuickTime movie file format can be found at developer .apple.com/techpubs/quicktime/qtdevdocs/RM/frameset.htm.

DV

For DV, the QuickTime movie import component supports NTSC and PAL video formats and 12-bit and 16-bit audio at 32, 44.1, and 48 kHz data rates, both locked and unlocked. The format is defined by *Specifications of Consumer-Use Digital VCRs*, published by the HD Digital VCR Conference. QuickTime 6.1 for Mac OS X also supports DVC-Pro (DVC-50) format.

MPEG Video

QuickTime provides different levels of support for MPEG-1, MPEG-2, and MPEG-4 audio and video.

MPEG-1

QuickTime supports playback of MPEG-1 video and layers 1, 2, and 3 audio.

QuickTime can play native .mpg files, as well as QuickTime movies with MPEG-1 audio and/or video.

QuickTime Player Pro cannot edit MPEG-1 video or export layer 2 audio multiplexed with MPEG-1 video, but other QuickTime media can be added to MPEG-1 video and layer 2 audio.

MPEG-1 video and audio encoding can be added to QuickTime by third-party software.

When opening an MPEG-1 movie file from a video CD, QuickTime creates a chapter list based on the chapter information stored there.

MPEG-2

QuickTime provides limited support for MPEG-2 audio and video. MPEG-2 playback can be added to QuickTime Player as a separate download from Apple ($19.99). This allows playback of native MPEG-2 files, as well as QuickTime movies with MPEG-2 encoded media.

MPEG-2 encoding can be added to QuickTime Player Pro as part of application software such as DV Studio Pro, but it is more common for applications that create DVDs to import QuickTime movies and export to MPEG-2 directly, often as VOB files or directly to DVD.

QuickTime Streaming Server can stream QuickTime movies with media compressed in MPEG-2 format.

MPEG-4

QuickTime provides full support for MPEG-4 video and MPEG-4 audio (also known as AAC audio).

QuickTime can import, play, edit, encode, and export MPEG-4 audio and video, in both native MPEG-4 file format and in QuickTime movies. MPEG-4 audio and video can be freely intermixed with other media types in QuickTime movies.

QuickTime Streaming Server can stream hinted MPEG-4 files, hinted QuickTime movies with MPEG-4 media, or reflected MPEG-4 streams, and QuickTime Broadcaster can encode and send MPEG-4 audio and video streams from live sources.

QuickTime can play protected MPEG-4 audio files (.mp4) purchased from the Apple music store, but it cannot copy, save, or edit these files.

OpenDML and AVI

QuickTime supports OpenDML and AVI formats as follows:

- All video compression types are copied directly with the following exceptions:
  - 0 maps to the Windows raw codec
  - dmb1 and MJPG map to the OpenDML JPEG codec
  - CRAM maps to the Microsoft Video codec
  - 0x01000000 maps to the BMP codec
  - dvsd maps to the DVC NTSC codec

- ACM sound compression types are mapped to QuickTime sound compression four-character codes by always putting ms in the high 2 bytes and the ACM 16-bit compression type in the low 2 bytes. Types already supported by QuickTime are mapped as follows:

- PCM (ACM 0x0001) maps to 8-bit offset binary format and 16-bit little-endian format
- aLaw (ACM 0x0006) maps to aLaw compression
- uLaw (ACM 0x0007) maps to uLaw compression

QuickTime contains video decompressors for all common Video for Windows video compression types, including Microsoft, Cinepak, Indeo, uncompressed, BMP, and Motion-JPEG.

Support for newer Windows Media compressors, such as DivX and various flavors of MS-MPEG4, can be added using downloadable third-party components.

All Microsoft-defined metadata is transferred to the imported movie's annotations. Metadata fields that have QuickTime equivalents are mapped as follows:

- 'ICOP' maps to Copyright

- 'ISBJ' maps to Information

- 'INAM' maps to Full Name

- 'ICRD' maps to Creation Date

- 'IMED' maps to Original Format

- 'ISRC' maps to Original Source

Where no QuickTime equivalent exists, the metadata item's four-character code is modified by replacing the initial *I* with ©, with all other characters remaining unchanged.

QuickTime can export to .avi format using any QuickTime compressor, but not all QuickTime compressors are supported by all .avi players. Use only common Video for Windows codecs to ensure maximum compatibility.

SDP

QuickTime supports the Session Description Protocol (SDP) format conforming to RFC specification 2327. QuickTime Player displays three lines of video annotations, as described in "Annotations" (page 695).

⏵ Digital Audio

QuickTime handles audio in AIFF, AIFC, AU, MPEG-1 layer 1 and 2, MPEG-1 layer 3 (MP3), MPEG-2 (with additional purchased download), MPEG-4 (AAC), Sound Designer II, and WAV files, as shown below. Files in all these audio formats open in place.

Media type	Macintosh file types	Filename extensions	MIME types
Audio Interchange File Format AIFF/AIFC	AIFF AIFC	.aif, .aiff, .aifc	audio/aiff audio/x-aiff
AU format	ULAW	.au, .snd, .ulw	audio/basic
MPEG-1, layer 1 and 2	MPEG MPGa MPGv MPGx	.m1s, .m15 .m1a, .m1v .m64, .mp2 .mpa, .mpg .mpm, .mpv .mpeg, .m75	video/mpeg audio/mpeg video/xmpeg audio/xmpeg
MPEG-1, layer 3 (MP3)	Mp3 SwaT MPEG PLAY MPG3 MP3	.mp3, .swa	audio/mpeg audio/xmpeg
MPEG-4 audio (AAC)	M4A	.mp4a, .m4a	audio/x-mpeg-4
Sound Designer II	Sd2f SD2	.sd2	audio/x-sd2
WAV	WAV .WAV	.wav	audio/wav audio/x-wav

AIFF and AIFC

The QuickTime movie import component supports all audio formats contained in AIFF/AIFC. However, it needs Macintosh Sound Manager 3.3 to handle the floating-point and aLaw formats. Supported formats include

- uncompressed 8-bit and 16-bit
- MACE 3:1 and 6:1
- IMA 4:1
- single-precision and double-precision floating point

- uLaw
- aLaw

The movie import component adjusts 1 to 7 bits per sample to 8 bits per sample, and 9 to 15 bits per sample to 16 bits per sample. This is consistent with the AIFC specification and allows proper playback of these AIFC files.

AU

The QuickTime movie import component supports AU, but it needs the Macintosh Sound Manager, version 3.3 or later, to handle the floating-point and aLaw formats. Supported formats include

- uncompressed 8-bit and 16-bit
- single-precision and double-precision floating point
- uLaw
- aLaw

MPEG-1, Layer 1 and 2

QuickTime supports playback of layer 1 and 2 sound, either alone or multiplexed with MPEG-1 video. QuickTime cannot export layer 2 sound.

Note Layer 1 sound is rarely used. Layer 2 sound is fairly common in MPEG-1 movies with video and sound. Layer 3 audio is popularly known as MP3.

MPEG-1, Layer 3 (MP3)

Starting with version 4, QuickTime supports the playback of MP3 files and MP3-encoded QuickTime audio. QuickTime 4.1 and later can also play MP3 streams and M3U playlists. QuickTime Streaming Server can stream MP3 playlists using IceCast (icy://) protocol.

Annotations from ID3v1-style MP3 files are imported into the Quick-Time movie's annotations, as follows:

- "title" is transferred to Full Name
- "artist" maps to Artist

- "album" maps to Album
- "year" maps to Creation Date
- "comment" maps to Comment
- "track number" maps to Description

MPEG-4

QuickTime supports import, playback, editing, encoding, export, and streaming of MPEG-4 (AAC) audio in native .mp4 format and as sound in QuickTime movies.

Sound Designer II

The QuickTime movie import component supports uncompressed 8-bit and 16-bit Sound Designer II audio format. This format relies heavily on its file having a resource fork; hence it is commonly used only on the Mac OS platform.

WAV

The QuickTime movie import component supports all WAV formats, including

- uncompressed 8-bit and 16-bit
- Microsoft ADPCM
- DVI/IMA
- aLaw

QuickTime handles ACM compression codes and metadata in WAV formats the same way as in OpenDML and AVI formats (see page 741). Macintosh Sound Manager, version 3.3 or later, is required to play Microsoft ADPCM, DVI/IMA, and aLaw audio files.

Still Images

QuickTime handles more than a dozen still image formats, as shown below. Files in all of these media types open in place.

Media type	Macintosh file types	Filename extensions	MIME types
BMP (Windows bitmap)	BMP, BMPf	`.bmp`	`image/x-bmp`
FlashPix	FPix	`.fpx`	`image/vnd.fpx`
GIF	GIFf, GIF	`.gif`	`image/gif`
JFIF/JPEG	JPEG	`.jpg`	`image/jpeg`
MacPaint	PNTG	`.pntg, .png, .mac`	`image/x-macpaint`
Photoshop	8BPS	`.psd`	`image/x-photoshop`
PNG	PNGf	`.png`	`image/png`
	PNG		`image/x-png`
PICT	PICT	`.pict`	`image/pict`
QuickDraw GX Picture	qdgx	*none*	*none*
QuickDraw Picture	PICT	`.pict, .pic, .pct`	`image/pict`
QuickTime image file	qtif	`.qtif, .qif, .qti`	*none*
Silicon Graphics image file	SGI	`.sgi, .rgb`	`image/x-sgi`
Targa image file	TPIC	`.tga`	`image/x-targa`
TIFF (Adobe)	TIFF	`.tif, .tiff`	`image/tiff`
			`image/x-tiff`

BMP

QuickTime's graphics import component supports bit depths of 1, 4, 8, and 24, plus 4-bit and 8-bit RLE compression.

FlashPix

Starting with QuickTime 4, the graphics import component supports FlashPix 1.0. The following annotations are transferred to the QuickTime movie:

- Copyright to Copyright
- Authorship to Artist
- Caption text to Full Name
- Content description notes to Information
- Camera manufacturer name to Make
- Camera model name to Model

GIF

QuickTime's graphics import component supports all GIF versions. The GIF comment field is transferred to the movie's Information annotation. The GIF image's color table is returned in the QuickTime image description.

A GIF with transparent pixels is rendered with those pixels transparent even in the copy and dither-copy graphics modes—it is not necessary to specify the transparent graphics mode.

Animated GIFs are opened as QuickTime movies, with each image as a separate frame.

JFIF/JPEG/JPEG2000

QuickTime's graphics import component supports grayscale, color, and all JFIF/JPEG subsampling ratios. It also supports progressive JPEG if there is enough memory. The JFIF comment field is transferred to the movie's Information annotation. QuickTime 6 and later for Mac OS X support JPEG2000 format as well.

MacPaint

QuickTime's graphics import component supports all Macintosh MacPaint formats.

Photoshop

QuickTime's graphics import component supports files created by Adobe Photoshop, version 2.5 or later, including bitmap, 8-bit indexed, grayscale, 3-channel RGB, and 4-channel aRGB (RGB + alpha) at 8 and 16 bits per channel.

Multilayer Photoshop files are opened as a series of still images, with higher-numbered layers loaded as subsequent frames.

Photoshop files store their metadata based on the IPTC-NAA Information Interchange Model and Digital Newsphoto Parameter Record. QuickTime places the entire ITPC-NAA record into a user data item of type 'iptc'. In addition, those metadata items defined by QuickTime are mapped directly to QuickTime types as follows:

- 116 maps to Copyright
- 120 maps to Information
- 105 maps to Full Name
- 55 maps to Creation Date
- 115 maps to Original Source

PNG

QuickTime's graphics import component supports the following PNG formats, with an optional alpha channel in all types:

- palette bit depths of 1, 2, 4, 8, and 16
- grayscale bit depths of 1, 2, 4, 8, and 16
- Truecolor, 8 and 16 bits per channel

PICT and Picture

QuickTime's graphics import component supports the Macintosh PICT, QuickDraw GX Picture, and QuickDraw Picture formats.

QuickTime Image File

QuickTime's graphics import component supports the QuickTime image file format. Text stored in a QuickTime image file metadata atom is copied directly to the movie's user data.

Silicon Graphics Image File

QuickTime's graphics import component supports SGI image files at depths of 8, 24, and 32 bits.

Targa Image File

QuickTime's graphics import component supports Targa (TrueVision) image files at depths of 8, 24, and 32 bits and at all defined orientations.

TIFF

QuickTime's graphics import component supports versions of TIFF with these characteristics:

- Compression formats: none, PackBits (RLE), and LZW (with or without horizontal differencing)
- Color spaces: B&W and grayscale (both white = 0 and black = 0), RGB, RGB and alpha, RGB palette, CMYK, and YCbCr
- Endian types: big and little
- Planar configurations: chunky and planar
- Data layouts: strips and tiles

QuickTime extracts TIFF metadata from standard tags and from the IPTC block.

▶ Animation

For animation, QuickTime handles Flash, QuickDraw 3D metafiles, animated GIFs, FLC files, and PICS files, as shown below. All these media types except PICS files open in place.

Media type	Macintosh file types	Filename extensions	MIME types
QuickDraw 3D Metafile	3DMF	.3dmf, .3dm, .qd3d, .qd3	x-world x-3dmf
Animated GIF	GIFf	.gif	image/gif
Flash	SWFL SWF	.swf	application/ x-shockwave-flash
FLIC (Autodesk Animator)	FLI	.flc, .fli	video/flc
PICS	PICS	*none*	*none*

QuickDraw 3D Metafile

QuickTime's movie import component supports Apple's QuickDraw 3D metafiles in both text and binary formats.

Animated GIF

QuickTime's movie import component supports all animated GIF versions, including images with transparent pixels. The GIF's global color table becomes QuickTime's image description's color table. The GIF comment field is transferred to an Information annotation in the resulting movie.

To correctly display animated GIFs in a QuickTime movie, the movie import component sets the graphics mode to force QuickTime to perform compositing.

Flash

The QuickTime movie import component and media handler supports Flash 5 animation format, both vector and bitmap. Sound and text are also supported.

FLC

QuickTime's movie import component supports all Autodesk FLC formats.

PICS

QuickTime's movie import component imports all PICS images, including those in frame-differenced files, into one video track. This format relies heavily on its file having a resource fork; hence, it is commonly used only on the Mac OS platform.

▶ MIDI, Audio CD, and Text

QuickTime handles several miscellaneous data types, including MIDI, karaoke, audio CD data, Macintosh System 7 sound data, and text, as shown below. None of these media types open in place.

Media type	Macintosh file types	Filename extensions	MIME types
Standard MIDI, karaoke, General MIDI	Midi	`.smf`, `.kar`, `.mifi`, `.mid`	`audio/midi` `audio/x-midi`
Audio CD data	trak	*none*	*none*
Macintosh System 7 sound	sfil	`.snd`	*none*
Text	TEXT	`.txt`	*none*

MIDI and Karaoke

QuickTime's movie import component imports MIDI data into a Quick-Time music track. With karaoke files, it imports the lyrics into a text track.

Audio CD

QuickTime's movie import component transfers digital data directly from an audio CD into a QuickTime movie file. This format is supported only on the Mac OS platform.

System 7 Sound

QuickTime's movie import component supports the following System 7 Sound Manager formats:

- uncompressed 8-bit and 16-bit
- MACE 3:1 and 6:1
- IMA 4:1
- single-precision and double-precision floating point

This format relies heavily on its file having a resource fork; hence it is commonly used only on the Mac OS platform.

Text

QuickTime's movie import component supports text as follows:

- On the Mac OS platform: all character sets defined by the Script Manager
- On the Windows platform: Windows 8-bit encoding
- On both platforms: Unicode

Descriptor markups are supported, as described in "Creating Text Tracks" (page 357).

QuickTime 6.1.1 adds support for 3GPP text import, playback, editing, and export.

⊙ Real-Time Streaming

QuickTime's real-time streaming technology can transmit a full range of the RTP payload types defined by the Internet Engineering Task Force (IETF). In addition, QuickTime's movie file format has been adopted as the basis for the MPEG-4 ISO standard.

QuickTime can deliver the following types of data as RTP payloads for real-time streaming:

- H.261 video
- H.263+ video
- Digital Video Interleaved (DVI audio)
- GSM audio (receive only)
- JPEG
- raw audio
- uLaw audio
- aLaw audio
- default QuickTime in RTP packing
- special QuickTime packing for Sorenson video
- special QuickTime packing for QDesign music
- Qualcomm PureVoice audio
- MPEG-1 video
- MP3 (also playlists using IceCast protocol)
- MPEG-4 audio (AAC) and video

Appendix F

Including QuickTime
on Your CD

This appendix discusses issues specific to putting QuickTime on a CD-ROM—what software to include, where to get it, licensing, and so on.

▶ QuickTime Software

If you put QuickTime content on a CD, your customers need to have QuickTime installed on their computers to experience it.

You don't have to include the QuickTime installation software on the CD, of course, but you probably want to, if only for the convenience of your customers. Besides, that way you know they have a version of Quick-Time compatible with your CD content.

There are two kinds of installers for QuickTime—the Web installer, which gets the latest version of QuickTime from Apple over the Internet, and the stand-alone installer, which installs QuickTime from a set of files that accompany the installer. For a CD-ROM, you generally want the stand-alone installer.

There are separate installers for Windows and Macintosh—if you're creating a cross-platform CD, you want both. You can either direct your customers to the proper folder or you can build the CD so that only the appropriate folder is visible for a given operating system; see "Making Cross-Platform CDs" (page 755).

You need a license from Apple to redistribute QuickTime. It doesn't cost anything—you just need to fill out a form. Then you download the installers you need, burn your CDs, and send two sample copies to Apple.

The exact details are subject to change, so go to

`developer.apple.com/mkt/swl/agreements.html#QuickTime`

Download the PDF agreement and the QuickTime CD-ROM installer for developers (you don't need a license to download the CD-ROM installer, only to redistribute it).

Fill out the form and follow the instructions on the PDF. That's it.

You can also apply for a license to include QuickTime Pro with your product. It's not free—it costs a few dollars per CD. Apple doesn't automatically grant a license to redistribute QuickTime Pro (after all, Apple sells it for $29.99). So you have to explain why you need it. If you need it, write to sw.license@apple.com.

Media Frameworks

QuickTime movies are presented by application software, such as QuickTime Player, the QuickTime browser plug-in, Adobe Acrobat, Tribeworks iShell, or Macromedia Director.

These applications also provide a framework for the media—a user interface of some kind, a way to navigate between multiple QuickTime movies, and often a way to integrate QuickTime movies with other types of content.

The simplest way to put QuickTime content on a CD is to use QuickTime Player as your framework. Just put a collection of movies on your disk and you're done. For a single movie, that's generally fine, but for a series of movies, or a combination of movies and other media, it has some shortcomings.

A more robust choice, and almost as simple, is to use the QuickTime browser plug-in to play your movies, using the browser to provide a framework. Navigation can be in HTML or through hotspots, HREFs, and wired sprite actions inside the movies. The combination of the QuickTime plug-in and the browser itself provides ample support for linking to HTML and other media.

This is an inexpensive and elegant cross-platform solution. You can currently license either Netscape Communicator or Microsoft Internet Explorer for redistribution on your CD at no cost, or you can simply assume that anyone with a CD-ROM drive in their computer also has a browser. All the tips and techniques in this book can be used in a browser framework on a CD.

If you want more control over the user interface than a browser provides, you need to pay—both in effort and in dollars.

You can create a customized user interface entirely in QuickTime—using wired sprites for navigation and control, and either media skins or full-screen mode to eliminate QuickTime Player's default interface—but there is a learning curve. The indispensable tool for creating a customized cross-platform user interface entirely in QuickTime is LiveStage Pro.

Two other good tools are Macromedia Director and Tribeworks iShell. Both allow you to create a customized user interface for delivering Quick-Time content on cross-platform CDs, adding their own code to display QuickTime and integrate it with other media. It's often a lot of work, and it isn't always cheap, but it can be worth it to provide exactly the user experience you want.

For a presentation that combines QuickTime content with carefully laid-out text and graphics, Adobe Acrobat's PDF format is an alternative worth considering. Acrobat Reader can be licensed for distribution on CD at no cost, supports QuickTime as well as scalable high-resolution text and graphics, and has an interface familiar to most Web users.

▶ Making Cross-Platform CDs

You can create CD-ROMs that are platform-specific, platform-indifferent, or cross-platform.

A platform-specific CD-ROM works on one kind of operating system, such as Mac OS or Windows. It won't play on other systems.

A platform-indifferent CD-ROM conforms to a standard, such as ISO-9660, and can be played on multiple platforms (such as Mac OS, Windows, or UNIX), but it takes no advantage of any operating system's features (such as custom icons and long filenames).

A cross-platform CD-ROM takes specific advantage of more than one operating system (showing different versions of a given folder to Mac OS and Windows users, for example).

You can make a platform-specific CD-ROM using just about any CD-R mastering software. Just create the CD on the platform you're targeting.

Most CD-R mastering software can also create ISO-9660 CD-ROMs. These play equally well on Mac OS and Windows systems. Stick to eight-character filenames with three letter extensions (.htm, not .html) if you go this route.

Cross-platform CD-ROMs (sometimes called hybrid CD-ROMs)—which can support the features of both Mac OS and Windows—are harder to make. The acknowledged champ in this department is Roxio Toast, which also adds MPEG-1 compression to QuickTime and enables you to create Video CDs (VCD format) that will play in most set-top DVD players. Highly recommended.

Appendix G
Work Flow Automation with AppleScript

This appendix discusses ways to automate your QuickTime work flow using AppleScript. On Macintosh computers, AppleScript can be used to automate many routine operations that use QuickTime Player, such as adding your logo or copyright information to movies. Starting with Quick-Time 5, you can use AppleScript do things that formerly required Plug-in Helper, such as adding an HREF to a movie. You can even do some things that formerly required third-party software, such as setting a movie to play back in full-screen mode. Over 100 useful example scripts are provided on the CD (in the AppleScript folder). This appendix includes a brief description of some of the scripts provided. Additional documentation can be found on the CD itself.

New useful scripts are constantly being added. To get the latest and greatest, go to www.apple.com/applescript/quicktime.

▶ What's AppleScript?

AppleScript is a scripting language with English-like syntax, used to write script files that can control your computer. AppleScript is part of the Mac OS and is included on every Macintosh.

More than a macro-language that simply repeats your recorded actions, AppleScript can make decisions—based on user input or by parsing and analyzing data, documents, or situations. AppleScript can automate much of what you do.

Applications and the Mac OS talk to each other and receive user input using a messaging protocol called Apple events. AppleScript provides a method for scripting Apple events, so you can control the Mac OS and many of the applications that run with it.

Scripts can be executed by double-clicking them, or they can be in the form of "droplets" that process files that are dragged onto them. Scripts can also be attached to folders, so that a script automatically executes when its folder is opened.

Scripts are written and edited using the Script Editor application. Every Macintosh comes with the Script Editor application installed. It's located in the AppleScript folder (inside the Apple Extras folder on your startup disk). The Script Editor's features and use are covered in the "Using the Script Editor" section of AppleScript Help. To open AppleScript Help, choose Help Center from the Help menu in the Finder, then click AppleScript Help.

The extent to which application programs are scriptable varies. Applications typically allow AppleScript to manipulate certain objects that belong to the application (such as words or data files), certain properties of those objects (such as a word's length or a file's name), and certain methods (such as writing a word to a file).

To see what objects, properties, and methods a given program exposes to AppleScript, run the Script Editor application, choose Open Dictionary from the File menu, and use the ensuing dialog box to select an application program.

QuickTime Player is highly scriptable for playing and editing movies. QuickTime Player's scriptability was greatly enhanced for QuickTime 5. It's actually possible to do things with QuickTime Player using AppleScript that you can't do manually, such as creating a movie that automatically closes or quits when done.

A complete AppleScript tutorial is outside the scope of this book. For more information, see www.apple.com/applescript/.

If you want to become truly proficient at writing AppleScript, you should probably get a good book on the subject, such as *Danny Goodman's AppleScript Handbook*.

You don't need to become proficient to use the AppleScript examples on the CD, however. They're easily mastered.

● AppleScript and QuickTime

The pro version of QuickTime Player exposes a complete set of objects, properties, and methods to AppleScript, allowing you to do a huge number of useful things such as opening, playing, editing, annotating, hinting, and exporting movies; adding media skins, logos, and hypertext links; and setting movie properties such as copy protection and full-screen presentation.

For repetitive tasks like branding your movies with a logo, adding the copyright annotation, and putting a link to your website on the last frame, AppleScript can be a great time-saver.

New and enhanced AppleScript commands are added as part of most QuickTime releases—QuickTime 6 introduces several. In addition, Quick-Time Player is a recordable application starting with QuickTime 6. This means you can record your actions and have a script written for you automatically. For a list of commands that are new or changed in QuickTime 6, and a bit more about recordability, see Appendix H, "New in QuickTime 6."

In general, scripts written for the pro version of QuickTime Player can also be used with the free version of QuickTime Player. Bear in mind, however, that the free version of QuickTime Player sometimes opens with a window suggesting that the viewer upgrade to QuickTime Pro (this happens once a week, currently). This window stays open until the viewer clicks a button, which could delay an overnight batch process until someone arrives in the morning.

Tip If you're automating important aspects of your work flow with AppleScript and Quick-Time Player, always run the scripts on a computer with QuickTime Pro installed.

The Scripts on the CD

To access the example scripts, just open the AppleScript folder on the CD. To see if new scripts have been made available, check the Web at www.apple.com/applescript/. There's a brief description of the scripts available in the file named readme.htm. A few of the more interesting scripts are also described in this appendix.

AppleScript Droplets

A droplet is a special AppleScript application that responds to files and folders dragged onto its icon. All of the following droplets can be used to process or play QuickTime files. Each droplet processes the files (or folders containing files and folders) dragged onto its icon.

Here's a brief description of some droplets and instructions for their use:

- **All Annotations**

  This droplet can be used to set the value of some or all possible annotations in a QuickTime file. If an annotation does not exist in the opened movie, the script creates it and sets its value. To set the values of the annotations, double-click the droplet and enter the values in the dialog boxes that appear.

- **Limited Annotations**

  This droplet can be used to set the value of a small number of annotations for QuickTime files. If an annotation does not exist, the script creates it.

  To use, select the droplet and press Command-I to open its Info window. In the Comments field, enter the name of each annotation followed by a colon and then the value for the indicated annotation. Each paragraph in the comment field is considered to be a separate annotation. For example:

  ```
  Copyright: (C) 2000 Apple Computer Inc.,
  Product: Apple iMac Television Commercial
  Author: TBWA Chiat/Day
  Performers: Jeff Goldblum - narrator
  ```

  The following are the names of the accepted annotations: Album, Artist, Author, Comment, Copyright, Creation Date, Description, Director, Disclaimer, Full Name, Host Computer, Information, Make, Model, Original Format, Original Source, Performers, Producer, Product, Software, Special Playback Requirements, Warning, Writer.

  The script has preferences for deleting any existing annotations and for retaining the Full Name annotation of the QuickTime file. To access the preferences dialog box, double-click the droplet.

- **Annotations & Credits**

  Removes any existing annotations from movies, sets new annotations, creates scrolling credits based on the added annotations, adds the rolling credits to the start of the movie, and saves a copy of the altered movie. This droplet requires the use of the AutoType OSAX, which is described in "OSA Menu Scripts" (page 763).

- **Convert to DV Stream**

  This droplet converts movie files to DV format, which can then be imported into iMovie. The original file is replaced by the newly created file.

- **Convert to QuickTime Format**

  This droplet opens a file and saves it as a QuickTime movie, with a file type of MooV and a creator type of TVOD. The original file is replaced and its name is not changed.

- **Save Copy as Hinted**

  This droplet opens a QuickTime movie and exports a copy to an indicated folder as a hinted QuickTime movie (ready for posting to a streaming server). Double-click the droplet to access the hint settings preferences.

- **Present Movies**

  This droplet presents movies dropped on it in sequential order. Double-click the droplet to access the playback preferences.

- **Create Slideshow From Folder**

  Drag a folder of images onto this droplet to create a slideshow movie file. Options include making the file self-presenting and self-closing; auto display of images (movie mode) or manual advancing (slideshow mode); seconds per image or images per second; and saving the file as a reference movie pointing to the original images or as a self-contained movie.

- **Save As Un-Editable**

  Saves a movie file so that it cannot be edited or saved by QuickTime applications. After setting the saveable property to false, the original movie file is exported as a self-contained movie. The original file is deleted, so use this droplet only on copies.

- **Set Controller Type**

  Sets the type of controller displayed for the movie. Double-click the droplet to access the preferences for controller type.

- **Set HREF Property**

  Assigns a URL to a movie so that when the movie is clicked, a Web page or movie is opened.

- **Media Skin**

  Automates the process of adding a QuickTime media skin to a movie. The droplet prompts you for a source movie, an image to use as a skin, a window mask, and a drag mask. There are options to put the image behind the movie (default) or on top of the movie with transparent areas. You can also specify x and y offsets to position the movie relative to the skin image.

Note The Media Skin droplet does not work with VR movies. You must change the controller of a VR movie to the Movie Controller, apply the droplet, then restore the controller to the VR Controller.

- **Save As Presentation File**

  Sets the playback properties so that a movie will automatically play in full-screen mode and close or quit when completed. Double-click the droplet to set the preferences for presentation size, display mode (movie or slideshow), and the completion action (none, auto close, auto quit).

- **Send & Play Remote Movie**

  When a single movie file is dragged onto this droplet, this script does the following:

  1. Turns on file sharing on a specified remote computer.

  2. Connects to the startup disk of the remote computer over TCP/IP.

  3. Finds or creates a folder named Movies on the root level of the mounted volume.

  4. Copies the movie file into the Movies folder, replacing any existing copies.

  5. Unmounts the shared volume and turns off file sharing on the remote computer.

  6. Instructs the remote computer to play the newly copied movie file.

  This script requires Mac OS 9.0 and QuickTime Player on the remote computer. Both computers must have active connections on the same IP network.

  To set up the droplet, double-click it to access the preferences dialog box. Enter the IP address of the target computer, the name of the governing keychain, and whether the movie should be looped.

  Before using this script, you must set up the remote computer by doing the following in the File Sharing control panel:

  1. In the Users & Groups panel, create a user and password, to be used by the sending computer, with assigned privileges of program linking and file sharing.

2. In the Start/Stop panel, select "Enable File Sharing Clients to connect over TCP/IP" but leave File Sharing off.

3. Turn on Program Linking and select "Enable Program Linking clients to connect over TCP/IP."

To enable file sharing on the startup disk of the remote computer, open the Info window for the startup disk and choose Sharing from the pop-up menu. Click "Share this item and its contents." In the User/Group pop-up menu, choose the user you created and give it Read & Write privileges.

The keychain on the sending computer must contain an AppleShare Key (file sharing) and an Application Key (program linking) for the remote computer. The user name and password must match those of the created user on the remote computer.

For a detailed explanation of remote computer access and control, see the AppleScript GuideBook Module for Program Linking Over IP, available at `www.apple.com/applescript/help_mods.html`.

OSA Menu Scripts

The following scripts are installed in the Scripts folder in the System Folder and are accessible via the OSA Script menu. If you don't have the OSA Menu extension, you can use the OSA Menu Lite 1.2.2 installer (included on the CD).

These scripts are meant to be copied, edited, and adapted for your requirements. Brief descriptions of each script and instructions for its use follow.

- **Set Name of Front Movie**

  This script allows the user to set the Full Name annotation of the front movie.

- **Copy Selection to New Movie**

  This script copies the current selection from the front movie, opens a new movie, and pastes the selection from the Clipboard into the new movie.

- **Create Chapter Track**

  This script creates a chapter track for the front movie. Use the "Add Chapter at Current Time" script to add individual chapters once this script has created the chapter track.

- **Add Chapter at Current Time**

  This script adds a chapter at the current time of the front movie. A chapter track must already exist.

- **Start Movie 2 with Movie 1**

  This script copies the front movie and places it at the start of the movie behind it.

- **Merge Movie 2 with Movie 1**

  This script copies the front movie and adds it to the movie behind it so that the timelines overlap.

- **Open & Export as Hinted Movie**

  This script prompts you to locate a movie file, which is then exported as a hinted movie.

- **Play Front Movie at X% Speed**

  This script prompts you for a speed percentage at which to play the front movie. For example, an input of 150 plays the front movie at one and one half the normal rate.

- **Step Thru Front Movie**

  This script steps incrementally through the front movie with one-second delays between each step.

- **Auto-Play of Front Movie**

  This script displays the current value of the autoplay property of the front movie. There is a button that toggles the current setting.

- **Path to Front Movie**

  This script displays the file path of the front movie. There is a button that reveals the source file on the desktop.

- **<EMBED> Tag Wizard**

  This script prompts you to answer a series of questions in order to create the appropriate <EMBED> tag for displaying a QuickTime movie in a Web page. The correct HTML tag is placed on the clipboard or written to a file on disk.

- **Create Thumbnail Link Movie**

  This script automates the process of creating a poster movie in a Web page that opens another movie in QuickTime Player when clicked.

The script prompts for the width and height of the desired poster movie. The script copies the current frame into a new movie and scales the image to the requested dimensions. The script then generates the HTML `<EMBED>` tag for the poster movie.

- **SMIL Sequence Wizard**

  This script creates SMIL movies that play sequences of QuickTime movies composed of files or remote streams. The user answers a series of questions and the script generates the appropriate QuickTime SMIL movie.

- **SMIL Slideshow w/ Bckgnd Audio**

  This script creates a SMIL slideshow with background audio. Run the script and select a folder containing JPEG, GIF, or PICT images and an audio file to be played in the background.

- **HREF for Movie End**

  This script prompts you for a target URL to assign to the end of the front movie. Successive dialog boxes determine whether to open the URL automatically or by user click, and whether to do so in a new window or the current window.

  This script creates a new movie containing the HREF track to embed in the target movie. To add this track to the target movie:

  1. Bring the HREF movie to the front. Select the entire HREF movie (Command-A) and then copy it to the clipboard (Command-C).

  2. Bring the target movie to the front. Select the entire target movie (Command-A) and then add the track on the clipboard using Add Scaled (Command-Shift-Option-V).

- **HREF for Movie Selection**

  This script prompts you for a target URL to assign to the selection of the front movie. Successive dialog boxes determine whether to open the URL automatically or by user click, and whether to do so in a new window or the current window.

  This script creates a new movie containing the HREF track to embed in the target movie. To add this track to the target movie:

  1. Bring the HREF movie to the front. Select the entire HREF movie (Command-A) and then copy it to the clipboard (Command-C).

  2. Bring the target movie to the front. The part of the movie timeline you want to associate with the HREF should already be selected. Add

the HREF track from the clipboard using Add Scaled (Command-Shift-Option-V).

- **Rolling Credits for Front Movie**

  This script creates scrolling credits for the front movie based on the Full Name annotation, entered or imported credits, and prompted copyright information. The credits are created as a new movie. You can import credits from a text file with each paragraph treated as a separate credit.

  The script stores default fonts and sizes to be used for the credits. These styles can be changed by clicking the Set Prefs button in the opening dialog box.

Note The font names must be spelled exactly as they appear inside their respective font suitcases. For example, Apple Garamond Light must be input as AppleGaramond Lt.

- **Import & Position Image Track**

  This script imports and positions an image into the front movie. Great for adding a logo or button.

- **Set Layer of Track(s)**

  This script allows the user to set the layer of tracks of the front movie.

  Again, this is just a sampling of the over 100 scripts you can find on the CD. Enjoy!

Appendix H

New in QuickTime 6

This appendix covers all the new features of QuickTime 6. Most of these features are integrated into the parts of the book where they belong, such as audio compressors, video enhancements, or <EMBED> tag extensions. So why this appendix?

Mainly for the convenience of loyal readers familiar with QuickTime 5 and earlier, who want a quick guide to the new additions.

But also because, as QuickTime evolves, new features and capabilities are added that don't always fit in existing categories. It's becoming clear, for example, that MPEG, XML, and scripting are going to need their own sections. I resisted the temptation to completely reorganize the third edition of *QuickTime for the Web* and settled for putting a few of the new features here. These aren't duck-billed platypus features in a Miscellaneous bin, however; they're fish with feet and lungs, and they're opening up new environments that will call for new classifications.

Hey, building the future is messy work at the edges, but it's exciting.

These are the new features of QuickTime 6:

- MPEG-4 import, playback, editing, encoding, streaming, and export
- New media types, audio and video codecs from outside Apple
- Flash 5 import, playback, and editing
- New wired actions and events
- ActiveX and plug-in scriptable in IE/Windows and Mozilla
- AppleScript recordability and enhancements
- QuickTime menu in Windows system tray
- New XML importer to test for QuickTime components

▶ All About MPEG-4

To say that MPEG-4 is an important addition to QuickTime would be a major understatement. QuickTime doesn't just play MPEG-4 files. It imports, plays, edits, encodes, exports, and streams MPEG-4. It works with MPEG-4 audio and video both in native .mp4 file format and as media in QuickTime movies. Consequently, MPEG-4 is discussed in several parts of this book.

These sections contain additional information about MPEG-4:

- "MIME Types and File Extensions" (page 128)
- "Checking for QuickTime Components" (page 163)
- "Recorded Music on the Web" (page 187)
- "I Want My MP3" (page 193)
- "Audio Codecs" (page 215)
- "Popular Audio Formats" (page 229)
- "Compressing Your Movie" (page 317)
- "Other Movie Formats" (page 347)
- All of Chapter 14, "Gently down the Stream" (page 407)

What's So Great about MPEG-4?

Three things: the file format, the codecs, and the open standard.

MPEG-4 is both a file format and an expandable set of compressors and media types. It's based on the QuickTime file format, and has the same robust expandability and modular flexibility. It's designed for the future.

MPEG-4 provides new high-quality audio and video codecs that work beautifully for local, Fast Start, video-on-demand streaming, and live streaming, from slow dial-up to fast DVD data rates.

MPEG-4 video compares well to the latest efforts from Sorenson, Microsoft, and Real. MPEG-4 audio (AAC) is better and faster than MP3, delivering higher quality at lower bandwidths. It's even designed to handle 5.1 surround sound for home theaters. These are outstanding codecs for Web, CD, DVD, or LAN delivery.

You can use MPEG-4 audio and video in QuickTime movies, or you can use the native .mp4 file format—you can export to .mp4 from QuickTime, stream hinted .mp4 files from QuickTime Streaming Server, and play .mp4 files and streams in QuickTime Player or the QuickTime browser plug-in.

MPEG-4 is an open standard that puts all the streaming audio and video players on a level playing field—you can stream MPEG-4 from QuickTime and play it in QuickTime, Real, Envivo, and other players, or stream from any ISO-compliant source and play in QuickTime or any other player.

The Tricky Bit

The only tricky thing about MPEG-4 is remembering that .mp4 files *aren't* QuickTime movies, even though they're quite similar. QuickTime imports and exports .mp4 files, and can also use MPEG-4 compression for media in QuickTime movies, but those are two different things. You can't change a file from one format to the other by changing the file extension—you need to convert the actual file.

Important Never give a QuickTime movie the .mp4 file extension, even if it contains only MPEG-4 audio and/or video. Never give an MPEG-4 file the .mov file extension, even though it plays in QuickTime. They are separate file types. Mislabeling them will cause you nothing but heartache and grief (well, heartburn and gripes, at the very least).

.mov or .MP4?

If you want to mix MPEG-4 video or audio with other QuickTime media, you should use the QuickTime file format (.mov files) for final delivery. A skinned QuickTime movie makes a great customized player for MPEG-4 streams, and MPEG-4 audio makes a great sound track for QuickTime movies.

If streaming audio and video are enough, and you want to reach the broadest possible audience, use the .mp4 file format—it will reach anyone with QuickTime, Real, Envivo, or any of the new MPEG-4 players coming out.

Tip Have you noticed how many new DVD players (MPEG-2 encoding) now play MP3 CD-Rs as well? Don't be surprised if new MP3 and DVD players start handling MPEG-4.

Of course, you may want to use the .mp4 file format and still play Web content in QuickTime. That way your audience can transfer your file to other MP4 players (if you allow it), but you still control the appearance and behavior of the media; you can use the QuickTime <EMBED> parameters to define the presentation's look and feel. And QuickTime supports progressive download (Fast Start) as well as streaming, so your .mp4 can go a little (or a lot) over the bandwidth limit without causing worry.

If you want to be sure your .mp4 files play in QuickTime, use SRC and QTSRC (and optionally <OBJECT> with ClassID and Codebase) to direct the browser to use QuickTime. It's the same technique you'd use to play an MP3 file in QuickTime. For details, see "Using QuickTime to Play Files in Other Formats" (page 30).

Creating .mp4 Files

To create .mp4 files from QuickTime Player, choose Export (File menu), Movie to MPEG-4, (pop-up menu), and click the Options button. This opens a dialog box with tabs for General, Video, Audio, Streaming, and Compatibility.

General

The General settings allow you to export audio, video, or both. You can make some choices about audio and video compressor settings here as well. One of your compression choices is Pass Through. Use this setting to export a QuickTime movie with MPEG-4 compression to the .mp4 file format without recompressing the data. This is a very fast operation and doesn't degrade audio or video quality at all.

The Size pop-up menu gives you three choices in the current release of QuickTime 6—Current, 320 x 240, and 160 x 120. If you need a different frame size, you can resize the movie and choose Current.

Note In QuickTime Player, you can resize a movie by opening the properties window (Movie menu, Get Movie Properties), choosing a video track from the left pop-up menu, and choosing Size from the right pop-up. Click the Adjust button and resize the track by dragging with the mouse (the Properties pane shows the pixel dimensions as you drag). Click the Done button when you have the correct size. If there are multiple video tracks, resize the largest track and repeat as necessary until all the tracks are within the desired bounds.

Video

The Video settings allow you to set a video bit rate limit, frame rate, and key frame rate. QuickTime 6.1 and later have a pop-up menu selection for Basic or Improved video compression as well.

Audio

The Audio settings allow you to set an audio bit rate limit, quality, sampling rate, and number of channels. You're currently limited to the low-complexity audio compressor and a choice of stereo or mono, but the MPEG-4 specification allows for more advanced audio compression, special voice compression, and 5.1 surround sound (among other things).

You'll find that MPEG-4's simple audio compressor allows only certain sampling rate and bit rate combinations. If you choose a bit rate inconsistent with your sampling rate, you'll see the sampling rate change; this causes your audio to be resampled during compression.

Tip Resampling sometimes degrades audio noticeably; you might get better sound by selecting a lower bit rate compatible with your actual sampling rate.

Compatibility

Text at the bottom of all the panels changes as you choose settings, to help you understand your choices and monitor ISO compliance. The Compatibility pane lets you override the selected audio and video settings to ensure ISO compliance. For more information, see "ISO Compliance" (below).

Streaming

The Streaming settings let you create a Fast Start or streaming .mp4. If you choose streaming, QuickTime will add a hint track. You can choose this option with the codecs set to Pass Through to turn a Fast Start movie with MPEG-4 compression into a hinted .mp4 without recompressing. For more information, see "Hinting for MPEG" (page 415).

You can stream .mp4 files using the QuickTime Streaming Server (version 4 or later), the Darwin Streaming Server (version 4 or later), or any ISO-complaint streaming server. QuickTime 6 can also play MP4 streams from any ISO-compliant source.

ISO Compliance

QuickTime will happily play any .mp4 file it can create. When you choose to make your .mp4 file ISO-compliant, you ensure that it can be played by any complaint MP4 player, not just by QuickTime. This restricts you to certain combinations of features that correspond to the feature sets defined for MP4 players.

The MPEG-4 specification covers more than just a video codec or an audio codec. It defines a rich set of multimedia, including such things as text and facial animation. No software is currently able to display all the different media described in the MPEG-4 specification, and the MPEG-4 specification is designed to grow. Consequently, MPEG-4 also defines feature sets, called Profiles, that list the subset of MPEG-4 features a particular player is guaranteed to support. This profile is also used to describe the feature set needed to play a particular movie.

A Profile 0 player, for example, can play simple MPEG-4 video at speeds up to 64 Kbits/sec and AAC audio at 44.1 and 48 kHz in mono or stereo. A Profile 0 movie doesn't require any other features for correct playback. Therefore, a Profile 0 player can play any Profile 0 movie.

A Profile 1 player has a larger required feature set that includes everything in Profile 0 as well as features such as voice compression and higher-bit rate video (up to 1.544 Mbits/sec).

QuickTime 6 is a Profile 0 player. It can play any Profile 0 movie.

QuickTime 6 also has some features of a Profile 1 player, such as the ability to handle higher bit rate video and improved video compression, so it can create and play many ISO-compliant Profile 1 movies. But it doesn't have the full Profile 1 feature set, so there are some Profile 1 movies QuickTime 6 can't play.

Similarly, you can create MPEG-4 files in QuickTime Player with video encoded at higher-bit-rates than 1.544 Mbits/sec. These files are not ISO-compliant Profile 1 movies, but if you know they're going to be played in QuickTime, you can use them anyway.

To ensure full interoperability with other players, create only ISO-compliant MP4 files, and use only profiles supported by your target audience's players—if your target is a Profile 0 MP4 player on a game machine, create only Profile 0 .mp4 files.

▶ New Media Types and Codecs

The component download program and modular architecture of QuickTime are beginning to pay huge dividends. People and companies outside of Apple are adding surprising new capabilities to QuickTime even as you read this.

There are interactive 3D modeling media types, interactive ray-trace rendering media types, immersive 360° movie media types, advanced audio and video codecs, multiple-resolution codecs that download visual detail on demand, popular Windows Media codecs, open source codecs—

the list just keeps growing. Some are part of the QuickTime component download program; others are completely independent.

The media types and codecs on the component download program have copies of their decompressors (and sometimes more) on Apple's Internet file servers. If someone in your audience tries to play a movie that needs the component, and they don't already have it, QuickTime offers to get it, install it, and let them play the movie. This lets you author and distribute movies with these new media types and codecs without worrying about whether your audience has them—if they need them, QuickTime will get the components for them.

For a current list of components on the QuickTime component download program, visit the Web at www.apple.com/quicktime/products/qt/components/.

Other components need to be either downloaded by your audience ahead of time or distributed by you. Even so, this lets you add anyone with QuickTime to your possible audience, without having to write your own player applications or browser plug-ins for Windows and Macintosh, and it makes it possible to add sound, still images, video, text, and any other QuickTime media to your specialized content without having to do any of that yourself.

For a partial list of third-party components now available, see

- "QuickTime-Compatible Codecs" (page 339)
- "Vector Graphics" (page 470)
- "Popular Audio Formats" (page 229)
- "Creating QTVR Panoramas" (page 621), especially "Zoomify It?" (page 638)

Flash 5

QuickTime 6 allows you to add Flash 5 (and earlier, of course) .swf files to your QuickTime movies as Flash tracks. This includes the greatly expanded set of Flash actions and action scripts in Flash 5. With additional software, such as LiveStage Pro, you can add QuickTime actions and event handlers to Flash media.

There's also a new "Enable Mouse Capture" checkbox in the Properties panel for Flash tracks (QuickTime Player > Movie Menu > Get Movie Properties). Because some new Flash actions capture mouse events that take place outside their track areas, it's possible to create obstructions between Flash tracks, QuickTime sprites, and movie controllers. If you find one track is blocking access to an underlying track, you can try rearranging the layers. If that doesn't resolve things, use the new Properties entry for your Flash track to disable mouse capture.

For more about QuickTime and Flash, see

- "Vector Graphics" (page 470), especially "Flash Vectors" (page 471)
- "Flash Sprites" (page 481)
- "Flash Tracks" (page 487)
- "Shocking Behavior with Flash Tracks" (page 522)

New Wired Actions

QuickTime 6 adds some significant new wired actions.

Note You need either prebuilt wired sprites ("widgets") or software that supports QuickTime scripting to create movies that use these actions.

- Dynamic image loading for sprites

  Wired actions now allow QuickTime movies to load and unload sprite images dynamically. For example, if you superimpose your sponsor's logo on the corner of a video track using a sprite, you can specify the sprite image as `http://yourserver.com/TodaysSponsor.psd`. The image can be in any format that QuickTime can read.

- Mouse capture

  Sprite tracks, as well as individual sprites, can now have mouse-event capture turned on or off. This allows you to capture mouse events or pass them through on a track-by-track or sprite-by-sprite basis. A track will capture mouse events only over a sprite in that track; a sprite will capture mouse events only over its own display area.

- Bit depth

  You can set the preferred bit depth for a sprite track using the Properties 2 panel (in the Movie Properties window), to tell QuickTime to use 8-bit, 16-bit, 24-bit, or 32-bit pixels. Animated GIFs, for example, can be set to 8 bits to conserve memory and guarantee proper color, while images that contain alpha channels need 32 bits. QuickTime generally does the right thing automatically, but this setting lets you tell QuickTime your preferred bit depth. Once in a while, QuickTime fails to take the hint; in that case, hold the Option key (Mac OS) or Alt key (Windows) when you open the sprite track's Properties 2 panel. This lets you specify the actual bit depth in QuickTime 6 and later. (The setting reads "Actual" instead of "Preferred.") Sometimes you have to be firm when you're talking to a machine.

- Chapter actions

  QuickTime 6 introduces new actions that allow you to go to a chapter by name, number, or relative position (next, previous, first, last).

JavaScript Control of ActiveX and Plug-in

The QuickTime plug-in has been scriptable using JavaScript since Quick-Time 4.1, but only using the LiveScript interface developed by Netscape. You couldn't control QuickTime using JavaScript from Internet Explorer for Windows. QuickTime 6 adds scriptability to the QuickTime ActiveX control using Microsoft's COM interface, and also adds scriptability of the plug-in using the XPCOM interface supported by Mozilla.

You can now control QuickTime using JavaScript from Netscape or Mozilla type browsers on the Mac OS or Windows, or from Internet Explorer on Windows—any browser that supports scripting of plug-ins using the COM, XPCOM, or LiveScript interface. For details, see "Quick-Time and JavaScript" (page 534).

AppleScript Enhancements

QuickTime Player is now a recordable application in Mac OS X. This means you can open the AppleScript editor, hit the Record button, perform a series of actions in QuickTime Player, then hit the Stop button and save your actions as an editable AppleScript. Letting QuickTime Player and AppleScript write your scripts for you can save a lot of time and trouble.

There are also several new and enhanced Applescript commands:

- EnterFullScreen
- ExitFullScreen
- Replace (same as Replace command in player's Edit menu)
- Invert (inverts a black and white or color image)
- Save export settings

- Export has been enhanced to include Fast Start QTVR, MPEG-4, inter-frame-compressed VR object movies, and QuickTime Media Links

- Make has been enhanced to make a new movie, new track, or new favorite item

QuickTime 6 adds movie properties that can be read and/or set using AppleScript:

- bass gain
- treble gain
- audio gain
- audio balance
- current chapter track (there can be alternate language tracks)
- current movie matrix
- current alternate (which of a group of alternates is selected)
- track mask, matrix, and transfer mode (graphics mode)

▶ QuickTime Menu in Windows System Tray

There is a new QuickTime menu in the Windows system tray. The menu includes the following items in QuickTime 6:

- **About QuickTime**—opens the About QuickTime dialog box
- **QuickTime Website**—opens the Apple QuickTime website in a browser
- **QuickTime Preferences**—opens Browser Plug-in control panel
- **QuickTime Info**—launches QTInfo
- **Open QuickTime Player**—launches QuickTime Player
- **Open Picture Viewer**—launches picture viewer
- **Check for QuickTime Updates**—opens QuickTime Update control panel
- **Favorites**—hierarchical menu of your favorites
- **Open Recent**—menu of recently opened items
- **Exit QuickTime Task**—quits the `qttask.exe` background task that checks for changes in the MIME type registry

There is also a new item in the control panel: a QuickTime system tray icon. If unchecked, the tray icon will never appear. If you choose to exit from the menu, it will exit, and when you reboot your computer, it will re-appear.

XML Importer for Component Check

QuickTime can open certain XML files and create movies based on their contents. These XML files are simply text files that use XML syntax and are saved with the .mov file extension. Your browser and the filing system for your OS treat these files as QuickTime movies, which allows you to direct them to the QuickTime browser plug-in or QuickTime Player. You generally create these XML files using a text editor or a script, but Quick-Time Player can generate some of these files for you using the Export command in the File menu.

Any XML file that QuickTime has an importer for can be saved using the .mov file extension. The XML file for a particular importer may be save-able using an alternate file extension as well. For example, a SMIL file can be saved as a .mov file or a .smil file. Browsers and operating systems often treat the file differently based on this file extension.

For example, QuickTime Player will happily open a SMIL file, whether its file extension is .mov or .smil. Your operating system will launch Quick-Time Player when you double-click a .mov file, but may open a .smil file using a different application, and your browser will probably pass the .mov file to the QuickTime plug-in but not the .smil version. The file extension doesn't matter to QuickTime, but it often determines whether QuickTime is used to handle the file.

SMIL is just one kind of XML file that QuickTime can import. There are currently three XML importers included with QuickTime Player:

- SMIL importer (.mov, .smil)

  This importer tells QuickTime to create a movie containing a set of movie tracks. The movie track contents are specified by URLs, and the track characteristics are passed as SMIL attributes. For details, see Chapter 18, "SMIL for the Camera."

- Media link importer (.mov, .qt1)

  This importer tells QuickTime to open a movie located at a particular URL and play it using the specified settings (autoplay, full-screen mode, and so on). QuickTime 6 adds a simple way to generate .qt1 files automatically using QuickTime Player. For details, see "Making a QuickTime Media Link (.qt1) File" (page 102).

- Component Preflight Importer (.mov)

  You can use the component preflight importer to test for the presence of specific QuickTime components. QuickTime will offer to automatically download and install any that are needed. This can be a useful filter if your website includes movies that use components not included in the minimal QuickTime installation or components introduced in a recent release of QuickTime. For details, see "Checking for QuickTime Components" (page 163).

Glossary

AAC Advanced audio codec specified for MPEG-4. Low-complexity AAC is roughly 30% more efficient than MP3, so the same audio quality can be achieved with a 30% smaller file, or the same size file can contain more audio detail.

ADPCM (Adaptive Differential Pulse Code Modulation) A compression technology used mainly in digital telephone systems.

AIFF (Audio Interchange File Format) An audio file format, widely used on the Web, that supports several compression formats.

aLaw A compression format used mainly for voice.

alpha channel The upper bits of a display pixel encoding, which control its opacity.

alternate track A movie **track** that contains alternate data for another track. QuickTime chooses one track to be used when the movie is played. The choice may be based on such considerations as language.

anti-alias To smooth the edges of an image by mixing its boundary pixels with the **background color.**

API (application programming interface) The set of function calls, data structures, and other programming elements by which a structure of code (such as a system-level toolbox) can be accessed by other code (such as an application program).

applet A **Java** program or code snippet that can be transmitted over a network and executed in a browser.

ASF (Advanced Streaming Format) A file format developed by Microsoft for **streaming.**

aspect ratio The ratio between the height and the width of an image.

asymmetric codec A **codec** that compresses relatively slowly and decompresses rapidly.

AU A digital audio format often used by **UNIX** systems.

AVI (Audio Visual Interleave) A file format used by Video for Windows.

background color The color of the background behind a sprite or other image.

bandwidth The rate (in **bits** or **bytes** per second) at which data can be transmitted over a connection.

bit A single piece of information, with a value of either 0 or 1.

bit depth The number of bits used to encode the color of each pixel in a graphic image.

bitmapped Stored in memory by assigning a numeric value to each **pixel** of an image.

blend matte A **pixel** map that defines the blending of video and digital data. The value of each pixel in the map governs the relative intensity of the video data for the corresponding pixel in the resulting image.

BMP A **bitmapped** graphics format used for still images in the **Windows** environment.

broadcaster Software that encodes audio and/or video in real time and sends at least one stream over an IP network.

byte Eight **bits.**

C programming language A higher-level compiled programming language. The QuickTime API is written in C.

CD-R A recordable CD.

cel-based Animation that consists of displaying a series of still images (from the acetate *cel* used in film animation).

CGI (Common Gateway Interface) script An interface to scripting languages used on Web servers.

chapter list   A list of named entry points into a **movie**. The user selects a chapter list item to go to that part of the movie.

choke speed   A limit to a movie's **bandwidth**, which you set to prevent its delivery from monopolizing the connection.

clipping   Restricting the boundaries of a graphics area. Parts of an image that fall outside the clipping region are not displayed.

codec   Any compression/decompression software tool.

compositing   The process of combining visual tracks in a movie to produce the final user experience.

control settings   In **QuickTime VR**, instructions that tell the VR controller what to do when it reaches a **viewing limit**.

controller   In QuickTime, the control bar that usually appears under a movie window.

current selection   The part of a QuickTime movie that has been selected for an operation.

DAT (digital audio tape)   A high-quality medium for recording sound.

delivery codec   A lossy codec used to compress media for final delivery to the viewer.

descriptor   A text tag that defines some part of the text's appearance, such as its typography.

dithering   A technique used to improve picture quality when you are attempting to display an image that exists at a higher bit-depth representation on a lower bit-depth device. For example, you might want to dither a 24-bits-per-pixel image for display on an 8-bit screen.

DNS (Domain Name System)   A server that converts **URL** descriptions into **IP addresses**.

D1   A class of high-quality video equipment.

DSL (digital subscriber line)   A medium-speed data transmission technology that operates over telephone lines at 300 to 2,000 Kbytes/sec.

DVD (digital video disc)   A disc that records data using a technology similar to that of a CD.

DVI (Digital Video Interlace)   A video compression standard.

effect track   A modifier **track** that applies an effect (such as a wipe or a dissolve) to a movie.

Fast Start   A technique of composing and delivering a movie so that it can start playing before its file is fully downloaded.

Favorites   A list of user-selected movies maintained by QuickTime Player.

firewall   An Internet filtering system that regulates traffic into or out of a network.

FireWire   A hardware technology for exchanging data with peripheral devices, defined by IEEE Standard 1394. Also called *iLink*.

Flash animation   A standard format for animated vector graphics.

FlashPix   A **pixel**-based still image format that breaks large arrays into sets of smaller files.

flattening   The process of copying all of the original data referred to by reference in QuickTime tracks into a QuickTime **movie** file. Flattening is used to bring in all of the data that may be referred to from multiple files after QuickTime editing is complete. It makes a QuickTime movie stand-alone—that is, it can be played on any system without requiring any additional files or tracks, even if the original movie referenced hundreds of files.

FLIC   An animation format. Also called *FLC*.

frame   A single image in a **movie** or sequence of images.

frame animation   In **QuickTime VR**, the technique of playing all the frames of the current view.

frame differencing   A form of temporal compression that involves examining redundancies between adjacent frames in a moving image sequence. Frame differencing can improve compression ratios considerably for a video sequence.

frame rate   The rate at which a movie is displayed—that is, the number of frames per second that are actually being displayed. In QuickTime the frame rate at which a movie was recorded may be different from the frame rate at which it is displayed. Frame rates may be fractional.

FTP (File Transfer Protocol)   A **protocol** for efficiently transporting files over the Internet.

gamma The relationship between the brightness range of an image displayed by one system and the same range in the image displayed by another system.

GIF (Graphics Interchange Format) A still image file and lossless compression format that is common on the Web.

graphics mode A modification of an image that determines how it blends with its background.

GSM A compressed audio format optimized for speech.

H.261, H.263 Video compression standards for streaming.

hint track In a movie sent by **streaming**, a track that specifies how the movie's content is to be packetized for transmission.

hot spot A place in a virtual reality **scene** where the software recognizes cursor actions.

HSV Short for hue, saturation, and value (or *brightness*), a way of defining colors.

HTML (Hypertext Markup Language) The principal language in which Web pages are written.

HTTP (Hypertext Transport Protocol) A **protocol** for sending Web pages and other hypertext material over the Internet.

HTTP streaming The process of sending a movie file over the Internet, using HTTP, so that it starts playing before the entire file has arrived. See **Fast Start**.

IETF (Internet Engineering Task Force) A group that sets standards for Internet technology.

IMA A lossless audio compression standard that provides 4:1 compression.

immersive imaging See **virtual reality**.

IP address A numeric address that identifies a computer on the Internet.

IRIX A version of **UNIX** developed by Silicon Graphics.

ISDN A medium-speed data connection technology. Single ISDN runs at 64 Kbits/sec, double ISDN at 128 Kbits/sec.

ISO (International Standards Organization) A group that establishes standards for multimedia data formatting and transmission, such as **JPEG**.

ISP (Internet service provider) A vendor that provides connections between computers and the Internet.

Java An object-oriented programming language that is widely used to write multiplatform programs that can be transmitted over a network and run on a variety of platforms. A version of the QuickTime **API** is implemented in Java as a set of classes and methods.

JavaScript A scripting language used to add interactivity to Web pages. Do not confuse JavaScript with **Java**.

JFIF A still image format essentially identical to JPEG.

JPEG (Joint Photographic Experts Group) Refers to an international standard for compressing still images. This standard supplies the algorithm for image compression. The version of JPEG used with QuickTime complies with the baseline **ISO** standard bitstream, version 9R9.

karaoke A **movie** and file type in which text is synchronized with music.

key frame A sample in a sequence of temporally compressed samples that does not rely on other samples in the sequence for any of its information. Key frames are placed into **temporally compressed** sequences at a frequency that is determined by the **key frame rate**.

key frame rate The frequency with which **key frames** are placed into temporally compressed data sequences.

keyed text Text on a transparent background, which may be **composited** over a still image or motion video.

LAN (local area network) A network maintained within a facility, as opposed to a WAN (wide area network) that links geographically separated facilities. A LAN typically supports data transfer at 10 or 100 Mbits/sec.

layer A mechanism for prioritizing the tracks in a movie or the overlapping of sprites. When it plays a movie, QuickTime displays the movie's images according to their layer—images with lower layer numbers are displayed on top; images with higher layer numbers may be obscured by images with lower layer numbers.

Linux A **UNIX**-like operating system with public source code.

lossless compression   A compression scheme that preserves all of the original data.

lossy compression   A compression scheme that does not preserve the data precisely; some data is lost, and it cannot be recovered after compression.

LZW compression   A patented lossless compression algorithm, used to compress **GIF** files.

Mac OS   The operating system that Apple provides for Macintosh computers.

Mac OS X   The latest version of the **Mac OS**.

Mac OS X Server   A version of the **Mac OS** based on Free BSD Unix. Includes software for serving Web pages, QuickTime movies, and real-time streams over a LAN or the Internet.

MACE (Macintosh Audio Compression and Expansion)   An older audio **codec** sometimes used on Macintosh computers.

matrix   See **transformation matrix**.

matte   A defined region of a movie display that can be clipped and filled with another image source.

MBone   Short for Multicast Backbone, a virtual network for real-time **streaming** over the Internet.

MIDI (Musical Instrument Digital Interface)   A standard format for sending instructions to a musical synthesizer.

MIME type   A type designation that browsers use to identify file formats and compression standards.

modifier track   A track in a movie that modifies the data or presentation of other tracks. For example, a **tween track** is a modifier track.

movie   A structure of time-based data that is managed by **QuickTime**. A QuickTime movie may contain sound, video, animation, or a combination of data types. A QuickTime movie contains one or more **tracks**; each track represents a single data stream in the movie.

movie file   A QuickTime file that contains a movie data structure. It may or may not contain the media data that the movie displays.

MP3 (MPEG layer 3)   A popular format for compressing music and transmitting it over the Web.

MPEG-4 Expandable multimedia file format based on the QuickTime file format. Current specification includes video and audio codecs. AAC audio is the current MPEG-4 audio codec. Do not confuse MPEG-4 video compression and AAC audio compression with the MPEG-4 file format (.mp4).

multicast The one-to-many form of **streaming**. Users can join or leave a multicast but cannot otherwise interact with it.

NAT (Network Address Translation) A technique sometimes used so that multiple computers can share a single **IP address**.

node In **QuickTime VR**, a position from which an object or panorama can be viewed.

NTSC (National Television System Committee) Refers to the color-encoding method adopted by the committee in 1953. This standard was the first monochrome-compatible, simultaneous color transmission system used for public broadcasting. This method is used widely in the United States.

object image array In **QuickTime VR**, a two-dimensional array that stores images of an object from various angles.

object node In **QuickTime VR**, a position for viewing an object from the outside.

object view In **QuickTime VR**, a description of the angle and other characteristics for viewing an object from a **node**.

PAL (Phase Alternation Line) A color-encoding system used widely in Europe, in which one of the subcarrier phases derived from the color burst is inverted in phase from one line to the next. This technique minimizes hue errors that may result during color video transmission. Sometimes called *Phase Alternating Line*.

palindrome looping Running a movie in a circular fashion from beginning to end and end to beginning, alternating forward and backward.

panorama A structure of QuickTime VR data that forms a virtual-world environment within which the user can navigate.

panorama view In **QuickTime VR**, a part of a panorama seen from a particular angle.

panoramic node In **QuickTime VR**, a position from which a surrounding panorama is viewed.

partial panorama In **QuickTime VR**, a panorama that runs less than 360 degrees.

PDF (Portable Document Format) A common file format for page-oriented documents.

Pentium A common microprocessor type used in computers that run **Windows**.

PICS file A file type used for animation.

PICT A still image format widely used on Macintosh computers.

pixel A single dot in a graphic image.

PKZip A compression program used in the **Windows** environment.

plug-in Software that you attach to a browser to enable it to display specific data formats.

PNG (Portable Network Graphics) A format for still images, similar in many respects to GIF, but newer and unencumbered by patent.

poster A still image, often a frame taken from a **movie,** used to represent the movie to the user.

PowerPC A microprocessor type used in Macintosh computers.

preferred rate The default playback rate for a QuickTime **movie**.

preferred volume The default sound volume for a QuickTime **movie**.

premultiplication A variation of certain **graphics modes** in which the **alpha channel** value becomes part of the value of each pixel in an image.

protocol A set of messaging standards for transmitting data.

QScript A scripting language used to add custom actions to QuickTime sprites.

QTI or QTIF (QuickTime Image File) A file format used to store QuickTime images.

QTSS (QuickTime Streaming Server) Apple's server software for real-time **streaming.**

QuickTime A set of Macintosh system extensions or a Windows dynamic-link library that supports the composition and playing of **movies**.

QuickTime for Java A set of **Java** classes and methods that implements the **QuickTime API**.

QuickTime Player An application, included with the QuickTime system software, that plays QuickTime **movies**.

QuickTime Pro A registered version of **QuickTime** with advanced features, primarily the addition of editing capabilities to **QuickTime Player**.

QuickTime VR A QuickTime media type that lets users interactively explore and examine photorealistic three-dimensional virtual worlds. QuickTime VR data structures are also called **panoramas** or object movies.

RAID (Redundant Array of Inexpensive Disks) A technology for combining multiple disks into one large, fast drive.

RGB Stands for red-green-blue, a way of representing colors.

RLE compression A lossless compression standard.

RTP (Real-Time Protocol) The transport protocol for sending real-time **streaming** content.

RTSP (Real-Time Streaming Protocol) A protocol that provides interactivity for movies sent by **streaming**.

scene In **QuickTime VR**, a collection of **nodes** that creates a virtual reality effect.

SCSI (Small Computer System Interface) A hardware connection technology for peripheral devices such as disk drives.

SDK (Software Developers Kit) A set of interfaces, available by download or CD-ROM from Apple, for C and Java developers who want to call QuickTime from their programs.

SDP (Session Description Protocol) file A text file that describes a **streaming** session and gives the user's computer instructions for tuning in.

SECAM (Système Electronique Couleur avec Memoire) A color-encoding system in which the red and blue color-difference information is transmitted on alternate lines, requiring a one-line memory in order to decode green information. Also called *Sequential Color with Memory*.

SGI image file A still image format developed by Silicon Graphics.

SIT A lossless file compression standard common on Macintosh computers.

SMIL (Synchronized Multimedia Integration Language) A standard for describing multimedia presentations using text files.

SMPTE (Society of Motion Picture and Television Engineers) An organization that sets video and movie technical standards.

SMTP (Simple Mail Transport Protocol) A protocol for sending email.

SND A Macintosh sound file format.

Solaris An operating system developed by Sun Microsystems.

spatial compression Image compression that is performed within the context of a single **frame**. This compression technique takes advantage of redundancy in the image to reduce the amount of data required to accurately represent the image. Compare **temporal compression**.

sprite An animated image that is managed by QuickTime. A sprite is defined once and is then animated by commands that change its position or appearance. See also **wired sprite**.

sprite track A movie **track** populated by **sprites**.

stitching In **QuickTime VR**, the process of combining still images into a **panorama**.

streaming Delivery of video or audio data over a network in real time, as an indefinite stream of numbered packets instead of a single file download.

S-video A video format in which color and brightness information are encoded as separate signals. The S-video format is component video, as opposed to composite video, which is the NTSC standard.

TCP/IP (Transmission Control Protocol/Internet Protocol) A low-level Internet transport technology that supports retransmission of lost packets.

telecine The process of inserting extra frames when transferring a film movie to video, to compensate for differences in frame rates.

temporal compression Image compression that is performed between **frames** in a sequence. This compression technique takes advantage of redundancy between adjacent frames in a sequence to reduce the amount of data that is required to accurately represent each frame in the sequence. Sequences that have been temporally compressed typically contain **key frames** at regular intervals. Compare **spatial compression**.

text descriptor A markup tag that contains text formatting commands.

TGA   A still image format.

TIFF (Tagged Image File Format)   A format often used to transport **bit-mapped** images between graphics applications.

tiling   A technique, used in **virtual reality**, for breaking an image into pieces so it can be played back without loading the entire image into memory.

timecode track   A movie track that stores external timing information, such as **SMPTE** timecodes.

Time slider   The part of the QuickTime **controller** that lets you move along a movie's timeline.

time stamp   A data structure that describes a text sample's starting time and duration in a movie.

T1   A relatively high speed (1.5 Mbits/sec) data connection technology.

track   A QuickTime data structure that represents a single data stream in a QuickTime **movie**. A movie may contain one or more tracks. Each track is independent of other tracks in the movie and represents its own data stream.

transfer codec   A high-quality or lossless **codec** used for transferring data during content creation.

transformation matrix   A 3-by-3 matrix that defines how to map points from one coordinate space into another coordinate space. It can be used to scale, rotate, or reposition an image.

tweening   The process of interpolating new data between given values in conformance to an algorithm. It is an efficient way to expand or smooth a movie's presentation between its actual frames.

tween track   A **track** that modifies the display of other tracks by **tweening**.

UDP (User Datagram Protocol)   A very low-level data transport protocol that does not support retransmission of lost packets, sometimes used instead of **TCP/IP**.

UFS (UNIX File System)   A file system used by **UNIX**.

uLaw   A type of audio compression.

unicast   The one-to-one form of **streaming**. If **RTSP** is provided, the user can move freely from point to point in a unicast movie.

Unicode   A two-byte standard for text encoding that covers most of the world's writing systems, including Chinese.

UNIX   An extensive operating-system technology used mainly by servers and work stations.

URL (Uniform Resource Locator)   A uniform way of specifying locations on the Internet or a local file system.

USB (Universal Serial Bus)   A hardware technology by which computers communicate with keyboards and other low-speed peripheral devices.

user data   Auxiliary data that your application can store in a QuickTime movie, track, or media structure. The user data is stored in a **user data list**; items in the list are referred to as **user data items**. Examples of user data include a copyright, date of creation, name of a movie's director, and special hardware and software requirements.

user data item   A single element in a **user data list**, such as a modification date or copyright notice.

user data list   The collection of **user data** for a QuickTime movie, track, or media. Each element in the user data list is called a **user data item**.

VBR (variable bit rate)   A way of compressing data that takes advantage of changes in the media's data rate.

viewing limits   In **QuickTime VR**, the limits of pan and tilt angle from which an object or panorama can be viewed.

virtual reality   The effect achieved by **QuickTime VR**, where users appear to be manipulating real objects or environments.

WAV or WAVE   A **Windows** format for sound files.

Windows   An operating system developed by Microsoft Corporation.

wired sprite   A **sprite** that initiates actions in response to events, such as telling other software when the user has clicked its image or passed the cursor over it.

XML   An extensible markup language, similar to **HTML** but more formal and more flexible.

ZIP   A lossless technology for compressing files of all types.

Index

Q

Interactive QuickTime
Authoring Wired Media

by Matthew Peterson
University of California, Berkeley; M.I.N.D. Institute; Tekadence, U.S.A.

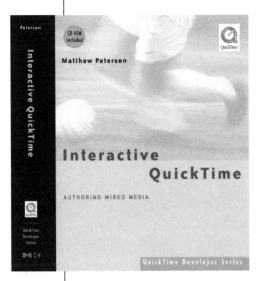

Designing interactive digital media is one of the most significant challenges for today's online community. It is a fast-growing field pushed by the rapid development and dispersion of Java, QuickTime, Shockwave, and Flash. While several good books are available for developers to learn the interactive capabilities of Java, Shockwave, and Flash, this is the first book about QuickTime interactivity. A logical follow-up to *QuickTime for the Web 3E,* this much-anticipated book by Matthew Peterson details the power of QuickTime's wired media technology and provides a resource for professionals developing and deploying interactive QuickTime content that can act as application user interfaces, educational multimedia, scientific display panels, musical instruments, games and puzzles, etc., and that can interact with you, your browser, a server, or with other movies.

Features

- Describes concepts and techniques of interactivity applicable to technology beyond QuickTime—including Flash.

- Features real-world, hands-on projects of progressive sophistication, allowing developers to start with a project appropriate to their own level of QuickTime experience.

- A companion CD-ROM contains the book's source code, tutorials, demo software, and QT installers.

ISBN 1-55860-746-3 • Paperback • 650 pages

Email: custserv.mkp@elsevier.com
Phone: 800.545.2522 / 314.453.7010
Fax: 800.535.9935 / 314.453.7095

MORGAN KAUFMANN PUBLISHERS
AN IMPRINT OF ELSEVIER

WWW.MKP.COM

Apple Computer, Inc.
Software License Agreement

English—Apple Computer, Inc. Software License

Français—Apple Computer, Inc. Contrat de Licence Logiciel

Español—Licencia de Software de Apple Computer, Inc.

Deutsch—Apple Computer, Inc. -Software-Lizenzvertrag

Italiano—Apple Computer, Inc. Licenza Software

Svensk—Apple Computer, Inc. Licensavtal

Nederlands—Apple Computer, Inc. Software-licentie

日本語—アップルコンピュータ・インクソフトウェア使用許諾契約

If for any reason a court of competent jurisdiction finds any provision, or portion thereof, to be unenforceable, the remainder of this License shall continue in full force and effect.

9. Complete Agreement. This License constitutes the entire agreement between the parties with respect to the use of the Apple Software and supersedes all prior or contemporaneous understandings regarding such subject matter. No amendment to or modification of this License will be binding unless in writing and signed by Apple.

APPLE COMPUTER, INC.
INTERNATIONAL SALES SUBSIDIARY LIST

COUNTRY	SUBSIDIARY
Austria	Apple Computer Gesellschaft m.b.H.
Brazil	Apple Computer Brasil Ltda.
Canada	Apple Canada Inc.
France	Apple Computer France S.A.R.L.
Germany	Apple Computer GmbH
Hong Kong	Apple Computer International Ltd
India	Apple Computer International Pte. Ltd.
Ireland	Apple Computer (UK) Limited
Italy	Apple Computer S.p.A.
Japan	Apple Japan, Inc.
Mexico	Apple Computer Mexico, S.A. de C.V.
Netherlands, Belgium	Apple Computer Benelux B.V.
Singapore	Apple Computer South Asia Pte Ltd
South Africa	Apple Computer (Proprietary) Limited
Spain	Apple Computer Espana, S.A.
Sweden, Norway, Denmark	Apple Computer AB
Switzerland	Apple Computer AG (SA) (Ltd.)
Taiwan	Apple Computer Asia, Inc.
United Kingdom	Apple Computer (UK) Limited

EA0054

FRANCAIS
Apple Computer, Inc. Contrat de Licence Logiciel

LISEZ SOIGNEUSEMENT CE CONTRAT DE LICENCE LOGICIEL "LICENCE" AVANT D'UTILISER LE LOGICIEL. EN UTILISANT LE LOGICIEL, VOUS ACCEPTEZ D'ETRE LIE PAR LES TERMES DE CETTE LICENCE. SI VOUS N'ETES PAS D'ACCORD AVEC LESDITS TERMES, N'UTILISEZ PAS LE LOGICIEL APPLE ET (LE CAS ECHEANT) RETOURNEZ LE A L'ENDROIT OU VOUS L'AVEZ OBTENU. SON PRIX VOUS SERA ALORS REMBOURSE.

1. Licence. Apple Computer, Inc. ou le cas échéant, sa filiale locale ("Apple") vous concède une licence sur, et en aucun cas ne vend, le logiciel, les outils, les utilitaires, la documentation et les polices de caractères accompagnant la présente Licence, qu'ils soient sur disquette, sur mémoire morte (ROM) ou sur tout autre support (le "Logiciel Apple"). Vous êtes propriétaire du support sur lequel le Logiciel Apple est enregistré mais Apple et/ou les concédant(s) d'Apple restent propriétaire(s) du Logiciel Apple. Le Logiciel Apple contenu dans l'emballage ainsi que les copies, que la présente Licence vous autorise à réaliser, sont régis par les termes de la présente Licence.

2. Utilisations Permises et Limitations. La présente Licence vous autorise à utiliser le Logiciel Apple pour (i) tester le Logiciel Apple, et (ii) développer des applications logicielles. Vous pouvez réaliser toutes les copies du Logiciel Apple nécessaires à l'utilisation du Logiciel Apple dans les limites fixées par la présente Licence et distribuer ces copies aux seuls employés pour lesquels l'utilisation du Logiciel Apple est indispensable et dans les limites des utilisations permises par la présente Licence. Afin de développer ces applications logicielles, vous pouvez également utiliser, copier, modifier (sauf restrictions figurant dans le dossier comprenant les informations sur les Licences), intégrer et compiler aux logiciels dont vous êtes propriétaire, diffuser (exclusivement sous forme de code objet) et seulement en association avec les logiciels dont vous êtes propriétaire, le Logiciel Apple décrit dans le dossier comprenant les informations sur les Licences, à la condition que vous reproduisiez sur chaque exemplaire les mentions de droit d'auteur d'Apple de même que les autres indications de propriété contenues sur l'original du Logiciel Apple. Vous ne pouvez pas diffuser le Logiciel Apple que conformément à un accord valide qui soit aussi protecteur des droits d'Apple pour le Logiciel Apple que la présente Licence. Sauf et dans les limites où la loi ou la présente Licence l'autorise, vous ne pouvez pas, en tout ou en partie, décompiler, désosser, désassembler, modifier, louer, prêter, concéder des licences, diffuser ou créer des produits dérivés à partir du Logiciel Apple ou transmettre le Logiciel Apple par un réseau ou vers un autre ordinateur. La présente Licence sera résiliée immédiatement et de plein droit, sans notification préalable de la part d'Apple, si vous ne vous conformez pas à l'une quelconque de ses dispositions. Apple pourra également résilier la présente Licence dans le cas où une nouvelle version du Mac OS serait incompatible avec le Logiciel Apple.

3. Garantie des Supports (le cas échéant). Apple garantit les supports sur lesquels le Logiciel Apple est enregistré contre tout vice de matière et de main d'oeuvre, sous condition d'une utilisation normale, pendant une période de quatre-vingt-dix (90) jours à compter de la date d'achat initiale. Votre seul recours, au titre du présent article se limite, et ceci au choix d'Apple, soit au remboursement du prix du produit contenant le Logiciel Apple, soit au remplacement du Logiciel Apple, lorsqu'il est retourné à Apple ou à un représentant autorisé d'Apple avec une copie de la facture. CETTE LIMITATION DE GARANTIE ET TOUTES GARANTIES IMPLICITES CONCERNANT LE SUPPORT Y COMPRIS LES GARANTIES IMPLICITES DE QUALITE MARCHANDE ET D'ADEQUATION À UN USAGE PARTICULIER SONT LIMITEES À UNE DUREE DE QUATRE-VINGT-DIX (90) JOURS À COMPTER DE LA DATE D'ACHAT INITIALE. CERTAINES LEGISLATIONS NE PERMETTENT PAS DE LIMITER LA DUREE D'UNE GARANTIE IMPLICITE, IL EST DONC POSSIBLE QUE LA LIMITATION MENTIONNEE CI-DESSUS NE S'APPLIQUE PAS A VOUS. CETTE LIMITATION DE GARANTIE TELLE QU'EXPRIMEE CI-DESSUS EST EXCLUSIVE DE TOUTE AUTRE GARANTIE QUELLE QUE SOIT SA FORME, ORALE, ECRITE, EXPRESSE OU TACITE. APPLE EXCLUT EXPRESSEMENT L'APPLICATION DE TOUTE AUTRE GARANTIE. CETTE GARANTIE VOUS DONNE DES DROITS SPECIFIQUES. VOUS POUVEZ EGALEMENT AVOIR D'AUTRES DROITS QUI VARIENT SELON LES LEGISLATIONS.

La disposition qui suit n'est applicable que pour la France : l'application de la présente garantie ne pourra vous priver de vos droits à la garantie légale (en cas de défauts ou de vices cachés).

4. Exclusion de Garantie sur le Logiciel Apple. Certains des Logiciels Apple peuvent être identifiés comme des versions du Logiciel Apple de type alpha, bêta, développement, pré-version, non-testées ou partiellement testées. De tels Logiciels Apple peuvent contenir des dysfonctionnements qui sont susceptibles de provoquer des erreurs et des pertes de données et peuvent se révéler incomplets ou contenir des inexactitudes. Vous reconnaissez et admettez expressément que l'utilisation du Logiciel Apple est à vos risques et périls. Le Logiciel Apple est fourni "TEL QUEL" sans garantie d'aucune sorte, et Apple et le(s) concédant(s) d'Apple (aux fins des dispositions des paragraphes 4 et 5, l'expression "Apple" désigne collectivement Apple et le(s) concédant(s) d'Apple) EXCLUENT EXPRESSEMENT TOUTE GARANTIE, EXPLICITE OU IMPLICITE, Y COMPRIS DE FACON NON LIMITATIVE LES GARANTIES IMPLICITES DE QUALITE MARCHANDE ET D'ADEQUATION A UN USAGE PARTICULIER ET TOUTE GARANTIE DE NON-CONTREFACON. APPLE NE GARANTIT PAS QUE LES FONCTIONS CONTENUES DANS LE LOGICIEL APPLE CORRESPONDRONT A VOS BESOINS OU QUE LE FONCTIONNEMENT DU LOGICIEL APPLE SERA ININTERROMPU, EXEMPT D'ERREUR OU QUE TOUT DEFAUT DU LOGICIEL APPLE SERA CORRIGE. DE PLUS, APPLE NE GARANTIT PAS NI NE FAIT AUCUNE DECLARATION CONCERNANT L'UTILISATION OU LES RESULTATS DE L'UTILISATION DU LOGICIEL APPLE OU DE LA DOCUMENTATION Y AFFERENT EN CE QUI CONCERNE LEUR EXACTITUDE, FIABILITE OU AUTREMENT. AUCUNE INFORMATION OU AUCUN CONSEIL, COMMUNIQUES VERBALEMENT OU PAR ECRIT PAR APPLE OU PAR UN DE SES REPRESENTANTS AUTORISES NE POURRA CREER UNE GARANTIE OU AUGMENTER DE QUELQUE MANIERE QUE CE SOIT L'ETENDUE DE LA PRESENTE GARANTIE. SI LE LOGICIEL APPLE S'AVERAIT DEFECTUEUX, VOUS ASSUMERIEZ SEUL (ET NON PAS APPLE NI UN REPRESENTANT AUTORISE D'APPLE) LE COUT TOTAL DE TOUT ENTRETIEN, REPARATION OU MODIFICATION NECESSAIRE. CERTAINES LEGISLATIONS NE PERMETTENT PAS L'EXCLUSION DE GARANTIES IMPLICITES, IL EST DONC POSSIBLE QUE L'EXCLUSION MENTIONNEE CI-DESSUS NE S'APPLIQUE PAS A VOUS.

La disposition suivante n'est applicable que pour la France : les présentes ne pourraient vous priver de vos droits à la garantie légale (en cas de défauts ou de vices cachés), dans la mesure où elle trouverait à s'appliquer.

5. Limitation de Responsabilité. EN AUCUN CAS, Y COMPRIS LA NEGLIGENCE, APPLE NE SERA RESPONSABLE DE QUELQUES DOMMAGES INDIRECTS, SPECIAUX OU ACCESSOIRES RESULTANT OU RELATIF A LA PRESENTE LICENCE. CERTAINES JURIDICTIONS NE PERMETTENT PAS LA LIMITATION OU L'EXCLUSION DE RESPONSABILITE POUR DOMMAGES INDIRECTS OU ACCESSOIRES, IL EST DONC POSSIBLE QUE L'EXCLUSION OU LA LIMITATION MENTIONNEE CI-DESSUS NE S'APPLIQUE PAS A VOUS. La seule responsabilité d'Apple envers vous au titre de tout dommage n'excédera en aucun cas la somme de deux cent cinquante francs (250FF).

6. Engagement Relatif aux Exportations. Vous ne pouvez pas utiliser ou autrement exporter ou réexporter le Logiciel Apple sauf autorisation par les lois des Etats-Unis et les lois du pays dans lequel vous avez obtenu le Logiciel Apple. En particulier mais sans limitation, le Logiciel Apple ne peut être exporté ou réexporté (i) dans tout pays soumis à embargo des Etats-Unis (ou à tout résident ou ressortissant de ce pays) ou (ii) à toute personne figurant sur la liste "Specially Designated Nationals" du Ministère des Finances des Etats-Unis ou sur le classement "Table of Denial Orders" du Ministère du Commerce des Etats-Unis. En utilisant le Logiciel Apple, vous déclarez et garantissez que vous n'êtes pas situé, sous le contrôle de, ou ressortissant ou résident d'un pays spécifié ci-dessus ou inscrit sur les listes mentionnées ci-dessus.

7. Gouvernement des Etats-Unis. Si le Logiciel Apple est fourni au Gouvernement des Etats-Unis, le Logiciel Apple est classé "restricted computer software" tel que ce terme est défini dans la clause 52.227-19 du FAR. Les droits du Gouvernement des Etats-Unis sur le Logiciel Apple sont définis pas la clause 52.227-19 du FAR.

8. Loi Applicable et Divisibilité du Contrat. Si une filiale Apple est présente dans le pays où vous avez acquis la licence du Logiciel Apple, la présente Licence sera régie par la loi du pays dans lequel la filiale est installée. Dans le cas contraire, la présente Licence sera régie par les lois des Etats-Unis et de l'Etat de Californie. Si pour une quelconque raison, un tribunal ayant juridiction juge qu'une disposition de la présente Licence est inapplicable, en totalité ou en partie, les autres dispositions de la présente Licence resteront entièrement applicables.

9. Entente Complète. Cette Licence constitue l'intégralité de l'accord entre les parties concernant l'utilisation du Logiciel Apple et remplace toutes les propositions ou accords antérieurs ou actuels, écrits ou verbaux, à ce sujet. Aucune modification de cette Licence n'aura quelque effet à moins d'être stipulée par écrit et signée par un représentant dûment autorisé d'Apple.

APPLE COMUTER, INC.
LISTE DES FILIALES

Pays	Filiales
Canada	Apple Canada Inc.
Afrique du Sud	Apple Computer (Proprietary) Limited
Royaume Uni	Apple Computer (UK) Limited
Suède, Norvège, Danemark, Finlande	Apple Computer AB
Suisse	Apple Computer AG (SA) (Ltd.)
Taiwan	Apple Computer Asia, Inc.
Pays Bas, Belgique	Apple Computer Benelux B.V.
Brésil	Apple Computer Brasil Ltda.
Espagne	Apple Computer Espana, S.A.
France	Apple Computer France S.A.R.L.
Autriche	Apple Computer Gesellschaft m.b.H.
Allemagne	Apple Computer GmbH
Hong Kong	Apple Computer International Ltd
Irlande	Apple Computer (UK) Limited
Mexique	Apple Computer Mexico, S.A. de C.V.
Italie	Apple Computer S.p.A.
Singapour	Apple Computer South Asia Pte Ltd
Japon	Apple Japan, Inc.

ESPAÑOL
Licencia de Software de Apple Computer, Inc.

ROGAMOS LEA DETENIDAMENTE EL PRESENTE CONTRATO DE LICENCIA DE SOFTWARE (EN ADELANTE DENOMINADO "LICENCIA") ANTES DE UTILIZAR EL SOFTWARE. EN EL SUPUESTO DE QUE UTILICE EL SOFTWARE, ELLO SE INTERPRETARÁ COMO UN HECHO INEQUÍVOCO DE SU ACEPTACIÓN A LOS TÉRMINOS Y CONDICIONES DE ESTA LICENCIA. SI VD. NO ACEPTA LOS TÉRMINOS Y CONDICIONES DE ESTA LICENCIA, NO UTILICE EL SOFWARE Y (EN SU CASO) DEVUELVA EL SOFTWARE AL ESTABLECIMIENTO DONDE LO ADQUIRIÓ PARA SU REEMBOLSO.

1. Licencia. Apple Computer Inc. ("Apple") le concede una licencia (sin que ello suponga su venta) para el uso del software, herramientas, utilidades, documentación y cualquier material complementario objeto de esta Licencia, ya sea en disco, en disco compacto, en memoria de lectura de ordenador o en cualquier otro soporte o de cualquier otra forma (el "Software Apple"). El Software Apple contenido en este paquete y cualesquiera copias, modificaciones y distribuciones que la presente Licencia le autorice a realizar están sujetos a esta Licencia.

2. Usos Permitidos y Restricciones. Esta Licencia le permite utilizar el Software Apple para (i) probar el Software Apple y (ii) desarrollar aplicaciones de software. Vd. puede hacer tantas copias del Software Apple como razonablemente sean necesarias para utilizar el Software según lo expresamente permitido por esta Licencia. Igualmente, Vd. puede distribuir estas copias a sus empleados siempre y cuando el trabajo de estos empleados requiera que utilicen el Software y, siempre y cuando, se cumplan los límites permitidos por la presente Licencia. Con sujeción a lo previsto en los términos complementarios de esta Licencia contenidos en la carpeta informática de Licencia ("Licensing Info Folder") que forma parte integrante de la presente Licencia y del Software Apple, el Software Apple podrá ser usado, copiado, modificado para poder desarrollar aplicaciones del software, así como incorporarlo o decompilarlo en combinación con sus propios programas, y distribuirlo (siempre en forma codificada) únicamente junto con todos sus propios programas y, siempre y cuando en todo caso se reproduzca en cada copia los derechos de Apple y cualquier otra leyenda en relación a los derechos de Apple que estuviesen en la copia original del Software Apple. Vd. puede también distribuir este Software Apple siempre que celebre con los terceros que lo reciban o utilicen un contrato que al menos proteja el Software Apple en los mismos términos que la presente Licencia. Salvo lo expresamente permitido por esta Licencia o por el derecho aplicable, no podrá Vd. descompilar, cambiar la ingeniería, desensamblar, modificar, alquilar, arrendar, prestar, distribuir, sublicenciar o crear trabajos derivados o basados en el Software de Apple o transmitir el Software Apple a terceros a través de una red o de un ordenador. Sus derechos bajo esta Licencia dejarán de estar en vigor de forma automática y sin necesidad de notificación de Apple en el supuesto de que Vd. incumpla cualesquiera término(s) de esta Licencia. Además, Apple se reserva el derecho de resolver la presente Licencia en el supuesto de comercializar una nueva versión del Mac Os que sea incompatible con el Software Apple.

3. Garantía Limitada sobre los Soportes. Apple garantiza que los soportes en los cuales está grabado el Software Apple carecen de defectos sobre materiales y mano de obra en circunstancias normales de uso y durante un plazo de noventa (90) días desde el momento de la adquisición inicial al por menor. Su único derecho bajo este apartado será, a opción de Apple, el reembolso del precio de compra del producto que contenía el Software Apple o la sustitución del Software Apple. ESTA GARANTÍA LIMITADA Y CUALESQUIERA GARANTÍAS IMPLÍCITAS Y/O CONDICIONES RELATIVAS A LOS SOPORTES, INCLUYENDO GARANTÍAS IMPLÍCITAS Y/O CONDICIONES DE COMERCIABILIDAD O CALIDAD SATISFACTORIA E IDONEIDAD PARA UN FIN DETERMINADO ESTÁN LIMITADAS A LA DURACIÓN DE NOVENTA (90) DÍAS DESDE LA FECHA DE ADQUISICIÓN AL POR MENOR. ALGUNAS

LEGISLACIONES NO PERMITEN LAS LIMITACIONES RESPECTO A LA DURACIÓN DE LAS GARANTÍAS IMPLÍCITAS, POR LO CUAL EN DICHO CASO ESTA LIMITACIÓN PODRÍA NO SER DE APLICACIÓN A VD. LA GARANTÍA LIMITADA PREVISTA EN ESTE APARTADO ES EXCLUSIVA Y SUSTITUYE A CUALESQUIERA OTRAS, SEAN VERBALES O ESCRITAS, EXPRESAS O IMPLÍCITAS. APPLE EXCLUYE EXPRESAMENTE TODAS LAS OTRAS GARANTÍAS. ESTA GARANTÍA LIMITADA LE CONFIERE DERECHOS ESPECÍFICOS. VD. PUEDE TAMBIÉN TENER OTROS DERECHOS EN FUNCIÓN DEL DERECHO IMPERATIVO APLICABLE.

4. Exclusión de Garantía en relación con el Software Apple. Algunos de los Software Apple pueden ser versiones designadas como alfa, beta, desarrollo, prototipo, sin probar o no probados completamente. Este Software Apple puede contener errores que causaren fallos o pérdida de información y pueden ser incompletos o contener inexactitudes. Vd. reconoce y acepta expresamente que el uso del Software Apple se realiza a su exclusivo riesgo. El Software Apple se suministra TAL Y COMO SE PRESENTA, sin garantía de ninguna clase y Apple y/o su(s) Licenciador(es) (a los efectos de las estipulaciones 4 y 5, Apple y el/los Licenciador(es) de Apple se denominarán de forma conjunta como "Apple") EXCLUYEN EXPRESAMENTE TODAS LAS GARANTÍAS EXPRESAS O IMPLÍCITAS, INCLUYENDO, CON CARÁCTER MERAMENTE ENUNCIATIVO Y NO LIMITATIVO, LAS GARANTÍAS DE COMERCIABILIDAD O CALIDAD SATISFACTORIA E IDONEIDAD PARA UN FIN DETERMINADO. APPLE NO GARANTIZA QUE LAS FUNCIONES CONTENIDAS EN EL SOFTWARE APPLE SATISFAGAN SUS NECESIDADES NI QUE EL SOFTWARE APPLE FUNCIONE ININTERRUMPIDAMENTE O SIN ERRORES O QUE LOS DEFECTOS DEL SOFTWARE APPLE SERÁN CORREGIDOS. ASIMISMO, APPLE NO GARANTIZA NI FORMULA DECLARACIÓN ALGUNA RELATIVA A LA UTILIZACIÓN O A LOS RESULTADOS DE LA UTILIZACIÓN DEL SOFTWARE APPLE O DE LA DOCUMENTACIÓN EN CUANTO A LA INEXISTENCIA DE ERRORES, EXACTITUD, FIABILIDAD U OTROS. NINGUNA INFORMACIÓN O ASESORAMIENTO ESCRITO O VERBAL FACILITADOS POR APPLE O POR UN REPRESENTANTE AUTORIZADO DE APPLE CONSTITUIRÁN GARANTÍA ALGUNA Y NO AUMENTARÁN EN MODO ALGUNO EL ÁMBITO DE LA PRESENTE GARANTÍA. EN EL SUPUESTO DE QUE EL SOFTWARE APPLE RESULTARA SER DEFECTUOSO, VD. (Y NO APPLE NI UN REPRESENTANTE AUTORIZADO DE APPLE) ASUMIRÁ EL COSTE ÍNTEGRO DE TODOS LOS SERVICIOS, REPARACIONES Y CORRECCIONES NECESARIOS. LOS HONORARIOS DE LA PRESENTE LICENCIA YA INCLUYEN ESTA DISTRIBUCIÓN DE RIESGOS. HABIDA CUENTA DE QUE LA NORMATIVA IMPERATIVA DE ALGUNOS PAÍSES NO PERMITE LA EXCLUSIÓN DE GARANTÍAS IMPLÍCITAS, LA ANTERIOR EXCLUSIÓN PUEDE NO SERLE APLICABLE.

5. Límite de responsabilidad. APPLE NO SERÁ RESPONSABLE EN NINGÚN CASO, INCLUYENDO POR NEGLIGENCIA, DEL LUCRO CESANTE O DAÑO EMERGENTE, DIRECTO O INDIRECTO, QUE PUDIERA DERIVARSE O ESTAR RELACIONADO CON LA PRESENTE LICENCIA, ELLO AUNQUE APPLE O REPRESENTANTE AUTORIZADO POR APPLE YA HAYAN AVISADO DE LA EXISTENCIA DEL POSIBLE DAÑO. ALGUNOS PAÍSES NO PERMITEN LA LIMITACIÓN DEL LUCRO CESANTE O DAÑO EMERGENTE, DIRECTO O INDIRECTO, POR LO CUAL ESTA LIMITACIÓN PUEDE NO SERLE APLICABLE A VD. La responsabilidad total de Apple frente a Vd. por daños y perjuicios no excederá, en ningún caso, de la cantidad de cincuenta dólares de EE.UU. (50 dólares).

6. Restricciones a la exportación. Vd. no podrá utilizar o, de otra forma, exportar o reexportar, el Software Apple, salvo en la forma permitida por la legislación de los Estados Unidos y del país en el cual se obtuvo el Software Apple. En particular, pero sin estar limitado a ello, el Software Apple no podrá ser exportado o reexportado (i) a ningún país que haya sido objeto de embargo por parte de los EE.UU. (o a ningún nacional o residente en ese país), (ii) a nadie que figure en la lista de Ciudadanos Especialmente Designados del Departamento del Tesoro de EE.UU. o en la Tabla de Órdenes de Denegación del Departamento de Comercio de EE.UU. La utilización por su parte del Software Apple se considerará un hecho inequívoco de su manifestación y garantía de no estar situado, no estar bajo control y no ser nacional de ninguno de tales países y de que no figura en ninguna de tales listas.

7. La Administración como usuario final. Si el Software Apple es suministrado al Gobierno de los Estados Unidos, el Software Apple se calificará como "software informático restringido", tal como se define en la cláusula 52.227-19 del FAR. Los derechos de la Administración de los Estados Unidos respecto del Software Apple serán los definidos en la cláusula 52.227-19 del FAR.

8. Ley aplicable e independencia de las estipulaciones. En el supuesto de existir una filial de Apple en el país en el cual fue obtenida la Licencia de Software Apple, esta licencia se regirá por el derecho de dicho país. En caso contrario, la presente Licencia se regirá por las leyes de los Estados Unidos y del Estado de California. Si por cualquier razón un tribunal competente declarara no exigible o ineficaz cualquier disposición de la presente Licencia o parte de la misma, el resto de la presente Licencia conservará plena vigencia y efecto.

9. Contrato Íntegro. La presente Licencia constituye el acuerdo completo entre las partes respecto a la utilización del Software Apple y sustituye todos los acuerdos anteriores o contemporáneos relativos a su objeto. La presente Licencia únicamente podrá ser modificada mediante acuerdo escrito firmado por Apple.

APPLE COMPUTER, INC.
LISTA DE FILIALES A NIVEL INTERNACIONAL DEDICADAS A LA VENTA

PAÍS	FILIAL
Austria	Apple Computer Gesellschaft m.b.H.
Brasil	Apple Computer Brasil Ltda.
Canadá	Apple Canada Inc.
Francia	Apple Computer France S.A.R.L.
Alemania	Apple Computer Gmb H
Hong Kong	Apple Computer International Ltd.
India	Apple Computer International Pte. Ltd.
Irlanda	Apple Computer (UK) Limited
Italia	Apple Computer S.p.a.
Japón	Apple Japan, Inc
México	Apple Computer Mexico, S.A. de C.V.

Holanda, Bélgica	Apple Computer Benelux, B.V.
Singapur	Apple Computer South Asia Pte Ltd
Sudafrica	Apple Computer (Proprietary) Limited
España	Apple Computer España, S.A.
Suecia, Noruega, Dinamarca	Apple Computer AB
Suiza	Apple Computer AG (SA) (Ltd.)
Taiwan	Apple Computer Asia, Inc.
Reino Unido	Apple Computer (UK) Limited

DEUTSCH
Apple Computer, Inc. -Software-Lizenzvertrag

BITTE LESEN SIE DIESEN LIZENZVERTRAG SORGFÄLTIG DURCH, BEVOR SIE DIE SOFTWARE BENUTZEN. WENN SIE DIE SOFTWARE BENUTZEN, ERKLÄREN SIE DAMIT IHR EINVERSTÄNDNIS MIT DEN BESTIMMUNGEN DES FOLGENDEN LIZENZVERTRAGES. EINER GESONDERTEN MITTEILUNG AN APPLE ODER IHREN HÄNDLER BEDARF ES NICHT. WENN SIE MIT DEM LIZENZVERTRAG NICHT EINVERSTANDEN SIND, BENUTZEN SIE DIE SOFTWARE NICHT UND — SOFERN ANWENDBAR — GEBEN SIE DIE SOFTWARE DORT ZURÜCK, WO SIE SIE ERWORBEN HABEN.

1. Lizenz. Die Apple Computer, Inc., Cupertino, California, USA, ("Apple"), erteilt Ihnen hiermit das Recht zur Benutzung der beigefügten Software, Software – Werkzeuge und Dienstprogrammen, einschließlich der beigefügten Dokumentation und sonstiger Materialien (im folgenden "Apple-Software"), unabhängig davon, ob diese auf einer Diskette, einem ROM oder einem anderen Datenträger gespeichert ist. Alle sonstigen Rechte an der Apple-Software bleiben vorbehalten. Auch alle Kopien und Bearbeitungen sowie der Vertrieb der Apple-Software unterliegen dieser Vereinbarung.

2. Nutzung und Beschränkungen. Apple erteilt Ihnen hiermit das Recht zur Installation und Benutzung der Apple-Software auf der Festplatte eines Computers. Sie sind berechtigt, die Apple-Software zu benutzen, um (a) die Apple-Software zu testen und (b) Anwendungs- Programme zu entwickeln. Sie sind berechtigt, Kopien der Apple Software im nach diesem Lizenzvertrag notwendigen Umfang zu erstellen und an ihre Mitarbeiter zu verteilen, sofern diese die Apple Software zur Erfüllung ihrer dienstlichen Aufgaben benötigen und sofern die Einhaltung der Bestimmunge dieses Lizenzvertrages sichergestellt ist. Zum Zwecke der Entwicklung von Anwendungs – Software sind Sie berechtigt, die Apple Software zu benutzen, zu kopieren, nach Maßgabe der in der Apple Software im Ordner Licensing Info enthaltenen Bedingungen zu modifizieren, in Ihre eigenen Programme einzufügen oder in Kombination mit Ihren Programmen zu kompilieren sowie in maschinenlesbarer Form nur mit Ihren eigenen Programmen zu vertreiben, vorausgesetzt, daß Sie gleichzeitig als Teil Ihrer eigenen Programme auf jeder Kopie den Apple-Urheberrechtshinweis und alle anderen Schutzrechtshinweise, die auf dem Original der Apple-Software enthalten sind, reproduzieren. Sie verpflichten sich ferner, sofern Sie die so entwickelte Anwendungssoftware vertreiben, mit dem Endbenutzer einen rechtsgültigen Lizenzvertrag zu schließen, der sämtliche Rechte von Apple an der Apple Software nach Maßgabe der Bestimmungen dieses Lizenzvertrages in vollem Umfang berücksichtigt. Alle sonstigen Rechte an der Apple-Software bleiben vorbehalten. Sie verpflichten sich, es zu unterlassen, die Apple-Software zu dekompilieren, zurückzuentwickeln, zu disassemblieren oder in sonstiger Weise in eine für Personen wahrnehmbare Form zu bringen, zu modifizieren, zu adaptieren, zu übersetzen, von der Apple-Software ganz oder teilweise abgeleitete Werke zu erstellen, die Apple-Software über ein Netzwerk von einem Computer auf einen anderen zu übertragen oder diese zu verkaufen oder Dritten auf sonstige Weise unentgeltlich oder gegen Bezahlung zum Gebrauch zu überlassen, soweit dies nicht nach diesem Vertrag oder zwingenden gesetzlichen Vorschriften ausdrücklich gestattet ist. Sollten Sie diese Einschränkungen nicht beachten, sind Sie nicht mehr berechtigt, die Apple-Software zu benutzen, auch wenn der Apple diesen Vertrag noch nicht gekündigt haben sollte. Darüber hinaus behält sich Apple das Recht vor, diesen Lizenzvertrag zu kündigen, wenn eine neue Version von MacOS freigegeben wird, die mit der Apple Software nicht kompatibel ist.

3. Gewährleistung. Fehler in der Apple-Software können nicht ausgeschlossen werden; dies gilt insbesondere für solche Versionen der Apple-Software, die als Alpha-, Beta-, Development-, Pre-Release-, ungetestete oder nicht vollständig getestete Versionen der Apple-Software bezeichnet sind. Apple übernimmt eine Gewährleistung nur im Rahmen der gesetzlichen Vorschriften. Es gilt eine Verjährungsfrist von sechs Monaten ab Lieferung der Apple-Software. Die Gewährleistung erfolgt ausschließlich nach Wahl des Lizenzgebers durch Nachbesserung oder Ersatzlieferung. Bleiben Nachbesserung und/oder Ersatzlieferung erfolglos, können Sie nach Ihrer Wahl Herabsetzung der Lizenzgebühr oder die Rückgängigmachung des Vertrages verlangen. Für Apple-Software, die geändert, erweitert oder beschädigt wurde, wird keine Gewähr übernommen, es sei denn, daß die Änderung, Erweiterung oder Beschädigung für den Mangel nicht ursächlich war.

4. Schadenersatz. Eine vertragliche oder außervertragliche Schadensersatzpflicht seitens des Lizenzgebers sowie seiner Angestellten und Beauftragten besteht nur, sofern der Schaden auf grobe Fahrlässigkeit oder Vorsatz zurückzuführen ist. Eine weitergehende zwingende gesetzliche Haftung bleibt unberührt. Die Haftung des Lizenzgebers ist auf die Vermögensnachteile begrenzt, die er bei Abschluß des Vertrages als mögliche Folge der Vertragsverletzung hätte voraussehen müssen, es sei denn, daß der Schaden auf grobe Fahrlässigkeit eines Organs oder eines leitenden Angestellten des Lizenzgebers oder auf Vorsatz zurückzuführen ist. Für den Verlust von Daten wird keinesfalls gehaftet, es sei denn, daß dieser Verlust durch regelmäßige - im kaufmännischen Geschäftsverkehr tägliche - Sicherung der Daten in maschinenlesbarer Form nicht hätte vermieden werden können. Ferner wird keinesfalls für Schäden gehaftet, die durch sonstige Fehlleistungen der Apple-Software entstanden sind und die durch regelmäßige, zeitnahe Überprüfungen der bearbeiteten Vorgänge hätte vermieden werden können. Soweit Schadensersatzansprüche nicht nach den gesetzlichen Vorschriften früher verjähren, verjähre ist - mit Ausnahme von Ansprüchen aus unerlaubter Handlung und nach dem Produkthaftungsgesetz - spätestens mit dem Ablauf von zwei Jahren ab Erbringung der mangelhaften Leistung.

5. Export. Sie stehen dafür ein, daß die Apple-Software nur unter Beachtung aller anwendbaren Exportbestimmungen des Landes, in dem Sie die Apple-Software erhalten haben, und der Vereinigten Staaten von Amerika ausgeführt wird. Insbesondere darf die Apple-Software nicht (i) in ein Land exportiert oder reexportiert werden, über das die Vereinigten Staaten ein Embargo verhängt haben, oder einem Staatsangehörigen oder Bewohner eines solchen Landes überlassen werden oder (ii) einer Person überlassen werden, die auf der Liste der Specially Designated Nationals des U.S. Treasury Department oder dem Table of Denial Orders des U.S. Department of Commerce verzeichnet sind. Indem Sie die Apple-Software benutzen, erklären Sie, daß Sie weder in einem dieser Länder wohnhaft sind noch seiner Kontrolle unterliegen noch ein Staatsangehöriger oder Bewohner eines dieser Länder sind noch auf einer der vorstehend erwähnten Listen genannt werden.

6. US-Behörden. Wenn die Apple-Software für Behörden der Vereinigten Staaten von Amerika erworben wird, gilt sie als "restricted computer software" nach Maßgabe der Bestimmung Nr. 52.227-19 der FAR. Die Rechte der Behörden der Vereinigten Staaten von Amerika an der Apple - Software werden in der Bestimmung Nr. 52.227-19 der FAR geregelt.

7. Anwendbares Recht und Teilnichtigkeit. Dieser Lizenzvertrag unterliegt deutschem Recht. Die Unwirksamkeit einzelner Bestimmungen berührt die Wirksamkeit des Vertrages im übrigen nicht.

8. Vollständigkeit. Dieser Lizenzvertrag enthält die gesamte Vereinbarung zwischen den Parteien in Bezug auf die Lizenz und tritt an die Stelle aller diesbezüglichen früheren mündlichen oder schriftlichen Vereinbarungen. Änderungen und Ergänzungen dieses Vertrages sind schriftlich niederzulegen.

APPLE COMPUTER, INC.
LISTE DER INTERNATIONALEN TOCHTERGESELLSCHAFTEN

LAND	TOCHTERGESELLSCHAFT
Österreich	Apple Computer Gesellschaft m.b.H.
Brasilien	Apple Computer Brasil Ltda.
Kanada	Apple Canada Inc.
Frankreich	Apple Computer France S.A.R.L.
Deutschland	Apple Computer GmbH
HongKong	Apple Computer International Ltd.
Indien	Apple Computer International Pte. Ltd.
Irland	Apple Computer (UK) Limited
Italien	Apple Computer S.p.A.
Japan	Apple Japan Inc.
Mexiko	Apple Computer Mexico, S.A. de C.V.
Niederlande, Belgien	Apple Computer Benelux B.V.
Singapur	Apple Computer South Asia Pte. Ltd.
Südafrika	Apple Computer (Proprietary) Ltd.
Spanien	Apple Computer Espana, S.A.
Schweden, Norwegen, Dänemark	Apple Computer AB
Schweiz	Apple Computer AG (SA) (Ltd.)
Taiwan	Apple Computer Asia, Inc.
England	Apple Computer (UK) Limited

ITALIANO
Apple Computer, Inc. Licenza Software

SI PREGA DI LEGGERE QUESTA LICENZA CON LA MASSIMA ATTENZIONE PRIMA DI FARE USO DEL SOFTWARE. L'USO DEL SOFTWARE SI CONFIGURA COME ACCETTAZIONE DA PARTE VOSTRA DELLE CONDIZIONI E DEI TERMINI DI QUESTA LICENZA. QUALORA NON SIATE D'ACCORDO CON DETTE CONDIZIONE E DETTI TERMINI, VORRETE RESTITUIRE PRONTAMENTE IL SOFTWARE DOVE LO AVETE ACQUISTATO ED IL PREZZO VERSATO VI SARA' RESTITUITO.

1. Licenza. Il Software, gli strumenti, le utilità, la documentazione e tutti i fonts relativi a questa Licenza sia su disco, su compact disc o a memoria di sola lettura o in altro supporto, la relativa documentazione e altri materiali (collettivamente il "Software Apple") Vi vengono dati in licenza, e non venduti, da Apple Computer Inc. ("Apple"). Il Software Apple che si trova in questo pacchetto e le eventuali copie, modificazioni e distribuzioni autorizzate dalla presente Licenza sono soggetti a questa Licenza.

2. Usi consentiti e restrizioni. Questa Licenza Vi consente di usare il Software Apple per (i) testare il Software Apple e (ii) sviluppare applicazioni software. Vi é consentito di effettuare il numero di copie del Software Apple che siano ragionevolmente necessarie a farne uso nei modi consentiti dalla presente Licenza e distribuire dette copie ai Vostri dipendenti i quali, per ragioni di ufficio, debbano fare uso del Software semprechè detto uso sia limitato agli usi consentiti dalla presente Licenza. Al fine di sviluppare applicazioni software Vi è consentito di usare, copiare, modificare (subordinatamente alle restrizioni descritte nel folder Licensing Info che è parte integrante del Software Apple), incorporare e compilare unitamente ai Vostri programmi e distribuire (solo in forma di codice oggetto) esclusivamente con i Vostri programmi il Software Apple descritto nel folder Licensing Info sul supporto purché riproduciate su ciascuna copia tutti i dati relativi al copyright Apple contenuti nell'originale ed ogni altra informazione sulla proprietà industriale e distribuiate detto Software Apple in forza di un valido contratto altrettanto protettivo dei diritti di Apple nel Software quanto lo é questa Licenza. Salvo quanto consentito dalla legge applicabile e dalla presente Licenza, non Vi é consentito di decompilare, disassemblare, assemblare a riverso, modificare, dare in locazione, in leasing, dare in prestito, sublicenziare, distribuire o ricavare entità derivate dal Software Apple, in tutto o in parte, o trasmettere detto Software in rete o da un computer ad un altro. I Vostri diritti in forza di questa Licenza cesseranno automaticamente, senza onere di comunicazione da parte di Apple, qualora vi sia inadempimento da parte Vostra delle condizioni indicate nella Licenza stessa. Apple si riserva inoltre il diritto di risolvere la presente licenza qualora venga prodotta una nuova versione di Mac™ OS che sia incompatibile con il Software Apple.

3. Garanzia limitata dei Media. Apple garantisce che i supporti sui quali il Software Apple é stato registrato sono immuni da difetti di materiali e manodopera, in condizioni normali d'uso, per un periodo di novanta (90) giorni dalla data di acquisto originario al dettaglio. L'unica garanzia in forza del presente paragrafo potrà essere, a scelta di Apple, il rimborso del prezzo di acquisto o la sostituzione del Software Apple. LA PRESENTE GARANZIA E QUALSIASI ALTRA GARANZIA IMPLICITA RIGUARDANTE I SUPPORTI, IVI INCLUSA QUELLA RIGUARDANTE LA COMMERCIABILITà E L'IDONEITà A SCOPI PARTICOLARI é LIMITATA IN DURATA A NOVANTA (90) GIORNI DALLA DATA DELL'ACQUISTO ORIGINARIO AL DETTAGLIO. Gli esoneri di responsabilità che precedono avranno efficacia nella misura massima consentita dalle norme in vigore. LA PRESENTE GARANZIA LIMITATA E' ESCLUSIVA E SOSTITUISCE OGNI ALTRA SCRITTA OD ORALE, ESPRESSA O IMPLICITA. APPLE ESPRESSAMENTE DISCONOSCE OGNI ALTRA GARANZIA. Dette norme possono altresi' contemplare altri vostri diritti oltre a quelli espressamente citati.

4. Esonero dalla garanzia del Software Apple. Parte del Software Apple potrà essere designato come alpha, beta, sviluppo, pre-release, non testato o potranno essere versioni non pienamente testate del Software Apple. Detto Software Apple potrebbe contenere errori che potrebbero causare errori o perdite di dati e potrebbe essere incompleto o contenere inaccuratezze. Voi espressamente accettate che l'uso del Software Apple avviene a Vostro esclusivo rischio. Il Software Apple viene fornito nello Stato in cui si trova e senza garanzia di sorta da parte di Apple. Sia Apple, sia il licenziante di Apple, ai fini di cui ai Par. 4 e 5, collettivamente denominati "Apple", si esonerano espressamente da ogni garanzia, espressa o implicita, ivi inclusa, ma senza limitazioni, la garanzia implicita di commerciabilità ed idoneità del prodotto a soddisfare scopi particolari. Apple non garantisce che le funzioni contenute nel Software Apple siano idonee a soddisfare le Vostre esigenze né garantisce un'operazione ininterrotta o immune da difetti né che i difetti riscontrati nel Software APPLE vengano corretti. Apple non garantisce altresì né dà affidamento alcuno relativamente all'uso o ai risultati derivanti dall'uso del Software Apple, né sotto il profilo della loro correttezza, accuratezza, affidabilità o sotto altri profili. Le eventuali informazioni orali o scritte o le eventuali consulenze da parte di esponenti o incaricati o di rappresentanti di Apple non possono in ogni caso configurarsi come affidamenti o garanzie o comunque inficiare questo esonero di garanzia. Nel caso di difettosità del Software Apple, saranno a vostro esclusivo carico tutti i costi e le spese per gli interventi, correzioni e ripristini che dovessero occorrere. IL PREZZO DELLA LICENZA PER IL SOFTWARE APPLE RIFLETTE L'ALLOCAZIONE DI RISCHI COME SOPRA. L'esonero di garanzia qui contemplato é da interpretarsi secondo quanto previsto dalla legge applicabile ed é pertanto da ritenersi inefficace nella parte che dovesse risultare incompatibile con le prescrizioni inderogabili della legge applicabile.

5. Limiti di responsabilità. IN OGNI CASO Apple é espressamente sollevata da ogni responsabilità, anche nell'eventualità di sua colpa, per qualsiasi danno, diretto o indiretto, di ogni genere e specie derivante O COLLEGATO all'uso del Software Apple, anche NELL'EVENTUALITà in cui apple sia stata avvertita della POSSIBILITà del verificarsi del danno stesso. I limiti di responsabilità contemplati in questo paragrafo possono essere diversamente regolati dalle norme in vigore nel Vostro ordinamento giuridico. In nessun caso il limite di responsabilità nei Vostri confronti a carico di Apple per il complesso di danni, delle perdite o per ogni altra causa, potrà superare l'importo di USA **$** 50.

6. Impegno all'osservanza delle norme relative all'esportazione. Varrà la presente quale Vostro impegno a non esportare il Software Apple se ciò non è espressamente consentito dalle norme degli Stati Uniti d'America e dalle leggi del paese in cui il Software Apple é stato ottenuto. In particolare, ma senza limitazioni, il Software Apple non potrà essere esportato o riesportato (i) in nessun Paese che si trovi sotto embargo statunitense né a residenti di detti Paesi o (ii) a chicchessia compreso nell'elenco dell'U.S. Treasury Department denominato Specially Designated Nationals o dell'U.S. Department of Commerce's Table denominato Denial Orders. Usando il Software Apple, Voi date espressamente atto e garantite di non essere cittadino o residente, anche solo di fatto, di un Paese compreso negli elenchi sopra citati, ovvero sotto il controllo di uno di detti Paesi.

7. Utilizzatori Finali Enti Governativi. Nel caso in cui il Software Apple venga fornito al Governo degli Stati Uniti d'America, il Software Apple viene classificato come "Software riservato" in base alla definizione di cui alla Clausola 52.227-19 del FAR. I diritti del Governo sul Software Apple sono quelli di cui alla Clausola 52.227-19 del FAR.

8. Legge regolatrice ed eventuale nullità di una o più clausole. Qualora nel Paese in cui avete acquistato il Software Apple vi sia una consociata Apple, in tale eventualità la legge del luogo dove si trova detta consociata regolerà questa Licenza. In caso diverso questa Licenza sarà regolata ed interpretata secondo le leggi degli Stati Uniti d'America e particolare e dello Stato della California. Se per qualsiasi ragione il giudice competente dovesse ritenere inefficace uno o più clausole o parti di clausole di questa Licenza, le altre clausole o parti di clausole rimarranno efficaci.

9. Interezza dell'Accordo. Questa Licenza costituisce l'intero accordo tra le parti relativamente all'uso del Software Apple e supera ed assorbe ogni eventuale precedente o contemporanea intesa o proposta riguardante quanto in oggetto. Le eventuali modifiche o integrazioni di questa Licenza dovranno essere effettuate, per essere efficaci, in forma scritta e dovranno essere sottoscritte da Apple.

APPLE COMPUTER INC.
LISTA DELLE CONSOCIATE LOCALI A LIVELLO INTERNAZIONALE

PAESE	CONSOCIATA
Austria	Apple Computer Gesellschaft mbH
Brasile	Apple Computer Brasil Ltda.
Canada	Apple Canada Inc.
Francia	Apple Computer France S.A.R.L.
Germania	Apple Computer GmbH
Hong Kong	Apple Computer International Ltd.
India	Apple Computer International Pte. Ltd.
Irlanda	Apple Computer (UK) Limited

Italia	Apple Computer S.r.l.
Giappone	Apple Japan, Inc.
Messico	Apple Computer Mexico, S.A. de C.V.
Olanda, Belgio	Apple Computer Benelux B.V.
Singapore	Apple Computer South Asia Pte Ltd
Sud Africa	Apple Computer (Proprietary) Limited
Spagna	Apple Computer Espana, S.A.
Svezia, Norvegia, Danimarca	Apple Computer AB
Svizzera	Apple Computer AG (SA) (Ltd.)
Taiwan	Apple Computer Asia, Inc.
Regno Unito	Apple Computer (UK) Limited

SVENSK
Apple Computer, Inc. Licensavtal

LÄS DETTA LICENSAVTAL ("LICENSAVTAL") NOGGRANT INNAN DU ANVÄNDER PROGRAMPRODUKTEN. GENOM ATT ANVÄNDA PROGRAMPRODUKTEN SAMTYCKER DU TILL OCH BLIR AUTOMATISKT BUNDEN AV VILLKOREN I DETTA LICENSAVTAL. OM DU INTE SAMTYCKER TILL DESSA VILLKOR, SKALL DU INTE ANVÄNDA PROGRAMPRODUKTEN OCH (OM TILLÄMPLIGT) ÅTERLÄMNA PROGRAMPRODUKTEN TILL FÖRSÄLJNINGSSTÄLLET, VAREFTER DINA PENGAR KOMMER ATT ÅTERBETALAS.

1. Licens. Programprodukten, verktygen, hjälpmedlen, dokumentationen och typsnitten som levereras med detta Licensavtal, på diskett, CD, ROM eller på annat medium, tillämplig dokumentation och annat material (nedan gemensamt kallat "Apple Programprodukten"), licensieras till Dig av Apple Computer Inc.(nedan "Apple"). Både den Apple Programprodukt som finns i förpackningen och eventuella kopior, modifieringar och distribution som Du har rätt att göra enligt detta Licensavtal regleras av detta Licensavtal.

2. Tillåten användning och restriktioner. Detta Licensavtal ger Dig rätt att använda Apple Programprodukten för (i) test av Apple Programprodukten, och (ii) utveckling av tillämpningar. Du får göra så många kopior av Apple Programprodukten som är rimligt för att kunna använda Apple Programprodukten på det sätt som tillåts enligt detta Licensavtal, och distribuera dessa kopior till de av Dina anställda vars arbetsuppgifter kräver att de skall kunna använda Apple Programprodukten, under förutsättning att sådan användning ligger inom ramen för vad som är tillåtet enligt detta Licensavtal. För att utveckla tillämpningar får Du använda, kopiera, förändra (under förutsättning att sådan förändring inte står i strid med de restriktioner som anges i Licensierings Informations mappen i Apple Programprodukten), införliva med och sammanställa med Dina egna tillämpningar och distribuera (endast i objektkodsform), dock endast tillsammans med Dina egna tillämpningar, den Apple Programprodukt som beskrivs i Licensierings Informations mappen på mediet, under förutsättning att Du på varje kopia återge alla upplysningar om upphovsrätt som finns på originalet av Apple Programprodukten, och distribuerar sådan kopia av Apple Programprodukten tillsammans med ett giltigt licensavtal som skyddar Apples rättigheter till Apple Programprodukten i minst lika hög grad som detta Licensavtal. Du får inte, på annat sätt än som uttryckligen tillåts av detta Licensavtal, dekompilera, dekonstruera, bryta ner, förändra, hyra ut, leasa, låna ut, underlicensiera, distribuera, skapa härledda produkter helt eller delvis baserade på Apple Programprodukten eller överföra Apple Programprodukten från en dator till en annan via ett nätverk. Dina rättigheter enligt detta licensavtal kommer automatiskt, utan varsel från Apple, att upphöra om Du bryter mot bestämmelserna i detta Licensavtal. Apple förbehåller sig vidare rätten att säga upp detta Licensavtal om en ny version av MacOs™, vilken inte är kompatibel med Apple Programprodukten, lanseras.

3. Begränsad garanti för medium (om tillämpligt). Apple garanterar att det medium på vilket Apple Programprodukten är lagrat vid normal användning är fritt från defekter i material och utförande under en period av nittio (90) dagar från det första slutanvändarinköpet. Apples enda skyldighet i enlighet med denna garanti skall vara att, efter eget skön, antingen återbetala köpeskillingen för produkten som innehöll Apple Programprodukten eller att leverera en ny Apple Programprodukt. ALLA EGENSKAPER ELLER GARANTIER SOM UNDERFÖRSTÅTT KAN ANSES TILLFÖRSÄKRADE MEDIA INKLUSIVE EGENSKAPEN ATT VARA FUNKTIONELLT OCH ÄNDAMÅLSENLIGT, BEGRÄNSAS HÄRMED I TIDEN TILL EN PERIOD AV NITTIO (90) DAGAR FRÅN LEVERANS. DENNA GARANTI SKALL INTE TOLKAS SOM EN INSKRÄNKNING AV DE RÄTTIGHETER SOM KAN TILLKOMMA DIG ENLIGT TVINGANDE TILLÄMPLIG LAGSTIFTNING. APPLE FRISKRIVER SIG HÄRIGENOM UTTRYCKLIGEN FRÅN ALLT ÖVRIGT ANSVAR FÖR APPLE PROGRAMPRODUKTEN.

4. Ingen garanti för Apple Programprodukten. Vissa Apple Programprodukter kan vara angivna som sk alpha- eller beta-versioner, utvecklingsversioner, icke testade-versioner eller inte helt testade versioner av Apple Programprodukten. Dessa Apple Programprodukter kan innehålla brister som kan förorsaka felaktigheter eller resultera i att data förloras, de kan även vara ofullständiga eller innehålla felaktigheter. Du förklarar Dig uttryckligen medveten om detta förhållande och att all användningen av Apple Programprodukten sker på Din egen risk. Apple Programprodukten tillhandahålles i befintligt skick och utan några som helst garantier. Apple och Apples Licensgivare (i denna punkt 4 och punkt 5 kollektivt benämnda "Apple") FRISKRIVER SIG HÄRIGENOM FRÅN ALLA, SÅVÄL UTTRYCKLIGA SOM UNDERFÖRSTÅDDA, GARANTIER, SÅLEDES OCKSÅ UNDERFÖRSTÅDDA GARANTIER AVSEENDE KVALITET, FUNKTIONALITET OCH ÄNDAMÅLSENLIGHET FÖR VISST SPECIFIKT SYFTE, SAMT PROGRAMPRODUKTENS EVENTUELLA INTRÅNG I ANNANS IMMATERIELLA RÄTTIGHETER. APPLE KAN EJ HELLER GARANTERA ATT PROGRAMPRODUKTEN UPPFYLLER DINA FÖRVÄNTNINGAR, ÄR FELFRI ELLER KAN ANVÄNDAS UTAN AVBROTT ELLER ATT FEL OCH BRISTER I PROGRAMPRODUKTEN KOMMER ATT ÅTGÄRDAS. APPLE GER INGA GARANTIER VAD GÄLLER ANVÄNDNING ELLER RESULTATET AV ANVÄNDNINGEN AV PROGRAMPRODUKTEN OCH DOKUMENTATIONEN, DESS PÅLITLIGHET, NOGGRANNHET, ELLER ÖVRIGA EGENSKAPER. DENNA BEGRÄNSADE GARANTI KAN EJ UTÖKAS GENOM MUNTLIGA ELLER SKRIFTLIGA UTSAGOR FRÅN VARE SIG APPLE ELLER APPLES REPRESENTANTER. OM PROGRAMPRODUKTEN SKULLE VARA FELAKTIG ELLER BRISTFÄLLIG FRISKRIVER SIG APPLE FRÅN ALLA KOSTNADER FÖR SERVICE, REPARATION ELLER ANNAT AVHJÄLPANDE. VID ÅSÄTTANDE AV LICENSAVGIFTEN FÖR PROGRAMPRODUKTEN HAR HÄNSYN TAGITS TILL DENNA RISKALLOKERING. I HÄNDELSE AV ATT DENNA BESTÄMMELSE STRIDER MOT TVINGANDE LAG ÄR BESTÄMMELSEN I DENNA DEL EJ TILLÄMPLIG.

5. Ansvarsbegränsning. APPLE ÄR INTE, OBEROENDE AV VÅLLANDE, ANSVARIG FÖR SKADA, VARKEN DIREKT ELLER INDIREKT SÅDAN, VILKEN ORSAKATS AV ELLER ÄR RELATERAD TILL DENNA LICENS. I HÄNDELSE AV ATT DENNA BESTÄMMELSE STRIDER MOT TVINGANDE LAG ÄR BESTÄMMELSEN I DENNA DEL EJ TILLÄMPLIG. I inget fall skall Apples totala skadeståndsansvar, oberoende av vållande, överstiga ett belopp motsvarande US$ 50.

6. Försäkran avseende export. Försäkran avseende export. Du har inte rätt att exportera eller vidareexportera Apple Programprodukten förutom på sådant sätt som är i enlighet med gällande exportlagstiftning i USA och gällande lagstiftning i det land där Apple Programprodukten förvärvades. I synnerhet (dock inte begränsat till) gäller att Apple Programprodukten inte får exporteras eller vidareexporteras till i) något av de länder som lyder under USAs embargo (eller till en medborgare eller innevånare i sådant land), eller ii) någon som anges på US Treasury Departments lista över sk Specially Designated Nationals eller US Department of Commerces sk Table of Denial Orders. Genom att använda Apple Programprodukten försäkrar Du att Du inte bor i, lyder under, är medborgare eller bosatt i något sådant land eller finns upptagen på någon av de ovan angivna listorna.

7. Amerikanska statliga slutanvändare. Om Apple Programprodukten distribueras till amerikansk statlig myndighet är Apple Programprodukten klassificerad som " restricted computer software" som denna term definieras i punkt 52.227-19 av FAR. Den amerikanska myndighetens rättigheter till programprodukten kommer i detta fall att regleras av punkt 52.227-19 av FAR.

8. Gällande lag och genomförbarhet. Om det finns ett dotterbolag till Apple i det land där licensrättigheterna till denna Apple Programprodukt förvärvades, skall detta lands lag tillämpas på denna licens. I annat fall skall USAs och delstaten Kaliforniens lagstiftning tillämpas. För den händelse att något villkor i detta licensavtal av domstol eller administrativ myndighet inte bedöms giltigt eller verkställbart, skall övriga delar av avtalet ändock gälla fullt ut och tolkas på sådant sätt som skulle gällt om den exkluderade delen av avtalet gällde.

9. Fullständigt avtal. Detta licensavtal innehåller allt som avtalats mellan parterna med avseende på användningen av Apple Programprodukten och ersätter samtliga tidigare skriftliga eller muntliga avtal, utfästelser eller överenskommelser parterna emellan. Ändring i detta licensavtal kan endast ske genom särskild upprättad och av behörig representant för Apple undertecknad handling.

APPLE COMPUTER, INC.
INTERNATIONELLA DOTTERBOLAG

LAND	DOTTERBOLAG
Kanada	Apple Canada Inc.
Sydafrika	Apple Computer (Proprietary) Limited
England	Apple Computer (UK) Limited
Sverige, Norge, Danmark, Finland	Apple Computer AB
Schweitz	Apple Computer AG (SA) (Ltd.)
Taiwan	Apple Computer Asia, Inc.
Holland och Belgien	Apple Computer Benelux B.V.
Brasilien	Apple Computer Brasil Ltda.
Spanien	Apple Computer Espana, S.A.
Frankrike	Apple Computer France S.A.R.L.
Österrike	Apple Computer Gesellschaft m.b.H.
Tyskland	Apple Computer GmbH
Hong Kong	Apple Computer International Ltd
Irland	Apple Computer (UK) Limited
Mexico	Apple Computer Mexico, S.A. de C.V.
Italien	Apple Computer S.p.A.
Singapore	Apple Computer South Asia Pte Ltd
Japan	Apple Japan, Inc.
Indien	Apple Computer International Pte. Ltd.

NEDERLANDS
Apple Computer, Inc. Software-licentie

LEES DEZE SOFTWARE-LICENTIE-OVEREENKOMST ("LICENTIE") AANDACHTIG DOOR VOOR U DE PROGRAMMATUUR GEBRUIKT. DOOR DE PROGRAMMATUUR TE GEBRUIKEN VERKLAART U ZICH AKKOORD MET DE VOORWAARDEN VAN DEZE LICENTIE. INDIEN U HET NIET EENS BENT MET DE VOORWAARDEN VAN DEZE LICENTIE, DIENT U DE ONGEBRUIKTE PROGRAMMATUUR TE RETOURNEREN AAN DE PLAATS WAAR U DEZE HEBT AANGESCHAFT. DE DOOR U BETAALDE PRIJS ZAL IN DAT GEVAL WORDEN TERUGBETAALD.

1. Licentie. De programmatuur, tools, hulpprogramma's, documentatie en lettertypen bij deze Licentie, hetzij op schijf, op compact disc, in "read only"-geheugen of op enig ander medium (de "Apple programmatuur"), worden aan u in licentie gegeven, en niet verkocht, door Apple Computer, Inc. ("Apple").

Deze Licentie is van toepassing op de Apple programmatuur in dit pakket en op eventuele kopieën, gewijzigde versies of te distribueren versies die u krachtens deze licentie maakt.

2. Toegestaan gebruik en beperkingen. Krachtens deze licentie is het u toegestaan de Apple programmatuur te gebruiken ten einde (i) de Apple programmatuur te testen en (ii) applicatiesoftware te ontwikkelen. Het is u toegestaan zoveel kopieën van de Apple programmatuur te maken als redelijkerwijs noodzakelijk is om de programmatuur te kunnen gebruiken zoals beoogd in deze Licentie, en deze ter beschikking te stellen aan werknemers wier taak het gebruik van deze programmatuur vereist, op voorwaarde dat dit gebruik niet strijdig is met de voorwaarden van deze Licentie. Ten einde applicatiesoftware te ontwikkelen is het u toegestaan de Apple programmatuur zoals beschreven in de Licensing Info-informatie op het medium waarop de programmatuur is geleverd, te gebruiken, te kopiëren, te wijzigen (mits wordt voldaan aan de beperkingen die worden vermeld in de Licensing Info-informatie), te integreren in en te compileren in combinatie met uw eigen programma's, te distribueren, op voorwaarde dat u op elke kopie de volledige auteursrechtvermelding en alle andere mededelingen betreffende het eigendomsrecht welke op het origineel van de Apple programmatuur vermeld zijn, overneemt, en u de Apple programmatuur distribueert voorzien van een geldige overeenkomst die voorziet in minimaal dezelfde bescherming van de rechten van Apple met betrekking tot de Apple programmatuur als deze Licentie. Behalve voor zover uitdrukkelijk toegestaan krachtens deze Licentie is het u niet toegestaan de Apple programmatuur te decompileren, van ontwerp te herleiden, te ontmantelen, aan te passen, te (doen) verhuren, in gebruik te (doen) geven, in sublicentie te geven, te distribueren, geheel of gedeeltelijk van de Apple programmatuur afgeleide werken te creëren of de Apple programmatuur te verspreiden via een netwerk of over te dragen van de ene naar de andere computer. Uw rechten ingevolge deze Licentie vervallen automatisch zonder voorafgaande kennisgeving van Apple indien u een van de voorwaarden van deze Licentie niet nakomt. Daarnaast behoudt Apple zich het recht voor deze Licentie te beëindigen indien een nieuwe versie van het Mac OS wordt geïntroduceerd die niet compatibel is met de Apple programmatuur.

3. Beperkte garantie op media. Apple garandeert dat de media welke de Apple programmatuur bevatten bij normaal gebruik gedurende een periode van negentig (90) dagen na de oorspronkelijke datum van aankoop in de detailhandel, vrij zijn van materiaal- en fabrikagefouten. U kunt krachtens deze paragraaf uitsluitend aanspraak maken, naar keuze van Apple, op terugbetaling van de aankoopprijs of op vervanging van de Apple programmatuur. DEZE BEPERKTE GARANTIE EN ELKE IMPLICIETE GARANTIE OP DE MEDIA, INCLUSIEF DE IMPLICIETE GARANTIE VAN VERHANDELBAARHEID EN GESCHIKTHEID VOOR EEN BEPAALD DOEL, IS BEPERKT TOT EEN PERIODE VAN NEGENTIG (90) DAGEN NA DE OORSPRONKELIJKE DATUM VAN AANKOOP IN DE DETAILHANDEL. IN BEPAALDE RECHTSGEBIEDEN IS BEPERKING VAN DE DUUR VAN EEN IMPLICIETE GARANTIE NIET TOEGESTAAN, WAARDOOR DE BOVENSTAANDE UITSLUITING VOOR U MOGELIJK NIET VAN TOEPASSING IS. DE HIER BESCHREVEN BEPERKTE GARANTIE IS EXCLUSIEF EN KOMT IN DE PLAATS VAN ALLE ANDERE GARANTIES, HETZIJ MONDELING OF SCHRIFTELIJK, HETZIJ EXPLICIET OF IMPLICIET. APPLE SLUIT UITDRUKKELIJK ALLE ANDERE GARANTIES UIT. DEZE BEPERKTE GARANTIE GEEFT U SPECIFIEKE JURIDISCHE RECHTEN. BOVENDIEN KUNNEN AFHANKELIJK VAN HET RECHTSGEBIED ANDERE RECHTEN GELDEN.

4. Beperking van garantie. Bepaalde Apple programmatuur kan zijn aangeduid als alfa-, bèta-, pre-release-, ontwikkel-, niet geteste of gedeeltelijk geteste versie van de Apple programmatuur. Dergelijke Apple programmatuur kan fouten bevatten die kunnen resulteren in storingen of het verlies van gegevens, en kan incompleet zijn of onjuistheden bevatten. U erkent en aanvaardt uitdrukkelijk dat gebruik van de Apple programmatuur uitsluitend voor uw eigen risico is. De Apple programmatuur wordt "IN DE STAAT WAARIN DEZE OP HET MOMENT VAN AANKOOP VERKEERT" (op "as is"-basis) en zonder enige garantie geleverd en Apple en Apple's Licentiegever(s) (voor het doel van paragraaf 4 en 5 hierna gezamenlijk te noemen "Apple") SLUITEN HIERBIJ UITDRUKKELIJK ALLE GARANTIES UIT, EXPLICIET OF IMPLICIET, DAARONDER BEGREPEN DOCH NIET BEPERKT TOT ALLE DENKBARE GARANTIES VAN VERHANDELBAARHEID EN GESCHIKTHEID VOOR EEN BEPAALD DOEL. APPLE GARANDEERT NIET DAT DE FUNCTIES WELKE IN DE APPLE PROGRAMMATUUR ZIJN VERVAT AAN UW EISEN ZULLEN VOLDOEN OF DAT MET DE APPLE PROGRAMMATUUR ONONDERBROKEN OF FOUTLOOS ZAL KUNNEN WORDEN GEWERKT OF DAT GEBREKEN IN DE APPLE PROGRAMMATUUR GECORRIGEERD ZULLEN WORDEN. VERDER VERLEENT APPLE GEEN GARANTIES BETREFFENDE HET GEBRUIK OF DE RESULTATEN VAN HET GEBRUIK VAN DE APPLE PROGRAMMATUUR TERZAKE VAN CORRECTHEID, NAUWKEURIGHEID, BETROUWBAARHEID OF ANDERSZINS. GEEN ENKELE MONDELINGE OF SCHRIFTELIJKE INFORMATIE OF KENNISGEVING VAN DE ZIJDE VAN APPLE OF EEN DOOR APPLE GEAUTORISEERDE VERTEGENWOORDIGER KAN EEN GARANTIE INHOUDEN OF DE OMVANG VAN DEZE GARANTIE UITBREIDEN. MOCHT DE APPLE PROGRAMMATUUR GEBREKEN VERTONEN, DAN KOMEN ALLE KOSTEN VAN ALLE NOODZAKELIJKE REVISIE, HERSTEL OF CORRECTIE VOOR UW REKENING (EN NIET VOOR DIE VAN APPLE OF EEN DOOR APPLE GEAUTORISEERDE VERTEGENWOORDIGER). DE LICENTIEVERGOEDING VOOR DE APPLE PROGRAMMATUUR WEERSPIEGELT DEZE OVERDRACHT VAN RISICO. IN BEPAALDE RECHTSGEBIEDEN IS UITSLUITING VAN IMPLICIETE GARANTIES NIET TOEGESTAAN, WAARDOOR DE BOVENSTAANDE UITSLUITING VOOR U MOGELIJK NIET VAN TOEPASSING IS.

5. Beperking van aansprakelijkheid. ONDER GEEN ENKELE OMSTANDIGHEID, WAARONDER BEGREPEN ONACHTZAAMHEID, ZAL APPLE AANSPRAKELIJK ZIJN VOOR SECUNDAIRE, SPECIALE OF GEVOLGSCHADE VOORTVLOEIEND UIT HET GEBRUIK OF DE ONMOGELIJKHEID GEBRUIK TE MAKEN VAN DE APPLE PROGRAMMATUUR, ZELFS INDIEN APPLE OF EEN DOOR APPLE GEAUTORISEERDE VERTEGENWOORDIGER VAN DE MOGELIJKHEID VAN DERGELIJKE SCHADE OP DE HOOGTE IS GESTELD. IN BEPAALDE RECHTSGEBIEDEN IS BEPERKING VAN OF UITSLUITING VAN AANSPRAKELIJKHEID VOOR SECUNDAIRE OF GEVOLGSCHADE NIET TOEGESTAAN, WAARDOOR DEZE BEPERKING VOOR U MOGELIJK NIET VAN TOEPASSING IS. In geen geval zal Apple's totale aansprakelijkheid voor alle schade, verliezen en juridische procedures (hetzij voortvloeiend uit een contractuele relatie, onrechtmatige daad - waaronder begrepen onachtzaamheid - of anderszins) ooit meer bedragen dan $50 (vijftig Amerikaanse dollar).

6. Bepaling betreffende de Amerikaanse exportwetten. Het is u niet toegestaan de Apple programmatuur te gebruiken of anderszins te exporteren of te herexporteren behalve voor zover toegestaan krachtens de wetten van de Verenigde Staten en van het rechtsgebied waarin u de Apple programmatuur hebt verkregen. In het bijzonder, maar zonder beperking, is het u niet toegestaan de Apple programmatuur te exporteren of te herexporteren (i) naar (een staatsburger of ingezetene van) een land waarvoor door de Verenigde Staten een embargo is ingesteld of (ii) enige persoon die voorkomt op de door het U.S. Treasury Department samengestelde lijst van "Specially Designated Nationals" of op de door het U.S. Department of Commerce samengestelde "Table of Denial Orders". Door de Apple programmatuur te gebruiken, verklaart u dat u zich niet bevindt in, onder controle staat van of staatsburger of ingezetene bent van een dergelijk land of op een van de bovengenoemde lijsten voorkomt.

7. Eindgebruikers binnen de Amerikaanse overheid. Indien de Apple programmatuur wordt geleverd aan de Amerikaanse overheid, wordt de Apple programmatuur aangemerkt als "restricted computer software" zoals omschreven in paragraaf 52.227-19 van de FAR. De rechten van de Amerikaanse overheid met betrekking tot de Apple programmatuur zullen zijn als omschreven in paragraaf 52.227-19 van de FAR.

8. Toepasselijk recht en deelbaarheid. Indien in het land waar de Apple programmatuur-licentie is aangeschaft, een lokale dochteronderneming van Apple aanwezig is, zal deze licentie onderworpen zijn aan het lokale recht. Indien geen lokale dochteronderneming aanwezig is, zal deze licentie onderworpen zijn aan de wetten van de Verenigde Staten en de staat Californië. In het geval dat enige bepaling van deze overeenkomst of een gedeelte daarvan door een bevoegde rechter nietig geacht zal worden, zullen de overige bepalingen van deze licentie onverkort van kracht blijven.

9. Volledige overeenkomst. Deze licentie vormt de volledige overeenkomst tussen partijen met betrekking tot het gebruik van de Apple programmatuur en gaat uit boven alle voorgaande of gelijktijdige overeenkomsten betreffende dit onderwerp. Aanpassingen of wijzigingen van deze Licentie zijn slechts geldig voorzover deze zijn opgesteld in schriftelijke vorm en zijn ondertekend door Apple.

APPLE COMPUTER, INC.
INTERNATIONALE DOCHTERONDERNEMINGEN

LAND	DOCHTERONDERNEMING
Brazilië	Apple Computer Brasil Ltda.
Canada	Apple Canada, Inc.
Duitsland	Apple Computer GmbH
Frankrijk	Apple Computer France S.A.R.L.
Hongkong	Apple Computer International Ltd.
Ierland	Apple Computer (UK) Limited
India	Apple Computer International Pte. Ltd.
Italië	Apple Computer S.p.A.
Japan	Apple Japan, Inc.
Mexico	Apple Computer Mexico, S.A. de C.V.
Nederland, België	Apple Computer Benelux B.V.
Oostenrijk	Apple Computer Gesellschaft m.b.H.
Singapore	Apple Computer South Asia Pte. Ltd.
Spanje	Apple Computer Espana, S.A.
Taiwan	Apple Computer Asia, Inc.
Verenigd Koninkrijk	Apple Computer (UK) Limited
Zuid-Afrika	Apple Computer (Proprietary) Limited
Zweden, Noorwegen, Denemarken	Apple Computer AB
Zwitserland	Apple Computer AG (SA) (Ltd.)

日本語
アップルコンピュータ・インクソフトウェア使用許諾契約

　本ソフトウェアを御使用になる前に本使用許諾契約をよくお読みください。本ソフトウェアを使用されることにより、本使用許諾契約の各条項に拘束されることに同意したことになります。本使用許諾契約の条項に同意されない場合には、本ソフトウェアを御使用にはならず、購入された場所にご返却下さい（適用ある場合）。そうすれば代金は返却されます。

1. 使用許諾　ディスク、コンパクトディスク、読み出し専用メモリー、その他の記録媒体又は他の一切のフォーム上の、本使用許諾契約書が添付されているソフトウェア、ツール、ユーティリティー、書類及びすべてのフォント、関連する書類及びその他のマテリアル（以下「アップルソフトウェア」という）は、アップルコンピュータ・インク（以下「アップル社」という）がお客様に使用許諾するものです。お客様は、アップルソフトウェアが記録されている媒体自体の所有権を有しますが、アップルソフトウェアに対する権利はアップル社及び／又はアップル社への許諾者に留保されます。本使用許諾契約は、本パッケージ中のアップルソフトウェア及び本使用許諾契約に基づく複製物、修正及び販売に適用されるものとします。

2. 使用方法及びその制限　本使用許諾契約により、お客様は、アップルソフトウェアを(i)アップルソフトウェアをテストするため及び(ii)アプリケーションソフトウェアを開発するために、使用することができます。お客様は、本許諾契約書による許諾に基づきソフトウェアを使用するために合理的に必要な限度の部数につきアップルソフトウェアの複製物を作成することができ、かかる複製物を、お客様の従業員に対して、業務上ソフトウェアを利用する必要のある従業員の方に限定してこれを配付することができます。但し、かかる従業員の方は、本許諾契約書により許諾された限りにおいてのみこれを使用することができます。アプリケーションソフトウェアの開発のため、お客様は、媒体の「ライセンス情報」フォルダーに記載されたアップルソフトウェアを使用、複製、変更（但し、アップルソフトウェアの一部である「ライセンス情報」フォルダーに記載された制限に服します）、お客様自身のプログラムに組み込み若しくはお客様自身のプログラムと共にコンパイルし、お客様自身のプログラムと共にする場合に限り販売（但し、オブジェクトコード形式に限ります）することができます。但し、アップルソフトウェアのオリジナルに表示されているアップル社の著作権表示及びその他一切の権利表示を付することを要し、本許諾契約書と少なくとも同程度にアップルソフトエアに対するアップルの権利を保護する有効な契約に基づいて販売することを要します。本使用許諾契約により明確に許可される場合を除き、お客様は、アップルソフトウェア又はその一部を、逆コンパイルし、リバースエンジニアし、逆アッセンブルし、修正し、賃貸し、リースし、貸与し、再使用許諾し、頒布し、二次的著作物を創作してはならず、かつ、

アップルソフトウェアをネットワークを通じて、またはあるコンピューターから別のコンピューターへ送ってはなりません。お客様が本使用許諾契約の一条項にでも違反した場合、本使用許諾契約に基づくお客様の権利は、アップル社からの通知なく、自動的に終了するものとします。さらにアップル社は、アップルソフトウェアと互換性のないニューバージョンのマックOSがリリースされた場合、本使用許諾契約を終了させる権利を保有します。

3. 媒体についての限定保証　アップル社は、通常の使用下において、最初の購入日より90日間、アップルソフトウェアが記録されている媒体に材質上及び製造上の瑕疵がないことを保証します。本条に基づくお客様に対するアップル社の唯一の保証実行方法は、アップル社の選択により、アップルソフトウェアを含む製品の代金の返還またはアップルソフトウェアの交換に限定されるものとし、お客様は、当該交換を受けるためには、アップルソフトウェアにその領収書をそえてアップル社又はアップル社の権限ある代表者に返却する必要があります。商品適格性および特定目的への適合性に関する黙示的保証を含む媒体に対する本限定的保証および一切の黙示的保証は、最初の購入日より90日間に限定されます。黙示的保証の継続期間に対する限定が許されない地域では、当該期間限定がお客様に適用されないことがあります。本書中に規定された限定的保証は唯一の保証であり、口頭または文書によるか、明示もしくは黙示によるとを問わず、他の一切の保証に代わるものです。アップル社は、他の一切の保証の責任を負いません。本限定的保証は、媒体についてお客様に対し特別の法的権利を賦与するものであり、お客様はその地域により認められるその他の権利も行使できます。

4. アップルソフトウェアに関する保証の放棄　アップルソフトウェアは、アルファバージョン、ベータバージョン、開発バージョン、未リリースバージョン、未テストバージョン、または十分にテストが行われていないバージョンのアップルソフトウェアが指定されることがあります。かかるアップルソフトウェアには、故障やデータ損失の原因となりうるエラーが含まれていることがあり、不完全であったり正確性に欠けることがあります。お客様は、アップルソフトウェアの使用に係わる全ての危険はお客様が負担することを明示的に確認し、同意するものとします。アップルソフトウェアは、一切の保証を伴わない「現状渡し」で提供されるものとし、アップル社及びアップル社に対する使用許諾者（第4条及び第5条において、アップル社及びアップル社に対する使用許諾者を総称して「アップル社」といいます）は、商品適格又は満足できる品質、特定目的への適合性及び第三者の権利の不侵害性に関する黙示的保証及び又は条件等を含む一切の明示的及び黙示的保証及び又は条件の責任を明示的に放棄します。アップル社は、アップルソフトウェアに含まれた機能がお客様の要求を満足させるものであること、アップルソフトウェアが支障なく若しくは誤作動なく作動すること、アップルソフトウェアの瑕疵が修正されること、のいずれも保証いたしません。また、アップル社は、アップルソフトウェアの使用、又はその使用の結果に係る確性、正確性若しくは信頼性等に関し、何らの保証若しくは表明もいたしません。アップル社又はアップル社の権限ある代表者の口頭又は書面によるいかなる情報又は助言も、新たな保証をおこなうものではなく又はその他いかなる意味においても本保証の範囲を拡大するものではありません。アップルソフトウェアに瑕疵が発見された場合、お客様（アップル社又はアップル社の権限ある代表者ではなく）が、すべてのサービス、修理又は修正に要する一切の費用を負担するものとします。アップルソフトウェアの使用許諾料には、この危険分担が反映されています。黙示的保証の免責を認めていない地域においては、上記の保証免責規定はお客様に適用されない場合もあります。

5. 責任の限定　過失を含むいかなる場合であっても、アップル社は、アップルソフトウェアの使用または使用不能に起因する若しくは関連する付随的、特別、間接又は結果損害について一切の責任を負いません。たとえアップル社又はアップル社の権限ある代表者がかかる損害発生の可能性につき助言されていたとしても同様とします。付随的又は結果損害に対する責任の限定を認めていない地域においては、この当該限定がお客様に適用されない場合もあります。いかなる場合も、お客様の一切の損害、損失、訴訟原因（契約上、過失を含む不法行為その他何であるかを問わない）に対するアップル社の賠償責任額は、５０米ドルを上限とします。

6. 輸出規制法に関する保証　お客様は、アメリカ合衆国の法律及びアップルソフトウェアを購入した国の法律により認められている場合を除き、アップルソフトウェアを使用せず、輸出または再輸出しないことに同意するものとします。特に、アップルソフトウェアは、(i)アメリカ合衆国の通商禁止国（またはその国民もしくは居住者）または(ii)アメリカ合衆国財務省の特別指定国リストもしくはアメリカ合衆国商務省の拒否命令表上に記載される一切の者に輸出または再輸出されないものとします。アップルソフトウェアを使用することにより、お客様は、上記国家に居住を定めておらず、上記国家の支配に服しておらず、かつ上記国家の国民もしくは居住者ではないこと、及び上記リストに該当するものではないことを表明し、かつ保証するものとします。

7. エンドユーザーがアメリカ合衆国政府である場合　アップルソフトウェアがアメリカ合衆国政府機関に対して提供される場合、アップルソフトウェアは、FAR第52.227-19条に定める「制限されたコンピュータソフトウェア」に分類されます。アメリカ合衆国政府のアップルソフトウェアに対する権利は、FAR第52.227-19条に定めるとおりです。

8. 準拠法及び契約の分離性　お客様がアップルソフトウェア使用権を許諾された国にアップルの子会社が存在する場合、当該子会社が所在する地域の法律を本使用許諾契約の準拠法とします。その他の場合、アメリカ合衆国及びカリフォルニア州の法律が適用されるものとします。何らかの理由により、管轄権を有する裁判所が本使用許諾契約のいずれかの条項又はその一部について執行力がないと判断した場合であっても、本使用許諾契約の他の条項は依然として完全な効力を有するものとします。

9. 完全な合意　本使用許諾契約は、アップルソフトウェアの使用について、お客様とアップル社の取り決めのすべてを記載するものであり、本件に関する、従前または同時期になされる一切の合意に優先して適用されるものです。本使用許諾契約の改訂又は変更は、アップル社が署名した文書による場合を除き効力を一切生じません。